# Brazil and Climate Justice

# International Environmental Law

*Series Editor*

Makane Moïse Mbengue

VOLUME 21

The titles published in this series are listed at *brill.com/iel*

# Brazil and Climate Justice

*Pioneering Climate Litigation for a Global Cause*

*Editors*

Maria Antonia Tigre
Armando Rocha
Délton Winter de Carvalho

BRILL | NIJHOFF

LEIDEN | BOSTON

Library of Congress Cataloging-in-Publication Data

Names: Tigre, Maria Antonia editor | Rocha, Armando Luis Silva editor | Carvalho, Délton Winter de editor
Title: Brazil and climate justice / edited by Maria Antonia Tigre, Armando Rocha, Délton Winter de Carvalho.
Description: Boston, Massachusetts : Brill, 2025. | Series: International environmental law, 1873-6599 ; 21 | Includes bibliographical references and index.
Identifiers: LCCN 2025010142 (print) | LCCN 2025010143 (ebook) | ISBN 9789004690813 hardback | ISBN 9789004690974 ebook
Subjects: LCSH: Liability for climatic change damages–Brazil | Liability for environmental damages–Brazil | Climate justice–Brazil | Climatic changes–Law and legislation–Brazil
Classification: LCC KHD3423 .B73 2025 (print) | LCC KHD3423 (ebook) | DDC 344.8104/6–dc23/eng/20250307
LC record available at https://lccn.loc.gov/2025010142
LC ebook record available at https://lccn.loc.gov/2025010143

Typeface for the Latin, Greek, and Cyrillic scripts: “Brill”. See and download: brill.com/brill-typeface.

ISSN 1873-6599
ISBN 978-90-04-69081-3 (hardback)
ISBN 978-90-04-69097-4 (e-book)
DOI 10.1163/9789004690974



This book is printed on acid-free paper and produced in a sustainable manner.

*To all the lives in Brazil affected by the impacts of climate change,*
*to those who suffer the consequences of deforestation and its ripple effects on the land, air, and water,*
*and especially to the vulnerable communities—Indigenous peoples, quilombolas, traditional populations, women, children, and future generations—who bear the brunt of these challenges.*
*This book is dedicated to your resilience, your voice, and the fight for justice in a rapidly changing world.*
*May your stories inspire the action and accountability that is urgently needed.*

# Contents

Foreword XI
*Michael B. Gerrard*
Acknowledgments XIII
List of Figures XIV
List of Tables XV
List of Abbreviations XVI
List of Contributors XVIII

1 Climate Change Litigation in Brazil: an Introduction 1
*Maria Antonia Tigre, Armando Rocha and Délton Winter de Carvalho*

**SECTION 1**
***Challenges in Climate Litigation in Brazil***

2 A Panorama of Climate Litigation in Brazil 47
*Danielle de Andrade Moreira*

3 The Separation of Powers Principle and the Role of Different Bodies in Climate Action 67
*Enéas Xavier and Letícia Simo Veras*

4 The Role of Science in Climate Litigation 85
*Juliana de Augustinis*

**SECTION 2**
***Climate Litigation and Human Rights***

5 Recognizing the Paris Agreement as a Human Rights Treaty: the *Climate Fund* Case and Brazilian Courts 111
*Carolina de Figueiredo Garrido*

6 The Obligation to Protect the Stability of the Climate System under the Right to a Healthy Environment in Brazil 125
*Délton Winter de Carvalho and Armando Rocha*

7 Brazil and Advisory Opinions before International Courts and Tribunals: Participation and Impact of Advisory Opinions in Domestic Courts 140
*Paula Wojcikiewicz Almeida*

8 Access to Justice and Climate Litigation in Brazil 169
*Luciana Gross Cunha and Maria Cecília de Araujo Asperti*

**SECTION 3**
***Climate Litigation and Vulnerabilities***

9 Vulnerabilities in Climate Litigation: the Role of Gender, Race, and Poverty 185
*Mariana Belmont and Nauê Bernardo Pinheiro de Azevedo*

10 Decolonizing Climate Litigation: an Analysis of Indigenous Climate Litigation in Brazil 200
*Gabriel Mantelli, Maurício Terena, Isabela Bicalho and Marie-Louise Siemons*

11 Future Generations and Climate Litigation in Brazil 223
*Luciana Bauer*

**SECTION 4**
***Climate Litigation and Biodiversity***

12 The Protection of the Marine Environment through Litigation in the Context of the Climate Crisis in Brazil 245
*Julia Cirne Lima Weston*

13 The Protection of the Amazon Forest as a Central Aspect of Climate Mitigation 260
*Maria Antonia Tigre and Anna Maria Cárcamo*

14 The Rights of Nature: Another Legal Avenue for Climate Litigation in Brazil? 294
*Fernanda Cavedon-Capdeville, José Rubens Morato Leite, Humberto Filpi and Tônia Dutra*

## SECTION 5
## *Beyond the State: Climate Litigation and the Energy Transition*

15 The Role of Financial Institutions in Climate Litigation in Brazil 317
*Alessandra Lehmen*

16 The State's Duty to Pursue the Highest Possible Ambition 336
*Guilherme J. S. Leal*

17 Climate Damage and Tort Law in Brazilian Climate Litigation 360
*Rafaela Martins da Rosa*

18 Just Transition Litigation in Brazil 389
*Luiz Ormay Jr*

Appendix: Table of Cases 400
Index 423

# Foreword

It is a great pleasure to introduce this timely and significant volume on climate litigation in Brazil. At a moment when the world is witnessing an unprecedented surge in climate-related legal actions, this book offers invaluable insights into one of the most active and consequential areas of climate litigation. Brazil, with its vast natural resources and critical role in global environmental stability, has become a key battleground for the future of climate governance, and this volume comes at an opportune time.

Over the past few years, Brazil has seen a notable increase in climate litigation, largely in response to a troubling trend of deregulation and weakening of environmental and climate laws. This period of the rollback in environmental governance has demonstrated the crucial role that courts play in safeguarding the environment, compelling governmental accountability, and ensuring compliance with both domestic climate legislation and international climate commitments. Through strategic litigation, civil society, public prosecutors, and other key actors have mobilized the judiciary to uphold the rule of law and protect fundamental rights.

The Brazilian experience of using the courts to counterbalance deregulation offers important lessons for a global audience. The cases analyzed in this book illustrate not only the power of climate litigation to fill governance gaps but also the potential of judicial oversight in the fight against climate change. As countries around the world grapple with similar challenges—whether due to inadequate climate policies, insufficient enforcement, or shifting political priorities—the Brazilian example demonstrates how courts can be harnessed as a crucial mechanism in holding governments and corporations accountable.

For scholars, practitioners, and policymakers interested in understanding the evolving landscape of climate litigation, this volume provides rich and relevant case studies. The lessons emerging from Brazil resonate beyond its borders, offering strategies and legal frameworks that will undoubtedly inspire further action across jurisdictions. It is not only a book for Brazilian readers but a vital contribution to the global conversation on climate justice, underscoring the importance of courts as arenas for advancing climate action worldwide.

This collection serves as both a record of Brazil's unique journey in climate litigation and a resource for anyone invested in the growing international movement to confront the climate crisis through the rule of law.

*Michael B. Gerrard*
Andrew Sabin Professor of Professional Practice
Faculty Director, Sabin Center for Climate Change Law
Columbia Law School

# Acknowledgments

The editors would like to thank Andrea Longo, Antoine de Spiegeleir, Beatriz Garcia, Carla Amado Gomes, Felix Martin Lockman, Heloísa Oliveira, Jorge Carrillo Bañuelos, Maria José Alarcon, and Natalia Urzola for their expert insights into early stage presentations of the chapters contained in this volume in an online workshop held in March 2024. Furthermore, we would like to thank Columbia's Global Center in Rio de Janeiro for hosting a fruitful event discussing climate litigation in Brazil in February 2024.

All climate litigation cases mentioned in this edited volume are included in the Global Climate Litigation Database maintained by the Sabin Center for Climate Change Law. To help update the wide berth of climate cases, the Sabin Center partners with the Brazilian Climate Litigation Platform developed by researchers from PUC-Rio (JUMA Platform), which regularly maintains information on climate litigation in Portuguese. In particular, we are grateful to Danielle de Andrade Moreira, Carolina Garrido, Luciana Tse Chaves Garcia Rego, and Ana Paula Ricci for helping translate the summaries of all climate cases to English to be accessible to a broader audience.

We are thankful to Brill, in particular Marie Sheldon and Beth Derr, for believing in this project.

# Figures


1.1 Periodization of climate litigation in Brazil 14
4.1 The number of rulings referring to scientific evidence or empirical data about appropriate mitigation measures to limit global warming (green bar) and that did not refer to expert information (red bar) in the sample of 49 judgments 102
4.2 List of rulings including the date of judgment that appraised the complexity, trustworthiness, uncertainty, or consistency of evidence about mitigation measures 103
4.3 List of rulings including the date of judgment which used at least one criterion to assess the complexity, trustworthiness, uncertainty, or consistency of evidence about mitigation measures 104
7.1 Classification of actors submitting statements to the ITLOS 146
7.2 States' position on matters of jurisdiction before ITLOS advisory opinion on climate change 147
7.3 Brazilian participation in advisory opinions before the Inter-American Court of Human Rights 158
7.4 Comparative analysis of actors submitting *amicus curiae* to the Inter-American Court of Human Rights in advisory opinions 23/2017 and 32/2023 158
7.5 Inter-American Court of Human Rights' advisory opinions most cited in Brazilian supreme court's decisions 159
7.6 Judges from the Brazilian Supreme Court who mentioned the Inter-American Court of Human Rights' advisory opinions in their votes 159
10.1 Indigenous people protesting against the Guaíba coal mine project 215
10.2 Indigenous people protesting against the temporal framework thesis 218
13.1 Development of Brazilian climate cases related to the Amazon rainforest 268
13.2 Status of Brazilian climate cases related to the Amazon rainforest 268
13.3 Categories of Brazilian climate cases related to the Amazon rainforest 275

# Tables

4.1 List of Brazilian cases selected for analysis, filing date, summary, and case outcome as of November 2023 91
4.2 List of criteria used in the rulings to assess trustworthiness, consistency, or uncertainty of the evidence about mitigation measures to combat climate change 104
7.1 State and non-State actors authorized to participate in ICJ advisory opinion on climate change 160
7.2 Brazilian participation in ICJ advisory opinions 162
7.3 List of Brazilian participation at the Inter-American Court of Human Rights 165
7.4 List of ICJ contentious cases and advisory opinions mentioned in decisions by the Brazilian Supreme Court 166
10.1 Table of cases related to Indigenous groups' rights and climate change 208
13.1 Deforestation-related goals in Amazon countries' NDCs 264
13.2 Cases related to carbon credits and land grabbing 276
13.3 Cases related to climate damages for illegal deforestation 280
13.4 Cases related to illegal deforestation policy 283
13.5 Cases related to administrative omissions 286
13.6 Cases related to activity regulation 288
13.7 Cases related to forest fires 290

# Abbreviations

| | |
|---|---|
| ACHR | American Convention on Human Rights |
| ACP | *Ação Civil Pública* (Public Civil Action) |
| ADI | *Ação Direta de Inconstitucionalidade* (Direct Action of Unconstitutionality) |
| ADO | *Ação Direta de Inconstitucionalidade por Omissão* (Direct Action of Unconstitutionality for Omission) |
| ADPF | *Arguição de Descumprimento de Preceito Fundamental* (Claim for Noncompliance with a Fundamental Provision) |
| AR6 | IPCC's Sixth Assessment Report |
| BACEN | *Banco Central do Brasil* (Central Bank of Brazil) |
| CBAM | Carbon Border Adjustment Mechanism |
| CBDR-RC | common but differentiated responsibilities and respective capabilities |
| CFC | *Conselho Federal de Contadores* (Federal Council of Accountants) |
| CNJ | Conselho Nacional de Justiça (Brazilian National Council of Justice) |
| CoP | Conference of the Parties |
| CRD | Capital Requirements Directive |
| CS3D | Corporate Sustainability Due Diligence Directive |
| CSRD | Corporate Sustainability Reporting Directive |
| DFI | Development financial institution |
| CVM | *Commissão de Valores Mobiliários* (Brazilian securities regulator) |
| ECD | European Union Environmental Crime Directive |
| ESG | Environmental, Social, and Governance |
| ESRS | European Sustainability Reporting Standards |
| EU | European Union |
| ECHR | European Convention on Human Rights |
| ECtHR | European Court of Human Rights |
| EIA | Environmental Impact Assessment |
| EUDR | European Union Regulation for Deforestation-Free Products |
| EUST | European Union Sustainability Taxonomy |
| FEBRABAN | *Federação Brasileira de Bancos* (Brazilian Federation of Banks) |
| FPIC | Free, Prior, and Informed Consent |
| GCD | Green Claims Directive |
| GCF | Green Climate Fund |
| GHG | Greenhouse gas |
| GRSAC | Relatório de Riscos e Oportunidades Sociais, Ambientais e Climáticas (Social, Environmental and Climate Risks and Opportunities Report) |
| GST | Global Stocktake |
| HRC | United Nations Human Rights Committee |

| | |
|---|---|
| IFRS S1 | International Financial Reporting Standards Foundation General Requirements for Disclosure of Sustainability-related Financial Information |
| IFRS S2 | International Financial Reporting Standards Foundation Climate-related Disclosures |
| ISSB | International Sustainability Standards Board |
| IACtHR | Inter-American Court of Human Rights |
| IAHRS | Inter-American Human Rights System |
| ICJ | International Court of Justice |
| *IEA* | *Instituto de Estudos Amazônicos* |
| ITLOS | International Tribunal for the Law of the Sea |
| IPCC | Intergovernmental Panel on Climate Change |
| LDC | Least developed countries |
| NCQG | New Collective Quantified Goal |
| NDC | Nationally Determined Contribution |
| NGO | Non-Governmental Organization |
| OAS | Organization of American States |
| OASTS | Organization of American States Treaty Series |
| SDG | Sustainable Development Goal |
| SEEG | *Sistema de Estimativas de Emissões e Remoções de Gases de Efeito Estufa* (System for Estimating Greenhouse Gas Emissions and Removals) |
| STF | *Supremo Tribunal Federal* (Federal Supreme Court) |
| STJ | *Superior Tribunal de Justiça* (Superior Court of Justice) |
| UNCLOS | United Nations Convention on the Law of the Sea |
| UNFCCC | United Nations Framework Convention on Climate Change |
| UNGA | United Nations General Assembly |
| UNTS | United Nations Treaty Series |

# Contributors

## Editors

*Armando Rocha*
is a Professor of International Law, Law of the Sea, and Climate Change Law at *Universidade Católica Portuguesa* and researcher at the Católica Research Centre for the Future of Law. He is also an invited Professor at the Catholic University of Lille (France), member of the Young Scientists Seminar of the Academy of Sciences of Lisbon, member of the International Law Association Committee on the Protection of Persons at Sea, and coordinator of the Law Schools Global League research group on Environmental Regulation.

*Maria Antonia Tigre*
is the Director for Global Climate Change Litigation at the Sabin Center for Climate Change Law at Columbia Law School. She previously worked as a Senior Attorney at the Environment Program of the Cyrus R. Vance Center for International Justice. She served as the Deputy Director for the Global Network for Human Rights and the Environment (GNHRE). She has authored numerous publications on regional and international environmental law, specifically focusing on environmental rights, the evolution of international environmental law, and climate litigation. Her research also encompasses the protection of the Amazon rainforest ecosystem. She has three sons.

*Délton Winter de Carvalho*
is a Professor of Environmental Law, Disaster Law and Climate Change Law at *UNISINOS*, Brazil. Attorney at Law. He has taught at the University of California, Berkeley and UC Berkeley. He is a research grantee of CAPES's Climate Emergency Program. His main publications include 'Climate Litigation to Protect the Brazilian Amazon: Establishing a Constitutional Right to a Stable Climate' (co-written with Joana Setzer) (2021) 30 *Review of European, Comp, & Int'l Environmental Law* 197–206 and 'The Ore Tailings Dam Rupture Disaster in Mariana, Brazil 2015: What Do We Have to Learn from Anthropogenic Disasters' (2019) 59(2) *Natural Resources Journal* 281–300.

## Authors

*Paula Wojcikiewicz Almeida*
is a Full Professor of International Law at FGV Rio Law (since 2008). She is the Director of the Centre for Global Law and director of the Jean Monnet Centre of

Excellence on EU-Latin America Global Challenges, sponsored by the European Commission (2023-2026). She is also the Director of the Jean Monnet Centre of Excellence on EU-South America Global Governance (2019-2023) and an Associate Researcher at the Institute of International and European Law at the Sorbonne (IREDIES). Paula has a doctorate with honors summa cum laude in International and European Law at the Université Paris 1 Panthéon-Sorbonne. She is the Director of Studies of the French-speaking section, 6th edition of the Winter Courses on International Law, organized by the Hague Academy of International Law (2024).

*Maria Cecília de Araujo Asperti*
is a Professor at the São Paulo Law School of the Getúlio Vargas Foundation (FGV Direito SP). She has a Ph.D. in Procedural Law from the University of São Paulo. Maria Cecília is the coordinator of the Access to Justice, Process, and Alternative Dispute Resolution Methods Center (NAJUPMESC).

*Juliana de Augustinis*
is a doctoral researcher at Tilburg University in the Department of Public Law and Governance. She conducts research in the Sectorplan Project "Judicial Law-making in a Global Legal Order: Rationalization, Participation and the Role of Scientific Evidence", funded by the Dutch Ministry of Education, Culture, and Science. She is also a member of the Transformative Effects of Globalization in Law (TEGL) research project, a collaboration between law faculties in the Netherlands. Her primary research interests concern constitutional and administrative law, public interest litigation, climate protection, comparative approaches, and empirical legal studies.

*Nauê Bernardo Pinheiro de Azevedo*
is a lawyer and political scientist from the University of Brasília. He has a specialization in Public Law from the Higher School of Magistracy of the Federal District. He holds a Master's degree (LL.M.) in European Private Law from the Università degli Studi "Mediterranea" di Reggio Calabria (2022) and a Master's degree in Constitutional Law from the Brazilian Institute of Teaching, Development, and Research of Brasília (IDP) (2023). He is a partner at De Jongh Martins Advogados.

*Luciana Bauer*
is a member of Judges for Democracy Brazil. She is a lecturer in Climate Change, Democracy and Human Rights and a global lawyer. A former federal judge at the 4th Brazilian Federal Circuit, Luciana is a Ph.D. candidate in Legal Science at the University of Vale do Itajaí—Univali (Brazil), in a Dual Degree with Widener University at Delaware Law School (United States). She is a guardian of future generations.

*Mariana Belmont*
is a journalist, born in Parelheiros (the southernmost part of the city of São Paulo), working in coordination and communication of public policies. She has held government positions on environmental and housing issues in São Paulo. Mariana worked as the communication coordinator for the Bocaina Mosaic of Protected Areas at the Chico Mendes Institute for Biodiversity Conservation (ICMBio). She served as Superintendent of Programs and Director of Climate and City at the Peregum Black Reference Institute. Mariana was a columnist for UOL and currently writes monthly for the Gender and Number portal. She is also an activist, involved in environmental and peripheral movements. Recently, she was a guest editor for the "Socio-Environmental Dialogues: Environmental Racism" magazine at the Federal University of ABCD. She is the organizer of the book "Environmental Racism and Climate Emergencies in Brazil" (Oralituras, 2023). Mariana currently works as an advisor on climate and environmental racism at Geledés—Black Women's Institute.

*Isabela Bicalho*
is pursuing a Master's degree in Public International Law at the University of São Paulo (USP). She graduated with a degree in Law from the Federal University of Uberlândia (UFU) and participated in a paid international mobility program at Lusófona University of Humanities and Technologies through the Associação das Universidades de Língua Portuguesa (AULP). She is currently a Legal Assistant at Hotta Advocacia, in collaboration with Pogust Goodhead.

*Fernanda Cavedon-Capdeville*
is a postdoctoral researcher at the Federal University of Santa Catarina (UFSC, Brazil). She was previously a postdoctoral researcher at the University of Limoges (France). Fernanda has a Ph.D. in Environmental Law at the University of Alicante (Spain); a Ph.D. in Juridical Sciences at the University of Itajaí Valley (UNIVALI, Brazil); a D.E.A. in Environmental Law at the University of Alicante (Spain). She is a member of the International Centre for Comparative Environmental Law (CIDCE, France). She has over 25 years of research experience on ecological law, human rights, disaster risk reduction and climate change, authoring distinct articles and book chapters. She is an independent consultant for international organizations on issues related to climate migration.

*Anna Maria Cárcamo*
is a Brazilian-qualified lawyer with a focus on environmental and climate change law and policy through a climate justice lens. She graduated in Law

from the Pontifical Catholic University of Rio de Janeiro and earned a Master's in Environmental Management from the Yale School of the Environment. Anna has extensive experience with civil society and international organizations, including the United Nations Climate Change Secretariat.

*Délton Winter de Carvalho*
is a Professor of Environmental Law, Disaster Law and Climate Change Law at *UNISINOS*, Brazil. Attorney at Law. He has taught at the University of California, Berkeley and UC Berkeley. He is a research grantee of CAPES's Climate Emergency Program. His main publications include 'Climate Litigation to Protect the Brazilian Amazon: Establishing a Constitutional Right to a Stable Climate' (co-written with Joana Setzer) (2021) 30 *Review of European, Comp, & Int'l Environmental Law* 197-206 and 'The Ore Tailings Dam Rupture Disaster in Mariana, Brazil 2015: What Do We Have to Learn from Anthropogenic Disasters' (2019) 59(2) *Natural Resources Journal* 281-300.

*Luciana Gross Cunha*
is a Professor at the São Paulo Law School of the Getulio Vargas Foundation (FGV Direito SP). She holds a Ph.D. in Political Science from the University of São Paulo. She is the coordinator of the Justice and Constitution Center (NJC) and the Access to Justice, Process, and Alternative Dispute Resolution Methods Center (NAJUPMESC).

*Tônia Dutra*
is a professor and researcher, with a Post-Doctorate in Law at the Federal University of Santa Catarina by CNPq. She is a member of the Research Group Environmental Law and Political Ecology in the Risk Society—GPDA/UFSC, and the Speak4Nature Project: interdisciplinary approaches on ecological justice (Horizon Europe—Research and innovation programme MSCA Staff Exchanges).

*Humberto Filpi*
is a Ph.D. candidate and Master in Law at the Federal University of Santa Catarina (UFSC), in the area of International Law and Sustainability. He holds a Master's degree from the Federal University of Santa Catarina (UFSC). He is a specialist in civil procedure. Humberto is a researcher at Environmental Law in the Risk Society Research Group (GPDA/UFSC). He is a member of the Global Network for Human Rights and the Environment (GNHRE) and LACLIMA (Latin American Climate Lawyers Initiative for Mobilizing Action). He is the author of the book "Litigância Climática Ecologizada: Contribuições da América Latina" (2021).

*Carolina de Figueiredo Garrido*
is a member of the research group Law, Environment and Justice in the Anthropocene (JUMA/NIMA/PUC-Rio) and a research fellow at the Interdisciplinary Observatory of Climate Change (OIMC) of the State University of Rio de Janeiro (UERJ). She holds a master's degree in State Theory and Constitutional Law and a post-graduate diploma in Brazilian Environmental Law from the Pontifical Catholic University of Rio de Janeiro (PUC-Rio). She also acts as a Rapporteur for Brazil at the Sabin Center's Peer Review Network of Climate Litigation. Her research focuses on climate litigation and the mobilization of the law to promote climate justice.

*Guilherme J. S. Leal*
is an environmental lawyer with over 20 years of practice. He holds a master's degree in Energy Law from the University College London, UK, and in Environmental Law from George Washington University, USA. He lectures Environmental Law in postgraduate courses at the Pontifical Catholic University of Rio de Janeiro, Brazil. He is also co-leader of the Climate, Energy and Sustainable Finance Chamber of the Brazilian Business Council for Sustainable Development—CEBDS (2024/2026 biennium).

*Alessandra Lehmen*
is a lawyer admitted in New York and Brazil, as well as President of the Brazilian Bar Environmental Law Commission, Rio Grande do Sul State. She is a Post-doctoral Laureate, Make Our Planet Great Again Program, Presidency of France; and holds a Ph.D. from the Federal University of Rio Grande do Sul and an LL.M. from Stanford Law School. She is a W50 Leadership Scholar, London School of Economics and Political Science; a Stanford Woods Institute Rising Environmental Leaders Fellow; a Law Professor at Caxias do Sul University, Brazil; Head of ESG at 30% Club Brazil; a member of the IUCN World Commission on Environmental Law; Brazil Country Rapporteur at the Climate Change Legal Initiative; and a Legal Fellow at the Centre for International Sustainable Development Law.

*Gabriel Mantelli*
is a Ph.D. candidate in Legal Theory at the University of São Paulo (USP) and recently undertook a visiting research period at the Geneva Graduate Institute. He holds a Master's degree in Law and Development from the Getúlio Vargas Foundation (FGV), where he also completed a visiting research period at Kent Law School, and a Bachelor's degree in Law from USP. He has served as a Lecturer at São Judas University (USJT) and is a Senior Associate at Hotta Advocacia, in collaboration with Pogust Goodhead.

*José Rubens Morato Leite*
is a Full Professor at the Federal University of Santa Catarina. He is the former president of the Institute 'Law for a Green Planet' (2013-2018) and coordinator of the Research Group on Environmental Law and Political Ecology in the Risk Society at CNPq/UFSC. José Rubens is an elected member of the governing board of the IUCN Academy of Environmental Law (2015 to 2018).

*Danielle de Andrade Moreira*
is the founder and coordinator of the Research Group "Law, Environment, and Justice in the Anthropocene" (JUMA), which integrates the Environmental Law Division of the Interdisciplinary Center for the Environment (NIMA-Jur) at the Pontifical Catholic University of Rio de Janeiro (PUC-Rio). She has a Doctorate and Master's in Law from the State University of Rio de Janeiro (UERJ). Professor at PUC-Rio, working with the Postgraduate Program in Law and NIMA-Jur. She is the academic coordinator of the Association of Environmental Law Professors in Brazil (APRODAB) and the director of the Institute "The Law for a Green Planet". She was legal Vice-President of the Deliberative Council of the Brazilian Fund for Biodiversity (FUNBIO) and legal advisor to FUNBIO, the Rio de Janeiro's Environmental Protection Agency (currently INEA), and the State Institute of Forestry Foundation (IEF/RJ, currently INEA). Danielle is the mother of Bruna, Tiago, and Flora.

*Enéas Xavier*
is a Ph.D. candidate at the University of Montreal, and a researcher at LACLIMA (Latin American Climate Lawyers Initiative for Mobilizing Action) and the NETI-USP (Centre for the Study of International Courts at the University of São Paulo's Faculty of Law). His research focuses on civil society participation in the UN conferences on climate change, the monitoring of climate negotiations, and the enforcement of States' engagements to tackle climate change. As an environmental lawyer, he works for NGOs in environmental litigation and has recently contributed to the development of written opinions submitted to the Inter-American Court of Human Rights.

*Luiz Ormay Jr*
is a lawyer and Ph.D. candidate at the University of Brasília, whose research is focused on constitutional and social and environmental law. Luiz holds graduated from the Federal University of Mato Grosso do SUL (UFMS) and holds a Master's in Law from the same university. He has a vast experience in environmental and climate litigation.

*Armando Rocha*
is a Professor of International Law, Law of the Sea, and Climate Change Law at *Universidade Católica Portuguesa* and researcher at the Católica Research Centre for the Future of Law. He is also an invited Professor at the Catholic University of Lille (France), member of the Young Scientists Seminar of the Academy of Sciences of Lisbon, member of the International Law Association Committee on the Protection of Persons at Sea, and coordinator of the Law Schools Global League research group on Environmental Regulation.

*Rafaela Martins da Rosa*
is a Federal Judge in Brazil. Ph.D. in Law from Unisinos. Visiting Researcher at the University of California, Berkeley Law. Judge Trainer at the National School of Magistrate Training in Brazil (ENFAM). Professor of Environmental Law and Climate Change in Brazilian Judiciary Schools. Collaborator at the National Council of Justice to implement the National Policy of the Judiciary for the Environment.

*Marie-Louise Siemons*
is a final-year Law undergraduate at the Pontifical Catholic University of São Paulo (PUC-SP). She was awarded a PIBIC-CNPq scholarship, under which she conducted scientific research on mining activities on Indigenous lands in Brazil. She was also a member of the Environmental Law Clinic Paulo Nogueira Neto at the University of São Paulo (CPaNN/USP) and contributed to the research team at the NGO World's Youth for Climate Justice. She is a Legal Intern at Hotta Advocacia, in collaboration with Pogust Goodhead.

*Maurício Serpa França (Maurício Terena)*
is an Indigenous lawyer, the Legal Coordinator at the Articulation of Indigenous Peoples of Brazil (APIB), and a lawyer for the Council of the Terena People. He holds a degree in Law and a Master's in Education, with a research focus on the criminalization of Indigenous leaders and territorial conflicts. He is a Ph.D. candidate in Social Anthropology at the University of São Paulo (USP).

*Maria Antonia Tigre*
is the Director for Global Climate Change Litigation at the Sabin Center for Climate Change Law at Columbia Law School. She previously worked as a Senior Attorney at the Environment Program of the Cyrus R. Vance Center for International Justice. She served as the Deputy Director for the Global Network for Human Rights and the Environment (GNHRE). She has authored numerous publications on regional and international environmental law, specifically

focusing on environmental rights, the evolution of international environmental law, and climate litigation. Her research also encompasses the protection of the Amazon rainforest ecosystem. She has three sons.

*Letícia Simo Veras*
is an International lawyer. Professor of International Law, Political Economy and Extension at the Methodist University of Piracicaba. Master's student in Public International Law at the University of São Paulo. Graduate in International Law from CEDIN/MG. President of the International Law Commission of the 8th Subsection of the São Paulo Bar Association. Member of GEDC/USP—Comparative Law Study Group. Former volunteer in the Mediation and Conflict Resolution Project for Refugees and Immigrants, an initiative between IPB—Instituto Pro Bono de São Paulo and ProMigra. She holds a Bachelor's degree in Law from UNIMEP and studied Public International Law with an emphasis on the Legal Institutions of the European Union, International Criminal Law, and International Justice at the University of Seville in Spain. As a researcher in International Refugee Law, she develops projects in the field of public policies for the reception of migrants, and human rights, as well as comparative studies on Law and Public Policies for Refugees in Brazil and Spain. Lecturer on public and private international law.

*Julia Cirne Lima Weston*
is a Ph.D. candidate and researcher at the Católica Research Centre for the Future of Law at Universidade Católica Portuguesa in Lisbon. She holds an LL.M. in International Law from University College London and a Bachelor's degree in Law from Pontifícia Universidade Católica do Rio Grande do Sul. Her previous work experience includes the International Tribunal for the Law of the Sea and the United Nations Division for Ocean Affairs and the Law of the Sea.

CHAPTER 1

# Climate Change Litigation in Brazil: an Introduction

*Maria Antonia Tigre**, Armando Rocha*** *and Délton Winter de Carvalho****

## 1 Introduction

If 'life is a dangerous business,' as João Guimarães Rosa wrote in *Grande Sertão: Veredas* [*The Devil to Pay in the Backlands*: 1956], climate change and its related effects are likely to make life conditions much harder than today. According to the scientific assessment produced by the Intergovernmental Panel on Climate Change (IPCC), global emissions of greenhouse gasses (GHGs) and their excessive concentration in the atmosphere are responsible for an increase in the average temperature on the Earth's surface (global warming), which disrupts the delicate balance of our climate system (climate change) and is responsible for a set of consequences that affect the conditions that sustain life as we know in our planet.

In this scenario, States' action to mitigate and adapt to climate change is urgently needed. Still, the rhythm of GHG emissions is actually increasing[1] as a result of the lack, poor design, or poor implementation of climate mitigation policies. Just like Cassandra, a character from Greek mythology who received the gift of seeing the future but was cursed with the fate of never being believed, the warnings of climate scientists also seem not to be a priority for policymakers.[2] Unsurprisingly, hence, 'climate litigation' is increasing

* *Sabin Center for Climate Change Law*, Columbia Law School, https://orcid.org/0000-0003-4308-1958, email: mb4913@columbia.edu

** *Universidade Católica Portuguesa*, School of Law, Católica Research Centre for the Future of Law, https://orcid.org/0000-0002-8181-1512, email: armandorocha@ucp.pt

*** *Universidade do Vale do Rio dos Sinos*, School of Law, https://orcid.org/0000-0001-9469-5779, email: delton@deltoncarvalho.com.br

1. United Nations Environment Programme, *Emissions Gap Report 2023: Broken Record—Temperatures Hit New Highs, Yet World Fails to Cut Emissions (Again)* (UNEP 2023), available at <https://doi.org/10.59117/20.500.11822/43922>, accessed 31 August 2024.
2. Armando Rocha, 'Conclusions: Courts as Agents of Change', in D'Alessandro & Castagno (eds), *Reports and Essays on Climate Change Litigation* (Università di Torino 2024) 217, 217.

 | DOI:10.1163/9789004690974_002

worldwide as a means to pressure States to adopt and implement (more) ambitious climate mitigation measures that may guide societies into a carbon-neutral future. This pivotal shift to litigation results from the initiative of concerned individuals, civil society movements, and some affected States, and the shift is noticeable in the docket of a vast array of domestic, regional, and international courts and tribunals.

The Global South is no exception to this trend, where a particular notable expansion is visible more recently.[3] In this geographic context, Brazil stands out as a particularly important case study. For several reasons (Eg the reliance on coal for energy production purposes, the need to socially and economically assist a wide sector of its population, or the geographic distribution of its population), Brazil is a relevant GHG emitter per capita (although not in absolute terms).[4] As a result, reducing GHG emissions is a priority for Brazil, notwithstanding the need to protect the vulnerable sectors of society and enhance social and economic development. Furthermore, the forecasts of future weather patterns suggest that Brazil will likely be affected by varied climate change-related events (from sea level rise to desertification). More particularly, the unique biome and rich biodiversity lying in Brazil are of core importance for the balance of the world's biosphere, but seem to be threatened by climate change-related impacts. Nonetheless, Brazil also holds pivotal tools to cope with climate change, namely by protecting and preserving natural sinks such as the Amazon or the Pantanal forests, or the mangroves in marine habitats. In this seemingly quixotic fight for mitigating climate change, Brazil is a key 'emitter,' 'victim,' and 'part of the solution' at the same time.

Hence, climate litigation in Brazil is evolving in a manner that incorporates all these dimensions. This introductory chapter does not explore in detail the Brazilian experience of climate litigation, which is spread throughout this edited book. Still, it aims to explain the *global* importance of climate litigation in Brazil (Section 2), discuss the role played by the Brazilian Judiciary, within the limits of their competence under the separation of powers principle, to pressure the federal State and other public authorities to enhance climate policies

---

3 See, among others, Melanie Jean Murcott & Maria Antonia Tigre, 'Developments, Opportunities, and Complexities in Global South Climate Litigation: Introduction to the Special Collection' (2024) 16 *Journal of Human Rights Practice* 1; Jacqueline Peel & Jolene Lin, 'Transnational Climate Litigation: The Contribution of the Global South' (2019) 113 *AJIL* 679, 723.

4 For a brief overview of Brazil's emissions, see the country report in 'Climate Transparency,' available at <https://www.climate-transparency.org>, and more specifically, Brazil—Climate Transparency Report: Comparing G20 Climate Action (Climate Transparency, 2022), available at <https://www.climate-transparency.org/wp-content/uploads/2022/10/CT2022-Brazil-Web.pdf>, last accessed 31 August 2024.

(Section 3), provide a periodization of climate litigation in Brazil to understand how and why courts' activism has been growing more recently (Section 4), explore the reasons why climate litigation in Brazil has been mostly a rights-based experience (Section 5), and provide an overview of this book's structure (Section 6). A more in-depth analysis of each topic specific to climate litigation in Brazil is found in this book's chapters. For the purpose of this analysis, the notion of 'climate litigation' used here and throughout this book is the Sabin Center for Climate Change Law's operational definition, which focuses on cases where 'climate change law, policy, or science must be a material issue of law or fact.'[5] This broad definition is intended to cover a wide range of cases that either directly or indirectly engage with climate change-related law, policy, or science. Cases and numbers were updated until September 2024.

## 2 A Climate Litigation Experience of Global Interest

Despite the surge of climate litigation in the Global South, its involvement had barely received any attention prior to 2019, with a significant discrepancy in the scholarly and media notice given its experience compared to climate litigation in the Global North.[6] As such, an edited book focused on climate litigation in Brazil, targeted at an audience beyond the Brazilian context, would be unimaginable a few years ago. Yet, the visibility of climate litigation research about and from the Global South is increasing.[7] This focus is crucial because climate litigation in these regions often addresses transnational issues that impact global climate policies and practices. The strength and effectiveness of judicial rulings in the Global South, as noted by Setzer and Benjamin, demonstrate the significance of these cases in shaping global climate governance.[8] By providing a new angle of analysis to common problems, and often innovative legal solutions to address such concerns, rulings from the Global South can be a useful inspiration for courts worldwide.

In fact, one reason to study the stocktake of judicial decisions from the Global South is explained by the distinction, in the theory of law, between legal concepts and conceptions. Legal concepts aim to crystalize a normative

5 'About—Climate Change Litigation' (Sabin Center for Climate Change Law) available at <https://climatechart.com/about/>, accessed 31 August 2024.

6 Peel & Lin (n 3) 723.

7 Murcott & Tigre (n 3).

8 Joana Setzer & Lisa Benjamin, 'Climate Change Litigation in the Global South: Filling in Gaps' (2020) 114 *AJIL Unbound* 56.

experience of the past in a phrasal formulation,[9] and they work as an epistemological tool for the categorization of facts as a result of a particularly distinctive note such facts share.[10] In the theory of law, concepts differ from conceptions—and one concept can be shared universally at the abstract level, although individuals share different conceptions of the same concept.[11] Conceptions, in fact, refer not to semantics or a phrasal formulation of a concept or idea, but rather to how one's worldview and cultural affiliation shape the understanding of that concept. For instance, there is no significant divergence among Brazilian, North American, or European courts regarding the concepts of 'separation of powers' and 'judicial discretion'—but the practice of these courts shows that they share a different understanding of what their role in society is and thus how they perceive the limits of their competence, although using the same phrasal formulation for those legal concepts. Differences in courts' practice do not result from the spell of a concept, but rather from judges' belongingness to different cultural worldviews that shape their understanding of the law as a social system and the courts' position in a legal system. Studying an experience from the Global South (and, more specifically, from Brazil), and focusing on these nuances, provides the ingredients to test, explore, and transplant innovative solutions to different parts of the world.

The experience of courts from other jurisdiction, when facing what one could call 'clone' disputes (ie disputes that raise the application of the same body of rules and principles, related to climate change mitigation and/or adaptation, to comparable facts) can be helpful for a judge who needs to provide a solution for a case that challenges the very fabric of the legal system. Yet, more often than not, the assessment of 'global' climate litigation was not truly global. Instead, it focused on cases and experiences from the Global North, leaving much of the 'rest of the world' on the periphery of a global experience. For scholars around the world, the stocktake of judicial decisions from the Global South seemed to form an exo-planet not belonging, or relevant, to the practice of the Global North. Nonetheless, with the growth of a recent body of scholarship focused on the Global South, these 'other' experiences become more shared and discussed.

9 Niklas Luhmann, *Law as a Social System* (OUP 2004) 340.

10 Karl Larenz & Claus-Wilhelm Canaris, *Methodenlehre der Rechtswissenschaft* (3rd edn, Springer 1995) 267.

11 On the difference between concepts and conceptions, see Ronald Dworkin, *Law's Empire* (Hart 1998) 70 ff.

Latin America (LATAM), in particular, is 'quietly leading a revolution' in climate litigation, as noted by Tigre et al.[12] This experience relies on the fact that the region has (i) a growing number of cases, (ii) based on environmental and human rights, (iii) that ground claims for climate justice and (iv) facilitate the understanding of the nature and extent of climate threats.[13] Indeed, Latin America and the Caribbean encompassed, as of April 2024, 70 percent of cases from the Global South. That totaled 154 cases spread across nine jurisdictions.[14] The promise and significance of climate litigation in the region is, as explained by Auz, due to (i) widespread recognition of the constitutional right to a healthy environment, (ii) the region's generally permissive legal standing provisions, (iii) its monist constitutional architecture, (iv) and the role of the Inter-American Human Rights System (IAHRS) in promoting progressive standards at the domestic level[15]—where a standalone right to a healthy environment is recognized both in Article 11 of the San Salvador Protocol[16] and in the case law of the Inter-American Court of Human Rights (IACtHR) that sees in Article 26 of the American Convention on Human Rights (ACHR)[17] the same right to a healthy environment.[18] This promise becomes even more significant with the advent of the forthcoming advisory opinion on climate change by the IACtHR requested by Chile and Colombia.[19] Within this regional context, Brazil is both an example and a lesson for countries within the region and beyond.

---

12 Maria Antonia Tigre, Natalia Urzola & Alexandra Goodman, 'Climate Litigation in Latin America: Is the Region Quietly Leading a Revolution?' (2023) 14 *Journal of Human Rights and the Environment* 67, 69.

13 ibid 69.

14 Maria Antonia Tigre, *Climate Litigation in the Global South: Mapping Report* (Sabin Center for Climate Change Law 2024) 82, available at <https://scholarship.law.columbia.edu/cgi/viewcontent.cgi?article=1231&context=sabin_climate_change>.

15 Juan Auz, 'Human Rights-based Climate Litigation: A Latin America Cartography' (2022) 13(1) *Journal of Human Rights and the Environment* 114, 116.

16 Additional Protocol to the ACHR in the Area of Economic, Social and Cultural Rights (adopted 17 November 1988, entered into force 16 November 1999) OASTS No 69. However, pursuant to Article 19(6) of the San Salvador Protocol, *a contrario sensu*, the right to a healthy environment under Article 11 of this protocol is non-justiciable.

17 American Convention on Human Rights (adopted 22 November 1969, entered into force 18 July 1978) OASTS No 36.

18 *Environment and Human Rights (State Obligations in relation to the Environment in the context of the Protection and Guarantee of the Rights to Life and to Personal Integrity—Interpretation and Scope of Articles 4(1) and 5(1) of the American Convention on Human Rights)*, Advisory Opinion OC-23/17, IACtHR Series A No 23 (15 November 2017).

19 Request for an Advisory Opinion on the Climate Emergency and Human Rights submitted to the Inter-American Court of Human Rights by the Republic of Colombia and

Significantly, Brazil has recently experienced a political process of deregulation, which aimed at reducing and/or removing environmental- and climate-related legal barriers to the development of economic projects. Ironically, the reaction against this deregulation helps explain Brazil's upsurge in climate litigation, which now stands at the forefront of the global climate litigation movement, reflecting a broader trend in emerging economies. Unfortunately, the experience of deregulation is not isolated, and a similar 'trend' is already observed and expected in Argentina.[20] Mirroring such a litigation upsurge in response to a (political) deregulation process in climate change could, therefore, provide a fighting stance for climate change mitigation and adaptation regionally, with Brazil as an example for Argentina and possibly other countries.

Unsurprisingly, scholars are now paying close attention to developments from Brazilian courts and singling out features unique to climate litigation in Brazil[21]—such as qualifying the Paris Agreement as a part of the genre of human rights treaties. As expertly detailed in Chapter 2 by Danielle de Andrade Moreira, the first climate case in Brazil was filed in 2007, but Brazil's climate litigation landscape has accelerated and diversified significantly since 2018.[22] As of September 2024, the country is home to 88 climate cases.[23] According to the Grantham Institute's 2024 report on global climate litigation, Brazil ranked third globally in the number of cases filed in 2023, trailing only the United

the Republic of Chile (9 January 2023) <https://www.corteidh.or.cr/docs/opiniones/soc_1_2023_en.pdf> accessed 12 August 2023.

20 Maxwell Radwin, 'Sweeping reform package threatens environmental protections in Argentina, critics say,' *Mongabay* (28 June 2024), available at https://news.mongabay.com/2024/06/sweeping-reform-package-threatens-environmental-protections-in-argentina-critics-say/.

21 Eg Letícia Albuquerque et al, 'Emergência Climática e Direitos Humanos: O Caso do Fundo Clima no Brasil e as Obrigações de Direito Internacional' (2022) 19 *Revista de Direito Internacional* 126; Danielle de Andrade Moreira, Ana Lucia Nina, Carolina de Figueiredo Garrido & Maria Eduarda Segovia Neves, 'Rights-Based Climate Litigation in Brazil: An Assessment of Constitutional Cases before the Brazilian Supreme Court' (2024) 16 *Journal of Human Rights Practice* 7; Joana Setzer & Délton Winter de Carvalho, 'Climate Litigation to Protect the Brazilian Amazon: Establishing a Constitutional Right to a Stable Climate' (2021) 30 *RECIEL* 197; Maria Antonia Tigre & Joana Setzer, 'Human Rights and Climate Change for Climate Litigation in Brazil and Beyond: An Analysis of the Climate Fund Decision' (2023) 54 *Georgetown JIL* 593.

22 See Danielle de Andrade Moreira (Chapter 2).

23 Brazil—Climate Change Litigation' (Sabin Center for Climate Change Law) available at <http://climatecasechart.com/non-us-jurisdiction/brazil/>, accessed 16 September 2024.

States and the United Kingdom.[24] Additionally, Brazil holds the fourth-highest aggregate number of climate cases worldwide, following the United States, Australia, and the United Kingdom.[25] Within the Global South, Brazil leads with the highest number of cases, accounting for 39% of climate litigation in Latin America.[26] There is strength in numbers. This rapid rise underscores Brazil's pivotal role in the global climate justice movement and highlights its significant contribution to the broader trend of increasing climate-related legal action. Significantly, numbers are constantly changing and only tell part of the story. The chapters in this edited book were written and finalized in different months and might have different numbers or rankings. Regardless, Brazil shows an upward trend in the number of cases, which justifies the focus of this book.

The dynamic nature of climate litigation in Brazil reflects an evolving legal landscape where the number of decided and pending cases rapidly increases. This surge in climate-related litigation mirrors broader trends in Latin America, where the recognition of environmental rights and the push for stronger climate action are gaining momentum.[27] As these cases continue to unfold, they have the potential to reshape legal frameworks and influence climate policies across the region. The outcomes of pending cases may lead to significant shifts in legal precedents, affecting both national and regional approaches to climate governance.

While these statistics show the relevance of climate litigation within Brazil, the significance of Brazil's climate litigation extends beyond national borders. This importance underscores its global prominence due to the critical role of Brazil's biodiversity worldwide, especially the Amazon rainforest, and the substantial GHG emissions captured annually that are crucial for global stability. The Amazon, often referred to as the 'lungs of the Earth,' plays a crucial role in regulating the planet's climate by absorbing carbon dioxide and generating oxygen. The Amazon rainforest absorbs roughly 2 billion tons of $CO_2$eq

24 See Joana Setzer & Catherine Higham, *Global Trends in Climate Litigation: 2024 Snapshot* (Grantham Research Institute on Climate Change and the Environment 2024) available at <https://www.lse.ac.uk/granthaminstitute/wp-content/uploads/2024/06/Global-trends-in-climate-change-litigation-2024-snapshot.pdf>.

25 ibid 2.

26 Tigre (n 14) 82.

27 See Maria Antonia Tigre, 'International Recognition of the Right to a Healthy Environment: What Is the Added Value for Latin America and the Caribbean?' (2023) 117 *AJIL Unbound* 184.

annually, but deforestation and degradation have diminished its capacity, contributing to increased global carbon emissions.[28] Brazil, home to approximately 60% of the Amazon, is at the center of this issue.

Additionally, according to data regarding 2021 emissions, Brazil is among the top ten global emitters of GHG, responsible for the emission of 1531.51 $MtCO_2eq$.[29] Studies also suggest that the oceans are the major global GHG sink, which explains the current process of ocean acidification, sea-level rise, or the destruction of fragile marine habitats and ecosystems.[30] In this sense, the oceans are a 'victim' of climate change, but sea-level rise and the destruction of coastal habitats and ecosystems are also a concern in terms of adaptation. In the advisory opinion recently rendered by the International Tribunal for the Law of the Sea (ITLOS), the tribunal emphasized that coastal States have an obligation to protect, preserve, and ameliorate the marine environment—which is especially important in the case of Brazil, which holds a long coastline, extensive maritime zones, and marine ecosystems of global significance such as mangroves, thus requiring immediate preservation measures.[31]

Given these factors, Brazil's climate litigation is not only pivotal for its domestic climate policies but also for the global climate system. The country's actions in this arena have far-reaching implications, influencing international climate negotiations and strategies due to its significant environmental and carbon footprint. Therefore, Brazil's proactive stance in climate litigation highlights its crucial role in global climate governance and underscores the interconnectedness of national and global climate efforts. So far, the importance of the Amazon rainforest for global efforts to mitigate GHG has put a spotlight on climate litigation related to the protection of this ecosystem—but, in fact, the overall significance of Brazil to the global effort of mitigation and adaptation extends much beyond the importance of the Amazon.

---

28 See, among others, Luciana V Gatti et al, 'Amazonia as a Carbon Source Linked to Deforestation and Climate Change' (2021) 595 *Nature* 388–393; Thaís M Rosan et al, 'Synthesis of the Land Carbon Fluxes of the Amazon Region between 2010 and 2020' (2024) 5 *Communications Earth & Environment*.

29 See 'Historical GHG Emissions' (Climate Watch Data) available at <https://www.climatewatchdata.org/ghg-emissions>, accessed 16 September 2024.

30 Eg Hans-Otto Pörtner et al, *IPCC Special Report on the Ocean and Cryosphere in a Changing Climate* (CUP 2022).

31 *Request for an Advisory Opinion submitted by the Commission of Small Island States on Climate Change and International Law* (Advisory Opinion of 21 May 2024) Case No 31, available at <https://www.itlos.org/fileadmin/itlos/documents/cases/31/Advisory_Opinion/C31_Adv_Op_21.05.2024_orig.pdf>. See Julia Weston (Chapter 9).

Publishing this analysis now, even as several cases remain unresolved, is crucial for several reasons. First, it offers a timely snapshot of the current state of climate litigation, highlighting emerging patterns and challenges that could define the future of climate law in Brazil, Latin America, and beyond. Second, it underscores the importance of understanding the evolving role of the judiciary in addressing climate change, particularly as courts become key arenas for advancing climate justice.[32] Finally, as the number of cases continues to grow, this publication serves as an essential resource for scholars, practitioners, judges, and policymakers, providing insights that can inform ongoing and future legal strategies in the fight against climate change. Historically, legal analysis and theory have thrived on preliminary decisions and the filing of cases, which already offer valuable insights and drive critical discussions about the global scope of climate litigation. This proactive approach ensures that critical lessons are drawn from current legal strategies, reinforcing the importance of early intervention and continuous legal innovation in the fight against climate change.

Furthermore, these cases can wield global influence for several other compelling reasons. First, Brazil underwent a period of environmental and climate deregulation, partly explaining the upsurge in litigation before domestic courts.[33] Second, the rights-based interpretation of the Paris Agreement by the Brazilian Federal Supreme Court (STF) in a groundbreaking decision adopted in 2022, in the *PSB v Brazil (on Climate Fund)* case, tested the limits of the separation of powers principle and provided a unique, human rights-oriented interpretation of the Paris Agreement.[34] Finally, the procedural rules of litigation and how these apply to principles of public participation and access to justice provide a model for expanding procedural requirements in mass climate litigation, which often limit the scope and reach of cases worldwide.[35]

---

32 Armando Rocha, 'Suing States—The Role of Courts in Promoting States' Responsibility for Climate Change', in Garcia & Cortês (eds), *Blue Planet Law* (Springer 2023) 99.

33 For more on this topic, and how it has influenced climate litigation in Brazil, see Danielle de Andrade Moreira (Chapter 2); Danielle de Andrade Moreira et al (n 4); Maria Antonia Tigre, 'The "Fair Share" of Climate Mitigation: Can Litigation Increase National Ambition for Brazil?' (2023) 16 *Journal of Human Rights Practice* 25.

34 *Partido Socialista Brasileiro (PSB), Partido Socialismo e Liberdade (PSOL), Partido dos Trabalhadores (PT) e Rede Sustentabilidade v União Federal.* ADPF 708, Judgment of 7 January 2022 (Rapporteur: Minister Luís Roberto Barroso) available at https://climatecasechart.com/non-us-case/psb-et-al-v-federal-union/ (*PSB et al v Brazil (on Climate Fund)*). See Tigre & Setzer (n 21). See, also, Enéas Xavier and Letícia Simo Veras (Chapter 3), Carolina de Figueiredo Garrido (Chapter 5), Délton Winter de Carvalho and Armando Rocha (Chapter 6).

35 Maria Cecília de Araújo Asperti and Luciana Gross Cunha (Chapter 8).

This is possible because less legal formalism and a different understanding of courts' societal function allow them to have a different angle to analyze existing black letter provisions. Judges' different cultural imprints and worldview, and their affiliation to a different legal tradition, explains why courts in the Global South (and in Brazil more specifically) seem to be more comfortable with testing innovative legal solutions. These factors, along with broader themes in Brazilian climate litigation, are intricately interwoven throughout this book.

In this context, the goal of this book is to assess the experience of Brazilian climate litigation regarding different topics—ranging from the mainstream analysis of the separation of powers principle, passing by the role of financial institutions, the importance of just transition in pending litigation, or how Brazilian courts take into account future generations and vulnerable groups such as Indigenous peoples. The purpose of the book, however, is not just to collect information about the uniqueness of the Brazilian experience—but rather to see how the activism of Brazilian courts can be legally transplanted into different domestic courts (or even international bodies), namely in Latin America and in the Global South, where the Brazilian experience is likely to be taken as a benchmark.

Nonetheless, perhaps due to language barriers, the attention placed by legal scholarship on climate litigation in Brazil remains extremely limited, with a missed opportunity for lessons from a comparative perspective. In fact, as of 2025, there has yet to be a book or research article focusing specifically on what can be learned from the progressive case law of Brazilian courts in the context of climate litigation. Finding piecemeal research articles focused on specific aspects of climate litigation in Brazil is not difficult. However, a comprehensive and systemically cohesive approach to the Brazilian experience on climate litigation published in English was still missing. This angle is innovative in international legal scholarship, and this book aims to close that gap by contributing to further advance comparative studies in climate litigation.

## 3 Empowering Courts and Empowered by Courts: the Importance of Litigating for a Stable Climate

It is often said that litigation serves two purposes: it settles a dispute in a peaceful manner (private function); and it provides an opportunity for courts to clarify (and thus to develop) the existing law, enlightening the players in a system about what is courts' authoritative reading of a rule or principle (public function).[36] Litigation, however, also has another function: it can be used as a tool for pressuring for societal changes (strategic function).[37] Climate litigation certainly fits in all these categories of litigation's functions.

In fact, there is no doubt that litigating for a stable climate or a healthy atmosphere is likely to result in a clarification and development of the existing climate change law; and for sure that, irrespective of the direction of the decision, will settle that specific dispute. Strategic climate litigation, however, also aims to target States' systematic non- or under-performance in achieving their climate goals and pressure States to properly regulate their GHG emissions and implement these latter laws and regulations.[38] Strategic litigation, to some extent, does not square well with an orthodox understanding of the traditional (private) function assigned to courts, since the use of courts to pressure for the adoption of specific policies seems to be an endorsement of a particular message or interference with the political branch of the government. However, regardless of one's opinion on the role of courts and litigation in our society, the fact is that courts' decisions carry a particular sociological authority that allows them to promote societal advances. Selecting and assessing facts, and selecting, interpreting, and applying norms, are the intellectual operations through which courts can make a 'meaningful contribution'[39] to clarify and develop the law on climate change. They may not be able to micro-manage a State's climate mitigation policy, but they can establish facts, flag a State's non- or under-performance of its climate goals, provide innovative legal solutions to be taken into account by the legislator, or give a sense of direction to the entire legal system.[40] In Brazil, where a process of deregulation took place between 2019 and 2022, performing any of these tasks was strategic to pressure State authorities to enhance climate policies: as can be seen throughout this book, acknowledging the existence of a human right to a stable climate in *PSB et al v Brazil* (*on Climate Fund*) and qualifying the Paris Agreement as part of the genre of human rights treaties were instrumental to establish a sense of direction for the entire political and administrative branch of the government, as well as to highlight the need to enhance climate mitigation and adaptation policies in Brazil. *PSB et al v Brazil* (*on Climate Fund*) show how courts can be empowered in strategic climate litigation and, thus, how

36 Eg Vaughan Lowe, 'The Function of Litigation in International Society' (2012) 61 *ICQL* 209.
37 Jules Lobel, 'Courts as Forums for Protest' (2004) 52 *UCLA Law Review* 477.
38 Rocha (n 32) 100 ff.
39 Brian Preston, 'The Contribution of Courts in Tackling Climate Change' (2016) 28 *JEL* 11, 11.
40 Rocha (n 32) 101.

they can contribute decisively to establishing a State's obligation to enhance its climate policies.[41]

This links with another idea. From a sociological standpoint, when the STF ruled, in *PSB et al v Brazil* (*on Climate Fund*), on Brazil's obligation to adopt mitigation measures crafted to secure a stable climate, it also exercised an empowerment function by endorsing a specific cause and message. This results from the fact that, in the manner our societies are organized, courts are a forum where States, individuals, non-governmental organizations (NGOs), civil society movements, and corporations bring and discuss their claims. This is what Lobel calls the 'protest role' of courts, meaning that courts can be viewed as 'arenas where political and social movements agitate for, and communicate, their legal and political agenda.'[42] As stated by Sands, when courts endorse a particular cause or message (even though within the limits of their action as third-party dispute settlement bodies), they act as 'purveyors of legitimacy,' namely by 'rais[ing] consciousness on a particular matter' and 'help[ing] us understand what needs to be done, or what is being done inadequately or not at all.'[43] The use of courts in Brazil to counter the deregulation that occurred between 2019 and 2022—led by some political parties and NGOs in Brazil—is the ultimate example of the strategic use of litigation, which is aimed at pressuring the State and at disseminating a message to inform society on the urgency and need to mitigate and adapt to climate change.

## 4 Periodization of Climate Litigation in Brazil

Courts can hence contribute to enhancing a State's climate policies. However, assessing the adequacy of a State's climate regulation dents the separation of powers principles, as it requires a certain judicial activism, as explained in Chapter 3 by Enéas Xavier and Letícia Vero Simas. As such, the contribution of courts to enhancing climate change law does not happen overnight, but rather unfolds through small but decisive steps. A periodization of climate litigation in Brazil helps understand how courts became increasingly more ingenious in the pursuit of legal solutions and to hint at future developments and needs.

41 ibid.

42 Lobel (n 37) 479.

43 Philippe Sands, 'Climate Change and the Rule of Law: Adjudicating the Future in International Law' (2016) 28 *JEL* 19, 24.

As a tool, 'periodization' is the technique of grouping cases in blocks of time for the purpose of scientific analysis, assuming that cases in the same time period (might) share a set of core similar characteristics. Segmentation of time, however, is merely pedagogic: on the one hand, because the beginning and the end of blocks of time, as well as their fundamental features, are defined arbitrarily; on the other hand, because the segmentation of time is only possible by over-simplifying reality. In the case of climate litigation in Brazil, for instance, cases are so diverse that different angles of study can lead to different categorizations of time. However, periodization is also a very useful tool to provide an understanding of what was, or what is, the lay of land in each period of time, as well as to provide a sense of direction to hint at future developments. Having in mind all these difficulties, this book follows a periodization of climate litigation in Brazil suggested by Tigre and Setzer.[44]

In their proposed periodization, the first period of climate litigation in Brazil started in the late 1990s and early 2000s. This was a period of 'agnosticism' since climate change was only invoked 'discretely' and 'marginally' before courts, but not as an essential part of the legal argument.[45] *Maia Filho v IBAMA*[46] is a prime example: in a case referring to deforestation and the burning of 600 hectares of land to clear it for livestock grazing, the Superior Court of Justice (STJ) referred to the importance of protecting the environment, 'especially in a period of climate change.' But adding this short sentence was the most the STJ could do. The exact same sentence was written in *Public Prosecutor's Office v Schneider*,[47] referring to the burning of a mangrove to build a landfill (an especially fragile habitat, although highly resilient and thus relevant to cope with sea level rise). Accordingly, in this period, the STJ was aware of the significance of climate change. Still, it did not address it directly, mainly because litigators (who define the scope of a case) did not bring climate change as a central part of their legal argument.

44 Tigre & Setzer (n 21) 616–622.

45 Tigre & Setzer (n 21) 616; Joana Setzer, Guilherme Leal & Caio Borges, 'Climate Change Litigation in Brazil: Will Green Courts Become Greener?', in Alogna, Bakker & Gauci (eds), *Climate Change Litigation: Global Perspectives* (Brill Nijhoff 2021) 143, 147–148.

46 *Maia Filho v Instituto Brasileiro do Meio Ambiente e dos Recursos Naturais*, Special Appeal No 1000.731-RO, STF Judgment of 25 August 2009, available at https://climatecasechart.com/non-us-case/maia-filho-v-environmental-federal-agency-ibama/.

47 *Public Prosecutor's Office v H Carlos Schneider S/A Comércio e Indústria et al*, Special Appeal No 650.728-SC, Judgment of 2 December 2009, available at https://climatecasechart.com/non-us-case/public-prosecutors-office-v-h-carlos-schneider-sa-comercio-e-industria-others/.

FIGURE 1.1 Periodization of climate litigation in Brazil

A second period of climate litigation in Brazil started to emerge in 2010, when the Public Prosecutor's Office filed 35 lawsuits against several airlines operating at Guarulhos (ie São Paulo's international airport), seeking compensation for the GHG emissions associated with landing and take-off of airplanes. These lawsuits showed that the Public Prosecutor's Office and Brazilian courts were able to single out climate change as an environmental problem and to articulate legal solutions to compensate for its effects. Nonetheless, the turning point that allowed for the emergence of a second period (a period of 'challenge' and 'growth') was the reaction in courts against the climate and environmental deregulation that took place during President Bolsonaro's term (2019–2022).[48] During this term, at least 30 lawsuits were filed challenging the State's inaction and deregulation.[49] Even though deregulation aimed to remove legal obstacles to the development of economic projects (namely, those obstacles aimed at protecting or preserving the environment or the climate), ironically, deregulation also provided fertile ground for the emergence of a diverse case law that fleshed out the bedrocks of climate change law and the limits to economic

48 Tigre & Setzer (n 21) 616–18.

49 ibid 617.

activities resulting from the need to protect a stable climate. In this sense, deregulation created the conditions for a turning point in climate litigation in Brazil. According to Tigre and Setzer, climate litigation in this period had three major goals:[50] first, to fight illegal deforestation; second, to reduce Brazil's GHG emissions; and third, to bring and normalize the use of climate change arguments before courts.[51] Furthermore, in this period, litigators fit and benefited from the experience of litigation in the Global South, aimed at challenging States' absence, poor design, or poor enforcement of climate mitigation policies, and at challenging the absence or inadequate implementation of a State's NDC submitted pursuant to the Paris Agreement.[52]

A third period (a phase of 'maturity') started in 2022 with the STF's ruling in *PSB et al v Brazil* (*on Climate Fund*).[53] In this judgment, the STF first acknowledged that the protection of a stable climate is a human right—namely a right of the present and for future generations.[54] Moreover, this judgment brought the Paris Agreement into the cluster of human rights treaties,[55] as it is concerned with guaranteeing a carbon-neutral, human (rights)-friendly future. *PSB et al v Brazil* (*on Climate Fund*) is a masterpiece of legal innovation, coupled with a refined and highly qualified line of arguments and an avant-garde understanding of the societal function of courts. In this judgment, the STF espoused more sophisticated legal arguments and took lessons and methodologies from international law, comparative climate litigation, and human rights law.[56] The immediate consequence of pinpointing a human right to a stable climate under the Brazilian Constitutional and qualifying the Paris Agreement as a human rights treaty is to equip courts with the power to order the cessation of inaction and the adoption of measures aimed at curbing down GHG emissions and to fulfill the commitments under the Paris Agreement. In other words, it is 'the' tool that empowers courts and tests the limits of the separation of powers principle.

In this period, 'empowerment of courts' and 'empowered by courts' are the keywords to understand climate litigation in Brazil. *PSB et al v Brazil* (*on Climate Fund*) was also a symbolic decision—and symbols matter if one aims

50 ibid.
51 See also Setzer & Winter de Carvalho (n 21) 198.
52 See Peel & Lin (n 3) 679; Setzer & Benjamin (n 8) 86–87; or Tigre & Setzer (n 21) 618.
53 *PSB et al v Brazil* (*on Climate Fund*).
54 Tigre & Setzer (n 21) 618.
55 *PSB et al v Brazil* (*on Climate Fund*) §17. See also Carolina de Figueiredo Garrido (Chapter 5), Délton Winter de Carvalho & Armando Rocha (Chapter 6) and Tigre & Setzer (n 21) 596.
56 Tigre & Setzer (n 21) 618–622.

to deepen climate action.[57] Symbols raise awareness and encourage action. Court's decisions, if properly drafted and substantiated, are taken seriously and thus create a buzz in public opinion and boost litigation in general. They show that resorting to judicial remedies can be a successful tool for exercising pressure upon States. In this sense, a symbolic decision such as *PSB et al v Brazil (on Climate Fund)* are a symbol of courts' empowerment, but they also empower civil society and enhance climate action.[58]

Unsurprisingly, new cases are piling up in courts' dockets in this third period. However, whereas in the second period, litigation was mostly reactive to State inaction and deregulation, in this latter third phase, litigants bring more sophisticated legal arguments and are more comfortable challenging each detail of economic projects and public decisions directly based on climate change arguments. For instance, in *Instituto Verdeluz et al v Portocem et al (on installation of a thermoelectric plant in Pecém)*,[59] plaintiffs asked for the annulment of the environmental license of a thermoelectric power plant based on the lack of an environmental impact assessment (EIA) study that properly analyzed the climate impacts driving from the operation of the plant. Climate change was not marginal but instrumental to the legal argument and targeted the details of a specific economic project. This newly acquired boldness is also visible in the use of science and scientific language before courts in order establish the violation of fundamental rights and compel further climate action from governments, as is better explained by Juliana de Augustinis in Chapter 4. Similarly, after a change in the government, a series of cases were filed by the Brazilian federal environmental protection agency, IBAMA, against large landowners and companies who have for long been responsible for massive deforestation in Brazil, especially in the Amazon rainforest. These cases have called for large awards for climate damages, which are slowly being awarded by courts.

In this third period, the diversity of, and among, cases resulted from a rights-based methodology, which resorted to the grammar of human rights (including, but not exclusive of, the standalone right to a healthy environment or the rights of Indigenous peoples). Framing climate litigation in human-rights terms implies that the protection of a stable climate is 'not a matter of free

57 Rocha (n 32) 101.

58 ibid 102.

59 *Instituto Verdeluz, Conselho Indígena do Povo Anacé de Japiman and Associação Indígena do Povo Anacé da Aldeia Planalto Cauipe v Portocem Geração de Energia, S.A., Secretaria do Meio Ambiente do Estado do Ceará (SEMACE), Instituto Brasileiro do Meio Ambiente (IBAMA) and Fundação Nacional do Índio (FUNAI)*, ACP 5003643-89.2022.4.02.5116, filed in 2022 before the Federal Court in Ceará (Brazil), available at https://climatecasechart.com/non-us-case/instituto-verdeluz-and-others-v-portocem-geracao-de-energia-sa-and-semace/.

political choice,'[60] but rather a mandatory obligation pursuant to the Constitution and international instruments such as the Paris Agreement or the ACHR. For instance, with a view of protecting the Amazon forest and its biodiversity, courts linked that protection with the human right to a stable climate, namely by saying that the protection of the Amazon is an integral part of the State's obligations to protect, respect, and secure the human right to a stable climate.[61] To some extent, this helps explain why, in *IEA v Brazil*, the court acknowledged that, compared with mainstream environmental litigation, climate litigation is an autonomous strand, as mentioned by Carolina Figueiredo de Garrido (Chapter 5) and Délton Winter de Carvalho and Armando Rocha (Chapter 6).

*IEA v Brazil* was the first time a court ruled on the commonalities and differences between environmental and climate litigation.[62] The court acknowledged that climate change is a special form of environmental risk and harm, which can fit in the traditional approach of environmental law and litigation, since both forms of litigation arise from the same foundation (ie the right to a healthy environment)—but highlighted that climate litigation is broader in terms of time and space, meaning that it entails a necessarily intergenerational and global analysis. This explains why climate litigation is more susceptible to resort to legal transplant, ie to resort to the case law from other jurisdictions (domestic, supranational, or international) in order to seek for innovative legal solutions. Unsurprisingly, *IEA v Brazil* is expressly informed by precedents from the Netherlands (*Urgenda Foundation v State of the Netherlands*), Pakistan (*Leghari v Federation of Pakistan*), and the USA (*Massachusetts v EPA*)[63]—the same way that the European Court of Human Rights (ECtHR), although not quoting *IEA v Brazil* directly, replicated the exact same idea of a special nature of climate litigation vis-à-vis environmental litigation.[64]

Hand in hand with climate litigation in Brazilian courts, it is also worth analyzing Brazil's participation in litigation before international and regional

60 *PSB et al v Brazil (on Climate Fund)* §27.

61 ibid.

62 Maria Antonia Tigre, Délton Winter de Carvalho & Joana Setzer, 'IEA v. Brazil: When a Court Accepts the Legally Disruptive Nature of Climate Change' (Climate Law—A Sabin Center Blog, 2021) <https://blogs.law.columbia.edu/climatechange/2021/12/21/iea-v-brazil-when-a-court-accepts-the-legally-disruptive-nature-of-climate-change/>, accessed 27 August 2024.

63 *Instituto de Estudos Amazónicos (IEA) v União Federal.* §5. ACP No. 5048951-39.2020.4.04.7000, filed on 8 October 2020 before the 4th Federal Regional Court of Curitiba, Decision of 7 December 2021, §§15–16, available at https://climatecasechart.com/non-us-case/institute-of-amazonian-studies-v-brazil/.

64 *Duarte Agostinho et al v Portugal et al* (App no 39371/20) ECtHR [GC] 9 April 2024, §189; *Verein KlimaSeniorinnen Schweiz et al v Switzerland* (App no 53600/20) ECtHR [GC] 9 April 2024, §422.

courts—including contentious and advisory proceedings before the IACtHR, the International Court of Justice (ICJ), or the International Tribunal for the Law of the Sea (ITLOS). In Chapter 9, Paula Wojcikiewicz Almeida tracks Brazil's participation in environmental- and/or climate-related proceedings before these courts, as well as the impact of their judgments and advisory opinions in the case law of domestic courts in Brazil. Curiously, it shows that the judgments and advisory opinions from international and regional courts are used as 'authorities' in climate litigation in Brazil (ie they strengthen legal arguments, and thus embolden domestic courts to test innovative legal solutions)—but also that there seems to be a mismatch between a more innovative and activist stance adopted by courts at the domestic level and a more cautious and conservative stance of Brazilian representatives in regional and international judicial proceedings.

## 5 A Rights-Based Experience

Brazil, just like other States, has ratified the Paris Agreement and submitted its NDC pursuant to Article 4 of the latter; and has adopted a set of national laws and regulations addressing climate change in general, or sectoral aspects related to it (Eg regarding just transition). All these measures are aimed to curb down GHG emissions and align Brazil's aggregate of emissions with the NDC it has submitted to the UNFCCC Secretariat. Hence, if climate goals established by Brazil are not met, or if Brazil is non- or under-performing its obligations under the Paris Agreement or domestic norms, climate litigation could (and perhaps should) aim to target the mitigation effort of Brazil more directly: ie to challenge whether climate goals binding upon Brazil are met, in line to be met, or not in line at all.[65]

However, data suggests that climate litigation worldwide (at the domestic, supranational, or international level) is not based on the (non-)performance of climate goals directly, but rather on the use of other rights protected by the legal system—namely the standalone human right to a healthy environment, or other 'greened' human rights.[66] Brazil is no exception to this trend, as explained by Danielle de Andrade Moreira,[67] Carolina de Figueiredo Garrido,[68] Délton Winter de Carvalho, and Armando Rocha.[69] This explains the

65 See Tigre (n 33).
66 Setzer & Higham (n 24).
67 Danielle de Andrade Moreira (Chapter 2).
68 Carolina de Figueiredo Garrido (Chapter 5).
69 Délton Winter de Carvalho and Armando Rocha (Chapter 6).

core importance of *PSB et al v Brazil* (*on Climate Fund*), a true turning-point in climate litigation in Brazil, where the STF established and adumbrated the human right to a stable climate under Article 225 of the Constitution, the ACHR, and the Paris Agreement. Based on this understanding of the right to a stable climate as a human right, a rights-based litigation can seek different purposes: to challenge the allocation of budget resources[70] or the licensing of thermoelectric plants,[71] assess compliance with Brazil's NDC, or order the cessation of an activity or the adoption of protective measures of natural sinks such as

---

70 *PSB et al v Brazil* (*on Climate Fund*), or *Partido Socialista Brasileiro* (*PSB*), *Partido Socialismo e Liberdade* (*PSOL*), *Partido dos Trabalhadores* (*PT*) *e Rede Sustentabilidade v União Federal*. ADO 59, Judgment of 16 August 2023 (Rapporteur: Minister Rosa Weber) available at https://climatecasechart.com/non-us-case/psb-et-al-v-brazil/.

71 *Instituto Internacional Arayara e Colônia de Pescadores Z-5 v Copelmi Mineração Ltda e Fundação Estadual de Proteção Ambiental* (*FEPAM*) ACP 5044993-20.2019.8.21.0001 / 5125450-05.2020.8.21.0001, filed on 27 September 2019 before the 10th Public Court of Porto Alegre, available at https://climatecasechart.com/non-us-case/instituto-internacional-arayara-and-fishermens-colony-z-5-v-copelmi-mineracao-ltda-and-fepam-mina-guaiba-project-and-affected-communities/; *Instituto Arayara de Educação e Cultura, Associação Indígena Poty Guarani, Conselho de Articulação do Povo Guarani and Comunidade da Aldeia Guarani Guajayvi v Copelmi Mineração Lda., Fundação Nacional do Índio* (*FUNAI*) *and Fundação Estadual de Proteção Ambiental Henrique Luis Roessler* (*FEPAM*), ACP 5069057-47.2019.4.04.7100 (Federal Court), filed on 1 October 2019 before the 9th Federal Court of Rio Grande do Sul, Judgment of 1 February 2022, available at https://climatecasechart.com/non-us-case/arayara-association-of-education-and-culture-and-others-v-funai-copelmi-mineracao-ltda-and-fepam-mina-guaiba-project-and-affected-indigenous-communities/; *Associação Gaúcha de Proteção ao Ambiente Natural* (*AGAPAN*), *Instituto Gaúcho de Estudos Ambientais* (*INGÁ*), *Instituto Preservar, Cooperativa Agroecológica Nacional Terra e Vida Lda, Coonattera, Bionatur and Centro de Educação Popular e Agroecologia* (*CEPPA*) *v Copelmi Mineração Lda. and Instituto Brasileiro do Meio Ambiente e dos Recursos Naturais e Renováveis* (*IBAMA*), ACP 5030786-95.2021.4.04.7100, filed on 19 May 2020 before the 9th Federal Court of Rio Grande do Sul, available at https://climatecasechart.com/non-us-case/instituto-preservar-et-al-v-copelmi-mineracao-ltda-and-ibama/; *Instituto Arayara de Educação e Cultura v Copelmi Mineração Lda., Fundação Estadual de Proteção Ambiental Henrique Luis Roessler* (*FEPAM*) *and Agência Nacional de Águas* (*ANA*), ACP 5069057-47.2019.4.04.710, filed on 10 September 2020 before the Court of Justice of Rio Grande do Sul, available at https://climatecasechart.com/non-us-case/arayara-association-of-education-and-culture-vs-copelmi-mineracao-ltda-and-fepam-guaiba-mine-project-and-hydrological-risks/; *Instituto Verdeluz, Conselho Indígena do Povo Anacé de Japiman and Associação Indígena do Povo Anacé da Aldeia Planalto Cauipe v Portocem Geração de Energia, S.A., Secretaria do Meio Ambiente do Estado do Ceará* (*SEMACE*), *Instituto Brasileiro do Meio Ambiente* (*IBAMA*) *and Fundação Nacional do Índio* (*FUNAI*), ACP 5003643-89.2022.4.02.5116, filed in 2022 before the Federal Court in Ceará (Brazil), available at https://climatecasechart.com/non-us-case/instituto-verdeluz-and-others-v-portocem-geracao-de-energia-sa-and-semace/.

the Amazon or the Pantanal rainforests.[72] In common, all these lawsuits share the fact that the legal argument used to challenge a State's policy is not the climate goal binding upon Brazil, or its NDC, but rather (non-)compliance with a human right to a healthy environment.

In fact, save for a few exceptions, all cases analyzed in this book follow a rights-based matrix, relying on the standalone fundamental right to a healthy environment, from which one can infer a right to a stable climate or a healthy atmosphere. Moreover, since climate change is a form of environmental risk and harm, climate litigation in Brazil also relies on other human rights (namely, procedural rights related to the environment, such as the right to environmental information or the right to file a lawsuit irrespective of being personally affected by a decision); and other fundamental rights that, although not directly linked to the environment, can be used (or 'greened') if their enjoyment is affected by climate change (Eg the rights to life, health, or physical integrity).[73]

Being rights-based, however, can be elusive: it is easy to find a proper basis for a legal obligation to mitigate and adapt to climate change (be it in the Constitution, statutory norms, or international law), but it can be challenging for individuals to face all procedural obstacles to enforce their right to a stable climate, starting with proving their victimhood capacity, the causation link between acts and omissions and the damage suffered, or their judicial *locus standi* in general. To cope with such challenges (which are also visible in all jurisdictions), rights-based climate litigation in Brazil has been led by three clusters of entities: first, public authorities entrusted with the protection of the rule of (environmental) law, namely the Public Prosecutor's or the Public Defender's Office; second, environmental NGO s; and third, political parties. In common, all these entities share a capacity to file an action on the interest of the general public and without any need to invoke being personally affected by an action or omission.

In fact, Article 5 of the Brazilian Constitution guarantees access to justice as a human right. According to this provision, para XXXV, 'the law shall not exclude from the Judiciary the assessment of any injury or a threat to any right.'[74] To guarantee this constitutional mandate, both the constitutional

72 Maria Antonia Tigre and Anna Maria Cárcamo (Chapter 13.)

73 In general, about the 'greening' of human rights, see 'Report of the Special Rapporteur on the Issue of Human Rights Obligations relating to the Enjoyment of a Safe, Clean, Healthy and Sustainable Environment, John Knox' UN Doc A/HRC/73/188 (19 July 2018) (Report of the Special Rapporteur) paras 12ff.

74 See Constitution, Article 5, para XXXV.

and the procedural law in Brazil offer a wide range of remedies to safeguard individual and collective rights. To begin with, collective rights such as the right to a healthy and sustainable environment or the right to a stable climate can be protected under the so-called *Ação Civil Pública* (Public Civil Action), which is ruled by Law No 7.347/95. Pursuant to Article 5 of this latter statute, legal standing to file a public civil action is granted to the Public Prosecutor's Office, the Public Defender's Office, the Federal Union, the federated states, the Federal District, municipalities, or an association constituted pursuant to civil law for at least one year, which seeks the protection of collective interests such as the environment (in other words, an NGO). Public civil actions are filed against public authorities before first instance courts;[75] and applicants may ask for monetary compensation for damages caused to the environment, or to the court to declare an obligation of *facere* (ie an obligation to adopt an action) or *non-facere* (ie an obligation to not adopt a certain action) binding upon the respondent.[76]

On the other hand, the Brazilian Constitution establishes a broad range of remedies to protect fundamental rights from violation, namely the *Ação Direta de Inconstitucionalidade* (Direct Action of Unconstitutionality, or ADI),[77] which is a lawsuit filed before the STF to get a declaration of unconstitutionality of a law or a federal norm. According to Article 103 of the Constitution, legal standing is granted to the President of the Republic, the Presidency of the Senate, the Presidency of the Chamber of Representatives, the Presidency of the Legislative Assembly or of the Legislative Chamber of the Federal District, a State or the Federal District Governor, the Federal Public Prosecutor's Office, the Federal Council of the Bar Association of Brazil, a political party represented in the national congress (ie the Senate or the Chamber of Representatives), or a trade union of national scope reach. For its turn, the *Ação Direta de Inconstitucionalidade por Omissão* (Direct Action of Unconstitutionality for Omission, or ADO) follows the exact same matrix, but targets an omission from public authorities at the Union or the federated state level of a statute whose adoption is imposed constitutionally.

Finally, Article 102, para 1, of the Constitution, and Law No 9.882/99 also establish an *Arguição de Descumprimento de Preceito Fundamental* (Claim for Noncompliance with a Fundamental Provision, or ADPF), ie an action aimed at avoiding or repairing damage to a fundamental provision (thus including the healthy and sustainable environment according to Article 225 of the

75 Law No 7.347/95, Article 2.

76 Law No 7.347/95, Article 3.

77 Constitution, arts 102(I)(a), 103 and 103-A.

Constitution), provided that the damage results from an act attributable to a public authority.[78] This lawsuit is also filed before the STF[79] and may be instituted by the same entities having legal standing to file a direct action of unconstitutionality (ADI).[80] In their complaint, the applicant must identify which constitutional provision was breached; which public authority infringed this latter provision and how; and which remedies should be adopted to avoid or repair such infringement.[81]

In this scenario, a bedrock of the Brazilian legal system is that the Public Prosecutor's Office (and, in some cases, the Public Defender's Office) is in charge of the protection of the rule of law.[82] In other words, in cases where a personal affection may be missing (as may happen in climate change-related cases), the diffuse interest of the general public is guaranteed by the Public Prosecutor's Office through public civil actions or any of the remedies directly established in the Constitution. While NGO s are often at the forefront of bringing climate cases worldwide, this scenario is different in Brazil,[83] where the majority of cases were traditionally brought by the Public Prosecutor's Office. Although the Public Prosecutor's Office is a branch of the Brazilian justice system, it is an independent institution, and, therefore, not subordinated to the executive, legislative, or judiciary.[84] The use of the Public Prosecutor's Office has significant advantages for climate litigation in Brazil. As noted by Medici-Colombo and Ricarte, practitioners from other jurisdictions in their comparative study 'criticized the (absent) role of public entities, such as public prosecutors and ombudsmen, in advocating (*ex officio* or at request) for environmental and climate matters through the judicial system.'[85] This absence leads to a disproportionate dependence on initiatives of civil society organizations and individuals for the judicial protection of the environment and the climate, in spite of their limited resources. Furthermore, Medici-Colombo and Ricarte observed that private actors, who are willing and able to file an environmental (let alone a climate) claim, are usually located in big cities, leaving 'distant' communities with constrained access to justice. In this scenario, the Public

78 Law No 9.882/99, art 1.
79 Law No 9.882/99, art 1.
80 Law No 9.882/99, art 2(I).
81 Law No 9.882/99, art 4.
82 Constitution, art 127.
83 Setzer & Higham (n 24) 2.
84 Constitution, art 127(§1).
85 Gáston Medici-Colombo & Thays Ricarte, 'The Escazú Agreement Contribution to Environmental Justice in Latin America: An Exploratory Empirical Inquiry through the Lens of Climate Litigation' (2024) 16 *Journal of Human Rights Practice* 160, 165.

Prosecutor's Office emerges as a major climate advocate and litigator before domestic courts, especially considering that they are funded by the State itself, and therefore lack the constraints of funding that NGO s often face.

Furthermore, the Brazilian legal system also acknowledges that environmental NGO s (who aggregate knowledge and human and financial resources, and have a wider and more comprehensive understanding of community concerns regarding environmental or climate risks and harms) have guaranteed access to courts in order to protect and preserve the environment. Although these NGO s do not have legal standing to initiate the constitutional remedies referred to before, they have been able to keep a thriving activity in instituting climate change-related public civil actions. *IEA v Brazil* was referred to in this chapter as a landmark in climate litigation in Brazil and is a prime example of how NGO s (in this case, the *Instituto de Estudos Amazônicos*) can use this form of lawsuit to help shape courts' ingenuity and creative mindset in bringing climate-related cases. Finally, the Brazilian legal system allows political parties represented in Congress to file lawsuits arguing the unconstitutionality of a law.[86] Although their legal standing is minor compared to the latter entities, some political parties rank among the major plaintiffs in climate litigation in Brazil, especially with respect to challenging the climate and environmental deregulation that took place between 2019 and 2022. This chapter has also referred to the role of *PSB et al v Brazil* (*on Climate Fund*), which is a fine work of ingeniousness in reading the Constitution and understanding of courts' role in our societies. The case was filed by a group of political parties in reaction to the deregulation that occurred between 2019 and 2022. A simple look at the table of cases (Annex I) shows that NGO s and political parties have been active in bringing climate change into courts' dockets in Brazil.

## 6 Book Structure

In order to provide an in-depth analysis of the climate litigation experience from Brazil, this edited book is divided into five parts, each focusing on distinct yet interconnected themes related to climate litigation in Brazil.

Part 1 (*Challenges in Climate Litigation*) sets the stage by exploring the various obstacles faced in this evolving legal field. It begins with a comprehensive overview of climate litigation in Brazil, providing a panorama of the current landscape. The subsequent chapters delve into the critical issues of the

86 Constitution, art 103, para VIII, and Law No 9.882, of 3 December 1999, art 2, para I.

separation of powers and the role of different branches of the government in climate action, the roles of the local, state, and federal levels of action, and the pivotal role that science plays in shaping legal arguments and decisions.

Part 2 (*Climate Litigation and Human Rights*) examines the intersection between climate change and human rights law, since climate litigation in Brazil is largely a rights-based experience. The chapters in this section discuss the qualification of the Paris Agreement by Brazilian courts as a human rights treaty (and thus its potential to align climate action in Brazil with the country's international commitments and obligations), highlighting the obligation to protect the stability of the climate under the right to a healthy environment (which is protected under Article 225 of the Brazilian Constitution and Article 26 of the ACHR). Having in mind the advisory opinions rendered (and yet to be rendered) by the IACtHR, the analysis extends to the influence of advisory opinions in domestic litigation in Brazil and Brazil's position in international judicial proceedings related to climate change. Additionally, this part addresses the crucial topic of access to justice in the context of climate litigation, emphasizing the importance of ensuring that legal avenues are available to all affected parties.

Part 3 (*Climate Litigation and Vulnerabilities*) addresses the social dimensions of climate litigation, particularly the vulnerabilities experienced by marginalized groups. The chapters cover the role of gender, race, and poverty in climate litigation, the rights of Indigenous communities, and the legal considerations for future generations. Although climate change is universal and affects every single person on the planet, individuals are not equally exposed to climate change-related effects. Vulnerability here is self-reinforcing. As such, this section underscores the importance of recognizing and addressing the disproportionate impacts of climate change on vulnerable groups and populations within the legal framework.

In Part 4 (*Climate Litigation and Biodiversity*), the book shifts focus to the critical relationship between climate change and the protection of biodiversity. Chapters in this section explore the legal mechanisms for safeguarding biodiversity, the marine environment, and the Amazon rainforest—each of which plays a central role in climate mitigation. The discussion also examines the rights of nature as a potential legal avenue for advancing climate litigation, offering a broader perspective on how environmental and climate laws intersect.

Finally, Part 5 (*Beyond the State: Climate Litigation and the Energy Transition*) explores the broader implications of climate litigation beyond state actions. The chapters discuss the role of (and the litigation against) financial institutions in securing financial flows that encourage carbon-neutral projects while discouraging the conduction of high carbon-led activities; the development of a just transition branch of climate litigation, which seeks to balance the needs of workers and communities in the shift towards a low-carbon economy; the potential and limitations of corporate climate litigation in Brazil in bridging the gap between GHG emitters and victims; and the use of tort law in climate damage cases, highlighting how procedural obstacles are read creatively to guarantee access to climate justice in relations among private actors. These separate parts are briefly discussed next.

### 6.1 *The Challenges in Climate Litigation*

Chapter 2, '*A Panorama of Climate Litigation in Brazil*,' by Danielle de Andrade Moreira, provides a bird's-eye view of climate litigation in Brazil. As noted in her chapter, 'climate cases in Brazil cover a wide range of topics, all of which are in some way directly related to climate change mitigation and adaptation. Although it is clear that climate change is beginning to be explicitly litigated before the Brazilian courts, it is not yet possible to dissociate it from environmental litigation itself.'[87] Moreira highlights four crucial points to understanding climate litigation in Brazil, namely (i) integration with mainstream environmental litigation, (ii) impact of political and environmental changes, (iii) diverse range of climate litigation topics, and (iv) constitutional and legal foundations.

First, many early and recent climate cases are structurally similar to traditional environmental lawsuits, relying on established environmental legislation and case law. This reflects how climate issues are increasingly being addressed within the existing environmental legal framework. Indeed, earlier climate cases in Brazil, particularly those before 2018, treated climate concerns as peripheral to broader environmental issues. However, since 2018, there has been a noticeable shift. Recent cases explicitly focus on climate change, although they often intersect with other environmental themes. The doctrines and legal instruments used (Eg the conduction of EIA studies or the monitorization of GHG emitting activities) may be shared with general environmental law, but there is a visible trend to look to climate change as a phenomenon requiring special rules and methodologies to be coped with.[88]

87 See Chapter 2 ('A Panorama of Climate Litigation in Brazil').

88 See ie *IEA v Brazil* (n 63) §§15–16.

Second, the rise in climate litigation is partly driven by recent political and environmental shifts, including setbacks in Brazilian environmental policy during President Bolsonaro's tenure and the heightened urgency of climate issues. The recent Brazilian experience shows how fragile political consensus can be if some of the electorate perceives mitigation measures as detrimental to social and economic development. However, it also shows that courts can be used to keep the domestic legislation aligned with a carbon-neutral future, the preservation of biodiversity and natural sinks, or the protection groups more vulnerable to climate-related events. In the end, it shows that setbacks to climate action are also an opportunity to highlight or provide proper foundations to climate change law, namely in terms of rights and obligations. The result is a more explicit focus on climate stability in recent legal cases.

Third, recent climate cases in Brazil cover a wide array of topics, from constitutional matters related to the limits and contours of a standalone right to a healthy environment, to the protection of the Amazon and the existing biodiversity, passing by the protection, preservation, and amelioration of the marine environment or the rules applicable to financial institutions. Such diversity of topics is unsurprising. As an economist would say, 'global warming is the Goliath of all externalities,'[89] since it affects every single aspect of our lives and requires action in every single social and economic domain; it requires decisive action affecting all actions in our daily lives. This diversity in themes and legal strategy is explored in depth throughout this book, and highlights the multifaceted nature of climate-related legal challenges in Brazil.

Fourth, Brazilian cases benefit from a robust constitutional and legal framework. These cases rely upon Article 225 of the Brazilian Constitution, which guarantees a standalone right to an ecologically balanced environment. They further rely on the integration of international treaties like the ACHR and the Paris Agreement into national law, which provide a strong foundation for addressing climate issues. This grounding enhances Brazil's capacity to tackle climate challenges through legal means.

Moreira's overview is critical for understanding the judiciary's evolving role in addressing climate change in Brazil. A decade ago, courts had minimal involvement in climate protection, but this has changed dramatically globally and within Brazil. Climate litigation has emerged as a distinct category, addressing issues of mitigation, adaptation, and loss and damage. Claimants increasingly turn to national, regional, and international courts to enforce climate laws, compel more ambitious measures from legislators, policymakers,

89 William Nordhaus, *The Climate Casino—Risk, Uncertainty, and Economics of a Warming World* (Yale University Press 2013) 18.

and businesses, and seek compensation for climate-related harms. As these cases progress through the Brazilian legal system, including the STF, they have prompted a critical reassessment of the judiciary's role in the climate crisis. This reassessment encompasses discussions on judicial independence, the possible political function of courts, the separation of powers principle, and the cultivation of climate expertise and knowledge within the judiciary. Transparency and public participation are also crucial elements of this discussion. While the Brazilian judiciary's role in the climate crisis is deeply interconnected with its legal framework, it also offers valuable lessons from a comparative perspective. Given the widespread insufficiency of national climate goals and the failure to meet existing targets, the question arises: how can courts bridge the gap in climate action and climate justice?

In this vein, Chapter 3, '*The Separation of Powers Principle in Brazil and the Role of Different Bodies in Climate Action*,' by Enéas Xavier and Letícia Simo Veras, critically examines the extent to which executive and legislative decisions on climate issues are subject to judicial review. While courts in common law countries like the United States, Canada, and some in Europe have often been reluctant to review such decisions, citing the separation of powers principle, Brazilian courts have taken a markedly different approach. As discussed in Chapter 3, the Brazilian Constitution clearly delineates the distribution of powers for environmental and climate protection across federal, state, and municipal levels, explicitly mandating harmony and independence among the executive, legislative, and judicial branches.

Yet recent cases have clarified and reinforced the judiciary's crucial role in the climate crisis. For example, Justice Carmen Lúcia emphasized that the judiciary must ensure the effectiveness of constitutional environmental protections[90]—and, on that basis, has argued for more participation of the judiciary in reviewing domestic legislation. Moreover, in *PSB et al v Brazil* (*on Climate Fund*), Justice Barroso asserted that the judiciary has both the authority and the obligation to oversee the executive and legislative branches to ensure compliance with legal norms and principles.[91] This emphasis helps to

90 *Partido Socialista Brasileiro* (*PSB*), *Rede Sustentabilidade, Partido Democrático Trabalhista* (*PDT*), *Partido Verde, Partido dos Trabalhadores* (*PT*), *Partido Socialismo e Liberdade* (*PSOL*) *e Partido Comunista do Brasil* (*PCdoB*) *v União Federal*. ADPF 760, Judgment of 6 April 2022 (Rapporteur: Minister Cármen Lúcia), at 153, available at https://climatecasechart.com/non-us-case/brazilian-socialist-party-and-others-v-brazil/.

91 *PSB et al v Brazil* (*on Climate Fund*) §34.

state that judicial oversight is not to be seen as interfering with other government branches, but rather as a constitutional duty. The rationale for this judicial role is that judges are not evaluating the merit or political expediency of actions but ensuring adherence to legal standards. This finding aligns with Tigre and Setzer, who also noted that Justice Barroso's clarifications addressed vital aspects of the separation of powers and expanded the Court's interpretative framework in climate litigation contexts.[92]

Chapter 4, '*The Role of Science in Brazilian Climate Litigation*,' by Juliana de Augustinis, discusses the role of science in climate litigation. It explores Brazil's lessons and insights regarding public participation and the use of scientific evidence in climate litigation. The chapter highlights the Brazilian judiciary's receptiveness to participatory mechanisms, such as *amicus curiae* and public hearings, and its willingness to consider expert input and information from interest groups through these channels.

De Augustinis observes that, in contrast to global trends where courts seldom rely on expert assistance to interpret scientific evidence and data related to GHG mitigation—often defaulting to IPCC reports and national studies on climate science—Brazilian courts actively engage with these tools to enhance their understanding of complex scientific issues beyond the judges' expertise. This proactive approach reflects the Brazilian judiciary's commitment to incorporating scientific knowledge into its climate-related rulings. It allows us to bridge the gap between climate science and one local and specific climate change-related harm. This practice is particularly instructive for climate litigation in the Global South, where relevant studies are often less abundant due to limited funding and research resources. The Brazilian example highlights the importance of judicial openness to expert input, especially in regions where scientific data on the effects of climate change is scarce.

De Agustinis' study aligns with Gastón Medici-Colombo and Thays Ricarte's comparative research on procedural rules and arrangements that govern litigation in Latin America.[93] They argue that these 'are not necessarily well-suited to the protection of collective interests, such as the environment,' a fact that is made worse by the added complexities of climate change.[94] Medici-Colombo and Ricarte identified that one of the main challenges in climate litigation in Latin America relates to 'difficulties in fully understanding cases involving complex scientific facts and innovative legal arguments (such as those related to climate change) or lack of appropriate enforcement or monitoring mechanisms

92 Tigre & Setzer (n 21) 630–631.

93 Medici-Colombo & Ricarte (n 85).

94 ibid 160.

for judgment compliance … as possible causes of delayed responses by courts in climate cases.'[95] This matter is being addressed with the innovative ways the Brazilian judiciary is using expert data in climate litigation, setting an example for other jurisdictions worldwide facing similar problems.

### 6.2 *Climate Litigation and Human Rights*

Chapter 5, '*Recognizing The Paris Agreement as a Human Rights Treaty: The Climate Fund Case and Brazilian Courts*,' by Carolina de Figueiredo Garrido, analyzes *PSB et al v Brazil* (*on Climate Fund*) and how the STF 'humanized' the Paris Agreement in this ruling. For this purpose, 'humanizing' climate and environmental treaties is symmetric to the 'greening' of human rights treaties: it corresponds to a process of identifying human rights, or a human rights basis, under treaties legally qualified as climate or environmental treaties. To our knowledge, this doctrine espoused in *PSB et al v Brazil* (*on Climate Fund*) is still unparalleled.

In fact, regardless of the never-ending debate about the fragmentation of international law and how its particular fields operate according to their own grammars, the fact is that treaties do not live in a vacuum: they need to be interpreted and balanced against other rules and principles that exist in the international *and* domestic legal orders alike. Therefore, it should not come as a surprise that a court interprets the Paris Agreement in a systemically integrated manner. However, what is surprising is that the Paris Agreement has been brought into the gamut of human rights treaties. As far as one can guess, the STF was concerned with tunneled readings that may produce distortive interpretations of a rule. As a result, the rationale implicit in the STF's ruling in *PSB et al v Brazil* (*on Climate Fund*) is that reducing GHG concentration in the atmosphere is not an end in itself, just as the Paris Agreement is not a mere sum of numerical targets and deadlines. Quite the opposite, complying with the goals of the Paris Agreement, as expressed in Article 2(1)(a), is a means towards securing the possibility of human life in the future.

A naïf interpretation of *PSB et al v Brazil* (*on Climate Fund*) is that the STF aimed at providing a human face to the Paris Agreement. A more cynical reading, however, emphasizes the fact that, by qualifying it as 'part of the genre of human rights treaties,' the STF 'upgraded' the Paris Agreement in the hierarchy of norms within the Brazilian legal system: whereas, as an ordinary climate or environmental treaty, it would rank at the same level as statutory norms, as a

95 ibid 165.

human rights treaty it ranks above statutory norms and can be used by a court to qualify a human right to a healthy atmosphere and a stable climate.

Based on this assumption, Chapter 6, '*The Obligation to Protect the Stability of the Climate System under the Right to a Healthy Environment in Brazil*,' by Délton Winter de Carvalho and Armando Rocha, elaborates on the development of a constitutional obligation to protect the stability of the climate under the human right to a healthy environment. In fact, apart from the obligations pursuant to the UNFCCC,[96] the Paris Agreement, or soft law instruments such as UN General Assembly (UNGA) resolutions,[97] no Constitution or human rights treaty refers explicitly to an obligation to protect the stability of the climate system. The period in which these hard law documents were written explains this absence of a reference to climate change. Nonetheless, since climate change is the downstream result of GHG emissions (ie a form of environmental pollution), Article 225 of the Brazilian Constitution and Article 26 of the ACHR[98] (guaranteeing the human right to a healthy environment) can be used to support an obligation to protect the stability of the climate system.

Carvalho and Rocha explain how this obligation was developed in *PSB et al v Brazil* (*on Climate Fund*) and in *IEA v Brazil*. Furthermore, the authors also elaborate on the importance of finding such an obligation in the Constitution or in the ACHR, since it implies that pursuing a set of policies aimed at reducing GHG emissions is not a matter of discretion, but rather mandatory for the other branches of the government. This conclusion is particularly relevant in relation to the adoption of climate change laws and policies—a domain often said to belong to the realm of political discretion and societal value-based judgements and trade-offs, ie a domain that lies outside the traditional function of courts. Political discretion, however, does not mean 'immunity from judicial oversight' and cannot be used as an excuse to postpone the adoption of mitigation measures. As such, finding a constitutional and human rights obligation to protect the stability of the climate equates, on the one hand, to flag to decision-makers that climate policies are subject to judicial oversight and, on the other hand, that the lack, poor design, or poor implementation of climate

96 United Nations Framework Convention on Climate Change (adopted 9 May 1992, entered into force 21 March 1994) 1771 UNTS 107.

97 UNGA 'The Human Right to a Clean, Healthy and Sustainable Environment' UN Doc A/RES/76/300 (28 July 2022), which expressly voices a concern with the protection of a healthy atmosphere and the stability of the climate system.

98 Although the ACHR does not refer to it directly, the case law of the IACtHR has asserted the protection of the right to a healthy environment under Article 26 of the ACHR. See OC-23/17 (n 18).

policies is likely to be viewed as an infringement of the obligation to protect the stability of the climate system.[99]

A pivotal tool in Brazilian climate litigation seems to be the hinge linking the Brazilian and the international legal systems. As seen before, the text of the ACHR and the case law of the IACtHR were key to backing the development of a cutting-edge domestic case law on the right to a healthy environment and its derivative obligation to protect the stability of the climate system. In this light, Chapter 7, '*Brazil and Advisory Opinions before International Courts and Tribunals: Participation and Impact of Advisory Opinions in Domestic Courts*,' by Paula Wojcikiewicz Almeida, analyzes how Brazilian courts have been using prior judgments and advisory opinions from the IACtHR to inform their own decisions. Based on a careful empirical assessment, Almeida shows that Brazilian courts do more than a mere quote in support of the existing domestic case law—they are actually open to using the IACtHR's case law as a 'persuasive authority,' ie as an interpretative element that can imply or lead to a change in those courts' case law. In this sense, data suggests a certain (although limited) link between the IACtHR's case law and advances in the case law of Brazilian courts. What is unclear is whether that use is not selective, in the sense that Brazilian courts may cherry-pick the IACtHR's judgments or advisory opinions in order to back their own decision on more sensitive issues.

Furthermore, Almeida also analyzes Brazil's participation in international judicial proceedings related to the environment and climate change. Curiously, Almeida unveils an entirely different picture: Brazil adopts a more conservative stance in these judicial proceedings, irrespective of its type of intervention. Even though there is no study or official explanation for this, it might be that Brazilian authorities do not oppose more ambitious policies or legal innovation but seek to preserve a national margin of discretion.

Finally, Chapter 8, '*Access to Justice and Climate Litigation in Brazil*,' by Cecília Asperti and Luciana Gross Cunha, elaborates on access to justice and climate litigation in Brazil. Their concern lies with climate change-related disasters and the need to enhance adaptation, preparedness, accountability, and reconstruction actions. As such, Chapter 8 is focused on the micro-implementation of human rights in the event of climate change-related disasters, when vulnerability is naturally enhanced. As Asperti and Cunha state in this chapter, there is no case in Brazil (pending or decided) where such issues

99 For instance, the facts in *PSB et al v Brazil* (*on Climate Fund*) that led to the finding of this obligation referred to the non-allocation of funds to cope with climate change-related effects in 2019 and 2020. As such, the ruling of the STF was adopted not in face of the lack or poor design of a regulatory framework, but rather in face of its lack of implementation.

were specifically discussed. Yet, the chapter relies on the 'Protocol on Access to Justice and Disasters: Recommendations Developed for the Justice System for Action in Disaster Cases' (*Protocolo Acesso à Justiça e Desastres: Recomendações Elaboradas para o Sistema de Justiça para Atuação em Casos de Desastres*), a study developed in 2023 by the São Paulo School of Law of *Fundação Getúlio Vargas* and aimed at devising parameters of preparation and (re)action in case of natural disasters related to climate change. These parameters build upon the stages of the disasters' risk management cycle, since they seem to be more suited to address the effects of climate change-related events. In their assessment, Asperti and Cunha argue for a greater centrality of vulnerable groups and individuals in the mechanisms for preparing and reacting to natural disasters; for an emphasis on the concrete action needed during an event; for fostering mechanisms of accountability for and reconstruction after an event; and for opening the justice system to receive and decide complaints related to the preparation and (re)action in case of climate change-related natural disasters.

### 6.3 *Climate Litigation and Vulnerabilities*

Zooming into the human rights of particular groups, Section 3 addresses how human rights have or could be used in climate litigation to protect groups and individuals in a situation of vulnerability. Scientific data on climate change proves that climate-related events will enhance the stress of the enjoyment of the full gamut of human rights. However, 'being all affected' does not equate to 'being all equally affected.' Some individuals, as a result of belonging to a particular group, are likely to face more and more dangerous climate change-related effects.[100] Chapter 9, '*Vulnerabilities in Climate Litigation: The Role of Gender, Race, and Poverty*,' by Mariana Belmont and Nauê Bernardo Pinheiro de Azevedo, analyzes how gender, race, and poverty can enhance a person's vulnerability in the face of these climate change-related effects. This chapter's narrative and line of arguments differ from the rest of the book: lawyers are used to discuss gender, race, or poverty in a legal argument based on enhanced vulnerability or discrimination. What is still missing is an understanding of how belonging to a specific gender, racial, or social group enhances a person's exposure to climate change-related events, and how legally relevant that enhanced exposure is. This explains, for instance, why a non-lawyer was in charge of co-writing this chapter. The chapter, therefore, uses a storytelling

100 See Maria Antonia Tigre, Melanie Murcott & Susan Ann Samuels, 'Introduction: Global South Perspectives on Litigation and Vulnerability Amidst Intersectional Climate Justice' in Tigre, Murcott and Ann Samuels (eds), *Climate Litigation and Vulnerabilities: Global South Perspectives* (Routledge forthcoming 2025).

narrative to address the issue of environmental and climate racism through the lens of climate (in)justice and litigation.

Chapter 10, *'Decolonizing Climate Litigation: an Analysis of Indigenous Climate Litigation in Brazil,'* by Gabriel Mantelli, Maurício Terena, Isabela Bicalho and Marie-Louise Siemons, assesses the experience of climate litigation by, or related to, Indigenous groups. In particular, this chapter analyzes how Indigenous groups are bringing lawsuits into the Brazilian judiciary to protect their territories and way of living in confronting climate change. The lens adopted is the Indigenous groups' way of living as connected with Nature and its cycles. Being part of a particular ecosystem (such as the Amazon) is, on the one hand, also part of the very identity and culture of an Indigenous group. On the other hand, Indigenous groups' lives and presence in that ecosystem are vital components of its preservation. Therefore, securing the rights of Indigenous peoples also contributes to protecting, preserving, and building resilience of ecosystems vital to the balance of the climate system, as is the case of the Amazon. For that reason, the Paris Agreement perceives the knowledge shared by Indigenous groups as a vital tool for promoting adaptation policies.[101]

This type of climate litigation in Brazil is in line with the IACtHR's environmental case law, which was inaugurated and largely developed in cases related to the protection of Indigenous groups' rights.[102] In this case law, the IACtHR acknowledges that the particular way of living of an Indigenous group involves a certain relation and connection with Nature and its cycles—a way of living that is at risk because of the detrimental harms to the environment that are caused or enhanced by climate change-related events. Unsurprisingly, Indigenous groups are singled out in the Paris Agreement as a vulnerable group of particular concern for policymakers.[103]

To explore the role of Indigenous communities in Brazilian climate litigation, Chapter 10 focuses on the cases related to the Guaíba Mine project,[104] *Fundação Nacional do* Índio *v IMA*,[105] and the *Indigenous Genocide Law Case,*[106]

101 Paris Agreement, art 7(5).

102 Eg *Indigenous Communities of The Lhaka Honhat (Our and) Association v Argentina.* Judgment of Feb 6, 2020, IACtHR Series C No 420.

103 Paris Agreement, Preamble, para 1.

104 *Arayara et al v Copelmi Mineração et al (Mina Guaíba project)*, and *Arayara et al v Copelmi et al (Mina Guaíba project and affected communities)*.

105 *Fundação Nacional do Índio (FUNAI) v Instituto do Meio Ambiente de Santa Catarina (IMA)*. Special Appeal No 1017365 SC, Judgment of 27 September 2023, Rapporteur: Edson Fachin, available at https://www.conjur.com.br/dl/fa/fachin-indios1.pdf

106 *Articulação dos Povos Indígenas do Brasil (APIB), Partido Socialismo e Liberdade (PSL) e Rede Sustentabilidade v União Federal,* ADI 7582, filed in December 2023 before the

where climate litigation related to Indigenous groups' rights resorts to a broad and varied spectrum of human rights, including mainstream human rights (such as the rights to life or health), the right to Free, Prior, and Informed Consent (FPIC), and the emerging rights for Nature[107]—that sibling of the rights of Nature, which is not a synonym of it but leads to similar interpretative results. Moreover, Chapter 10 explains how climate litigation, in relation to Indigenous groups' rights, is inherently intertwined with the broader discussion about historical reparations for Indigenous groups as a result of past human rights infringements, such as their expulsion from ancestral lands.

Chapter 11, '*Future Generations and Climate Litigation in Brazil*,' by Luciana Bauer, analyzes how the rights of future generations have been, or can be, used in the context of climate litigation in Brazil. The chapter first explores the legal and philosophical existence of, and the rights possibly held by, future generations. In fact, the scientific projections for the future behavior of the climate system suggest that the most harmful consequences resulting from GHG emissions will take place in the future. Accordingly, future generations are likely to be more affected than past or current generations—even though, for the simple fact that they are unborn, they have not contributed yet to global warming. Conscious of an ethical commandment to protect the future generations' right of enjoying a climate system that allows them to sustain the conditions for life with dignity, the UNFCCC states that States 'should [but not shall] protect the climate system for the benefit of present and future generations of humankind'[108]—although the same concern is not voiced in the Paris Agreement.

In this context, Chapter 11 provides insights from Brazilian climate litigation, where legal arguments related to 'future' and 'future generations' are being formulated by plaintiffs, although still in a very timid manner. In any case, Bauer explains how invoking the right to the 'future' and 'future generations' rights allows courts to discuss intergenerational equity within the (human) rights' grammar. Perhaps because no judicial proceeding was formally instituted by a representative of future generations, a curious note from the Brazilian experience so far is that it seems that courts and plaintiffs are more comfortable with legal arguments regarding the right to the 'future' or, in another formulation, the right to the perpetuation of the Earth and life itself—an argument that benefits from the climate and environmental litigation regarding the Indigenous'

Federal Supreme Court, available at https://climatecasechart.com/non-us-case/adi-7582-indigenous-genocide-law/.

107 See also Maria Antonia Tigre, 'Climate Change and Indigenous Groups: The Rise of Indigenous Voices in Climate Litigation' (2022) 9 *e-Publica* 211, 256.

108 UNFCCC, art 3(1).

groups rights, as highlighted by Bauer in her chapter. Taking into account cases such as *IEA v Brazil*,[109] *Costa Legal et al v Florianópolis et al*,[110] and the execution of the 2018 IACtHR judgment in the *Case of the Xucuru Indigenous People and their Members v Brazil*,[111] Bauer notes how Article 225 of the Brazilian Constitution can be used, even if only limitedly, in a manner that incorporates the legal protection of the continuity of life for present and future generations.

### 6.4 *Climate Litigation and Biodiversity*

Chapter 12, '*The Protection of the Marine Environment through Litigation in the Context of the Climate Crisis in Brazil*,' by Julia Cirne Lima Weston, delves into cases related to the marine environment and aims to link the legal obligation to protect, preserve, and ameliorate the marine environment with the efforts of mitigation and adaptation to climate change. The science produced in the last years has emphasized the role of oceans in regulating the global climate system, as well as how oceans are affected by GHG emissions and global warming, and how this can ultimately create more stress to our societies—namely to, but not exclusive of, coastal communities. The ITLOS endorsed and emphasized this science in its advisory opinion on climate change and international law,[112] and further qualified GHG emissions as a form of pollution of the marine environment under Article 1(1)(4) of the United Nations Convention on the Law of the Sea (UNCLOS).[113] In the case of Brazil, the configuration of its coastline, the large extension of the maritime areas under its spatial jurisdiction, and the marine habitats lying therein (fragile, but also key to building coastal resilience) explain the importance of protecting, preserving, and ameliorating the state of the marine environment.

---

109 *IEA v Brazil* (n 63).

110 *ONG Costal Legal, Associação Florianopolitana das Entidades Comunitárias (UFECO) e Associação Pachamama v Município de Florianópolis, Fundação Municipal do Meio Ambiente (FLORAM), Estado de Santa Catarina, Instituto do Meio Ambiente de Santa Catarina (FATMA), Companhia Catarinense de Águas e Saneamento (CASAN) e Agência de Regulação de Serviços Públicos de Santa Catarina (ARESC)*. 6th Federal Court of Santa Catarina, ACP No. 5012843-56.2021.4.04.7200, filed on 19 May 2021, available at https://climatecasechart.com/non-us-case/ong-costa-legal-and-others-vs-municipality-of-florianopolis-and-others/.

111 *Case of the Xucuru Indigenous People and their Members v Brazil*. Judgment of Feb 5, 2018, IACtHR Series C No 346.

112 *Request for an Advisory Opinion submitted by the Commission of Small Island States on Climate Change and International Law* (Advisory Opinion of 21 May 2024) Case No 31, §§46–66.

113 ibid, 159–179. See United Nations Convention on the Law of the Sea (UNCLOS) (adopted 10 December 1982, entered into force 16 November 1994) 1833 *UNTS* 3.

In this light, in Chapter 12, Weston first notes that climate litigation in relation to the marine environment is still uncommon and under-researched, both in Brazil and internationally. Weston discusses lessons from two cases that reached Brazil's Superior Court of Justice (STJ), identifying critical lessons for comparative climate litigation related to the marine environment. For example, in *Federal Public Prosecutor's Office v Brazil et al* (*Sea advance and coastal erosion*),[114] involving illegal bar constructions and coastal erosion at Boa Viagem beach, the STJ emphasized that coastal erosion due to climate change is foreseeable and should be considered in legislative, administrative, and judicial decisions. The STJ's decision underscores the undeniable reality and anthropogenic causes of climate change, emphasizing its widespread and devastating impacts, especially on vulnerable populations. The court highlights the scientific consensus on climate change and cautions judges to avoid being swayed by irrational, denialist views often driven by unsustainable economic interests. The ruling reinforces the courts' duty to uphold environmental (and climate) laws against such interests. Specifically, the STJ deemed it unfeasible for lower courts to ignore technical evidence regarding climate-induced coastal erosion and sea-level rise (enhanced by the destruction of marine habitats such as mangroves) and warned against trivializing these issues as isolated or temporary phenomena. The decision is remarkable on many levels, but also because it seems not only to settle a dispute between two parties but also to target and influence lower courts' stance on environmental issues. This is also in line with *IEA v Brazil*, where the autonomous nature of climate change and climate litigation vis-à-vis other environmental issues was stated for the first time. While in *Federal Public Prosecutor's Office* (*MPF*) *v Brazil and Others* (*Sea Advance and Coastal Erosion*), the court did not go that far, the STJ dealt with climate change impacts on the marine environment as a special form of environmental harm deserving a differentiated attention from policy-makers and judges.

In Chapter 13, '*The Protection of the Amazon Forest as a Central Aspect of Climate Mitigation in Brazil*,' Maria Antonia Tigre and Anna Maria Cárcamo delve into the wide range of climate cases that specifically relate to the Amazon rainforest. The chapter, therefore, discusses 34 cases pertaining to the Amazon biome. The fact that over 40 percent of climate cases in Brazil relate to the Amazon rainforest reinforces its role as central in climate mitigation and adaptation. First, the authors provide a broad overview of these cases according

114 *Ministério Público Federal v União Federal, Instituto Brasileiro do Meio Ambiente e dos Recursos Naturais Renováveis, Estado do Sergipe, Agência Ambiental do Sergipe e Outros*. ACP 0800002-72.2014.4.05.8502, filed on 29 January 2024 before the Sergipe 5th Federal Court, available at https://climatecasechart.com/non-us-case/federal-public-prosecutors-office-mpf-v-brazil-and-others-sea-advance-and-coastal-erosion/.

to the year they were filed and their status and specifically discuss the cases that were already decided. Second, the chapter identifies themes related to climate litigation in the Amazon rainforest, several of which intersect with other chapters in this book. The themes identified are: (i) carbon credits and land grabbing, (ii) climate damages, (iii) illegal deforestation, (iv) administrative omissions, (v) project-specific authorization, (vi) forest fires. And third, the chapter discusses a few examples of transnational cases related to the Brazilian Amazon rainforest, namely *Envol Vert et al. v. Casino*,[115] a case related to illegal deforestation and human rights infringements by the cattle industry in Brazil and Colombia, and *Notre Affaire à Tous Les Amis de la Terre, and Oxfam France v BNP Paribas*,[116] which relates to the lack of transparency and clarity in the bank's plans and information regarding its investments and loans, which includes a commitment to cease all financial support to companies producing oil and gas reserves in the Amazon. These cases further showcase the potential of climate litigation related to Brazil to expand beyond the country's borders.

Chapter 14, '*The Rights of Nature: Another Legal Avenue for Climate Litigation in Brazil?*,' by Fernanda Cavedon-Capdeville, José Rubens Morato Leite, Humberto Filpi, and Tônia Dutra, covers the topic of the rights of Nature and how they can be recognized in the context of climate litigation: ie how pursuing the protection of the rights of Nature can contribute to enhancing mitigation and/or adaptation policies. In particular, Chapter 14 takes *Costa Legal et al v Florianópolis et al*[117] as a case study, since this is the only case before the courts in Brazil where a legal argument related to the rights of Nature was formulated.

As the authors mention in this chapter, the emergence of a discourse on the rights of Nature is not made in a vacuum—the theoretical and philosophical foundations have been discussed for a while, and the legal formulations for the rights of Nature have also been tested by the IACtHR and legally transplanted into the Brazilian legal system. The authors also emphasize that, to be strictly objective, 'rights of Nature' as such have not been recognized by the IACtHR or Brazilian courts yet. Nonetheless, the manner in which the IACtHR has

---

115 *Envol Vert, Sherpa, Canopée, Notre Affaire à Tous, France Nature Environnement, Mighty Earth, Comissão Pastoral da Terra* (CPT), *Coordenação das Organizações Indígenas da Amazônia Brasileira* (COIAB), *Federação dos Povos Indígenas do Pará* (FEPIPA), *Federação das Organizações e Povos Indºigenas do Mato Grosso* (FEPOIMT) *& Organización Nacional de los Pueblos Indígenas de la Amazonia Colombiana* (OPIAC) *v Casino*, filed before the Saint-Étienne Judicial Court, available at https://climatecasechart.com/non-us-case/envol-vert-et-al-v-casino/

116 *Notre Affaire à Tous, Les Amis de la Terre, and Oxfam France v BNP Paribas*, filed in 2023 before the Judicial Court of Paris (France), available at https://climatecasechart.com/non-us-case/notre-affaire-a-tous-les-amis-de-la-terre-and-oxfam-france-v-bnp-paribas/

117 *Costa Legal et al v Florianópolis et al* (n 110)

interpreted the right to a healthy environment in THE ADVISORY OPINION 23/17, and how the Sixth Federal Court of Santa Catarina has interpreted the right to a healthy environment in *Costa Legal et al v Florianópolis et al* (in cases detached from the rights of Indigenous groups' rights) come closer to such recognition of the rights of Nature. In a nutshell, the question refers to whether the right to a healthy environment (as a *human* right) only protects human interests, ie human life or health, or whether it can also protect environmental components irrespective of the harm produced to human beings. In *Costa Legal et al v Florianópolis et al*, the court recognized the intrinsic value of nature and thus endorsed this second view. Adopting a more pronounced ecocentric nuance does not equate to affirming the existence of the rights of Nature, but it allows us to state that the rights of natural components in themselves are directly protected under the right to a healthy environment and Article 225 of the Brazilian Constitution. This ecocentric view is also found in apex courts, where an *in dubio pro nature* principle has been affirmed.

### 6.5 *Beyond the State: Climate Litigation and the Energy Transition*

Chapter 15, '*The Role of Financial Institutions in Climate Litigation in Brazil*,' by Alessandra Lehmen, discusses the role of financial institutions in climate litigation in Brazil. The underlying assumption of this chapter is that climate change must also be viewed through economic and financial lenses: on the one hand, because Brazil's economy is highly carbon-led, meaning that GHG emissions are the driving force behind our societies; on the other hand, because to secure a transition to a carbon-neutral society and economy, financial markets must be prepared to channel funds to finance such transition. A perfunctory reading of the Paris Agreement already shows how the treaty drafters were concerned with bringing the financial markets into the spotlight of climate mitigation policies.

Lehmen provides an insight into what counts as climate finance—a matter of terminology, but having in mind that one can only align all types of investments and financial products and activities with climate goals, if all of us share a common understanding of what counts as climate finance as a result of its contribution to the pursuit of such climate goals. The experience from Brazilian courts is still short, but cases such as *AMOREMA e AMORETGRAP v Sustainable Carbon and others*[118] and *Conectas Direitos Humanos v BNDES and BNDESPAR*[119]

118 *Associação dos Moradores da Reserva Extrativista Mapuá (AMOREMA) and Associação dos Moradores da Reserva Extrativista Terra Grande-Pracuúba (AMORETGRAP) v Sustainable Carbon (on voluntary carbon markets)*. ACP 1045416-11.2021.4.01.3900, filed in 2021 before the Federal Court of Pará, available at https://climatecasechart.com/non-us-case/amorema-e-amoretgrap-vs-sustainable-carbon-and-others-carbon-credits-and-extractive-reserves/

119 *Conectas Direitos Humanos v BNDES Participações S.A. (BNDESPAR) and Banco Nacional de Desenvolvimento Econômico e Social (BNDES)*, Federal Court of the Federal District,

provide a hint of what the future climate litigation against financial institutions in Brazil can be; and show how non-binding environmental, social, and governance (ESG) standards can be a powerful tool, if they inform the interpretation of hard law statutory instruments binding upon financial institutions.

Chapter 16, '*The State's Duty to Pursue the Highest Possible Ambition by Filling Regulatory Gaps on Corporate Climate Responsibilities*,' by Guilherme Leal, explores the government's role in regulating domestic mitigation measures. The chapter discusses the regulatory challenges and gaps in addressing climate change in Brazil, particularly the reliance on voluntary commitments by private companies due to the lack of comprehensive regulation. It highlights the growing influence of ESG policies and Corporate Environmental Responsibility (CER) initiatives, which are often motivated by external pressures rather than genuine commitment to climate action, jeopardizing the effectiveness and credibility of measures, and effectively risking greenwashing claims due to the lack of enforceability.

Leal further examines Brazil's regulatory framework's limitations in compelling private companies to mitigate GHG emissions, noting the absence of economy-wide rules and the fragmented nature of sector-specific regulations. Market-driven regulations, such as integrating climate-related financial disclosures in the financial sector and adopting international standards like those set by the International Sustainability Standards Board (ISSB) and the Task Force on Climate-related Financial Disclosures (TCFD), could possibly fill this gap until Brazil adopts clear and comprehensive guidelines for energy transition and climate neutrality.

Still, Leal argues that climate litigation has further acted as this gap-filler. In terms of state responsibility for climate change, *PSB et al v Brazil* (*on Climate Fund*), as noted before, is a landmark case—akin to the U.S. Supreme Court's decision in *Massachusetts v. EPA*. The STF then reinforced its position in overseeing effective regulatory action concerning deforestation and GHG reduction in *PSB et al v Brazil* (*on Amazon Fund*). The next step would be the *Renovabio Case* (ADI 7596),[120] which may further clarify the government's obligations in setting emission reduction targets for the private sector.

Chapter 17, '*Climate Damage and Tort Law in Brazilian Climate Litigation*,' by Rafaela Martins da Rosa, takes an in-depth look into climate damage and tort law in Brazil. Understanding what 'climate damage' is is vital in litigation

Process No. 1038657-42.2022.4.01.3400, filed on 21 June 2022, available at https://climatecasechart.com/non-us-case/conectas-direitos-humanos-v-bndes-and-bndespar/

120 *ADI 7596* (*RenovaBio and Unlawful Interference in Economic Activity*), filed on 5 February 2024 before the STF, available at https://climatecasechart.com/non-us-case/adi-7596-renovabio-and-unlawful-interference-in-economic-activity/.

against States and non-state actors alike, namely in cases where a plaintiff asks compensation for such damages under tort law. However, climate damages—just as climate litigation in itself—are unique if compared with other environmental damages, for instance, as a result of its planetary scale and the fact that it is the downstream result of an excessive concentration of GHG in our atmosphere, which for their turn are attributable to several States at the same time. In Brazil, tort actions and the legal regime for liability for environmental damages are perceived autonomously with regard to personal or property damages but include damages produced to the atmosphere. Nonetheless, in a very audacious move, the National Council of Justice (CNJ) issued its Resolution No 433/2021, which states the obligation of national courts to single out climate damage as a special kind within the genre of environmental damage. With this background, Chapter 17 explores how Brazilian courts have been conceptualizing climate damages in the context of tort law—having in mind that the fate of a claim for reparation for damages related to climate change is inherently linked to the plaintiff's capacity to overcome procedural obstacles related to legal standing and victimhood, causation, or shared responsibility. To this end, emphasizing the autonomy of climate damage—as endorsed by the CNJ—may be perceived as an attempt to lower the standard of reading of these procedural concepts.

Finally, Chapter 18, '*Just Transition Litigation in Brazil*,' by Luiz Ormay Jr, explores the topic of just transition litigation in Brazil. Based on the need to shift our economies from carbon-led to carbon-neutral, 'just transition' is the concept that aims to match this transition in energy sources with the need to protect vulnerable groups, foster employment, and social protection, secure fairness in energy access and use, and guarantee a politically informed and participated decision-making process.[121]

However, geographical features can make the transition from carbon- to green or clean energy-led economies more complex. Brazil is a prime example of population dispersion and a severe dependency on coal, oil, and gas for the production of energy. Accordingly, a fair just transition regime must reconcile and accommodate apparently incompatible and contradictory measures, such as subsidizing renewable energies and securing a stable energy production and supply flux. This balance was sought by Brazilian legislation—both at the Federal Union level and in the state of Santa Catarina. However, taxonomy is also relevant in this context, because labeling a law as pursuing a 'just

121 Denton et al (eds), *IPCC, 2022: Climate Change 2022: Mitigation of Climate Change. Contribution of Working Group III to the Sixth Assessment Report of the Intergovernmental Panel on Climate Change* (CUP 2023).

transition' can be deceptive, namely if, as a result of a complex political bargain, just transition measures end up encouraging, or at least supporting, the resort to fossil fuels. In these cases, just transition litigation—ie lawsuits that challenge the justice, equity, proportionality, or adequacy of measures aimed at encouraging a transition from fossil fuel to green energy sources (Eg challenging subsidies to the use of fossil fuels)—is an avenue open to litigants who question the 'deceptiveness' of such measures. Chapter 18 analyzes two cases from Brazilian courts—*Rede Sustentabilidade v State of Santa Catarina* (*on Just Energy Transition*)[122] and *Rede Sustentabilidade et al v Brazil* (*on Jorge Lacerda Thermoelectric Complex*)[123]—where political parties filed an application for a direct action of unconstitutionality (ADI), arguing that just transition laws from the Federal Union and the state of Santa Catarina were not adequate, and therefore infringed the human right to a healthy environment protected under Article 225 of the Brazilian Constitution.

## 7 Wrapping Up

As the chapter has outlined, this book focuses on analyzing the evolving landscape of climate litigation in Brazil, a country at the forefront of the global climate justice movement. Brazil's unique position as both a significant GHG emitter and a key player in global mitigation efforts, with its vast natural resources like the Amazon rainforest and the coastal mangroves, makes it a critical case study.

As this book was being written and finalized in 2024, Brazil experienced a series of devastating, unprecedented climate events. In the state of Rio Grande do Sul, catastrophic floods swept through an area the size of the United Kingdom, while fires in the Amazon rainforest scorched land equivalent to the size of Costa Rica, shrouding vast regions of South America in smoke. The magnitude of these climate-related disasters underscores Brazil's critical role in the global fight against climate change. It highlights the urgent need for collective action to address this escalating crisis.

---

122 *Rede Sustentabilidade v Estado de Santa Catarina*. ADI 7332, filed on 29 December 2022 before the Federal Supreme Court, available at https://climatecasechart.com/non-us-case/adi-7332-policy-for-just-energy-transition-of-the-state-of-santa-catarina/

123 *Rede Sustentabilidade, Partido Socialismo e Liberdade* (PSOL) *e Partido Socialista Brasileiro* (PSB) *v União Federal* (*on Jorge Lacerda Thermoelectric Complex*). ADI 7095, filed on 10 March 2022 before the Federal Supreme Court, available at https://climatecasechart.com/non-us-case/adi-7095-complexo-termeletrico-jorge-lacerda/

The evolving landscape of climate litigation in Brazil reflects the country's complex position as both a contributor to, a victim of, and part of the solution to climate change, while also holding unique tools for mitigation and adaptation. The rapid increase in climate cases, many of which are grounded in human rights claims, underscores the growing importance of judicial intervention in addressing environmental deregulation and pushing for more robust climate policies. The Brazilian experience, particularly the judicial lawsuits driven by human rights-based claims, offers valuable insights into how courts can influence climate policy in emerging economies. By honing in on Brazil, this book provides a nuanced analysis of climate litigation that reflects both the challenges and the potential for legal innovation in the Global South.

The specific scope of this book—centered on climate litigation in Brazil—has been deliberately chosen to provide readers with an in-depth understanding of a jurisdiction that is increasingly pivotal in global climate governance. This focus allows for a more thorough examination of the interplay between environmental and climate law, human rights, and the judiciary's role in advancing climate justice. The Brazilian context, as discussed, presents a unique convergence of environmental deregulation and judicial activism, offering lessons that can be applied beyond its borders, especially within the Global South.

Brazil's climate litigation experience is not only relevant domestically but also holds valuable lessons for the Global South and beyond. Its innovative legal approaches, particularly the rights-based interpretation of international agreements like the Paris Agreement and unique approaches to climate damages, offer new perspectives that can inspire courts worldwide. This surge of cases, often overlooked in the broader discourse dominated by Global North litigation, highlights the need for more attention to the contributions of Global South jurisdictions in shaping global climate governance.

The chapters that follow delve deeper into the specific dimensions of Brazil's climate litigation, exploring the judicial, legal, and socio-political factors that have shaped this movement. By doing so, this book aims to shed light on the broader implications of Brazil's legal actions, offering a comprehensive and cohesive analysis that contributes to a more inclusive understanding of global climate litigation. Ultimately, Brazil's experience demonstrates that climate litigation is not only a tool for environmental protection but also a means of advancing social justice, ensuring that vulnerable communities and future generations are safeguarded from the worst impacts of climate change.

Readers are invited to explore the diverse chapters of this book, each delving into a different aspect of climate litigation in Brazil. From judicial rulings and the separation of powers to issues surrounding just transition, vulnerable groups, and financial institutions, these chapters collectively contribute to a broader understanding of how Brazil is shaping the future of climate law. The effort to compile these analyses reflects the collective contributions of scholars, legal practitioners, and policymakers dedicated to advancing the field of climate litigation in Brazil.

In sum, this book offers not only a detailed exploration of Brazil's climate litigation landscape but also an invitation to engage with the growing global discourse on climate justice. This book aims to inspire further comparative studies and foster a deeper understanding of how legal frameworks can drive meaningful climate action by providing a comprehensive overview of Brazil's judicial efforts to tackle climate change.

# SECTION 1

## *Challenges in Climate Litigation in Brazil*

CHAPTER 2

# A Panorama of Climate Litigation in Brazil

*Danielle de Andrade Moreira**

## 1 Introduction

The urgency and gravity of the climate issue in the Anthropocene[1] have led to the filing of legal actions worldwide aimed at addressing the problem, directly or indirectly. Climate litigation has intensified in recent years, both in the Global North and South, presenting itself as a promising path for addressing the emergency caused by climate change.[2] This trend has also been observed in Brazil, particularly since 2018,[3] due to the recent deepening of legislative setbacks in social and environmental matters and in the administrative structure responsible for environmental protection.

* Associate Professor at the Pontifical Catholic University of Rio de Janeiro (PUC-Rio), Brazil, Law School and Interdisciplinary Center for the Environment. Coordinator of the Research Group 'Law, Environment, and Justice in the Anthropocene' (*Direito, Ambiente e Justiça no Antropoceno*, JUMA/PUC-Rio). ORCID No. 0000–0001-8860-7963.1

1 See Jordi Jaria Manzano, 'El Dret, l'antropocè i la justícia' (2016) VII *Revista Catalana de Dret Ambiental* 1; Will Steffen, Paul Crutzen & John McNiell, 'The Anthropocene: Are Humans Now Overwhelming the Great Forces of Nature' (2007) 36 *AMBIO: A Journal of the Human Environment* 614; Maristella Svampa, 'El antropoceno como diagnóstico y paradigma' (2019) 24 *Utopia y praxis latinoamericana* 33.

2 Joana Setzer & Catherine Higham, *Global Trends in Climate Change Litigation: 2024 Snapshot* (Grantham Research Institute on Climate Change and the Environment and Centre for Climate Change Economics and Policy 2024) 2, 13–14; Maria Antonia Tigre, *Climate Litigation in the Global South: Mapping Report* (Sabin Center for Climate Change Law 2024). See also Joana Setzer & Catherine Higham, 'Global Trends in Climate Change Litigation: 2023 Snapshot' (Grantham Research Institute on Climate Change and the Environment and Centre for Climate Change Economics and Policy 2023) 11–18; Michael Burger & Maria Antonia Tigre, 'Global Climate Litigation Report: 2023 Status Review' (Sabin Center for Climate Change Law and UNEP 2023) 6–21.

3 Danielle de Andrade Moreira, Carolina de Figueiredo Garrido, Juliana Chermont Pessoa Lopes, Paula Máximo de Barros Pinto, Victória Lourenço de Carvalho e Gonçalves, Luciana Tse Chaves Garcia Rego, Maria Eduarda Garambone Sydenstricker & Ana Paula Ricci, *Panorama da Litigância Climática no Brasil: Relatório de 2024* (JUMA/PUC-Rio, 2024) 16. See also Danielle de Andrade Moreira, Juliana Lopes, Paula Pinto, Carolina Garrido, Victoria Gonçalves & Luciana Rego, *Brazilian Climate Litigation Bulletin 2023* (JUMA/PUC-Rio, 2023) 18–19.

 | DOI:10.1163/9789004690974_003

Brazil is among the six major greenhouse gas (GHG) emitters in the world.[4] Around 75% of Brazilian emissions are from land use change and agriculture (crop and livestock).[5] Brazil is Party to the Paris Agreement and has, since 2009, a National Policy for Climate Change that sets forth principles, goals, guidelines, and instruments to fight climate change. The Federal Constitution (1988) and the National Environmental Policy (1981) also provide for broad protection of the environment, being broad enough to encompass the current threats to the climate, biodiversity, water, air, soil, human health, and culture-related matters (all these elements related to each other within a holistic approach).

Climate change raises complex issues within this regulatory framework. Its multifaceted nature requires the systemic interpretation and application of the regulatory structure.[6] Climate litigation requires connecting climate change with mainstream environmental regulatory framework, entailing that climate litigation in Brazil fits within the legal framework, and case-law already paved by mainstream environmental litigation.

This chapter presents an overview of climate litigation in Brazil based on a diagnosis derived from the analysis and classification of climate litigation brought before the Brazilian judiciary. The analysis centers on cases included in the Brazilian Climate Litigation Platform (hereinafter, 'JUMA Platform'), which was created and is directed by the author of this chapter.[7] Section 2 aims

4 'China, the United States, India, the EU, Russia, and Brazil were the six world largest GHG emitters in 2022. Together they account for 50.1% of global population, 61.2% of global Gross Domestic Product (GDP), 63.4% of global fossil fuel consumption and 61.6% of global GHG emissions.' Monica Crippa et al, 'GHG emissions of all world countries' (Publications Office of the European Union, 2023) available at <http://doi:10.2760/235266> accessed 27 December 2023.

5 According to the System for Estimating Greenhouse Gas Emissions and Removals (*Sistema de Estimativas de Emissões e Remoções de Gases de Efeito Estufa*—SEEG), in 2022, 'land-use changes, including the devastation of all Brazilian biomes, accounted for 1.12 billion gross tons of carbon dioxide equivalent ($CO_2$eq), or 48% of the national total. The agriculture sector comes second, with 617 million tons of $CO_2$eq, a 3% increase from 2021, representing 27% of the country's gross emissions. Energy is third, with 412 Mt$CO_2$eq, a 5% decrease following a record 24% increase in the previous year. The waste (91 Mt$CO_2$eq, a 1% downward fluctuation) and industrial processes (78 Mt$CO_2$eq, a 6% decrease) sectors represent 4% and 3% of the country's total emissions, respectively'. David Tsai et al, 'Análise das emissões de gasses de efeito estufa e suas implicações para as metas climáticas do Brasil 1970–2022' (SEEG 2023) 5, available at <https://oc.eco.br/wp-content/uploads/2023/11/Relatorio-SEEG_gases-estufa_2023FINAL.pdf> accessed on 27 December 2023.

6 See Richard Lazarus, 'Super Wicked Problems and Climate Change: Restraining the Present to Liberate the Future' (2009) 94 *Cornell Law Review* 1153.

7 The database is only available in Portuguese at <https://www.juma.nima.puc-rio.br/base-dados-litigancia-climatica-no-brasil>. For the purpose of this chapter, all 80 cases introduced

to show that climate litigation in Brazil fits within the legal avenues already paved by environmental litigation. Section 3 presents a snapshot of the set of legal cases included in the Platform based on analytical categories established to identify the profile of the climate litigation movement in the country.[8] These categories include: (i) whether the climate is a central or a contextual argument; (ii) the nature of the suit (systemic or routine lawsuit); (iii) the profile of the litigants as plaintiffs and defendants; (iv) explicit or implicit references to environmental or climate justice; (v) whether the case seeks a defense of a stable climate or climate deregulation; (vi) identification of the sector that contributes to GHG emissions and the Brazilian biome involved in the case; and (vii) remedies sought (mitigation, adaptation, climate risk assessment or climate damage repair measures). Section 4 illustrates how pre-existing and already tested legal tools dedicated to environmental protection have been applied to address the climate crisis in Brazilian courts.

## 2 Climate and Environmental Litigation in Brazil

Climate litigation in Brazil is a branch of overall environmental litigation. This is evidenced by the fact that many early and numerous recent climate cases are structurally akin to cases related to the protection of the environment, thus also based on environmental legislation, case law, and scholarship. Out of the 80 cases cataloged in the JUMA Platform until 31 March 2024, a total of 74 involve the application of Article 225 of the Brazilian Constitution (hereinafter, 'Constitution'), which guarantees the right to an ecologically balanced environment.[9]

The earlier cases, especially those filed before 2018, only reference climate concern in a peripheral or indirect way within the high court's rulings, since

in the platform until 31 March 2024 were analyzed. Due to the partnership established between JUMA/PUC-Rio and the Sabin Center for Climate Change Law, Brazilian climate litigation cases included in the JUMA Platform have been translated and are also available on the Global Climate Change Litigation Database, available at <https://climatecasechart.com/non-us-climate-change-litigation/>.

8 For a better understanding of the methodology regarding selection criteria and classification of cases, see Danielle de Andrade Moreira, Letícia Lima, Juliana Lopes, Carolina Garrido & Maria Eduarda Segovia, *Plataforma de Litigância Climática no Brasil: Metodologia para Seleção e Categorização de Casos Climáticos Brasileiros* (Lucas Melara 2022).

9 Out of the 80 cases examined, only 6 do not refer to Article 225. Most of these 6 cases raise issues related to carbon markets, such as the illegal appropriation and trade of carbon credits in the voluntary carbon market, the obligation to meet decarbonization credit acquisition goals, or the blending of biodiesel with fossil diesel.

climate change does not appear directly in the authors' complaints. These cases were not brought forward as climate litigation per se, but rather as environmental lawsuits wherein climate-related issues were cited alongside a variety of other environmental concerns.[10] For example, some of the recurrent issues present in judicial decisions of this set of previous cases are those related to:

1. the protection of mangroves, the coastal zone, and beaches;
2. sugar cane straw burning and forest firing, in which the climate change is mentioned in the context of the air pollution;
3. water pollution or water crisis, considering that the risk of water shortage is increased by climate change;
4. the failure to comply with the Forest Code (Law No. 12.651/2012) in cases that do not expressly mention climate change, but still consider the harmonious coexistence of the forest system with the related systems as the climate system; and
5. the discussion on the (un)constitutionality of the Forest Code, mentioning that climate change is increased by illegal deforestation.

There is a significant change in the profile of the most recent cases, especially those filed after 2018. In this recent wave of cases, laws and facts related to climate change are addressed in a more explicit, direct, and central way, although arguments still come together with environmental law-based reasoning. It is also worth noting that the setbacks and dismantling of the Brazilian environmental policy (which occurred especially between 2019 and 2022, during the government of President Bolsonaro)[11] also drove the focus to climate issues, bolstering the climate litigation movement in Brazil.

---

10 Among these earlier cases, there is a subset that stands out as an exception in Brazilian climate litigation prior to 2018, as they specifically addressed climate change from the outset. In 2010, the Public Prosecutor of São Paulo initiated 35 lawsuits against airline companies operating at the international airport of São Paulo. These lawsuits sought compensation for the $CO_2$ emissions resulting from the daily landing and take-off of aircrafts. The court dismissed the suits against several of the airlines on the grounds of lack of jurisdiction over the claims. See Joana Setzer, Guilherme Leal & Caio Borges, 'Climate Change Litigation in Brazil: Will Green Courts Become Greener?', in Alogna, Bakker & Gauci (eds), *Climate Change Litigation: Global Perspectives* (Brill Nijhoff 2023) 152–4.

11 'Brazil's environmental regulatory regime has been under significant attack, especially from 2019 to 2022. Through budget cuts imposed on regulatory agencies, modification of the regulatory structure, and deliberate policies impacting fragile environmental areas, the government under President Bolsonaro sought to dismantle its environmental policy'. Danielle de Andrade Moreira, Ana Lucia Nina, Carolina Garrido & Maria Eduarda Segovia, 'Rights-based Climate Litigation in Brazil: An Assessment of Constitutional Cases before the Brazilian Supreme Court' (2024) 48 Journal of Human Rights Practice, 16. See also Maria Antonia Tigre & Joana Setzer, 'Human Rights and Climate Change for

Following this trend, the majority of the recent cases were filed with the specific purpose of protecting climate stability. Nevertheless, the approach to addressing climate issues varies. Among the 80 cases recorded on the JUMA Platform, 45 cases take the climate as a/the major issue, whilst 35 cases address the climate only contextually.[12]

This set of recent cases covers a range of topics, for example, cases questioning or related to:

1. the shutdown of the Amazon Fund and the Climate Fund, the non-execution of the Action Plan for the Prevention and Control of Deforestation in the Amazon, and the Federal Government omission in combating the Amazon deforestation and its inaction to control environmental illegal agents in at least the ten main hotspots of environmental illicit activities in the Amazon;[13]
2. flaws and insufficiencies in the EIA or environmental licensing process of relevant GHG emitters projects (Eg opencast coal mining projects, thermoelectric plants, and chemical hubs);[14,15]

---

Climate Litigation in Brazil and Beyond: An Analysis of the Climate Fund Decision' (2023) 54 *Georgetown Journal of Int'l Law* 593, 595.

12 While the JUMA Platform is the most comprehensive database available on Brazilian climate cases, it is not exhaustive. Although the JUMA Platform encompasses cases explicitly related to climate change, they can refer to climate change as the main issue (or one of the main issues) or only as a contextual argument. Climate is considered a contextual argument when the lawsuit addresses climate change only in a secondary or accessory manner, or with the objective of contextualizing the discussion, without the climate issue being central and essential to the action. Cases in which climate concerns are brought only as a context for legal arguments that are not directly related to climate issues 'are included only if they are considered relevant due to their media and/or academic impact and their potential to effectively contribute to the development of climate litigation in Brazil'. Moreira et al, *Brazilian Climate Litigation Bulletin 2023* (n 3) 3.

13 Before the STF, see *PSB et al v Brazil* (*on Climate Fund*) [STF] ADPF 708, 7 January 2022; *PSB et al v Brazil* (*on deforestation and human rights*) [STF] ADPF 760, 6 April 2022; or *PSB et al v Brazil* (*on Amazon Fund*) [STF] ADO 59, 16 August 2023. For other jurisdictions, see *IEA v Brazil*, ACP filed in the State of Paraná; or *Ministério Público Federal v Brazil* (*on deforestation hotspots in the Amazon*), ACP filed in 2020 in the State of Amazonas.

14 In the State of Rio Grande do Sul, *Arayara et al v Copelmi Mineração et al* (*Mina Guaíba project*) ACP ACP 5069057-47.2019.4.04.7100 [Federal Court] filed in 2019, and ACP 5069057-47.2019.4.04.7100 [Court of Justice] filed in 2020; *Ministério Público v Estado de Rio Grande do Sul et al* (*on carbochemical complex*) ACP 9065931-65.2019.8.21.0001, filed in 2019; *Associação Gaúcha et al v Copelmi Mineração et al* (*Nova Seival Thermal Power Plant*) ACP 5030786-95.2021.4.04.7100, filed in 2020; *Arayara v. Copelmi Mineração et al* (*on hydrological risks*) ACP 5069057-47.2019.4.04.710 (Court of Justice) filed on 2020. In the State of Ceará, *Instituto Verdeluz et al v Portocem et al* (*on installation of a thermoelectric plant in Pecém*).

15 See Guilherme Leal (Chapter 16) in this book.

3. civil liability for unauthorized GHG emissions from illegal deforestation, requiring compensation for the corresponding climate-environmental damage;[16,17,18]
4. the unconstitutionality of subnational just energy transition policies and changes in the Brazilian energy planning, providing subsidies to the use of coal for energy generation and establishing mandatory contracting of energy from natural gas-fired thermoelectric plants, which will increase GHG emissions;[19,20]
5. the lack of rules for assessing the climate impacts of lending activities carried out by financial institutions, violating Brazil's commitments under the Paris Agreement and the National Climate Change Policy;[21,22] and
6. the sale of carbon credits generated within or around extractive reserves located in the Amazon region without proper compensation to the communities that have worked to preserve forests in the project areas and the enforcement of contractual obligations related to carbon credits generated by a REDD+ (Reducing Emissions from Deforestation and Forest Degradation) project.[23]

---

16 In accordance with Article 14 of the Resolution No. 433/2021, issued by the National Council of Justice (CNJ), climate-environmental damage refers to the climate dimension of environmental damage.

17 In the State of Amapá, *IBAMA v Souza Brilhante (on illegal wood storage)*, ACP 1003478-16.2018.4.01.3100, filed in 2018. In the State of Amazonas, *IBAMA v. Seringal (on illegal wood storage)*, ACP 1000364-26.2019.4.01.3200, filed in 2019; *Federal Public Prosecutor's Office et al v Rezende (on deforestation and climate damage)*, ACP 1005885-78.2021.4.01.3200, filed in 2021; *IBAMA v. Dirceu Kruger (on illegal wood storage)*, ACP 1037196-19.2023.4.01.3200, filed in 2023. In the State of Minas Gerais, *IBAMA v Siderúrgica* São Luiz et al (on coal irregular origin), filed in 2019. In the State of Pará, *IBAMA v. Madeireira Madevi (on illegal wood storage)*, ACP 1000656-73.2018.4.01.3902, filed in 2018, *IBAMA v Gabriel Madeiras (on illegal wood storage)*, ACP 1000185-42.2018.4.01.3907, filed in 2018; *IBAMA v Silmar Gomes Moreira (on illegal wood storage)*, ACP 1000469-62.2018.4.01.3903, filed in 2018; *IBAMA v Madeira Nova Aliança (on illegal wood storage)*, ACP 1000275-31.2019.4.01.3902, filed in 2019; *IBAMA v Floresta Verde (on illegal wood storage)*, ACP 1000083-80.2019.4.01.3908, filed in 2019. In the State of Roraima, *IBAMA v Madelin Madeireira Linhares (on illegal wood storage)*, ACP 1001659-42.2018.4.01.4200, filed in 2018. In the State of Mato Grosso, *IBAMA v Alto Norte (on illegal wood storage)*, ACP 1000200-41.2018.4.01.3606, filed in 2018.

18 See Maria Antonia Tigre & Anna Maria Cárcamo (Chapter 13) in this book.

19 *PSB et al v Brazil (on Electrobras Privatization)* [STF] ADI 6932, filed in 2021; *Rede Sustentablidade et al v Brazil (on Jorge Lacerda Thermoelectric Complex)* [STF] ADI 7095, filed in 2022; *Rede Sustentabilidade v State of Santa Catarina (on Just Energy Transition)* [STF] ADI 7332, filed in 2022.

20 See Luiz Ormay Jr. (Chapter 18) in this book.

21 *Conectas Direitos Humanos v BNDES and BNDESPAR*, filed in 2022 in the Federal District.

22 See Alessandra Lehmen (Chapter 15) in this book.

23 *AMOREMA and AMORETGRAP v Sustainable Carbon at al*, ACP filed in 2021 in the State of Pará; *Carbonext v Amazon Imóveis (Voluntary Carbon Market)*, filed in 2021 in the State of São Paulo.

Indeed, climate cases in Brazil cover a wide range of topics, all of which are in some way directly related to climate change. Although it is clear that climate change is beginning to be explicitly litigated before the Brazilian courts,[24] it is not yet possible to dissociate it from the environmental litigation itself.

The nature of climate litigation in Brazil aligns with the broad concept of the related movement in the Global South.[25] Considering that there is no precise or unique definition to the expression climate litigation, it can be understood as the set of 'judicial, administrative or extrajudicial actions directly or indirectly related to climate change, which unfold at the following levels: (i) cases in which climate change constitutes the central issue to be analyzed, appearing as the main and express ground of the lawsuit; (ii) cases in which climate change explicitly appears as one of the grounds discussed, being articulated, however, together with other environmental and/or technical arguments ; (iii) cases in which climate change is not explicitly mentioned, but which have clear implications for climate regulation more broadly.'[26]

This comprehensive definition is consistent with the characteristics of climate disputes submitted before Brazilian courts, including the overlap between climate and environmental litigation, which led the National Council of Justice to categorize climate litigation as a specialized branch within environmental law and litigation.[27]

Undoubtedly, a notable feature of climate litigation in Brazil is its alignment with the pre-existing framework of environmental law, especially as outlined in Article 225 of the Constitution. This provision establishes a collective right to an ecologically balanced environment, assigning duties to both the government and society to uphold its protection for present and future generations.[28]

---

24 As Délton Winter de Carvalho and Armando Rocha explain in Chapter 6, in the *IEA v Brazil* case, the court considered that climate litigation is a special form of litigation, which shares a certain genetic code with mainstream environmental litigation but should be autonomized nonetheless (paras 14–5). This approach has not *yet* been replicated in other decisions from Brazilian courts.

25 See Tigre (n 2) and Jaqueline Peel & Jolene Lin, 'Transnational Climate Litigation: The Contribution of the Global South' (2019) 113(4) *AJIL* 679; Joana Setzer & Lisa Benjamin, 'Climate Litigation in the Global South: Constraints and Innovations' (2020) 9(1) *Transn'l Env'l Law* 77.

26 Danielle de Andrade Moreira (ed), *Litigância Climática no Brasil: Argumentos Jurídicos para a Inserção da Variável Climática no Licenciamento Ambiental* (Editora PUC-Rio 2021) 39. Despite the broad scope of the term climate litigation, which includes cases directly or indirectly related to climate change, the inclusion of cases is restricted to those that expressly mention the climate issue to enable the construction of a climate litigation database in Brazil.

27 Resolution No. 433/2021 of the National Council of Justice (CNJ), art 3(4).

28 See Carolina Garrido (Chapter 5) and Délton Winter de Carvalho & Armando Rocha (Chapter 6) in this book.

The link between environmental law and climate litigation allows to use Article 225 of the Constitution in climate litigation, hand in hand with the general framework of environmental law. In fact, the evolution of environmental law in response to environmental hyper complexities has created a fertile ground for climate litigation, paving the way for further progress in protecting climate stability. The disruptive nature of environmental law continuously propels shifts across legal doctrines, statutory enactments, and case law. This disruption creates opportunities for innovative approaches to climate litigation and underscores the importance of preexisting legal mechanisms in addressing environmental and climate challenges in Brazil. With its robust constitutional and legal system applicable to environmental and climate issues, Brazil has a solid foundation for addressing climate stability.

In this regard, the recognition of the collective right to a balanced environment under Article 225 of the Constitution, which includes a stable climate as a fundamental human right, is a significant milestone in the case law of the STF.[29] Indeed, climate litigation is increasingly focused on the defense of human rights, with the STF more frequently emphasizing the link between the right to a healthy environment and the enjoyment of other human rights[30]—in manner that places climate litigation in Brazil at the forefront of an expanding wave of rights-based climate litigation in Latin America.[31]

Brazil is also Party to the Paris Agreement, which was internalized through Legislative Decree 140/2016 and Executive Decree 9,073/2017. This means that the Paris Agreement holds direct effect in the Brazilian legal system, thus being binding upon individuals and companies, and invokable before courts. Since the right to an ecologically balanced environment is a human right,

---

29 Moreira et al (n 11) 50, and Moreira et al (n 26) 34. See Carolina Garrido (Chapter 6) and Délton Winter de Carvalho and Armando Rocha (Chapter 6) in this book. See also Danielle de Andrade Moreira, Letícia Lima, Juliana Lopes, Carolina Garrido, Maria Eduarda Segovia & Paula Barros Pinto, *Litigando a Crise Climática no Brasil: Argumentos Jurídicos para se Exigir do Estado a Implementação Doméstica do Acordo de Paris* (Pimenta Cultural 2022); Alessandra Lehmen, 'Advancing Strategic Climate Litigation in Brazil' (2021) 22 *German Law Journal* 1471, 1471–83.

30 Moreira et al (n 11) 4.

31 'Through the use of creative approaches including the elevation of green rights to fundamental rights, the use of expedited procedures to protect human rights, and the (re)interpretation of traditional rights and recognition of new ones, climate litigation in LATAM [Latin America] is making a pivotal contribution towards global efforts to tackle climate change. Rights-based climate litigation is an additional layer to this emerging trend.' Maria Antonia Tigre, Natalia Urzola & Alexandra Goodman, 'Climate Litigation in Latin America: Is the Region Quietly Leading a Revolution?' (2023) 14 *Journal of Human Rights and the Environment* 67, 69.

international treaties related to the environment, including the Paris Agreement, also pertain to the matter of human rights.[32]

The STF has validated this interpretation on various occasions, including one notable instance during the adjudication of the *PSB et al v Brazil* (*on Climate Fund*).[33] In this case, Minister Luís Roberto Barroso (acting as rapporteur) equated environmental treaties (such as the Paris Agreement) to human rights treaties, thus assigning them a supra-legal *status* within the domestic legal hierarchy. Given this supra-legal standing, these human rights treaties are positioned above ordinary statutory norms yet remaining subordinated to the Constitution. Hence, the STF dispelled all doubt concerning the incorporation of climate issues into the breadth of Article 225 of the Constitution, confirming their connection with a fundamental human right.[34] In its decision on *PSB et al v Brazil* (*on Climate Fund*), the STF underlined that the executive branch bears a 'constitutional, supra-legal, and legal duty' to protect the environment and undertake action to address climate change. These duties are considered binding and are not a matter of 'political choice.'[35] In a constitutional order that requires the economic system to be informed by environmental principles,[36] explains why, using the words of Minister Herman Benjamin, Brazil went 'from misery to opulence' in terms of constitutional protection of the environment.[37]

At the level of statutory norms, a National Environmental Policy Act (NEPA, Law No. 6,938/1981) and a National Climate Change Policy Act (NCCPA, Law No. 12,187/2009) are in place in Brazil. The enactment of the NEPA in 1981 was a significant step, as it recognized the importance of taking a holistic and systemic approach to environmental protection: instead of viewing ecological elements (Eg air, fauna, flora, water, or biodiversity) in isolation (ie as if they were not related to each other), these statutes acknowledge the interconnection

32 Moreira et al (n 11) 62–3. See also Carolina Garrido (Chapter 5) in this book.

33 *PSB et al v Brazil* (*on Climate Fund*). On this topic, see Carolina Garrido (Chapter 5) in this book.

34 Moreira et al (n 26) 3 and 14.

35 Moreira et al (n 11) 59–60. 'By recognizing the Paris Agreement as a human rights treaty, the Supreme Court would likely be favorable to a claim that calls for an increase in mitigation ambition consistent with the 1.5°C goal of the Paris Agreement, the (human rights) obligation to mitigate GHG emissions through progressive commitments, and a science-based approach to establishing these obligations, relying on fair share and the zero-deforestation goal'. Maria Antonia Tigre, 'The "Fair Share" of Climate Mitigation: Can Litigation Increase National Ambition for Brazil?' (2023) *Journal of Human Rights Practice*, huad032, 17.

36 Constitution, art 170(VI).

37 Antonio Herman Benjamin, 'Direito Constitucional Ambiental Brasileiro', in Canotilho & Leite (eds), *Direito Constitucional Ambiental Brasileiro* (Saraiva 2007) 57, 84.

between ecological factors, and further relate the environment with social, economic, and cultural aspects. The NEPA establishes a legal framework which in abstract is able to deter the practice of activities detrimental to the environment,[38] such as the mandatory nature of environmental licensing and EIA studies,[39] the adoption of a broad notion of 'polluter'[40] hand in hand with a regime of strict and objective liability for environmental damage.[41]

For its turn, the NCCPA, adopted in 2019, targets climate change more specifically. Nonetheless, its foundational concepts, strategic directions, goals, and guiding principles have profound ties with general environmental law. For instance, the NCCPA's guiding principles include the prevention, the precautionary, and the sustainable development principle, common to general environmental law.[42] Moreover, 'the assessment of environmental impacts on the microclimate and macroclimate' and 'the establishment of environmental standards and quantifiable and verifiable goals for the reduction of anthropogenic emissions from sources and the enhancement of anthropogenic removals by sinks of GHG' are listed among the NCCPA instruments.[43] Article 11 of NCCPA confirms the link with NEPA, while stating that the 'principles, objectives, guidelines, and instruments of public policies and governmental programs shall align with the principles, objectives, guidelines, and instruments of this National Policy on Climate Change.'

The reason for spending these lines on statutory norms is because both instruments reveal Brazil's commitment to environmental protection and climate action, providing a solid foundation for mobilizing legal tools to protect climate stability. More specifically, these instruments may be used in a climate-related constitutional lawsuit, a 'public civil action' (*ação civil pública*), or a 'citizen suit' (*ação popular*). Nevertheless, the actual application and enforcement of environmental regulations still faces several challenges, 'including weak and fragmented institutions, incomplete legal foundations, and limited political will, budgetary constraints, inappropriately staffed agencies, as well as strong industrial and commercial lobbies.'[44] The improvements seen in the case law (namely, in overall environmental litigation) provide some

38 See Danielle de Andrade Moreira & Stela Luz Andreatta Herschmann, 'The Awakening of Climate Litigation in Brazil: Strategies Based on the Existing Legal Toolkit' (2021) 59 *Direito, Estado e Sociedade* 172, 181–3.
39 Law No. 6,938/1981, art 9 (III and IV).
40 Law No. 6,938/1981, art 3 (IV).
41 Law No. 6,938/1981, art 14 (para 1).
42 Law No. 12,187/2009, art 3.
43 Law No. 12,187/2009, art 6, XVII and XVIII.
44 Setzer & Benjamin (n 25) 6.

hope. Indeed, the 'green' jurisprudence, particularly established in the higher courts, has affirmed and reinforced environmental protection through innovative interpretations of constitutional and statutory provisions.[45]

In fact, as an evolving field, environmental law depends on, and fosters, a series of 'reinterpretations' of conventional legal mechanisms to make them suitable for dealing with the unique challenges of environmental issues, including the intricate nature of climate-related challenges. Reflecting on the disruptive path already taken by environmental law in legislative, doctrinal, and jurisprudential terms, this chapter argues that the Brazilian environmental legal framework already includes the normative tools to deal with climate risk (preventively) and its unwanted consequences (from a reparatory or compensatory perspective). The following section outlines the main traits of the climate actions presented to the Brazilian justice system.

## 3 Brazilian Climate Litigation Profile

The JUMA Platform is dedicated to gathering information on the country's climate cases. The platform disseminates information that enables research and action in Brazil's fight against environmental and climate injustices. By focusing on judicial cases directly related to climate change, the platform allows the analysis of climate litigation's peculiarities in Brazil. The climate approach must be explicit in the cases analyzed, as the central or one of the main issues addressed, or only as a contextual argument.

The classifications in the platform aim to identify parameters that allow the analysis of climate litigation peculiarities in Brazil. The *Climate Litigation in Brazil: 2024 Report*[46] presents the results of the quantitative and qualitative analysis of 80 cases registered on the JUMA Platform until March 2024.[47]

While there may still be a higher concentration of cases in the Global North, the increasing number of cases in the Global South, including Brazil, is an encouraging trend. In Brazil, this trend can be seen in the recent increase in the number of cases, particularly since 2018. Since the end of 2017, the volume

45 Moreira et al (n 11) 49-50; Setzer, Leal & Borges (n 10) 149–150; Nicholas S Bryner, 'Brazil's Green Court: Environmental Law in the Superior Tribunal de Justiça (High Court of Brazil)' (2012) 29 *Pace Env'l Law Review* 470, 476, 485–6, 536.

46 Danielle de Andrade Moreira, Carolina de Figueiredo Garrido, Juliana Chermont Pessoa Lopes, Paula Máximo de Barros Pinto, Victória Lourenço de Carvalho e Gonçalves, Luciana Tse Chaves Garcia Rego, Maria Eduarda Garambone Sydenstricker & Ana Paula Ricci, 'Executive Summary—Climate litigation in Brazil: Report 2024' (JUMA/PUC-Rio 2024).

47 The text of this section draws significantly on the mentioned report.

of such cases had surged to nearly ninefold over the course of five years.[48] By documenting and analyzing these cases, the JUMA Platform plays a role in creating awareness, promoting accountability, and supporting efforts to protect the climate stability in Brazil.

With the increasing evidence of the gravity of climate change effects, it is not surprising that individuals, organizations, and even governments are seeking legal avenues to address its consequences and hold responsible parties accountable. Climate litigation can be crucial in shaping policies, driving systemic change, and encouraging the adoption of sustainable practices to further mitigate climate-environmental damage. As climate litigation continues to gain momentum, one can expect more diverse cases and novel legal arguments to emerge, ultimately shaping how societies and legal systems address climate change and its consequences.

Brazil's upward trend in climate litigation and the diverse array of stakeholders engaged in these legal proceedings is indeed a fascinating development. The data revealed that the Public Prosecutor and NGO s are the leading actors responsible for presenting climate cases. While the Public Prosecutor remains at the forefront of climate litigation in Brazil, it is a notable development that civil society initiatives almost match these governmental bodies in terms of litigation volume.[49] The NGO's role in bringing forth climate cases reveals a new trend in Brazil, considering that, until recently, civil society did not had an active role in mainstream environmental litigation.[50] This also indicates a growing recognition of the need to address climate-related issues within the country's legal system.

Climate litigation in Brazil is mostly directed at governmental entities: federative entities, Government agencies, State officials, and the legislative branch comprise 82 instances within the 80 cases documented. This data suggests that the upsurge in climate litigation is related to the setbacks promoted by the federal government, especially from 2019 to 2022. Legal action appears to be taken against those considered responsible for these setbacks. Yet, within the current landscape of climate litigation in Brazil, there is a rising trend in lawsuits targeting the private sector: 31 out of the 80 cases documented are directed at private companies and 16 at individuals.

---

48 Moreira et al *Brazilian Climate Litigation Bulletin 2023* (n 3) 4; Tigre (n 2).

49 The Federal Public Prosecutor's Office and State Public Prosecutor's Offices cumulatively are involved in 22 cases, whereas civil society groups have reached a comparable level of engagement, being involved in 21 cases.

50 Although in Brazil NGO s have the standing to file environmental lawsuits since 1985 (Law No. 7.347/1985), their engagement before the judiciary has not been consistent.

It is worth noting that nearly half of the cases (37) are classified as systemic cases, suggesting a strategic and comprehensive approach to climate litigation in Brazil. Systemic cases 'are those that seek adjustments or changes to public or private policies, organizations, or institutions.'[51] This approach not only aims to address current setbacks but also seeks to combat future challenges related to climate change.[52] However, it should be noted that routine cases make up 43 of the 80 cases listed on the JUMA Platform. These cases 'are those that discuss a particular act or venture, with some cases that can be considered as models of more routine litigation, using replicable strategies and arguments, especially in environmental disputes, to discuss and include the climate issue.'[53] Furthermore, routine cases can play a crucial role in shaping future outcomes. By challenging specific projects that contribute to high GHG emissions or questioning climate impact assessments in environmental licensing processes, significant changes in specific sectors of the economy can be fostered. Similarly, imposing civil liability for climate-environmental damage can drive accountability and encourage more responsible practices.

Among the 80 cases recorded in the JUMA Platform, over half of them (50 cases) are public civil actions.[54] The vast majority of cases documented seek to contribute to the better regulation and implementation of climate protection measures (76 out of 80). However, climate litigation can also be used to avoid, question, or delay advances in climate regulation. This is evidenced by the four cases identified as unfavorable to climate protection, thereby indirectly exacerbating the climate crisis scenario.[55]

Some specificities of climate litigation in Brazil merit attention. It is worth examining whether environmental or climate justice issues are present in litigation. It is also worth evaluating what specific biomes are impacted and what

---

51 Danielle de Andrade Moreira, Letícia Lima, Paula Pinto, Carolina Garrido, Juliana Lopes, Maria Eduarda Neves, Luciana Rego, João Victor Rosa & Maria Eduarda Sydenstricker, *Boletim da Litigância Climática no Brasil 2022* (JUMA/PUC-Rio 2022) 22.

52 As highlighted in the 2024 report on climate litigation in Brazil, 'among the 37 systemic cases, the vast majority (at least 30) challenge setbacks, such as the dismantling of the environmental and climate regulatory framework or failure, insufficiency, or ineptitude in the implementation of public policies.' 'Between 2019 and 2022, during the Bolsonaro administration, 32 systemic cases were filed, representing more than one-third of all cases on the Platform, and the majority of those classified as systemic (37 cases in total)'. Moreira et al (n 46) 8.

53 Moreira et al (n 51) 22.

54 Law No. 7,347/1985.

55 All four cases unfavorable to climate protection registered on JUMA Platform challenge policies, administrative acts, and public measures related to programs for reducing GHG emissions within the energy sector.

sectors of the economy are involved. Such analysis can provide a deeper understanding of the legal strategies employed and their potential impact on various ecosystems and economic sectors within the country.

As interconnected concepts, climate justice and environmental justice play crucial roles in tackling the unequal distribution of the burdens and benefits of climate change and other environmental impacts. While the debate about advancing climate justice has gained momentum, more than half of the cases (44 out of 80) do not engage with these issues. However, there are 17 cases that explicitly mention the term 'environmental (in)justice' or 'climate (in)justice', highlighting the importance of these concepts in the legal discussions. Environmental and climate justice concepts or grounds are implicitly discussed as a relevant foundation in other 19 cases.

With regard to the Brazilian biomes, the prominence of the Amazon in the climate litigation aligns with its importance for the country's climate and socio-environmental challenges. Addressing the issues related to increasing deforestation in the Amazon is crucial for preserving the region's ecological integrity and for the sinking of global GHG emissions. The Amazon biome appears in 34 cases documented on the JUMA Platform.[56] Conversely, the fact that another 34 cases do not specify any particular biome underscores the breadth of environmental issues being tackled through litigation in Brazil.

As for the GHG emission sectors, a considerable number of cases are associated with land use change and forests, mirroring Brazil's emissions profile. Among the 80 cases cataloged, 47 address issues related to land use change and forests. This is followed by the energy sector, which features in 25 cases. Since land use change and forestry constituted a major fraction of Brazil's GHG emissions (constituting 48% of its emissions in 2022),[57] tackling the issues within this sector is crucial and has the potential to influence the country's effort to reduce overall emissions substantially.

Within the scope of measures addressed in climate litigation, mitigation remains predominant, evidenced by its mention in 44 out of 80 cases. Civil liability for climate-environmental harm and the requirement for climate risk assessment are being more frequently invoked, as indicated by their appearance in 24 and 19 cases, respectively.

Thus, climate litigation in Brazil presents opportunities to contribute to better regulation and implementation of climate protection measures. As with any predictions, monitoring developments and observing how these trends unfold in practice is essential. Climate litigation plays an essential role in

56 See Tigre and Cárcamo, Chapter 13.

57 Tsai et al (n 5) 5.

driving environmental awareness and accountability, and it will be crucial to see how the legal landscape evolves in Brazil in the near future. The following section illustrates the application of established legal instruments, originally intended for environmental protection in general, to address the climate crisis within the Brazilian judicial system.

## 4 Strategies based on Existing Legal Tools

Data regarding climate litigation in Brazil show how pre-existing and already tested legal tools regarding environmental protection can be applied to address climate change. For example, environmental licensing and EIA studies are a preventive measure within the ambit of the NEPA[58] and mentioned in Article 225 of the Constitution. These tools stem from the prevention and the precautionary principles and require a prior assessment of the environmental impacts of activities that are either effectively or potentially pollutant. Conducting an EIA aims to look to direct and indirect, short-, medium-, and long-term effects; temporary and permanent consequences; and cumulative and/or synergistic effects. Ultimately, it aims to assess the environmental feasibility of an activity or project that potentially causes substantial environmental degradation and the prescriptive measures necessary to avoid, mitigate, or compensate adverse impacts.

Although these tools have been part of the Brazilian legal system for over four decades, there is a vast array of legal bases and specific legal arguments that may be leveraged to demand the consideration of direct and indirect GHG emissions from private companies within EIA studies and related environmental licensing procedures.

In the context of EIA studies, qualifying GHG emissions as an outcome detrimental to the environment requires the delineation of (i) the applicable mitigating measures, (ii) the project phase at which these measures will be applied, (iii) the targeted environmental component (whether physical, biological, or socioeconomic); (iv) the temporal extent of the application of such measures (short-, medium-, or long-term); (v) the responsibilities of the entrepreneur

58 Law No. 6,938/1981, art 9(III and IV). According to the Constitution, art 225, para 1(IV), 'In order to ensure the effectiveness of this right [to an ecologically balanced environment], it is incumbent upon the Government to: (...) IV—demand, in the manner prescribed by law, for the installation of works and activities which may potentially cause significant degradation of the environment, a prior environmental impact study, which shall be made public.'

and of public authorities; and (vi) the projected cost of implementation; further to (vii) the identification and offset of impacts that are irremediable or immitigable, alongside the oversight and systematic monitoring of foreseen environmental impacts. All these factors can thus be litigated before courts.

In a study conducted throughout the year 2020, a group of researchers concluded the following regarding climate within the environmental licensing context:

'There are, therefore, a significant number of norms, principles, and legal arguments capable of supporting the understanding that the climate variable must be effectively considered in the planning phase of activities subject to environmental licensing, resulting in the reduction and/or compensation of the respective GHG emissions. Such incorporation of climate concerns allows society to face the climate crisis and guarantee the fundamental human right to an ecologically balanced environment (and a stable climate). Conversely, neglecting to consider climate impacts subjects society and the ecological system, of which it is a part, to unacceptably serious—and avoidable—risks.'[59]

Notably, of the 80 cases listed in the JUMA Platform, 19 include climate risk assessment as one of the addressed measures. Among these cases, 13 specifically tackle environmental licensing in the context of climate-related concerns, addressing these issues either as a basis for litigation or as a part of the remedy requested. These cases might be related to a particular project or enterprise (thus qualified as routine cases) or deal with broader regulatory issues connected to environmental or climate policies as they apply to environmental licensing procedures (thus constituting systemic cases).

The doctrine of environmental civil liability is another critical legal instrument for holding polluters accountable for the environmental and climate-related risks and damages they produce and improperly externalize.[60] Its

---

59 Danielle de Andrade Moreira, Letícia Lima, Juliana Lopes, Bruno Manzolillo, Carolina Garrido & Maria Eduarda Segovia, *Summary of Rationales for Climate Litigation in Brazil: Legal Arguments for the Inclusion of the Climate Variable in Environmental Licensing* (1st edn, Editora PUC-Rio 2022) 27.

60 The polluter-pays principle 'mandates that activities potentially causing environmental degradation internalize all the environmental costs resulting from their operation. Thus, it refers to the internalization of negative environmental externalities, incorporating the external environmental costs into the production costs. Under this principle, the aim is to attribute to the polluter the social cost of the pollution they have generated or are capable of generating'. Danielle de Andrade Moreira, 'Responsabilidade Ambiental Pós-Consumo: Prevenção e Reparação de Danos à luz do Princípio do Poluidor-Pagador' (1st edn, Editora PUC-Rio, 2015) 85.

distinct features from the civil liability traditional theory are justified due to the unique nature of the harm caused to the environment.

Initially, civil liability aimed to compensate patrimonial and individual damages in situations where it was easy to identify the victim, the harm, the offender, and the culpable conduct. Its primary function was reparatory, aiming to restore the status quo after the damage. With the advent of industrial society and the multiplication of associated risks, civil liability evolved, eliminating the need for fault in some cases, such as environmental damage, and thus adopting strict liability. The adoption of strict liability, along with other changes in the structure of civil liability, proved essential, given that environmental damage often results from multiple and diffuse actions, making it difficult to prove the causal link.[61] Climate-related environmental damages are even more complex due to global climate changes caused by diverse factors with broad, indirect and difficult-to-measure effects. These challenges require a reinterpretation of environmental civil liability to address the specificities of climate damage, which affect multiple victims, including future generations.

Among the environmental civil liability unique traits, there are (i) the strict and joint and several liability among polluters;[62] (ii) the so-called 'full risk theory';[63] (iii) the expanded concept of the polluter and the far-reaching concept of causation; (iv) the broad concept and the need to comprehensive remediation of environmental damage, covering not only the ecological damage, but also related cultural, social, and economic aspects of the reparation, comprehending individual and collective harm, and including material and moral damages, *interim* damage and the residual damage; (v) reversing the burden of proof; (vi) the absence of statutory limitation period for civil reparation of environmental damage claims.[64]

All these aspects are recognized by the judiciary and have been widely used in actions seeking civil reparation for environmental damage. Moreover, many of these arguments are based on the polluter-pays principle, which can be identified as 'an important driver of change and subsequent consolidation of more protective understandings of the environment concerning the reparation

61 See Moreira (n 60) 254–68.

62 Law No. 6,938/1981, art 14(1) and Civil Code, art 942.

63 In line with this theory, typical defenses based on intervening causes (such as third-party conduct or acts of God, whether or not foreseeable) are not admitted as an argument to exclusion of liability.

64 Moreira & Herschmann (n 38) 181–3.

of environmental damages, promoting the refinement of the interpretation of the main features of environmental civil liability.'[65]

Indeed, environmental damage has multiple dimensions. In an opinion rendered in the 'High Court of Brazil' (*Superior Tribunal de Justiça*) Judge Herman Benjamin states the environmental damage 'is multifaceted (ethically, temporally, ecologically, and monetarily speaking, and it is still sensitive to the diversity of a vast universe of victims, ranging from the isolated individual to the community, future generations, and the ecological processes themselves considered).'[66] Therefore, the reparation of climate-environmental damage falls within this broad and multidimensional perspective of environmental harm, necessitating that all its repercussions be taken into account.

The nature of climate-environmental damage presents unique traits due to its hyper-complexity. Proving causation, for example, is challenging, since damage can be caused by concurrent, simultaneous, or successive events impacting a multiplicity of victims, including future generations. Tackling such damage challenges the traditional contours of civil liability law and calls for an in-depth analysis geared towards adapting the legal mechanisms to better address this multifaceted issue.[67]

Civil liability for climate-environmental damage is a remedy or one of the remedies discussed in 24 out of the 80 climate cases listed in the JUMA Platform. Although some of these lawsuits are based on questioning GHG emissions, when they pursue reparations for associated harm, they often reference environmental damage in general terms without constructing a detailed argument to distinguish its specific climate dimension (climate damage). Nevertheless, these litigations can be regarded as exemplifying legal actions that address climate-environmental damage within the Brazilian context.

The vast majority of cases are linked to deforestation in the Amazon region and the consequent emission of GHGs into the atmosphere, and suppression of carbon sinks.[68] Land use change and forestry is the GHG emission sector accounting for 19 of the 24 cases of reparation for climate-environmental

---

65 Danielle de Andrade Moreira, Letícia Lima & Izabel Moreira, 'O Princípio do Poluidor-Pagador na Jurisprudência do STF e do STJ: Uma Análise Crítica' (2019) 16 *Revista Veredas do Direito* 367, 399.

66 Superior Tribunal de Justiça (STJ) Judgment of 14 August 2012, Special Appeal No. 1.198.727/MG, Judge Rapporteur: Minister Herman Benjamin.

67 Note that, given the scope constraints of this analysis, this chapter does not aim to address the challenges that the climate crisis presents to the legal framework of civil liability.

68 See Maria Antonia Tigre & Anna Maria Carcamo (Chapter 13) in this book.

damage. The energy sector accounts for five instances, followed by the agriculture sector with four, and the industrial processes sector with only two.[69]

The way in which the analyzed cases are based on traditional environmental civil liability depends upon the specific factual circumstances unique to each legal action. However, all 24 cases are grounded on strict liability and incorporate into their legal arguments at least one other feature of the civil liability regulatory framework, such as the broad concept of polluter (encompassing both direct and indirect polluters), joint and several liability, as well as the multifaceted nature of environmental harm. Additionally, these lawsuits recognize the duty of full restitution for damage caused, hence necessitating a consideration that goes beyond simple restoration *in natura*, which might be expected in deforestation cases. They also entail the potential for claiming *interim* damages, compensating for residual harm, seeking collective moral damages, and in certain instances, demanding the disgorgement of unjust profits gained from the damaging activities. Damage valuation is challenging in many of Brazil's legal actions on climate-environmental damage.[70]

As exemplified by environmental licensing and environmental civil liability tools, Brazil's advanced environmental legal framework has been extensively debated and applied doctrinally and jurisprudentially, having the polluter-pays principle as an important guide. Moreover, as the backdrop for the mobilization and application of these legal tools is the Constitution, which ensures a balanced environment for the present and future generations and imposes correlated duties on both the Public Power and the community.

The Brazilian legal system has been the stage for actions aimed at preserving a stable climate. In most of these cases, the legal framework designed for environmental protection has been strategically and coherently assembled and specifically applied to the issue of climate change. The fundamental task of addressing global environmental changes, like climate change, relies on the ability of the law to provide adequate responses to the uncertainties and complexities in a world that is already witnessing dramatic shifts.

---

69 Danielle de Andrade Moreira, Victória Gonçalves & Maria Eduarda Segovia, 'Aspectos Conceituais e Práticos da Responsabilização Civil por Dano Ambiental-Climático no Brasil' (2024) 113 *Revista de Direito Ambiental* 341.

70 On this topic, see Danielle de Andrade Moreira; Victoria Gonçalves & Fernanda Barbosa, 'Valoração da Dimensão Climática do Dano Ambiental no Brasil' (2024) 113 *Revista de Direito Ambiental* (2024).

## 5 Conclusion: Perspectives for Climate Litigation in Brazil

In recent years, there has been an increasing focus by society as a whole on climate change and a noticeable rise in climate litigation in Brazil. Whilst earlier cases only peripherally addressed climate-related issues in decisions, a second wave of cases explicitly addresses climate change since the claim's conception.

The key to understanding this evolution lies in the link between climate and environmental litigation. Because climate change not only introduces new risks but also worsens existing environmental threats such as coastal erosion, air pollution, water scarcity, and deforestation, it is crucial to consider both climate change and the environment in an integrated manner. Furthermore, acknowledging climate change as a central and decisive factor in environmental litigation favors the recognition of the growing importance and urgency of addressing these issues through the judicial system. To that end, the use of the constitutionally protected human right to a healthy environment has been instrumental in shaping the contours of the Brazilian rights-based climate litigation within mainstream environmental litigation.

The increase in climate litigation in Brazil can initially be perceived as a reaction to the socio-environmental regressions promoted by the previous federal administration. In this sense, it shows civil society's commitment to seeking legal remedies to address environmental and climate challenges. The change in the federal government since 2023, however, may hint a reduction of new climate-related lawsuits being filed in the coming years, although any setback by the Legislative Power is likely to be litigated. Furthermore, an increase in cases against private companies is also expected, which requires a detailed analysis of their role at the roots of climate change; and more cases related to civil liability for climate-environmental damage and to the assessment of climate-related impacts within the scope of environmental licensing procedures are likely to become more frequent.

The growing role of civil society in fighting climate change in Brazil will probably consolidate the role of NGOs in bringing new and innovative climate cases before courts.

Overall, the trends in Brazil's climate litigation landscape indicate a growing recognition of the need to address climate change through legal means, involving diverse actors and focusing on current setbacks and long-term strategic issues. In this context, in Brazil, the strategy of climate litigation finds means and instruments to thrive and produce results, especially if directed towards the promotion of climate justice.

CHAPTER 3

# The Separation of Powers Principle and the Role of Different Bodies in Climate Action

*Enéas Xavier* and Letícia Simo Veras***

## 1 Introduction

Separation of powers is one of the fundamental principles of the political organization of modern states. It was conceived as a response to the arbitrariness of absolutism in the past to provide legal ground for enabling the effectiveness of fundamental rights by ensuring limits between the distinguished branches of power (executive, legislative, and judicial) in performing their duties and functions.

Separation of powers is also a cornerstone of the Brazilian Constitution. Regarding environmental matters, the Constitution establishes the allocation of competence to be performed by each federative entity in a cooperation system.[1] Nonetheless, the lines that define the role to be played by each political body are not always clear, which may lead not only to the breach of the separation of powers principle but also to the violation of fundamental rights. Furthermore, the challenges arising from climate change may potentially aggravate these conflicts. In this regard, this chapter proposes a reading of the application of the principle of the separation of powers for tackling climate change from the perspective of climate litigation.

First, the chapter analyzes the separation of powers doctrine in the Brazilian legal system. Second, it discusses the Brazilian legal and constitutional order, specifically on the protection of the environment and climate change.

* Ph.D. candidate at the University of Montréal. Researcher at the Latin American Climate Lawyers Initiative for Mobilizing Action (LACLIMA) and at Centre for the Study of International Courts at the University of São Paulo's Faculty of Law (NETI-USP). ORCID ID: 0009-0009-1604-7501.

** Law Professor at the Methodist University of Piracicaba. Master's degree in International and Comparative Law at the University of São Paulo. Postgraduate in International Law from CEDIN/MG. Bachelor's degree in Law from the Methodist University of Piracicaba, PIBIC/CNPq Scientific Initiation Scholarship 2015/2017. ORCID ID: 0000–0002-0956-3438.

1 Constitution, art 23 (VI, VII and sole paragraph).

 | DOI:10.1163/9789004690974_004

It addresses the allocation of competence in environmental matters and the roles played by every federative entity.

The chapter approaches the separation of powers in Brazilian law from the perspective of STF's decisions in climate litigation. It introduces the main environmental and climate topics through which conflicts between federative entities take place, detailing the reasoning behind each decision. Suggestions on possible roles to be developed and issues of conflicts between different bodies for tackling climate change are also considered.

In environmental protection and climate change, the rule of law is critical in ensuring that governmental actions are grounded in legal principles and that there is accountability for failure to act. The rule of law dictates that all actions the state takes, including those related to climate policies, must adhere to established legal norms and frameworks. This is especially pertinent considering climate change, which requires long-term, consistent policy measures that transcend political cycles and immediate interests.

The Brazilian legal system, emphasizing cooperative federalism, exemplifies the complexities of implementing climate policies within a multi-level governance framework. The Constitution mandates a collaborative approach to environmental protection, assigning responsibilities to the Union, (federated) states, and municipalities. However, this division of responsibilities often leads to ambiguities and conflicts, particularly in the enforcement and execution of climate policies.

Furthermore, the judiciary's role, especially the STF, becomes crucial in resolving disputes and ensuring that environmental and climate laws are upheld. The court's interpretations and rulings on climate litigation cases clarify legal ambiguities and reinforce the rule of law by holding governmental bodies accountable for their environmental obligations. These judicial decisions play a pivotal role in shaping Brazil's climate governance landscape, ensuring that constitutional mandates for environmental protection are met.

Addressing climate change within the framework of the rule of law requires continuous adaptation and evolution of legal norms to keep pace with emerging scientific understanding and socio-economic realities. The principles of the rule of law must guide the development and implementation of climate policies, ensuring that they are just, equitable, and effective in mitigating the impacts of climate change. This approach upholds the integrity of the legal system and fosters public trust in governmental actions related to climate governance.

## 2 The Separation of Powers Principle in the Brazilian Legal System

The modern state is a political organization necessary to form the rule of law principle. To confront the absolute State power concentrated in the hands of a single person perpetuating self-interests, a new ideal of governance founded on the rule of law is conceived, comprising 'a number of principles of a formal and procedural character, addressing how a community is governed.'[2]

The rule of law provides clear guidance in the liberal State, where public action is strictly performed. Thus, there was a need to distribute the formerly absolute power in various forms, promoting the creation of laws and establishing the jurisdictional function of agents not belonging to the nobility, with powers limited to the laws. In this sense, the figure of the tripartite state powers emerged to dissolve absolutist power and make public functions efficient and sectorized.

The separation of powers doctrine is often attributed to Montesquieu.[3] The philosopher from the Enlightenment asserts that 'when the legislative and executive powers are united in the same person, or (...) body of magistrates, there can be no liberty; because apprehensions may arise, lest the same monarch or senate should enact tyrannical laws, to execute them in a tyrannical manner.'[4] Furthermore, he asserts that 'there is no liberty, if the judiciary power be not separated from the legislative and executive.'[5] Madison expresses the same concern, as he stresses that 'the accumulation of all powers, legislative, executive and judiciary in the same hands, whether of one, a few or many, and whether hereditary, self-appointed, or elective, may justly be pronounced the very definition of tyranny.'[6]

As one can realize, the main concern in the separation of powers principle is to restrain the abuse of power. To prevent it, 'it is necessary from the very nature of things that power should be a check to power.'[7] For this matter, a system of checks and balances is introduced, through which the functions entrusted and performed by one branch avoid the abuse of power that might be eventually perpetrated by the other.

The checks and balances system has become a paradigm adopted worldwide by modern States. However, one must consider that the State is a

---

2 Jeremy Waldron, 'The Rule of Law', in Zalta & Nodelman (eds), *The Stanford Encyclopedia of Philosophy* (2023), available at <https://plato.stanford.edu/archives/fall2023/entries/rule-of-law/> accessed on 15 January 2024.

3 Steven G Calabresi, Mark E Berghausen, Skylar Albertson, 'The Rise and Fall of the Separation of Powers' (2012) 534 *Northwestern University Law Review* 106.

4 Charles de Secondat, Baron de Montesquieu, *The Spirit of Laws* (Batoche Books 2001 translated by Thomas Nugent) Book XI, Chapter 6.

5 ibid, Book XI, Chapter 6.

6 Alexander Hamilton, James Madison & John Jay, *The Federalist* (Jacob E Cooke ed, Wesleyan University Press 1961) 10 <http://press-pubs.uchicago.edu/founders/documents/v1ch10s14.html>, accessed 21 January 2024.

7 Montesquieu (n 4) Chapter 4.

political-social concept that may vary materially depending on the historical and cultural context in which a society is immersed. Therefore, there are oscillations in respective allowances entrusted to each power within different legal orders. This circumstance has become self-evident in Brazilian law throughout its political history until the adoption of the 1988 Constitution, in which the harmony between powers is formally established in its current form.[8] This provision is acknowledged as a *permanent clause*, which means it is an unalterable and unmodifiable constitutional provision that cannot be reformed or derogated from,[9] thus safeguarding the powers of the republic and their harmonious functioning with one another.[10]

However, the Constitution entrusts the judiciary to perform a particular duty in this system by stating that 'the law shall not exclude any injury or threat to a right from review by the judiciary.'[11] In this matter, Moraes stresses that the jurisdictional activity 'shall avoid the threat or injury to rights, freedoms or prerogatives (…) arising from the omission of the competent power, declaring the existence of omission and allowing the injured to enjoy the constitutional norm, as provided for in the decision.'[12]

## 3 The Environmental Protection and Climate Change in the Constitution

Environmental provisions within constitutional texts are quite usual, mainly under the influence of international conferences organized by the United Nations.[13] The Brazilian Constitution is an example,[14] in which the environment is conceived in its unitary concept through an innovative approach, transversal and interdisciplinary, covering fundamental rights, procedural obligations for sustainable development, legal jurisdiction, and State activities,

8 Constitution, art 2., which states that 'The Legislative, the Executive and the Judicial, independent and harmonious among themselves, are the powers of the Union.'

9 Constitution, art 60(III).

10 Cícero José Barbosa Nery Júnior, 'Breve História do Princípio da Separação dos Poderes nos Paradigmas do Estado de Direito' (2020) 12/14 *Revista de Ciências do Estado* 12.

11 Constitution, art 5(XXXV).

12 Alexandre de Moraes, *Direito Constitucional* (30th edn Atlas 2014) 189. [free translation]

13 Pierre-Marie Dupuy & Jorge E Viñuales, *International Environmental Law* (2nd edn, CUP 2018) 375.

14 For further details on the recognition of environmental rights as constitutional rights notably in Latin America, see Maria Antonia Tigre, 'The Right to a Healthy Environment in Latin America and the Caribbean: Compliance through the Inter-American System and the Escazú Agreement' (2024) *International Courts versus Non-Compliance Mechanisms* 262.

among other subjects through the constitutional order, toward the enjoyment of the right to an ecologically balanced environment.[15]

Article 225 states that 'all have the right to an ecologically balanced environment, which is an asset of common use and essential to a healthy quality of life, and both the Government and the community shall have the duty to defend and preserve it for present and future generations.' This provision is the cornerstone of environmental protection in the constitutional order and establishes a complex legal structure in two simultaneous directions.[16]

On the one hand, it acknowledges the right to an ecologically balanced environment as an intergenerational fundamental right.[17] On the other hand, it determines that protecting the environment is not a choice but rather an irrefutable duty to be fulfilled by both the State and society for the benefit of present and future generations.[18] For the effectiveness of Article 225 of the Constitution, paragraph 1, a series of commands are determined to be carried out by legislative and administrative authorities, such as the exigence of prior environmental impact study for the development of 'activities which may potentially cause significant degradation of the environment.'[19]

Climate change is referred to in the Constitution only on tax matters. It is expressly mentioned in Article 155(V), as it prohibits the taxation on 'donations destined, within the Executive Power of the Union, to social and environmental projects or aimed at mitigating the effects of climate change and federal educational institutions.'[20] In addition, the recently enacted tax reform determined the maintenance of a 'favorable tax regime for biofuels and low-carbon hydrogen in the form of a complementary law, to ensure that they are taxed at a lower rate than fossil fuels.'[21] A proposed constitutional amendment is currently under discussion in the Federal Congress, seeking to expressly recognize climate security as a fundamental right and to enforce the adoption of mitigation and adaptation actions by the State.[22] However, the current constitutional order offers sufficient ground for tackling climate change.

The intergenerational perspective of entitlement to a healthy environment enshrined in the Constitution[23] also underlies the concept of sustainable

15 Paulo Affonso Leme Machado, *Direito Ambiental Brasileiro* (21st edn Malheiros 2013) 145.

16 *Asibama Nacional v Presidente da República* [2022] STF ADIN 4.757 DF.

17 See Luciana Bauer, Chapter 11 in this book.

18 Herman V Benjamin, 'Responsabilidade Civil pelo Dano Ambiental' (1998) 24 *Revista de Direito Ambiental* 3, 9.

19 Constitution, art 225(paragraph 1, IV).

20 Constitution, art 155(V). [free translation]

21 Constitution, art 225(paragraph 1, VIII). [free translation]

22 Proposta de Emenda à Constituição PEC 37/2021 [2021].

23 Constitution, art 225.

development.[24] The right to life and an ecologically balanced environment are entwined. Machado explains that 'it is not enough to live, nor to conserve life; it is fair to pursue and obtain the quality of life,' and therefore, the essential ecological processes, whose preservation and restoration is a duty imposed on all federative entities[25] must be in a state conducive to such an end.[26] Sarlet and others highlight that 'the climate system is undoubtedly an essential ecological process elementary to safeguarding the ecological integrity and multiple (sub) interdependent natural systems (water and rainfall regime, soil, biodiversity, etc.)'[27] and it is inherent to the concept of environment.

Federal Law No 6,938, of October 31, 1981, also known as the National Environmental Policy (PNMA), provides a comprehensive definition of the *environment* as 'the set of conditions, laws, influences and interactions of physical, chemical and biological order, which allows, shelters and governs life in all its forms;' and *pollution* as the 'degradation of environmental quality.'[28] Federal Law No 12,187, of 29 December 2009, defines *adverse effects of climate change* as alterations in the 'environment and the biota resulting from climate change with significant deleterious effects on the composition, resilience or productivity of natural and managed ecosystems or the operation of socio-economic systems or on human health and welfare.'[29]

Setzer and others highlight that, in the Brazilian context, 'climate change law is generally understood within the broader context of environmental law … [as its] issues have been incorporated, explicitly and implicitly, into national and subnational legislation, as either a central or incidental element.'[30] Therefore, the current Brazilian constitutional order establishes duties for the State to provide minimum environmental protection standards and guarantee fundamental environmental rights that comprise the stability of the climate system and the adverse impacts of climate change.[31]

---

24 Ingo Wolfgang Sarlet, Gabriel Wedy & Tiago Fersterseifer, *Curso de Direito Climático* (Thomson Reuters Revista dos Tribunais 2023) RB 2.2, 1.1.

25 Constitution, art 225 (paragraph 1, II).

26 Machado (n 15) 69.

27 Sarlet et al (n 24) at RB 2.2, 1.1. [free translation]

28 Law No 6.938 [1981] art 3(I). [free translation]

29 Law No 12.187 [2009] art 2(I). [free translation]

30 Joana Setzer et al, 'Climate Change Litigation in Brazil: Will Green Courts Become Greener?', in Alogna et al (eds), *Climate Change Litigation: Global Perspectives* (2021) 143, 145.

31 Ingo Wolfgang Sarlet & Tiago Fensterseifer, *Direito Constitucional Ambiental* (5th edn, Revista dos Tribunais 2017) 60.

## 4 The Allocation of Power for the Protection of the Environment and Tackling Climate Change in Brazilian Law

The political-administrative organization of the Federative Republic of Brazil is formed by the federal union, 26 federative states, a federal district, and 5,571 municipalities.[32] Thus, the allocation of competence in Brazilian law must comply with the decentralization of power, where the different federative entities perform administrative, legislative, and judicial activities according to the Constitution. Silva explains that, following the predominance of general interest, 'the Union will be responsible for those matters and issues of predominant general, national interest, while the States will stress the matters and subjects of predominant regional interest, and Municipalities concern matters of local interest.'[33]

Legal competence to protect the environment and tackle climate change meets this concept of general interest and is subject to different duties to be performed by all federative entities. Despite being considered a transboundary concern, the impacts of climate change must be addressed by all federative entities, even the local municipal authority, as required by constitutional and infra-constitutional order. A cooperative ecological federalism is established through which actions performed by all federal entities are coordinated, and autonomy is strengthened for the enhanced protection of the environment[34] and for tackling climate change.[35]

Regarding legislative actions, the Constitution adopts the concurrent competence of the legislature. Article 24 establishes the power of the Union, states, and the federal district to concurrently legislate on environmental matters. In this modality of competence, the Union is responsible for enacting general rules (Article 24, para 1), which States can complement or even supplement whenever legislation is absent. Despite not being mentioned in Article 24, municipalities may exercise this competence too, according to Article 30(II) of the Constitution. However, the performance of this duty shall never be directed to weaken environmental requirements but rather to enhance them.[36] Among the federative states, 19 have enacted legal norms on climate change policies,

32 Instituto Brasileiro de Geografia e Estatística, 'Estimativas da População' (IBGE 2020), available at <https://biblioteca.ibge.gov.br/visualizacao/livros/liv101747.pdf> accessed on 16 December 2023.

33 José Afonso da Silva, *Curso de Direito Constitucional Positivo* (37th edn, Malheiros 2014) 482. [free translation]

34 Sarlet & Fensterseifer (n 31) 165.

35 Federative Council Resolution No 3 [2024].

36 Machado (n 15) 339–340.

representing a considerable percentage.[37] Brazilian municipalities, however, still struggle to incorporate climate change matters into their normative frame.[38]

Regarding administrative actions, the Constitution adopted the common competence of the executive power. Article 23 establishes that 'the Union, the states, the Federal District and the Municipalities, in common, have the power: (...) to protect the environment and to fight pollution in any of its forms.'[39] The main goal of the constitutional legislator was to seek coordination between federative entities for the protection of the environment instead of being subject to separate and excluding actions of each of them.[40] For this matter, the Constitution conceived that 'supplementary laws shall establish rules for the cooperation between the Federal Government and the states, the Federal District, and the municipalities, aiming at the attainment of balanced development and well-being on the nationwide scope.'[41] The infra-constitutional legislation further details how these duties are performed, with important implications for tackling climate change.

## 5 Climate Litigation and the Role of the STF

Despite the explicit disposition of harmony and independence between powers expressed in the Constitution, one must acknowledge the judicial branch's unique role. The jurisdictional activity is no longer limited to the mechanical application of the law but rather as a primary legal remedy in ensuring the effectiveness of constitutional dispositions and enforcing each federative entity to comply with their legal duties.[42] Therefore, it falls under the STF's competence to analyze 'the interpretation that best maximizes the effectiveness of constitutional rules' and exercise the control of public policies in environmental matters.[43]

37 Danielle de Andrade Moreira et al., *Summary of Rationales for Climate Litigation in Brazil* (2022) 14.

38 Isabela Battistello Espíndola & Wagner Costa Ribeiro, 'Cities and Climate Change: Challenges to Brazilian Municipal Master Plans' (2020) 22 *Cadernos Metrópole* 365.

39 Constitution, art 23(VII). [free translation]

40 Machado (n 15) 182–183.

41 Constitution, art 23.

42 Nery Júnior (n 10) 5 .

43 *Partido Progressista v Presidente da República*, ADC 42, Judgment of 21 February 2018.

In Brazil, the STF has been increasingly active in tackling climate change. According to the JUMA's database, 80 climate cases had been identified within Brazilian jurisdiction by June 2024, 37 of which had reached the STF.[44] In March 2022, the STF initiated procedures for adjudicating a body of lawsuits labelled by its members as the *green docket*.[45] These cases have drawn the attention of Brazilian society due to their potential repercussion on shaping the State's action on climate and environmental matters through jurisdictional activity.[46] Rulings were concluded by March 2024.[47]

Not all of these cases address climate change at its core,[48] as climate litigation may encompass subjects other than climate change law and science that might 'have a serious impact on the volume of greenhouse gas emissions or on a community's resilience to climate change.'[49] In the cases composing the green docket and others related to climate and environmental matters, the STF must address requirements for granting environmental permits, deforestation, budgetary funding, and human rights violations, such as the right to life and an ecologically balanced environment or the right to participate in environmental stewardship, are also addressed in climate litigation cases that reach the STF, whose grounds seek a closer connection between these constitutional fundamental rights and climate change concerns.[50] This set of rights is often

44 Danielle de Andrade Moreira et al, *Brazilian Climate Litigation Bulletin 2024* (JUMA/PUC-Rio 2024).

45 Supremo Tribunal Federal, 'Confira a pauta de julgamentos do STF para esta quarta-feira (30)' (30 March 2022), available at <https://noticias.stf.jus.br/postsnoticias/confira-a-pauta-de-julgamentos-do-stf-para-esta-quarta-feira-30/> accessed on 15 April 2024. Supremo Tribunal Federal, 'Confira a pauta de julgamentos do STF para esta quarta-feira (4)' (04 May 2022), available at <https://portal.stf.jus.br/noticias/verNoticiaDetalhe.asp?idConteudo=486333&ori=1> accessed 15 April 2024.

46 Brenda Dutra France & Clara Barradas, 'Litigância climática estratégica e a Pauta Verde do STF' (*LACLIMA* 2022), available at <https://laclima.org/paperseries/litigancia-climatica-estrategica-e-a-pauta-verde-do-stf/> accessed on 16 April 2024.

47 Ricardo Cintra Torres de Carvalho, 'Supremo Tribunal Federal conclui julgamento da pauta verde' (*Consultor Jurídico*, 6 April 2024), available at <https://www.conjur.com.br/2024-abr-06/supremo-tribunal-federal-conclui-julgamento-da-pauta-verde/> accessed on 16 April 2024.

48 Danielle de Andrade Moreira et al, *Litigando a Crise Climática no Brasil—Argumentos Jurídicos para se Exigir do Estado a Implementação Doméstica do Acordo de Paris* (Pimenta Cultural 2022) 39. Jacqueline Peel & Hari M Osofsky, 'Climate Change Litigation' (2020) 23 *Annual Review of Law and Social Science* 16.

49 Joana Setzer & Catherine Higham, *Global trends in climate change litigation: 2024 snapshot* (London School of Economics and Political Science 2024) 8.

50 Danielle de Andrade Moreira et al, 'Rights-Based Climate Litigation in Brazil: An Assessment of Constitutional Cases Before the Brazilian Supreme Court' (2023) 16 *Journal of Human Rights Practice* 47.

referred to as climate rights, which 'encompass the ways in which national constitution, human rights law and other laws in general, imbue individuals and communities with rights to climate mitigation and adaptation action.'[51]

The jurisprudence delivered by the STF paves the way for establishing the boundaries of competence allocation and shaping the extension of each political power body's role in climate matters.[52] Silva highlights that it has become increasingly difficult to distinguish and identify the boundaries of competence allocation between different federative entities in the Modern State.[53] This conflict is widely acknowledged as one of the most controversial matters in Brazilian environmental law,[54] often requiring the intervention of the STF.[55]

STF's precedents have long consolidated the jurisprudence that 'normative acts, expressions of the normative function, whose species comprise the regulatory function (of the Executive) (...) and the legislative function (of the Legislature) are subject to the concentrated constitutionality control.'[56] Similarly, the Court has already ruled that 'judicial review of discretionary administrative act understood as unlawful and abusive does not represent a breach of the separation of powers principle.'[57] Analyzing the rulings in the green docket, Moreira points out trends in the court's approach that will influence the allocation of competence of each federative entity in climate matters: legal reasoning developed on the separation of powers principle and the right to a healthy and balanced environment; State's duty to protect the environment; interrelation between national and international law.[58] In the same sense, building from a survey conducted on decisions delivered by the STF addressing environmental licensing, Farias and others highlight a trend in the jurisprudence of the court for the unconstitutionality of legal norms implying the renunciation or

51 Michel Burger & Maria Antonia Tigre, *Global Climate Litigation Report: 2023 Status Review* (UNEP 2023) 26.

52 Supremo Tribunal Federal, 'Decisões do STF contribuíram para políticas públicas de meio ambiente no país' (05 June 2024), available at <https://portal.stf.jus.br/noticias/verNoticiaDetalhe.asp?idConteudo=544577&ori=1> accessed 20 June 2024.

53 Silva (n 33), 482 [free translation].

54 Terence Trennepohl, *Manual de Direito Ambiental* (8th edn, Saraiva, 2020) 65.

55 *Public Prosecutor's Office v Governor of the State of Santa Catarina*, ADI 6650 SC, filed on 18 December 2020, Judgment of 27 April 2021, available at <https://www.jusbrasil.com.br/jurisprudencia/stf/1203199122/inteiro-teor-1203199189>.

56 *Public Prosecutor's Office v Governor of the State of Rio de Janeiro*, AgReg ADI 2950–9 RJ, Judgment of the Federal Supreme Court of 6 October 2004.

57 *Comercial Cesa S/A v Public Prosecutor's Office*, AgReg-AgIn 777.502 RS, Judgment of the Federal Supreme Court of 28 September 2010 [2] [free translation].

58 Moreira et al (n 50) 5.

weakening of legal parameters of environmental protection within the scope of the cooperative ecological federalism.[59]

## 6 The Separation of Powers Principle and Competence Allocation in Climate Litigation

In *PSB et al v Brazil (on Climate Fund)*,[60] the Federal Government was charged with omitting financial resources for funding mitigation actions, compromising the effectiveness of the Climate Fund, and breaching constitutional dispositions and Brazilian commitments in international treaties. Justice-rapporteur Luís Roberto Barroso asserted that certain legal obligations for the specific allocation of funds fall on the legal authority of Congress, which the Federal Government shall not ignore and must carry out its duties under penalty of violation of the separation of powers principle.[61] In its concurring opinion, Justice Edson Fachin stated that 'one cannot speak of the separation of powers when public policies are used to empty environmental protection, whereas the constituent legislator has ordered the environmental protection to public authorities and collectivity.'[62] Furthermore, Justice Edson Fachin added that the 'respect for state duties of climate protection is imperative [and] no administrative discretion allows public policies neither government programs to ignore such duties, which arise from the constitutional text.'[63]

In *PSB et al v Brazil (on deforestation and human rights)*,[64] the plaintiffs sought the effective execution of public policies to fulfill Brazilian international climate engagements. The Federal Government faced charges of adopting a series of illegal administrative actions that resulted in the rise of deforestation in the Amazon Forest. The defendant unsuccessfully evoked the separation of powers principle to dismiss the case. The opinion delivered by

59 Talden Faris et al, 'O entendimento do STF quanto à simplificação do licenciamento ambiental' (*Consultor Jurídico*, 05 September 2022), available at <https://www.conjur.com.br/2022-set-05/farias-stallivieri-andrade-licenciamento-pauta-stf2/> accessed 20 June 2024.

60 *PSB et al v Brazil (on Climate Fund)*, ADPF 708, Judgment of 7 January 2022, available at <https://climatecasechart.com/non-us-case/psb-et-al-v-federal-union/>, para 1.

61 ibid, 28.

62 ibid, 40.

63 ibid, 8.

64 *PSB et al v Brazil (on deforestation and human rights)*, ADPF 760, Judgment of 6 April 2022, available at <https://climatecasechart.com/non-us-case/brazilian-socialist-party-and-others-v-brazil/>.

Minister Cármen Lúcia (acting as judge-rapporteur) explicitly acknowledged the *unconstitutional matter of things in environmental stewardship*[65] due to the exponential rise in deforestation and the government's omission in protecting the ecologically balanced environment. According to the reasoning, 'the separation of powers principle is not a *room divider* for breach of the Constitution,' and this scenario requires the Judiciary to ensure the effectiveness of the constitutional environment protection.[66]

These cases highlight the jurisprudence of the STF, which states that 'the constitutional duty of environmental protection reduces the room for public authority discretion.'[67] This precedent is self-evident in cases where environmental protection standards are lowered, breaching the allocation of competence and the constitutional right to a healthy environment. On this matter, Santa Catarina State Law No 14,675 of 13 April 2009 exempted certain mining activities from the environmental assessment process.[68] This rule was challenged before the STF and held unconstitutional. According to the decision delivered, State Law No 14,675 establishes a 'subversion of the systemic logic of national general rules by the Legislative Assembly' for introducing such a waiver, violating Articles 24 and 225 of the Constitution, therefore affronting the efficiency of balanced environmental protection.[69] A similar decision was delivered in a case challenging the Mato Grosso State Complementary Law No 38 of 21 November 1995, which exempted specific hydroelectric dam projects from the previous environmental impact assessment.[70] The STF asserted that the State of Mato Grosso breached the limits of its constitutional competence by adopting lower environmental protection standards than those established by federal law, violating Article 24 of the Constitution.[71]

On the other hand, the jurisprudence of the STF has previously upheld legislative acts, as they either enhanced environmental standards or addressed

---

65 The unconstitutional state of things theory is described as a 'massive and persistent violation of fundamental rights, resulting from structural failures and failure of public policies and whose modification depends on comprehensive measures of a normative, administrative and budgetary nature' (*PSL v Brazil et al (on Arrest Warrant)*, ADPF 347 DF, Judgment of the Federal Supreme Court of 9 September 2015, at 8) [free translation].

66 *PSB et al v Brazil (on deforestation and human rights)* 153.

67 ibid, 5.

68 Santa Catarina State Law No 14,675 [2009].

69 *Public Prosecutor's Office v Governor of the State of Santa Catarina,* 1. [free translation]

70 Mato Grosso State Complementary Law No 38 [1995].

71 *Public Prosecutor's Office v Governor of the State of Mato Grosso, Procurador-Geral da República v Governador do Estado de Mato Grosso,* ADI 4.529 MT, Judgment of the Federal Supreme Court of 22 November 2022 (Rapporteur: Minister Rosa Weber), available at <https://redir.stf.jus.br/paginadorpub/paginador.jsp?docTP=TP&docID=764658040>.

regional or local challenges.[72] For example, the Bahia State Law No 12.377 of 28 December 2011, created new modalities of environmental permits and allowed the development of certain activities through a simplified licensing process.[73] The law was challenged before the STF on the grounds that it violated constitutional competence allowance and preempted federal general regulation on exigences for grating environmental permits. Despite the relevance of the arguments, the decision delivered by the STF asserted that federative states might complement general rules created by the Union, especially to meet regional and local peculiarities and that the law challenged fell into the concurrent competence established by the Constitution.[74] Furthermore, Minister Dias Toffoli, acting as judge-rapporteur, acknowledged that state legislation may address simplified procedures on licensing activities of lower environmental impact. At the local level, the STF has consolidated favorable jurisprudence to recognize the municipality's competence to legislate on environmental issues to safeguard fundamental rights, such as the health of its citizens and the ecologically balanced environment.[75] In Belo Horizonte City, Municipal Law No 4,253[76] established pollution standards and sanctioned fines for vehicle smoke emissions. The norm was challenged unconstitutional on the grounds of breaching the allocation of competence by establishing more restricted environmental rules. The STF ruled, however, that regulating environmental pollution from toxic gases emitted by vehicles in the urban perimeter falls into the local sphere of municipal competence.[77]

While these examples relate to environmental cases, the subjects addressed are crucial for tackling climate change and provide more critical lessons for

---

72 See *Public Prosecutor's Office v Governor of the State of Ceará*, ADI 4615 CE, Judgment of the Federal Supreme Court of 20 September 2019, available at <https://redir.stf.jus.br/paginadorpub/paginador.jsp?docTP=TP&docID=751257523>; *PSL v Ceará State Council of the Environment*, ADI 6288 CE, Judgment of the Federal Supreme Court of 23 November 2020, available at <https://redir.stf.jus.br/paginadorpub/paginador.jsp?docTP=TP&docID=754566819>.

73 Bahia State Law No 12,377 [2011].

74 *Public Prosecutor's Office v Governor of the State of Bahia*, ADI 5014 BH, Judgment of the Federal Supreme Court of 13 November 2023, available at <https://redir.stf.jus.br/paginadorpub/paginador.jsp?docTP=TP&docID=774332617>.

75 *Public Prosecutor's Office of the State of São Paulo v Sindicato da Indústria de Material Plástico do Estado de São Paulo*, Special Appeal No RE 732.686 SP, 19 Judgment of the Federal Supreme Court of October 2017, available at <https://jurisprudencia.stf.jus.br/pages/search/repercussao-geral9422/false>.

76 Belo Horizonte Municipal Law No 4,253 [1985].

77 São Bernardo Ônibus *Ltda v Belo Horizonte Environment Secretary*, Special Appeal RE 194.704 MG, Judgment of the Federal Supreme Court of 24 October 2017.

climate litigation. Brazilian cities have recently led the worst global air quality charts due to extreme heat waves and pollution. Mining activities are significant problems in Brazilian society as they contribute to deforestation.[78] Water dam construction generates substantial impacts, as it floods vast forest areas, opens new frontiers for agribusiness, and becomes a source of greenhouse gases.[79] Emissions from the energy sector, mainly concentrated in the transport category, as well as deforestation and land-use changes, represent a considerable share of the Brazilian national inventory.[80]

## 7 The Separation of Powers Principle and the Implementation of International Human Rights Treaties

The national implementation of human rights treaties often challenges the separation of powers, requiring joint legal action by the executive and legislative branches.[81] The Constitution affirms that the President of the Republic has the exclusive power to 'conclude international treaties, conventions and acts, *ad referendum* of the National Congress,'[82] which means that the Congress must confirm the presidential act, as it holds the 'exclusive power to decide conclusively on international treaties, agreements or acts that result in charges or commitments.'[83] Also, the Brazilian constitutional order comprises rights and guarantees established in international treaties ratified by the country. Furthermore, the STF has already ruled that human rights treaties shall enjoy a *supra-legality* status in Brazilian law, whose effects and obligations are hierarchically equivalent to constitutional dispositions.[84] Besides that, as Brazil

78 J Siqueira-Gay et al, 'Strategic Planning to Mitigate Mining Impacts on Protected Areas in the Brazilian Amazon' (2022) 5 *Nat Sustain* 853, 854.

79 Philip M Fearnside, 'Impacts of Brazil's Madeira River Dams: Unlearned lessons for Hydroelectric Development in Amazonia' (2014) 38 *Environmental Science & Policy* 164, 168.

80 *Fourth National Communication of Brazil to the UNFCCC* (2021), available at: <https://www.gov.br/mcti/pt-br/centrais-de-conteudo/publicacoes-mcti/quarta-comunicacao-nacional-do-brasil-a-unfccc/executive_summary-_4nc_brazil_web.pdf> accessed on 15 June 2024.

81 Nuno Manoel Morgadinho dos Santos Coelho, 'Do possível reconhecimento de status de supralegalidade aos tratados internacionais em matéria ambiental: análise da ADPF n.º 708' (2023) 11 *Revista Direitos Humanos e Democracia* e13827.

82 Constitution, art 49 (I).

83 ibid, art 84 (VIII).

84 *Banco Bradesco S/A v Vera Lúcia B de Albuquerque et al*, Special Appeal No RE 466.343-1 SP, Judgment of 3 December 2008 (Rapporteur: Minister Gilmar Mendes).

integrates the Inter-American System for the Protection of Human Rights, the conventionality control doctrine requires full compliance by the national legal order with the jurisprudence of the Inter-American Court of Human Rights (IACtHR).[85] In other words, international treaties ratified by the Brazilian State on human rights and environmental matters and decisions taken by the IACtHR are legally binding and have implications for the domestic legal body's activities.[86]

In *PSB et al v Brazil* (*on Climate Fund*), the STF acknowledged the Paris Agreement as a human rights treaty,[87] asserting the constitutional and *supra-legal* duty of the Union to tackle climate change.[88] Furthermore, the STF addressed the intersectionality between climate change impacts and human rights violations by endorsing the IACtHR's recognition of the 'undeniable relationship between the protection of the environment and the realization of other human rights' and that 'the environmental degradation and the adverse effects of climate change affect the real enjoyment of human rights,' as expressed in *Kawas-Fernández v Honduras*[89] and the Advisory Opinion OC-23/17.[90]

In *PSB et al v Brazil* (*on deforestation and human rights*), Minister Cármen Lúcia (acting as judge-rapporteur) underscored that the violation of the fundamental right to a healthy environment 'produces irreversible effects on all human beings, the present and future generations, impacting the right to health and life of indeterminate numbers of people, affecting entire ecosystems, animals, air quality, soil and water and mineral resources.'[91] In *PSB et al*

---

85 For this matter, the STF has already ruled that 'international treaties and conventions with human rights content, once ratified and internalized, while directly creating rights for individuals, operate the suppression of the effects of other infra-constitutional State acts that oppose their full effectiveness' (*ADEPOL-Brasil v President of the Court of Justice of the State of São Paulo*, ADI 5240 SP, Judgment of the Federal Supreme Court of 20 August 2015, available at <https://redir.stf.jus.br/paginadorpub/paginador.jsp?docTP=TP&docID=10167333>).

86 Moreira et al (n 50) 60.

87 See Carolina Garrido (Chapter 5), Délton Carvalho and Armando Rocha (Chapter 6) in this book.

88 *PSB et al v Brazil* (*on Climate Fund*) 3.

89 *Kawas-Fernández v Honduras* (*Merits, Reparations and Costs*). Judgment of April 3, 2009, IACtHR Series C No 196, available at <https://www.corteidh.or.cr/docs/casos/articulos/seriec_196_ing.pdf>, para 148.

90 *Environment and Human Rights* (*State Obligations in relation to the Environment in the context of the Protection and Guarantee of the Rights to Life and to Personal Integrity—Interpretation and Scope of Articles 4(1) and 5(1) of the American Convention on Human Rights*), Advisory Opinion OC-23/17, IACtHR Series A No 23 (15 November 2017) available at <https://www.corteidh.or.cr/docs/opiniones/seriea_23_ing.pdf>, para. 47.

91 *PSB et al v Brazil* (*on deforestation and human rights*) 3.

*v Brazil* (*on Amazon Fund*), Minister Rosa Weber (acting as judge-rapporteur) asserted that the 'environmental degradation in the Legal Amazon has caused continuous damage to the health, life and dignity of people.'[92]

Furthermore, the STF has also addressed the fundamental right to public participation in decision-making in two other cases, following the IACtHR jurisprudence that the exercise of procedural rights as an appropriate venue to 'support better environmental policymaking' and 'allow for the realization of other treaty-based rights, including the rights to health, life and personal integrity.'[93] In the ADPF 623,[94] the Presidential Decree No 9,806[95] of 28 May 2019, which reduced the number of representatives from civil society in the National Environmental Council, was declared unconstitutional. The Court asserted that 'dismantling organic structures that enable democratic participation of heterogeneous social groups in decision-making processes has the effect of implementing a hegemonic system, concentrated and non-responsive,' incompatible with the constitutional democratic architecture.[96] The OC-23/17 was mentioned by Justice-Rapporteur Rosa Weber in her opinion.[97] In another similar decision delivered in the ADPF 651,[98] the Federal Decree No 10,224, of February 5, 2020, which excluded civil society participation in the National Environmental Fund Council, was also considered unconstitutional. The STF affirmed that 'the exclusion of popular participation in the composition of environmental bodies frustrates the constitutional option for the presence of civil society in formulating environmental public policies.'[99]

Arguments brought by the Federal Government to justify the limitation or exclusion of civil society participation often refer to the rationalization of decision-making processes and—of course—the discretion of its public authority to freely choose public policies.[100] The protection of the environment is an obligation to be carried out by society, as determined by Article 225 of the Constitution. This provision must be interpreted not only from a perspective of

---

92 *PSB et al v Brazil* (*on Amazon Fund*), ADO 59, Judgment of 16 August 2023, available at <https://climatecasechart.com/non-us-case/psb-et-al-v-brazil/>.

93 Advisory Opinion OC-23/17, at 211.

94 *Public Prosecutor's Office v President of the Republic,* Judgment of the Federal Supreme Court of 22 May 2023, available at <https://redir.stf.jus.br/paginadorpub/paginador.jsp?docTP=TP&docID=769273788>.

95 Presidential Decree No 9,806 [2019].

96 *Public Prosecutor's Office v President of the Republic*, at 4. [free translation]

97 ibid, 40.

98 *Rede Sustentabilidade v Brazil* (*on the 'Pacote Verde'*), ADPF 651, Judgment of 28 April 2022.

99 ibid.

100 *Public Prosecutor's Office v President of the Republic*, at 10; *Rede Sustentabilidade v Brazil* (*on the 'Pacote Verde'*), at 2.

duty assignment but also as a democratic fundamental right of participation entrusted to civil society to be fully observed by authorities. In international law, the Rio Declaration[101] asserts that 'environmental issues are best handled with participation of all concerned citizens (...);' and that it shall be granted to individuals 'the opportunity to participate in decision-making processes.'

In addition to the jurisprudence of the IACtHR, the Escazú Agreement[102] provides substantial obligations on climate change, human rights, and procedural rights standards to be observed at the domestic level by all Parties.[103] The treaty has already been referred to in decisions by the IACtHR addressing national policies and administrative acts of environmental and climate concern.[104] Brazil has not yet ratified the treaty. Furthermore, a broad request for an advisory opinion on the climate crises before the IAcHR is pending to be delivered.[105] The ratification of the Escazú Agreement and the advisory opinion to be delivered by the IACtHR may profoundly impact public policies and shape the role of all federative entities in the different branches on climate change, as it will require the adequacy of the domestic legal order with international standards adopted under the Inter-American System for the Protection of Human Rights and the conventionality control.

## 8 Conclusions

Brazilian law provides sufficient and robust legal ground for tackling climate change. The Constitution establishes the competence of each federative entity

101 *Report of the United Nations Conference on Environment and Development* (1992). United Nations General Assembly, A/CONF.151/26 (Vol. I), principle 10.

102 Regional Agreement on Access to Information, Public Participation and Justice in Environmental Matters in Latin America and the Caribbean (adopted 4 March 2018, entered into force 22 April 2021) 3397 *UNTS*.

103 ECLAC, *Regional Agreement On Access To Information, Public Participation And Justice In Environmental Matters In Latin America And The Caribbean—Implementation Guide* 9 [2022].

104 *Baraona Bray v Chile* (*Preliminary Objections, Merits, Reparations and Costs*). Judgment of Nov 24, 2022, IACtHR, Series C No 481, available at <https://www.corteidh.or.cr/docs/casos/articulos/seriec_481_ing.pdf>; *Habitantes de La Oroya v Peru* (*Excepciones Preliminares, Fondo, Reparaciones y Costas*). Judgment of Nov 27, 2023, IACtHR Series C No 511, available at <https://www.corteidh.or.cr/docs/casos/articulos/seriec_511_esp.pdf>.

105 *Request for an Advisory Opinion on the Climate Emergency and Human Rights submitted to the Inter-American Court of Human Rights by the Republic of Colombia and the Republic of Chile.* Request filed by Chile and Colombia on 9 January 2023, available at <https://www.corteidh.or.cr/docs/opiniones/soc_1_2023_en.pdf>.

and how they complement and supplement one another in performing administrative and legislative activities. In addition, the Constitution encompasses an intergenerational perspective of rights and duties to be performed by different legal bodies. Whenever the limits of these legal allocations are breached, or legal obligations to safeguard fundamental rights are not adequately fulfilled, the STF may be provoked to resolve eventual threats or violations.

The STF plays a decisive role in interpreting and applying constitutional dispositions in environmental and climate matters in Brazil. Under the ecological cooperative federalism system, the STF frequently faces jurisdictional conflicts between federative entities, addressing a fragmented and complex legal system where responsibilities may overlap. The STF's jurisprudence strengthens national response to the adverse effects of climate change as it rules over the allocation of competencies among federative entities, shaping their roles according to constitutional dispositions.

The highlighted precedents affirm the interpretation of climate change from the perspective of fundamental environmental rights already established in Brazilian law. The STF's jurisdictional activity analyzes normative acts from the Executive and Legislative Powers to ensure compliance with the constitutional precepts of the right to an ecologically balanced environment and climate stability. A similar dynamic is observed concerning international human rights treaties. The interpretation that climate change falls under the concept of supra-legality opens new perspectives for climate actions to be demanded from the constituted powers, especially within the scope of the Inter-American Human Rights System.

The STF's jurisprudence, therefore, consolidates the understanding that the separation of powers must serve the effectiveness of fundamental rights in environmental and climate matters—rather than be used as a subterfuge to evade constitutional obligations imposed to all federative entities to protect the environment and tackle climate change. No political entity is entitled to authority discretion to freely decide not to comply with the duty to tackle climate change nor to weaken environmental protection standards. Otherwise, the jurisdictional activity may be provoked. In this sense, the STF lies as an open venue in climate litigation in Brazilian law and for further developments on the allocation of competence and role of each political entity from the perspective of the separation of powers, considering the growing adverse impacts of extreme climate events and the internalization of international commitments on the matter assumed by Brazil.

CHAPTER 4

# The Role of Science in Climate Litigation

*Juliana de Augustinis**

## 1 The Scientific Dimension of Framework Climate Litigation against Governments and the Brazilian Experience

Scientific matters and supporting evidence often permeate climate disputes. 'Systemic mitigation'[1] or 'government framework'[2] climate cases, in which petitioners claim failures in governmental responses to climate change, are a telling example. Judicial decisions in well-known cases such as *Leghari v Federation of Pakistan*,[3] *Urgenda Foundation v State of the Netherlands*,[4] *Friends of the Irish Environment v The Government of Ireland et al*,[5] and *Greenpeace v Instituto Nacional de Ecología y Cambio Climático et al*,[6] reveal a variety of topics, such as the adverse impacts of climate change, the urgency to mitigate greenhouse gas (GHG) emissions, and appropriate GHG mitigation levels.

* Ph.D. candidate at Tilburg Law School, email: J.Augustinis@tilburguniversity.edu.

1 The expression refers to litigation challenging the adequacy of a government's overall approach to reducing GHG emissions. See Joana Setzer & Catherine Higham, *Global Trends in Climate Change Litigation: 2024 Snapshot* (Grantham Research Institute on Climate Change and the Environment and Centre for Climate Change Economics and Policy 2024); Joana Setzer & Catherine Higham, *Global Trends in Climate Change Litigation: 2021 Snapshot* (Grantham Research Institute on Climate Change and the Environment and Centre for Climate Change Economics and Policy 2021). The 2024 report 'Climate Litigation in Brazil' published by the Research Group on Law, Environment, and Justice in the Anthropocene (JUMA) brings a slightly more comprehensive definition to systemic cases as those 'aimed at prompting changes to public and private policy, filed by organisations or institutions and involving complex, broad discussions.' See Danielle de Andrade Moreira et al, *Executive Summary—Climate Litigation in Brazil: Report 2024* (JUMA/PUC-Rio 2024).

2 Setzer and Higham define government framework disputes as 'cases that challenge the implementation or ambition of climate targets and policies affecting the whole of a country's economy and society' or differently put, cases that dispute a government's overall climate policy response. Joana Setzer & Catherine Higham, *Global Trends in Climate Change Litigation: 2022 Snapshot* (Grantham Research Institute on Climate Change and the Environment and Centre for Climate Change Economics and Policy 2022) 18.

3 *Asghar Leghari v Federation of Pakistan* [2015] WP No 25501/201 (Lahore High Court).

4 *Urgenda Foundation v State of the Netherlands* [2015] HAZA C/09/00456689.

5 *Friends of the Irish Environment v Ireland* [2017] No 793 JR (Supreme Court of Ireland).

6 *Greenpeace v Instituto Nacional de Ecología y Cambio Climático et al* [2021] RA(I) 81 (11th Collegiate Court of the 1st Circuit in Administrative Matters).

 | DOI:10.1163/9789004690974_005

While scholars highlight the influence of scientific knowledge in climate litigation,[7] judicial interaction with empirical data and science in climate disputes that aim for broad policy changes still requires more attention to Global South practices and perspectives.[8] In this context, Brazil emerges as a meaningful case-study for leading the number of reported climate cases in the Global South,[9] ranking fourth worldwide.[10] It also serves as a possible source of inspiration for other jurisdictions for presenting multiple pending climate cases that can use methods such as *amicus curiae* and public hearings to inform judges.

To introduce the state of knowledge on the topic and underexplored research pathways, in Section 2, I look at existing studies on the influence of climate science on judicial reasoning. In Section 3, I explore how Brazilian courts, with several ongoing climate cases, engage with scientific evidence. In Section 4, I present relevant findings from a systematic content analysis of climate rulings in 14 countries conducted to map the judicial interaction with climate science concerning GHG mitigation. I conclude in Section 5 with a reflection on what we can learn from the Brazilian experience compared to the global trends.

The existing judgments in climate lawsuits in Brazil suggest a judicial openness not only to participatory instruments such as *amicus curiae* and public hearings but also to address information provided by experts and groups of interest through these tools. Global trends point to an infrequent reference in court decisions to the assistance of experts for understanding scientific evidence and empirical data concerning GHG mitigation. Contrastingly, Brazilian rulings used tools to gather and grasp scientific aspects unfamiliar to judges. Such an approach, remarkable in cases such as *PSB et al v Brazil (on Climate Fund)*, could favour a more complete and transparent consideration of climate

7 The existing literature is better developed in Section 2.

8 While recognising the diversity within overarching groups like the Global South and Global North, these categories remain relevant in discussions around climate litigation. Specifically, considering that countries in the Global South generally emit fewer GHG historically compared to their Global North counterparts but are disproportionately affected by climate change. For a more in-depth analysis of the usefulness of such classifications, see, for instance, Melanie Jean Murcott & Maria Antonia Tigre, 'Developments, Opportunities, and Complexities in Global South Climate Litigation: Introduction to the Special Collection' (2024) 16 *Journal of Human Rights Practice* 1.

9 As reported by the 2024 *Climate Litigation in the Global South: Mapping Report*, 'Brazil has the highest proportion of cases at 39%, followed by Mexico at 10.5%, Indonesia at 7.1%, and Colombia at 6.7%.' See Maria Antonia Tigre, *Climate Litigation in the Global South: Mapping Report* (Sabin Center for Climate Change Law 2024).

10 According to the 2024 report on 'Climate Litigation in Brazil', the country would lag behind only the USA, Australia, and the United Kingdom in the total number of reported climate cases. Danielle de Andrade Moreira et al (n 2).

science by courts and inspire other jurisdictions. The richness of procedures that encourage public participation and the consideration of information in Brazilian cases, along with diverse pending decisions in influential public interest cases, highlight the relevance of studying new climate judgments in Brazil and other Global South countries.

## 2 The Influence of Climate Science on Judicial Reasoning

Legal scholars discuss the entanglement of scientific and normative questions on climate change litigation, pointing out, for instance, how scientific findings can provide the factual background for the litigants' arguments and influence judicial decisions. Beauregard et al provide examples from Colombia, the Netherlands, and the United States to illustrate how scientific evidence concerning present and future likely harmful impacts of climate change is fuelling plaintiffs' arguments. Science has supported claims that governmental (in)actions aggravated climate change and violated citizens' fundamental rights. In cases like *Urgenda Foundation v State of the Netherlands*[11] and *Future Generations v Ministry of the Environment (of Colombia) et al*,[12] science has informed the allegations of human rights violations and supported judicial orders, including injunctions against governments. In the *Urgenda* case, the Dutch Supreme Court ordered the State to reduce GHG emissions by 25% in 2020 compared to 1990. In the case of *Future Generations,* the Colombian Supreme Court held the government accountable for failing to meet its commitment to reach net zero deforestation by 2020.[13]

Several publications focus, in particular, on the influence of climate science on the judicial reasoning in the *Urgenda* case. Remarkably, the Intergovernmental Panel on Climate Change (IPCC) has a crucial role in the judicial determination that the Dutch Government should pursue more ambitious GHG emission reductions to meet its international obligations under the Paris Agreement.[14]

11 *Urgenda Foundation v State of the Netherlands* (n 5).

12 *Future Generations v Ministry of the Environment et al* (2018) Process No 11001 22 03 000 2018 00319 00, Decision of 5 April 2018 (Supreme Court of Colombia), available at <https://climatecasechart.com/non-us-case/future-generation-v-ministry-environment-others/>.

13 Charles Beauregard, D'Arcy Carlson, Stacy-Ann Robinson, Charles Cobb & Mykela Patton, 'Climate Justice and Rights-Based Litigation in a Post-Paris World' (2021) 21 *Climate Policy* 652.

14 See, for instance, KJ de Graaf & JH Jans, 'The Urgenda Decision: Netherlands Liable for Role in Causing Dangerous Global Climate Change' (2015) 27 *Journal of Environmental Law* 517; Jennifer Huang & Maria Antonia Tigre, 'Trends in Climate Justice Litigation:

Minnerop, for example, explains that scientific evidence assisted Dutch courts in acknowledging a duty of care to reduce GHG emissions and helped to translate this duty of care into a specific standard of care (25% reduction) for the government. The author highlights that the decision by the Hague Court of Appeal ' (...) reveals that the concrete content of this duty of care is not derived from human rights, but from scientifically proven and internationally endorsed [GHG] emission reduction targets which are imperative to achieve the temperature goal of the Paris Agreement.'[15] In a similar direction, Beauregard et al comment that, in the *Future Generations* case, the Supreme Court of Colombia 'used the scientific evidence of the climate impacts of deforestation to hold the Colombian Government accountable to its NDC commitment of net zero deforestation by 2020.'[16]

### 2.1 *Understudied Research Pathways*

Existing studies about courts' engagement with climate science reveal judges' hesitation to rely on the latest scientific insights establishing causation and attributing responsibility for climate change,[17] as well as long-term projections for climate impacts.[18] In the context of international environmental adjudication, Sulyok notices, on the one hand, the use of judicial avoidance strategies towards scientific knowledge. On the other hand, the contrary tendency of judges to be too deferent towards the evidence without scrutinising its quality can also be found in certain cases.[19] Whereas courts disregarding scientific

---

The Dutch Case and Global Repercussions', in Abate (ed), *Climate Justice—Case Studies in Global and Regional Governance Challenges* (Environmental Law Institute 2016) 571; Jaap Spier, '"The «Strongest» Climate Ruling Yet": The Dutch Supreme Court's Urgenda Judgment' (2020) 67 *Netherlands ILR* 319; Lucy Maxwell, Sarah Mead & Dennis van Berkel, 'Standards for Adjudicating the Next Generation of *Urgenda*-Style Climate Cases' (2022) 13 *Journal of Human Rights and the Environment* 35; Heather Colby et al, 'Judging Climate Change: The Role of the Judiciary in the Fight Against Climate Change' (2020) 7 *Oslo Law Review* 168.

15 Petra Minnerop, 'Integrating the "Duty of Care" under the European Convention on Human Rights and the Science and Law of Climate Change: The Decision of The Hague Court of Appeal in the *Urgenda* Case' (2019) 37 *Journal of Energy & Natural Resources Law* 149, 149.

16 Charles Beauregard et al (n 13) 657.

17 Rupert F Stuart-Smith et al, 'Filling the Evidentiary Gap in Climate Litigation' (2021) 11 *Nature Climate Change* 651.

18 Maria L Banda, *Climate Science in the Courts: A Review of U.S. And International Judicial Pronouncements* (Environmental Law Institute 2020).

19 Katalin Sulyok, 'Introduction to a Comparative Study on Judicial Engagement with Science', in Sulyok (ed), *Science and Judicial Reasoning: The Legitimacy of International Environmental Adjudication* (CUP 2020).

knowledge can bring the risks of overlooking scientifically valid arguments or relying on claims unsupported by science, deferential approaches could also lead to uncritical acceptance of scientific knowledge. That raises questions about whether courts have the procedural capacity to understand scientific aspects of climate cases or perhaps need new tools for this purpose.

One research gap concerns how courts in different jurisdictions consider scientific knowledge when judging claims for stronger climate action. In particular, evidence about appropriate measures to limit global warming to certain temperature thresholds is a potentially relevant factor for such decisions. Connected questions in this respect are: do rulings in different countries consider the scientific basis of this question in climate cases that seek broader policy change? Do rulings assess qualitative aspects of the evidence, such as trustworthiness, its consistency with the parties' arguments, or the degree of uncertainty? Do they use established methods or criteria to appraise these qualitative aspects of the evidence?

From another angle, scholars also discuss the relevance of studying practices from the Global South, which often bring innovative approaches to environmental protection that challenge legal formalism.[20] For instance, climate cases from Latin America have developed the notions of intergenerational equity and rights of nature that connect to climate governance.[21] Moreover, climate lawsuits keep expanding in the region, diversifying this scenario and bringing increased attention to climate protection.

## 3 Global South in Perspective: Judicial Engagement with Science in Climate Lawsuits in Brazil

Hereafter, I analyse how several climate lawsuits in Brazil engaged with expert knowledge and scientific evidence. For this purpose, I selected Brazilian cases involving broad challenges to climate change governance. I excluded, therefore, lawsuits regarding challenges to policies in specific sectors and not overall climate policies—Eg, cases concerning decarbonisation credits for fuel

20 Joana Setzer & Lisa Benjamin, 'Climate Litigation in the Global South: Constraints and Innovations' (2020) 9 *Transnational Environmental Law* 77.

21 Maria Antonia Tigre, Natalia Urzola & Alexandra Goodman, 'Climate Litigation in Latin America: Is the Region quietly Leading a Revolution?' (2023) 14 *Journal of Human Rights and the Environment* 67.

distributors,[22] norms on the export of wood products,[23] and changes to electricity plans in Brazil.[24] Moreover, the selection comprised claims not only about mitigation and adaptation policies but also climate cases challenging national deforestation policies and the allocation of resources of climate funds.

To identify relevant cases for the project scope, I reviewed pertinent categories in the Sabin Climate Litigation Database in November 2023. Accordingly, I filtered results into the following sub-categories within 'Global litigation—Suits against governments': (a) GHG emissions reduction and trading, (b) Protecting biodiversity and ecosystems, (c) Human rights, (d) Energy and power, and (e) Failure to adapt. In addition, I screened 75 results in the search 'Global litigation—by jurisdiction—Brazil'. Based on this process, I selected five cases for analysis, as listed in the table below. Rather than intending to cover all possible relevant disputes, the criteria for selection referred to disputes with potential significant policy impacts.[25]

After selecting relevant cases in Brazil, I analysed them by looking at whether and how judgments considered empirical data and scientific evidence and which role this evidence possibly played in the decision according to the judicial motivation. In addition, I looked at other procedural documents available on the courts' websites, such as the parties' submissions and accompanying evidence, preliminary orders, *amici curiae* submissions, and public hearings transcripts, also available on the Brazilian tribunals' webpages.

The screening of climate cases in Brazil within the scope of the present analysis shows at least five climate cases with potential considerable impacts

---

22 Eg *Brasilcom et al v Ministério de Minas e Energia*, MS 27093/DF (2020/0306047), filed on 18 November 2020 before the Superior Court of Justice, Decision of 10 December 2022, available at <https://climatecasechart.com/non-us-case/brasilcom-et-al-v-ministerio-de-minas-e-energia/>.

23 *ISA et al v Brazil et al* (*Wood exportation*), ACP 1009665-60.2020.4.01.3200, filed on 4 June 2020 before the 7th Federal Environmental and Agrarian Court of the Judiciary Section of Amazonas, available at <https://climatecasechart.com/non-us-case/isa-abrampa-and-greenpeace-v-brazil/ and at https://judicialportal.informea.org/sites/default/files/court-case/ACP-ISA-1009665-60.2020.4.01.3200.pdf>.

24 Eg *PSB et al v Brazil* (*on Electrobras Privatization*), ADI 6932, filed on 15 July 2021, available at <https://climatecasechart.com/non-us-case/adi-6932-eletrobras-privatization/>.

25 The 2024 *Climate Litigation in the Global South: Mapping Report* highlights, for instance, the significance of two Federal Supreme Court (STF) rulings in cases included in the study for their potential impact on the interpretation of climate laws in the country. Namely, in *PSB et al v Brazil* (*on Climate Fund*) and *PSB et al v Brazil* (*on Amazon Fund*). See Maria Antonia Tigre (n 9).

TABLE 4.1 **List of Brazilian cases selected for analysis, filing date, summary, and case outcome as of May 2024**

| Case name | Filing date | Original court | Summary | Case outcome (as of May 2024) |
|---|---|---|---|---|
| *PSB et al v Brazil (on Climate Fund)* | 5 June 2020 | Federal Supreme Court | Four political parties filed a lawsuit against the Brazilian state alleging the federal government's failure to meet its constitutional duty to allocate resources of the Climate Fund to projects to mitigate and adapt to climate change. | **Decided.** The Federal Supreme Court ruled in favour of the plaintiffs on 30 June 2022. |
| *IEA v Brazil* | 8 October 2020 | Federal District Court of Curitiba | The Institute of Amazonian Studies sued the Brazilian state arguing the federal government's failure to comply with the Climate Change National Policy Act. The plaintiff sought recognition, under the Brazilian Constitution, of a fundamental right to a stable climate for present and future generations and an order directing the State to comply with climate legislation. | **Pending.** |
| *PSB et al v Brazil (on deforestation and human rights)* | 11 November 2020 | Federal Supreme Court | Seven Brazilian political parties, supported by NGOs, filed a lawsuit against the Brazilian state asserting constitutional rights violations due to the federal government's failure to implement Brazil's Action Plan for Prevention and Control of the Legal Amazon Deforestation. That would lead to increased deforestation thereby contributing to dangerous climate change. The plaintiffs plead for benchmarks for compliance and stronger enforcement measures. | **Pending.** Favourable opinion of Supreme Court Justice-rapporteur on 6 April 2022. |

TABLE 4.1 **List of Brazilian cases selected for analysis, filing date, summary, and case outcome as of May 2024** (*cont.*)

| | | | | |
|---|---|---|---|---|
| *Six Youths v Minister of Environment et al* | 13 April 2021 | 14th Federal Civil Court of Sao Paulo | Young activists filed a lawsuit against Brazilian government officials, alleging the updated 2020 Nationally Determined Contributions (NDCs) are regressive compared to previous climate commitments, in violation of the Paris Agreement. The plaintiffs seek the NDCs' nullification and an injunction for a more ambitious reduction target. | **Pending.** A preliminary decision rejected a claim for urgent relief on 27 May 2021. On November 21st, 2023, an out-of-court settlement was reached and the government updated the Brazilian NDCs previously reduced during Bolsonaro's government. |
| *Laboratório do Observatório do Clima v Minister of Environment et al* | 26 October 2021 | 7th Federal Environmental and Agrarian Court of the Judiciary Section of Amazonas | Laboratório do Observatório do Clima, a network of 71 civil society organisations, filed a lawsuit against the Brazilian government, seeking to align the National Climate Change Policy with the latest science and IPCC reports to ensure Brazil's GHG mitigations match a 1.5°C scenario. The plaintiffs argue that the updated NDCs retreat from earlier goals, contravening the Paris Agreement and Brazil's climate laws. | **Pending.** Case admitted on 13 May 2022. |

on national climate governance. A look at the case outcomes as of May 2024 also reveals that the cases are mostly still pending a decision on the merits. One might argue that the low number of decisions substantially limits more comprehensive analyses of judicial approaches to expert data and scientific knowledge. However, a closer look at the existing judgments and other documents in the process, such as submissions by the litigants and *amici curiae*, evidence filed, and other judicial documents, provided a surprisingly extensive amount of relevant information. Moreover, many Brazilian courts make the procedural documents publicly available on their websites. Therefore, I considered a broader variety of records accessible in each case.

### 3.1 *Engagement with Science in PSB et al v Brazil (on Climate Fund)*

The case of *PSB et al v Brazil (on Climate Fund)*[26] stands out from the other selected Brazilian disputes for being the first initiated and the only one with a final decision on the merits at the time of writing. This case involved four political parties challenging the federal government's reluctance to manage the Climate Fund. The latter is an essential financial instrument of the Brazilian National Policy on Climate Change. Established by Law in 2009, the Fund aims to support projects, studies, or activities that contribute to reducing GHG emissions or promote the development of adaptation strategies to the adverse effects of climate change. In the dispute, the plaintiffs argued that despite the aggravation of the climate crisis and the Federal statutory duties of presenting an annual plan for using the Fund's resources, the Climate Fund became inoperant entirely during 2019 and partially during 2020. This mismanagement would result from the lack of appointment of the Fund Management Committee following the 2018 presidential elections. The Federal Supreme Court ruled in favour of the plaintiffs, acknowledging the Federal Union's unconstitutional omission in not allocating the Climate Fund resources and ordering the government to make the Fund operate with the required assignment of resources to climate protection.[27]

---

26 *PSB et al v Brazil (on Climate Fund)* [STF] ADPF 708, Judgment of 7 January 2022.

27 To establish the omission, Justice-rapporteur Luís Roberto Barroso considers in his opinion, for instance, the Federal Senate's Environment Committee 'Assessment of the National Policy on Climate Change' pointing out that the Fund's inactivity was due to the lack of appointment of the Fund Management Committee because the Executive intended to change its composition before allocating the resources. Also, according to the document, the new composition of the Committee privileged the representation and participation of the private sector to the detriment of the organised civil society, unlike the old composition. ibid para 21.

In the judge rapporteur's motivation, the main grounds for the decision were the constitutional right to a healthy environment and the duty to comply with internationally assumed rights and commitments. However, it is interesting to note the role climate science played in a partially concurring opinion by Justice Edson Fachin with reservations on two points. Namely, the decision should also order the Federal Union to publish periodic quarterly statistical reports concerning the Climate Fund spending in the different sectors and formulate a National Inventory of GHG Emissions and carbon removals. In his opinion, Justice Edson Fachin engaged with the findings of the latest IPCC reports and large-scale scientific studies about the anthropogenic causes, impacts, and the need to take mitigation and adaptation measures. Based on this information, he affirmed the urgent need to take action to mitigate emissions to safeguard the fundamental right to environmental protection established in the constitution. To assert that such action would be based on 'the best available scientific knowledge,'[28] the Justice considered the fact that there is massive support from scientists throughout the globe explaining what is necessary concerning GHG reductions. In this vein, the scientific dimension seemed to be an inherent part of the concurring opinion in favour of additional protective measures compared to the rapporteur's opinion. The opinion also mentioned two Federal Supreme Court understandings from previous rulings relevant to the decision. The first position is that public authorities should base their decisions on technical and scientific criteria when their acts have ecological consequences. The second Federal Supreme Court's view is that courts should apply the precautionary principle to environmental matters in case of scientific uncertainty.

Another relevant aspect of the case relates to the procedural use of public hearings and the intervention of *amicus curiae*. In the aftermath of the Brazilian 1988 Constitution, Federal statutes regulating judicial review instruments[29] designed such deliberative practices to counter-balance the Federal Supreme Court's democratic legitimacy deficit, as Justices do not hold elective mandates.[30] Additionally, one can praise this openness to public participation for reinforcing the quality of the decisions. Namely, by allowing civil society members, mainly those with expertise on the subject under discussion, to bring relevant information to the process, clarify technical aspects of the

28 *PSB et al v Brazil* (*on Climate Fund*) (n 24), 'Opinion of Minister Edson Fachin', para 3.

29 Eg Law No 9,868, of 10 November 1999, or Law No 9,882, of 3 December 1999.

30 Thiago Luis Sombra, 'Why Should Public Hearings in the Brazilian Supreme Court be Understood as an Innovative Democratic Tool in Constitutional Adjudication?' (2016) 17 *German Law Journal* 657.

dispute, and potentially influence decisions that inevitably affect the public interest.

Accordingly, the Federal Supreme Court invited several public authorities, civil society organisations, research institutes, and private sector entities but also published a call to anyone interested in contributing to the debate. The court admitted participation according to the criteria of representativeness, technical expertise, and plurality of perspectives and allotted time to all participants to present their points. The admitted entities should send any audiovisual materials beforehand to the court and, preferably, a summary of their presentation's main points. The audience was recorded and made publicly available. In addition, specialised persons and entities with sufficient representativity were admitted as *amici curiae* to offer expertise or insights on the case—Eg, through *amicus* briefs.

The organisations admitted as *amici curiae* in the process provided the court with a range of evidence about both global and regional sources and impacts of climate change[31] and data about the mismanagement of the Climate Fund.[32] Complementarily, in the public hearing held on 21 September 2020, numerous experts commented on scientific information conveyed in the IPCC reports[33] and studies about more localised climate-related events, especially concerning the Amazon rainforest region.[34] Specialists also clarified aspects concerning increasing illegal deforestation in Brazil and its severe implications for global

31 For instance, Instituto Alana (a social and environmental impact group) presented extensive data from Brazilian research institutes reports. Eg, information about deforestation in the Amazon biome being the main factor for GHG emissions in Brazil and numbers about the steady increase in deforestation rates in the Amazon region between 2019 and 2021. It also conveyed information in the IPCC reports about the more intense impacts of climate change in Global South countries. Manifestation of Instituto Alana as *amicus curiae* in *PSB et al v Brazil (on Climate Fund)*.

32 Put forward, for instance, by Laboratório do Observatório do Clima, a network of 71 civil society organisations admitted as *amicus curiae*. Manifestation of Laboratório do Observatório do Clima in *PSB et al v Brazil (on Climate Fund)*.

33 In the public hearing, Thelma Krug, elected Vice-Chair of the IPCC for the Sixth Cycle of Panel (October 2015—October 2022), presented scientific information about the global impacts of climate change. See *Public hearings in PSB et al v Brazil (on Climate Fund) ADPF 708—Operation of the National Fund for Change Climate (Climate Fund) and public policies on environmental matters* (Federal Supreme Court 2020) paras 415–425.

34 Maurício Voivodic, executive director of WWF Brazil, has presented, for instance, information about the risks of a 'savannization' process of the Amazon rainforest, which would increase the risks of fires and biodiversity loss. ibid paras 217–226.

warming,[35] the government's lack of protection for Indigenous lands,[36] and deficient environmental oversight.[37] This information has directly influenced, for instance, the opinion on the necessity of additional judicial determinations to ensure the alignment of the allocation of the Fund's resources with the National Climate Policy. Justice Fachin's opinion explicitly mentioned, in this regard, that it reached this conclusion based on 'the extremely relevant public hearing convened by the Justice-rapporteur.'[38]

The main decision, by the Justice-rapporteur, also referred to allegations by *amici curiae* on the suboptimal allocation of resources by the government after the Fund activities were resumed. Those objections would concern the destination of resources mainly to the urban environment when a relevant amount of GHG emissions results from deforestation and soil modifications in the rural environment. Nevertheless, the Justice included the remark as an *obiter dictum* for exceeding the scope of the case.[39]

On the one hand, the case exemplifies the influence of scientific knowledge in judicial orders for stricter protective climate measures—notably the opinion by Justice Edson Fachin. On the other hand, it illustrates the intensive use of public hearings and *amicus curiae* as procedural tools to collect and assess scientific data. Therefore, the court's commitment to inclusivity and expert input might inspire jurisdictions that lack or avoid using procedural methods to understand specialised knowledge. Another remarkable aspect of the case relative to other jurisdictions concerns the enhanced transparency in the judicial process, with all documents publicly available on the Supreme Court's website, including the full transcript of the hearing with over 600 pages.

### 3.2 *Engagement with Science in Pending Cases in Brazil*

There are also a few pending climate cases in Brazil that fit the scope of this analysis. *IEA v Brazil*[40] draws attention in this regard as the plaintiffs seek, in

35 For instance, in the presentations by Castro Simnovic, representing the environmental protection institute Chico Mendes and Fabiana Ferreira Alves, Climate Justice Coordinator of Greenpeace Brazil. ibid paras 100–111, 180–187.

36 See, Eg, the speech of Sônia Guajajara, Coordinator of the Association of Indigenous People of Brazil—APIB. ibid paras 187-195.

37 See, Eg, the speech of Fabiana Ferreira Alves, Climate Justice Coordinator of Greenpeace Brazil. ibid paras 180–187.

38 *PSB et al v Brazil* (*on Climate Fund*) (n 24) 'Opinion of Minister Edson Fachin', para 8.

39 *PSB et al v Brazil* (*on Climate Fund*) (n 24) 'Opinion of Minister Luís Roberto Barroso', paras 32–35.

40 *IEA v Brazil*, ACP No. 5048951-39.2020.4.04.7000, filed in 2020 before the 4th Federal Regional Court of Curitiba.

addition to an order to compel the government to comply with deforestation control policies as part of the National Climate Change Policy, the recognition of a fundamental right to a stable climate as an implicit fundamental right.[41] It also raises interest in future decision-making in the court's engagement with the extensive scientific evidence submitted by the plaintiffs. This evidence includes, Eg, officially available data on the occurrence of deforestation and its national and regional effects, and a technical report by a climate expert, lead author for the Intergovernmental Panel on Climate Change.[42] On top of that, the plaintiffs also requested the governmental agency responsible for satellite deforestation monitoring in the country to function as an *amicus curiae*. Now that the agency declined the invitation, the court can still request technical information from the institute to understand complex technical evidence. In March 2022, the court also allowed the parties to bring experts to clarify specific points of the case at the hearing. The case underscores, therefore, the potential role of experts in Brazil in providing specialised knowledge and insights that can aid in resolving disputes with significant scientific or technical components.

*PSB et al v Brazil (on deforestation and human rights)*[43] is also a striking climate case pending on the Federal Supreme Court, bringing about as petitioners both political parties and NGO s and admitting in the procedure many civil society organisations as *amici curiae*. In April 2022, the Justice-rapporteur Cármen Lúcia issued an extensive ruling on the merits in favour of the plaintiffs, acknowledging a 'state of unconstitutional affairs' regarding the illegal deforestation of the Amazon Forest and ordering the Federal Government to present an appropriate Action Plan for Prevention and Control of the Legal Amazon Deforestation. The Plan should, for instance, specify the measures undertaken to protect the rights of Indigenous people and other people living in Conservation Units and Indigenous Lands and combat crimes committed in the ecosystem.

The opinion goes over comprehensive official data about deforestation and the efficacy of the Action Plan for the Prevention and Control of Deforestation in the Legal Amazon between 2004 and 2012, provided by governmental agencies. Expert knowledge was, therefore, essential to support the conclusion about the occurrence of repeated unconstitutional omissions by the Federal

41 Joana Setzer & Délton Winter de Carvalho, 'Climate Litigation to Protect the Brazilian Amazon: Establishing a Constitutional Right to a Stable Climate' (2021) 30 *RECIEL* 197.

42 ibid.

43 *PSB et al v Brazil (on deforestation and human rights)* [STF] ADPF 760, Judgment of 6 April 2022.

Government in the control of deforestation and management of environmental protection in Brazil. Furthermore, such a situation of unconstitutional affairs would constitute a grave offence against fundamental rights. In this regard, it is interesting to note the Justice's inspiration in a jurisprudential construction from the Colombian Constitutional Court as she explains the origins of the notion of the unconstitutional state of affairs. Notwithstanding the forward-looking opinion, one of the Justices requested the case files for inspection and a possibly dissenting opinion.

The cases of *Laboratório do Observatório do Clima v Minister of Environment et al*[44] and *Six Youths v Minister of Environment et al*[45] also show how climate disputes in Brazil are highly informed by scientific information provided either by the parties or interested organisations admitted as *amici curiae* or presenters in public hearings. Such procedural instruments reveal a large potential to inform courts about unclear aspects of the evidence. The first case, still pending as of May 2024, presents a significant perspective for the courts' engagement with empirical data and scientific evidence given the plaintiffs' submissions, bringing a possibility for future comparative research. The latter dispute, although also admitted by a Federal Court, has been terminated by an out-of-court settlement between the parties in 21 November 2023.[46] This development happened during President Luis Inacio Lula da Silva's mandate, when the Federal Government corrected the country's Nationally Determined Contribution (NDC), resuming the national goal of cutting GHG emissions by up to 48% by 2025 and by 53% by 2030 compared to the emission levels recorded in 2005. Thereby, remedying the less ambitious goal that resulted from increased net emissions allowed for 2025 and 2030 during Jair Bolsonaro's presidential mandate. This legal modification of net emissions rather than the reduction targets became known as 'climatic stepover'

44 *Laboratório do Observatório do Clima v Minister of Environment et al*, ACP 1027282-96.2021.4.01.3200, filed on 26 October 2021 before the 7th Federal Environmental and Agrarian Court of the Judiciary Section of Amazonas, available at <https://climatecasechart.com/non-us-case/laboratorio-do-observatorio-do-clima-v-environmental-ministry-and-brazil/>.

45 *Six Youths v Minister of Environment et al*, Popular Action No 5008035-37.2021.4.03.6100, filed on 13 April 2021 before the 14th Federal Civil Court of São Paulo, Judgment of 7 June 2024, available at <https://climatecasechart.com/non-us-case/six-youths-v-minister-of-environment-and-others/>.

46 Observatório do Clima, 'Conciliação encerra embate sobre "pedalada" climática de 2020' (Observatório do Clima 2023) available at <https://www.oc.eco.br/conciliacao-encerra-embate-sobre-pedalada-climatica-de-2020/> accessed on 6 August 2024.

('*pedalada climática*'), an analogy to a Brazilian soccer trick in which one player rolls their foot over the top of the ball without touching it to deceive an opposing player.[47]

## 4 Global Trends in the Judicial Treatment of Scientific Evidence and Data about Mitigation

In this Section, I present findings from a systematic content analysis of case law to investigate judicial interaction with scientific aspects of climate change disputes against governments involving mitigation policies, also known as 'systemic mitigation' climate cases. More specifically, I analyse the extent to which climate rulings referred to scientific evidence and data regarding what GHG emissions reductions would be suitable for limiting global warming to temperature thresholds that are deemed safer by science. Additionally, I aim to show whether and how courts assessed the validity of this evidence.

As pointed out by Verbruggen et al, 'systematic case law analysis' describes the application of a range of data analysis methods from social science that share the aims of finding meaningful relationships or patterns in a data set (in this case judicial decisions) in a replicable and reliable manner. Accordingly, content analysis entails the systematic selection, coding, and analysis of texts, possibly via data analysis software.[48] In a 2008 seminal study, Hall and Wright identified the potential of 'structured content analysis' to lay the foundations of a 'unique legal empirical methodology' that generates replicable knowledge about 'what courts do and how and why they do it'.[49]

The research design for this study applied general coding techniques described, for instance, by Saldaña[50] and Schebesta.[51] Accordingly, the coding

47 Advocacia Geral da União, 'AGU, Ministério do Meio Ambiente e Mudança do Clima e jovens ambientalistas fazem acordo em ação que discutia "pedalada climática" do governo anterior" (AGU 2023) available at <https://www.gov.br/agu/pt-br/comunicacao/noticias/agu-ministerio-do-meio-ambiente-e-mudanca-do-clima-e-jovens-ambientalistas-fazem-acordo-em-acao-que-discutia-pedalada-climatica-do-governo-anterior> accessed on 6 August 2024.

48 Paul Verbruggen (ed), *Methoden van systematische rechtspraakanalyse: Tussen juridische dogmatiek en data science* (Boom juridisch 2021).

49 Mark A Hall & Ronald F Wright, 'Systematic Content Analysis of Judicial Opinions' (2008) 96 *California Law Review* 63.

50 Johnny Saldaña, *The Coding Manual for Qualitative Researchers* (4th edn, SAGE 2021)

51 Hanna Schebesta, 'Content Analysis Software in Legal Research: A Proof of Concept Using ATLAS.TI' (2018) 23 *Tilburg Law Review* 23.

process involved a first exploratory stage to create a set of codes connected to the research questions. Namely: to what extent do climate rulings across jurisdictions consider scientific evidence and data about appropriate mitigation policies and government action against climate change? How, if at all, do courts approach qualitative aspects of this evidence?

A pilot study of 23 rulings served as a basis for inductively finding relevant codes and developing explicit rules for the coding process.[52] Accordingly, in February 2023, I reviewed the selection of the rulings and systematically coded a more extensive list of judgments according to my coding protocol. For coding and carrying out the content analysis, the qualitative data analysis software Atlas.ti was used. In addition, qualitative notes were taken during the coding process, to gather additional insights on possible explanations for courts' engagement with scientific knowledge.

The final study comprised 49 rulings in systemic mitigation cases,[53] ie, disputes in which the petitioners challenge the implementation or ambition of the government's mitigation policies, issued between 2015 and 2022 across 14 countries. Namely: Australia, Belgium, Canada, Czech Republic, France, Germany, India, Ireland, Mexico, New Zealand, Pakistan, the Netherlands, the United Kingdom, and the United States. To draw this sample, I first filtered climate cases concerning challenges to governments' overall climate change mitigation policies in the Sabin Center for Climate Change Law database at Columbia Law School (Sabin) and the Climate Rights and Remedies (CRRP) database.[54] I selected judgments that could address more than merely procedural questions[55] and, therefore, potentially approach the substance of the claim to change mitigation approaches and deal with empirical questions around these policies. I also selected rulings issued after both parties provided arguments to the process, excluding preliminary judgments before the defendant's contestation. For the analysis of the verdicts on Atlas.ti, I

52 Juliana de Augustinis, 'The Science Behind Climate Change Litigation: Are Courts Shying Away from Expert Aid?' (*Institutions for Conflict Resolution* 2023) available at <http://institutionsforconflictresolution.net/NEWS-COMMENTS/COMMENT-The-Science-Behind-Climate-Change-Litigation-Are-Courts-Shying-Away-From-Expert-Aid/#wbb1> accessed 29 January 2024.

53 See definition in footnote 2.

54 The selection did not involve lawsuits about curbing deforestation for only indirectly addressing climate change policies. It also did not include cases challenging the inappropriate use of climate funds for not corresponding to a general climate policy or legislation but consisting of an instrument for it.

55 Eg excluding rulings limited to discussing jurisdiction or the exhaustion of administrative remedies.

systematically coded the following categories. (i) reference to scientific evidence or empirical data about mitigation pathways that governments could follow to stabilise the global temperature in levels deemed as safer by science and international commitments under the UN Framework. That is, well below 2°C or 1.5°C compared to pre-industrial levels. (data about mitigation measures). (ii) courts' qualitative assessments of data about mitigation measures. (iii) criteria to perform the qualitative assessments of this evidence.

### 4.1 *Reference to Data about Mitigation Measures*

The content analysis revealed that 27 of 49 rulings (approximately 55%) alluded to scientific information or empirical data about mitigation measures to limit global warming to safer temperature thresholds, such as evidence about proper GHG emissions mitigation in general, or according to specific rates and trajectories. Therefore, the findings show that the majority of rulings referred to the scientific basis of appropriate mitigation action. Several rulings mentioned the scientific findings voiced in the IPCC Reports, Eg global carbon budget recommendations for 1.5°C and 2°C relative to pre-industrial times, but were not limited to this source. Some judgments have also referred to more 'local' evidence in scientific reports authored by governmental or independent entities, expert groups, or individual experts. For instance, regarding GHG emission reduction targets for specific countries or regions[56] or the compatibility of regional emissions trajectory with holding global warming to 1.5°C above pre-industrial levels.[57] Notwithstanding, almost half of the judgements (approximately 45%) did not mention any evidence about appropriate mitigation measures.

Therefore, the findings suggest that most rulings did not overlook the science behind what action governments could take. Yet, a considerable number did not consider technical information in this respect.

56 See, for instance, the reference to the report of the Expert Group on Climate and Sustainable Development to determine the GHG emission reduction targets for the Federal State of Belgium and its Regions in *VZW Klimaatzaak v Kingdom of Belgium et al, 2015/4585/A* (French-speaking Court of First Instance of Brussels) 82.

57 In this regard, see expert opinions about emissions in the Australian state of New South Wales in *Bushfire Survivors for Climate Action Incorporated v Environmental Protection Authority* [2021] NSWLEC 92; [2020] NSWLEC 152 (leave granted to BSCA to file and serve expert evidence on climate change science) paras 85–87.

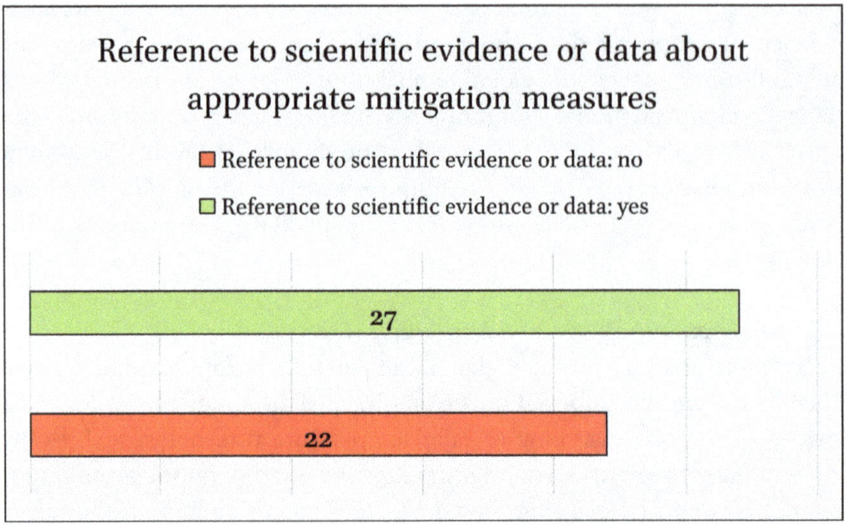


FIGURE 4.1 The number of rulings referring to scientific evidence or empirical data about appropriate mitigation measures to limit global warming (green bar) and that did not refer to expert information (red bar) in the sample of 49 judgments

### 4.2 *Judicial Assessments of Scientific Findings: Do Courts Need More Expert Aid?*

The frequency of judicial reference to scientific evidence or empirical data about adequate mitigation measures to combat climate change tells us to what extent the examined climate rulings considered expert knowledge about what states could do to reduce emissions and tackle climate change. Follow-up questions concern whether and how courts engaged with this information. Did courts, for instance, approach qualitative aspects of scientific evidence about mitigation measures against climate change? Did they use any assessment criteria for that?

For that purpose, the content analysis included judicial appraisals of (scientific) evidence in four categories: complexity, trustworthiness, uncertainty, and consistency. According to the coding scheme, the category complexity entails any explicit mention in the rulings of evidence being complex or not—Eg, statements such as 'evidence is technically complex.' Trustworthiness includes the judicial consideration of the evidence's soundness, authoritativeness, novelty, persuasiveness, or clarity. For instance, statements about the evidence representing 'the best available science' or containing 'credible scientific information.' Uncertainty comprises any consideration about scientific uncertainty or the probabilistic feature of the evidence—Eg, observations that science entails an inherent degree of uncertainty or that the evidence does not

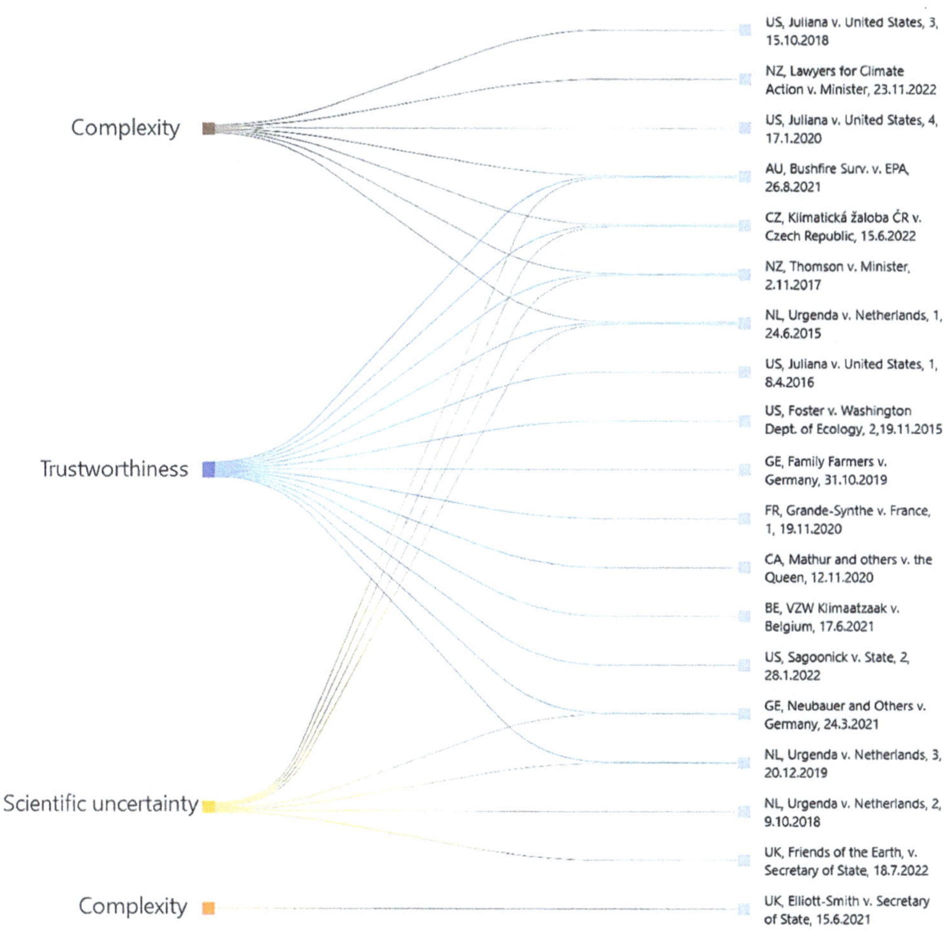


FIGURE 4.2 List of rulings including the date of judgment that appraised the complexity, trustworthiness, uncertainty, or consistency of evidence about mitigation measures

provide certainty enough to formulate a duty of care. Consistency relates to assessments about the evidence supporting claims in the process—Eg, about the evidence not providing a specific mitigation level by individual states to support the claim that the state should reduce emissions to a certain extent. The analysis of these codes shows that 19 of 49 rulings (38,78%) made at least one of these qualitative assessments.

The next question addressed in the study connects to assessment criteria eventually used in the judgments to evaluate the described aspects of non-legal information. The inductive coding process identified different criteria represented in the table below.

TABLE 4.2 List of criteria used in the rulings to assess trustworthiness, consistency, or uncertainty of the evidence about mitigation measures to combat climate change

| **Criteria to assess evidence's trustworthiness** | **Criteria to assess the consistency of complex evidence** | **Criteria to assess scientific uncertainty** |
|---|---|---|
| Consideration of IPCC features that make it a reliable source. Eg, composition, type of organisation, and findings considered in international decision-making processes. | Direct consideration of scientific evidence. | Consideration, in the evidence, of explanations of degrees of uncertainty, such as a scientific report. |
| Consideration of quality assurance process in the evidence. Eg, extensive evaluations of scientific research or peer review. | Consideration of comments or explanations in an expert's affidavit, testimony, or report. | |
| Consideration that evidence drew information from the IPCC report, which contains credible information. | | |
| Consideration of expert opinions about the credibility of the evidence | | |

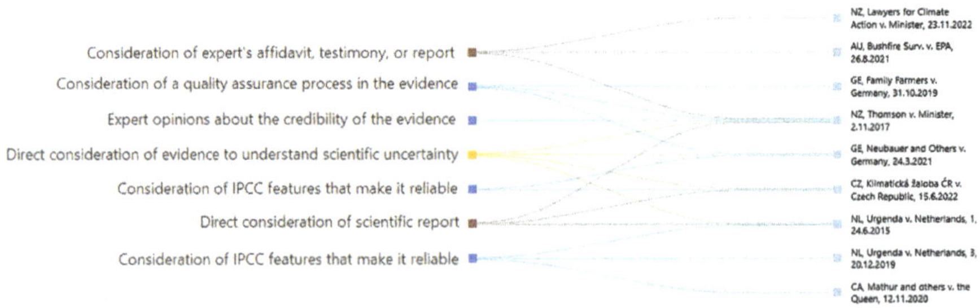


FIGURE 4.3 List of rulings including the date of judgment which used at least one criterion to assess the complexity, trustworthiness, uncertainty, or consistency of evidence about mitigation measures

Moreover, the analysis showed that only 9 decisions used at least one criterion to assess these aspects, corresponding to 18,37% of the sample of 49 rulings.

These findings indicate that courts rarely used criteria to assess the quality of the evidence. Of the 49 decisions studied, only 4 out of 49 decisions (8.2%) explicitly mentioned the help of experts, provided through opinions, affidavits, testimony, or reports, to understand the evidence about appropriate mitigation measures to limit global warming. At the same time, one can imagine a range of procedural tools, such as appointing committees of experts, commissioning expert reports, conducting reliability tests, requesting public audiences, asking the parties to clarify points, and instituting focus groups, among others, that could have been used in theory. The results also raise questions like: why did courts rarely invoke the help of experts to understand qualitative aspects of the scientific evidence brought by the litigants? Further qualitative research might reveal whether this avoidance relates to courts' lack of procedures, the parties' behaviour in the process, Eg, defendants not challenging the quality of the evidence, judges' active choices to circumvent these evidentiary aspects, Eg, to avoid costs, delays, or adding complexity to the process, or even implicit views about science and its role in the judicial sphere.

Another emerging research path, implemented in this study, connects to comparing this identified trend with climate rulings not included in the systematic content analysis,[58] remarkably in jurisdictions that might bring innovative judicial approaches, such as Brazil.

## 5 Conclusions: Lessons from Brazilian Climate Litigation in Perspective with Global Trends

The Brazilian experience shows that many cases with potentially significant societal impacts are still pending. The existing decisions reveal, however, that expert knowledge offered by the parties and entities admitted in the process has assisted courts in establishing the violation of fundamental rights and ordering governments to take further climate action. Ongoing cases also show the potential of procedural tools like public hearings and *amicus curiae* to elucidate formal or substantive aspects of the evidence—Eg, the reliability of

58 For instance, for being judged after 2022 or for not precisely fitting the scope of the study—Eg, for involving a challenge to one instrument of the climate policy, and not the overall climate policy.

scientific findings or the meaning of statistical figures and margin of errors. Publicly available information on the lawsuits provides large amounts of data for analysis. *PSB et al v Brazil (on Climate Fund)*[59] illustrates, for instance, that scientific knowledge played a relevant role to support the conclusion of Justice Edson Fachin in favour of an injunction compelling the Federal Government to resume the activities of the Climate Fund and provide information on GHG emissions, avoiding the violation of fundamental rights. The concurring decision also explicitly addresses the importance of public agents considering scientific knowledge in their decision-making. *PSB et al v Brazil (on deforestation and human rights)*[60] illustrates, likewise, the dialogue with empirical data and scientific evidence in the opinion of Justice Cármen Lúcia. There, extensive official data about deforestation supported the conclusion about an unconstitutional state of affairs regarding deforestation and the environment in Brazil.

The systematic content analysis of climate rulings in systemic mitigation cases against governments in various jurisdictions suggests, in turn, a few global trends in judicial approaches to empirical data and climate science. It shows, for instance, that more than half of the verdicts referred to expert knowledge about appropriate mitigation measures to combat climate change. Nevertheless, rulings appraised the trustworthiness, the uncertainty, or the consistency of the evidence with the parties' claims less often, namely in 38,78% of the cases. Moreover, a strikingly lower percentage of judgments, ie, 18,37%, used a tool or criterion to assess the evidence's trustworthiness, uncertainty, or consistency. Instruments such as reliability tests and expert clarifications about the evidence's trustworthiness or degree of uncertainty were infrequent. The numbers raise concerns about superficial engagements with expert knowledge posing risks to the justification and transparency of the rulings. It also poses new questions, such as: why did courts rarely invoke the help of experts to understand qualitative aspects of the evidence? Could methodologies for assessing scientific information assist judges in climate change litigation? It also sparks interest in whether courts in specific countries use procedural tools to engage with expert knowledge.

Comparing judicial involvement with science in Brazilian climate lawsuits with the content analysis findings yields some noteworthy insights. The Brazilian cases revealed, for instance, an openness from procedural law and judges to societal participation through the institutes of *amicus curiae* and public hearings. On one side, that allowed multiple voices and civil society

---

59 *PSB et al v Brazil* (*on Climate Fund*) (n 24).
60 *PSB et al v Brazil* (*on deforestation and human rights*) (n 41).

interests to bring relevant and diverse information to the process. This knowledge comprised scientific information on climate change global causes and impacts in the IPCC reports, along with more localised evidence about regional biomes and communities, Eg, on impacts on the Amazon rainforest and the severe implications of illegal deforestation for global warming. Additionally, public hearings enabled experts to clarify aspects of scientific evidence and quantitative data with which judges and the general public, as a rule, are not familiar. Without denying the use of hearings in other jurisdictions or more indirect judicial approaches to evidence, not explicitly mentioned in the decisions, the Brazilian experience sheds light on the direct engagement in the judicial decisions with the information provided in these participatory fora, and a more explicit influence in the judges' opinions. The *PSB et al v Brazil (on the climate fund)* case, concerning the failure of Bolsonaro's government to run the National Climate Fund and channel its resources into mitigation and adaptation initiatives, illustrates how the information conveyed at the public hearing greatly influenced the Justices' opinions compelling the Federal Union to make the Climate Fund operative again. In this regard, Justice Fachin mentioned that the public hearing convened by the justice rapporteur was 'extremely relevant' to reaching his decision. The case also illustrates a distinguishing feature compared to other jurisdictions. Namely, the remarkable transparency of the legal proceedings, with all documents concerning the case available to the public on the Supreme Court's website. From this perspective, the Brazilian jurisdiction brings, in different respects, an innovative approach to expert knowledge in climate lawsuits compared to the generally identified trends.

As presented in the chapter, decisions are expected in many promising cases. *IEA v Brazil*[61] draws attention, for instance, to whether the court will consider all the evidence brought about by the plaintiffs and use experts to clarify technical aspects of it. *PSB et al v Brazil (on deforestation and human rights)*[62] raises questions on whether other Justices will follow the Justice-rapporteur opinion. The richness of information and participatory tools in Brazilian climate cases also raises awareness about the importance of observing the ongoing developments in climate change litigation in Global South countries. New judgments in climate litigation are, thus, on the rise, bringing multiple opportunities for comparative and empirical research on the topic.

61 *IEA v Brazil* (n 38).

62 *PSB et al v Brazil* (*on deforestation and human rights*) (n 41).

### Acknowledgements

I am immensely grateful for the sharp remarks and suggestions for improvement by Professor Armando Rocha and commentators from the Global Network for Human Rights and the Environment (GNHRE). I also thank my PhD supervisors, Rob van Gestel and Jurgen de Poorter, for encouraging me to write this chapter and for Rob van Gestel's careful feedback and valuable insights throughout the text.

# SECTION 2

## *Climate Litigation and Human Rights*

CHAPTER 5

# Recognizing the Paris Agreement as a Human Rights Treaty: the *Climate Fund* Case and Brazilian Courts

*Carolina de Figueiredo Garrido**

## 1 Introduction

This chapter addresses the interdependence between the environment, climate, and human rights, drawing on the Paris Agreement and its interpretation by Brazilian courts as a human rights treaty.

The 2015 Paris Agreement seeks to strengthen the global response to climate change. Its main objective is to limit the increase in the average global temperature to well below 2°, preferably to 1.5°C.[1] This is a fundamental threshold, because the current increase in the planet's average temperature is already causing several detrimental effects on the environment—the magnitude of which also severely impacts the very enjoyment of human rights.

The UN Special Report 'Safe Climate' affirms that climate change affects a series of human rights (e.g., the right to life, health, food, water and sanitation, and rights of the child), including the right to a healthy environment.[2] In Brazil, a full list of fundamental rights is protected constitutionally, also including the right to an ecologically balanced environment, which is considered a human right to be secured by the State and the public as a whole.[3] In fact, as climate change has a detrimental impact on the environment, the stability of the climate system is increasingly recognized as an essential part of the right to an ecologically balanced environment under the Brazilian Constitution,[4] also concerning the enjoyment of other fundamental rights thereunder.

* Researcher at the Research Group Law, Environment and Justice in the Anthropocene (JUMA/NIMAJUR/PUC-Rio) and at the Interdisciplinary Observatory on Climate Change (OIMC/IESP/UERJ). ORCID: https://orcid.org/0000-0001-5180-0524.

1 UNFCCC, art 2(1)(a).

2 Special Rapporteur on Human Rights and the Environment, 'Safe Climate' (UN Doc A/74/161, United Nations General Assembly 74th Session, 22 July 2019).

3 See Délton Winter de Carvalho & Armando Rocha, 'The Obligation to Protect the Stability of the Climate System under the Right to a Healthy Environment in Brazil', Chapter 6 in this book.

4 Danielle de Andrade Moreira et al, *Litigando a Crise Climática no Brasil: Argumentos Jurídicos para se Exigir do Estado a Implementação Doméstica do Acordo de Paris* (Pimenta Cultural 2022) 15.

 | DOI:10.1163/9789004690974_006

Based on this premise, the Brazilian Federal Supreme Court (hereinafter referred to as 'STF') affirmed in 2022, in *PSB et al v Brazil (on Climate Fund)*,[5] that environmental treaties, such as the Paris Agreement, are a species of the broader genre 'human rights treaties'. This statement is particularly relevant in the Brazilian legal context, in which human rights treaties have at least supra-legal status and only rank below constitutional provisions, therefore taking precedence over infra-constitutional statutory norms. This chapter highlights the importance and innovation of this interpretation by the STF, that can inspire climate litigation worldwide.

The ruling was celebrated in Brazil as a central precedent for climate litigation.[6] However, *PSB et al v Brazil (on Climate Fund)* was not widely discussed outside Brazil, unlike comparable high-profile cases from the Global North.[7] Only a limited number of scholars—mainly from Brazil—have analyzed the *PSB (on Climate Fund)* ruling and its impacts.[8] This might bring implications for global climate litigation, as developments in the Global South—with potential to inspire similar decisions—are frequently slipping under the radar.[9] This is particularly relevant in this case, considering that the Paris Agreement has been mobilized as a reference to inform the interpretation and application of domestic laws and policies in several climate cases throughout the globe.[10]

Given this context, this chapter highlights the advancements brought by the STF's recognition of the Paris Agreement as a human rights treaty for Brazilian climate litigation and beyond. Section 2 gives a brief overview of the

---

5 *PSB et al v Brazil (on Climate Fund)* [STF] ADPF 708, Judgment of 7 January 2022, available at <https://climatecasechart.com/non-us-case/psb-et-al-v-federal-union/>.

6 Maria Antonia Tigre & Joana Setzer, 'Human Rights and Climate Change for Climate Litigation in Brazil and Beyond: An Analysis of the Climate Fund Decision' (2023) 54(4) *Georgetown JIL* 593, 596–597.

7 ibid, 596–597.

8 ibid. Examples of analyses in English are Danielle de Andrade Moreira, Ana Nina, Carolina de Figueiredo Garrido & Maria Eduarda Neves, 'Rights-based Climate Litigation in Brazil: An Assessment of Constitutional Cases before the Brazilian Supreme Court' (2023) 16(1) *Journal of Human Rights Practice* 7; Maria Antonia Tigre, 'Advancements in Climate Rights in Courts Around the World', Climate Law: A Sabin Center blog (1 July 2022); Joana Setzer & Catherine Higham. *Global Trends in Climate Change Litigation: 2023 Snapshot.* (Grantham Research Institute on Climate Change and the Environment and Centre for Climate Change Economics and Policy 2023); and Angelica Rutherford & Flavianne Fernanda Bitencourt Nóbrega, 'The Paris Agreement as a Human Rights Treaty: The Ruling in *PSB et al v Brazil (on Climate Fund)*' (2022) 3(2) *Jus Corpus LJ* 456.

9 Tigre & Setzer (n 6) 597.

10 Moreira et al (n 4) 32–33; Brain Preston, 'The Influence of the Paris Agreement on Climate Litigation: Legal Obligations and Norms (Part I)' (2021) 33(1) *JEL* 1, 5.

International Climate Change Regime, focusing on the Paris Agreement and its importance in linking the international and domestic spheres and its relations with international human rights law. Section 3 connects the protection of a healthy environment, a stable climate, and human rights, presenting the Paris Agreement in its importance to protect human rights. Section 4 analyzes the Paris Agreement as a human rights treaty, drawing lessons from Brazilian environmental, climate and human rights litigation. Section 4.1 analyzes precedents on the supra-legal status of human rights treaties and on the right to an ecologically balanced environment as a human right. Section 4.2 focuses on climate litigation in Brazil and *PSB et al v Brazil* (*on Climate Fund*), and on how these precedents were applied for the affirmation of the Paris Agreement as a human rights treaty. Section 5 provides a forward-looking analysis of what can the recognition of the supra-legal status of the Paris Agreement mean for future litigation in Brazil and the influence of its interpretation as a human rights treaty for overall litigation. This chapter concludes that this is a central precedent in rights-based climate litigation that brings lessons to litigation worldwide.

## 2 The Paris Agreement and the International Climate Change Regime: a Brief Overview

From an international law point of view, conceiving the Paris Agreement as a human rights treaty might be surprising, although the link between human rights and climate change is clear. The history leading to its adoption could not anticipate that a domestic court would qualify it as a human rights treaty.

In fact, although the environment and the climate system are among the prominent concerns of the international community, it took a long time for them to be framed as a matter of human rights. The increased attention paid to climate change in the scientific community and international concern about global environmental issues led to the recognition of the need for cooperation between States to address them under the regulation of International Environmental Law.

In 1990 the IPCC requested, at the Second World Climate Conference, for a response to climate change from the international community through a treaty.[11] As a result, the UNFCCC was adopted in 1992, providing the basis for multilateral action by States to fight climate change.[12] The Convention stipulated

11 UN, 'UNFCCC—25 Years of Effort and Achievement: Key Milestones in the Evolution of International Climate Policy'.

12 UN, 'UNFCCC eHandbook: A Guide to the UNFCCC and its Processes'.

that the ratifying States should meet annually at the Conferences of the Parties (CoP) to take stock of their progress, monitor the implementation of their obligations, and continue negotiations.[13] In this sense it

> … followed the common model of international environmental protection regimes, whereby the Framework Conventions are the founding stones of systems that are subsequently consolidated by Protocols, Amendments, Annexes and decisions adopted by the Meetings or Conferences of the Parties, based on greater scientific information about the problem and the possibility of consensus between the Parties to agree on more concrete obligations.[14]

Following, in 2015, the Paris Agreement was adopted during CoP21. Its core goal (set out in Article 2) is an average temperature goal of limiting warming to 1.5°C or, at most, to well below 2°C. All Parties must contribute to this goal by submitting their NDC s.[15]

Regulated in Articles 3 and 4, the NDC s are the heart of the Paris Agreement, containing States' climate pledges. Article 3 affirms that Parties must make ambitious and timely efforts to fulfill them, in line with the core goal, and Article 4 states that they must progress over time and reflect the greatest possible ambition. It also establishes that actions must be taken at the domestic level so that the NDC s are implemented, stressing the interconnectedness between international and domestic climate action.[16]

From an international law point of view, obligations arising from treaties, and especially the Paris Agreement, can be divided into hard law, soft law and recommendatory content.[17] However, in litigation at the domestic level, international law divisions are sometimes surpassed and procedural obligations, when read from different legal frameworks, require effective action to be taken.[18]

In this sense, the Paris Agreement is a powerful basis for climate litigation,[19] largely due to its innovative feature of integrating national commitments—

13 ibid.

14 Lívia Gaigher Bósio Campello & Rafaela de Deus Lima, 'O Regime Internacional de Mudanças Climáticas: uma análise da cooperação internacional solidária no Acorde de Paris' (2018) 19(3) *Revista Argumentum* 670 (author's translation).

15 Moreira et al (n 4) 26.

16 ibid 26–27.

17 Daniel Bodansky, 'The Legal Character of the Paris Agreement' (2016) 25(2) *RECIEL* 142.

18 Moreira et al (n 4) 31–32.

19 ibid 24.

provided for in a State's NDCs—into an international instrument that binds them to the common goal of preventing warming above the temperature limits of 1.5°C and 2°C.[20] The treaty allows for the identification of gaps between existing policies and those needed in order to achieve its mitigation and adaptation objectives. In this context, parties in domestic litigation can back up their claims against public authorities with the argument that their governments' 'easy political statements' must be accompanied by 'hard political measures.'[21]

Although being part of International Environmental Law, the Paris Agreement was also the first climate treaty to explicitly mention 'human rights'.[22,23] However, this mention was relegated to the preamble that states that Parties should take action to address climate change while respecting, promoting, and considering their respective human rights obligations. Therefore, the preamble links human rights to the possible negative side of mitigation measures and not, as one would expect, to the impacts of climate change. Despite this timid inclusion, the recognition remains a crucial development, representing the culmination of years of civil society advocacy and scholarly progress.[24] It also contributes to the consolidation of a narrative that associates climate action with human rights obligations.[25]

John Knox, former UN special rapporteur on human rights and the environment, upheld that the Paris Agreement is 'not a human rights treaty in the usual sense,' since it does not 'define rights or create mechanisms to review and promote their compliance.'[26] Nevertheless, he also mentions that the Paris

20 UN, *The Status of Climate Change Litigation—A Global Review* (UNEP 2017) 17.

21 ibid 17.

22 Susana Borràs & Beatriz Felipe Pérez, 'El régimen jurídico del cambio climático: entre la justicia climática y los derechos humanos' (Working paper 2, Universitat Rovira i Virgili, Tarragona, March 2016), 22.

23 Sam Adelman, 'Human Rights in the Paris Agreement: Too Little, Too Late?' (2018) 7 *Transnational Environmental Law* 17.

24 Eg see Stephen Humphreys, *Human Rights and Climate Change* (2010); Ottavio Quirico & Mouloud Boumghar, *Climate Change and Human Rights: An International Law Perspective* (2015); Sam Adelman, 'Rethinking Human Rights: The Impact of Climate Change on the Dominant Discourse', in Humphreys (ed), *Human Rights and Climate Change* (CUP 2010) 159; Sam Adelman, 'Human Rights and Climate Change', in DiGiacomo (ed), *Human Rights: Current Issues and Controversies* (University of Toronto Press 2016) 411; John H Knox, 'Linking Human Rights and Climate Change at the United Nations' (2009) 33(2) *Harvard Environmental Law Review* 477; Derek Bell, 'Does Anthropogenic Climate Change Violate Human Rights?' (2011) 14(2) *Critical Rev. International Social Political Philosophy* 99.

25 Benoit Mayer, 'Human Rights in the Paris Agreement' (2016) 6 *Climate Law* 109.

26 John H Knox, 'The Paris Agreement as a Human Rights Treaty', in Akande, Kuosmanen, McDermott & Roser (eds.), *Human Rights and 21st Century Challenges: Poverty, Conflict, and the Environment* (OUP 2020) 323.

Agreement should be seen as a milestone for its integration of human rights safeguards and the first environmental treaty to recognize human rights as part of its framework.[27] In this sense, STF's interpretation of the Paris Agreement as a human rights treaty—the first of this kind in the world—is a strong breakthrough in clarifying the link between the Paris Agreement and the protection of human rights.[28]

## 3 The Paris Agreement and the Protection of Human Rights: the Interdependence between the Environment, Climate, and Human Rights

Parallel to the development of the International Climate Change Regime, climate change also started to be analyzed under International Human Rights Law. This convergence enabled major advances in the association between these two protection regimes and laid the foundations for the recognition of the Paris Agreement as a human rights treaty by the STF.

Various bodies within the UN (such as the Human Rights Council, special procedures, treaty bodies) and Regional Human Rights Protection Systems (such as the European and Inter-American systems) have explored the relationship between climate change and human rights. They lead to the conclusion that: (i) climate change threatens a series of human rights and, consequently, (ii) States' obligations and private actors' responsibilities regarding human rights must inform measures to combat the climate crisis.[29]

The adoption of Resolution No 7/23 by the Human Rights Council in 2008 was a first milestone in this process. The resolution mandated that a study should be carried out on the relationship between climate change and human rights. The resulting report recognized that climate change, in addition to affecting the environment and the economy, also affects specific human rights (Eg the rights to life, adequate food, drinking water, health, adequate housing, and self-determination). It also warned that vulnerable groups will face the greatest risks.[30]

After that, the Human Rights Council adopted a series of other resolutions expressing that climate change is an immediate and far-reaching threat to the

27 ibid.
28 Tigre (n 8).
29 Special Rapporteur on Human Rights and the Environment (n 2) 26.
30 Borràs & Pérez (n 22) 19.

enjoyment of human rights.[31] Also, reports have been produced by several Special Rapporteurs, stressing some vulnerabilities that intersect with climate impacts, including those on (i) the right to food, (ii) adequate housing, (iii) the human rights of migrants, (iv) the rights of indigenous peoples, (v) extreme poverty and human rights, (vi) the human rights of internally displaced persons, (vii) human rights and the enjoyment of a safe, clean, healthy and sustainable environment.[32]

Already in 2021, the Human Rights Council issued Resolution No 48/14, determining the creation of a special rapporteur specifically dedicated to the promotion and protection of human rights in the context of climate change. The first rapporteur appointed, Ian Fry, listed eight key themes that would guide his mandate, including climate litigation and the links with other special rapporteurs. This demonstrates the relevance of discussions on climate litigation mobilizing—various—human rights.

The relationship between human rights and environmental protection was also confirmed at the international level by the UN Human Rights Council through Resolution No 48/1310 (also adopted in 2021), stating that a clean, healthy, and sustainable environment is a human right. The resolution recognizes that climate change is one of the most pressing and serious threats to the enjoyment of human rights for present and future generations. This prepared the room for the General Assembly to acknowledge, in 2022, the right to a healthy environment as a human right, reaffirming the centrality of climate change.

Although at the level of soft law, these recognitions reinforce the link between the environment, climate change, and human rights, they are especially relevant considering that the recognition of human rights in the Paris Agreement's Preamble has significant limitations: (i) it fails to create rights or obligations on its own, (ii) a recognition in a preamble means that no concrete measures were identified and it mentions only the impact of climate action on the protection of human rights,[33] thus (iii) it fails to adequately acknowledge the immense impacts of climate change itself on human rights.[34,35]

In this sense, rights-based climate litigation that mobilizes the Paris Agreement is a path—already being paved—to strengthen the link between

31 Examples include Human Rights Council Resolutions Nos 7/23, 10/4, 18/22, 26/27, 29/15, 32/33, 35/20 and 38/4.

32 Special Rapporteur on Human Rights and the Environment (n 2) 27–28.

33 Mayer (n 25) 115.

34 Adelman (n 23) 18.

35 Tigre & Setzer (n 6) 624.

International Environmental Law and Human Rights Law, and to require its application at the domestic level. The recognition of the Paris Agreement as a human rights treaty, as done by the STF in *PSB et al v Brazil* (*on Climate Fund*) ruling, is a major step in this process.

## 4 The Paris Agreement as a Human Rights Treaty: Lessons from Brazilian Climate Litigation

### *4.1 Precedents: Brazilian Case Law on Human Rights and the Right to an Ecologically Balanced Environment*

In Brazil, internalized treaties can have the status of statutory norms, supra-legal status, or constitutional status. Constitutional Amendment (EC) 45/2004 added paragraph 3 to Article 5 of the Federal Constitution, which says that human rights treaties approved by a qualified majority (of 3⁄5) have the status of constitutional amendments. However, in 2008, the STF ruled in the Special Appeal (Recurso Extraordinário—RE) 349.703 that human rights treaties incorporated in the Brazilian legal system (if not adopted by that majority) still have a supra-legal status.[36] This means that they rank below the Constitution, but above statutory norms, given that they secure the fundamental rights provided for in the Constitution.[37]

This interpretation was later applied by the STF to environmental treaties, since the right to an ecologically balanced environment is conceived of as a fundamental right in the Brazilian constitutional system.[38] The logical conclusion, reinforced in *PSB* (*on Climate Fund*), is that treaties that aim to secure a healthy environment—and, therefore, the preservation of life—should be qualified as human rights treaties and benefit from their special status,[39] even if formally they are not qualified as such.

The first time the STF applied the supra-legal status for a specific environmental treaty was in 2017, in the ruling in *ANPT et al v Brazil*.[40] The Court held that the Basel Convention on the Control of Transboundary Movements of Hazardous Wastes and their Disposal and the Conventions 139 and 162 of the International

36 Judgment of 13 December 2008 (STF) Special Appeal No 349703, Rapporteur: Minister Carlos Britto, available at <https://redir.stf.jus.br/paginadorpub/paginador.jsp?docTP=AC&docID=595406>.

37 Moreira et al (n 4) 13.

38 Moreira, Nina, Garrido & Neves (n 8) 14; Winter de Carvalho & Rocha (n 3).

39 Moreira et al (n 4) 17.

40 *ANPT et al v Brazil*, ADI 4066, Judgment of 24 August 2017, available at <https://redir.stf.jus.br/paginadorpub/paginador.jsp?docTP=TP&docID=14452232&prcID=2607856>.

Labor Organization have supra-legal status, since they aim to protect human rights, more specifically the right to health and to a healthy environment.[41] In 2021, in *Rede Sustentabilidade v National Environmental Council* (*on* CONAMA *Resolutions*), the STF acknowledged the supra-legal status of the Ramsar and the Biodiversity Conventions, and stated that they must be respected by domestic decisionmakers, since they 'shape the content' of the fundamental right to an ecologically balanced environment.[42] Once again, the recognition of the role of environmental treaties was based on their understanding as human rights treaties.[43]

As climate stability is part of the essential core of the human right to an ecologically balanced environment, a treaty that is essentially climate-related is also obviously related to—this and other—human rights. Thus, the Paris Agreement should also enjoy a supra-legal status,[44] as recognized by the STF in *PSB et al v Brazil* (*on Climate Fund*) *when the court first recognized this status in broad terms, applying to all environmental treaties.*

### 4.2 *The Recognition of the Paris Agreement as a Human Rights Treaty in* PSB et al v Brazil (on Climate Fund)

The facts in *PSB et al v Brazil* (*on Climate Fund*) concerned the State's omission in the face of the Climate Fund's inoperativeness during the years 2019 and 2020, a period in which it failed to allocate resources to tackle climate change without adequate justification. It also questioned the failure of public policies in relation to Brazil's climate commitments and targets, mentioning international treaties such as the Paris Agreement.

The case began with four political parties (PSB: Partido Socialista Brasileiro, P-SOL: Partido Socialismo e Liberdade, PT: Partido dos Trabalhadores, and Rede Sustentabilidade) filling, in June 5, 2020, a complaint before the STF challenging the State's failure to adopt appropriate administrative measures for the functioning of the Climate Fund.[45] The plaintiffs sought from the STF a declaration of 'unconstitutional omission', given that the changes in the Fund's governance rules led to the suspension of its operations and funding for climate change

41 ibid, 45.

42 *Rede Sustentabilidade v National Environmental Council* (*on* CONAMA *Resolutions*), ADPF 747, 748 and 749, filed on 2 October 2020 before the Federal Supreme Court, Judgment of 14 December 2021, available at <https://climatecasechart.com/non-us-case/workers-party-vs-national-environment-council-adpf-749-on-conama-resolutions/>, at 44.

43 Moreira, Nina, Garrido & Neves (n 8) 14.

44 Moreira et al (n 4) 22.

45 *PSB et al v Brazil* (*on Climate Fund*) (n 5).

mitigation and adaptation measures. The plaintiffs also requested an injunction compelling the government to reactivate the Climate Fund.[46]

To that end, the plaintiffs claimed that the Federal Government neglected Brazil's climate-related obligations and responsibilities, and failed to follow the policies mandated by federal law—especially the National Climate Change Policy (Law No 12.187/2009)—despite having ample funds available. This failure was presented as part of a larger pattern of non-compliance with climate obligations—stated in domestic and international law—leading to increased deforestation in Brazil. They argued that, despite Brazil's international commitments outlined in its NDC submitted to the UNFCCC Secretariat, the government implemented measures that actually weakened forest policies and hindered deforestation control efforts. By referencing new legislation and policies enacted during the relevant period, the plaintiffs highlighted the significant increase in deforestation rates, leading to human rights violations.[47]

Concerning international law, they argued that the failure to mobilize resources for climate mitigation threatened Brazil's compliance with the Paris Agreement. As requested remedies, the plaintiffs sought an injunction mandating the Government to take specific administrative actions, aiming (i) the reactivation of the Climate Fund's operations and the availability of its resources; (ii) the presentation of appropriate annual plans for the allocation of the Fund's resources; and (iii) for the Government to refrain from imposing new contingencies on the Climate Fund's resources in the future. For final remedies, they requested the STF to confirm the injunction and declare the unconstitutional nature of the Government's omissions regarding the Climate Fund's proper functioning.[48]

On June 30, 2022, the STF reached its final decision, following the vote of Minister Barroso, working as Judge Rapporteur in the case.[49] The STF stated that the Government is constitutionally bound to carry out the allocation and execution of Climate Fund resources to mitigate climate change, based on the constitutional right to a healthy environment and the principle of separation of powers.[50]

The Court ruled in favor of the plaintiffs and refuted the arguments of the Government, which stated that the management and allocation of the Climate Fund's resources was a discretionary competence of the Executive. The ruling emphasized that:

---

46 ibid, 37.

47 ibid, 5–8, 22–30.

48 ibid, 37–38.

49 ibid.

50 Tigre & Setzer (n 6) 614.

> … the issue of climate change is a constitutional matter. Along these lines, Article 225 … of the Constitution expressly establishes the right to an ecologically balanced environment, imposing on the Public Power the duty to defend, preserve and restore it, for present and future generations. Therefore, environmental protection does not fall within the political judgment—of convenience and opportunity—of the Chief Executive. It is an obligation to which compliance is binding.[51]

The STF also explained that Brazil recognizes the supra-legal nature of human rights treaties and that 'there is no doubt that environmental matters fall within this category.'[52] It stated that 'environmental treaties are a species of the genre of human rights treaties,'[53] and, precisely for this reason, 'there is no legally valid option to simply omit to fight climate change.'[54]

The ruling concluded that there is a constitutional, supra-legal, and legal duty to protect the environment and to fight climate change, considering the supra-legal status of the Paris Agreement. However, this interpretation was grounded not in the Paris Agreement itself, but in the Brazilian Constitution, which acknowledges the supra-legal status of human rights treaties ratified by Brazil, and that the right to a healthy environment is a fundamental right.[55] In this sense, Tigre and Setzer stress that the STF:

> … missed an opportunity to advance the interpretation of the very nature of the Paris Agreement as a human rights treaty based on its own preambular recognition of human rights. Given the wide adoption of the Paris Agreement, further engaging with this aspect of climate law would have proven useful for building a transnational climate regime, as it would facilitate cross-reference between this decision and other rights-based cases worldwide.[56]

On the other hand, the *PSB et al v Brazil* (*on Climate Fund*) case is also a part of a broader trend that shows that climate litigation in Brazil centers on the protection of human rights. The STF is ready—and eager—to use the right to a healthy environment, hand in hand with other human rights, in the context of climate litigation.[57] In this sense, interpreting the Paris Agreement as a human

51 *PSB et al v Brazil* (*on Climate Fund*), 22–23 (author's translation).
52 ibid, 22.
53 ibid, 22.
54 ibid, 22.
55 Tigre & Setzer (n 6) 626.
56 ibid, 626.
57 Moreira, Nina, Garrido & Neves (n 8) 2.

rights treaty is the result of using its own case law on fundamental rights combined with applying international law principles in novel ways.

Overall, the *PSB et al v Brazil* (*on Climate Fund*) ruling is an important precedent for climate change litigation in Brazil since it established the importance of climate protection under the Constitution, and clarified that a stable climate system is inherent to the right to an ecologically balanced environment. As such, it has been widely reported as the most important decision on climate litigation in Brazil.[58] By recognizing environmental and climate protection as a constitutional obligation and courts' role in overseeing government actions, it also marks a significant advancement for climate litigation in the Global South.[59]

## 5 Looking Ahead: What Can the Recognition of the Paris Agreement as a Human Rights Treaty Mean for Future Litigation?

Brazil has a long and well-established history of human rights and environmental litigation. In comparison, climate litigation is a recent phenomenon gaining traction.[60] With already 80 cases at the time of the writing of this chapter, Brazil is one of the top countries in cumulative numbers and the first between Global South jurisdictions.[61] However, most of the climate cases are still pending.[62] In this sense, the ruling of the STF in *PSB et al v Brazil* (*on Climate Fund*) and its recognition of the supra-legal status of the Paris agreement may deeply influence future climate litigation cases and decisions in the country.[63]

The 'supra-legality' of climate and environmental treaties grants them a hierarchical precedence over ordinary laws. Hence, any Brazilian legislation or decree conflicting with the Paris Agreement, possibly including Brazil's NDC, could be nullified. Any (in)action opposing this safeguard constitutes a direct breach of both the Constitution and an internalized human rights treaty. Hence, the recognition of supra-legal status to the Paris Agreement gives plaintiffs the power to demand the State to enforce the obligations contained thereunder domestically.[64]

58 ibid, 13–14.

59 Tigre & Setzer (n 6) 615.

60 ibid, 615.

61 Danielle de Andrade Moreira et al, *Executive summary: climate litigation in Brazil 2024 report*. (Grupo de Pesquisa Direito, Ambiente e Justiça no Antropoceno: 2024), 5.

62 ibid, 5. See also *Brazil*, Climate Case Chart, http://climatecasechart.com/non-us-jurisdiction/brazil/ (last accessed 3 February 2024).

63 Tigre & Setzer (n 6), 637.

64 ibid, 615.

Since they secure human rights also protected constitutionally, treaties with supra-legal status make the constitutional text itself more effective. They also have an interpretative role in relation to infra-constitutional legislation, in this specific case confirming that the objective of limiting global warming and the commitments contained in the Paris Agreement need to be observed in the application of Brazilian environmental regulations.[65] These points, although not deeply explored by the STF ruling in *PSB et al v Brazil* (*on Climate Fund*), can be developed in future cases.

In fact, some of the more recent cases before Brazilian courts already mention the *PSB et al v Brazil* (*on Climate Fund*) ruling. One example is *Rede Sustentabilidade v State of Santa Catarina*, targeting the 'Policy for Just Energy Transition of the State of Santa Catarina.'[66] The case was filed in January of 2023 by the political party Rede Sustentabilidade arguing that a federate State policy that provides incentives for the mineral coal production chain contradicts emission reduction objectives—and thus violates the Paris Agreement. Therefore, the plaintiff argues, it runs against the ruling in *PSB et al v Brazil* (*on Climate Fund*), 'which recognized that international treaties relating to the defense of the environment are treaties of human rights, having, consequently, a supra-legal nature within our legal system.'[67]

As far as one can predict, the ruling can be used to advance climate litigation in Brazil and be a lesson to courts from other jurisdictions. In fact, Tigre and Setzer mention that, based on this precedent, 'judges could then further engage with the Paris Agreement more clearly, clarifying what this recognition means in terms of the obligations contained in it.'[68] The authors also believe that this ruling might have influence beyond the Brazilian legal system, considering that Brazil is becoming a 'hub' for global climate litigation, with 'innovative cases, procedural advancements, and rulings that have the potential to inspire and influence litigants and courts worldwide.'[69]

This is especially relevant considering that cross-fertilization between courts is frequent in climate litigation. Courts often draw cross-border inspiration when faced with novel legal dilemmas, citing rulings from other jurisdictions

---

65 Moreira et al (n 4) 22.

66 *Rede Sustentabilidade v State of Santa Catarina* (*on Just Energy Transition*), ADI 7332, filed on 29 December 2022 before the Federal Supreme Court, available at <https://climatecasechart.com/non-us-case/adi-7332-policy-for-just-energy-transition-of-the-state-of-santa-catarina/>.

67 ibid, Petition filed on 29 December 2022, available at <https://climatecasechart.com/wp-content/uploads/non-us-case-documents/2022/20221229_Acao-Direta-de-Inconstitucionalidade-7332_petition.pdf> at 56 (author's translation).

68 Tigre & Setzer (n 6) 630.

69 ibid, 598.

to support their reasoning. This practice is especially vital in areas where domestic legal precedents are scarce, yet similar climate-related challenges have been tackled by other courts. Considering this context, it would not be surprising if courts worldwide relied on the *PSB et al v Brazil* (*on Climate Fund*) ruling to reach analogous conclusions within their own legal frameworks, or if plaintiffs cited the decision to bolster their claims.[70]

Moreira and others also highlight how the STF has connected the domestic and international legal regimes for the protection of fundamental rights and 'clearly signaled that international law incorporated in Brazil has teeth: international obligations must be respected' and climate obligations bound government actions. The authors understand that the court placed itself in dialogue with actors in various parts of the world by drawing on international organizations' opinions, scientific data, and comparative law cases.[71] This example could and should be followed worldwide.

## 6 Conclusion

The urgency of the climate crisis cannot be overstated, as it continues to exacerbate and threaten human rights globally. The international community addressed this concern developing, since 1992, the International Climate Change Regime, which culminated in the adoption of the Paris Agreement in 2015. Although its importance in linking the international and domestic spheres, the treaty itself failed to deepen the recognition of the interplay between climate change and human rights law.

However, given the abundant recognition of the human rights ramifications of climate change—acknowledged by international bodies and courts worldwide—and the rise of rights-oriented climate litigation, it is a natural development to interpret the Paris Agreement through a human rights lens. Within this broader context, the STF stands out as taking an innovative stance and being the first court in the world to recognize the Paris Agreement as a human rights treaty.

This recognition not only holds implications for Brazil but also carries potential impacts for the global climate litigation community. As such, the *PSB et al v Brazil* (*on Climate Fund*) ruling is a milestone and represents a breakthrough in acknowledging the interplay between the environment, climate change, and human rights.

70 ibid, 629.

71 Moreira, Nina, Garrido & Neves (n 8) 19.

CHAPTER 6

# The Obligation to Protect the Stability of the Climate System under the Right to a Healthy Environment in Brazil

*Délton Winter de Carvalho* and Armando Rocha***

## 1 Introduction

Climate change is 'the defining issue of our age. It is defining our present. Our response will define our future:'[1] it affects the planetary ecological equilibrium and threatens the survival of species, including humankind. As a result, mitigating and adapting to climate change should be a priority for policymakers worldwide—but perhaps because mitigating and adapting to climate change entails deep changes for individuals and political communities (which affect our social interaction, our political thinking and structures, our economies, and even our life choices), climate change policies are lacking in ambition, or lacking altogether.

In this context, resorting to the grammar of human rights to bring climate change issues to the attention of human rights bodies does not amount to a panacea—but it does help in prioritizing and giving moral status to the need for stronger climate policies. The question, therefore, is which human right(s) can be mobilized in order to identify an obligation to protect the stability of the climate system, and namely if a standalone right to a healthy environment can be identified and used to that end.

To understand how an obligation to protect the stability of the climate system has been fostered by Brazilian courts, this chapter first assesses the emergence of a right to a healthy environment in the system of the American Convention on Human Rights (ACHR)[2] (Section 2). Then, based on these

* *Universidade do Vale do Rio dos Sinos*, School of Law, https://orcid.org/0000-0001-9469-5779.

** *Universidade Católica Portuguesa*, School of Law, Católica Research Centre for the Future of Law, https://orcid.org/0000-0002-8181-1512.

1 Ban Ki Moon, 'Opening Remarks at the 2014 Climate Summit', 23 September 2014, available at <https://www.un.org/sg/en/content/sg/speeches/2014-09-23/opening-remarks-2014-climate-summit>.

2 American Convention on Human Rights (adopted 22 November 1969, entered into force 18 July 1978) 1144 UNTS 123. Ratified by Brazil through Presidential Decree No 678 of 6 September 1992.

 | DOI:10.1163/9789004690974_007

findings, this chapter assesses how a right to a healthy environment is also set out in the Brazilian Constitution (Section 3), so that we can assess what is the State's obligation to protect the stability of the climate system under the Brazilian constitutional system (Section 4). To this end, two main cases decided by Brazilian courts are here analyzed in more detail.

## 2 The International Law Framework

### *2.1 The Right to a Healthy Environment under International Law*

Most human rights treaties—which predate the 1972 Stockholm Declaration—do not refer to the right to a healthy environment.[3] This helps explaining why the ACHR is silent on this regard, even though Article 11 of the 1989 San Salvador Protocol[4] (an optional protocol adopted with a view of incorporating social, economic, and cultural rights into the ACHR system) sets out that 'Everyone shall have the right to live in a healthy environment,' and thus that 'The States Parties shall promote the protection, preservation, and improvement of the environment.' In this sense, as a State Party to the San Salvador Protocol, Brazil committed internationally to adopt measures aimed at securing a healthy environment, which includes the protection of natural components such as the atmosphere and the stability of the climate. This provision could be key in climate litigation, but Article 19(6) of the San Salvador Protocol sets out that the right to a healthy environment is non-justiciable—which precludes of the Inter-American Court of Human Rights (IACtHR) jurisdiction (but not necessarily that of domestic courts).

In any case, because 'environmental degradation and the adverse effects of climate change affect the real enjoyment of human rights,'[5] the IACtHR declared that a standalone right to a healthy environment is *also* protected

---

3 See, *inter alia*, Pierre-Marie Dupuy & Jorge E Viñuales, *International Environmental Law* (2nd edn, CUP 2018) 366; Malgozia Fitzmaurice, Meagan S Wong & Joseph Crampin, *International Environmental Law—Text, Cases and Materials* (Elgar 2022) 118.

4 Additional Protocol to the American Convention on Human Rights in the Area of Economic, Social, and Cultural Rights (adopted 17 November 1988, entered into force 16 November 1999) OASTS No 69 (hereinafter referred to as 'San Salvador Protocol'). Ratified by Brazil through Presidential Decree No 3.321 of 30 December 1999.

5 Advisory Opinion OC-23/17 (IACtHR 15 November 2017) *The Environment and Human Rights (State Obligations in Relation to the Environment in the Context of the Protection and Guarantee of the Rights to Life and to Personal Integrity—Interpretation and Scope of Articles 4(1) and 5(1) of the American Convention on Human Rights)* §47.

under Article 26 of the ACHR,[6] which affirms that States Parties must adopt the necessary measures for 'achieving progressively ... the full realization of the economic, social, educational, scientific and cultural standards set forth in the Charter of the Organization of American States.' To that end, the IACtHR mentioned that Article 29(d) of the ACHR also refers to the protection of the rights derived from the American Declaration of the Rights and Duties of Man and other international acts of the same nature, which includes the San Salvador Protocol and the right to a healthy environment thereunder.[7]

As such, the 'green shift' in the IACtHR's case-law was the recognition of a justiciable and standalone right to a healthy environment directly under the ACHR,[8,9] which can be used in a broad spectrum of cases where State conduct affects natural components without, or even irrespective of, affecting the enjoyment of other human rights. In this context, the IACtHR has also stated that 'Environmental degradation may cause irreparable harm to human beings [and not only to human rights]; thus, a healthy environment is a fundamental right for the existence of humankind.'[10] Moreover, it highlighted that States' obligation to protect natural components is not limited to the utilities provided to humankind, but also as a value in itself.[11] Implied is the idea that if environmental degradation makes human beings more vulnerable—by putting at risk values such as (the possibility of) human life, physical integrity, health or well-being—, then human dignity itself is at risk, and thus the necessity of its protection through human rights mechanisms.

As a result, because environmental degradation creates and enhances vulnerability, a standalone right to a healthy environment was asserted by the IACtHR as implied in Article 26 of the ACHR. The potential use of such standalone right is immense, especially in climate litigation, where applicants

---

6 ibid §57; *Indigenous Communities of The Lhaka Honhat (Our Land) Association v Argentina, Merits, Reparations, and Costs*, IACtHR Series C No 420 (6 February 2020) §202.

7 OC-23/17 (n 5) §§56–59.

8 Armando Rocha & Rômulo Sampaio, 'Climate change before the European and Inter-American Courts of Human Rights: Comparing Possible Avenues before Human Rights Bodies' (2023) 32 *RECIEL* 279, 281; Maria Antonia Tigre & Natalia Urzola, 'The 2017 Inter-American Court's Advisory Opinion: Changing the Paradigm for International Environmental Law in the Anthropocene' (2021) 12 *Journal of Human Rights and the Environment* 24, 44.

9 Although recognizing a standalone human right to a healthy environment 'does not mean that other human rights will not be violated as a result of damage to the environment' (*Lhaka Honkat* (n 6) §203). See also OC-23/17 (n 5) §54.

10 OC-23/17 (n 5), §59.

11 *Habitantes de La Oroya v Peru (Excepciones Preliminares, Fondo, Reparaciones y Costas)*, IACtHR Series C No 511 (27 November 2023), §118.

using other human rights usually face procedural obstacles related to questions of victimhood status, causation, or legal standing. To that end, one must first assess whether an obligation to protect the stability of the climate system can derive from the human right to a healthy environment. If that is the case, then the domestic legal system of Brazil, as a State Party to the ACHR, must be interpreted in line with the obligations stemming from the ACHR, including the view of the 'healthy environment' as a standalone human right.

### 2.2 *The Obligation to Protect the Stability of the Climate System*

Since the atmosphere is a natural component of our global environment, and since a healthy atmosphere and a stable climate system are necessary conditions for securing a broader ecological planetary equilibrium, identifying a right to a healthy environment under Article 26 of the ACHR helps to reveal the States' obligation to protect the stability of the climate system. In addition, a healthy atmosphere and a stable climate system are also a necessary condition for the full realization of human rights, since climate change-related events expose individuals to greater vulnerability and strain their physical means of subsistence, whether or not any other human rights are directly affected.[12]

Accordingly, the right to a healthy environment entails States' obligations under Article 26 of the ACHR to protect and preserve a healthy atmosphere and to secure a stable climate,[13] namely by reducing GHG emissions from their jurisdiction and improving the condition of their natural carbon sinks (Eg by protecting and preserving the existing rainforests and by adopting reforestation measures).

Although there is still no direct precedent from the IACtHR on this issue, the approach adopted in Advisory Opinion OC-23/17—which specifically mentioned climate change in connection with the right to a healthy environment—suggests the ACHR is 'fertile ground' for future climate-related litigation.[14] A good indicator of such use is the *La Oroya* case, in which the Inter-American Commission on Human Rights[15] resorted to Article 26 of the ACHR to establish the States' obligation to continuously and progressively reduce GHG emissions in accordance with their international obligations and commitments, and to design and implement adaptation policies.[16] Afterwards, the IACtHR

---

12 In this sense also, see OC-23/17 (n 5), §47.

13 Rocha & Sampaio (n 8) 281.

14 Maria Antonia Tigre, 'Climate Change and Indigenous Groups: The Rise of Indigenous Voices in Climate Litigation' (2022) 9 *e-Publica* 214, 235.

15 Hereinafter referred to as 'IACommHR'.

16 *Comunidad de La Oroya v Peru* (IACommHR Decision of 19 November 2020) §142.

emphasized the link between human rights and climate change and mentioned that the obligation to protect the environment is even more important in this context, since climate change puts at risk the very survival of species.[17] Implied in the words of the IACtHR is a human right to stable system as a consequence of the human right to a healthy environment.

Furthermore, aware of the difficulty of fleshing out specific human rights' obligations, the IACommHR adopted Resolution No 3/2001, which aims to assist States and sets out a non-binding framework of States' obligations under the ACHR in relation to climate change.[18] In spite of its non-binding nature, this resolution provides a sense of direction in terms of what policies may be adopted by States—and despite the use of the verb mode 'should' instead of 'shall' with respect to each suggested obligation, it clearly indicates that adopting mitigation and adaptation policies is an obligation pursuant to the right to a healthy environment implicit to Article 26 of the ACHR.

As a result, under Article 26 of the ACHR, one can identify a human right to a healthy environment and a stable climate system, which implies a State's obligation to protect and preserve the stability of the atmosphere. The next question, therefore, is to what extent does this view of a right to a stable climate system informs the domestic legal order of Brazil, namely at the constitutional level, having in mind that, according to what was expressly mentioned in the case *IEA v Brazil*, international environmental agreements prevail over domestic statutory norms in Brazil.[19]

## 3 The Right to a Healthy Environment in the Brazilian Constitution

Climate litigation before domestic courts is naturally influenced by the ACHR and the findings of the IACtHR and the IACommHR—but unsurprisingly, the first port of call used by domestic courts is their own Constitution. In any case, it is worth mentioning that, in 2022, the National Council of Justice (a body responsible to oversee the conduct of courts in Brazil) issued its Recommendation No 123, where it explicitly 'recommends that bodies of the Brazilian

---

17 *La Oroya* (n 11) §119.

18 IACommHR, 'Resolution No 3/2021, Climate Emergency: Scope of the Inter-American Human Rights Obligations (31 December 2021).

19 *IEA v Brazil*, 4th Regional Federal Court of Curitiba, Decision of 7 December 2021, §§1–2; *PSB et al v Brazil (on Climate Fund)* STF 7 January 2022, §17.

judiciary comply with international human rights treaties and conventions and use the rulings of the Inter-American Court of Human Rights.'[20]

In the case of Brazil, Title II of the 1988 Constitution lists the fundamental rights and guarantees protected thereunder but does not refer to the 'environment' or the 'climate system'. However, Article 225 of the Constitution explicitly refers that all persons hold a right to an 'ecologically balanced environment,'[21]—which amounts to saying that, from a purely formal standpoint, it sets out a fundamental right to a healthy environment,[22] representative of the so-called third generation of fundamental rights. The question, thus, is not whether there is a fundamental right to a healthy environment under the Brazilian Constitution, but rather what its anatomy is and what its implications downstream are, including if one can unveil an obligation of protecting and preserving the stability of the climate system. This latter question specifically was discussed by the Federal Supreme Court, as is discussed below.

### 3.1 *An Autonomous or Standalone Fundamental Right*

As seen, the right to a healthy environment is regarded as a standalone or autonomous fundamental right under Article 225 of the Brazilian Constitution. Establishing an 'autonomous legally protected right'[23] implies that the protection of the environment is neither dependent, nor conditional upon the protection of other fundamental rights, such as the rights to life, physical integrity, private property, or health. While the link between the environment and these fundamental rights is undeniable (and may be triggered in cases where these human rights are also put at risk or infringed by an environmental harm), the right to a healthy environment is considered an autonomous, unitary, and collective fundamental right under the Constitution. This idea was further fleshed out by the Federal Supreme Court, which held that:

---

20 Conselho Nacional de Justiça, 'Recommendation No 123, of 7 January 2022' (recommending the organs of the Brazilian Judiciary to observe the international human rights treaties and to use the case law of the Inter-American Court of Human Rights). Available at https://atos.cnj.jus.br/atos/detalhar/4305.

21 'All persons have the right to an ecologically balanced environment, which is an asset of common use and essential to a healthy quality of life, and both the Government and the collectivity shall have the duty to defend and preserve it for present and future generations.'

22 Délton Winter de Carvalho, *Gestão Jurídica Ambiental* (2nd edn, Revista dos Tribunais, 2020) 133–140.

23 JJ Gomes Canotilho, *Estudos sobre Direitos Fundamentais* (2nd edn, Coimbra Editora, 2008) 183.

> '[the] right to environmental integrity—a typical third generation right—constitutes a legal prerogative of collective ownership, and reflects, within the process of human rights' affirmation, the significant expression of a power attributed not to any individual identified in his or her singularity, but, in a truly broader sense, to the social collectivity itself.'[24]

Therefore, as mentioned by Minister Luís Roberto Barroso, a major contribution of the Brazilian Constitution is the 'recognition of the environment as an autonomous legal asset, to which everyone has a right'—which 'is not a typical subjective right, which can be divided, singled out or exercised individually,'[25] but rather a 'transindividual' right.

The practical consequence is that the protection of the environment is based on the idea of ecological balance, rather than being conditioned on the prior demonstration of damage to other fundamental rights.[26] This does not amount to enshrining a right of Nature, but—in line with the subsequent case law of the IACtHR—it favors the emergence of environmental obligations aimed to protect and preserve natural components irrespective of their utilities for human beings. In terms of climate litigation, this allows to bypass procedural obstacles relating to the victim status, causation, or legal standing.

### 3.2 *The 'Anatomy' of the Fundamental Right to a Healthy Environment under the Brazilian Constitution*

One dogmatic question that is often raised is whether there can be a stand-alone right to a healthy environment, since the environment itself cannot be 'appropriated' individually—in contrast with what happens to other rights such as the right to life or physical integrity. On this regard, it should be noted that the Brazilian Constitution was deeply influenced by the German constitutional tradition,[27] including the idea that fundamental rights have a parallel subjective and objective dimension: whilst the subjective dimension refers to

---

24 *Antônio de Andrade Ribeiro Junqueira v Presidente da República*, STF Decision of 17 November 1995.

25 Luís Roberto Barroso, 'A Proteção do Meio Ambiente na Constituição Brasileira' (1992) 44 *Revista de Direito da Procuradoria Geral do Rio de Janeiro* 41, 51.

26 For an analysis of judicial application by higher or constitutional courts in comparative constitutional law as an independent, dependent, derivative, or dormant right, see James R May & Erin Daly, *Global Environmental Constitutionalism* (Cambridge University Press, 2015) 109–127.

27 Konrad Hesse, *Elementos de Direito Constitucional da República Federal da Alemanha* (Fabris, 1998) 228–244; Gilmar Ferreira Mendes & Paulo Gustavo Gonet, *Curso de Direito Constitucional* (13th edn, Saraiva, 2018).

the rights-based view of claims opposable between persons (which translate into subjective rights, whose 'object' can be 'appropriated' individually or by collections of individuals), the objective dimension refers to the duty-based perspective of obligations deriving from, and necessary to secure, the enjoyment of a fundamental right (which also translate into claims formulated by individuals, although the 'object of protection' is not subject to individual 'appropriation').

The best example of a fundamental right having that dual character is precisely the right to a healthy environment under Article 225 of the Constitution—a fundamental right whose claims refer not to the impacts that may affect the life or health of an individual, but rather to the impacts that affect an individual enjoyment of the environment, hand in hand with a collective and more diffuse enjoyment of the same environment. Because the environment, as a legal good, cannot be individualized into as many parts as its potential rights-holders, it entails that objective character where individuals, as the beneficiaries of the enjoyment of a healthy environment, can submit claims even though they are not the holders of the environment or a parcel of it. In this sense, the standalone right to a healthy environment is the best example of a fundamental right with this dual character, allowing individuals to submit claims based on a subjective and/or an objective dimension of such fundamental right—and this view is aligned with, and informed by, the IACtHR's understanding of a human right to a healthy environment as autonomous to other human rights and freedoms.

This point is key, since the protection of the stability of the climate system (being diffuse and not susceptible of individual appropriation) is more likely to be recognized as implicit to the objective dimension of fundamental rights. In the next section, we analyze how courts have acknowledged that the Brazilian Constitution secures the protection of the stability of the climate system based precisely on this objective dimension of fundamental rights, in line with the views espoused by the IACtHR.

## 4 The Obligation to Protect the Stability of the Climate System in the Brazilian Constitution

According to the theory of constitutional law, an objective character of a fundamental right is the immediate result of conceiving a specific value as an object of protection—thus allowing individuals to make claims based on the obligation of public authorities to secure the protection of such value, irrespective of holding a subjective right[28] (ie irrespective of being able to appropriate, either partially or entirely, the protected good). As a result, one must first understand how the Brazilian Constitution conceives the stability of the climate system as an 'object of protection', so that one can better understand how courts have been fleshing out an obligation to protect it under that same Constitution.

This exercise is to be made in light of the international obligations binding upon Brazil, including those under the UNFCCC.[29] In this regard, one cannot ignore that Brazil is qualified as a developing State for the purposes of the UNFCCC, but Article 2 still conceives the climate system as an object of protection, inspiring the domestic legal systems of all States Parties to secure the protection of the climate system. In this light, some statutes adopted in Brazil aim to implement the UNFCCC and to pursue its goals, and thus share its view of the climate system as an object of protection. For instance, the National Policy on Climate Change (Law No 12.187/2009) explicitly refers to the climate system as a protected legal object,[30] whilst the Forest Code (Law No 12.651/2012) expressly refers to the 'integrity of the climate system' as one of the core principles of the Brazilian legal framework governing forests.[31]

At the top of the normative pyramid, however, lies the Brazilian Constitution, which qualifies the 'environment' in terms of an ecological balance required for a healthy quality of life. To this end, the environment is treated as 'an asset for the common use of society', that is, an asset of public domain and diffuse interest. Therefore, Article 225 of the Brazilian Constitution squares well with the idea of a 'subjective' right (as protecting a value or good that can be 'appropriated' individually) but is especially fit for claims based on an 'objective' right held by all those who are members of the same community or are affected by a detrimental harm caused to the environment. This 'objective' right is derived, for instance, from paragraph I(1) of that Article 225, which expressly states that in order to ensure the effectiveness of this right, public authorities must 'preserve and restore the essential ecological processes,' having in mind that the climate system is necessarily included in the notion of 'essential ecological processes.' Furthermore, the language, here, is perfectly aligned with the views espoused by the IACtHR regarding the right to a healthy

28 Délton Winter de Carvalho & Rafaela Santos Martins da Rosa, 'Premissas para a Configuração do Sistema Climático como Bem Jurídico' (2021) 104 *Revista de Direito Ambiental* 299.

29 Ratified by Brazil through Presidential Decree No 2.652, of 1 July 1998.

30 Eg Article 3(I).

31 Article 1(I).

environment, and namely on the protection of natural components as a value in itself.[32]

As such, in our view, Article 225 of the Brazilian Constitution enshrines a right to a healthy environment and a right to a stable climate, encompassing both a 'subjective' and an 'objective' character. On this regard, we follow the view of Ademola Jegede, according to whom the right to a safe climate can be perceived of as a 'new' fundamental right, because it (1) reflects a fundamental social value, as the effects of climate change negatively affect human dignity;[33] (2) presents relevance at the level of the world value system, as climate change-related impacts are universal;[34] (3) is recognized as an interpretation consistent with the UN Charter obligations, customary law or general principles of law;[35] (4) does not repeat the existing body of international human rights law, as it underlines the connection between several other human rights and does not replicate an existing right;[36] (5) is able to attain a high degree of consensus at the international level, as seen by the overarching international commitment under the 2015 Paris Agreement;[37] (6) is compatible with State practice, as can be seen in both the strong judicialization of climate change issues in several countries and the overarching commitment to the Paris Agreement;[38] and (7) is sufficiently precise regarding claims and duties that can be derived from it.[39]

In this light, this chapter can now assess how courts have explored these subjective and objective characteristics of the right to a stable climate, namely in *IEA v Brazil* and in *PSB et al v Brazil*, having in mind that courts' pronouncements are key to clarify the existence and extent of a right and an obligation to protect the stability of the climate system.

### 4.1 *IEA v Brazil*

In light of the rising deforestation of the Brazilian Amazon, on October 8, 2020, the Institute of Amazonian Studies (*Instituto de Estudos Amazônicos—IEA*) filed a public civil action (class action) against the Federal Government of Brazil, seeking, among other requests, (i) a court order enforcing the federal

---

32 Eg *La Oroya v Peru* (n 11), §118.

33 Ademola Jegede, 'Arguing the Right to a Safe Climate under the UN Human Rights System' (2020) 9 *International Human Rights Law Review* 185, 211–212.

34 ibid 197.

35 ibid 198.

36 ibid 199, 212.

37 ibid 199–200.

38 ibid 200.

39 ibid 200–201.

government to comply with its own climate policies; (ii) a guarantee that if the 3.925 $km^2$/year limit for deforestation in the Amazon for 2020 is not met, the federal government will be required to reforest the equivalent area exceeding the limit set out in its policy (PPCDAm); and (iii) a court order mandating the defendant to allocate sufficient resources for this purpose (to avoid deforestation and/or to promote reforestation), as well as to use all available resources for this purpose.

In addition to these requests, the most significant innovation of the case is that it seeks the recognition of a fundamental right to a stable climate, which is, according to the applicants, implicitly entrenched in the Brazilian Constitution.[40] According to the applicants, the right to a stable climate for present and future generations is a logical consequence of providing a constitutional status to the right to a healthy environment, without prejudice of other human rights which also entail, in the views of the applicants, an obligation to protect the stability of the climate system: the dignity of the human person (Article 1); the rights to life, freedom, equality, security, and property (Article 5); and the rights to health, food, and housing (Article 6).

However, the applicants also argued that the right to a stable climate system is a new fundamental right implicit to the Brazilian Constitution. Here lies the main contribution of this case to the understanding of an obligation to protect the stability of the climate system. In fact, based on the magnitude of the climate crisis and the negative repercussions that climate change imposes on so many fundamental rights, they alleged that there is a need to recognize a new and autonomous right that guarantees a stable climate system capable of sustaining human life. Accordingly, the applicants claim that, in the context of the climate crisis, the stability of the climate system is a value protected at the constitutional level—a protection that is afforded under both individual (dignity of the human person) and collective rights (ecologically balanced environment), but which must be also protected through a new and autonomous fundamental right to a stable climate.

The court's decision cannot be underestimated: relying in the above-mentioned case law of the IACtHR, but also in decisions from other jurisdictions (Eg USA, the Netherlands, or Pakistan), the 4th Regional Federal Court ruled for the first time in Brazil (and perhaps worldwide)[41] that a distinction

40 Joana Setzer & Délton Winter de Carvalho, 'Climate Litigation to Protect the Brazilian Amazon: Establishing a Constitutional Right to a Stable Climate' (2021) 30 *RECIEL* 204.

41 Maria Antonia Tigre, Délton Winter de Carvalho & Joana Setzer, 'IEA v Brazil: When the Court Accepts the Legally Disruptive Nature of Climate Change' (*Climate Law—A Sabin Center Blog*, 21 December 2021), available at https://blogs.law.columbia.edu/climate

must be made between environmental and climate litigation—thus autonomizing the latter while acknowledging the common ground between them.[42] The geographic and urgency scale of climate litigation, therefore, justify using different lenses to assess climate litigation cases.[43] To that end, however, the court needed to build upon a prior premise: that of a standalone fundamental right to a stable climate, entailing a corresponding obligation to protect and preserve the stability of the climate system, guaranteed under Article 225 of the Brazilian Constitution. With this in mind, the court also emphasizes the need to prioritize the resource to transnational authorities (namely, decisions from other jurisdictions and international law instruments) and to use of special lenses in the analysis of a climate case (namely, by adopting a disruptive reading of the existing law, concepts, and doctrines).

### 4.2 *PSB et al v Brazil (on Climate Fund)*

On June 5, 2020, four Brazilian political parties filed a Direct Action of Unconstitutionality by Omission against the Federal Government before the Federal Supreme Court (ie Brazil's highest judicial instance). The lawsuit targeted the federal government's failure to adopt administrative measures to allocate resources and maintain the operations of the Climate Fund (created by Law No 12.114/2019). This fund is a financing instrument provided for in Brazil's National Climate Change Policy Law, being its purpose to guarantee financial resources for projects, studies, or activities to mitigate and adapt to climate change and its effects.[44] In this process, the applicants claimed that, in spite of the Ministry of the Environment's obligation to prepare an annual plan, this fund had remained inoperative since 2019.

More specifically, the applicants alleged that the suspension of the Climate Fund's operational maintenance activities is a violation of Article 225 of the

change/2021/12/21/iea-v-brazil-when-a-court-accepts-the-legally-disruptive-nature-of-climate-change/.

42 *IEA v Brazil* (n 19) §§15–16.

43 A similar, although more cautious, approach was adopted by the European Court of Human Rights (ECtHR), who mentioned that 'climate change cases present several specific characteristics distinguishing them from "classic" environmental cases', (*Duarte Agostinho et al v Portugal and 32 Other States* (App no 39371/20) ECtHR [GC] 9 April 2024, §189) implying that 'it would be neither adequate nor appropriate to follow an approach consisting in directly transposing the existing environmental case-law to the context of climate change.' (*Verein KlimaSeniorinnen Schweiz and Others v Switzerland* (App no 53600/20) ECtHR [GC] 9 April 2024, §422) It is not likely that the ECtHR was inspired by the decision in *IEA v Brazil*, but it still shows how the 4th Regional Federal Court was pioneer and anticipated what would be the following evolution in the case-law.

44 *PSB et al v Brazil* (n 19) §17.

Brazilian Constitution, having in mind the State's constitutional obligation to preserve and restore 'essential ecological processes,' to promote the ecological management of the ecosystems, to define territorial spaces and their components to be specially protected, and protect fauna and flora.

In a preliminary decision, the Federal Supreme Court accepted the case, but changed its form to an Action for Failure to Comply with a Fundamental Precept (ADPF), whose main goal is to secure fundamental constitutional values and principles. On July 1, 2022, the Federal Supreme Court handed down a historic decision, which, to date, is Brazil's most important precedent on climate litigation. Here, Minister Luís Roberto Barroso carefully drafted the reasons why, in accordance with a right to a healthy environment, the Federal Executive Branch is constitutionally obliged to carry out the allocation and execution of resources from the Climate Fund to mitigate climate change. To that end, Minister Luís Roberto Barroso first flagged the constitutional, supra-legal, and legal nature of the obligation to protect the stability of the climate system (as treaties such as the UNFCCC or the Paris Agreement are akin to human rights treaties) in order to set out the basis for the court's decision under the separation of powers principle. As a result, the court further concluded that the maintenance of the Climate Fund by the Federal Executive is mandatory, and 'not a matter of free political choice.'[45] Similarly, Minister Luís Roberto Barroso explained that using the resources of the Climate Fund for other purposes is prohibited pursuant to the constitutional obligation to protect the environment and Brazil's international commitments.[46]

To understand this decision, one must single out some aspects:

1. *Constitutional Obligation to the Environment and the Climate System.* It can be seen from the decision that the Federal Supreme Court considered the maintenance of the Climate Fund primarily as a constitutional obligation arising from the subjective and objective dimensions of the standalone fundamental right to an ecologically balanced environment[47]—namely, 'the constitutional duty to protect and restore the environment (and the other interdependent fundamental rights).'[48] Nonetheless, the Federal Supreme Court did not refer to an autonomous fundamental right to a stable climate system; and apparently did not

45 ibid §27.

46 ibid §37.

47 Ingo Wolfgang Sarlet & Tiago Fensterseifer, 'O Direito Fundamental ao Clima Limpo, Saudável e Seguro e os Deveres Estatais de Proteção Climática à luz da Constituição Federal de 1988' (2023) 24 *Cadernos Jurídicos da Escola Paulista da Magistratura* 41.

48 *PSB et al v Brazil* (n 19) §30.

follow the line adopted in *IEA v Brazil* regarding the different matrix of climate litigation *vis-à-vis* mainstream environmental litigation. In any case, Minister Luís Roberto Barroso still mentioned that the fundamental right to an ecologically balanced environment imposes on the public authorities the 'duty to defend, preserve and restore the environment for present and *future generations*;'[49] and implied from it a constitutional obligation to protect the stability of the climate system, which is covered by the subjective (right) *and* the objective (duty) characteristics of the right to a healthy environment. Finally, it is also worth mentioning that Minister Luís Roberto Barroso highlighted the idea that a 'principle of the prohibition of retrogression is especially prominent when it comes to environmental protection'[50]—which is infringed whenever the level of environmental or climate protection decreases, either through inaction or the suppression of public policies without due replacement by others that are equally adequate. This doctrine was key to declare that the Executive Branch's decision of de-funding the Climate Fund was unconstitutional, since it constituted a step backwards in the realization and implementation of the right to the environment.

2. *The Paris Agreement as a source of a supra-legal obligation.* In the ruling of *PSB et al v Brazil*, the Federal Supreme Court was the first court worldwide to recognize the Paris Agreement as a human rights treaty.[51] To that end, it implicitly assumed that, from a formal angle, the Paris Agreement would not be part of the acquis of international human rights law for the purposes of Article 5(3) of the Brazilian Constitution—but explicitly mentioned that, in light of the deep link between a stable climate and the realization and enjoyment of human rights in general, the Paris Agreement is part of the genre of human rights treaties for the said purposes of Article 5(2) of the Brazilian Constitutional. This means, for instance, that to protect the stability of the climate system is a supra-legal obligation (even though not a constitutional obligation); and that complying with this latter obligation is mandatory, not optional:[52] holding a supra-legal nature means that ordinary statutory norms need to comply with international treaties, or risk being nullified.

49 ibid §16 (emphasis added).
50 ibid §18.
51 ibid §17. See Maria Antonia Tigre & Joana Setzer, 'Human Rights and Climate Change for Climate Litigation in Brazil and Beyond: An Analysis of the Climate Fund Decision' (2023) 54 *Georgetown JIL* 593, 596.
52 ibid.

Finally, one must note that the *PSB et al v Brazil* decision goes a step further in that it correlates the 'supra-legal' hierarchy with its 'supranational' source. As such, 'supra-legality' is presented by the Federal Supreme Court as the internal normative repercussion resulting from the international character of the human rights treaties ratified by Brazil and the transnational characteristics of climate disputes—which is evidence of that normative openness pointed out in the *IEA v Brazil* case. The immediate legal effect of the supra-legal status of the Paris Agreement (as a human rights treaty) is that any legislation or decree that violates the climate obligations set out thereunder (including the commitments under the NDC submitted by Brazil to the UNFCCC Secretariat) is unconstitutional and is susceptible of nullification.[53]

## 5 Conclusion

In sum, Brazilian courts have been able to forge a cutting-edge doctrine regarding the State's obligation to protect and preserve the stability of the climate system. To that end, both *IEA v Brazil* and *PSB et al v Brazil* show how courts are open-minded towards international law treaties and the case law from the IACtHR or other domestic jurisdictions—and use these instruments in order to inform and buttress their decisions. In *IEA v Brazil*, the court elaborated on the autonomy of the right to a stable climate system (and its corresponding State's obligation to protect and preserve the climate system) in order to suggest that cases relating to climate change effects have a different matrix and require an approach autonomous to the mainstream environmental litigation. For its turn, in *PSB et al v Brazil*, the Federal Supreme Court forged a more robust doctrine regarding the obligation to protect, preserve, and restore the stability of the climate system (although intrinsic to the right to a healthy environment, not autonomous to it). To that end, it qualified the Paris Agreement as akin to a human rights treaty for the purposes of Article 5(2) of the Brazilian Constitution, which allows to find a constitutional and a supra-legal basis for the obligation to protect and preserve the stability of the climate system, as well as to nullify domestic measures which risk achieving the goals set out in the UNFCCC or which damage the stability of the climate system, and *ergo* the right to a healthy environment.

53 Tigre & Setzer (n 51) 615.

CHAPTER 7

# Brazil and Advisory Opinions before International Courts and Tribunals: Participation and Impact of Advisory Opinions in Domestic Courts

*Paula Wojcikiewicz Almeida**

## 1 Introduction

Climate change represents a prominent example of 'common interest,' 'collective interest' or 'common concern.'[1] It reflects a fundamental value that cannot be left to the free disposition of individual States but is instead a matter of concern to all States.'[2] The notion of community interests is recognized by international law and does not remain limited to those norms possessing a specific normative status, such as *jus cogens* or obligations *erga omnes*.[3]

Therefore, the fight against the effects of climate change reflects a common concern, since the existence of an institutional structure on a global level depends upon its protection and amelioration.[4] However, the limits of the current international political scenario have led to limited accomplishment of global achievements related to climate change,[5] since there is no supranational authority capable of effectively enforcing States' obligations related to

* FGV Direito Rio, https://orcid.org/0000-0002-5899-9254

1 Bruno Simma, 'From Bilateralism to Community Interest in International Law' (1994) 250 *Collected Courses of the Hague Academy of International Law* 217, 233.

2 'A first, very tentative, definition of 'community interest' could perceive it as a consensus according to which respect for certain fundamental values is not to be left to the free disposition of States individually or inter se but is recognized and sanctioned by international law as a matter of concern to all States.' Simma, ibid.

3 Markus Benzing, 'Community Interests in the Procedure of International Courts and Tribunals' (2006) 5 *Law & Prac. Int'l Cts. & Tribunals* 369, 371.

4 Simma (n 1) 285.

5 Benzing (n 3) 372; Fabrizio Cafaggi & David Caron, 'Global Public Goods amidst a Plurality of Legal Orders: A Symposium' (2012) 23 *EJIL* 643, 645; Thomas Cottier, 'The Emerging Principle of Common Concern: A Brief Outline', in Petersmann (ed), *Multilevel Governance of Interdependent Public Goods: Theories, Rules and Institutions for the Central Policy Challenge in the 21st Century* (2012) EUI Working Papers, RSCAS No 23, 185–186, available at <https://cadmus.eui.eu/bitstream/handle/1814/22275/RSCAS_2012_23final.pdf?sequence=2&is> accessed 22 August 2024; Anna Pitaraki, 'Can the "Development Dimension" of the WTO Be Secured Without Stronger Synergies Between the WTO and the World Bank?', in Petersmann (ed), ibid, 100.

 | DOI:10.1163/9789004690974_008

community interests.[6] As a component of the international governance structure, international courts and tribunals (ICTs) can be considered a key element to the promotion of the international rule of law,[7] including the provision of global public goods.[8]

Advisory opinions are increasingly being used to address common interests. This trend is evident at the International Court of Justice (ICJ), where several opinions have sparked a growing demand for participation of States, international organizations, and civil society.[9] Similarly, the International Tribunal for the Law of the Sea (ITLOS) not only acknowledges the embedded community interests on the cases brought before it but has also noted the binding and *erga omnes* character of the obligation to protect and preserve the marine environment.[10] This highlights that inter-State courts, like the ICJ and the ITLOS, are increasingly using advisory opinions to address issues that impact the global community.

This chapter examines three advisory opinions submitted to ICTs regarding climate change.[11] The recent request to the ICJ by the UN General Assembly (UNGA) is a key focus.[12] This request, driven mostly by non-State actors (NSAs), seeks an advisory opinion on legal obligations of States concerning climate change and consequences of breaching them.[13] Specifically, the request aims to clarify the existence and scope of these obligations under international law, focusing on protecting the climate system, the marine environment,

---

6 Benzing (n 3) 372; Cafaggi & Caron (n 5) 645; Cottier (n 5) 185–186; Pitaraki (n 5) 100.

7 Geir Ulfstein, 'International Courts and Judges: Independence, Interaction and Legitimacy' (2014) 46 *NYU Journal of Int'l Law & Politics* 849, 859–860.

8 André Nollkaemper, 'International Adjudication of Global Public Goods: The Intersection of Substance and Procedure' (2012) 23 *EJIL* 769.

9 Two recent advisory opinions on *Legal Consequences arising from the Policies and Practices of Israel in the Occupied Palestinian Territory, including East Jerusalem* and on *Obligations of States in respect of Climate Change* reflect this emerging trend.

10 *Responsibilities and obligations of States sponsoring persons and entities with respect to activities in the Area* (*Request for Advisory Opinion submitted to the Seabed Disputes Chamber*), International Tribunal for the Law of the Sea, 1 February 2011, 17, <https://www.itlos.org/index.php?id=109> accessed 4 April 2024.

11 For a brief overview of the requests, see Maria Antonia Tigre, '*It Is (Finally) Time for an Advisory Opinion on Climate Change: Challenges and Opportunities on a Trio of Initiatives* (2024) 17 *Charleston LR* 623.

12 Jack Kenny & Constantinos Yiallourides, *Promoting Climate Justice through International Law: Climate Litigation & Climate Advisory Opinions* (BIICL 2023) 5.

13 *The General Assembly of the United Nations requests an advisory opinion from the Court on the obligations of States in respect of climate change* (No 2023/20, International Court of Justice 2023) xxxx <www.icj-cij.org/sites/default/files/case-related/187/187-20230419-PRE-01-00-EN.pdf> accessed 4 April 2024.

and addressing potential legal remedies for violations, particularly regarding human rights.[14]

In parallel, small island States Antigua and Barbuda and Tuvalu established a commission ('COSIS') with the power to request advisory opinions from the ITLOS.[15,16] Their request focused on clarifying States' obligations under international law to protect the marine environment (Part XII of UNCLOS), particularly in the face of climate change's existential threat to its survival.[17]

The Inter-American Court of Human Rights (IACtHR) was the first ICT to address climate change.[18] Advisory Opinion 23/2017, for instance, recognized the right to a healthy environment and States' obligations to prevent environmental harm across borders, making a special reference to climate change.[19] In January 2023, Chile and Colombia requested an advisory opinion on climate change and its impact on human rights,[20] which seeks to clarify States' duties regarding due diligence, environmental defenders' rights, and other human rights issues arising from climate change.

Therefore, the simultaneous requests for advisory opinions may, conversely, promote a thorough clarification of international law and contribute to the development of climate governance.[21] There is considerable scope for procedural

---

14 Aditi Shetye, 'It Is So Decided: Promoting Climate Justice through International Law' (*BIICL*, 12 April 2023) <https://www.biicl.org/blog/56/it-is-so-decided-promoting-climate-justice-through-international-law?utm_content=bufferdf348&utm_medium=social&%E2%80%A6> accessed 12 June 2023.

15 Agreement for the Establishment of the Commission of Small Island States on Climate Change and International Law (hereinafter 'COSIS Agreement') adopted and entered into force 31 October 2021.

16 Benoit Mayer, 'International Advisory Proceedings on Climate Change' (2023) 44 *Michigan JIL* 41.

17 ITLOS, 'Request for an Advisory Opinion submitted by the Commission of Small Island States on Climate Change and International Law', ITLOS Case No 31 (12 December 2022) (hereinafter 'COSIS Request').

18 *Environment and Human Rights (State Obligations in relation to the Environment in the context of the Protection and Guarantee of the Rights to Life and to Personal Integrity—Interpretation and Scope of Articles 4(1) and 5(1) of the American Convention on Human Rights)*, Advisory Opinion OC-23/17, IACtHR Series A No 23 (15 November 2017) (hereinafter 'Advisory Opinion OC-23/17').

19 ibid.

20 IACtHR, 'Request for an Advisory Opinion on the Climate Emergency and Human Rights submitted by Colombia and Chile' (9 January 2023) (hereinafter 'Request to the IACtHR on the Climate Emergency').

21 Juan Auz and Thalia Viveros-Uehara, 'Another Advisory Opinion on the Climate Emergency? The Added Value of the Inter-American Court of Human Rights' (*EJIL Talk!*, 2 March 2023) <https://www.ejiltalk.org/another-advisory-opinion-on-the-climate-emer-

and substantive cross-fertilization of findings between the ICTs.[22] Taking this context into account, this chapter focuses on the Brazilian participation and contribution in the referred advisory proceedings (Section 2) and assesses the potential application of these opinions by Brazilian domestic courts, notably Brazilian apex courts (Section 3).

## 2 Brazilian Participation in Advisory Proceedings before ICTs

*Amicus curiae* encompasses actors discretionarily authorized by the ICTs—whether by invitation or by their own request—to participate without acquiring the status of a party.[23] They 'do not themselves have a legally protected interest in the particular case and yet want to intervene,'[24] thereby opening bilateral litigation to issues of public or general interest.[25] The purpose of such interventions 'is to assist the court, to contribute a unique perspective or specialized knowledge that will enrich and improve the court's decision.'[26] Their goal is to 'introduce public interest considerations into the decision—and, indirectly, to impact the development of international law.'[27]

Whereby human rights courts found fertile ground to properly develop *amicus curiae* participation, the ITLOS and the ICJ still struggle with the

gency-the-added-value-of-the-inter-american-court-of-human-rights/> accessed 12 June 2023.

22 See the *Chagos Advisory Opinion*, in which the ICJ affirmed that it 'will consider any relevant judicial or arbitral decision' when answering a question submitted to the Court. *Legal Consequences of the Separation of the Chagos Archipelago from Mauritius in 1965* (Advisory Opinion) [2019] ICJ Rep 95, §81.

23 Lance Bartholomeusz, 'The Amicus Curiae before International Courts and Tribunals' (2005) 5 *Non-State Actors & IL* 273.

24 Armin von Bogdandy & Ingo Venzke, 'On the Democratic Legitimation of International Judicial Lawmaking' (2011) 12 *German Law Journal* 1341, 1366–7; See also Philippe Sands & Ruth Mackenzie, 'International Courts and Tribunals, Amicus Curiae', *Max-Planck Encyclopedia of Public International Law* (ed. Rüdiger Wolfrum) (2009); Hervé Ascensio, 'L'Amicus Curiae devant les Juridictions Internationales' (2001) 105 *RGDIP* 897.

25 Dinah Shelton, 'The Participation of Nongovernmental Organizations in International Judicial Proceedings' (1994) 88 *AJIL* 611, 612.

26 Avidan Kent & Jamie Trinidad, 'Amicus Curiae Participation in International Proceedings: Forever Friends?', in Kent, Skoutaris & Trinidad (eds), *The Future of International Courts* (Routledge 2019), 235, 242.

27 Yaël Ronen & Yael Naggan, 'Third Parties', in Romano, Alter & Yuval Shany (eds), *The Oxford Handbook of International Adjudication* (OUP 2013) 806, 821.

traditional State-to-State approach to international dispute settlement. Being inter-State courts, their position towards *amicus curiae* participation closely resembles one another.[28]

### 2.1 *ICJ and ITLOS*

There is scholarly support for the acceptance of NGO *amicus curiae* submissions, notably in cases involving obligations *erga omnes* or broad public interests that are not restricted to national borders.[29] The treatment and acceptance of *amicus curiae* briefs varies in ICTs. Each adjudicative body formulates its own response to encompass broader participation, some being more receptive to *amicus curiae* and to the participation in different phases of the proceedings by NSAs, while others remain still reluctant to incorporate different views concerning supposed bilateral disputes being submitted to ICTs, as is the case of the ICJ.[30] Therefore, ICTs have different approaches as to who may participate in proceedings in the quality of *amicus curiae*. The extent of participation as *amicus curiae* will depend on factors,[31] such as the existence of an express provision, the nature, jurisdiction, and competence of the court or regime to which it is part, the court's powers and the parties' stance.[32]

This section intends to, on the one hand, address the procedural rules concerning participation before the ICTs provoked in their advisory function concerning climate change, notably the ICJ and the ITLOS, as well as evaluate Brazil's participation before these courts in the advisory opinions concerning climate change.

#### 2.1.1 Participation Mechanisms Applied to States and NSAs

The ICJ Statute and Rules of Court contain no provision for allowing non-party participation (except for State intervention) in contentious cases. While not explicitly allowed, States and international organizations can submit written or oral statements in both contentious and advisory proceedings (Article 66 ICJ Statute). The presentation of *amicus curiae* briefs by nongovernmental

28 Bartholomeusz (n 23) 226.
29 Shelton (n 25) 627.
30 Bartholomeusz (n 23) 275.
31 Astrid Wiik, *Amicus Curiae Before International Courts and Tribunals* (Nomos/Hart 2018) 121.
32 Bartholomeusz (n 23) 275–6.

organizations in contentious cases is not formally envisaged in the ICJ, except in the context of advisory proceedings (Article 66(2) ICJ Statute).[33]

Similarly to the ICJ, Article 133 ITLOS Rules allows State Parties and international organizations to furnish information in advisory proceedings.[34] Unlike the ICJ, however, all State Parties to the UNCLOS automatically have the right to submit information in ITLOS advisory proceedings,[35] and international organizations can also be invited by the Tribunal or submit information on their own initiative. However, in contentious proceedings, ITLOS has not allowed participation from NGOs as *amicus curiae*, similar to the ICJ's practice.[36] The limited number of advisory requests submitted to ITLOS so far has also restricted the development of practices regarding non-party participation in its proceedings. To date, only three requests for advisory opinions have been submitted to ITLOS.[37]

In the most recent *COSIS Request,*[38] 32 States,[39] 11 international organizations[40] and 10 NSAs[41] have submitted written statements (see Figure 7.1). However, according to Article 133 ITLOS Rules, only States and international organizations invited by the Registrar can be accepted as being part of the case file.[42]

33 See Practice Direction XII. See also Bartholomeusz (n 23) 220–4.
34 Bartholomeusz (n 23) 227–8.
35 Bartholomeusz (n 23) 230–1.
36 Rozemarijn J Roland Holst, 'Taking the Current when it Serves: Prospects and Challenges for an ITLOS Advisory Opinion on Oceans and Climate Change' (2023) 32 *RECIEL* 217.
37 See <https://www.itlos.org/en/main/cases/advisory-proceedings/> accessed 22 August 2024.
38 COSIS Request (n 17).
39 The States that sent written statements were Democratic Republic of the Congo; Poland; New Zealand; Japan; Norway; Germany; Italy; China; European Union; Mozambique; Australia; Mauritius; Indonesia; Latvia; Singapore; Republic of Korea; Egypt; Brazil; France; Chile; Bangladesh; Nauru; Belize; Portugal; Canada; Guatemala; United Kingdom; The Netherlands; Sierra Leone; Micronesia; and Djibouti.
40 The International Organizations invited to submit their considerations on the case were United Nations; International Union for the Conservation of Nature (IUCN); International Maritime Organization (IMO); Commission of Small Island States on Climate Change and International Law (COSIS); Pacific Community (SPC); United Nations Environment Programme (UNEP); African Union; and International Seabed Authority (ISA).
41 Holst (n 36) 217.
42 See Maria Antonia Tigre & Korey Silverman-Roati (eds), 'ITLOS Advisory Opinion on Climate Change: Summary of the Briefs and Statements submitted to the Tribunal' (Sabin Center for Climate Change Law 2023), available at <https://scholarship.law.columbia.edu/cgi/viewcontent.cgi?article=1209&context=sabin_climate_change> accessed 22 August 2024.

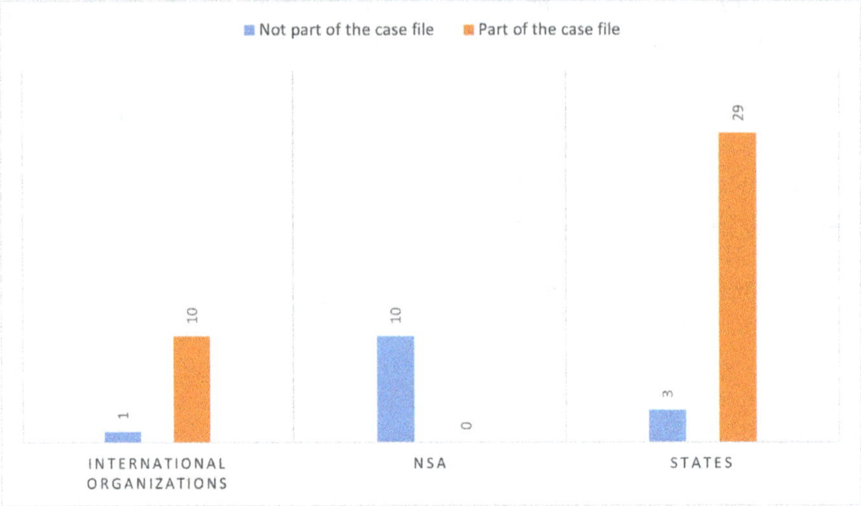


FIGURE 7.1 Classification of actors submitting statements to the ITLOS

### 2.1.2 Brazilian Use of Participation Mechanisms

Before the ICJ, the only instance in which Brazil acted as a party to contentious proceedings concerns the case brought by Honduras on *Certain Questions concerning Diplomatic Relations* (*Honduras v Brazil*).[43] The case, however, was dismissed by a request from Honduras. As far as advisory opinions are concerned, Brazil's participation has been limited: Brazil only submitted information in six out of 31 proceedings.[44] Despite this limited participation, Brazil has consistently emphasized its commitment to promoting international law and upholding the ICJ as the UN's primary judicial body.[45]

Historically, Brazil has not been active in the proceedings of the ITLOS. In 2023, it sent for the first time a written statement to the request for an advisory opinion submitted by the COSIS on Climate Change and International Law.[46]

43 *Certain Questions Concerning Diplomatic Relations* (*Discontinuance*) [Order of 12 May 2010] ICJ Rep 303.

44 *Legal Consequences arising from the Policies and Practices of Israel in the Occupied Palestinian Territory* (Advisory Opinion) [2023]; *Chagos Advisory Opinion* (n 22); *Accordance with International Law of the Unilateral Declaration of Independence in respect of Kosovo* (Advisory Opinion) [2017] ICJ Rep 403; *Legal Consequences of the Construction of a Wall in the Occupied Palestinian Territory* (Advisory Opinion) [2004] ICJ Rep 136.

45 *Legal Consequences arising from the Policies and Practices of Israel in the Occupied Palestinian Territory, including East Jerusalem*, 'Written Statement of the Federative Republic of Brazil' (2023).

46 *COSIS Request* (n 17) 'Written Statement of Brazil', 2023.

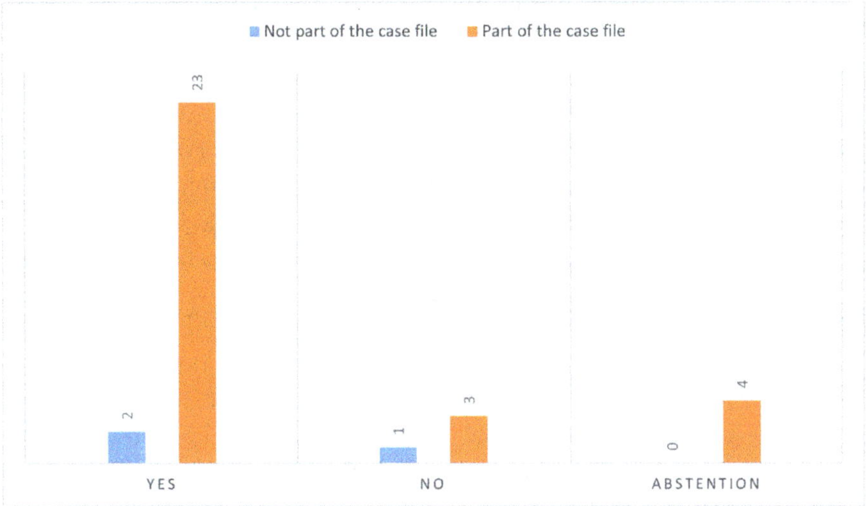


FIGURE 7.2 States' position on matters of jurisdiction before ITLOS advisory opinion on climate change

In its written statement, Brazil submitted that ITLOS does not have jurisdiction to issue the requested advisory opinion. Alternatively, Brazil argues the Tribunal's advisory jurisdiction should be limited *ratione materiae* to the requesting organization's scope of activities. This does not reflect a majoritarian position, as depicted in Figure 7.2. Only three of the 30 States submitting written statements (India, China, and Brazil) questioned ITLOS' advisory jurisdiction.

## 2.2 *Inter-American Court of Human Rights*

### 2.2.1 Participation Mechanisms Applied by State and NSAs

Unlike its European counterpart,[47] the IACtHR did not explicitly allow for *amicus curiae* participation in its proceedings.[48] However, although the 1980

47 For instance, 1981 marked the first time that the ECtHR allowed the admission of an NGO that was not a party to the proceedings, in the case *Young, James & Webster v the United Kingdom* (Apps no 7601/76 & 7806/77). Subsequently, in 1982, the court amended its rules to formally provide for *amicus curiae* participation. Then, the practice was officially recognized in Article 36(2) of the European Convention on Human Rights through Protocol 11, which was enacted in 1998. The amendment permitted those making amicus curiae participation requests to take part in oral submissions and excluded *ratione materiae* limitations on their contribution (Wiik (n 31) 103–4).

48 'The Court's first Rules of Procedure in 1980 made no explicit mention of *amici* briefs. However, Article 34(1) of the 1980 Rules stated that the "Court may … decide to hear … in any … capacity, any person whose … statements seem likely to assist in carrying out its

Rules of Procedure did not explicitly authorize *amici* submissions, the IACtHR routinely accepted such briefs in both its advisory and contentious jurisdictions. In its first advisory opinion,[49] it used the existing rules to invite and receive written submissions, including those from NGOs. In 2009, the Court defined the term '*amicus curiae*' under the definitions listed in Article 2 and explicitly allowed *amici* briefs for proceedings such as compliance, monitoring, and provisional measures. Under Article 44(1) IACtHR Rules, 'any person or institution seeking to act as amicus curiae may submit a brief to the Tribunal,' which includes not only written submissions from interested parties, but also allows for participation in public hearings.

*Amicus curiae* submissions can constitute not only the opinion of an expert,[50] either factual or legal, but also 'opinions from sociological, psychological, historical and other perspectives, according to the needs of the case.'[51] While *amicus curiae* submissions are not binding upon the Court,[52] they must comply with the Court's procedures.[53] This includes providing identifying information, a summary of the case, in-depth analysis, and recommendations relevant to the specific issues.

### 2.2.2 Brazilian Use of Participation Mechanisms

The far-reaching nature of the questions raised in the Request for an Advisory Opinion on Climate Emergency and Human Rights prompted an exceptional number of briefs offering relevant observations.[54] As of August 2024, the Request to the IACtHR has received 261 statements from States, OAS organs, international organizations, non-governmental organizations, academic institutions, and civil society, all of which were invited to participate in the public hearings.[55]

---

function" presumably, this included *amici* briefs, since the IACtHR received and accepted submissions from dozens of *amici* in cases controlled by the 1980 Rules.' Francisco Rivera Juaristi, 'The Amicus Curiae in the Inter-American Court of Human Rights (1982–2013)' (1 August 2014) https://papers.ssrn.com/abstract=2488073 (accessed 1 April 2024) 7.

49 Some sources suggest an earlier case in 1981.

50 Fabián Novak, 'Amicus Curiae: Inter-American Court of Human Rights (IACtHR)' *Max Planck Encyclopedias of International Law* (2020).

51 ibid.

52 ibid.

53 ibid.

54 Request for an Advisory Opinion on Climate Emergency and Human Rights, 'Written Statement of Brazil'.

55 See Maria Antonia Tigre, Advisory Opinion on Climate Change: Summary of Written Observations submitted to the Inter-American Court of Human Rights (Part 1)' (Sabin

After a period of relative passivity in international legal proceedings, Brazil has recently demonstrated a more engaged approach. In the Request for an Advisory Opinion on Climate Emergency and Human Rights, Brazil participated by submitting written observations.[56] While acknowledging the Court's jurisdiction and the legitimacy of the request from other countries, Brazil emphasized the heightened ecological and socioeconomic vulnerabilities faced by Latin America due to climate change. By participating in these proceedings, Brazil not only highlighted its regional concerns but also advocated for a solution that considers the varying capacities of different countries in addressing this global challenge.

In its written statement, Brazil underscored the fundamental principles of international environmental law, such as the precautionary principle, the polluter-pays principle, and the principle of sustainable development. These principles, it argued, are essential for addressing the global climate crisis. Brazil emphasized the inextricable link between climate change and human rights and highlighted that the impacts of climate change disproportionately affect vulnerable populations, particularly children, women, indigenous peoples and environmental activists. Brazil reiterated its commitment to equality and non-discrimination, asserting that all individuals, regardless of their socioeconomic status, race, ethnicity, or gender, have the right to a healthy environment. The statement acknowledged the intergenerational nature of climate change and the imperative to protect the rights of future generations.

Brazil outlined the general duties of States in the context of climate change and emphasized the importance of international cooperation in addressing climate change, highlighting the need for global solidarity and the importance of multilateral agreements, such as the Paris Agreement, in coordinating efforts to mitigate and adapt to climate change. Brazil discussed the substantive obligations of states in relation to climate change, including the obligation to prevent climate change, mitigate its impacts, and adapt to its effects. Finally, Brazil addressed the procedural obligations of states, including the obligation to ensure access to justice, access to information, and participation in decision-making processes related to climate change.

---

Center for Climate Change Law 2024) <https://scholarship.law.columbia.edu/cgi/viewcontent.cgi?article=1222&context=sabin_climate_change> accessed 22 August 2024.

56 'Written Statement of Brazil' (n 54).

## 3 The Application of ICTs' Advisory Opinions by Brazilian Domestic Courts

This section assesses the influence of ICTs' advisory opinions within Brazilian apex courts. It delves into the possibilities of a judicial dialogue between international and domestic courts in Brazil, while also assessing the dynamics of judicial dialogue between the Brazilian Federal Supreme Court (STF) and advisory opinions issued by the ICJ, the ITLOS, and the IACtHR.

### 3.1 *Judicial Dialogue between ICTs and Brazilian Domestic Courts*

Brazil's STF has increasingly cited the IACtHR in recent decades. This trend aligns with the concept of 'judicial dialogue,' which can be broadly understood as judicial interaction and encompasses not only an exchange of views between courts on a given subject but also a referral of the decisions of other courts.[57] Indeed, court interactions often involve citing external decisions, but they somewhat resemble more of a monologue than a genuine dialogue, since the cited court does not have a chance to respond or engage in a meaningful exchange of views.[58]

However, this one-directional flow of citations can still serve valuable functions, as highlighted by Slaughter's concept of 'transjudicial dialogue.'[59] Slaughter emphasizes two key functions: (i) general cross-fertilization, where courts can get inspiration for solutions to complex legal problems within their own jurisdictions by referencing international pronouncements (such as the IACtHR's advisory opinions); (ii) enhancing persuasiveness and legitimacy, by which citations to authoritative interpretations of international human rights (from specialized supranational human rights bodies) can boost the persuasive force and legitimacy of a court's own decisions.

To examine how advisory opinions produce impact in national case law, we adopt the following definition of 'impact': 'the intended or unintended effects on practices, structures, and social outcomes stemming from adjudicatory and non-adjudicatory actions by international bodies.'[60] According to Ocaña and Pérez-Liñán, the impact of international pronouncements can be measured

57 Paula Wojcikiewicz Almeida, 'The Asymmetric Judicial Dialogue Between the ICJ and the IACtHR: An Empirical Analysis' (2020) 11 *Journal of Int'l Dispute Settlement* 2.

58 ibid.

59 See Anne-Marie Slaughter, 'A Typology of Transjudicial Communication' (1994) 29 *University of Richmond LR* 1, 113.

60 Maya Ortiz Ocaña & Aníbal Pérez-Liñán, 'Transformative Impact: A Framework for Analysis', in von Bogdandy, Piovesan, Ferrer McGregor & Morales Antoniazzi (eds), *The Impact of the Inter-American Human Rights System* (OUP 2024) 176.

using a three-stage scale: (i) 'appropriation,' (ii) 'institutional response,' and (iii) 'transformation on the ground.'[61] This study focuses on the second stage, which examines how domestic tribunals (in our case, Brazilian apex courts) incorporate advisory opinions from the ICT s. Essentially, this judicial dialogue between domestic courts and the IACtHR contributes to the development of a coherent legal framework.[62]

In this context, data suggests that the most suitable way to measure judicial influence lies in analyzing citation patterns within Brazilian jurisprudence. This approach focuses on how Brazilian apex courts engage with the IACtHR's pronouncements. By examining these reference dynamics, we can gauge the extent to which the IACtHR shapes legal reasoning and potentially influences future court decisions in Brazil.[63]

Exemplifying a limited dialogue with ICT s, decisions of the ICJ have been cited only eleven times by the STF. The sole reference to an ICJ advisory opinion was made by Justice Gilmar Mendes in RE 466.343,[64] in which the 1970 Advisory Opinion on Namibia was cited to underscore the applicability of the 1969 Vienna Convention on the Law of Treaties as part of international customary law.[65] Additionally, the case law of the STF reveals no references to decisions or opinions from the ITLOS.

### 3.2 *The Dynamics of Judicial Dialogue between the STF and Advisory Opinions Issued by the IACtHR*

In this subsection, advisory opinions rendered by the IACtHR are analyzed in order to provide for an exploration of the judicial dialogue between the STF and the IACtHR. Building on Slaughter's take on judicial dialogue, we propose

---

61 ibid.

62 For further readings on causal relations, process tracing and case studies see: Sandra Botero, *Courts that Matter: Activists, Judges, and the Politics of Rights Enforcement* (CUP 2023); Alexander George & Andrew Bennet, *Case Studies and Theory Development in the Social Sciences* (MIT Press 2005); Andrew Bennett, 'Process Tracing and Causal Inference', in Brady & Collier (eds), *Rethinking Social Inquiry: Diverse Tools, Shared Standards* (Rowman & Littlefield 2010).

63 For further readings on the use of cross-citation to understand the impact on human rights legal order see: Ezequiel Gonzalez-Ocantos & Wayne Sandholtz, 'Constructing a Regional Human Rights Legal Order: The Inter-American Court, National Courts, and Judicial Dialogue, 1988–2014' (2021) 19 *Int'l J Constitutional Law* 1559.

64 Judgment of 3 December 2008 (STJ), Special Appeal No 466.343-1, Rapporteur: Justice Gilmar Mendes, 11.

65 *Consequences for States of the Continued Presence of South Africa in Namibia (South West Africa) notwithstanding Security Council Resolution 276 (1970)* (Advisory Opinion) [1971] ICJ Rep 16.

a classification system to analyze how the STF uses IACtHR advisory opinions. This system categorizes references based on their relative importance to the outcome of the judgment, whether presenting a substantial (1) or minimal impact (2). By analyzing the impact of IACtHR advisory opinions on the STF, we can gain a deeper understanding of how this judicial interaction functions in practice.

#### 3.2.1 Substantial Impact

The first category in our proposed classification system focuses on situations where the STF substantively engages with the IACtHR advisory opinions. This means the STF decision demonstrably references the advisory opinion in a way that impacts the national case's outcome. In some instances, the STF resorted to the advisory opinion to introduce new legal standards or interpretations within the Brazilian legal system. This involves incorporating the opinion's reasoning to broaden the scope of existing human rights protections or to tackle a legal issue not previously addressed by domestic law.

A prime example is IACtHR's advisory opinion on gender identity, equality, and non-discrimination for same-sex couples (OC-24/17), which played a relevant role in a number of cases.[66] In a case before the Superior Court of Justice,[67] Justice Edson Fachin integrated the advisory opinion into his case summary as a precedent and repeatedly cited it throughout his vote. Furthermore, he drew upon the IACtHR's definition of gender identity as a core concept. This extensive application of the opinion's concepts exceeds Justice Fachin's vote as Justices Rosa Weber, Luís Fux, and Gilmar Mendes also relied upon the opinion to bolster their arguments. In this instance, the STF's engagement with the IACtHR pronouncement transcended mere citation, reflecting its use as a relevant element in the Court's deliberations.

Advisory Opinion OC-24/17 was again referenced by the STF in *PPS v Brazil*,[68] which centered on the vulnerability of the LGBT+ community to human rights violations. Notably, Minister Fachin not only incorporated Advisory Opinion OC-24/17 as a legal precedent in his case summary, but also engaged with it extensively throughout his analysis and final vote. Further solidifying the

66 *Gender Identity, and Equality and Non-Discrimination of Same-Sex Couples—State Obligations concerning change of Name, Gender Identity, and Rights Derived from a Relationship between Same.Sex Couples (Interpretation and Scope of Articles 1(1), 3, 7, 11(2), 13, 17, 18 and 24 in relation to Article 1, of the American Convention on Human Rights,* Advisory Opinion OC-24/17, IACtHR Series A No 24 (24 November 2017) (hereinafter 'Advisory Opinion OC-24/17').

67 Judgment of 1 March 2018 (STJ) ADI 4.275, Rapporteur: Justice Edson Fachin, 25.

68 *PPS v Brazil*, ADI 26, Judgment of 13 June 2019.

significance of Advisory Opinion OC-24/17, in a writ of injunction,[69] Minister Fachin—seeking to criminalize discrimination based on sexual orientation or gender identity—also extensively references the advisory opinion. Minister Fachin strategically positioned the opinion by listing it as a legal precedent in the case summary. He subsequently relied on the IACtHR's analysis, specifically its differentiation between sexual orientation and gender identity, a central argument of the writ.

The STF has also actively engaged with an IACtHR's advisory opinion on mandatory journalist registration (OC-05/85).[70] In an extraordinary appeal on a related topic, Minister Gilmar Mendes integrated that opinion into the STF's case-law.[71] This is evidenced not only by his direct citations to specific pages of the IACtHR pronouncement, but also by his decision to highlight the opinion as a key point within the case summary. This dual approach underscores the significant weight afforded to the advisory opinion in shaping the final judgment.

Our analysis consistently reveals Justice Fachin's use of the IACtHR's advisory opinions to inform his legal reasoning. Notably, he employs a twofold approach. First, as a rapporteur, he frequently incorporates them as precedents in his case summaries. Second, he uses the advisory opinion to bolster his understanding of key concepts. This qualitative finding aligns with our quantitative analysis demonstrating that Justice Fachin is the most frequent user of advisory opinions among the 14 decisions examined. Additionally, Advisory Opinion OC-24/17 is the most frequently cited opinion overall. Advisory Opinion OC-5/85 was cited three times and Advisory Opinions OC-18/03 and 23/17[72] were each cited twice, while Advisory Opinions OC-17/02, 07/86, and 02/82 were cited only once.

### 3.2.2 Minimal Impact

The second category in our classification system encompasses situations where the STF references an IACtHR advisory opinion in its judgment, but this

69 Writ of Injunction No 4.733, STF Process No 9942814-37.2012.1.00.000, Rapporteur: Minister Edson Fachin.

70 *Compulsory Membership in an Association Prescribed by Law for the Practice of Journalism (Articles 13 and 29 American Convention on Human Rights)*, Advisory Opinion OC-5/85, IACtHR Series A No 5 (13 November 1985) (hereinafter 'Advisory Opinion OC-5/85').

71 Judgment of 17 June 2009 (STF) Special Appeal No 511.961, Rapporteur: Minister Gilmar Mendes, 57.

72 Regarding Advisory Opinion OC-23/17, see *Rede Sustentabilidade v Brazil*, ADO 54, Judgment of 1 April 2022, para 83, 147–148; and Judgment of 17 December 2022 (STF) ADI 6957, Rapporteur: Minister Edson Fachin.

reference appears to have had minimal impact on the final outcome of the case. For instance, domestic decisions might simply acknowledge the existence of an opinion without engaging in a detailed analysis of its reasoning or principles. This could be a transcription or a brief overview of relevant international pronouncements. Alternatively, the STF might reference the opinion to bolster an argument already grounded in domestic legal principles or prior STF's decisions. In this case, the advisory opinion serves as a supplementary source of authority.

In 2009, ADPF 130 marked the first instance where the STF cited an advisory opinion from the IACtHR.[73] In his vote, Minister Celso de Mello referenced both Advisory Opinions OC-07/86 and 02/82 to address the freedom of press. However, his decision draws heavily on national case law and legislation, as he used the opinion merely to support his argument in favor of the right of reply for aggrieved parties in response to media publications or broadcasts. In 2021, in ADI 5418, the STF revisited that latter ADPF 130 judgment, having Minister Edson Fachin mentioned Advisory Opinion OC-07/86 as an accessory element of their reasoning in this case.

This trend continues in recent cases, as demonstrated by Minister Edson Fachin's vote on ADI 5.617,[74] which concerned the allocation of party funds for electoral campaigns. In his ruling, Minister Fachin drew on the IACtHR's Advisory Opinion OC-18/03 on undocumented migrants. However, he did not discuss this opinion further in the vote. This selective use of a reasoning from the advisory opinion exemplifies the nuanced approach Brazilian apex courts can adopt when interpreting international pronouncements.

Minister Edson Fachin's approach to incorporating international legal pronouncements is further exemplified in Habeas Corpus Order No 143.988.[75] As the Rapporteur in this case, Judge Fachin used IACtHR Advisory Opinion OC-17/2002 in a supporting role for his decision-making. Similar to the previous case, the IACtHR pronouncement was not extensively analyzed, but rather used to support a more protective interpretation of the United Nations Convention on the Rights of the Child, as posited by the opinion.

In Extraordinary Appeal 670.422,[76] Minister Dias Toffoli also refers to Advisory Opinion OC-24/17, which directly addresses the core issue of changing names and genders in civil registries. One might expect this case to prominently

73 Judgment of 20 March 1986 (STF) ADPF 130, Rapporteur: Minister Celso de Mello.

74 Judgment of 15 March 2018 (STF) ADI 5617, Rapporteur: Minister Edson Fachin.

75 Order of 24 August 2020, Habeas Corpus No 143988, Rapporteur: Minister Edson Fachin.

76 Judgment of 18 August 2018 (STF) Extraordinary Appeal No 670.422, Rapporteur: Minister Dias Toffoli.

feature the advisory opinion in its legal reasoning. However, Minister Toffoli instead relied primarily on the STF's established jurisprudence to support his vote. While the judgment acknowledges the existence of Advisory Opinion OC—24/17, it does so indirectly, referencing it through the apex court's own prior rulings.

While issuing his judgment in ADI 6.957,[77] Minister Fachin referred to Advisory Opinion OC-23/2017 to emphasize the State's obligation to prevent environmental harm, encompassing an extraterritorial dimension also. However, unlike his approach in other cases where he served as rapporteur, Minister Fachin did not engage in an in-depth analysis of the advisory opinion.

## 4 Conclusion

This chapter had a twofold objective. First, it aimed to analyze Brazil's engagement with advisory proceedings before ICTs, focusing on the ICJ, the ITLOS, and the IACtHR. The analysis revealed a more active role for Brazil in the IACtHR system compared to the ICJ and ITLOS.

Drawing on the concept of 'judicial dialogue,' this chapter concludes that a nascent but promising form of dialogue exists. Evidence of this dialogue emerges from instances where the STF references and integrates IACtHR pronouncements into their legal reasoning. Notably, Judge Fachin's prominent use of Advisory Opinion OC-24/17 on gender identity exemplifies this. The Court not only cited the opinion but also employed its definitions and reasoning as foundational elements in its decision. This suggests a willingness to engage with the IACtHR beyond mere citation and to use its pronouncements as persuasive authority.

Despite this, a growing openness to IACtHR opinions on human rights and the environment indicates a potential for a stronger dialogue in the future. Judges' backgrounds and philosophies also influence their openness to international law. Justices such as Edson Fachin, known for their frequent and in-depth engagement with international law, exemplify this phenomenon. Their legal training, prior experiences, and personal views on the role of international law all contribute to their approach.

Effective judicial dialogue offers several potential benefits. It allows the STF to leverage the expertise of the IACtHR on critical issues with well-developed international legal frameworks. Additionally, it fosters a more

77 Judgment of 17 December 2022 (STF) ADI 6957, Rapporteur: Minister Edson Fachin.

dynamic interpretation of domestic law, aligning it with evolving international human rights standards.[78] Ultimately, a more robust judicial dialogue between the STF and the IACtHR could contribute to a more just and equitable regional legal order.

In January 2023, Chile and Colombia jointly requested an advisory opinion for the IACtHR to clarify the obligations arising from the climate emergence and human rights—namely due diligence, right to life, children's rights, procedural rights, environmental defenders' rights and differentiated responsibilities.[79] The request seeks to clarify the duties of States concerning the Paris Agreements, the implementation of the obligations within the States' jurisdictions, as well as mitigation obligations, international cooperation, forced displacement, corporate accountability, among others.

The IACtHR advisory opinion on climate change has the potential to influence domestic climate change litigation worldwide. By clarifying States' legal obligations to address climate change, the Court can provide a powerful catalyst for action at the national level.

One of the most immediate effects of the advisory opinion could be to inspire legal advocates to amplify climate litigation in domestic courts. Although non-binding, the Court's decision could serve as a blueprint for litigants, providing them with a stronger legal foundation to argue for accountability.

The advisory opinion could also provide guidance to domestic courts in interpreting climate-related laws and regulations. By clarifying the legal principles applicable to climate change, the Court can help domestic judges to reach more informed and consistent decisions. National courts can elaborate comprehensively on the interpretation of existing human rights norms and apply them to the climate sphere, thus rendering a human rights framework applicable to the Inter-American human rights system.

The Court's decision is likely to be particularly influential due to its progressive approach to human rights law. By centering the experiences of victims,

78 In a significant move towards greater alignment with international human rights standards, Brazil's National Council of Justice (CNJ) issued Resolution No. 364, in 2021. This resolution recommends judges at all levels of the Brazilian judiciary to consider the IACtHR advisory opinions in their rulings. This recommendation reflects a growing recognition of the importance of 'transjudicial dialogue', where domestic courts engage with the jurisprudence of international human rights bodies. By encouraging judges to consider IACtHR pronouncements, the CNJ aims to ensure that Brazilian judicial decisions are informed by the latest interpretations of human rights law. For more information, see: https://atos.cnj.jus.br/atos/detalhar/3659.

79 *Request for an Advisory Opinion submitted by Colombia and Chile* 9 January 2023, IACtHR. See Mayer (n 16) 46.

the Court has established a precedent of recognizing the interconnectedness of human rights and environmental protection. This approach could lead to innovative interpretations of international law, such as the principle of common but differentiated responsibilities.

The request for an advisory opinion also presents a significant opportunity to deepen judicial dialogue between the STF and the IACtHR. This landmark decision offers a comprehensive framework for understanding the relationship between climate change and human rights, providing a rich source of legal reasoning for domestic courts grappling with climate litigation. In particular, the STF has the potential to employ inter-court dialogue as a strategy for developing a robust agenda of environmental and climate rights in Brazil. While it is premature to assess the full impact of the advisory opinion on environmental rights within the Brazilian legal framework, the efforts of the justices to foster connections with international courts are commendable.

# CHAPTER 7 Appendix

## Figures

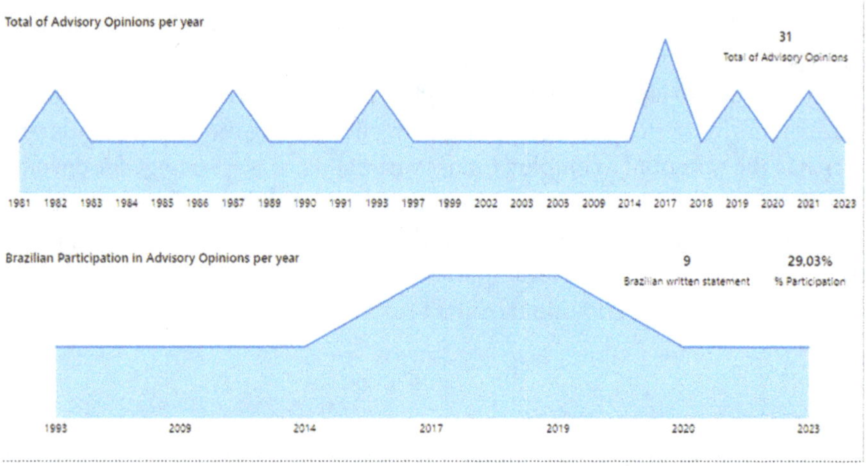


FIGURE 7.3 Brazilian participation in advisory opinions before the Inter-American Court of Human Rights

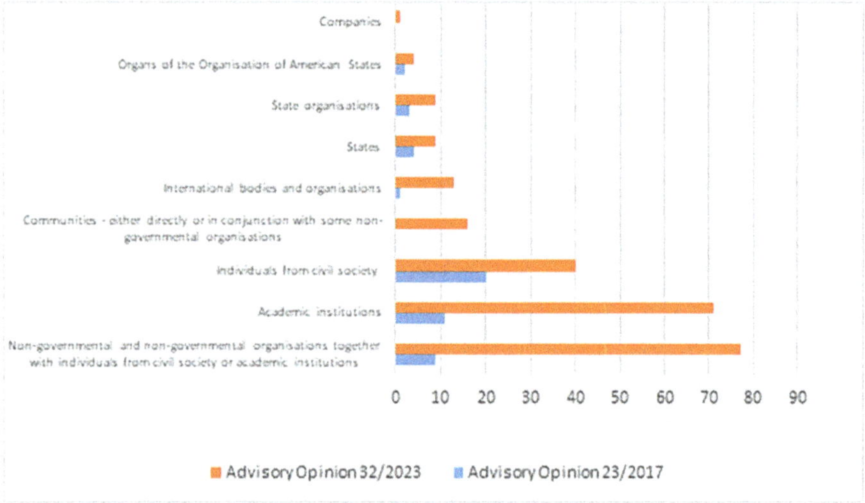


FIGURE 7.4 Comparative analysis of actors submitting *amicus curiae* to the Inter-American Court of Human Rights in advisory opinions 23/2017 and 32/2023

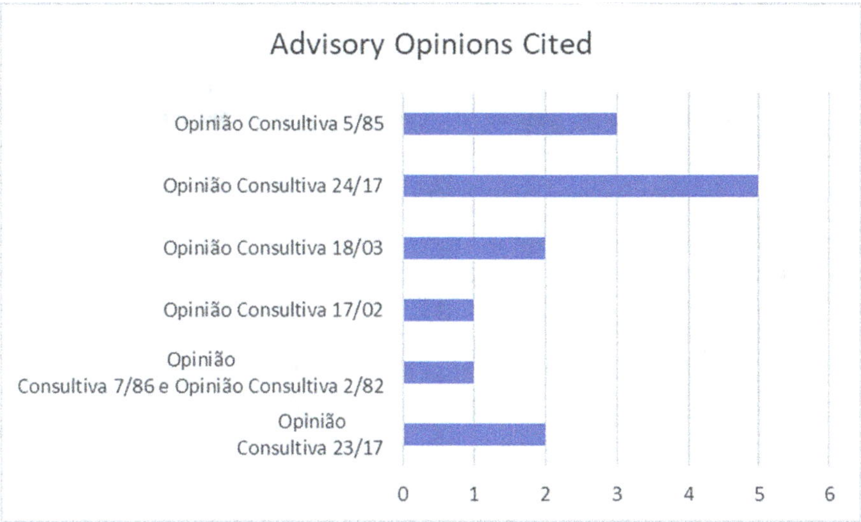


FIGURE 7.5 Inter-American Court of Human Rights' advisory opinions most cited in Brazilian supreme court's decisions

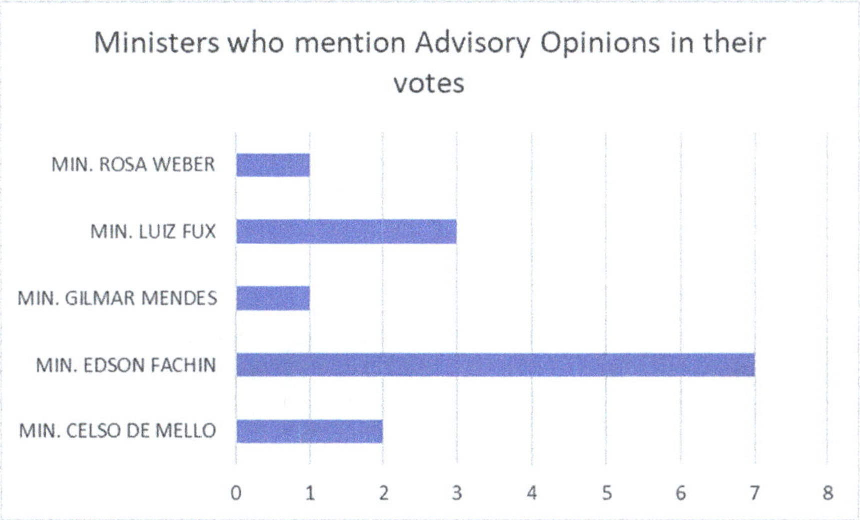


FIGURE 7.6 Judges from the Brazilian Supreme Court who mentioned the Inter-American Court of Human Rights' advisory opinions in their votes

## Tables

TABLE 7.1 State and non-State actors authorized to participate in ICJ advisory opinion on climate change based in the Article 66 of the statute of the court

| Actor | Type of actor | Composition | Date of acceptance |
|---|---|---|---|
| African Union | International Organization | Republic of Burundi; Republic of Cameroon; Central African Republic; Republic of Chad; Republic of the Congo; Republic of Equatorial Guinea; Gabonese Republic; Democratic Republic of São Tomé and Príncipe | 18/07/2023 |
| Alliance of Small Island States (AOSIS) | International Organization | Antigua and Barbuda; Bahamas; Barbados; Belize; Cuba; Dominica; Dominican Republic; Grenada; Guyana; Haiti; Jamaica; Saint Kitts and Nevis; Saint Lucia; Saint Vincent and the Grenadines; Suriname; Trinidad and Tobago; Cook Islands; Federated States of Micronesia; Fiji; Kiribati; Nauru; Niue; Palau; Papua New Guinea; Republic of the Marshall Islands; Samoa; Solomon Islands; Tonga; Tuvalu; Vanuatu; Cabo Verde; Comoros; Guinea Bissau; Maldives; Mauritius; Sao Tome and Principe; Seychelles; Singapore; Timor Leste | 20/12/2023 |
| Commission of Small Island States on Climate Change and International Law (COSIS) | International Organization | Antigua and Barbuda; Tuvalu; Palau; Niue; Vanuatu; ST. Lucia; ST Kitts and Nevis | 22/06/2023 |
| European Union (EU) | International Organization | Austria; Belgium; Bulgaria; Croatia; Cyprus; Czechia; Denmark; Estonia; Finland; France; Germany; Greece; Hungary; Ireland; Italy; Latvia; Lithuania; Luxembourg; Malta; Netherlands; Poland; Portugal; Romania; Slovakia; Slovenia; Spain; Sweden | 23/06/2023 |

TABLE 7.1 State and non-State actors authorized to participate in ICJ advisory opinion on climate change based in the Article 66 of the statute of the court (*cont.*)

| | | | |
|---|---|---|---|
| Forum Fisheries Agency (FFA) | International Organization | Cook Island; Federated States of Micronesia; Kiribati; Marshall Islands; Niue; | 20/09/2023 |
| International Union for Conservation of Nature (IUCN) | International Organization | 1,400 Members from over 170 countries | 14/06/2023 |
| Melanesian Spearhead Group (MSG) | International Organization | Fiji; Papua New Guinea; Front De Liberational De Nationale Kanak Et Solcialiste (FLNKS); Vanuatu; Solomon Islands; | 20/09/2023 |
| Organisation of African, Caribbean and Pacific States (OACPS) | International Organization | Angola, Antigua and Barbuda, Belize, Cape Verde, Comoros, Bahamas, Barbados, Benin, Botswana, Burkina Faso, Burundi, Cameroon, Central African Republic, Chad, Congo (Brazzaville), Congo (Kinshasa), Cook Islands, Côte d'Ivoire, Cuba, Djibouti, Dominica, Dominican Republic, Eritrea, Eswatini, Fiji, Gabon, Gambia, Ghana, Grenada, Republic of Guinea, Guinea-Bissau, Equatorial Guinea, Guyana, Haiti, Jamaica, Kenya, Kiribati, Lesotho, Liberia, Madagascar, Malawi, Maldives, Mali, Marshall Islands, Mauritania, Mauritius, Micronesia, Mozambique, Namibia, Nauru, Niger, Nigeria, Niue, Palau, Papua New Guinea, Rwanda, St. Kitts and Nevis, St. Lucia, St. Vincent and the Grenadines, Solomon Islands, Samoa, São Tomé and Príncipe, Senegal, Seychelles, Sierra Leone, Somalia, Sudan, Suriname, Tanzania, Timor Leste, Togo, Tonga, Trinidad and Tobago | 24/11/2023 |
| Organization of the Petroleum Exporting Countries (OPEC) | International Organization | Qatar; Indonesia; Libya; the United Arab Emirates; Algeria; Nigeria; Ecuador; Gabon; Angola; Equatorial Guinea; Congo | 01/09/2023 |

TABLE 7.1 State and non-State actors authorized to participate in ICJ advisory opinion on climate change based in the Article 66 of the statute of the court (*cont.*)

| | | | |
|---|---|---|---|
| Pacific Community | International Organization | American Somoa; Australia; Cook Island; Federated States of Micronesia; Fiji; France; French Polynesia; Guam; Kiribati; Marshall Islands; Nauru; New Caledonia; New Zealand; Niue; Northern Mariana Islands; Palau; Papua New Guinea; Piticairn Islands; Samoa; Solomon Islands; Tokelau; Tonga; Tuvalu; United Kingdom; United States of America; Vanuatu; Wallis and Futuna | 24/11/2023 |
| Pacific Islands Forum | International Organization | Australia; Cook Islands; Federated States of Micronesia; Fiji; French Polynesia; Kiribati; Nauru; New Caledonia; New Zealand; Niue; Palau; Papua New Guinea; Republic of Marshall Islands; Samoa; Solomon Islands; Tonga; Tuvalu; Vanuatu | 20/12/2023 |
| Parties to the Nauru Agreement Office (PNAO) | International Organization | Federated States of Micronesia; Kiribati; Marshall Islands; Nauru; Palau ; Papua New Guinea; Solomon Islands and Tuvalu; Tokelau. | 04/03/2024 |
| World Health Organization | United Nations Agency | All United Nations 193 states members | 26/03/2024 |

TABLE 7.2 Brazilian participation in ICJ advisory opinions

| Title | Introduction | Culmination | Status |
|---|---|---|---|
| Advisory Opinion | | | |
| Obligations of States in respect of Climate Change | 2023 | Pending | Pending |
| Legal Consequences arising from the Policies and Practices of Israel in the Occupied Palestinian Territory, including East Jerusalem | 2023 | Pending | Sent written statement |
| Legal Consequences of the Separation of the Chagos Archipelago from Mauritius in 1965 | 2017 | 2019 | Sent written statement |

TABLE 7.2 Brazilian participation in ICJ advisory opinions (*cont.*)

| | | | |
|---|---|---|---|
| Judgment No.2867 of the Administrative Tribunal of the International Labour Organization upon a Complaint Filed against the International Fund for Agricultural Development | 2010 | 2012 | Didn't send any written or oral statement |
| Accordance with international law of the unilateral declaration of independence in respect of Kosovo | 2008 | 2010 | send written statement |
| Legal Consequences of the Construction of a Wall in the Occupied Palestinian Territory | 2003 | 2004 | send written statement |
| Difference Relating to Immunity from Legal Process of a Special Rapporteur of the Commission on Human Rights | 1998 | 1999 | Didn't send any written or oral statement |
| Legality of the Use by a State of Nuclear Weapons in Armed Conflict | 1993 | 1996 | Didn't send any written or oral statement |
| Legality of the Threat or Use of Nuclear Weapons | 1995 | 1996 | Didn't send any written or oral statement |
| Applicability of Article VI, Section 22, of the Convention on the Privileges and Immunities of the United Nations | 1989 | 1989 | Didn't send any written or oral statement |
| Applicability of the Obligation to Arbitrate under Section 21 of the United Nations Headquarters Agreement of 26 June 1947 | 1988 | 1988 | Didn't send any written or oral statement |
| Application for Review of Judgment No. 333 of the United Nations Administrative Tribunal | 1984 | 1987 | Didn't send any written or oral statement |
| Application for Review of Judgment No. 273 of the United Nations Administrative Tribunal | 1981 | 1982 | Didn't send any written or oral statement |
| Interpretation of the Agreement of 25 March 1951 between the WHO and Egypt | 1980 | 1980 | Didn't send any written or oral statement |
| Western Sahara | 1974 | 1975 | Quoted in written procedures |

TABLE 7.2 Brazilian participation in ICJ advisory opinions (*cont.*)

| | | | |
|---|---|---|---|
| Application for Review of Judgment No. 158 of the United Nations Administrative Tribunal | 1972 | 1973 | Didn't send any written or oral statement |
| Legal Consequences for States of the Continued Presence of South Africa in Namibia (South West Africa) notwithstanding Security Council Resolution 276 (1970) | 1970 | 1971 | Didn't send any written or oral statement |
| Certain Expenses of the United Nations (Article 17, paragraph 2, of the Charter) | 1961 | 1962 | Didn't send any written or oral statement |
| Constitution of the Maritime Safety Committee of the Inter-Governmental Maritime Consultative Organization | 1959 | 1960 | quoted in written procedures |
| Admissibility of Hearings of Petitioners by the Committee on South West Africa | 1955 | 1956 | Didn't send any written or oral statement |
| Judgments of the Administrative Tribunal of the ILO upon Complaints Made against UNESCO | 1955 | 1956 | Didn't send any written or oral statement |
| Voting Procedure on Questions relating to Reports and Petitions concerning the Territory of South West Africa | 1954 | 1955 | Didn't send any written or oral statement |
| Effect of Awards of Compensation Made by the United Nations Administrative Tribunal | 1953 | 1954 | Quoted in written procedures |
| Reservations to the Convention on the Prevention and Punishment of the Crime of Genocide | 1950 | 1951 | Quoted in written procedures |
| Competence of the General Assembly for the Admission of a State to the United Nations | 1949 | 1950 | Sent written statement |
| International Status of South West Africa | 1949 | 1950 | Quoted in write statement and oral proceedings |

TABLE 7.2 Brazilian participation in ICJ advisory opinions (*cont.*)

| | | | |
|---|---|---|---|
| Interpretation of Peace Treaties with Bulgaria, Hungary and Romania | 1949 | 1950 | Didn't send any written or oral statement |
| Reparation for Injuries Suffered in the Service of the United Nations | 1948 | 1949 | Didn't send any written or oral statement |
| Conditions of Admission of a State to Membership in the United Nations (Article 4 of the Charter) | 1947 | 1948 | Quoted in oral statements |
| CONTENTIOUS CASES | | | |
| Certain Questions concerning Diplomatic Relations (Honduras v. Brazil) | 2009 | | Discontinued |

TABLE 7.3 List of Brazilian participation in Inter-American Court of Human Rights

| Title | Year | Brazil participation |
|---|---|---|
| Differentiated approaches to people deprived of their liberty OC-29/22 | 2019 | Brazil sent a written statement |
| The Human Rights Obligations Of A State That Has Denounced The American Convention On Human Rights And Tries To Withdraw From The Oea- Oc-26/20 | 2019 | Brazil sent a written statement |
| Gender identity and equality and non-discrimination of same-sex couples. State obligations in relation to name change, gender identity and rights arising from a same-sex relationship OC-24/17 | 2017 | Brazil sent a written statement |
| Rights and guarantees of children in the context of migration and/or in need of international protection. OC-21/14 | 2014 | Brazil took part in the submission |
| Article 55 of the American Convention on Human Rights. Advisory Opinion OC-20/09 | 2009 | Brazil sent a written statement |
| International Liability for Issuance and Enforcement of Laws Violating the Convention Oc-14/94 | 1993 | Brazil sent a written statement |

TABLE 7.4 List of ICJ contentious cases and advisory opinions mentioned in decisions by the Brazilian Supreme Court

| Reporting judge | Date of judgement | Date published | Place of mention | Advisory opinion | Contentious | Judge who mentioned it |
|---|---|---|---|---|---|---|
| Min.Marco Aurelio | 10/09/2003 | 03/09/2004 | Vote | | Nottebohm (Liechtenstein v. Guatemala) | Min. Marco Aurelio |
| Min.Edson Fachin | 01/03/2021 | 23/08/2021 | Docket | | Jurisdictional Immunities of the State (Germany v. Italy: Greece intervening) | |
| Min.Edson Fachin | 01/03/2021 | 23/08/2021 | Report | | Jurisdictional Immunities of the State (Germany v. Italy: Greece intervening) | |
| Min.Edson Fachin | 01/03/2021 | 23/08/2021 | Vote | | Jurisdictional Immunities of the State (Germany v. Italy: Greece intervening) | Min.Edson Fachin |
| Min.Edson Fachin | 01/03/2021 | 23/08/2021 | Vote | | Jurisdictional Immunities of the State (Germany v. Italy: Greece intervening) | Min. Gilmar Mendes |
| Min.Edson Fachin | 01/03/2021 | 23/08/2021 | Vote | | Jurisdictional Immunities of the State (Germany v. Italy: Greece intervening) | Min. Marco Aurelio |
| Min.Edson Fachin | 01/03/2021 | 23/08/2021 | Vote | | Jurisdictional Immunities of the State (Germany v. Italy: Greece intervening) | Min. Alexandre De Moraes |
| Min. Ricardo Lewandowski | 08/05/2012 | 24/09/2012 | Report | | Democratic Republic of the Congo v. Belgium, | |

TABLE 7.4 List of ICJ contentious cases and advisory opinions mentioned in decisions by the Brazilian Supreme Court (*cont.*)

| | | | | | | |
|---|---|---|---|---|---|---|
| Min. Ricardo Lewandowski | 08/05/2012 | 24/09/2012 | Vote | | Democratic Republic of the Congo v. Belgium, | Min. Ricardo Lewandowski |
| Min. Gilmar Mendes | 08/06/2011 | 05/10/2011 | Vote | Legal Consequences for States of the Continued Presence of South Africa in Namibia (South West Africa) notwithstanding Security Council Resolution 276 (1970) | | Min. Gilmar Mendes |
| Min. Edson Fachin | 11/10/2017 | 07/08/2018 | Vote | | Islamic Republic of Iran v. United States of America | Min. Alexandre De Moraes |
| Min. Cezar Peluso | 03/12/2008 | 05/06/2009 | Vote | Legal Consequences for States of the Continued Presence os South África in Namíbia (South West África) | | Min.Gilmar Mendes |

TABLE 7.4 List of ICJ contentious cases and advisory opinions mentioned in decisions by the Brazilian Supreme Court (*cont.*)

| Min. Edson Fachin | 29/09/2020 | 13/06/2019 | Vote | | Republic of Guinea v. Democratic Republic of the Congo | Min. Edson Fachin |
|---|---|---|---|---|---|---|
| Min. Edson Fachin | 09/11/2016 | 27/08/2018 | Vote | | Jurisdictional Immunities of the State (Germany v. Italy: Greece intervening) | Min. Edson Fachin |
| Min. Celso De Mello | 13/06/2019 | 06/10/2020 | Vote | | Ahmadou Sadio Diallo (Republic of Guinea v. Democratic Republic of the Congo) | Min. Edson Fachin |

CHAPTER 8

# Access to Justice and Climate Litigation in Brazil

*Luciana Gross Cunha* and Maria Cecília de Araujo Asperti***

## 1 Introduction

Climate litigation is usually associated with initiatives to resort to court to hold public and private entities accountable for the present consequences of climate change and demand mitigation and adaptation measures.[1] Experiences worldwide account for both practical and symbolic effects, as well as strategic possibilities for fostering economic and political changes through litigation.[2] Commonly cited examples, such as *Urgenda v Netherlands*,[3] *Colombian Citizens v Ministry of Environment*,[4] or *Leghari v Pakistan*,[5] are claims aimed at imposing targets for reducing States' GHG emissions or rates of deforestation, or even at demanding from the government the implementation of existing policies. These examples show that courts may become an arena to discuss, revise, implement, and monitor goals and plans related to climate change.[6]

Brazil is becoming a key player in climate change litigation. According to the Sabin Center's Global Climate Change Litigation report on climate change litigation in the Global South, 39% of the overall cases were filed before Brazilian courts.[7] Among several other paradigmatic climate litigation cases

* Fundação Getúlio Vargas, São Paulo School of Law, https://orcid.org/0000-0002-7396-1879.

** Fundação Getúlio Vargas, São Paulo School of Law, https://orcid.org/0000-0001-5945-9455.

1 Conectas Direitos Humanos, *Guia de Litigância Climática* (Conectas Direitos Humanos 2019) 12–18.

2 ibid; Catarina Vallejo & Siri Gloppen, 'A Busca pelo Efeito Borboleta na Litigância Climática', in Garavito (ed), *Litigar a Emergência Climática* (Editora FGV 2022) 165–184.

3 *Stichting Urgenda v State of the Netherlands*, ECLI:NL:HR:2019:2007, Hoge Raad, 19/00135, Supreme Court, Judgment of 20 December 2019.

4 *Liliana Andrea García Ávila et al v Ministerio de Ambiente y Desarrollo et al*, Process No 25000 2341 000 2023 00614 00, Administrative Court of Cundinamarca, Judgment of 7 July 2023.

5 *Asghar Leghari v Federation of Pakistan*, Process No WP 25501/201, Supreme Court, Judgment of 25 January 2018.

6 Conectas (n 1) 19–21. For the use of courts for pressuring States to pursue climate goals, see generally Armando Rocha, 'Suing States—The Role of Courts in Promoting States' Responsibility for Climate Change', in Garcia & Cortês (eds), *Blue Planet Law* (Springer 2023) 99.

7 Maria Antonia Tigre, 'Climate Litigation in the Global South: Mapping Report' (Sabin Center for Climate Change Law 2024) 2–3. The report also informs that of the 2,629 cases of the database (as of April 2024), Global South cases represent only 8.3% of cases.

 | DOI:10.1163/9789004690974_009

(further discussed in Section 2), two recent Federal Supreme Court (STF) cases are worth mentioning. Firstly, the ruling in which the court recognized the Federal Union's omission by not fully allocating funds to the '*Fundo Nacional sobre Mudança do Clima*' (National Climate Change Fund) and ordered the federal government to take the necessary steps for its operation, with the consequent allocation of resources.[8] Also, concerning the '*Fundo Amazônia*' (Amazon Fund), the STF ordered the adoption of measures for its reactivation and the invalidation of decrees that had changed its format, preventing the financing of new projects.[9] These rulings have a substantive political impact, as they come from the highest court in the Brazilian judiciary and express its views regarding the State's obligation to finance policies and measures on climate mitigation and adaptation.

As climate litigation gains greater resonance in institutional and academic debates, disasters related to climate change are becoming more frequent and with increasingly severe impacts, especially when it comes to vulnerable populations or those in situations of risk. It is no coincidence that lawsuits seeking accountability, remedies, and the protection of rights for vulnerable populations or those at risk are also becoming more common. Vulnerability is one of the keywords in climate litigation globally, and, unsurprisingly, also in Brazil. Alongside individual claims for remedy (usually more focused on monetary compensation), there are numerous and complex class actions filed by the Public Prosecutor's and the Public Defender's offices, both holding legal standing according to Brazilian legislation; and filed by civil society organizations, to primarily demand the redress of social, economic, and environmental damages, but also preventive measures through the implementation of public policies related to risk reduction and impact mitigation.

Disasters have been the subject of academic and technical studies for some time. In the field of social sciences, the sociology of disasters has focused on the development of concepts specific to disasters. In the legal field, recent research has mobilized the idea of creating a cluster of studies and teaching dedicated to 'Disaster Law,' which encompasses measures arising from ways to guarantee the rights of individuals and the environment that are somehow affected by disasters. Thus, terms such as 'affected individuals,' 'social, economic, and political vulnerabilities caused by disasters and risks,' 'environmental and climate racism,' 'environmental and climate refugees,' or 'responsibility' are

8 *PSB et al v Brazil* (*on Climate Fund*) ADPF 708, 7 January 2022, available at <https://climatecasechart.com/non-us-case/psb-et-al-v-federal-union/>.

9 *PSB et al v Brazil* (*on Amazon Fund*) ADO 59, 16 August 2023, available at <https://climatecasechart.com/non-us-case/psb-et-al-v-brazil/>.

increasingly discussed in academic and scientific circles. In some way, this literature appropriates and reinforces typical concepts of climate justice to portray the effects of disasters, especially those resulting from extreme climate events.[10]

Furthermore, the mechanisms presented by climate justice, through climate litigation, to safeguard rights and hold accountable those directly and indirectly responsible for climate-related events are closely aligned with measures already identified in the literature for dealing with disasters. For example, these mechanisms include climate risk assessment, adaptation, mitigation, and accountability, which, in the case of disasters, correspond to the disaster risk management cycle, comprising stages such as prevention and mitigation, response, compensation, and reconstruction.[11]

Another issue that links studies on disasters and climate justice (with an emphasis on the idea of 'access to justice') is the centrality and participation of vulnerable individuals—who suffer the most drastic effects of disasters and climate change—in defining, constructing, and implementing appropriate measures in response to these phenomena.[12]

Thus, for the purposes of this chapter, and with the aim of further bridging the fields, we consider disasters resulting from extreme weather events as *climate disasters*, which enables us to leverage the concepts and analytical frameworks developed from the perspective of both fields of knowledge. This also broadens the discussion on strategies and effects of climate litigation, as we could consider the judicialization of issues related to climate disasters as

---

10 Norma Valencio & Mariana Siena (eds), *Sociologia dos Desastres—Construção, Interfaces e Perspectivas no Brasil* (RiMa Editora 2009). To delve deeper into the discussion about disaster law in Brazil, see Délton Winter de Carvalho & Fernanda Dalla Libera Damacena, *Direito dos Desastres* (Livraria do Advogado 2013); Délton Winter de Carvalho & Fernanda Dalla Libera Damacena, 'A intensificação dos desastres naturais, as mudanças climáticas e o papel do Direito Ambiental' (2012) 49 *RIL* 83 97; Tiago Fensterseifer, 'A Responsabilidade do Estado Pelos Danos Causados às Pessoas Atingidas Pelos Desastres Ambientais Associados às Mudanças Climáticas: Uma Análise à Luz dos Deveres de Proteção Ambiental do Estado e da Proibição de Insuficiência na Tutela do Direito Fundamental ao Ambiente' (2011) 13 *Opinião Jurídica* 322 354; Mariana P Leitão, *Desastres Ambientais, Resiliência e a Responsabilidade Civil* (Lumens Juris 2018).

11 Daniel Farber, 'Catastrophic Risk, Climate Change, and Disaster Law' (2013) 16 *Asia Pacific Journal of Env'l Law* 37.

12 Fundação Getúlio Vargas, *Parâmetros para uma Abordagem Baseada em Direitos Humanos para a Resposta e Reconstrução Envolvendo Empresas* (FGV 2019) available at <https://repositorio.fgv.br/items/bb940f5b-90bd-4d00-9d02-b9432c1852e5> accessed 14 June 2024.

examples of what has conventionally been termed expressions of so-called climate litigation.

The goal is to discuss access to justice in climate litigation cases, especially in climate disasters, and the need to pay greater attention to the centrality and participation of those whose rights have been, or may be, violated. Mapping out who has access to courts and their claims can help understand how climate justice, and more specifically climate disasters, are addressed in the 'Brazilian justice system'—an expression used here in a broad sense to refer to institutions such as courts, the Public Prosecutor's Office and the Public Defender's Office[13]—to hold State agencies, private companies, or individuals accountable for their respective omissions or activities that have contributed to such events.

For climate litigation, lawsuits may aim at holding parties accountable for mitigation and/or reducing vulnerability, assessing and managing climate risks, repairing damages, as well as reducing or halting GHG emissions.[14] As previously indicated, these objectives may also involve claims related to disaster risk management and post-disaster remedies. To assess cases related to the pursuit of these goals, this chapter utilizes the database produced and made available by the JUMA Climate Litigation Platform ("JUMA a Platform"), which catalogs cases concerning climate-related issues.[15] Based on this data, this chapter systematizes the main characteristics of this kind of litigation according to the following metrics: (1) who is resorting to the judiciary, (2) which institutions of the justice system are involved, (3) what themes are being addressed, and (4) which cases are more linked to prevention and reconstruction in cases of climate disasters. As further detailed, data shows the role of the justice system in climate litigation in Brazil and highlights that, although climate disasters are becoming increasingly frequent in Brazil, the debate on climate change is not yet commonly featured in lawsuits addressing risk management and reparation in these cases.

Finally, to analyze central issues regarding access to justice for communities affected by climate disasters based on the roles of Brazilian justice system

---

13 Other agents and institutions (such as lawyers, the police, and registries) could also be included as part of the justice system (Maria Tereza Sadek, 'O Sistema de Justiça, in Sadek (ed), *O Sistema de Justiça* (Centro Edelstein de Pesquisas Sociais 2010) 9–10), but since the focus of this chapter is on access to justice in climate disaster cases, courts, the Public Prosecutor's Office, and the Public Defender's Office are the key players to discuss the demands for rights of those affected by disaster and climate change.

14 Conectas (n 1).

15 JUMA, *Grupo de Pesquisa Direito, Ambiente e Justiça no Antropoceno* (2024), available at <https://litigancia.biobd.inf.puc-rio.br> accessed 26 September 2024.

institutions, this chapter resorts to the study developed by the Fundação Getulio Vargas research group on Access to Justice, Disasters and Climate Change[16] to draw some of the parameters suggested to enhance the participation of affected communities and prioritize the centrality of affected individuals and address vulnerabilities in these cases.

## 2 Access to Justice and Climate Litigation in Brazil

In 2023, Brazil experienced a record number of climate disasters. According to the *Centro Nacional de Monitoramento e Alertas de Desastres Naturais*,[17] 1161 events were identified, with 716 occurrences linked to hydrological events and 445 cases of geological origin, such as landslides, not to mention the drought that affected the state of Amazonas in 2023. Regarding the effects of heavy rains, these events resulted in 132 deaths, leaving 9.2 thousand injured, 74.7 thousand homeless, and 525 thousand displaced persons.[18]

As populations increasingly feel the effects of global warming, there is a growing mobilization of different actors aiming to resort to national and international courts to seek recognition of the right to a sustainable environment, as well as accountability for GHG emissions and their climate consequences.

The JUMA Platform is a database with information on judicial proceedings directly or indirectly related to climate change.[19] This database does not include all cases in Brazilian courts that in any way concern environmental law or even climate-related issues: its scope is defined by cases considered paradigmatic, with media and academic repercussions, and that have the potential to contribute effectively to the development of climate litigation in Brazil.[20] For the

16 FGV DIREITO SP NAJUPMESC, *Protocolo Acesso à Justiça e Desastres: Recomendações Elaboradas para o Sistema de Justiça para Atuação em Casos de Desastres* (2023), available at <https://repositorio.fgv.br/items/616abe6c-b517-41de-be38-3023be78e7ad> accessed 30 March 2024.

17 CEMADEM—National Center for Monitoring and Alerts of Natural Disasters, an agency of the Ministry of Science, Technology, and Innovation.

18 CEMADEM (2024), *Reunião de Impactos do CEMADEM: Avaliação e Previsão de Impactos de Extremos de Origem Hidro-geo-climático em Atividades Estratégicas para o Brasil* (2024), available at <https://www.gov.br/cemaden/pt-br/assuntos/monitoramento/boletim-de-impactos/boletim-de-impactos-de-extremos-de-origem-hidro-geo-climatico-em-atividades-estrategicas-para-o-brasil-2013-17-01-2024-ano-07-no-62/62-reuniao-impactos-janeiro-2024.pdf/view> accessed 30 March 2024.

19 JUMA (n 15)

20 Danielle de Andrade Moreira (ed), *Plataforma de Litigância Climática no Brasil: Metodologia para Seleção e Categorização de Casos Climáticos Brasileiros* (Lucas Melara 2022) 5.

selection of judicial proceedings, the JUMA Platform defines climate justice as the recognition that the impacts generated by climate change affect different social groups in diverse ways, intensifying inequalities between those who produce the effects of climate change and those who are severely impacted by them.[21] Lawsuits in this database were filed before the Brazilian judiciary, namely (federated) state courts, federal courts, and higher courts (the Superior Court of Justice, STJ, and the Federal Supreme Court, STF).

As of March 2024, there was a total of 80 cases, which were compiled and further examined in terms of the involved parties, key issues, whether claims were somehow related to the field of disaster law—if they mentioned disaster events, claims for prevention, mitigation, response, reconstruction or rehabilitation—, and whether the focus was set in prevention and/or adaptation measures.[22]

Overall, there were 50 cases classified as '*Ações Civis Públicas*' (a type of class action) filed by one of the entities that hold legal standing according to the Public Civil Actions Law (Law No 7.347/1978) and the Consumer Protection Code (Law No 8.078/1990): i.e. the Public Prosecutor's Office, the Public Defender's Office, public entities of the Union (i.e. the Federal State), (federated States), Municipalities, and the Federal District, as well as civil society associations (provided that these latter have been established for at least one year and include in their institutional purposes the defense of collective rights).[23]

These class actions underscore the importance of the role played by justice system institutions in climate litigation in Brazil. Of the total cases, the Public Prosecutor's Office was involved in 22 cases, while the Public Defender's Office was involved in 5 cases. Civil society organizations are also important players, as they were involved in 12 cases.

Such lawsuits primarily deal with environmental issues, seeking injunctive relief to cease deforestation practices and construction of buildings causing environmental damage. There are also cases seeking to hold private companies and individuals accountable for environmental damages. When filed against the government, these lawsuits request the cancellation of licenses and authorizations for activities causing environmental damage, the suspension of legislation that relaxes rules on forest protection, conducting environmental

21 ibid 13.

22 See Danielle de Andrade Moreira (Chapter 2).

23 1978 Public Civil Actions Law 7947 (Brazil); 1990 Consumer Protection Code Law 8078 (Brazil).

impact studies, implementing policies to reduce air pollution and deforestation in the Amazon, and the publication of data on such deforestation.

In addition, there are four cases of '*Ações Populares*,' also considered class actions but which can be filed by citizens challenging the validity of acts deemed harmful to public assets.[24] These are cases in which the citizen plaintiffs question the validity of governmental acts such as the licensing of mining projects, raising concerns about the exacerbation of climate events resulting from them; a State program incentivizing the automotive industry; a normative act that mandated the reduction of the mandatory blend level of biodiesel in diesel oil; and the submission by the federal government, in 2020, of a NDC less ambitious than the previous one presented in 2015, in violation of Article 4(3) of the Paris Agreement. While these initiatives are quantitatively fewer, they represent significant mobilization by civil society organizations and activist groups in using litigation as a mechanism to pressure the government to adopt climate commitments in its public policies.

Although the analysis of cases compiled by the JUMA Platform demonstrates consistent and varied initiatives of mobilization by justice system institutions and civil society organizations in terms of climate litigation, there are few cases involving climate adaptation. Such results are aligned with overall data from climate litigation in the Global South, where 77,8% of cases were classified by the Sabin Center as related to climate mitigation and only 18.1% to climate adaptation actions.[25]

Regarding disaster risk management, adaptation, and mitigation initiatives are fundamental components to reducing the possibility of harm. When considering climate-related natural disasters, which are increasingly more frequent, implementing adaptation measures is urgent and necessary. Despite this, among the class actions qualified in this database as climate litigation, we identified only five actions addressing adaptation initiatives: one requesting the removal of constructions from environmentally protected areas;[26] one action requesting studies of urban impacts prior to granting licenses for the construction of large-scale residential and commercial buildings;[27] two constitutional actions before the STF demanding the government to present and implement policies to prevent fires in the Pantanal and Amazon rainforest, and establish a

24 1965 Popular Action Law No 4717 (Brazil).

25 Tigre (n 7) 19. The 4.1% of the remaining cases are related to loss and damage.

26 *Public Prosecutor's Office of the State of Rio de Janeiro v Niterói (Neighborhood Impact Study)* ACP No 0006155-57.2013.8.19.0002, filed on 31 January 2013 before the Civil Court of Niterói.

27 *Federal Public Prosecutor's Office v Brazil et al (Sea advance and coastal erosion)* ACP No 0800002-72.2014.4.05.8502, filed on 29 January 2024 before the Sergipe 5th Federal Court.

public health and veterinary medical treatment project in the region;[28] and one class action regarding the suspension of the licensing process of the Guaíba Mine Project, which includes a request for the preparation of an emergency action plan aimed at mitigating the consequences of potential environmental damage.[29] None of these cases specifically address the normative framework or legal and technical concepts related to disaster risk reduction, nor do they discuss extreme weather events resulting in disasters, which have been increasing drastically in recent years.

These results show that, when it comes to litigation, the agendas of climate litigation and disasters are not fully aligned. On the one hand, climate litigation rarely discusses risk reduction and remedy measures related to disasters. On the other hand, cases related to disasters are not compiled in the JUMA database, since they rarely incorporate the climate change agenda. However, strategies concerning climate change litigation can (and should) address claims related to risk management and recovery, especially considering the reality of the most climate-vulnerable communities in the Global South.

In terms of the disasters' risk management cycle, the stage of preparedness is closely linked with the idea of climate adaptation, and may include measures in locations already affected by climate change-related events in order to avoid or mitigate negative impacts or to compel the government to develop legal instruments and plans to deal with changes in rainfall patterns, more frequent droughts, and rising sea levels.[30] These measures, which can be the subject of climate litigation, are also extremely relevant in disaster litigation, particularly concerning claims to prevent future or recurrent damages in locations that are more vulnerable to climate change-related events. Also, in terms of climate adaptation, it is possible to seek measures for urban planning or environmental preservation policies, such as in lawsuits demanding the review of environmental licensing processes or actions to combat deforestation.

Regarding the response and recovery stages in disasters' risk management cycle, they should also influence urgent climate litigation strategies. Claims may address the liability of those who contributed to or omitted action regarding the occurrence of the disaster accountable for urgent measures and to provide full remedy to all social, economic, and environmental damages.

Most importantly, both fields recognize the protection of vulnerable populations, who are most affected both by the direct effects of climate change and

28 *PSL et al v Brazil et al* (*Pantanal Wildfires*) ADPF 857, filed on 22 June 2021 before the STF.

29 *Arayara v Copelmi Mineração et al* (*on hydrological risks*) ACP 5069057-47.2019.4.04.710, filed on 10 September 2020 before the Court of Justice of Rio Grande do Sul.

30 Conectas (n 1) 33, 46.

in disaster cases. Once these issues are more closely bridged, victims will certainly benefit from claims that will better address the consequences of climate change in their territories and livelihoods, facilitating their access to justice and the defense and guarantee of their rights.

## 3 Justice System and Access to Justice in Cases of Climate Disasters

The justice system plays a leading role in Brazil both in climate litigation, as seen in Section 2, and disaster litigation, including climate change-related disasters. The Public Prosecutor's Office and the Public Defender's Office are key players in seeking the implementation and/or changes of public policies aimed at disaster risk management, and in demanding from governments and companies an appropriate response, reconstruction, and rehabilitation of affected communities. These justice system institutions are also called upon to act in judicial actions brought by the government in cases of forced eviction motivated by risk evaluations, and they become invested in representing the interests of affected individuals to ensure their minimum rights in risk eviction proceedings. These entities also engage in out-of-court negotiations, administrative procedures, and '*Compromissos de Ajustamento de Conduta*,' i.e., conduct adjustment agreements, which hold executive force and coercive power according to Brazilian law.[31]

Concerning disaster litigation, most cases are class actions brought by the Public Prosecutor's Office and/or the Public Defender's Office, sometimes alongside civil society organizations, as also seen in climate litigation cases. These are often cases of structural litigation,[32] in which courts assume a significant role in technical and legal discussions regarding the adequacy of existing public policies and the roles of governments and/or companies. Courts become a crucial forum to assess risk, causality, and liability, and evaluate and monitor risk management and recovery actions. As decision-making is, therefore, shifted from the political to the judicial arena, the justice system faces the challenge of ensuring appropriate and effective procedural mechanisms for the effective participation of civil society and, most importantly, of the affected communities.

Having this reality as a premise, the research group '*Acesso à Justiça, Desastres e Mudanças Climáticas*' of the São Paulo Law School of Fundação Getúlio Vargas developed the *Protocolo Acesso à Justiça e Desastres: Recomendações*

31 1978 Public Civil Actions Law No 7947, art 5(6).

32 Owen Fiss, 'The Forms of Justice' (1979) 93 *Harvard Law Review* 1.

*Elaboradas para o Sistema de Justiça para Atuação em Casos de Desastres* ('Access to Justice Protocol'),[33] which is a policy paper aimed at supporting justice system institutions with minimum standards that they ought to demand from governments and companies in terms of prevention and response, reconstruction, and remediation contexts of disasters.

The Access to Justice Protocol draws from the premise that these institutions play a pivotal role in cases of climate change-related disasters (as defined in Section 1) and in disasters not directly related to extreme events. This policy paper consolidates normative and empirical research addressing disaster cases in Brazil in recent years. This section addresses some of these recommendations and discusses their importance in terms of climate litigation.

The Access to Justice Protocol addresses concerns related to the access to justice of groups and individuals in situations at risk and affected by disasters and the need to ensure not only their participation but effectively their agency in terms of decision-making processes. To this end, the Access to Justice Protocol adopts as a cross-cutting premise the attention to vulnerabilities, drawing from the definition that disasters occur when hazardous events interact with conditions of exposure, vulnerability, and capacity.[34] Vulnerabilities are a constitutive element of the very concept of disaster, as well as a factor that determines the severity and seriousness of the resulting impacts and influences the entire process of seeking prevention and remedies. As emphasized in the protocol, the vulnerability of individuals and territories causes them to suffer more intensively the impacts of the disaster, while also imposing additional obstacles to full reparation.[35]

The focus on vulnerabilities is also aligned with the concept of climate justice, as the movement that recognizes that measures to contain climate change must take into account the need for responses and legal and institutional structures that consider the inequalities of conditions among countries and individuals, prioritizing the realization of the rights of vulnerable people.[36] Regarding access to justice, this same perspective should guide the actions of institutions within and outside the justice system involved in

33 FGV Direito SP NAJUPMESC (n 16).

34 United Nations Office for Disaster Risk Reduction, *Report of the Open-Ended Intergovernmental Expert Working Group on Indicators and Terminology relating to Disaster Risk Reduction* (UN Doc. No A/71/644, 2016), available at <https://www.preventionweb.net/publication/report-open-ended-intergovernmental-expert-working-group-indicators-and-terminology> accessed 30 March 2024.

35 FGV Direito SP NAJUPMESC (n 16) 16.

36 Andréia Coutinho Louback & Letícia Maria Lima (eds), *Quem Precisa de Justiça Climática no Brasil?* (Hivos 2022).

recognizing and guaranteeing the rights of people in vulnerable situations, and to what extent markers of inequality, such as race, class, and gender, impact these individuals' experiences with the justice system and their participation in conflict resolution.[37]

Reflecting on measures to strengthen access to justice for communities affected by extreme climate events, the Access to Justice Protocol outlines a set of recommendations aimed at enhancing participation and victim's centrality in decision-making processes, both in terms of pre-disaster prevention and preparedness (and in terms of climate mitigation and adaptation), and of post-disaster response, reconstruction, and rehabilitation. If followed by the institutions within the justice system, these recommendations are likely to enhance access to justice for vulnerable communities and affected individuals.

In this regard, the Access to Justice Protocol recommends greater attention to social participation in risk mapping through means such as municipal conferences and public hearings for the development of risk prevention, mitigation, and response plans.[38] Although in a phase prior to litigation *proprio sensu*, they inform the idea of a material or substantive access to justice. It is also necessary that risk mapping policies consider the specific risks arising from the climate crisis and that the population participates in collective training on climate resilience topics so they can effectively contribute to the planning of climate adaptation actions. Concrete experiences highlight the importance of community knowledge about the territory and its socio-environmental dynamics in these planning efforts.[39] Given the core premises of community participation and the victim's centrality, climate adaptation measures that do not comply with these standards may be subject to judicial scrutiny.

Although the *Arayara v Copelmi Mineração et al (on hydrological risks)* case does not mention specific concepts and regulations related to disaster risk management, it is, among the cases analyzed on the JUMA platform, the one that most closely relates to discussions on climate disasters, as it raises concerns about the development of an emergency plan to address potential damages caused by the mine's activities. The claim for the suspension of the licensing process is based precisely on the lack of participation from the affected community, arguing that the absence of public hearings in affected

---

37 Rebecca L Sandefur, 'Access to Civil Justice and Race, Class, and Gender Inequality' (2008) 34 *Annual Review of Sociology* 339, 358.

38 FGV Direito SP NAJUPMESC (n 16) Recommendation 14.

39 Instituto Pólis and Council of Architecture and Urbanism, *Plano Comunitário de Defesa Civil e Adaptação à Crise Climática da comunidade caiçara de Ponta Negra*, available at <https://polis.org.br/projeto/plano-comunitario-de-ponta-negra-rj/> accessed 29 March 2024.

communities would render the mine's prior licensing process null and void. There is, therefore, a clear concern with ensuring prior community participation in preventive and mitigating actions, which aligns with the recommendations of the Access to Justice Protocol.

The Access to Justice Protocol also emphasizes the importance that the population has access to transparent, expedited, and accessible information,[40] which includes information about the causes of the disaster, its consequences, and the preventive and remedial measures taken by governments and/or companies. Recommendations also address the need for regular meetings so that governments and companies can direct their efforts to meet community needs and be held accountable by affected individuals for their actions.[41] These meetings are particularly important in the context of climate change-related disasters, given the recurrence of extreme events in the territory, such as floods, droughts, extreme temperatures (including heatwaves), and forest fires. The cyclical nature of these events and their increasing recurrence reinforce the need for constant dialogue with the community so that adequate measures are implemented and constantly reassessed.

To ensure adequate and effective participation in the judicial arena and out-of-court reparation programs and grievance mechanisms, affected populations must have access not only to legal services but also other forms of interdisciplinary and independent technical support. This is addressed in Recommendation No 32 of the Access to Justice Protocol, which explains the roles, guidelines, and some of the characteristics of the work carried out by this kind of organization in disaster cases. Victims and the justice system may demand that the State or companies finance these services in climate litigation cases, assuring that the community chooses which organization should be hired and defines its specific scope. Organizations that work with disasters' technical support usually engage in community mobilization, capacity building, and translation of legal documents and may also issue technical reports, provide support in negotiations for agreements, conduct damage assessments, and monitor and refer emergency cases, among others.

Participation also requires appropriate mechanisms to engage the affected communities in negotiations, agreements, and other decision-making processes.[42] Beyond the usual public hearings, complex climate-change-related disaster cases demand the design and implementation of specific governance structures, with permanent advisory and decision-making bodies

40 FGV Direito SP NAJUPMESC (n 16) Recommendation 21.

41 FGV Direito SP NAJUPMESC (n 16) Recommendations 22 and 23.

42 FGV Direito SP NAJUPMESC (n 16) Recommendation 35.

involving both public and private entities, and primarily the affected communities themselves—hence the importance of the mobilization and advisory activities carried out by technical support organizations. Whatever participatory arrangement is adopted, it is crucial that justice institutions, when representing affected communities, do not enter into agreements without their prior participation and final consent.

Finally, the measures outlined here require the strengthening and equipping of the justice system to address the claims associated with disasters,[43] including the need for training, data management, internal regulations, and coordination among various stakeholders—such as the Public Prosecutor's Office, Public Defender's Office, Brazilian Bar Association, and Civil Defense—through the creation of working groups for joint and coordinated action. As seen, these institutions play a crucial role in facilitating access to justice for the affected communities and in litigating rights related to climate change and disasters. It is interesting to reflect on how this increased engagement of these institutions in the climate agenda can also contribute to bridging the gap between the fields of disasters and climate justice, with greater attention to prevention, adaptation, and reparation measures in cases of disasters resulting from extreme climate change-related events.

## 4 Conclusions

The climate litigation upsurge in Brazil is leading to the creation and operationalization of new concepts and meanings aimed at mitigating and adapting to climate change while holding public and private actors accountable for their contribution to global warming. In the field of climate change-related disasters, the intensity and increased frequency of events and their impacts have drawn academic attention and mobilized the justice system through litigation aimed at holding involved parties accountable, recognizing and ensuring the rights of affected vulnerable populations, and recovering affected areas.

This chapter argues that the two fields—climate litigation and disaster law—share common approaches that range from focusing on the centrality of vulnerable people most affected by climate change and extreme weather events to the management stages of these phenomena. Also, in terms of access to justice, as well as access to the institutions of the justice system and their role in recognizing and ensuring the rights of vulnerable populations and a

43 FGV Direito SP NAJUPMESC (n 16) Recommendation 44.

healthier environment, their perspectives are remarkably similar. Thus, the importance of climate and disaster litigation and the role of civil society and justice system institutions in addressing these cases also suggest that both fields can and should be integrated.

The joint operationalization of the concepts and tools of both areas contributes to enhancing responses to climate change and the disaster management cycle, reducing their impact. When climate litigation addresses concerns related to disaster risk management, it mobilizes increasingly necessary adaptation measures based on parameters already established by the field of disaster law.

This chapter analyzed the JUMA database on climate litigation in Brazil and concluded that few cases deal with the stages of the disasters' risk management cycle, as their objectives are much more linked to responding to the effects of global warming, rather than to the preparation, adaptation, and mitigation stages aimed at reducing the effects related to climate change.

Data from the JUMA platform also indicates the protagonism of the justice system institutions in the legal mobilization against global warming, which connects with FGV's *Access to Justice Protocol*. This document contains recommendations for the Public Prosecutor's Office, the Public Defender's Office, and courts, to act in response, reconstruction, and reparation in disasters' contexts, considering the centrality of the affected vulnerable population in decision-making. Thus, the protocol recommends mobilizing social participation mechanisms from the stages of prevention and risk mapping, with the publicization of information for the involved population, to the adoption of decision-making instruments and instances that include the engagement of affected people in the accountability and reparation process.

According to the recommendations outlined in the Access to Justice Protocol, it is important to involve vulnerable populations in disaster risk management. This can be achieved by creating forums for information exchange, establishing consultative and decision-making bodies, and providing technical advice to ensure these populations can participate effectively. When examining climate litigation cases, it becomes clear that the challenges faced in prioritizing the affected population are closely related to disaster management.

The participation of affected communities in the decision-making process requires the strengthening and empowerment of the institutions within the justice system so that they can operationalize the instruments and concepts related to the climate agenda, from a human rights perspective. Such an approach may contribute with the mitigation of and adaptation to the impacts of extreme climatic phenomena that result in disasters.

# SECTION 3

## *Climate Litigation and Vulnerabilities*

CHAPTER 9

# Vulnerabilities in Climate Litigation: the Role of Gender, Race, and Poverty

*Mariana Belmont* and Nauê Bernardo Pinheiro de Azevedo***

## 1 Introduction

In 1989, Spike Lee released 'Do the Right Thing,' a film that reveals the daily life of a poor community in a suburban area of the United States. The coexistence of Blacks, Hispanics, Koreans, and Italians is far from harmonious, filled with constant tensions and relationships that tread the line between discord and endurance. In the film, at the Love Radio station, DJ Love Daddy advises his listeners about the approaching heatwave: "Stay home or you'll end up with a plastic helmet on your head." On the streets, the elderly, sitting on the sidewalk, talk about the extreme heat.

This heat, depicted by Spike Lee, drives the film's narrative and is part of what happened during the so-called 1988 Drought, a period when extreme heatwaves combined with dust storms devastated crops and caused numerous forest fires, resulting in significant financial loss for the U.S. government.

Climate change directly impacts public health,[1] and combating climate change could be the greatest opportunity to improve global health this century. However, discussions about the impact of climate change on health are often incomplete, with little attention given to structural discrimination and the need for racial justice. Together, racism and climate change interact and have disproportionate effects on the lives of Black populations. The impacts fall disproportionately on already disadvantaged groups.

Authorities' use of words like 'extreme' and 'nature' to justify landslides is nothing more than an attempt to explain their unjustifiable naturalization of death. Summer rains are expected. News of families losing everything, from their homes to their lives, is also expected. The blame is not on the rain. Civil

* Journalist and researcher, marianabelmont22@gmail.com, ORCID No. 0009-0005-3622-2961.

** PhD candidate in Law, State, and Constitution at the University of Brasília, nauebernardo@gmail.com, ORCID No. 0000-0003-1551-914X.

1 Letícia Leobet & Mariana Belmont, 'Mudanças Climáticas e os impactos na saúde da população negra' (7 December 2023) *Geledes*, https://www.geledes.org.br/mudancas-climaticas-e-os-impactos-na-saude-da-populacao-negra/.

 | DOI:10.1163/9789004690974_010

society, the federal government, and state and municipal governments can no longer act only on the day of the tragedy after lives are lost.

The precarious housing conditions in risk areas disproportionately affect Black communities, who are more vulnerable to living in risky areas due to residential segregation, economic inequality, and racial discrimination. According to the Institute for Applied Economic Research (IPEA), in 2018, about 70% of natural disaster victims in Brazil were Black. Moreover, environmental racism in housing in risk areas also manifests in how authorities and the media address these problems. Often, marginalized communities are blamed for the problems they face, being portrayed as responsible for living in risk areas or not taking sufficient preventive measures.

Both within and outside the United Nations (UN), Member States are advocating initiatives to develop solutions to the global ecological crisis. In this context, a racial justice approach to this crisis is urgent and necessary, yet within the global framework, it remains completely marginalized. Despite the significant efforts of global environmental justice advocates, the interests and concerns of non-White peoples have been successfully marginalized within the UN structures coordinating the global response to the ecological crisis. The prevailing global responses to environmental crises are characterized by the same forms of systemic racism driving these crises. Environmental, climate, and racial injustices are the institutionalized status quo.

According to Martine and Alves, the economic progress achieved by humanity in recent decades has been significant but has come at the cost of unsustainable use of natural resources, destruction of biological diversity, and large emissions of greenhouse gases (GHG), factors responsible for the current environmental crisis.[2] Layrargues notes a context of regression in the environmental institutionalization of Brazil and Latin America, determined by factors such as the renewal of development based on extractivism and the expectation of economic comparative advantage due to the abundance of natural resources.[3]

## 2 Environmental Deregulation

Environmental deregulation, therefore, moves contrary to the needs perceived by various academic and scientific sectors. It contributes to the dismantling

2 George Martine e José Eustáquio Diniz Alves, 'Economy, Society and Environment in the 21st Century: Three Pillars or Trilemma of Sustainability?' (2015) 32 *R. Bras. Est. Pop.* 433.

3 Philippe Pomier Layrargues, 'Anti Ecologismo no Brasil: Reflexões Ecopolíticas sobre o Modelo do Desenvolvimentismo-Extrativista-Predatório e a Desregulação Ambiental Pública' in M M D Oliveira, M Mendes, C M Hansel e S Damiani (eds), *Cidadania, Meio Ambiente e Sustentabilidade* (EDUCS 2017) 325.

of policies aimed at economic development with respect to a balanced environment and also endangers humanity's very survival. Achieving climate justice will require effective action on an interdisciplinary and global scale. This is because the lives of historically marginalized and impoverished populations are more broadly impacted.

In this context, national states seek to conclude supranational agreements for better environmental practices, the latest being the Paris Agreement. This agreement is responsible for implementing, in each signatory state, a system of nationally determined targets for reducing GHG emissions. However, many of these agreements and internal legislations are systematically ignored or violated.

Thus, the context associated with socio-environmental and climate litigation emerges. The inaction or deliberate actions of national states or individuals against a balanced environment and the relative scientific consensus on the risks posed by uncontrolled carbon and GHG emissions into the atmosphere, combined with national and supranational legal frameworks regarding climate and the environment, increasingly drive organized civil groups to seek judicial intervention to resolve these issues.

Climate and environmental litigation will be useless if climate justice is not its beginning, middle, and end. After all, we are talking about matters concerning fundamental and diffuse rights (such as food, health, and an ecologically sustainable environment, among others involved in this type of litigation). In Brazil, there have been undeniable advances regarding the flexibility of the judiciary in relation to the environment and climate, especially before the Supreme Federal Court. But how much of this has effectively yielded results for marginalized populations? Therefore, this chapter addresses socio-environmental and climate litigation from a justice perspective, initially focusing on conceptualizing environmental racism. Next, it discusses the current state of the art, addressing factors and consequences of the lack of justice for socially marginalized people. Finally, the text concludes.

## 3 Environmental and Climate Injustice

Every time the Alcântara Launch Center (CLA) launches a rocket into space, the residents of the Mamuna *Quilombo*[4] feel it. Not necessarily through an

4 The various Black communities that remained in their territories in the post-abolition period—rendered invisible by the State and suffering expropriations and violence of different kinds—are recognized as groups bearing ethnically differentiated rights through the constitutional text that establishes in Article 68 of the Transitional Constitutional Provisions that "the remaining members of the quilombola communities who are occupying their lands

announcement from the institute or news reports, but because the ground of the entire community shakes. It has been this way since 1990, the year of the first launch from the Alcântara aerospace base in the state of Maranhão. Of all the hundreds of people that make up the municipality, the Mamuna community is the closest to the area. The Brazilian Air Force, responsible for the CLA, claims that the risk of a rocket hitting the community is low. Even so, the *quilombo* residents are afraid.

According to a report by Folha de S. Paulo, using data from the São Paulo Civil Defense, 44 deaths have already been confirmed.[5] There are also 1,730 displaced people and 766 homeless. Among the dead is a 7-year-old child who died in a landslide in Ubatuba. The other 43 dead are from São Sebastião, the city most affected by the storm—31 deaths in Barra do Sahy, 2 in Juquehy, 1 in Camburi, and 1 in Boiçucanga. There was also flooding in the Ponta da Praia Community, in Rio Pequeno, Butantã region, and several families lost everything. Poor families.

You might have heard that this happens because poorer areas have many hills and slopes or because many are near rivers. But, to start with, it is essential to understand that living in steep areas is not synonymous with disaster. As Belmont[6] argues, just look at the Perdizes region in São Paulo, a middle-upper-class neighborhood where buildings do not slide with each storm—thanks to infrastructure investments made by the City Hall.[7]

Systemic racism has served as a fundamental organizing principle for the global systems and processes at the center of the climate and environmental crises. Understanding and addressing contemporary climate and environmental injustice within a racially discriminatory context requires a historical approach to how 'race' and racism have shaped the political economy of climate and environmental realities, as well as the legal structures and worldviews

---

shall have their definitive ownership recognized, and the State shall issue the respective titles to them." The use of the terms *quilombo*, remaining *quilombo* members, and *quilombolas*, in this sense, was part of a political movement to appropriate legal categories and also to recognize the existence of groups possessing specific ways of life associated with territoriality and ethnic differentiation. in.: IPHAN, 'Quilombo,' available at http://portal.iphan.gov.br/dicionarioPatrimonioCultural/detalhes/81/quilombo.

5 Mariana Belmont et al., 'Adaptação a Mudanças Climáticas em Territórios Negros e Políticas de Reparação' (16 May 2023) *Folha de S. Paulo*, available at https://www1.folha.uol.com.br/colunas/desigualdades/2023/05/adaptacao-as-mudancas-climaticas-em-territorios-negros-e-politica-de-reparacao.shtml.

6 Mariana Belmont, 'A Culpa Não é da Chuva, é do Racismo Ambiental' (21 February 2023), *Folha de S. Paulo*, available at https://www1.folha.uol.com.br/colunas/desigualdades/2023/02/a-culpa-nao-e-da-chuva-e-do-racismo-ambiental.shtml.

7 ibid.

those structures represent. At the heart of the climate crisis are the levels of GHG emissions resulting from centuries of natural resource extraction, industrialization, industrial processes, and consumption of the products of these processes. In their presentations, various experts summarized a rich body of research mapping the racist colonial regimes that underpinned the extraction of coal, gas, and oil, forging a global capitalist system dependent on maintaining racial hierarchies, which are, therefore, at the center of the global ecological crisis.

Within the broader environmental justice movement, climate justice seeks the historical accountability of nations and entities responsible for climate change. Climate justice also aims for the radical transformation of contemporary systems that enable the global ecological crisis and distribute the associated suffering in a racially discriminatory manner. As climate change is driven by the accumulation of GHG in the atmosphere, historical emissions are a contemporary existential problem. Between 1850 and 2002, industrialized countries produced three times more carbon dioxide than the entire Global South. However, it is the Global South and also the non-white, colonially marked regions of the world that are most affected and least able to mitigate and survive the global ecological crisis, significantly due to the colonial processes that caused historical emissions in the past.[8]

## 4 Environmental and Climate Racism and Their Present Effects

Racism, as a structural and widely disseminated phenomenon, interacts with most of the unequal distributions of burdens and benefits in societies worldwide. Therefore, environmental and climate racism are no different. Abimbola et al. associate the colonization process with the racist hierarchy that promotes the climate emergency.[9] According to the authors, this phenomenon facilitated and established the overexploitation of natural resources to fuel the industrialization of the Global North.[10] This process, according to the authors, was responsible for allowing the unfolding of the climate crisis as it is seen

8 Julia Dehm e Sarah Riley-Case, 'Redressing Historical Responsibility for the Unjust Precarities of Climate Change in the Present' in B. Mayer & A. Zahar (eds), *Debating Climate Law* (Cambridge University Press, 2021), pp. 170–89, at 171.

9 Olumide Abimbola et al, *Racism and Climate (In)Justice: How Racism and Colonialism shape the Climate Crisis and Climate Action* (Heinrich Böll-Stiftung 2021) https://us.boell.org/sites/default/files/2021-03/FINAL%20-%20Racism%20and%20Climate%20%28In%29Justice%20Framing%20Paper.pdf.

10 ibid, at 7.

today, bringing devastating impacts to humanity, especially in developing countries.

Environmental and climate racism reveal themselves as intricate phenomena that not only amplify existing inequalities but also disproportionately impact marginalized communities around the globe.[11] The history of international climate policy reflects a pattern of unfulfilled promises and inadequate commitments to protect the most vulnerable from the effects of climate change. From Eunice Foote's initial 1856 proposal on the role of $CO_2$ in atmospheric warming to subsequent global conferences and the formation of the UNFCCC in 1992, there has been a growing recognition of the need to mitigate anthropogenic interference in the global climate system.[12]

Recently, more than 1,800 municipalities and states in 33 countries have declared climate emergencies, many of them from local governments in the Global North, such as Australia, Belgium, Canada, France, Germany, the United Kingdom, and the United States.[13] However, the financial and political responses of developed countries to these emergencies have been insufficient, given the severity of the climate crisis. An example of this is the United Kingdom, which declared a climate emergency in 2019 but significantly reduced Official Development Assistance in 2020, exacerbating the urgent financial needs of developing countries to address the determinants of climate vulnerability, such as limited access to health and social protection.[14]

The emergency declared by political leaders in developed countries only occurred when the impacts of climate change began to affect their own territories, highlighting how white privileges within these countries influence the delayed response to climate crises.[15] The literature on climate change also emphasizes that vulnerabilities to climate impacts are deeply rooted in social structures prioritizing certain interests over others.[16] According to Sealey-Huggins, this vulnerability is shaped by the organizational forms of societies, resulting in higher levels of exposure and compounded risks to climate change.[17]

In Global North countries, minority communities face greater pollution, environmental degradation, and climate change impacts compared to white communities, demonstrating a differential racialized impact described as

11 ibid, at 5.
12 ibid, at 9.
13 ibid, at 11.
14 ibid, at 11.
15 ibid.
16 ibid, at 8.
17 ibid.

environmental racism.[18] Additionally, institutional racism continues to influence domestic responses to climate change, leaving minority communities more vulnerable and exposed to climate disasters.[19]

Indigenous communities in the Global North are among the most affected by climate change due to centuries of exclusion and marginalization.[20] Similarly, in the Global South, the colonial legacy continues to be a central factor in climate vulnerabilities, with historical patterns of underdevelopment, colonization, neocolonialism, and neoliberalism exacerbating the climate crisis in these regions.[21]

To combat environmental and climate racism, it is crucial to confront the racialized dimensions of social structures that perpetuate inequalities.[22] This requires a profound cultural shift in institutions and organizations based in the Global North, ensuring genuine participation and inclusion of diverse minority communities in climate policies.[23] The urgency to jointly address racial and climate injustice is evident, especially considering that Global South communities and people belonging to minority groups face specific challenges based on regional and contextual power imbalances.[24] There is no time to lose in transforming climate response systems and promoting true and responsible solidarity that challenges the predominance of the Global North in the global climate regime.[25]

## 5 Race, Ethnicity, National Origin, and 'Sacrifice Zones'

The term 'sacrifice zones' originates from a designation used during the Cold War to describe areas irradiated due to nuclear weapons production. Racially marginalized and formerly colonized peoples were among those whose communities were disproportionately 'sacrificed' to the demands of nuclear proliferation, as evidenced by the impacts of nuclear testing on the people of the Marshall Islands, as well as Indigenous peoples and ethnic minorities living in territories controlled by military superpowers. Today, a sacrifice zone can be understood as a place where residents suffer devastating physical and mental

18 ibid, at 17.
19 ibid, at 17–18.
20 ibid, at 18.
21 ibid.
22 ibid, at 20.
23 ibid.
24 ibid.
25 ibid.

health consequences and human rights violations as a result of living in pollution hotspots and contaminated areas. Climate change is driving the proliferation of sacrifice zones, which in many places are, in fact, racial sacrifice zones.

> In rural areas, forests, cities, or anywhere else, the violation of rights of the Black population is systemic. This population lives in areas most affected by pollution, biodiversity loss, and climate change. They are disproportionately concentrated in "sacrifice zones"—regions that have become dangerous and even uninhabitable due to environmental degradation. While sacrifice zones are concentrated in the formerly colonized territories of the Global South, the Global North is largely responsible for these conditions. These "sacrifice zones" are more accurately described as "racial sacrifice zones." Racial sacrifice zones include indigenous territories, quilombola communities, and are directly related to the racist extraction and economic exploitation that occurred during the colonial era, for which the colonial powers have not been held accountable.[26]

## 6 Race, Ethnicity, National Origin, and Climate-Induced Displacement

According to UNHCR, 90% of refugees[27] and most internally displaced persons come from countries highly vulnerable to climate change. At the same time, countries highly vulnerable to climate change host more than 40% of refugees, while internally displaced persons in conflict-affected and climate-vulnerable countries are often displaced to areas where they are exposed and vulnerable to climate-related risks. The risk for refugees and internally displaced persons is twofold: on the one hand, settlements are disproportionately concentrated in regions exposed to above-average warming levels and specific climate risks, including extreme temperatures and droughts; on the other hand, these populations often inhabit settlements and legal circumstances that are intended to be temporary but extend for generations, while facing legal and economic barriers to their ability to migrate away from climate impacts.

26 UN Human Rights Council, 'Report of the Special Rapporteur on Contemporary Forms of Racism, Racial Discrimination, Xenophobia and Related Intolerance' (A/75/49) (2020) https://www.ohchr.org/en/documents/thematic-reports/a77549-report-special-rapporteur-contemporary-forms-racism-racial.

27 UNHCR, 'Data on Refugees in Brazil and Worldwide,' available at https://www.acnur.org/br/sobre-o-acnur/dados-sobre-refugio-no-brasil-e-no-mundo.

The term 'environmental racism' describes institutionalized discrimination involving "environmental policies, practices, or directives that differentially affect or harm individuals, groups, or communities based on race or color.[28]" People of African and Asian descent, Indigenous peoples, Roma, refugees, migrants, stateless persons, and other racially and ethnically marginalized groups are all affected by environmental racism, which must be addressed as much as possible under international human rights law.

The Durban Declaration and Programme of Action (DDPA),[29] which remains the international community's most comprehensive plan to eliminate racism and racial discrimination, offers recommendations on combating environmental racism. For example, it calls for greater support for people of African descent to invest in 'environmental control measures' and offers various recommendations for "non-discriminatory measures to provide a safe and healthy environment for individuals and groups of individuals who are victims of or subject to racism, racial discrimination, xenophobia, and intolerance."[30]

Environmental racism and climate injustice interact with other forms of social exclusion, such as discrimination based on gender, age, and disability. Intersectional analyses of human rights violations related to the environment and climate must recognize that women, elderly people, people with disabilities, and gender and sexually diverse individuals who are members of racially marginalized groups face distinct human rights violations. Several presentations made this point explicit. Women, in particular, play important roles in rural and agricultural life and are often on the front lines of human rights violations related to the environment and climate. Regarding violence against women and girls, it was reported that climate change-induced violence against women is a distinct phenomenon caused by the feminization of intersecting vulnerabilities. The elderly and children are also vulnerable to climate harms, especially when living in economically marginalized communities or states with limited economic resources to meet their specific needs. Similarly, people with disabilities need resources to adapt and mitigate climate change damages, and these resources are typically denied to certain states and racially marginalized communities due to systemic discrimination.

Environmental justice and climate justice are often linked to the right to sustainable development. The right to development aims to ensure both the

---

28 NRDC, 'What is Environmental Racism?' https://www.nrdc.org/stories/what-environmental-racism. See also RD Bullard, 'Confronting Environmental Racism in the Twenty-First Century' (2002) 4(2) *Global Dialogue* 35.

29 Durban Action Programme, paras 5, 8(c) and 111.

30 ibid., at 84.

right to social and economic progress and the realization of all other human rights through self-determination and equal sovereignty. The Declaration on the Right to Development states that the right of peoples to self-determination includes exercising their inalienable right to full sovereignty over all their wealth and natural resources.[31]

In many national contexts, environmental injustice is often analyzed in terms of socioeconomic inequalities with limited attention to racial and ethnic inequalities, and there is widespread resistance to collecting disaggregated data based on race and ethnicity. Without discounting the importance of poverty, gender, age, and other social characteristics in exposing communities to environmental and climate change harms, discrimination based on race, color, descent, and national and ethnic origin remains a critical determinant of climate and environmental harms experienced by individuals and communities. Systemic racial discrimination results in economic marginalization, and in many places, racially, ethnically, and nationally marginalized groups are trapped in low-income brackets. The economic marginalization of racially marginalized people plays a significant role in restricting their control over the development of their communities and their exposure to toxic waste and climate disasters. Similarly, racially marginalized peoples often lack true self-determination over the economic development occurring in or near their communities, making them frequent victims of racial sacrifice zones created by national authorities or transnational corporations.

People of African descent in Brazil are disproportionately exposed to floods and landslides due to their economic marginalization and segregation into dangerous areas. Afro-Brazilians are disproportionately the victims of such disasters because of the socio-political structure in Brazil that places racialized people in more vulnerable living conditions, while public policymakers fail to address these precarious living conditions.

Environmental racism results in the routine persecution of human rights defenders and environmental protectors working to shield their communities from environmental harm. Worldwide, these defenders often come from indigenous communities or other racially marginalized groups. As previously discussed, racial marginalization implies economic and political marginalization. When marginalized groups make efforts to assert their rights in the face of exploitative governments and transnational corporations, they are heavily

31 UN Human Rights Council, 'Report of the Working Group of Experts on People of African Descent on its Mission to the United States of America' (2016), available at https://www.ohchr.org/sites/default/files/rtd.pdf.

persecuted. Often, accountability for the persecution of human rights defenders from racially and ethnically marginalized groups is limited.

In Brazil, Indigenous and Afro-descendant leaders have been targeted by public and private agents for their advocacy against large-scale public and private projects near their territories. Global Witness reports that Brazil has the fourth-highest number of murdered environmentalists in the world. Traditional peoples, *quilombolas,*[32] riverside communities, and Indigenous communities face constant pressure from various economic activities on their territories and have been threatened or cruelly murdered. In Pará, a region of escalating environmental conflicts, several cases of ordered assassinations of environmental activists have been reported. In these incidents, all victims were Black women fighting for a balanced way of life with forest conservation.

In Brazil, Sapê do Norte,[33] certified as a protected quilombo territory, has been home to *quilombola* communities since the 1960s. The inhabitants of this region have experienced a drastic reduction in biodiversity, large-scale deforestation, stream drying and spring silting, animal deaths, and high pesticide dumping in water and soil due to the construction of highways, agribusiness attacks, the installation of a gas pipeline by Petrobras, and the breaking of the 'Fundão Dam' operated by Samarco. The construction of the Alcântara Launch Center over the largest quilombo territory in Brazil resulted in the forced removal of 312 *quilombola* families, and more continue to be displaced across the country.

Several presentations noted that some 'green' solutions to climate change challenges actually reinforce or perpetuate racial marginalization and inequalities. The transition to alternatives to fossil fuels in some contexts results in 'green sacrifice zones,' meaning racially and ethnically marginalized groups are disproportionately exposed to human rights violations associated with the extraction or processing of these alternatives. They seek to maintain unsustainable consumption levels in the Global North through transitions that require tremendous destructive extraction from the Global South. As 'Green New Deals' proliferate in the Global North, their effectiveness depends on their ability to address the root causes of the ecological crisis and undo the systemic racism embedded in fossil fuel economies.

---

32 ACNUDH, 'Colombia: Extreme Risks for Rights Defenders Who Challenge Corporate Activity' (August 2022) A/HRC/46/35; IACHR, 'IACHR and UN Human Rights Condemn Murders of Environmental Activists and Quilombolas in Brazil' (2022).

33 Conflict Maps, 'Es Quilombo de Sape do Norte: Reduzidos a 10 em Pessoas e Território Continuam na Luta pela Titulação de Suas Terras,' https://mapadeconflitos.ensp.fiocruz.br/conflito/es-quilombo-de-sape-do-norte-reduzidos-a-10-em-pessoas-e-territorio-continuam-na-luta-pela-titulacao-de-suas-terras/.

Many climate-related initiatives are developed without the input, consideration, or leadership of racially marginalized people, and they may reinforce existing racial discrimination patterns in national and international economies. The over-reliance on technocratic knowledge and the exclusion of local communities from climate change leadership have worked to divert attention from the systemic changes demanded by frontline communities and are necessary to truly address the ongoing crisis.

Adopt a global approach that effectively responds to the fact that climate justice requires racial justice and that racial justice requires climate justice. The racially disparate impacts of environmental degradation and climate injustice require a fundamental reorientation of political institutions, economic systems, and legal principles to include racial justice and equality priorities. 'Green transitions' must also be racially just transitions. Transitions to cleaner forms of energy, climate adaptations, and other programs must take measures, including special measures, to ensure that responses to climate change do not continue patterns of racial marginalization and discrimination. True racial justice implies the end of environmental racism and also implies adaptation, mitigation, and loss and damage structures that uproot the systemic racism embedded in the global economy, political hierarchies, and legal structures. This includes mass decolonization of legal and economic systems to ensure racially marginalized peoples, including Indigenous peoples, have true self-determination, including sovereignty over their territories. As noted in a presentation, racial justice and climate justice require fiscal justice.

## 7 Vulnerabilities in Climate Litigation before Brazilian Courts

Today, Brazil can say that it has a Supreme Court that is sensitive to socio-environmental issues, although this sensitivity may be subject to debate regarding how and under what circumstances it was formed. However, it is a fact that there are precedents, some with binding force and others not, which can be used as examples of paths towards seeking environmental justice in the judiciary.

Among the precedents addressing climate issues, the first to mention is the understanding established in the case of *PSB et al v Brazil* (*on Climate Fund*),[34] which dealt with the reactivation of the Climate Fund, suspended by an act of

34 Partido Socialista Brasileiro (PSB), Partido Socialismo e Liberdade (PSOL), Partido dos Trabalhadores (PT) e Rede Sustentabilidade v União Federal, ADPF 708, Judgment of 7

the Brazilian federal government in 2019. The case was reported by Minister Roberto Barroso and judged in July 2022. From this judgment, it is noteworthy that "[a]mong the efforts Brazil should undertake to do its part in mitigating the problem is the reduction of deforestation, one of the main activities responsible for GHG emissions," and that "environmental protection should not be interpreted as discretionary political judgment, but as a binding obligation," by virtue of Article 225 of the Federal Constitution.[35] The prevailing vote also reaffirms the binding nature of the Paris Agreement as it is a human rights treaty ratified in Brazil. Nevertheless, it is necessary to reflect on what led to this judgment: the legal approach adopted by the reporting minister involved the issue of the separation of powers (arguing that the Climate Fund resources could not be withheld by an executive act due to Brazil's Fiscal Responsibility Law). The Executive Power's omission was acknowledged, and the Court ordered the reactivation of the Climate Fund.

Secondly, there is the case of the *PSB et al v Brazil* (*on Amazon Fund*),[36] which dealt with the reactivation of the Amazon Fund, also suspended by an act of the Brazilian federal government in 2019. The case was reported by Minister Rosa Weber and judged in November 2022.

Similarly to the *PSB et al v Brazil* (*on Climate Fund*) judgment, this case ended with the Supreme Federal Court's order for the reactivation of the Amazon Fund. It also focused on the technical aspects of the public policy's operation, finding unconstitutionality due to the policy's non-functioning as a result of Brazil's duty to maintain an ecologically balanced environment (Article 225 of the Federal Constitution). The legal reasoning addressed how the policy's suspension prevented funding actions that could reduce deforestation in the biome, thus violating the constitutional duty that must be followed by all, including the government. It is worth noting that, in the winning vote, the reporting minister referred to the Amazon Fund as a financial environmental public policy. It is mentioned that "[e]nvironmental degradation in the Legal Amazon has been causing continuous damage to health, life, and dignity of people, making it difficult for Brazil to achieve the objectives of building a free,

---

January 2022, Rapporteur: Minister Luís Roberto Barroso, avalaible in https://climatecasechart.com/non-us-case/psb-et-al-v-federal-union/.

35 Nauê Bernardo Pinheiro de Azevedo, 'A Atuação do Supremo Tribunal Federal na Arguição de Descumprimento de Preceito Fundamental 708—Reativação do Fundo Clima' (2023) 2(2) *Diálogos Soberania e Clima* 10.

36 Partido Socialista Brasileiro (PSB), Partido Socialismo e Liberdade (PSOL), Partido dos Trabalhadores (PT) e Rede Sustentabilidade v União Federal, ADO 59, Judgment of 16 August 2023, Rapporteur: Minister Rosa Weber, disponível em https://climatecasechart.com/non-us-case/psb-et-al-v-brazil/.

just, and supportive society, and also national development, which is only effective if sustainable, promoting the well-being of all and responsibly responding to the commitments made under the National Policy on Climate Change."[37]

These two cases are paradigmatic for two reasons: firstly, because they represent the effective handling of arguments regarding the climate crisis and its repercussions, and secondly, because not a single line in these two precedents specifically addresses the issue of environmental injustice. This highlights the increasing need for argumentative refinement in these actions to ensure the issue is effectively exposed, debated, and judged in the judiciary.

In the case of *PSB et al v Brazil* (*on Climate Fund*), in particular, the public policy comes with a historical gap regarding the provision of resources for mitigation and adaptation activities. According to Azevedo, up until 2023, there was insufficient provision of resources for these areas, despite the Fund having a financial allocation of about BRL 550 million.[38] Additionally, there was a geographic inequality in the distribution of resources, much more concentrated in wealthy states than in impoverished ones. The judicialization of its suspension was not sufficient to resolve this issue, as it was not the main object of the action.

As noted, despite progress in climate litigation in Brazil, with two important precedents from the Constitutional Court, there is still a long way to go for this litigation to address climate injustice incisively. Even with all the warnings raised by the most reliable scientific sources about the climate emergency, climate issues are still not at the center of judicial decision-making in Brazil, being a peripheral argument in the true decision-making motives.

Climate litigation cannot distance itself from socio-environmental litigation in Brazil, given the path already opened by the latter in Brazilian courts. Conversely, socio-environmental litigation cannot disregard the important arguments related to climate, as this is an issue gaining increasing importance in society, reflecting decision-making elements in the courts. Through this path, it will be possible, for example, to seek judicial solutions regarding the lack of adaptation policies in peripheral areas not covered by state infrastructure to prevent collapse risks in the event of extreme weather events.

The climate issue spans various aspects but should not be disconnected from the environment or society. After all, the exceptional heatwave and the enormous rainfall equally affect the prison, the community, the court, and the Chamber of Deputies, but with entirely different consequences in each of these environments. Environmental and climate justice are 'key' to overcoming the

37 ibid.

38 Nauê Bernardo Pinheiro de Azevedo, 'O Uso do Fundo Clima Enquanto Instrumento de Aceleração das Políticas de Adaptação e Mitigação' (2023) 2(5) *Diálogos Soberania e Clima* 5.

challenges inherent in these consequences, since one cannot progress without the other.

Scientific warnings treat environmental and climate issues as urgent and highly relevant. The consequences of human behavior, already identified and predicted by science, are also becoming visible. Not surprisingly, countries worldwide are adopting mitigation and adaptation measures as part of their respective climate policies, demonstrating the danger that the environmental crisis represents for humanity. That said, it is essential to recognize the phenomenon of environmental and climate racism as necessary to resolve the issue.

As discussed by Abimbola et al., eliminating racism in climate policies and actions requires institutional and individual coordination of multi-sectoral responses that include: (4.1) recognizing the history and legacy of colonialism in climate policies and actions; (4.2) promoting profound cultural change in institutions and organizations in the Global North, questioning current inclusion practices to foster effective participation and engagement of diverse ethnic-racial groups; (4.2.2) fulfilling human rights obligations under the International Convention on the Elimination of All Forms of Racial Discrimination and the Convention on the Elimination of All Forms of Discrimination Against Women; and (4.2.3) addressing collective trauma related to climate and racial injustice.[39] Additionally, it is essential to promote solidarity and accountability through structural and institutional reforms, focusing on ending the dominance of the Global North in the global climate regime.

The urgency of addressing racial and climate injustices together cannot be considered exaggerated. The Global South and social and ethnic minority groups face significant challenges based on regional and contextual power imbalances. However, these groups cannot wait for the slow process of reformulating international organization architectures while they continue to be tragically affected by climate change. If there was ever a moment for accelerated transformation, it is now.[40]

Climate and socio-environmental litigation need to address these issues, and their outcomes must serve as a means to tackle these problems. As long as discomfort with discussing this agenda continues to outweigh the need for effective measures to protect impoverished and marginalized populations, the concept of climate justice will serve only to sell books and works in some bookstores in a Global North country.

39 Olumide Abimbola et al, *Racism and Climate (In) Justice* (Heinrich Böll-Stiftung 2021) https://us.boell.org/sites/default/files/2021-03/FINAL%20-%20Racism%20and%20Climate%20%28In%29Justice%20Framing%20Paper.pdf, at 20.

40 ibid.

CHAPTER 10

# Decolonizing Climate Litigation: an Analysis of Indigenous Climate Litigation in Brazil

*Gabriel Mantelli*, Maurício Terena**, Isabela Bicalho*** and Marie-Louise Siemons*****

## 1 Introduction

In recent years, reports from the Intergovernmental Panel on Climate Change (IPCC) have emphasized the urgent need to reduce fossil fuel consumption and significantly cut greenhouse gas (GHG) emissions. They underscore the profound risks posed by climate change, particularly to vulnerable populations, and highlight the imperative to promote adaptation to mitigate its direct impacts.[1]

In 2022, for the first time in thirty years since its inaugural publication, the IPCC acknowledged colonialism not only as a catalyst for the climate crisis, but also as an ongoing issue exacerbating the vulnerability of communities to climate impacts. The incorporation of the term 'colonialism' marks a significant stride in the pursuit of climate justice, as it is imperative to recognize the ramifications of modern colonization on certain populations' susceptibility to vulnerability, shedding light on the disparity in experiencing climate change. Communities already grappling with inequality, poverty, inadequate sanitation, and various forms of oppression and violence are disproportionately susceptible to the severe ramifications of climate events, such as floods, droughts, access to contaminated water, and landslides. Acknowledging colonialism as

* PhD candidate in Legal Theory at University of São Paulo (USP). Master in Law and Development from FGV.

** Indigenous lawyer of the Terena ethnic group, Legal Coordinator at APIB, PhD candidate in Social Anthropology at University of São Paulo (USP).

*** Graduated in Law from UFU, Master's student in Public International Law at USP, Junior Lawyer at Gaia Silva Gaede Advogados.

**** Graduate in Law from PUC-SP.

1 Intergovernmental Panel on Climate Change, 'Climate Change 2022: Impacts, Adaptation and Vulnerability. Contribution of Working Group II to the Sixth Assessment Report of the Intergovernmental Panel on Climate Change' (CUP 2022).

 | DOI:10.1163/9789004690974_011

a factor amplifying the climate crisis entails understanding the current legacy from historical injustices.

As concerns over the climate crisis grow, litigation has become a potent tool used by civil society to hold governments and corporations accountable for their inaction on climate goals. Litigation is also crucial for safeguarding the right to a clean environment and a stable climate for present and future generations.[2] Globally, the climate litigation movement is gaining traction, evident in landmark cases like *Urgenda Foundation v State of the Netherlands*,[3] *Juliana v USA*,[4] and *Leghari v Pakistan*.[5] In Brazil, climate litigation is picking up pace, with over 80 documented cases, half of which target federal entities.[6]

Climate litigation thus occupies a pivotal role in the discourse on environmental justice, empowering marginalized communities to demand more ambitious climate action and targets. Central to this discussion are Indigenous communities, whose disproportionate vulnerability to climate change underscores their pivotal role in the climate justice movement. Indeed, Indigenous peoples often take active roles in climate litigation, advocating for their rights and demanding accountability from governments and corporations.

This chapter delves into the utilization of Indigenous peoples' rights in climate litigation with a specific focus on the experiences of Indigenous communities in Brazil. Indigenous climate litigation encompasses cases that center on the rights of Indigenous peoples, either through direct representation or with support of public and non-governmental organizations (NGOs). While the number of such cases remains relatively limited, it is crucial to recognize the significance of integrating climate justice with the protection of indigenous rights.

Section 2 explores the global context of Indigenous climate litigation, emphasizing how Indigenous communities are leveraging lawsuits to address

2 Joana Setzer & Catherine Higham, *Global Trends in Climate Change Litigation: 2022 Snapshot* (Grantham Research Institute on Climate Change and the Environment 2022) available at <https://www.lse.ac.uk/granthaminstitute/wp-content/uploads/2022/08/Global-trends-in-climate-change-litigation-2022-snapshot.pdf> accessed 29 February 2024.

3 *Stichting Urgenda v State of the Netherlands*, ECLI:NL:HR(2019(2007, Hoge Raad, 19/00135, Supreme Court, Judgment of 20 December 2019.

4 [2024] United States Court of Appeals [2015] 24–684

5 *Asghar Leghari v Federation of Pakistan*, Process No WP 25501/201, Supreme Court, Judgment of 25 January 2018.

6 Danielle de Andrade Moreira et al, *Panorama de Litigância Climática no Brasil* (Editora das Autoras 2024). See, also, Maria Antonia Tigre, Armando Rocha & Délton Winter de Carvalho (Chapter 1) and Danielle de Andrade Moreira (Chapter 2) in this book.

the impacts of climate change on their lands and cultures. It highlights key cases, such as those involving the Torres Strait Islanders and U.S. tribes, which challenge governments and corporations for failing to protect Indigenous rights and mitigate climate-related harms. The section underscores the importance of incorporating Indigenous perspectives and traditional knowledge into climate justice efforts, aiming for a more equitable and sustainable approach to environmental protection and adaptation.

For their turn, Section 3 provides an overview of Indigenous climate litigation in the Brazilian context, which has been growing significantly in recent years, whilst Section 4 seeks a more detailed analysis of the particularities of this context through the study of two paradigmatic cases: the climate litigation initiated by the Mbya Guarani Indigenous community regarding the environmental licensing of a coal mine in southern Brazil, and the broader Indigenous litigations aimed at securing the demarcation of Indigenous lands and challenging the temporal framework thesis. These cases highlight how Indigenous advocacy can enrich climate litigation, leveraging climate law to uphold Indigenous rights in innovative ways.

## 2 Context of Indigenous Climate Litigation in the World

To understand the urgency of bolstering Indigenous activism, we need to look at how Amerindian communities in the Global South resist colonialism. Amerindian thought emphasizes the intrinsic connection between humans and nature, as highlighted by scholars like Viveiros de Castro.[7] The diverse Amerindian ethnic groups offer alternative perspectives on the relationship between humans and nature, reshaping our understanding of the Anthropocene era and legal frameworks. This connection between beings and the environment gives rise to the concept of the 'Bem Viver' (living well), calling for a paradigm shift away from harmful practices toward environmental preservation and the recognition of Nature's rights for present and future generations.[8]

Indigenous activism is crucial for driving social change beyond colonial norms. It is urgent to shift the focus from Eurocentric views by placing Indigenous peoples at the forefront of environmental, climate, and human rights issues. The rise in climate litigation, demanding protection for Indigenous

7 Eduardo Viveiro de Castro, *A Inconstância da Alma Selvagem e Outros Ensaios de Antropologia* (Cosac Naify 2002).

8 Alberto Acosta, *O Bem Viver: Uma Oportunidade para Imaginar Outros Mundos* (1st edn, Elefante, 2016).

livelihoods and territories, reflects the need to rethink justice and the legal system. This involves moving away from Western perspectives and embracing diverse viewpoints. As Pazello suggests, we must incorporate new communal lifestyles, with law playing a reactive role in this process.[9]

The IPCC reports have underscored the heightened risks posed by climate change, particularly to communities whose lives depend on the environment, such as traditional rural populations and Indigenous peoples. In response to the escalating threats to their way of life, health, heritage, and survival resulting from climate change, Indigenous communities have turned to climate litigation to compel governments to fulfill their environmental and climate obligations and to urge companies to adopt more stringent climate measures for controlling and mitigating the effects of global warming.

In 2022, eight Indigenous individuals from the Boigu, Poruma, Warraber, and Masig communities residing in the Torres Strait Islands of Australia filed a petition with the United Nations Human Rights Committee against the Australian government. They argued that the government's failure to implement adequate adaptation and mitigation measures had adversely impacted their traditional livelihoods, culture, and means of subsistence. Notably, rising sea levels had destroyed ancestral burial grounds, severing cultural ties and disrupting customary practices. The petition cited violations of articles 27 (right to culture), 17 (right to privacy, family, and home), and 6 (right to life) of the International Covenant on Civil and Political Rights (ICCPR).

Despite the Australian government's initial dismissal of the petition, the UN Human Rights Committee acknowledged Australia's failure to protect the Indigenous peoples of Torres Islands from the worsening impacts of climate change, affirming violations of their rights to cultural heritage and traditional living spaces. The Committee emphasized the profound cultural and existential connection of these communities to their archipelago, stressing the imperative for robust national and international efforts to safeguard their cultural heritage and livelihoods.[10]

9 Ricardo Pazello, *Direito Insurgente e Movimentos Populares: O Giro Descolonial do Poder e a Crítica Marxista ao Direito* (Universidade Federal do Paraná 2014).

10 *Daniel Billy et al v Australia* (*Torres Strait Islanders Petition*) Views adopted on 23 September 2022, Communication No CCPR/C/135/D/3624/2019, submitted in 13 May 2019, available at <https://climatecasechart.com/non-us-case/petition-of-torres-strait-islanders-to-the-united-nations-human-rights-committee-alleging-violations-stemming-from-australias-inaction-on-climate-change/#:~:text=On%20September%2023%2C%202022%2C%20the,private%20life%2C%20family%20and%20home> accessed 26 September 2024.

The landmark decision in the Torres Strait Islands case holds significant implications for future Indigenous climate litigation cases. It underscores the urgent need for comprehensive measures and global collaboration to protect the cultural heritage and livelihoods of Indigenous peoples grappling with climate change impacts. By recognizing the rights of Indigenous communities and their vulnerability to environmental degradation, the decision sets a precedent for addressing similar challenges worldwide, emphasizing the imperative for meaningful dialogue and concrete actions to support Indigenous adaptation and preserve their way of life.

Another notable case involves a complaint filed by five Indigenous tribes in the United States before the United Nations, alleging the government's failure to address forced climate displacement.[11] The complaint, invoking special rapporteurs on the Human Rights of Internally Displaced Persons and the Rights of Indigenous Peoples, seeks interventions to address displacements caused by climate change-induced threats. The tribes demand recognition of their self-determination and sovereignty, federal recognition for unrecognized tribes, and measures to protect tribal lands and cultural heritage, among other remedies.

In September 2020, ten UN Special Rapporteurs addressed the U.S. government regarding human rights violations related to climate change impacts on indigenous communities, citing international human rights law. Despite the lack of response from the U.S. government, the Biden administration announced a $115 million commitment to a Voluntary Community-Driven Relocation Program during the White House Tribal Nations Summit in November 2022, aimed at assisting tribes affected by climate threats. However, it appears that none of the tribes involved in the UN complaint received funding from this commitment.[12]

In 2021, eleven NGOs, including four representing Indigenous peoples of the Brazilian and Colombian Amazon, filed a lawsuit against the French supermarket chain Casino for its involvement in deforestation of Indigenous lands for cattle ranching. The plaintiffs allege environmental damages and human rights abuses, demanding compliance with the French law on corporate vigilance and compensation for damages caused by the chain's activities.[13] The case underscores the importance of corporate responsibility in environmental protection and respect for Indigenous rights.

11 *Rights of Indigenous Peoples in Addressing Climate-Forced Displacement* [2020] United Nations USA 16/2020.

12 ibid.

13 *Envol Vert et al v Casino* [2021] Saint-Étienne Judicial Court.

While Indigenous communities continue to bear the brunt of the climate crisis, they are increasingly turning to litigation in pursuit of climate justice. As stated by Maria Antonia Tigre, the legal arguments commonly employed in Indigenous climate litigation cases cover a broad spectrum, including Indigenous rights, such as the right to Free, Prior, and Informed Consent (FPIC), traditional human rights like the right to life and health, and the emerging concept of rights for Nature.[14] These cases underscore the vital role of courts in addressing climate injustices and vulnerabilities. Many cases are still pending, but the recent ruling concerning the Torres Strait Islanders signifies a significant milestone in climate litigation, showcasing these communities' ability to amplify their voices.

## 3 Indigenous Climate Litigation in Brazil

### *3.1 Indigenous Law in Brazil*

The 1988 Brazilian Federal Constitution represented a significant advancement in determining the legal framework for Indigenous rights in Brazil. While the Indigenous Statute (Law No 6.001/1973) primarily provided for the 'integration' of Indigenous populations into the rest of society, the Constitution began to guarantee respect and protection for the culture of native populations.

For the first time in Brazil, the constitutional text defined a clear legal concept of Indigenous land, recognizing Indigenous peoples' original rights over the lands they traditionally occupy. According to the Constitution (art 231), Indigenous Lands are those permanently inhabited by Indigenous peoples, used for productive activities, and essential for preserving the environmental resources necessary for their well-being and physical and cultural reproduction, in accordance with their customs and traditions.

Indigenous communities are defined as distinct segments of the national society, which consider themselves historically continuous with pre-Columbian societies. They have legitimacy to defend their rights and interests in court, with the mandatory intervention of the Public Prosecutor's Office.[15] In the perspective of a permanent legal recognition and respect for Indigenous cultures, the constitutional text also recognizes to the Indigenous people

14 Maria Antonia Tigre, 'Climate Change and Indigenous Groups: The Rise of Indigenous Voices in Climate Litigation' (2022) 9 *e-Publica* 211, 256.

15 Constitution, art 232.

their rights over 'their social organization, customs, languages, beliefs, and traditions.[16]

Federal government is responsible for ensuring that each Indigenous group can live according to their own traditional forms of social organization and life, respecting the particularities of each community. This means that it is not up to the State to impose the official legal system of Brazilian society on Indigenous communities, since this system is often not suitable for their needs and specific realities.

Therefore, Brazilian law has come to recognize the existence of an 'independent normative system' of Indigenous peoples, granting them special rights permanently and independently of possible changes in their relations with society around them. Free access by Indigenous peoples to their lands is essential to guarantee the exercise of these rights, including the right to preserve their cultural characteristics.

Currently, Brazil harbors a remarkable diversity of Indigenous peoples, as revealed by official data. With over 266 identified groups, it is estimated that the Indigenous population totals 1,693,535 individuals across the national territory, representing nearly 1% of the total population. Regionally, they are concentrated in larger numbers in the North, parts of the Northeast, and the Midwest, specifically in states comprising the so-called Legal Amazon.[17] Indigenous lands comprise 774 areas, covering a total area of 118,258,133 hectares (1,182,581 km$^2$), thus constituting 13.9% of the Brazilian territory.[18]

A recent study conducted by the Socioenvironmental Institute highlights the significant contribution of Indigenous peoples and traditional communities to the preservation of Brazilian forests. One-third of Brazil's forests are protected through Indigenous lands, *Quilombola* territories, and environmental protected areas. Moreover, these areas have shown superior effectiveness in forest conservation compared to other forms of environmental protection.[19]

The relevance of these territories in forest preservation extends beyond national borders, reflecting on a global scale. A study conducted by scientists, policy experts, and indigenous leaders demonstrates that Indigenous lands

---

16 Constitution, art 231.

17 Instituto Socioambiental, '*Povos indígenas no Brasil*' [Indigenous Peoples in Brazil] available at <https://pib.socioambiental.org/pt/P%C3%A1gina_principal> accessed 01 may 2024.

18 'Informações gerais sobre Terras Indígenas no Brasil 2024' [General Information on Indigenous Lands in Brazil 2024] (Instituto Socioambiental 2024) available at <https://terrasindigenas.org.pt/pt-br/brasil> accessed 13 August 2024.

19 Antonio Francisco Perrone Oviedo and Juan Doblas, *As Florestas Precisam das Pessoas* (Instituto Socioambiental 2022) available at <https://acervo.socioambiental.org/acervo/documentos/florestas-precisam-das-pessoas> accessed 5 March 2024.

have maintained low deforestation rates compared to other areas of the Amazon over decades, playing a crucial role in climate regulation and global warming mitigation.[20]

However, while Indigenous lands can be seen as effective barriers against deforestation, these territories are among the most vulnerable to external pressures and climate impacts, while also consistently facing attacks. In this scenario, activist organizations for Indigenous rights, along with communities, have directed efforts towards strategic litigation, challenging traditional legal narratives to consolidate their rights.

### 3.2 *Brazilian (Indigenous) Climate Litigation*

Brazil has currently around 86 climate litigation cases according to research-led databases.[21] PUC-Rio's database (JUMA) identifies 86 cases, with 37 addressing climate as the main issue. Civil society leads the proposition of cases, having proposed 26 lawsuits, followed by public administration bodies and political parties.[22] It is worth noting that the most used instrument is the *ação civil pública* (public civil action) with 54 lawsuits, which in short seeks to protect diffuse, collective, consumer and environmental rights, according to Law No 7.347/1985.

These litigation cases reflect a growing trend of lawsuits aimed at addressing climate-related concerns in Brazil. With the increasing recognition of the urgent need to mitigate climate change impacts, stakeholders from various sectors are turning to the legal system to advocate for environmental protection and accountability. The prevalence of the public civil action demonstrates a concerted effort to safeguard diffuse, collective, consumer, and environmental rights, highlighting the multidimensional approach taken to address climate challenges within the legal framework. As the number of climate litigations continues to rise, it underscores the evolving role of the judiciary in shaping environmental policy and promoting sustainable development in Brazil.

In terms of Indigenous climate litigation, there are currently 13 climate litigation cases in Brazil. These cases reflect the ongoing struggle against large enterprises and policies that threaten their rights and territories. The cases focus on state omissions in environmental protection and disputes with companies in the energy, mining, and infrastructure sectors, which seek to exploit resources in areas traditionally occupied by Indigenous peoples or nearby

---

20 Wayne S Walkera et al, 'The Role of Forest Conversion, Degradation, and Disturbance' (2020) 117 *Proceedings of the national academy of sciences* 3015.

21 Moreira et al (n 6).

22 ibid.

TABLE 10.1 Table of cases related to Indigenous groups' rights and climate change

| Case name | Year filed | Status |
|---|---|---|
| Arayara et al v Copelmi Mineração et al (Mina Guaíba project)[a] | 2019 | Under appeal |
| Arayara et al v Copelmi et al (Mina Guaíba project and affected communities)[b] | 2019 | Under appeal |
| PSB et al v Brazil (on deforestation and human rights)[c] | 2020 | Decided |
| PSB et al v Brazil (Federal environmental sanctioning process)[d] | 2020 | Decided |
| Partido dos Trabalhadores v Brazil(Fires in the Pantanal and the Amazon Forest)[e] | 2020 | Decided |
| Federal Public Prosecutor's Office v Brazil et al (on deforestation hotspots in the Amazon)[f] | 2020 | Under judicial secrecy |
| PSB et al v Brazil (on Electrobras Privatization)[g] | 2021 | Pending |
| Jaci-Paraná Extractive Reserve and Guajará-Mirim State Park[h] | 2021 | Decided |
| Public Prosecutor's Office of the State of Rio Grande do Sul v Municipality of Eldorado do Sul et al (Eldorado Master Plan)[i] | 2021 | Decided |
| PSL et al v Brazil et al (Pantanal Wildfires)[j] | 2021 | Decided |
| Arayara et al v ANP et al[k] | 2023 | Pending |
| Indigenous Genocide Law Case[l] | 2023 | Pending |
| Instituto Verdeluz et al v Portocem et al (on installation of a thermoelectric plant in Pecém)[m] | 2023 | Pending |

a *Arayara et al v Copelmi Mineração et al (Mina Guaíba project)*, ACP 5069057-47.2019.4.04.7100, filed on 1 October 2019 before the 9th Federal Court of Rio Grande do Sul, Judgment of 1 February 2022.

b *Arayara et al v Copelmi et al (Mina Guaíba project and affected communities)*, ACP 5044993-20.2019.8.21.0001 / 5125450-05.2020.8.21.0001, filed on 27 September 2019 before the 10th Public Court of Porto Alegre.

c *PSB et al v Brazil (on deforestation and human rights)*, ADPF 760, STF Judgment of 6 April 2022.

d *PSB et al v Brazil (Federal environmental sanctioning process)*, ADPF 755, filed on 21 October 2020 before the STF.

e *Partido dos Trabalhadores v Brazil (Fires in the Pantanal and the Amazon Forest)*, ADPF 746, requested to the STF by Partido dos Trabalhadores on 1 September 2020.

f *Federal Public Prosecutor's Office v Brazil et al* (*on deforestation hotspots in the Amazon*), ACP 1007104-63.2020.4.01.3200, filed in 2020 before the 7th Federal Environmental and Agrarian Court of the Judiciary Section of Amazonas.
g *PSB et al v Brazil* (*on Electrobras Privatization*), ADI 6932, filed on 15 July 2021 before the STF.
h *Jaci-Paraná Extractive Reserve and Guajará-Mirim State Park*, State ADI 0804739-62.2021.8.22.0000, requested by the Public Prosecutor's Office on 1 May 2021 before the Rondônia Justice Court, Judgment of 1 November 2021,
i *Public Prosecutor's Office of the State of Rio Grande do Sul v Municipality of Eldorado do Sul et al* (*Eldorado Master Plan*), ADI 0007238-31.2021.8.21.7000, filed on 22 January 2021 before the Court of Justice of Rio Grande do Sul, Judgment of 10 December 2021.
j *PSL et al v Brazil et al* (*Pantanal Wildfires*), ADPF 857, filed on 22 June 2021 before the STF.
k *Arayara et al v ANP et al*, ACP 1049493-58.2023.4.01.3200, filed in December 2023 before the 3rd Federal Civil Court of the Judiciary Section of Amazonas.
l *Indigenous Genocide Law Case*, ADI 7582, filed in December 2023 before the STF.
m *Instituto Verdeluz et al v Portocem et al* (*on installation of a thermoelectric plant in Pecém*), ACP 5003643-89.2022.4.02.5116, filed in 2022 before the Federal Court in Ceará (Brazil).

areas, without proper consultation and respect for Indigenous rights as guaranteed by national and international legislation.

The case *Arayara et al v ANP et al* seeks to challenge the bidding process for oil exploration blocks promoted by the National Petroleum Agency (ANP). The blocks in question are in the Paraná and Amazonas Basins, in areas overlapping with places of influence or restriction of 23 Indigenous Lands. In addition, the lawsuit highlights the setback that the expansion of oil exploration represents, given that the climate crisis implies the need to promote the transition to clean energy sources. Judgment in the case is still pending.

At federal level, *Indigenous Genocide Law Case* concern Federal Law No 14.701/2023. This statute codified the 'temporal framework thesis,' which asserts that Indigenous peoples are only entitled to lands that have been under their possession or continuous occupation since the promulgation of the Constitution, excluding lands that were occupied or claimed thereafter. The lawsuit is pending judgment along with a series of cases in the STF involving Federal Law No 14.701/2023.

In the case *Instituto Verdeluz et al v Portocem et al* (*on installation of a thermoelectric plant in Pecém*), the lawsuit seeks to suspend and annul the environmental licensing process for Portocem Thermoelectric Power Plant. The plaintiffs allege that the Environmental Impact Study (EIA) failed to comply with legal standards and omitted significant aspects, such as the invisibility of nearby Indigenous communities, impacts on water resources, potential socioeconomic and health effects, as well as climate issues. A preliminary injunction to suspend the licensing was denied, and the lawsuit is awaiting judgment.

Another concentrated control action involving climate change and Indigenous peoples is *PSB et al v Brazil* (*on Electrobras Privatization*), which challenges Federal Law No 14.182/2021. This statute addresses the privatization of Eletrobras and introduces changes to the country's electricity sector framework. The statute includes measures that compromise the decarbonization of the energy matrix, violating international climate commitments. Additionally, it allows the construction of the 'Linhão de Tucuruí' transmission line without respecting environmental licensing processes and consultations with affected Indigenous communities, disregarding their rights and ongoing legal processes. Despite the adoption of an expedited procedural route for the lawsuit, it remains under consideration.

The *Jaci-Paraná Extractive Reserve and Guajará-Mirim State Park* case challenges the reduction of conservation areas in the Amazon under State Complementary Law No 1,089/2021. This statute reduces the area of the Jaci-Paraná Extractive Reserve and the Guajará-Mirim State Park, allowing environmental regularization of properties in the declassified areas. The declassification of these areas directly impacts the Indigenous Lands of Uru-eu-wau-wau, Karipuna, Igarapé Lage, Igarapé Ribeirão, and Karitina. In this context, the Organization of Indigenous Peoples of the Guarajá-Mirim Region (Oro Wari) filed a request to participate as *amicus curiae*. The final ruling declared the statute unconstitutional for declassifying a significant area of conservation unit without prior technical studies, violating the principles of precaution, prevention, and prohibition of environmental regression (a principle that is hardly recognized in other jurisdictions). It also acknowledged the public authority's duty to promote environmental protection as a diffuse good essential for healthy human life.

In the state of Rio Grande do Sul, *Public Prosecutor's Office of the State of Rio Grande do Sul v Municipality of Eldorado do Sul et al* (*Eldorado Master Plan*) was filed against changes to the Eldorado do Sul Master Plan that would permit urban expansion into environmental protection areas near Indigenous territories. The lawsuit was judged in favor, declaring the municipal statute unconstitutional.

With a further focus on the climate issue, *PSB et al v Brazil* (*on deforestation and human rights*) addressed the Federal Government's omission in implementing the Action Plan for the Prevention and Control of Deforestation in the Amazon (PPCDAm). The Articulation of Indigenous Peoples of Brazil (APIB) acted as *amicus curiae* in the case, emphasizing the importance of defending Indigenous rights for environmental protection. In April 2024, the STF recognized flaws in the Amazon Legal protection policy and mandated the Federal Union to make a significant commitment to combat illegal deforestation, implement the measures of the PPCDAm, to strengthen monitoring agencies, and to provide transparent information about its actions and results, ordering that data on these measures be submitted to the Environmental and Climate Change Observatory of the National Justice Council (CNJ).

*PSL et al v Brazil et al* (*Pantanal Wildfires*) was filed to hold the government accountable for its omission regarding the fires in the Pantanal, which severely affect Indigenous peoples and the environment. Similarly, *Partido dos Trabalhadores v Brazil* (*Fires in the Pantanal and the Amazon Forest*) addresses the Federal Government's omission concerning its duties to protect, prevent, precaution, supervise, conserve, monitor, and ensure environmental sustainability, particularly regarding its actions against fires that have impacted the Pantanal and the Amazon Rainforest. Both lawsuits were judged together, and the STF recognized structural flaws in the Amazon Legal protection policy, mandating that the Federal Union develop a plan to prevent and combat fires in the Pantanal and the Amazon.

PSB *et al v Brazil* (*Federal environmental sanctioning process*) seeks to recover an environmental sanctioning process at the federal level in response to environmental dismantling during the former President Bolsonaro administration. The decision was deemed extinguished without a resolution on the merits due to the subsequent loss of the object, as there were significant changes in the factual, political, and normative context since the initiation of the lawsuit, including the repeal of the provisions that introduced the changes questioned.

Another extremely relevant lawsuit is *Federal Public Prosecutor's Office v Brazil et al* (*on deforestation hotspots in the Amazon*), filed against the Federal Union, IBAMA, ICMBio, and FUNAI, seeking urgent implementation of measures to control environmental violations in the main hotspots of the Amazon. The lawsuit highlights the increase in deforestation, which breaches the National Climate Change Policy (PNMC) and the Action Plan for the Prevention and Control of Deforestation in the Amazon (PPCDAm), violating international commitments of Brazil such as the Paris Agreement. Additionally, it seeks to hold the Federal Union accountable for the damage caused to the environment and Indigenous peoples of the Amazon due to the lack of prompt and adequate actions to protect the environment and the health of these populations during the COVID-19 pandemic. As the case is under judicial secrecy, the current status of the lawsuit is unknown.

Finally, concerning the lawsuits *Arayara et al v Copelmi et al* (*Mina Guaíba project and affected communities*) and *Arayara et al v Copelmi Mineração et al* (*Mina Guaíba project*), the aim is to suspend and annul the environmental licensing process for the Guaíba Mine Project, an open-pit coal mining venture located in areas inhabited by traditional communities and Indigenous territories.

Indigenous peoples play a central role in climate litigation in Brazil, acting as parties or as *amicus curiae* in environmental lawsuits. Since the defense of their territories is intrinsic to environmental and climate protection, these cases reflect the growing resistance and mobilization of Indigenous communities to prevent the advancement of legislation and projects that violate their rights. Thus, they seek to ensure the preservation of the ecosystems they depend on, playing a fundamental role in curbing climate change.

## 4 Case Studies

Here we discuss two main cases in the context of protecting indigenous rights and their environmental and climate implications in Brazil. The first case involves the Guaíba Mine Project, where the Arayara Institute and the Poty

Guarani Indigenous Association sued FUNAI, Copelmi Mining, and the Henrique Luiz Roessler State Foundation for Environmental Protection (FEPAM).[23] The lawsuit sought to suspend and annul the environmental licensing of the project, alleging the lack of an Environmental Impact Assessment and the absence of free, prior, and informed consultation with the Guajayvi community of the Mbyá Guarani people. The court's decision suspended the licensing process until FUNAI analyzed the Indigenous Component Study (ECI), recognizing the need to include indigenous communities in decisions affecting their lives and cultures.

The second case involves the debate over the Temporal Framework, a legal concept that limits the recognition of indigenous lands to those under possession at the time of the 1988 Constitution's promulgation. The STF ruled this thesis unconstitutional in *Fundação Nacional do Índio v IMA*,[24] directly impacting the territorial rights of all indigenous peoples in Brazil. Additionally, Law No 14.701 attempted, through the legislative process, to reestablish the Temporal Framework, but it faces multiple direct actions of unconstitutionality (ADI s) and direct actions of constitutionality (ADC s) that question or defend this interpretation. The text also emphasizes the importance of a decolonial perspective to understand the relationship between indigenous rights and environmental protection, reinforcing that preserving indigenous lands is crucial for climate change mitigation and social justice.

### 4.1 *Guaíba Mine Case*

The first of these cases was jointly filed by the Arayara International Institute and the Poty Guarani Indigenous Association against the National Indigenous Foundation (FUNAI), Copelmi Mineração, and the Henrique Luiz Roessler State Foundation for Environmental Protection (FEPAM).[25] The aim was to suspend and annul the environmental licensing process for the Guaíba Mine Project, a Copelmi venture deemed the largest open-cast coal mining project in Brazil.[26]

The plaintiffs alleged that the project failed to comply with the obligation to conduct an Environmental Impact Assessment and that there had been no free, prior, and informed consultation with the Indigenous (TeKoá) Guajayvi community of the Mbyá Guarani people, who were affected by the project in Charqueado. Additionally, it was claimed that the Indigenous community

23 *Arayara et al v Copelmi Mineração et al (Mina Guaíba project)* (n 23).

24 *Fundação Nacional do Índio v IMA*, Special Appeal No 1017365/SC, STF Judgment of 27 September 2023.

25 *Arayara et al v Copelmi Mineração et al (Mina Guaíba project)* (n 23).

26 ibid.

expressed interest in commenting on the project after the initial public hearing but was not afforded the opportunity to do so.

Due to the failure to adhere to standards, notably Convention No 169 of the International Labour Organization (ILO), and the potential social, climatic, and environmental impacts such as atmospheric methane gas emissions, pollution of tributaries into rivers, and GHG emissions on nearby communities, the lawsuit sought to suspend the environmental licensing process for the project. It requested a comprehensive assessment of the technical and locational feasibility of the project and specific consultations with the indigenous peoples of the region.

A preliminary injunction suspended the environmental licensing process for the Guaíba Mine Project until FUNAI analyzed the Indigenous Component Study (ECI), to be included in the Environmental Impact Study/Environmental Impact Report (EIA/RIMA), as a means of complying with ILO Convention No 169. FUNAI and FEPAM later asserted that the licensing process for the Guaíba Mine was regular and posed no potential environmental harm. However, the court declared the project's licensing process null and void on the grounds that indigenous communities should participate in decisions affecting their way of life and culture.

Subsequently, Copelmi filed an appeal with a request for suspensive effect, contending that the court's decision was causing damage to the company. However, the request for suspensive effect was rejected by the court, and the appeal is still pending judgment.

Although the appeal is pending, the ruling recognizing the insufficient consultation of indigenous peoples in the licensing process for the Guaíba Mine marks a significant milestone in strengthening the rights of indigenous peoples. This recognition is based on the potential climatic, environmental, cultural, and social impacts that the project activities could have on indigenous life and ancestry.

The case of the Guaíba Mine gains relevance when examined in the context of climate change and environmental protection. Although it does not directly address climate issues, it underscores the urgent need to consider the long-term environmental impacts of industrial activities.

The extraction of natural resources, as in the case of mine, can have significant consequences for regional and global climates through GHG emissions and ecosystem degradation. Therefore, by recognizing the importance of consulting indigenous peoples and considering environmental impacts, this case establishes a crucial link between protecting the rights of local communities and efforts to mitigate the effects of climate change. This holistic approach not only promotes social justice but also contributes to building a more sustainable and resilient future in the face of global climate challenges.

FIGURE 10.1 Indigenous people protesting against the Guaíba coal mine project
Note: Fabiana Reinholz. Audiência reacende debate e críticas sobre Mina Guaíba e Polo Carboquímico no RS. [Hearing Reignites Debate and Criticism About Mina Guaíba and the Carbochemical Hub in RS] (*Brasil de Fato*, 1 October 2019) available at <https://www.brasildefators.com.br/2019/10/01/audiencia-reacende-debate-e-criticas-sobre-mina-guaiba-e-polo-carboquimico-no-rs> accessed 1 May 2024.

### 4.2 *Demarcation of Indigenous Lands*

In September 2023, the STF delivered a landmark ruling by a majority vote of 9 to 2, recognizing the unconstitutionality of the 'Marco Temporal' (Temporal Framework) legal thesis in *Fundação Nacional do Índio v IMA*.[27] This legal interpretation posited that indigenous peoples were entitled only to the lands they inhabited at the time of the Federal Constitution's promulgation on October 5, 1988. The Temporal Framework thesis originated from various legal proceedings and litigations, with indigenous peoples actively seeking protection and demarcation of their ancestral lands, including cases involving the Xokleng, Kaingang, and Guarani indigenous lands (as in *Fundação Nacional do Índio v IMA*), as well as the *Raposa Serra do Sol* case.

Article 231(1) to (4) of the Constitution recognize the inalienable, unavailable, and imprescriptible rights of indigenous peoples over their lands. In response to a decision by the Federal Regional Court of the 4th Region, which

27 *Fundação Nacional do Índio v IMA* (n 37).

ordered the repossession of an area occupied by the Xokleng indigenous people, FUNAI filed an extraordinary appeal in *Fundação Nacional do Índio v IMA*. This appeal contested the decision of the court of first instance, which recognized ownership as evidence of fair possession, which disregarded the traditional occupation of the land by indigenous peoples. The Superior Court of Justice (STJ) subsequently suspended all lawsuits on possession conflict over indigenous lands upon recognizing the general repercussion of the issue (following Theme 1.031, adopted by the STF in *Fundação Nacional do Índio v IMA*), therefore deferring jurisdiction to the STF.

The significance of *Fundação Nacional do Índio v IMA* extends beyond the specific case, as it directly impacts the territorial rights of all indigenous peoples in Brazil. The significance of *Fundação Nacional do Índio v IMA* extends beyond the specific case, as it directly impacts the territorial rights of all indigenous peoples in Brazil. Additionally, Law No 14.701 attempted, through the legislative process, to establish the Temporal Framework, even after the STF's ruling on its unconstitutionality. The approval of this statute represents a concerted effort by powerful sectors, such as agribusiness and the rural sector, to undermine the STF's decision and ensure the legal recognition of claims over lands that were disputed or occupied by non-indigenous individuals or entities after 1988.

To counter this legislative movement, multiple direct actions of unconstitutionality have been filed, challenging the constitutionality of Law No 14.701. These lawsuits argue that the statute violates the inalienable rights of indigenous peoples, as established in Article 231 of the Constitution. Conversely, direct actions of constitutionality have been submitted by supporters of the statute, aiming to affirm its legality and alignment with the Constitution. One of the most notable of these legal challenges is the *Indigenous Genocide Law Case*.[28] This lawsuit was recently added to the Juma database, reflecting its crucial role in the broader legal discourse surrounding the Temporal Framework. The inclusion of the *Indigenous Genocide Law Case* in the Juma database not only highlights the importance of the case but also underscores the intrinsic connection between this issue and the climate crisis, as the protection of indigenous territorial rights is fundamental to environmental preservation and climate change mitigation.

28 *Indigenous Genocide Law Case* (n 34).

The Temporal Framework thesis has faced widespread criticism from indigenous communities for violating historical and territorial rights, establishing a specific date for demarcating indigenous lands while ignoring centuries of occupations and forced displacements. Moreover, indigenous groups warn of the potential for the Temporal Framework to legitimize rights violations and instigate conflicts over indigenous lands.

It is important to note that the Temporal Framework thesis finds support in the *Raposa Serra do Sol* case, which was ruled by the STF in 2009. However, the STF's evolving understanding of the Temporal Framework reflects ongoing indigenous advocacy for territorial rights and environmental justice. Indigenous actions, including protests, political lobbying, and legal maneuvers, have been instrumental in challenging the Temporal Framework's injustices and rights violations.

Recognition and respect for indigenous territorial rights not only promote social justice and human rights but also contribute to global efforts to combat climate change and protect the planet for future generations. By acknowledging indigenous peoples' historical and ancestral connections to the land, one affirms their role as stewards of biodiversity and guardians of environmental sustainability.

Although the Temporal Framework is not strictly about climate change, it is necessary to recognize that the effects of instituting the temporal framework on indigenous lands can have severe impacts on the climate system. This is because protecting indigenous lands is linked to preserving an ecologically balanced environment for present and future generations and maintaining forests as carbon sinks. The possibility of restricting indigenous land tenure rights only to indigenous peoples who were in possession of the lands in 1988 increases the likelihood that lands originally preserved under the practices of traditional peoples may be used and deforested for large-scale production. This would be a driving force behind increased GHG emissions and consequently terrestrial temperatures. During the movements of indigenous peoples against the legal thesis of the Temporal Framework, various artworks were used to reinforce the possible consequences of the framework's enactment, many of which linked the legal thesis to the impossibility of achieving full climate justice.

In an interview during the Temporal Framework trial, the legal coordinator of the Articulation of Indigenous Peoples (APIB) stressed how the Temporary Framework trial is characterized as climate litigation because all the preservation and environmental protection that Indigenous Lands promote are strong

FIGURE 10.2 Indigenous protesting against the temporal framework thesis
Note: Richard Wera Mirim, Terra indígena é garantia de futuro para toda a humanidade [Indigenous Land is a Guarantee of a Future for All Humanity] (Le Monde Diplomatique, 09 August 2024) <Terra Indígena é garantia de futuro para toda a humanidade – Le Monde Diplomatique> accessed 13 august 2024.

allies in the fight against climate change.[29] In fact, a report produced by the World Resources Institute and Climate Focus pointed out that countries such as Brazil, Colombia, Peru, and Mexico were only able to achieve the goals of the Paris Agreement if they preserved and protected the lands occupied by indigenous peoples because these lands are more effective carbon sinks (meaning that they store more carbon than they emit) than non-indigenous lands due to the traditional and sustainable land management practices used by traditional peoples and the fact that they are largely untouched forested lands.[30]

---

29 Cristiane Fontes, 'Marco temporal de terras indígenas é um litígio climático, diz Maurício Terena' [Temporal Framework for Indigenous Lands is a Climate Litigation, Says Maurício Terena] *Folha de S.Paulo* (São Paulo, 30 May 2023) <www1.folha.uol.com.br/ambiente/2023/05/marco-temporal-de-terras-indigenas-e-um-litigio-climatico-diz-mauricio-terena.shtml> accessed 01 March 2024.

30 'Sink or swim: How Indigenous and community lands can make or break nationally determined contributions' (Forest Declaration Assessment March 2022) <https://forestdeclaration.org/resources/sink-or-swim> accessed 13 August 2024.

In addition, the Institute for the Protection of the Amazon (IPAM) has carried out research which identifies that the projected emissions from the change in the use of lands that are now indigenous territories is between 7.6 and 18.7 billion tons of $CO_2$eq, equivalent to 5 to 14 years of GHG emissions in Brazil.[31]

Despite the advancement of the doctrine of general repercussion established in *Fundação Nacional do Índio v IMA* compared to the prevailing understanding in the Supreme Court, certain limitations are still observed, which cater to the desires of the rural sector. The doctrine establishes a sort of inverted temporal framework, where possession, improvements, and titles are ensured for those who occupied indigenous lands since the promulgation of the Constitution of 1988, provided there was no indigenous occupation or continuous expropriation in the area on October 5, 1988.

## 5 Conclusion

Climate litigation has emerged as a crucial tool in the fight against climate change, especially in the context of Indigenous rights and the preservation of their territories. In Brazil, this discussion is intrinsically linked to the debate on the temporal framework, a legal thesis that limits the recognition of indigenous lands only to those that were under possession on the date of the promulgation of the 1988 Constitution.

This legal interpretation has been widely criticized for limiting the original rights of Indigenous peoples and for ignoring the historical reality of communities that, in many cases, were violently removed from their lands before this date. The recognition of these original rights should be based on the right to memory, truth, and reparation, considering the testimonies of elders, shamans, and wise figures from the villages, some of whom, almost centenarians, are still alive to bear witness to the massacres and expulsions their communities faced.[32]

---

31 Ana Alencar and others, 'Uma combinação nefasta—PL 490 e Marco Temporal ameaçam os direitos territoriais indígenas e colocam em risco a segurança climática da Amazônia e do país' [A Deadly Combination—PL 490 and the Temporal Framework Threaten Indigenous Territorial Rights and Endanger the Climate Security of the Amazon and the Country] (IPAM June 2023) <https://ipam.org.br/wp-content/uploads/2023/06/Uma-combinacao-nefasta-%E2%80%93-PL-490-e-Marco-Temporal-ameacam-os-direitos-territoriais-indigenas-e-colocam-em-risco-a-seguranca-climatica-da-Amazonia-e-do-pais.pdf.> accessed 13 August 2024.

32 Liana Amin Lima da Silva & Carlos Frederico Marés Souza Filho, 'Marco Temporal como Retrocesso dos Direitos Originários Indígenas e Quilombolas', in Tarrega, Wolkmer &

The analysis of the cases related to the Mina Guaíba project and *Indigenous Genocide Law Case* reveals that, although these issues appear as significant contextual elements, the associated climate discussion is still in its early stages of development. The impact of climate change on decisions related to these cases has not yet been fully explored, and the climate implications of these projects are only beginning to be reconfigured. The absence of an in-depth discussion on how climate issues influence and are influenced by these cases underscores the need to integrate these dimensions into future analyses. The conclusion about the climate impact of these cases has yet to be consolidated, requiring a more detailed examination of their long-term environmental and social repercussions.

Legal scholars in Brazil address the tension between the protection of Indigenous rights and prevailing legal frameworks, which often fail to fully recognize the significance of Indigenous lands. Such scholars argue that current legal interpretations can undermine the rights of Indigenous peoples, who play a crucial role in preserving vital ecosystems, such as the Amazon.[33] Aligning legal frameworks with indigenous rights makes the protection of these lands a crucial component of global environmental governance. This approach highlights that defending Indigenous territories is not just a matter of justice, but also essential for the survival of the planet.

This analysis connects to the broader relationship between climate litigation and the protection of Indigenous rights. The participation of indigenous communities in ecosystem preservation is fundamental to combating climate change, making the defense of their territorial rights a central piece both for environmental sustainability and social justice.

A decolonial perspective provides an essential theoretical framework for understanding and challenging the legal and political practices that sustain the temporal framework and other forms of oppression. Ailton Krenak and Luciana Gersen dos Santos emphasize the importance of land as an integral part of Indigenous identity and culture, countering the Western, mercantilist view of property.[34] They argue that the fight for Indigenous land rights is also a fight to preserve the memory and history of Indigenous peoples, which have been constantly erased or distorted by colonial and neocolonial processes.

---

Marés Souza Filho (eds), *Direitos Territoriais Quilombolas: Muito Além do Marco Temporal* (PUC-Goiás 2016).

33 See Maria Antónia Tigre and Anna Maria Cárcamo, Chapter 13 in this book.

34 Ailton Krenak, *Futuro Ancestral* (1st edn, Companhia das Letras 2022); Luciano Gersem dos Santos, *O Índio Brasileiro: O Que Você Precisa Saber sobre os Povos Indígenas no Brasil Hoje* (1st edn, LACED 2006) 101.

The Indigenous perspective on land and its relationship to climate justice offers a more comprehensive and integrative approach, challenging the limitations of the temporal framework and other forms of oppression. By recognizing land as a vital element of Indigenous identity and culture, this perspective not only counters a mercantilist and reductionist view but also opens space for a broader dialogue on environmental governance that respects and incorporates traditional knowledge.

The temporal framework, by restricting Indigenous territorial rights to a colonial view of possession, not only disregards the historical and cultural reality of these peoples but also undermines climate mitigation strategies. Indigenous land management practices, which include ecological knowledge and sustainable resource use, are crucial for preserving ecosystems vital for global climate regulation.

Adopting a decolonial perspective and strengthening climate litigation are fundamental steps to ensure that indigenous rights are respected and that climate mitigation strategies are truly inclusive and effective. Overcoming the Temporal Framework thesis and reaffirming original land rights are not just acts of social justice, but crucial necessities for the planet's survival. Integrating these Indigenous perspectives into climate discussions can broaden the scope of proposed solutions and promote a more just and sustainable future for all.

The idea of a future for Indigenous peoples is closely related to the concept of *buen vivir*, which critiques the colonial capitalist model and offers viable alternatives based on Indigenous values and resistance experiences.[35] Krenak emphasizes the need to build a future that rejects colonial discourse, stating that it is impossible to consider a history of homeland 'amid this continental graveyard;' it is crucial to continue insurgent through convergences.[36] Coloniality continues to influence the relationship between indigenous peoples and their lands, as Quijano argues, limiting the possibility of a just future.[37] Therefore, thinking beyond the Temporal Framework and adopting a decolonial perspective are essential to ensure that climate solutions are truly inclusive and respectful of the traditions and rights of Indigenous peoples. In the context of increasing recognition of Amerindian knowledge and the need to

---

35 Acosta (n 8) 264.

36 Krenak (n 46).

37 Anibal Quijano, Colonialidade do poder, eurocentrismo e América Latina [Coloniality of Power, Eurocentrism, and Latin America] in Edgardo Lander (org.) *A colonialidade do saber: eurocentrismo e ciências sociais*—perspectivas latino-americanas (3rd edn, Clacso 2005a).

confront colonial power structures, Indigenous climate litigation has emerged as a crucial tool for both resistance and protection. Colonialism has historically exploited and dispossessed Indigenous peoples, causing significant damage to their lands and traditional ways of life. Despite these adversities, the ancestral knowledge and sustainable practices of these communities offer essential insights for a more equitable and effective approach to environmental management. Indigenous climate litigation addresses the pressing need to safeguard not only territorial rights but also the ecological wisdom that contributes significantly to climate resilience.

By challenging legal and political systems that marginalize Indigenous rights, these litigations highlight the critical connection between protecting Indigenous territories and effective climate action. Incorporating Indigenous knowledge into environmental policies can enhance global climate strategies, emphasizing that the defense of Indigenous lands is integral to maintaining ecological balance and addressing climate change. This approach calls for a profound transformation in our environmental justice frameworks, advocating for a more inclusive and collaborative effort to tackle the climate crisis and ensure a sustainable future for all.

CHAPTER 11

# Future Generations and Climate Litigation in Brazil

*Luciana Bauer**

## 1 Introduction

John Rawls inaugurates his Theory of Justice[1] by presenting the hypothesis that the democratic consensus—with its principles of justice, priority of freedoms, and human dignity—is born out of a gathering of people who choose the best rules and rights for themselves and for future citizens. This marks the beginning of a new outlook: a system of justice in which a hypothetical and previous generation creates and perfects, with its political pluralism, a state of justice as equality and equity for future generations, preserving and improving the constitutional consensus, which becomes the foundation of the democratic state and its basic structure.

Rawls innovates by attributing to past generations the responsibility of making the best choices, through philosophical and moral reflection, which must ensure the equitable and fair distribution of legal assets and rights to present and future generations. While admitting that this distribution may not be equitable, Rawls points out that it is more beneficial for the majority, while maintaining political consensus and respecting minorities, since the unfolding of his theory of justice assimilates Kant's views on the need for perpetual peace and justice as equity also for nations and peoples.[2]

In light of the loss of biodiversity, alarming systematic pollution, and global warming with its extreme disasters,[3] this chapter assesses how constitutional democracies have solved their norm of intergenerational law to deliver the assets of life, security, and happiness to future generations, both human and non-human. In addition, this chapter considers intergenerational law and how

* Lecturer on Climate Change, Human Rights and Democracy. Former Federal Judge. This work is part of the International Research Program between Delaware Law School and the Stricto Sensu Graduate Program in Legal Science - PPCJ/UNIVALI. https://orcid.org/0000-0003-3037-8461.

1 John Rawls, *Uma Teoria da Justiça* [*A Theory of Justice*] (Almiro Pisatta & Lenita Maria Rimoli Esteves tr, Martins Fontes 2002).

2 John Rawls, *O Direito dos Povos* [*The Right of Peoples*] (Luis Carlos Borges tr, Martins Fontes, 2004).

3 Mary Christina Wood, *On the Eve of Destruction: Courts Confronting the Climate Emergency* (CUP 2021).

 | DOI:10.1163/9789004690974_012

it calls for a new approach to the legal protection of future generations, as well as the intersection between intergenerational law and climate law. Some lessons from environmental and climate litigation are also analyzed, as well as ways in which Brazil contributes to these new perspectives on climate and the environment as rights intrinsic to humanity.

## 2 Intergenerational Law

While the concept of intergenerational rights or concerns in legal standards was born in modern philosophy with Kant, later acquiring greater importance in the legal-philosophical forms of consensual democracy presented by Rawls, it is only with the advent of global environmental and climate jurisprudence that this concept takes on its current form.[4] New theorists such as Häberle, Jonas, and Brown Weiss offer a taxonomy of intergenerational law centered on the need for the Earth's assets and attributes to be preserved at their lowest common level, with a focus on the concept of human dignity.

Given the Chernobyl accident and the devastation caused by atomic weapons in previous wars, Häberle recognizes that a single generation would leave a trail of pollution equivalent to thousands of years of radioactive waste for subsequent generations to manage.[5] With this idea in mind, he outlines a new constitutional law with another form of social contract: the intergenerational contract, which would be the normal expression of the developmental phase of the Constitutional State. The basis would be a balance between the freedom of the current generation and the obligations regarding the interests of future generations. Jonas, in his work *Principle of Responsibility,* presents the philosophical argument of the finitude of nature and life.[6] He also questions the reasonableness of the destruction that the two great wars brought upon humanity (and all the technological apparatus that followed them, such as atomic energy), in the sense that nature might perhaps no longer be able to simply regenerate itself. This philosophical postulate—innovative because previous philosophers never questioned a man-made extinction or an ultimate nuclear extinction—entails the notion that future generations should

4 James May & Erin *Daly, Judicial Handbook on Environmental Constitutionalism* (UNEP 2017).

5 Peter Häberle, 'Un derecho constitucional para las presentes y futuras generaciones. The form of the social contract: the intergenerational contract' (2009) *Lecciones y Ensayos* 87, 17–37 (Milton Fellay & Leandro Ferreyra tr).

6 Hans Jonas, *O Princípio da Responsabilidade: Ensaio de uma Ética para a Civilização Tecnológica* [*Das Prinzip Verantwortung. Versuch einer Ethik für die Technologische Zivilisation*] (Marijane Lisboa & Luiz Barros Montez tr, PUC Rio 2011) 41.

not carry our waste and ill deeds on their shoulders. Any action can only be deemed legally acceptable if it is compatible with the permanence of human life on Earth. Brown Weiss discusses at length this Rawlsian question: 'Should we be kind to future generations?'[7] She answers with a pragmatic Theory of Intergenerational Equity, based on the idea that there is no hierarchy between past, present, or future generations since the current generation should never be considered the owner of natural assets (cultural heritage) but rather a precarious holder, who should return the same assets to the next precarious holders. For the scholar, the principle of intergenerational equity requires each generation to be able to satisfy its own needs by conserving access to planetary resources, as well as their diversity and quality, without depleting them.

Starting with the 1972 Stockholm Declaration,[8] which established the obligation to protect and improve the environment for future generations, followed by the 1992 Rio Declaration on Environment and Development,[9] which stated that development must equitably meet the needs of present and future generations, intergenerational law has evolved to include climate aspects. This is due to the intensification of climate litigation and its new approach on behalf of both current and future generations.

## 3 Future Generations and Climate Litigation

Only a handful of countries, including Brazil,[10] have enshrined the concept of future generations in their constitutional charters.

Just as the green amendments[11] are important as a way of consolidating political will and consensus on protecting the environment and the climate, devising constitutional provisions that ensure rights to future human generations—especially those with a climate focus—would also bring about

7 Edith Brown Weiss, 'Implementing Intergenerational Equity', in Fitzmaurice, Ong & Merkouris (eds), Research Handbook on International Environmental Law (Edward Elgar 2010) 100.

8 United Nations Conference on the Human Environment, 'Stockholm Declaration on the Human Environment' (16 June 1972) UN Doc A/CONF.48/14/Rev.1.

9 United Nations Conference on Environment and Development, 'Rio Declaration on Environment and Development,' (12 August 1992) UN Doc A/CONF.151/26.

10 Brazilian Constitution, art 225: 'All have the right to an ecologically balanced environment, which is an asset of common use and essential to a healthy quality of life, and both the Government and the community shall have the duty to defend and preserve it for present and *future generations*' (emphasis added).

11 Maya K Van Rossum, *The Green Amendment: Securing our Right to a Healthy Environment* (Disruption Books 2017).

a significant evolution in their protection, without the need to rely solely on the sequence of fortuitous events provided by the doctrines of public trust.[12]

For some years now, the United Nations (UN) has been proposing approaches to confer rights and legal certainty to future generations, either through its climate treaties or through effective mechanisms, such as the idea of implementing an *ombudsman* for future generations (Brundtland Commission).[13] This individual would be a specific UN high commissioner for future generations, possibly taking legal action in cases where future rights were at stake. In September 2024, *The Summit of the Future* will take place, a conference that aims to implement the rights of future generations through UNGA Decision No 77/568.[14] The UN has long considered a resolution to support global jurisprudence on the rights of future generations, adding ancestral knowledge from Indigenous peoples, as well as what has been learned so far in climate litigation. The aim is for the rights of future generations to be enshrined as a human right in international agreements, national legislation, and case law.[15]

Regardless of this transnational normative agenda currently in the making, legal action is already being taken on behalf of future generations—without waiting for a law or constitution to explicitly provide for this possibility. Significantly, future generations are not to be confused with children and young people,[16] who already account for 25% of plaintiffs in climate litigation.[17] Faced with the prospect of having future generations as plaintiffs in court, many judges are hesitant about how to proceed, and several national constitutional courts remain reluctant to accept future generations as parties. The judiciary sometimes diminishes or annuls their presence, often due to three reasons. Some understand that accepting parents as representatives of minors in court

---

12 Mary Wood & Michael C Blumm, *The Public Trust Doctrine in Environmental and Natural Resources Law* (3rd edn, Carolina Academic Press 2021).

13 United Nations World Commission on Environment and Development, *Our Common Future* (*Brundtland Report*) (OUP 1987).

14 UNGA Dec 77/568 'Scope of the Summit of the Future' (1 September 2023) UN Doc A//77/L.109.

15 Human rights are not aimed at protecting the current generation, or one single generation. Nonetheless, it is believed that a formal inscription in the body of constitutional letters brings greater effectiveness, especially for reluctant courts.

16 Elizabeth Donger, 'Children and Youth in Strategic Climate Litigation: Advancing Rights through Legal Argument and Legal Mobilization' (2022) 11(2) *Transnational Environmental Law* 263.

17 Michael Burger & Maria Antonia Tigre, *Global Climate Litigation Report: 2023 Status Review* (Sabin Center for Climate Change Law & UNEP 2023).

(such as in *Minors Oposa v Factoran*[18]) would already be sufficient for jurisdictional protection. Others note that accepting children makes it unnecessary to invoke future generations (such as in *Neubauer et al v Germany*[19]). Finally, some simply disqualify future generations, such as in *Urgenda Foundation v Netherlands*,[20] and remove them from the case. This occurs on the grounds that future generations do not exist procedurally, since they do not have a concrete legal asset that has suffered damage.

However, the uncertain scenario for future generations in court is changing. Judicial representatives from around the world gathered at the ECtHR for a meeting called '*Justice, Future Generations and Environment*',[21] which aimed at contributing to the preparation of the 'Declaration on Future Generations,' to be discussed at the 2024 Summit of the Future. The meeting marked a milestone in the international dialog between judges on justice for the next generations. Three issues in particular were addressed. First, the competence of the courts to judge actions brought in the interests of future generations, especially the legitimacy of the judge to examine claims in a legal field that

18 Supreme Court of the Philippines, *Minors Oposa v Factoran* (GR No 101083) Judgment of 30 July 1993, available at <https://cer.org.za/virtual-library/judgments/foreign-and-international-courts/oposa-v-factorian>, accessed on 12 February 2024.

19 Constitutional Court of the Federal Republic of Germany, *Neubauer et al v Germany* (1 BvR 2656/18, 1 BvR 78/20, 1 BvR 96/20 & 1 BvR 288/20) Order of 24 March 2021, available at <https://www.bundesverfassungsgericht.de/SharedDocs/Entscheidungen/DE/2021/03/rs20210324_1bvr265618.html>, accessed on 15 January 2024.

20 The Hague court expressly rejected future generations in paragraph 37 of the decision: 'It is not disputed between the parties that the claim of Urgenda, insofar as acting on behalf of the current generation of Dutch nationals against the emission of [GHGs] on Dutch territory, is admissible. However, the State argued, as understood by the Court, that Urgenda cannot act on behalf of future generations of Dutch nationals nor of current and future generations of foreigners. The State does not have an interest in this ground of appeal, because Urgenda's claim is already admissible insofar as Urgenda acts on behalf of the interests of the current generation of Dutch nationals and individuals subject to the State's jurisdiction within the meaning of Article 1 ECHR, respectively. After all, it is without a doubt plausible that the current generation of Dutch nationals, in particular but not limited to the younger individuals in this group, will have to deal with the adverse effects of climate change in their lifetime if global emissions of [GHGs] are not adequately reduced. Therefore, the Court does not have to consider the questions raised by the State in this ground of appeal.' The Hague District Court, *Urgenda Foundation v Netherlands* (Case No 19/00135) Judgment of 9 October 2018, para 37, available at <https://climatecasechart.com/wp-content/uploads/non-us-case-documents/2018/20181009_2015-HAZA-C0900456689_decision-4.pdf>, last accessed on 3 August 2024.

21 Constitutional Council France. *Justice, Future Generations and Environment https://www.conseil-constitutionnel.fr/sites/default/files/2024-02/generations-futures-programme-en.pdf.*

borders on the political field.[22] This will require determining which courts have jurisdiction, given the nature of the disputes and their location, depending on the legal systems and areas involved (whether regional or international). The second issue referred to the proposition of acting in the field of environmental justice. The third concerned the relation between national and supranational legal procedures.

Why are future generations a welcome innovation in court? Firstly, it allows for a deeper environmental and climate debate, including the critical notion of intergenerational equity. Secondly, there is a robust mobilizing component in invoking future generations and unborn beings as parties, thereby increasing the responsibility of the judge when pronouncing the concrete law on a case. Furthermore, it serves as an initiation for future citizens in the political art of democratic consensus, resulting in a greater gain for the community.

An initiative from various intellectuals, scientists, and entities linked to the climate and environmental struggle promulgated the *Maastricht Principles on The Human Rights of Future Generations*,[23] which seeks to consolidate the current state of international law with regard to the human rights of future generations, making a general compilation of all applicable legislations in force and creating a more comprehensive overview of all prevailing rights of future generations in the world. This consolidation is intended to assist in drafting a future treaty on such rights.

Recently, Special Rapporteur on the right to development, Surya Deva made a rapport about development of children and future generations,[24] reaffirming that the right of young children and future generations to sustainable development and to decisions about the future is an inalienable human right:

> In the present report, the Special Rapporteur focuses on realizing the right to development of children and future generations. Children are often referred to as the future of society. However, they are part of the

---

22 Constitutional Council France and Brazilian Supreme Court. *Justice, Future Generations and Environment. Note Presse. https://www.conseil-constitutionnel.fr/sites/default/files/2024-02/generations-futures-programme-en.pdf.*

23 UNHCHR, 'Maastricht principles on the Human Rights of Future Generations' (UNHCHR 2023), available at <https://www.ohchr.org/sites/default/files/documents/new-york/events/hr75-future-generations/Maastricht-Principles-on-The-Human-Rights-of-Future-Generations.pdf>, accessed on 4 March 2024.

24 UN A/HRC/57/43: Right to development of children and future generations—Report of the Special Rapporteur on the right to development, Surya Deva in https://www.ohchr.org/en/documents/thematic-reports/ahrc5743-right-development-children-and-future-generations-report.

> present generation of rights holders and should not be confused or conflated with future generations.2 The term 'future generations' should be understood to refer to all generations that do not yet exist, 3 but will exist and inherit the Earth in the future. The Special Rapporteur recommends that the concept of future generations should be understood to include all organisms, not merely human beings … The principle of intergenerational equity embodies 'a concept of fairness among generations in the use and conservation of the environment and its natural resources'. While this principle is often invoked in relation to environmental justice or sustainable development, the concept of equity has broader dimensions and can be applied to all decisions taken by present generations with impacts for future generations. Decision makers—including governments and businesses—often plan for the future. Such planning is generally based on forecasted numbers and abstract future needs, rather than the human rights of future generations. To act in line with the principle of intergenerational equity, that must change. Article 5 (4) of the Declaration on the Responsibilities of the Present Generations Towards Future Generations provides that 'the present generations should take into account possible consequences for future generations of major projects before these are carried out'. The foreseeability and severity of harm and the probability of its occurrence and irreversibility should be the key factors to consider.[25]

## 4 Going beyond Future Generations of Humans

Other important UN resolutions that have an even more revolutionary scope are being studied: they focus not only on the concept of intergenerational human rights, but on the right to the perpetuation of life itself and Earth.[26] One of the examples of these proposed resolutions is the concept of *Living Well in Balance and Harmony with Mother Earth and Mother Earth Centric Actions* presented to UNEP by the Republic of Bolivia at the beginning of 2024. This resolution recalled previous UN General Assembly resolutions related to the International Day of Mother Earth and highlights the diverse approaches available to countries for sustainable development. Although withdrawn, the document recognized the indigenous perspective on Living Well, emphasizing balance, harmony, and complementarity with all living beings on Earth.

25 ibid.
26 See Fernanda Capdeville et al (Chapter 14).

It underlined the importance of non-anthropocentric approaches, such as ecocentric, biocentric, and cosmocentric worldviews. The proposal acknowledged the global biodiversity framework and the role of biodiversity in human well-being and prosperity. It stressed the need to recognize Mother Earth as a living being with rights, incorporating this perspective into various international agreements. The proposal suggested specific actions, including policy instruments for nature protection, economic growth with wealth redistribution, educational initiatives, and promoting sustainable consumption and production. It encouraged integrating Mother Earth-centric actions into national policies, programs, and projects. Furthermore, the proposal called for financial and technical support for Mother Earth-centric actions, emphasizing their role in addressing climate and environmental crises. It suggested the creation of a web-based platform to exchange information on such actions. The proposal concluded by calling on member States to prioritize and implement Mother Earth-centric actions, emphasizing the involvement of Indigenous peoples and local communities.

In the same vein as Bolivia, Zaffaroni proposes an ecocentric approach that abandons the neglect with which animals and nature have been treated in philosophical thought and laws. He recalls the civilizational achievement represented by this vision of *Pachamama*[27] (Mother Earth, in Quechua) in the constitutions of Bolivia and Ecuador, which starts from the notion that the individual is not the only subject of rights, because the rights of *Pachamama* form the core of other rights. Only by respecting her can the lost balance and harmony be rebuilt. This line of thought is not unlike the view of Nussbaum, a disciple of Rawls, who holds that it is inexorable to defend the rights of disabled people, future generations, and animals as if they were our own rights.[28] If Rawls focuses on how to distribute assets fairly, Nussbaum breaks new ground by saying that not only humans have the right to this distribution of justice. The philosopher argues that the rights of animals will one day have the same weight as the environmental rights that people want for themselves, because it is a right to life itself and because it extends to future generations. Animals need a dignified life just as much as humans, which is also part of a necessary non-anthropogenic outlook.

So we have these two major concepts taking shape at the level of transnational normativity: (i) the concept of intergenerational law or intergenerationality, especially within climate law, in which future generations will also have their rights guaranteed by treaties; and (ii) the concept of *Pachamama*

---

27 Eugenio Raúl Zaffaroni, *La Pachamama y el humano* (Madres de Plaza de Mayo 2017).
28 Martha Nussbaum, *Justice for Animals* (Simon and Schuster 2022).

or *Nature Law*, which is beginning to take shape, of safeguarding assets and beings beyond the human, based on the ancestral concept of Mother Earth and collective human responsibility.

This creates a philosophical bridge between humanity's ancestral knowledge and the litigation and climate laws that we need, as Tigre wrote:

> Now that the right to a healthy environment and the complementing duty for the environment have been adopted at the international level, we can introduce additional progressive new rights and duties that take us even further in environmental protection. For example, the deep care for the Earth shared across religious and Indigenous beliefs promotes harmony with nature, which is already reflected in international environmental law. It reinforces that every person has a right to a healthy environment and relatedly shares a duty to care for the environment. These beliefs can similarly provide the pathway for evolving or emerging concepts such as intergenerational equity, ecojustice, rights of nature, and ecocide.[29]

## 5 The Cases of Intergenerational Law and Brazilian Intergenerational Climate Law

There is a difference between the Brazilian constitutional system[30] and other constitutional models adopting collective and diffuse rights. In the Brazilian model, there is a representative or a procedural substitution provided for by law for all rights of an intergenerational nature and of future generations brought before the courts.[31] Perhaps for this reason, the national climate

29 Maria Antonia Tigre, 'Exploring the Bedrock for Earth Jurisprudence' (2022) 22 *Rutgers Journal of Law & Religion* 223.

30 The Brazilian Constitution addresses future generations primarily in its Preamble and also in specific articles that establish principles and guidelines for sustainable development and environmental preservation. In fact, the Preamble mentions the commitment to building a free, just, and fraternal society, guaranteeing national development, eradicating poverty, and promoting the well-being of all, without distinction of origin, race, sex, color, age, and any other form of discrimination. Moreover, Article 170(VI) mentions that the economic order must observe the defense of the environment for present and future generations. Finally, Article 225 establishes that 'everyone has the right to an ecologically balanced environment, a common asset of the people and essential to a healthy quality of life, imposing on the Public Power and the community the duty to defend and preserve it for present and future generations.'

31 In the United States, for example, there is an extreme difficulty in advancing climate action or intergenerational action, due to the well-defined doctrine of standing, as

lawsuit databases do not contain any lawsuits in which future generations figure as autonomous entities.[32] Even though there is no mention of future generations plaintiffs in court, there is a lot being said about the rights of future generations in the environmental and climate fields in Brazilian courts.

Brazil has always been an ambitious country in environmental law, which is reflected in its climate law.[33] The Federal Supreme Court (STF) is an example of this in its Green Agenda,[34] in which it defined Brazil as an Ecological Constitutional State.[35] This concept of ecological democracy creates an intense link between the defense of life, human rights, and the rights of nature. The great legacy of these actions analyzed by the STF translates into public climate policies as part of the constitutional system of intergenerational protection due to climate change, based on the STF's interpretation of Article 225 of the Brazilian Constitution. All climate action must be interpreted in a way that respects the right to life, health, human dignity, cultural and environmental heritage, and provides for the continuity of life for current and future generations.

Three of the best illustrations of intergenerational (climate) cases currently before Brazilian courts will be decided on the basis of these constitutional interpretative points[36] given by the STF. These cases are: *IEA v*

---

discussed in Antonin Scalia, 'The Doctrine of Standing as an Essential Element of the Separation of Powers' (1983) 17(4) *Suffolk University LR* 881. In Brazil, however, the Public Prosecutor's Office has broad legitimacy to represent any collective legal interest. In fact, Article 129(III) and (IX) confers powers upon the Public Prosecutor's Office to act in the defense of collective and diffuse rights.

32 Jusclima2030 is the official climate action database of the Brazilian National Council of Justice and has bilingual access at JusClima2030 (jfrs.jus.br). In addition, the JUMA databases from PUC-Rio can be found at <https://www.juma.nima.puc-rio.br/en/base-dados-clima-licenciamento-ambiental>. Cases are also available in English at the Sabin Center's database.

33 Rafaela Martins da Rosa, *Dano Climático: Conceito, Pressupostos e Responsabilização* (2nd edn, Tirant lo Blanch, 2024).

34 James R May, Marcelo Buzaglo Dantas & Luciana Bauer, 'Climate Rights in Brazil and the United States: A Convergence in Contrasts' (2024) 56(1) *Case Western JIL* 439.

35 *PSB et al v Brazil (on deforestation and human rights)*, ADPF 760, Judgment of 6 April 2022, paras 19–25.

36 The Opinion by Justice Cármen Lúcia in *PSB et al v Brazil* (*on deforestation and human rights*), ADPF 760, STF 6 April 2022, defines these constitutional interpretative points, referring to Brazil as an Ecological Constitutional State and emphasizing that the protection of the environment is a matter of planetary scope and that it is the duty of the State and society to ensure ecological balance for present and future generations. Nature does not forgive man-made damage, and it is necessary to act responsibly to avoid irreparable damage. Environmental dignity is seen—in her opinion—as a central element of contemporary constitutionalism, which must take into account not only the dignity of the human person, but also the dignity of the human species and the preservation of

*Brazil*;[37] *Costa Legal et al v Florianópolis et al*;[38] and the execution of the 2018 judgment handed down before the IACtHR in *Case of the Xucuru Indigenous People and their Members v Brazil*.[39]

These cases illustrate the three main types of climate action in Brazil that have a connection with future generations by preserving biomes, natural rights, or cultural means of subsistence. These three types of climate actions are: The first are pure climate actions, with parties, content, and claims that fall under climate rights adopted by treaties or global jurisprudence.[40] This class has two subtypes: 1.1) climate action to prevent damage to the climate or

---

the environment as a whole. Environmental ethics is seen as an essential principle to ensure respectful coexistence between human beings and nature. The duty of the State to enforce the guarantee of environmental dignity is a direct consequence of the anthropocentric spirit of the Constitution. After all, the constitutional text, in its first article, third paragraph, establishes the dignity of the human person as one of the essential foundations of the Brazilian Republic. Article 225 of the Constitution, as already mentioned, includes the right to an ecologically balanced environment in the sphere of human dignity, elevating the protection of ecosystems to the status of an elementary purpose of the republic. Cármen Lúcia's vote goes exactly in this direction. For the Justice, by adhering to and ratifying the various environmental commitments related to the climate agenda, the Brazilian State included such objectives and targets in its internal obligations to protect ecosystems, reduce deforestation and control carbon emissions. Especially because, as a nation still in development, Brazil's role in limiting the greenhouse effect is much more about maintaining carbon sequestration spaces and less about reducing emissions. For this Justice, the following principles are taken from the Brazilian environmental and climate constitutional subsystem: (a) principle of environmental dignity (b) principle of environmental ethics (c) principle of solidarity in environmental matters (d) principle of environmental efficiency (e) principle of responsibility in environmental matters; (f) principle of non-retrogression in environmental and climate matters.

37 *IEA v Brazil*, ACP No. 5048951-39.2020.4.04.7000, filed in 2020 before the 4th Federal Regional Court of Paraná.

38 *Costa Legal et al v Florianópolis et al*, ACP No. 5012843-56.2021.4.04.7200, filed on 19 May 2021 before the 6th federal court of Santa Catarina.

39 *Case of the Xucuru Indigenous People and their Members v Brazil*. Judgment of Feb 5, 2018, IACtHR Series C No 346.

40 Generally in the concept of climate litigation adopted by UNEP in the report *Climate Change Report*: Status Review 2023. This report considers 'climate litigation' to be cases that raise material issues based on laws or facts related to climate change mitigation, adaptation or the science of climate change. These cases are brought before a range of administrative or judicial bodies. The lawsuits are usually identified with keywords such as 'climate change', 'global warming', 'global change', 'GHGs', and 'sea level rise', but cases that actually raise legal or factual issues related to climate change are considered, even if they do not use these specific terms. But in the Brazilian case, where GDP (PIB) basically comes from agricultural and mineral commodities, the conflict over land, and specifically over indigenous land, must also be considered a climate litigation many times, especially when it involves the conservation of key biomes that are in immemorial possession of

to guarantee the implementation of protocols that Brazil has adhered to and is responsible for with regard to carbon emissions and climate change; and 1.2) reparatory action for climate damage that has already been consolidated, as in the case of the public civil action brought by the representative of the Brazilian State's Department (AGU—*Advocacia Geral da União*) related to climate damage (such as that caused by deforestation) and against major deforesters (individuals and companies).[41] The second are nature rights actions with climate impact, whose primary focus is the protection of natural objects that are essential for future generations of humans and non-humans—their preservation and dignity—and which have a high climate impact.[42] The third is human rights actions with climate impact, whose primary focus is generally linked to human rights related to land and territory, both for Indigenous people and the autochthonous population, as well as for small farmers and extractivists in the sustainable economy of biomes, with a high climate impact. The latter generally come from regional human rights courts or the STF.

In the first category, exemplified by *IEA v Brazil*,[43] refers to future generations due to its primary purpose of preserving the climate through the preservation of a key biome for the regulation of the Earth's climate and life.[44] This lawsuit was filed in the city of Curitiba, state of Paraná, in 2020, and asks for compliance with the Action Plan for the Prevention and Control of Deforestation in

---

indigenous people according to the Brazilian Constitution. Therefore, a relaxation of this initial concept would be welcome.

41 *IBAMA v Dirceu Kruger* (*on illegal wood storage*) ACP 1037196-19.2023.4.01.3200, filed on 12 September 2023 before a Federal Court in Amazonas. This is a public civil action filed by the Brazilian Institute of the Environment and Natural Resources (IBAMA) against Dirceu Kruger, arguing for civil liability for climate damage due to the illegal deforestation of 5,600 hectares of Amazon Forest in areas located in the Municipalities of Boca do Acre and Lábrea, in the state of Amazonas. By judgment of 18 July 2024, the court accepted the arguments of the AGU and determined, among other measures, that the offender presents a compensation project within a period of 90 days, under penalty of a daily fine. The project should include the implementation of carbon sinks, and it should be considered for this purpose the emission of 901,600 tons of $CO_2$ and, for the purposes of slaughter, possible recovery/restoration verified in deforested areas. At the request of the AGU, the defendant was also prohibited from having access to financing in official establishments and from receiving tax benefits, as well as from acquiring, divesting, renting or lending chainsaws, tractors, chains, and associated instruments, as well as cattle or agricultural products. In relation to the areas subject to deforestation, the practice of any negotiating act that transfers the occupations to third parties.

42 See Fernanda Capdeville et al, Chapter 14.

43 *IEA v Brazil* (n 37).

44 We are more and more facing the sixth extinction, so yes, all climate disputes or otherwise that maintain key biomes for the maintenance of life are of interest to future generations.

the Legal Amazon (PPCDAm), linked to the National Policy on Climate Change (PNMC), stating that the maximum rate of illegal deforestation in the Amazon should not exceed 3,925.00 $km^2$ and demanding the federal government to carry out forest restoration of the entire area deforested in excess of the annual legal limit, among other measures. The request is based on the grounds that, by failing to meet the PPCDAm targets and the related emission reductions, the government is violating fundamental rights, the constitution, and infra-constitutional legislation. The plaintiffs are seeking an order obliging the federal government to comply with existing policies, reforest an area equivalent to that which has been deforested above the legal limit, and allocate sufficient budgetary resources for this purpose. They argue that the constitution guarantees a fundamental right to a stable climate and the government must comply with emission reduction and deforestation targets.

This lawsuit suffers the erratic effects that most pure climate lawsuits are subject to in lower courts in Brazil. This procedure makes it more flexible for the court to rule, adapting the complexity of the cases to the democratic and legal form that these large cases demand (such as several hearings, often of traditional peoples, extensive expert opinions, etc). In this lawsuit filed in 2020, the lower court initially did not accept the climate case, seeing it as just another environmental lawsuit. In a court of appeal decision, Judge Vania Hack (2021) ruled that it was indeed a climate lawsuit and drafted a vote establishing the court's jurisdiction and the nature of the lawsuit.[45] This vote is truly a lesson in climate law and how a judge should proceed. The case went back to the judge in the lower court, who did not rule on it for a year. Then, at the end of 2023, the lower court innovated and reopened discussions that had already been settled by the court of appeals' decision. This case serves as a perfect example, because it illustrates that we have very little pure climate litigation, and when it does reach the courts, such litigation is generally difficult to process due to the country's lack of climate culture.

Reparatory actions have been more successful, as an example of the recent decision (July 2024) in the case of *IBAMA v Kruger*, in which Federal Judge Rodrigo Melo condemned a major deforester of the Amazon rainforest and accepted the arguments of the AGU. The judge determined, among other measures, that the offender presents a compensation project within a period of 90 days, under penalty of a daily fine. The project should include the

45 *IEA v Brazil* (n 37) Opinion of Judge Vania Hack Almeida. Interlocutory Appeal No 5033746-81.2021.4.04.0000/PR. Rapporteur Vania Hack Almeida, Aug 19, 2021, available at https://jusclima2030.jfrs.jus.br/wp-content/uploads/2021/05/Decisa%CC%830-Agravo-de-Instrumento.pdf, accessed on 10 March 2024.

implementation of carbon sinks, considering the emission of 901,600 tons of $CO_2$ and recovery/restoration in deforested areas.

The second action is *Costa Legal et al v Florianópolis et al*,[46] filed in 2021. This case is classified as a nature rights case—one of the first in Brazil along the same lines as the Whanganui River,[47] Atrato River,[48] Yamuna[49] and Ganges Rivers[50] actions. In these cases, preserving natural environments, biomes, large rivers, and lakes, for example, ultimately has a high impact on achieving climate objectives and defending the rights of future generations. All cases of preservation of biomes, rivers, and oceans are intergenerational by nature.[51] By granting such entities the right to existence and legal personality, these are preserved as a last resort for future generations. Lagoa da Conceição was conceived by the Institutional Extension Project of the Center for Legal Sciences at the Federal University of Santa Catarina, which asked several renowned researchers the same question: 'Is it possible to attribute "autonomous rights"[52] to Nature and, in particular, to Lagoa da Conceição?' The leading theoretician behind this action was Professor José Rubens Morato Leite, who used his knowledge of the rights of nature to create a structural action that challenges the more traditional theoretical frameworks, and presented a new paradigm in intergenerational and climate litigation in defense of the protection of a diffuse ecological and intangible asset of the city of Florianópolis.

This case has a significant climate impact since the lagoon is a system that supports several microbiomes of the central coastal marine biome, which has not yet been safeguarded by law under the Brazilian legal framework. The island of Florianópolis, with almost a million inhabitants, is one of the

46 José Rubens Morato Leite, Melissa Ely Melo & Carolina Medeiros Bahia (eds), *Direito Ecológico na Prática—Ação Estrutural da Lagoa da Conceição* (1st edn, AmoLer Editora 2023).

47 New Zeland. Te Awa Tupua (Whanganui River Claims Settlement) Act 2017, available at https://www.legislation.govt.nz/act/public/2017/0007/latest/whole.html.

48 Colombia. *Case of ethnic communities that inhabit the basin of the river Atrato and manifest health effects as a consequence of illegal mining activities*, available at https://www.corteconstitucional.gov.co/relatoria/2016/t-622-16.htm.

49 *India DDA v Rajendra Singh & Others* (*Yamuna River case*), available at https://main.sci.gov.in/jonew/judis/35204.pdf.

50 *India A. Mohd. Salim Petitioner v State of Uttarakhand & Others* (*Ganges River case*), available at https://ecojurisprudence.org/wp-content/uploads/2022/02/IN_Second-Opinion-Salim-v.-State-of-Uttarakhand_126.pdf

51 Luciana Bauer, *Concept, Validity and Application of the Climate Intergenerational Law Rule in Contemporary Democracies* (forthcoming).

52 A variation on the question posed by philosopher Chistopher Stone in his book *Should Trees have Standing?* (OUP 2010).

territories most likely to be rendered non-viable by rising sea levels.[53] And the entire mangrove system[54] (one of the biomes that stores the most carbon and the island's marine life) depends on the Florianópolis's estuary and its interconnections. In this way, the Conceicao lagoon (the major Florianópolis's lagoon) not only provides drinking water and a breeding ground for various forms of life, but also regulates the island's own protection against erosion and rising seas.[55] Preserving the lagoon and, consequently, its population of fishermen and artisans, also prevents climate gentrification, along the lines of what we see in places like Miami in the United States, as it prevents occupation and real estate speculation in one of Brazil's most expensive cities, precisely because it is considered a natural paradise. The aim of this case is to recognize Lagoa da Conceição as a subject of rights and protect it from imminent collapse due to the inefficiency of public environmental policies.[56] The lawsuit was very well handled, and a technical committee that will implement a systemic approach to governance in order to prepare the lawsuit for its final judgment.

The third type of case, *Case of the Xucuru Indigenous People and their Members v Brazil* has already obtained a favorable ruling before the IACtHR.[57] This is a human rights case with equally extensive climate impact. The ruling, issued on February 5, 2018, unanimously declares the responsibility of the Brazilian state for violating the rights of the Xucuru people to collective property and judicial guarantees and protection. According to the IACtHR, Brazil acted with delay and disrespect in the demarcation of an Indigenous area in Pernambuco, destined for 2,300 Indigenous families spread across 24 communities, who suffered moral and physical damage, including death, as a result of Brazil's delay in demarcating the land and expelling non-Indigenous people who also inhabited the same land.

This is the face of Brazil's main climate problem: the struggle for land ownership and land title, mainly involving Indigenous[58] and *quilombola*[59] lands or

53 Climate Central. *Surging Seas: Sea Level Rise, Storms & Global Warming's Threat to the US Coast* (Climate Central 2012).

54 Larissa Trindade, 'Os Manguesais da Ilha de Florianópolis frente a Antropização da Paisagem' (LL.M. thesis, UFSC 2009) available at https://repositorio.ufsc.br/handle/123456789/93092.

55 José Rubens Morato Leite, Melissa Ely Melo & Carolina Medeiros Bahia (eds), *Direito Ecológico na Prática—Ação Estrutural da Lagoa da Conceição* (1st edn, AmoLer Editora 2023).

56 ibid.

57 *Xucuru Indigenous People v Brazil* (n 39).

58 See Gabriel Mantelli, Maurício Terena, Isabela Bicalho & Marie-Louise Siemons, Chapter 10.

59 *Quilombola* is the land occupied by former slaves in Brazil and the Constitution considers these lands territory belonging to Brazilian Afro-descendants.

that of small farmers and extractivist workers. The pressure for land in a country that is rich in mineral and agricultural commodities is the primary factor in violence and deforestation for the people who protect the forests the most: the ancestral peoples.[60] In March 2024, Brazil received yet another conviction in the *Case of Airton Honorato et al v Brazil,* filed in 2021, for having allowed the murder of a member of the Landless Movement (MST) go unpunished in 2000, precisely in a case of agrarian conflict over land.[61]

The STF accepted the unconstitutionality of the temporal landmark thesis,[62] reaffirming that indigenous and *quilombola* lands are immemorial, as provided for in the Constitution. The ruling of the Xucuru people, in this context of violated human rights, has brought enormous innovations to the Brazilian justice system, as the National Council of Justice, by Resolution No 544, instituted a system of compliance with the decisions issued by human rights courts, specifically the IACtHR.[63] This system will have a major impact on land disputes, which ultimately have a huge climate impact. The Federal Regional Court of the 5th Region (TRF5) will be the first in the country to set up a Unit for Monitoring and Supervision of Decisions, Deliberations and Recommendations of the Inter-American System for the Protection of Human Rights,[64] within the scope of the Federal Court of the 5th Region (UMF/JF5).[65] Its first

60 Food and Agriculture Organization (FAO) & Fund for the Development of the Indigenous Peoples of Latin America and the Caribbean (FILAC), *Forest Governance by Indigenous and Tribal Peoples: An Opportunity for Climate Action in Latin America and the Caribbean* (FAO 2021) available at <https://doi.org/10.4060/cb2953en>.

61 *Case of Airton Honorato et al v Brazil.* Judgment of Nov 27, 2023, IACtHR Series C No 508.

62 Federal Supreme Court, 'Tema 1031—Definição do estatuto jurídico-constitucional das relações de posse das áreas de tradicional ocupação indígena à luz das regras dispostas no artigo 231 do texto constitucional'. Judge Rapporteur: Minister Edson Fachin. Leading Case No RE 1017365, filed on 14 December 2016.

63 Brazil. Conselho Nacional de Justiça, Resolution No 544, adopted on 11 January 2024, whose Article 1 states that 'The Unit for Monitoring and Supervision of Decisions of the Inter-American Human Rights System (UMF/CNJ) involving the Brazilian State is hereby established within the scope of this Council, linked to the Department for Monitoring and Supervision of the Prison System and the System for the Execution of Socio-Educational Measures (DMF)'. Furthermore, the same provision sets that 'For the purposes of this Resolution, decisions of the Inter-American Human Rights System shall mean judgments, provisional measures, resolutions and advisory opinions issued by the [IACtHR] and recommendations, resolutions, reports and precautionary measures issued by the [IACommHR].'

64 See Paula Wojcikiewicz Almeida, Chapter 7.

65 'TRF5 é o primeiro tribunal do país a criar uma unidade para monitorar cumprimento das decisões da Corte IDH' (TR5, 19 August 2022) available at <https://www.trf5.jus.br/index.php/noticias/leitura-de-noticias?/id=324349>, accessed 19 March 2024.

task is to implement the ruling of the Xucuru people and, subsequently, adjust all similar demands that reach the same solution determined by the IACtHR. This will significantly impact all other claims regarding Indigenous and *quilombola* rights and lands. Today, this is the subject of dispute even in the Brazilian National Congress, since the temporal landmark thesis (despite the fact that it was declared unconstitutional by the STF), still underpins a number of bills currently before the Senate, and threatens several thousand square kilometers of forest in possession of indigenous and *quilombola* populations.[66] For all these reasons, this human rights action and this capillary system for implementing the rulings of human rights courts, such as the IACtHR, promises to revolutionize and secure the climate rights of a large portion of Brazilians and their future generations.

## 6 Climate Litigation as a Form of Overlapping Consensus

We can foresee that future generations will be increasingly present in climate actions, or actions aimed at protecting biodiversity and biomes, or actions that have a high degree of intergenerational and/or climate impact.[67] According to recent UN data, young people (people under 30 years old) represent only about 2.6% of seats in national parliaments around the world, and less than 1% hold leadership political positions.[68] The climate litigation and intergenerational climate litigation make a significant bridge in this political power vacuum for young people and future generations. Especially in view of the fact that the carbon market and various transnational climate pacts replicate the colony-metropolis binomial.[69]

66 In Brazil, we are currently experiencing a battle between agribusiness and indigenous people, in a thesis called the time frame, which has already been declared unconstitutional by the Supreme Court. And this big land issue is the biggest Indigenous climate and human rights issue that we have. APIB https://apiboficial.org/2024/07/12/what-is-pec-48-and-how-does-it-affect-indigenous-peoples-and-the-environment/?lang=en.

67 David W Orr (ed), *Democracy in the Hotter Times—Climate Change and Democratic Transformation* (MIT 2024).

68 See data available at https://dppa.un.org/sites/default/files/dppa_youth_peace_and_security_strategy_2024-2026.pdf.

69 We must keep an open mind in terms of climate litigation and future generations. For example, a lawsuit brought by a collective of farmers and their future generations against an agrochemical company, used extensively throughout the commodity-producing Global South, might not be found in a climate database. But this monoculture production system—with its reliance on endocrine disruptors and its view of food as a type of merchandise, its large-scale production of grain for livestock feed, its depletion of collective

But these young people need more effective measures outside the judicial sphere to have their political voice and their needs met, in what Rawls calls overlapping consensus. Rawls recognized that in modern democratic societies, there is an inevitable pluralism of overarching doctrines—religious, philosophical, and moral worldviews that people follow. Faced with this pluralism, Rawls introduced the concept of 'overlapping consensus' as a way to achieve stability in a just society. He wrote: 'A political conception of justice does not presuppose any particular comprehensive doctrine, but can be supported by reasons from different comprehensive doctrines.'[70] Thus, even with different conceptions, citizens can agree on political principles that regulate the basic structure of society, promoting social stability. But this is not a global reality for young people who do not have political representation.

Likewise, relying solely on climate litigation can be counterproductive as a single solution or single strategy. Politics matter. Judgments such the recent *Verein KlimaSeniorinnen*,[71] which recognize the urgent right to transition to a new energy matrix and compel their governments to take action, and which are impeccable sentences from the point of view of the climate struggle, have delays and difficulties to be implemented. And if one relies only on lawsuits, we also do not have a real consensus on climate change with other players in democracy as effectively as laws and political pacts would have.[72] Returning to Rawls and focusing on the essence of his theory, namely that only a democratic consensus of pluralisms can lead to national or transnational action, we find that the more effective actions can be the political actions that benefit from climate litigation. The Sustainable Taxonomy of Brazil—Action Plan,[73] announced in December by the Brazilian Minister of the Economy are the exemple, with its focus on finance and a sustainable economy. Or the recent

water resources, and its deterioration of health and biodiversity—is part of an unsustainable cycle from a climate point of view, as damaging as the carbon matrix of the oil industry itself.

70 John Rawls, *Political Liberalism* (Columbia University Press 1993) 144.

71 *Verein KlimaSeniorinnen Schweiz and Others v. Switzerland* (App no. 53600/20) ECtHR [GC] 9 April 2024.

72 In Brazil, as much as the Brazilian Supreme Court says that the Time Frame is unconstitutional, only a social-political agreement—an overlapping as Rawls said in his Political Pluralism—with various political entities can carry out a pacification and a solution that effectively leads to an ecological nation, as Justice Carmen Lúcia understood in her vote. ADPF 760.

73 Ministry of Finance, Sustainable Taxonomy of Brazil —Action Plan (Brasília 2023), available at https://www.gov.br/fazenda/pt-br/orgaos/spe/taxonomia-sustentavel-brasileira/arquivos-taxonomia/sustainable-taxonomy-of-brazil-december-v2.pdf, accessed on 30 April 2024.

approval by the European Parliament of the Corporate Sustainability Due Diligence Directive (CSDDD vote on April 24, 2024), which requires companies to exercise human rights and environmental due diligence in relation to their own operations.[74] Or the new reforestation European Politics and law (Regulation (EU) 2024/1991[75] of the European Parliament and of the Council of 24 June 2024 on nature restoration and amending Regulation (EU) 2022)[76] that imposes an effective and immediate solution to the biodiversity loss and the degradation of ecosystems for our climate crisis. Litigation should be a means for political pressure to achieve consensus and bring about swift action, and not an end in itself. We must create political mechanisms so that future generations have a voice. Political voice. This would be an unprecedented and absolutely climate-friendly measure of intergenerational justice.

## 7 Conclusion

We find ourselves in an era in which the *human right to a clean, healthy and sustainable environment* has been created. The rights of future generations and the related transnational norms on climate, biodiversity, and the maintenance of the Earth's habitability have amalgamated with other constitutional rights to form what is known as the *Rule of Intergenerational Climate Law*,[77]

---

74 Directive (EU) 2024/1760 of the European Parliament and of the Council of 13 June 2024 on corporate sustainability due diligence and amending Directive (EU) 2019/1937 and Regulation (EU) 2023/2859.

75 The European Parliament member who proposed the nature restoration measure, approved on June 24, 2024, was Eleonora Evi. She is a member of the European Parliament affiliated with the Italian political party Europa Verde. Eleonora Evi was born on November 20, 1983. She serves as an example of young leadership actively changing environmental legislation.

76 Regulation (EU) 2024/1991 of the European Parliament and of the Council of 24 June 2024 on nature restoration and amending Regulation (EU) 2022/869.

77 Consequently, the norm that arises from state and federal constitutions and protocols ratified by most countries in the transnational area (Rio Declaration, Kyoto Protocol and Paris Agreement), which we come to call due to a scientific need for greater definition and clarity as the 'norm of intergenerational climate law', has the following characteristics: (a) It is a norm that is born with the social pact, possessing the same fundamental and constitutive force of pacifying and organizing the social forces that unite in a State to develop common goals and for mutual benefit, and therefore essential for the stability of the pact. (b) Its object is to be a constitutional norm that conveys universal truths regarding human rights and scientific prognoses, for the survival of the current and future generations. (c) Because it is a constitutive norm of the State, it does not necessarily need to be written/positive in a national or state constitution to be followed. Its normative force comes

a standard that tests the democratic consensus of peoples—with its principles of justice, priority of freedoms and human dignity—to avoid extinction.

The national implementation of decisions from international human rights court systems is an excellent example of what Rawls meant by the rights of peoples: the pacification and perpetuation of civilization through treaties and their transnational mechanisms. Adopting Indigenous and *quilombola* rights to health and a dignified life into the judicial system has an immediate climate impact since the climate crisis is primarily a crisis of the capitalist mode of exhausting natural resources.

Decolonizing the vision of future generations inside and outside courts by listening to local populations who are their current guardians; adopting a more fluid conceptualization of what is defined by climate litigation, in a regional context in which intergenerational rights are mixed with territorial rights, cultural survival, and ancestral knowledge of Mother Earth; accepting this same Mother Earth as a real entity with legal standing—whether as *Pachamama* or as the enchanted spirits of Xucuru mythology—all of these are facets of an initial revolution that the philosophical and political principles of adopting an intergenerational right and an intergenerational climate right can bring us.

The legal norms built up so far allow us to defend life and the human legacy for our future generations and all future non-human generations with the same intensity. All that remains is to take the final step and ensure that these guarantees are put into practice. In the words of our philosopher and celebrated Brazilian writer Ailton Krenak: 'Tomorrow is not for sale'.[78]

---

from the universal right to life and also from transnational pacts that safeguard it at the international level, by the mere adherence of the signatory countries and ratification by national parliaments. The entry into transnational pacts already internally densifies in the signatory states the command of the rule of intergenerational climate law with which the national country has committed itself. Countries may be condemned for actions and omissions confronting the international agreement to which they have acceded. (d) Transnationality, which is an attribute of the rule of intergenerational climate law, it is undoubted that the interpretation registered by human rights courts or internal constitutional courts forms a global jurisprudence, accessible and applicable by legislators and judges, both internally and externally to the constitutional system of norms. (e) The rule of intergenerational climate law is part of a new branch of legal and social sciences, which is called intergenerational law, and which deals with the impact of legal norms and legislation on the responsibilities of the current generation to future generations and life itself. Luciana Bauer, Fábio da Silva Veiga & Paulo de Brito, *Future Law*, vol III (Instituto Iberoamericano de Estudos Jurídicos & Universidade Lusófona do Porto 2022) 316–3267.

78 Ailton Krenak, *O Amanhã* Não Está à Venda (Companhia das Letras 2020).

# SECTION 4

## *Climate Litigation and Biodiversity*

CHAPTER 12

# The Protection of the Marine Environment through Litigation in the Context of the Climate Crisis in Brazil

*Julia Cirne Lima Weston*[*]

## 1 Introduction

Brazil figures both amongst the countries with the most climate litigation cases submitted in 2023 and cumulatively thus far.[1] With the recent submission of an advisory opinion request to the International Tribunal on the Law of the Sea (ITLOS) concerning the obligations of States towards the marine environment in climate change,[2] it is important to approach this issue from a domestic climate litigation standpoint. This chapter then asks how Brazil has dealt with climate litigation concerning the protection of the marine environment.

In this sense, Brazil is a party to the UNCLOS and is therefore subject to its rules concerning the protection of the marine environment. Furthermore, it has constitutional provisions on the right to a healthy environment, as well as comprehensive environmental legislation. Brazil can, therefore, be subject to climate litigation on the issue and so it has been, with two cases decided thus far. The current chapter therefore seeks to examine how Brazil has dealt with climate litigation on the protection of marine environment. To do that, the chapter starts with a contextualization of the relevance of the marine environment in climate change. The lens then focuses on Brazil, with membership to relevant treaties as well as its relevant domestic legislation to climate litigation. It then moves on to analyzing the two cases which have been submitted on the issue of the marine environment.

* PhD Candidate at Universidade Católica Portuguesa, Researcher at Católica Research Centre for the Future of Law, funded by Fundação para a Ciência e a Tecnologia (FCT).

1 Joana Setzer and Catherine Higham, 'Global Trends in Climate Change Litigation: 2024 Snapshot' (Grantham Research Institute on Climate Change and the Environment 2024) <https://www.lse.ac.uk/granthaminstitute/wp-content/uploads/2024/06/Global-trends-in-climate-change-litigation-2024-snapshot.pdf> accessed 14 August 2024.

2 Request for Advisory Opinion submitted by the Commission of Small Island States on Climate Change and International Law, Order of 16 December 2022, ITLOS Reports 2022–2023, to be published.

 | DOI:10.1163/9789004690974_013

## 2 The Protection of the Marine Environment in Climate Change

Protecting and preserving the marine environment is of utmost importance in the context of climate change.[3] In fact, the oceans play an essential part in climate regulation by acting as a major carbon sink, having absorbed around a third of the world's carbon emissions,[4] which explains why the oceans are an immediate 'victim' (if one might say) of climate change.[5] Moreover, the oceans help regulate the Earth's average temperature and natural climate variations,[6] which, in turn, explains why the oceans (warmed, acidified, and generally disturbed) also enhance climate change and its effects. As a result, 'negative climate change impacts on the oceans are increasingly serious, including sea-level rise, ocean warming and ocean acidification.'[7] These harmful effects of climate change have been emphasized by the UN General Assembly in its yearly Oceans and Law of the Sea resolutions.[8]

Therefore, main climate change concerns to oceans include serious impacts such as warming, deoxygenation, acidification, and sea-level rise as a broader consequence of climate change. How to tackle these effects has been questioned by reference to Part XII of the UNCLOS,[9] which addresses the protection of the marine environment.[10] The inclusion of such climate change issues within the UNCLOS' framework, however, raises questions about their relevance to the convention and the possibility to apply it in conjunction with

3 Guifang Xue, 'Climate Change Challenges and the Law of the Sea Responses', in Ruppel, Roschmann & Ruppel-Schlichting (eds), *Climate Change: International Law and Global Governance*, vol. I, *Legal Responses and Global Responsibility* (Nomos 2013) 547.

4 Karen Scott, 'Ocean Acidification: A Due Diligence Obligation under the LOSC' (2020) 35 IJMCL 382.

5 Elijah Wolfson, 'The Ocean Is Climate Change's First Victim and Last Resort' *Time Magazine* (23 June 2022) available at <https://time.com/6190044/ocean-climate-change/> accessed 20 March 2024.

6 Stephen A Macko, 'Global Ocean Challenges', in Nordquist et al (eds), *Freedom of Navigation and Globalization* (Brill 2015) 303.

7 Catherine Redgwell, 'Treaty Evolution, Adaptation and Change: Is the LOSC "Enough" to Address Climate Change Impacts on the Marine Environment?' (2019) 34 IJMCL 440.

8 Eg 'Oceans and the Law of the Sea' UNGA Res 77/248 (30 December 2022) UN Doc A/RES/77/248.

9 United Nations Convention on the Law of the Sea (adopted 10 December 1982, entered into force 16 November 1994) 1833 UNTS 397.

10 Redgwell (n 7); Scott (n 5); Alan Boyle, 'Climate Change, Ocean Governance and UNCLOS', in Barrett & Barnes (eds), *Law of the Sea: UNCLOS as a Living Treaty* (British Institute of International Law 2016) 211; Seokwoo Lee & Lowell Bautista, 'Part XII of the United Nations Convention on the Law of the Sea and the Duty to Mitigate Against Climate Change: Making Out a Claim, Causation, and Related Issues' (2018) 45 Ecology Law Quarterly 129.

other international climate law treaties. This situation, therefore, pushes the law of the sea's ability to adapt to current topics.[11] In this sense, despite the oceans' undoubtable relevance to climate change mitigation and adaptation, they have not been widely featured within the climate law regime, with only a mention in the Paris Agreement's preamble.[12]

The link between the law of the sea and the oceans was the basis of a request for an advisory opinion to the ITLOS, submitted in December 2022,[13] and of a subsequent request to the International Court of Justice (ICJ), submitted in March 2023.[14] The decision on the advisory opinion requested to the ITLOS was issued on 21 May 2024 and the current chapter will briefly approach its relevant findings for the topic at hand.

First, it is important to highlight that the ITLOS concluded that greenhouse gas (GHG) emissions qualify as pollution within the concept provided in the UNCLOS.[15] This therefore brings GHG emissions into the UNCLOS, including the general obligation to protect and preserve the marine environment (Art. 192) and the duty to prevent, reduce and control marine pollution (Art. 194).[16] From these articles and subsequent ones in the UNCLOS, the ITLOS derived a few obligations to States Parties, namely to prevent that GHG emissions under their jurisdiction cause harm to other States; to adopt and enforce laws and regulations to prevent, reduce and control marine pollution from GHG emissions (from land-based, atmospheric and vessel-based sources) and to conduct environmental impact assessments to address marine pollution from GHG emissions.[17] In this context, the ITLOS refers to the UNFCCC framework as documents to be taken into account in taking measures and developing rules and regulations to prevent, reduce and control marine pollution from anthropogenic GHG emissions.[18]

11 Redgwell (n 7).

12 Millicent McCreath & Amber Rose Maggio, 'Introduction: Climate Change and the Law of the Sea: Adapting the Law of the Sea to Address the Challenges of Climate Change' (2019) 34 IJMCL 387.

13 Commission of Small Island States on Climate Change and International Law, 'Request for Advisory Opinion' <https://www.itlos.org/fileadmin/itlos/documents/cases/31/Request_for_Advisory_Opinion_COSIS_12.12.22.pdf> accessed 10 August 2023.

14 International Court of Justice, 'Obligations of States in Respect of Climate Change' (*International Court of Justice*, 2024) <https://www.icj-cij.org/case/187> accessed 19 March 2024.

15 Request for Advisory Opinion submitted by the Commission of Small Island States on Climate Change and International Law, Advisory Opinion, 21 May 2024, ITLOS Reports 2024, to be published.

16 ibid.

17 ibid.

18 ibid.

Considering the obligations clarified by the ITLOS in isolation, one might believe the Tribunal's understanding provides an opportunity for climate litigation to demand action from States domestically, as they should have rules and regulations and duly enforce them to address GHG emissions and marine pollution. Yet, it is important to stress that the ITLOS stated that the obligation was one of "due diligence", did not go into detail in the opinion itself what this would entail in practice, and that ' [...] the implementation of the obligation of due diligence may vary according to States' capabilities and available resources'.[19] This is a very important caveat, considering that Brazil is a developing State, albeit an upper middle income State according to the Organization for Economic Co-operation and Development.[20] All things considered, whereas the ITLOS' decision does establish a connection between climate change impacts and the protection of the marine environment, the theme of the current chapter, it does raise more questions than it answers them. This can therefore be an even more relevant time for domestic litigation in a sense to further develop the understanding of these obligations and their content. Furthermore, the other advisory opinion requested to the ICJ can also potentially help clarify the obligations of States in climate change. With these important new developments in mind, the current article moves on to analyzing the specific case of Brazil.

## 3 The Brazilian Context: Membership to International Treaties and National Legislation

In order to understand oceans-based climate litigation (both current and future) in Brazil, one needs to understand the international commitments binding Brazil. First, the bedrocks of the international legal regime on the marine environment are laid down in the UNCLOS—signed by Brazil on 10 December 1982 and ratified on 22 December 1988.[21] As this treaty sets out the 'constitutional order' of the oceans,[22] it is the starting point of any law of the

19 ibid.

20 OECD, 'DAC List of ODA Recipients' <https://www.oecd.org/en/topics/sub-issues/oda-eligibility-and-conditions/dac-list-of-oda-recipients.html>, accessed 13 August 2024.

21 United Nations Treaty Collection, '6. United Nations Convention on the Law of the Sea' <https://treaties.un.org/Pages/ViewDetailsIII.aspx?src=TREATY&mtdsg_no=XXI-6&chapter=21&Temp=mtdsg3&clang=_en>, accessed 14 August 2024.

22 Tommy Koh, 'A Constitution for Our Oceans' <https://www.un.org/depts/los/convention_agreements/texts/koh_english.pdf> accessed 10 February 2023.

sea-related climate litigation—although one must keep in mind that, having been adopted in 1982, it does not mention GHG emissions or climate change.[23]

Before the adoption of the UNCLOS, Brazil already participated in the UN Conference on the Human Environment in 1972, which resulted in the Stockholm Declaration;[24] and the 1992 UN Conference on Environment and Development, which resulted in the Rio Declaration.[25] These resolutions elaborated on essential principles and topics within international environmental law,[26] thus are immediately relevant in the context of climate change and marine environmental law.[27] Moreover, Brazil ratified other key international treaties related to the protection and preservation of the environment (marine or not).[28] Concerning climate change, Brazil is a party to the United Nations Framework Convention on Climate Change (UNFCCC) since 1994,[29] to the Kyoto Protocol since 2005,[30] and to the Paris Agreement since 2016.[31]

In 2023, Brazil updated its nationally determined contribution (NDC) under the Paris Agreement. However, its new NDC (like its predecessor) does not make any reference to the oceans or the marine and coastal environment.[32] The NDC only focuses on mitigation and adaptation measures to climate change in general and how the different biomes within Brazil are adversely

23 Alan Boyle, 'Law of the Sea Perspectives on Climate Change' (2012) 27 IJMCL 831.

24 United Nations General Assembly, 'A/CONF.48/INF.5/Rev.I' <https://documents-dds-ny.un.org/doc/UNDOC/GEN/NL3/217/10/PDF/NL321710.pdf?OpenElement> accessed 27 September 2023.

25 United Nations, 'Rio Declaration on Environment and Development' <https://www.un.org/en/development/desa/population/migration/generalassembly/docs/globalcompact/A_CONF.151_26_Vol.I_Declaration.pdf> accessed 12 September 2023.

26 Malcolm Shaw, *International Law* (Oxford University Press 2021), 740.

27 Foo Kim Boon, 'The Rio Declaration and Its Influence on International Environmental Law' [1992] Singapore Journal of Legal Studies.

28 For instance, Brazil is a party to the Convention on Biological Diversity, to the International Convention for the Prevention of Pollution from Ships, the International Convention for the Regulation of Whaling, among others.

29 United Nations Treaty Collection, '7. United Nations Framework Convention on Climate Change' (*United Nations Treaty Collection*, 2023) <https://treaties.un.org/pages/ViewDetailsIII.aspx?src=IND&mtdsg_no=XXVII-7&chapter=27&Temp=mtdsg3&clang=_en>.

30 United Nations Treaty Collection, 'Kyoto Protocol to the United Nations Framework Convention on Climate Change' (*United Nations Treaty Collection*, 2023) <https://treaties.un.org/pages/showDetails.aspx?objid=080000028002la16> accessed 12 September 2023.

31 United Nations Treaty Collection, '7. d Paris Agreement' (*United Nations Treaty Collection*, 2023) <https://treaties.un.org/Pages/ViewDetails.aspx?src=IND&mtdsg_no=XXVII-7-d&chapter=27&clang=_en>.

32 United Nations Framework Convention on Climate Change, 'Brazil First NDC 2023 Adjustment' <https://unfccc.int/documents/633022> accessed 8 January 2024.

affected by its impacts.[33] The coastal zone, however, is one of the focuses of the National Adaptation Plan to Climate Change (NAP), also adopted due to Brazil's commitments under the UNFCCC legal complex.[34]

Therefore, Brazil is a party to the main international legal instruments concerning both climate change and the law of the sea, having internalized them within its legal system. Climate change-related marine environment-focused litigation is only possible because, at the domestic law level, Brazil has adopted a set of constitutional and statutory norms,[35] together with formally non-binding public policy instruments, creating a legal background which judicial cases have relied on. First of all, Article 225 of the 1988 Brazilian Federal Constitution[36] establishes that 'All people have the right to an ecologically balanced environment, a good of common use of the people and essential to a healthy quality of life and it is imposed to the Public Administration and the community the duty to defend it and preserve it for current and future generations.'[37] Under this provision, one can identify several environmental-related constitutional responsibilities, such as the protection of ecosystems, fauna and flora, among others.[38] Although the Constitution is silent on the matter of a subjective right, some authors agree that this implies having a fundamental right to a healthy environment under the Constitution.[39] For instance, the Constitution sees the environment as a ' [...] common asset, essential for a good quality of life'.[40] Within this framework, Article 225 further establishes that the maritime coastal zone is a 'national patrimony' and shall be used in such a way as to

33 ibid.

34 Brazil, 'National Adaptation Plan to Climate Change: General Strategy, Vol. 1' <https://unfccc.int/sites/default/files/resource/Brazil-NAP-English.pdf> accessed 9 January 2024.

35 Édis Milaré, *Direito Do Ambiente: A Gestão Ambiental Em Foco, Doutrina, Jurisprudência, Glossário* (Revista dos Tribunais 2009).

36 Hereinafter referred to as the 'Constitution'.

37 Brazil, 'Constituição Da República Federativa Do Brasil de 1988' <http://www.planalto.gov.br/ccivil_03/constituicao/constituicaocompilado.htm> accessed 14 September 2023. In the original version: 'Todos têm direito ao meio ambiente ecologicamente equilibrado, bem de uso comum do povo e essencial à sadia qualidade de vida, impondo-se ao Poder Público e à coletividade o dever de defendê-lo e preservá- lo para as presentes e futuras gerações.'

38 ibid; Édis Milaré (n 35).

39 Délton Winter de Carvalho, *Gestão Jurídica Ambiental* (2nd edn, Revista dos Tribunais 2020); Ingo Wolfgang Sarlet, Luiz Guilherme Marinoni, and Daniel Mitidiero, *Curso de Direito Constitucional* (Saraiva Jur 2019).

40 Joana Setzer and Délton Winter de Carvalho, 'Climate Litigation to Protect the Brazilian Amazon: Establishing a Constitutional Right to a Stable Climate' (2021) 30 RECIEL 197.

ensure the preservation of its environment,[41] thus making more explicit the idea that the marine and coastal environment contained therein is an integral part of the overall 'environment.'[42]

Furthermore, the National Policy for the Environment seeks ' [...] the preservation, improvement and recovery of environmental quality that is favorable to life, seeking to ensure, within the country, conditions for socioeconomic development, national security interests and the protection of the dignity of human life [...].'[43] At the federated State level, some states have also adopted state policies on the environment. For instance, the State of Rio Grande do Sul's Environmental Policy emphasizes that the coastal zone is a "specially protected territorial space", in line with the Constitution's idea of a holistic link between marine and terrestrial environment.[44]

Moreover, the Forest Code establishes the so-called Permanent Preservation Areas (APPs or Áreas *de Preservação Permanente*),[45] which are areas ' [...] covered, or not, by native vegetation and with the environmental function to preserve hydric resources, the landscape, the geological stability and biodiversity, enable the genetic flow of fauna and flora, protect the soil and ensure the well-being of human populations."[46] Their relevance to the marine environment lies in the fact that some APPs are within the coastal environment, such as mangroves, which are vital to protecting the coast against climate change-related events. Although the Forest Code cannot be used to interpret a constitution, it confirms the idea of a broad understanding of what the environment is, which includes the marine environment.

In turn, the National Policy on Climate Change (NPCC) follows a more orthodox approach of not explicitly referencing the link between the marine environment and climate change. The NPCC establishes the general duty to act to reduce the impacts of anthropogenic acts interfering with the climate system to the benefit of current and future generations. It also sets out the obligation

41 Brazil, 'Constituição Da República Federativa Do Brasil de 1988' (n 37).

42 Délton Winter de Carvalho, 'A Zona Costeira Brasileira e o Gerenciamento de Danos Ambientais Futuros' (2011) Esp Direito e Ambiente 97.

43 Brazil, 'Lei Nº 6.938, de 31 de Agosto de 1981' <https://www.planalto.gov.br/ccivil_03/leis/l6938.htm> accessed 26 September 2023.

44 Brazil, 'Lei No 15.223, de 5 de Setembro de 2018' < https://leisestaduais.com.br/rs/lei-ordinaria-n-15223-2018-rio-grande-do-sul-institui-a-politica-estadual-de-desenvolvimento-sustentavel-da-pesca-no-estado-do-rio-grande-do-sul-e-cria-o-fundo-estadual-da-pesca> accessed 27 September 2023.

45 Brazil, 'Lei Nº 12.651, de 25 de Maio de 2012' <https://www.planalto.gov.br/ccivil_03/_ato2011-2014/2012/lei/l12651.htm> accessed 26 September 2023.

46 ibid.

to adopt measures to prevent, avoid, or minimize identified causes of climate change originating in Brazil.[47] Amongst the NPCCC's goals are those of strengthening GHG sinkholes, adapting measures to climate change, and consolidating and expanding legally protected areas.[48] The NPCCC is based on obligations under international climate change law (namely the UNFCCC legal complex) and aims to promote research on climate change mitigation, as well as observation of the national climate, including in its contiguous oceanic areas (the only explicit reference to the marine environment).[49]

Federated States have also issued specific legislation on their respective climate change policies. For instance, the State of Pernambuco details in its policy that it must create a research institute on the theme of oceans and climate to research, forecast, and monitor this issue permanently.[50] Being Pernambuco a coastal State, its State Policy also focuses on research, mitigation, and adaption strategies for marine and coastal management, such as promoting research on the ocean as a climate regulator, implementing monitoring for risk prevention in coastal areas, as well as the conservation and recovery of reefs.[51]

At the level of non-binding instruments, the Brazilian Ministry for the Environment adopted the NAP in 2016.[52] The main goal of the NAP is ' [...] to influence public-policy instruments and/ or governmental programs, [...] with a view to broadening the coherence of adaptation strategies among public policies'.[53] The NAP has different focus areas it deems relevant and affected by climate change in Brazil, such as urban infrastructure, and agriculture, among others. One of these focal points is the coastal zone.[54] In this context, the NAP does not differentiate amongst biomes in the coastal zone, which can refer both to coastal and marine environments, ranging from mangroves to coral reefs.[55]

---

47 Brazil, 'Lei Nº 12.187, de 29 de Dezembro de 2009' <https://www.planalto.gov.br/ccivil_03/_ato2007-2010/2009/lei/l12187.htm> accessed 26 September 2023.

48 ibid.

49 ibid.

50 Brazil, 'Lei No 14.090, de 17 de Junho de 2010' <https://legis.alepe.pe.gov.br/texto.aspx?tiponorma=1&numero=14090&complemento=0&ano=2010&tipo=&url=> accessed 27 September 2023.

51 ibid.

52 Brazil, 'National Adaptation Plan to Climate Change: General Strategy, Vol. 1' (n 34); Brazil, 'Plano Nacional de Adaptação à Mudança Do Clima: Estratégias Setoriais e Temáticas, Vol. II' <https://www4.unfccc.int/sites/NAPC/Documents/Parties/Brazil/Brazil%20PNA_%20Volume%202.pdf> accessed 9 January 2024.

53 Brazil, 'National Adaptation Plan to Climate Change: General Strategy, Vol. 1' (n 34).

54 ibid.

55 Brazil, 'Plano Nacional de Adaptação à Mudança Do Clima: Estratégias Setoriais e Temáticas, Vol. II' (n 52).

With respect to specific strategies, the NAP first provides an overview of the risks faced by the coastal zone as a result of climate change, to elaborate on what strategies work better to face climate change-related effects.[56] The risks identified in the NAP are in line with those listed in the UNGA resolution on Oceans and Law of the Sea, namely sea-level rise and ocean acidification, with some more specific considerations, such as the interaction between the coastal zone risks and infrastructure, or the impacts on biodiversity.[57] However, the NAP emphasized that it could not identify major risks and opportunities in climate change adaptation within the coastal zone without the necessary data.[58] As such, the proposed actions within the NAP cover issues such as data gathering and research projects on the coastal zone, establishing relevant monitoring systems, and integrating marine spatial plans throughout the coast.[59] Unsurprisingly, the goals based on those actions aim to establish reference centers and knowledge databases and further research in order to best determine adaptation measures for the coastal zone.[60] Although the NAP is not formally binding, it is the centerpiece of the entire building block of Brazil's policy and law-making regarding climate change and establishes long and short-term goals concerning adaptation measures to be adopted and developed with due public participation.[61]

Furthermore, the relevant framework in Brazil also includes legislation referring to the law of the sea. In this regard, as the constitution places the territorial sea, ocean beaches, oceanic islands, and resources of the continental shelf and the exclusive economic zone under the "public domain" of Brazil,[62] Law 8.617 of 4 January 1993 declares what the Brazilian maritime zones are in accordance with the UNCLOS.[63] These maritime zones are included in the concept of marine environment and in the scope of application of the following laws and non-binding instruments.

Law 7.661 of 16 May 1988 institutes the National Plan for Coastal Management (NPCM) as a part of the National Policy for the Environment.[64] The NPCM

56 ibid.
57 ibid.
58 ibid.
59 ibid.
60 ibid.
61 Brazil, 'National Adaptation Plan to Climate Change: General Strategy, Vol. 1' (n 34); Brazil, 'Plano Nacional de Adaptação à Mudança Do Clima: Estratégias Setoriais e Temáticas, Vol. II' (n 43).
62 Brazil, 'Constituição Da República Federativa Do Brasil de 1988' (n 37).
63 Brazil, 'Lei Nº 8.617, de 4 de Janeiro de 1993' <http://www.planalto.gov.br/ccivil_03/leis/l8617.htm> accessed 14 September 2023.
64 Brazil, 'Lei Nº 7.661, de 16 de Maio de 1988' <https://www.planalto.gov.br/ccivil_03/leis/l7661.htm> accessed 9 January 2024.

is thus subordinate to the principles of the National Policy for the Environment and is created to guide the rational use of coastal zone resources, contribute to its population's quality of life, and the protection of natural patrimony.[65] The NPCM regulates the uses and activities within the coastal zone while prioritizing the conservation and protection of natural resources within the coastal zone, such as reefs, coastal islands, beaches, bays, dunes, and mangroves, among others.[66] In other words, it prioritizes the preservation of natural resources that are key to climate adaptation. The NPCM was reviewed in 1996 (NPCM II) to mirror the commitments of Brazil under international treaties.[67]

Two instruments aim to implement the NPCM. First is Decree 5.300 of 7 December 2004, which regulates the NPCM,[68] and is more explicit in referring to the coastal zone as ' [...] the geographical space of interaction between air, sea, and earth, including its resources, renewable or not, comprising a maritime and a territorial strip [...].'[69] The second is the National Policy for the Environment, approved by Decree 5.377 of 23 February 2005, which aims to regulate activities which seek to explore, exploit and utilize the resources within the Brazilian maritime zones[70] and emphasizes the need to study 'climate variations.'[71] However, both instruments refrain from developing more on the link between climate change and the marine environment.

Decree 10.544 of 16 November 2020 approved the 'Sectorial Plan' for marine resources. One of its concerns is with the ' [...] environmental monitoring of the oceans, the marine biodiversity, the adjacent atmosphere and the climate within the maritime areas of national interest, to base the formulation of management policies and measures that promote sustainable development'.[72] This monitoring aims to understand the dynamic changes caused by climate change on the Brazilian coast.[73] There is also a focus on protecting biodiversity and the marine environment, as well as safeguarding from coastal vulnerabilities.[74]

65 ibid.

66 ibid.

67 Brazil, 'Plano Nacional de Gerenciamento Costeiro (PNGC II)' <https://gerenciamentocosteiro.furg.br/images/Materiais/PNGC-II.pdf> accessed 9 January 2024.

68 Brazil, 'Decreto Nº 5.300 de 7 de Dezembro de 2004' <https://www.planalto.gov.br/ccivil_03/_ato2004-2006/2004/decreto/d5300.htm> accessed 10 January 2024.

69 ibid.

70 Brazil, 'Decreto Nº 5.377 de 23 de Fevereiro de 2005' <https://www.planalto.gov.br/ccivil_03/_ato2004-2006/2005/decreto/d5377.htm> accessed 9 January 2024.

71 ibid.

72 Brazil, 'Decreto Nº 10.544, de 16 de Novembro de 2020'.

73 ibid.

74 ibid.

More recently, Decree 12.045 of 5 June 2024 established the National Program for the Conservation and Sustainable Use of Mangroves.[75] Unlike its preceding decrees and legislation which only contained passing mentions of climate change, this legislation specifically considers climate change as a relevant factor in the conservation of mangroves. It also emphasizes the role of mangroves in climate change mitigation and adaptation, the incorporation of climate risks in planning conservation initiatives, the need to increase mangrove habitats' resilience to reduce coastal vulnerabilities to climate change, and the need to promote climate justice.

This brief overview of the applicable legislation and policy clarifies a few issues. First, while there are national laws concerning the protection of the environment and climate change issues in general, these laws do not focus on the marine environment at any point. The scientific link between climate change and the marine environment is clear, but domestic laws build upon a fragmented regulation that separates the marine environment from other environmental and climate laws and regulations. Second, in the same way regulatory fragmentation did not preclude requesting advisory opinions to the ITLOS and ICJ on States' obligations under the UNCLOS in relation to climate change, also at the domestic level, cross-regime interaction can provide the legal grounds for climate litigation with regard to the marine environment. On the one hand, short mitigation or adaptation measures risk the state of the marine environment. On the other hand, not complying with the obligations concerning protecting and preserving the marine environment can contribute to enhancing climate change effects. This possibility of climate litigation supported by a systemic interpretation is addressed in the next session.

## 4 Brazilian Climate Litigation: What Has Been Done for the Marine Environment Thus Far

Relying on the Global Trends in Climate Change Litigation Report, Brazil is the third-ranked country in terms of documented climate litigation cases.[76] The cases analysed in this chapter rely on the database of the Sabin Center for

75 Brazil, 'Decreto Nº 12.045, de 5 de Junho de 2024'.

76 Joana Setzer and Catherine Higham (n 1), Maria Antonia Tigre, 'Climate Litigation in the Global South: Mapping Report' (Sabin Center for International Law 2024) <https://scholarship.law.columbia.edu/cgi/viewcontent.cgi?article=1231&context=sabin_climate_change> accessed 14 August 2024.

Climate Change Law updated until September 2023.[77] Out of the 63 cases identified within the database, two are relevant to the chapter's topic. One deals with the subject matter of coastal erosion, and another with the destruction of mangroves.

The first case (*Federal Public Prosecutor's Office* (MPF) *v. Brazil and Others* (*Sea Advance and Coastal Erosion*) was an ação *civil pública* ('public civil suit', which resembles public interest litigation brought by the public prosecutor) submitted by the *Ministério Público* (public prosecutor's office) in 2014 against Brazil, the State of Sergipe and the relevant environmental organs, concerning illegally built beach bars at Boa Viagem beach.[78] In this suit, the prosecution asked for the interdiction of the bars, as well as their destruction due to their negative impacts to the environment of a permanent preservation area within the coastal zone.[79] This was both due to the risk posed to customers due to the effects of coastal erosion on the constructions and the risk to the sensitive beach environment, including an aggravation of coastal erosion due to the location of the beach bars and the mitigation measures adopted to keep the constructions standing (e.g. use of sandbags to prevent the sea from advancing).[80] The Federal Justice of the State of Sergipe issued a decision determining the interdiction and demolition of the beach bars, using as basis the constitutional right to a healthy environment, Law 9.605/98 which establishes sanctions for environmental crimes, the National Plan for Coastal Management (identifying the relevant coastal biomes risking damage) and the relevant State of Sergipe laws determining the area a Permanent Preservation Area (APP).[81] The first decision issued by the Federal Justice did not mention climate change explicitly, only coastal erosion.[82]

The case was then appealed by the owners of the beach bars both to the Regional Federal Tribunal and to the Superior Court of Justice (STJ). Although the appeal to the STJ concerned a procedural issue (whether an appeal could

77 Climate Case Chart, 'About' (*Climate Case Chart*, 2023) <https://climatecasechart.com/about/> accessed 25 September 2023.

78 Climate Case Chart, 'Federal Public Prosecutor's Office (MPF) v. Brazil and Others (Sea Advance and Coastal Erosion)' (*Climate Case Chart*, 2023) <https://climatecasechart.com/non-us-case/federal-public-prosecutors-office-mpf-v-brazil-and-others-sea-advance-and-coastal-erosion/> accessed 25 September 2023.

79 Justiça Federal em Sergipe, 'Ação Civil Pública 0800372-46.2017.4.05.8502' < https://pje.jfse.jus.br/pjeconsulta/ConsultaPublica/DetalheProcessoConsultaPublica/listView.seam?signedIdProcessoTrf=d2a329088a6accf6198378dc4b42cebo#> accessed 14 August 2024.

80 ibid.

81 Ibid.

82 ibid.

be submitted), its content went beyond mere procedural issues.[83] The STJ dismissed the appeal due to procedural issues and further added that the destruction of the bars by coastal erosion was a foreseeable fact due to climate change.[84] This seems a minor remark, but the STJ elaborated on the idea that coastal erosion and sea-level rise cannot be seen as sporadic phenomena.[85] To that end, Justice Herman Benjamin upheld that:

> [...] may it be added that, currently, climate change represents an incontestable phenomenon: its consequences are everywhere and spare no one. It directly impacts and ruins millions of people, especially the poorest; threatens hundreds of millions of many others; incites the investigatory spirit of researchers; challenges the foresight of politicians and legislators; and, increasingly, makes itself present in the daily life of Tribunals. That said, there is no longer any uncertainty over the reality, anthropic causes and devastating effects of climate change on the community of planetary life and in humanity's daily life. [...] Faced with such a scientific consensus, judges must be vigilant not to be used as a resonating box for irrational ideas—negationist of facts and knowledge—positions which frequently are no more than a screen to hide powerful and unsustainable economic interests espoused by adversaries of the foundational values of the Environmental Rule of Law.[86]

Therefore, Justice Benjamin clearly affirmed that courts must recognize climate change as a fact and a phenomenon while recognizing climate change's deleterious impacts on the daily lives of human beings. This reference to climate change was short and lateral to the main argument, but still, the STJ upheld its sociological function of checking and confirming facts in the context of climate change (in this case, climate-induced coastal erosion and sea-level rise). The STJ's decision is rather short, as it is procedural, and does not directly cite the environmental legislation above. However, the first decision issued by the Federal Justice and upheld by STJ was importantly based on the constitutional right to a healthy environment, the National Plan for Coastal Management, as well as on the relevant criminal law. This can be

83 Climate Case Chart (n 78).

84 ibid.

85 Superior Tribunal de Justiça, 'AgInt No Agravo Em Recurso Especial No 2188380—SE (2022/0252968–6)' <https://climatecasechart.com/wp-content/uploads/non-us-case-documents/2023/20230324_ACP-n.-0800002-72.2014.4.05.8502_ruling-1.pdf> accessed 25 September 2023.

86 ibid.

undoubtedly seen as Brazil's coastal protection framework being successfully used to safeguard the coastal environment.

The second case refers to the importance of mangroves in climate mitigation, adaptation, and resilience-building, since mangroves have a great capacity to store and capture carbon (greater and more efficiently than other ecosystems) and they protect coastal environments from extreme weather events (e.g., cyclones).[87] This second case was also an *ação civil pública* submitted by the public prosecutor's office against a private company. The plaintiff argued that the company grounded and drained a mangrove habitat, demanding that it demolish edifications built on top of the mangrove and restoring it to its prior natural environment.[88] Once again, the case went on to the STJ, which confirmed the decision of the lower courts favorable to the plaintiff. In this decision, Justice Herman Benjamin stated that:

> [...] it is everyone's duty, proprietors or not, to work towards the preservation of mangroves, an ever-increasing need, especially in a time of climate change and sea-level rise. Destroying them for direct economic use, under the permanent incentive of easy profits and short-term benefits, draining them or grounding them for real estate speculation or soil exploitation, or transforming them into a trash deposit, characterize a serious offence to an ecologically balanced environment and to the collective well-being, a behavior that shall be promptly and energetically curbed and sanctioned by the Public Administration and the Judiciary.[89]

Therefore, Justice Benjamin highlighted the link between preserving coastal ecosystems and building resilience against severe climate change impacts and emphasized the collective damage resulting from this habitat's destruction. It is important to consider that unlike in the coastal erosion decision, here the STJ does refer to the constitutional right to a healthy environment, the National Policy on the Environment, and the Forest Code.[90] That can be explained by the fact that this was an actual appeal to the merits of the first decision which granted the public prosecutor's office's claims.

87 S. Sandilyan and K. Kathiresan, 'Mangroves as Bioshield: An Undisputable Fact' (2015) 103 Ocean & Coastal Management 94.

88 Superior Tribunal de Justiça, 'Recurso Especial No 650.728—SC (2003/0221786–0)' <https://climatecasechart.com/wp-content/uploads/non-us-case-documents/2009/20091202_Special-Appeal-No.-650.728-SC_ruling-1.pdf> accessed 25 September 2023.

89 ibid.

90 ibid.

In a nutshell, while most climate cases in Brazil do not directly address the oceans and marine environment, there are two cases where the state of the coastal environment was at issue: the destruction of important coastal habitats and sea-level rise. Both cases and their foundations evidence the Brazilian framework's readiness to deal with the specific topic of climate change and the marine environment. The content of the votes issued by Justice Herman Benjamin and their evident links between science, climate mitigation and the need for courts to recognize climate change and safeguard the marine environment can serve as an inspiration to further climate litigation on the issue at hand.

## 5 Conclusion

Brazil is no stranger to climate litigation yet has only decided on two cases on the marine environment thus far. However, we can draw significant lessons from how Brazilian courts have addressed these cases, especially concerning the protection of coastal habitats and the need to factor in coastal erosion and sea-level rise in urban settings. Although relatively few, the cases already decided by Brazilian courts regarding the marine environment took the side of the protection and preservation of the coastal environment and considered sea-level rise impacts as an increasingly frequent phenomenon. Therefore, there are comparative lessons from Brazilian marine environment litigation to other jurisdictions, with hopefully more cases in the future. Brazil is, after all, party to the relevant international treaties on the matter and has important national legislation and policies on the issue. This framework has been successfully put to the test in the analyzed case law. It will therefore be interesting to see how climate litigation in the marine environment sphere develops in Brazilian courts in the years to come and what kinds of suits will be used to bring these cases forward and how they can inspire future cases in other jurisdictions.

CHAPTER 13

# The Protection of the Amazon Forest as a Central Aspect of Climate Mitigation

*Maria Antonia Tigre* and Anna Maria Cárcamo***

## 1 Introduction

The Amazon rainforest stands as a vital pillar in the fight against climate change, functioning as a crucial GHG sink, a critical regulator of the global climate, and a reservoir of unparalleled biodiversity. Distributed among eight nations, the Amazon rainforest plays a crucial role in climate mitigation. It has the potential to sequester approximately two billion tons of $CO_2$ annually, accounting for about 20 percent of the carbon released into the atmosphere from fossil fuel combustion. As a global GHG reservoir, the Amazon regulates worldwide climate patterns. However, escalating deforestation in the Amazon countries jeopardizes this capacity, as the forest can only act as a carbon sink if it absorbs more $CO_2$ than it releases.[1] The ongoing increase in deforestation poses a threat to the Amazon's ability to stabilize global weather.

The consequences of deforestation are stark, with an estimated emission of 22,000 tons of $CO_2$ per square kilometer cut and burned. A complete clearance of the entire Amazon would release 366 billion tons of $CO_2$, equivalent to ten years of global emissions. Even a partial release of this magnitude would significantly accelerate global warming, leading to severe consequences. If human-induced climate change remains unaddressed, there is a looming risk

* *Sabin Center for Climate Change Law*, Columbia Law School, https://orcid.org/0000-0003-4308-1958, email: mb4913@columbia.edu

** Hotta Advocacia in Collaboration with Pogust Goodhead and Instituto Ação Climática, email: acarcamo@pogustgoodhead.com.

1 See i.e., Maria Antonia Tigre, *Regional Cooperation in Amazonia: A Comparative Envrionmental Law Analysis* (Brill Nijhoff 2017); Maria Antonia Tigre, 'Building a Regional Adaptation Strategy for Amazon Countries' (2019) 19(4) *Int'l Env't Agreements: Pol., L. and Econ.* 411.

 | DOI:10.1163/9789004690974_014

that the Amazon could become a net emitter of carbon rather than a vital carbon sink.[2]

The allure of its economic potential has engendered persistent challenges in safeguarding and preserving this precious ecosystem, notably in the face of encroachments by the cattle industry in Brazil. Insufficient governance mechanisms have exacerbated these challenges, leading to alarming deforestation rates and prompting a surge in domestic litigation contesting the inadequacy of existing measures.[3] According to data from the Monitoring of the Andean Amazon Project, an estimated 1.57 million hectares of the Amazon were deforested in 2021, growing to 1.98 million hectares of deforestation in 2022—an amount of land approximately equivalent to 370,000 football fields.[4] This represented the second-highest amount of deforestation on record and continued the upward trend in deforestation rates starting in the mid-2010s.[5]

Brazil holds around two-thirds of the Amazon rainforest. Therefore, the Brazilian government's policies towards protecting it significantly impact the rate of Amazonian deforestation in any given year. For example, commentators have attributed the increase in deforestation rates between 2019 and 2022 to the lack of enforcement of illegal logging, the deregulation of agricultural production in Amazon states, and other policies de-emphasizing environmental protection during the administration of the former Brazilian President, Jair Bolsonaro.[6] As of September of 2023, the pace of deforestation in Brazil, as measured by Brazil's National Institute for Space Research (INPE), has been dramatically lower than the same periods over the previous three years (approximately 4.3 million hectares of deforestation between January 2023 and September 2023, compared to approximately 8.6 million hectares of

2 Maria Antonia Tigre, 'Cooperation for Climate Mitigation in Amazonia: Brazil's Emerging Role as a Regional Leader' (2016) 5(2) Transnat'l Env't Law 401.

3 Danielle de Andrade Moreira, Chapter 2.

4 *Maap #187: Amazon Deforestation & Fire Hotspots 2022* (MAAP 2023). <www.maaproject.org/2023/amazon-deforestation-fire-2022/> accessed 18 March 2024; Olivia Munson, 'What Is the Biggest State in the US? The States from Largest to Smallest by Land Area' (*USA Today*, 26 February 2024) <https://www.usatoday.com/story/news/2022/12/09/what-largest-state-us-size-states-land-area/8083288001/> accessed 18 March 2024.

5 *Maap #187: Amazon Deforestation & Fire Hotspots 2022* (MAAP 2023) <www.maaproject.org/2023/amazon-deforestation-fire-2022/> accessed 18 March 2024.

6 'Deforestation in the Amazon' (*Council on Foreign Relations*) <www.cfr.org/amazon-deforestation/> accessed 18 March 2024.

deforestation between January 2022 and September 2022, 7 million hectares in the same period in 2021, and 7 million hectares in the same period in 2020).[7]

This chapter delves into the complex interplay between climate mitigation efforts and the protection of the Amazon rainforest. By scrutinizing 34 out of the 80 climate litigation cases in Brazil that specifically pertain to the Amazon biome,[8] it sheds light on the multifaceted legal strategies employed by litigants to safeguard this ecologically crucial region. Drawing insights from these cases, it offers a bird's-eye view of the current scenario and efficacy—for the few instances of decided cases—of climate litigation strategies related to the Amazon rainforest.

Furthermore, this chapter extends its purview to transnational climate cases, highlighting a few examples of cases pertaining to the Brazilian Amazon that have been filed in other jurisdictions. Ultimately, this chapter contributes to an initial exploration of the challenges faced in safeguarding the Amazon rainforest as an integral component of climate mitigation efforts in Brazil. It aims to inform policymakers, scholars, and advocates about the efficacy of climate litigation as a tool to protect this unique ecosystem, fostering broader discussions on international cooperation and legal measures to preserve the Amazon for present and future generations.

The chapter is structured as follows. Section II explores the intricate challenges posed by economic interests, particularly focusing on the influential cattle industry and its impact on the Amazon rainforest. The discussion delves into the factors contributing to escalating deforestation rates, emphasizing the insufficiency of existing measures and governance structures. The examination extends to the legal and regulatory gaps that have played a role in environmental degradation and the persistent issue of deforestation. Section III provides an overview of the climate litigation landscape in Brazil, as it pertains to the Amazon rainforest. The focal point is an in-depth examination of 34 climate cases specifically related to the Amazon biome. The analysis encompasses legal strategies, arguments, and outcomes in these cases, offering an initial understanding of the dynamic of climate-related legal battles in the Brazilian Amazon. Section IV examines a few transnational cases filed in other jurisdictions related to the Brazilian Amazon rainforest.

The concluding section summarizes the challenges encountered in protecting the Amazon rainforest and mitigating climate-related impacts. It reflects

---

7 André Carvalho, 'Sobre Terrabrasilis' (*Amazônia Legal—Avisos de Desmatamento*) <https://terrabrasilis.dpi.inpe.br/app/dashboard/alerts/legal/amazon/aggregated/> accessed 18 March 2024.

8 Data updated until 1 August 2024.

on the significance of climate litigation as a tool in safeguarding the Amazon biome, offering insights for future prospects. Recommendations for effective governance and conservation measures are presented, emphasizing the importance of international cooperation in preserving this vital ecosystem for future generations.

## 2 Deforestation Challenges in the Amazon Rainforest

All eight Amazon countries are parties to the UNFCCC[9] and have published Nationally Determined Contributions (NDCs) outlining their steps for meeting the goals of the Paris Agreement.[10] For many Amazon countries, carbon emissions resulting from deforestation make up a significant proportion of the total emissions produced by each country. For example, in Brazil, approximately 70% of total emissions are estimated to result from deforestation.[11] In Bolivia, approximately 78% of the country's total emissions resulted from deforestation in 2021.[12]

Because of the significance of the rainforest on the countries' carbon footprint, each NDC includes considerations on how the country intends to preserve or expand forested areas and/or reduce deforestation. However, none of the countries have committed to eliminating deforestation. Instead, they commit to reducing illegal deforestation, improving mining and agricultural efficiencies to reduce the impact on the Amazon, and employing diverse methods to reduce deforestation rates, including through increasing protected areas. The following chart summarizes the main goals highlighted in the NDCs relating to the Amazon rainforest.

---

9 'Parties to the United Nations Framework Convention on Climate Change' (*Unfccc.int*) <https://unfccc.int/process/parties-non-party-stakeholders/parties-convention-and-observer-states> accessed 18 March 2024.

10 Nationally Determined Contributions (NDCs)' (*United Nation Climate Change*) <https://unfccc.int/process-and-meetings/the-paris-agreement/nationally-determined-contributions-ndcs> accessed 18 March 2024.

11 Gregory Asner et al, *Measuring Carbon Emissions from Tropical Deforestation: An Overview* (Environmental Defense Fund 2012) <www.edf.org/sites/default/files/10333_Measuring_Carbon_Emissions_from_Tropical_Deforestation--An_Overview.pdf> accessed 18 March 2024.

12 Emissions from deforestation equaled about 21.9 $tCO_2$ per capita, out of total emissions of about 28 $tCO_2$ per capita (ie 78% of total emissions). Lykke Andersen, Luis Gonzales & Alfonso Malky, 'Bolivia's Net Zero Path: Investment Needs, Challenges, and Opportunities', 4 *Climate and Economics*, <https://www.frontiersin.org/articles/10.3389/fclim.2022.1026344/full> accessed 18 March 2024.

TABLE 13.1 Deforestation-related goals in Amazon countries' NDCs

| Country | Deforestation related goals |
|---|---|
| Bolivia | By 2030, reduce deforestation to 80% compared to the baseline and reduce deforestation in National Protected Areas by 100% |
| Brazil | Reach zero deforestation by 2030, according to the Action Plan for the Prevention and Control of Deforestation in the Legal Amazon (PPCDAm) |
| Colombia | Reduce emissions from deforestation equivalent to reducing deforestation to 50.000 ha/year in 2030, with the goal of reaching 0 ha/year by 2030 |
| Ecuador | Reduce 20% of GHG emissions by 2025 in the land use sector, with 16% conditioned to international cooperation |
| Guyana | Avoided deforestation and REDD+ program to reduce 48.7 $MtCO_2eq$ in emissions annually<br>Conserve additional 2 million hectares of forest |
| Peru | Reduce 30% of emissions by 2030, and 40% reduction conditioned to international cooperation (no specific target for deforestation) |
| Suriname | Maintain 93% forest cover<br>Increase protected forests and wetlands cover to at least 17% of terrestrial area by 2030 |
| Venezuela | Reduce emissions by 20% by 2030 (no specific target for deforestation) |

Note: NDCs updated until March 2024. ibid.

The State of Climate Action 2023 report underscores the critical role of climate action in addressing deforestation, particularly in countries like Brazil.[13] While the urgency to limit global warming to 1.5°C is apparent, the technical feasibility of achieving this goal remains viable, with substantial benefits for vulnerable communities and ecosystems worldwide. The report emphasizes the importance of cutting GHG emissions as a primary defense mechanism, reducing the frequency and severity of climate impacts and minimizing losses and damages.[14]

Agriculture, forestry, and other land uses are identified as key sectors, contributing significantly to net anthropogenic GHG emissions globally. This

13 Sophie Boehm et al, *State of Climate Action 2023* (System Change Lab 2023).

14 ibid.

sector is both a GHG source and sink, making it pivotal in climate mitigation efforts. Notably, recent positive developments, such as multilateral commitments and policy shifts, indicate a growing global momentum to address deforestation. The Glasgow Leaders' Declaration on Forests and Land Use, the Kunming-Montreal Biodiversity Framework, and specific actions by countries like Brazil signal a willingness to combat deforestation and promote sustainable land use practices.

However, the report highlights historical challenges in meeting interim targets and securing promised funds, emphasizing the need for sustained and effective action. Limiting global temperature rise to 1.5°C underscores the need for dramatic declines in permanent forest loss. Specifically, annual deforestation rates and associated GHG emissions must decrease by 70% by 2030 and 95% by 2050, relative to 2018 levels. Amazon countries, however, are nowhere near accomplishing these goals. This underlines the reason why climate litigation in forest-rich countries like Brazil is on the rise.

## 3 Brazilian Climate Change Legislation and the Amazon

Brazil has comprehensive environmental and climate legislation that can be utilized for climate litigation to protect the Amazon. The pillar of all socio-environmental legal protection lies in Article 225 of the Brazilian Constitution, which foresees that an ecologically balanced environment is a right of all present and future generations, and there is a duty of all, in particular of the state, to protect it. Article 225 highlights the Amazon as a national heritage that must be especially protected. The Constitution also includes the environment as a guiding principle for economic activity (Article 170), and establishes that properties must follow their social function, which includes environmental compliance (Article 186). As will be further discussed, based on this constitutional protection, the Federal Supreme Court (STF) has recognized that environmental treaties are *supra-legal*, and, thus, superior to regular legislation in the country.[15] Therefore, the Paris Agreement and the UNFCCC, internalized through Federal Decrees Nos 2.652/1998 and 9073/2017, can be invoked in domestic courts and should outweigh contradictory legislation.

15 *PSB et al v Brazil* (*on Climate Fund*) ADPF 708, Judgment of 7 January 2022. See Carolina de Figueiredo Garrido (Chapter 5) and Délton Winter de Carvalho & Armando Rocha (Chapter 6).

In addition, the Brazilian National Policy for Climate Change (*Política Nacional de Mudanças Climáticas*, PNMC)[16] establishes mitigation and adaptation goals and mechanisms. While the 2009 Law precedes the Paris Agreement, it included as one of its directives the future international commitments made by Brazil under the UNFCCC or related instruments.[17] Thus, the commitments in its NDC, including eliminating deforestation by 2030, should also be considered a directive of this law. Moreover, the PNMC established several mechanisms, including specific plans for protecting biomes against deforestation.[18] The Action Plan for the PPCDAm was updated in 2023 to include the objective of eliminating deforestation by 2030, as well as several other actions to guarantee the biome's protection.[19] Adequate implementation of this plan, especially monitoring and control, can be considered the reason for reductions in deforestation rates in the Amazon in 2023.[20]

Furthermore, the National Policy on the Environment (*Política Nacional do Meio Ambiente,* PNMA) defines a 'polluter' as any physical or legal person who directly or indirectly affects the environment.[21] The Amazon also receives special protection in the Law of Protection of Native Vegetation, known as the Forest Code, which established that 80% of the area of private lands in the Amazon rainforest must be protected.[22] Finally, Brazil has long-standing environmental litigation precedents that are relevant for climate change litigation, such as the theory of integral risk, which excludes *force majeure* from eliminating liability in cases of environmental impact, the inversion of the burden of proof, and the full reparation theory, which provides that the environment must be recovered to the full extent or the closest possible.[23] This framework provides the starting point for climate litigation in Brazil.

---

16 Law No 12.187, of 29 December 2009, *Política Nacional sobre Mudança do Clima* [National Climate Change Policy].

17 ibid, art 5(I).

18 ibid, art 4(VI) and art 6(III).

19 *Plano de Ação para Prevenção e Controle do Desmatamento na Amazônia Legal 5.ª Fase (2023–2027)* (2023) [Action Plan to Prevent and Control Deforestation in the Legal Amazon, 5th Phase], < www.gov.br/mma/pt-br/ppcdam_2023_sumario-rev.pdf> accessed 10 April 2024.

20 Minister of the Environment and Climate Change, 'Results of PRODES 2022–2023 in the Amazon, 2023', <https://www.gov.br/mma/pt-br/taxa-de-desmatamento-na-amazonia-cai-22-3-em-2023/coletiva-de-imprensa-prodes-22-23.pdf> accessed 14 August 2024.

21 Law No 6.938, of 31 August 1981, *Política Nacional do Meio Ambiente* [National Environmental Policy] art 2.

22 Law No 12.651, of 25 May 2012, *Código Florestal* [Forest Code].

23 Danielle de Andrade Moreira et al, 'Rights-Based Climate Litigation in Brazil: An Assessment of Constitutional Cases Before the Brazilian Supreme Court' (2024) 16 *Journal of Human Rights Practice* 7.

## 4 Climate Litigation in the Brazilian Amazon

Climate litigation in Brazil has grown significantly since 2020. As of August 2024, Brazil had 85 climate cases, based on the Sabin Center for Climate Change Law's Global Climate Litigation Database[24] and the Research Group on Law, Environment, and Justice in the Anthropocene (JUMA)'s Climate Litigation in Brazil Database.[25] There are a few early examples of climate litigation in Brazil in the 2000s and 2010s, but a rising trend began in 2018.[26] Given Brazil's portfolio of GHG emissions, the vast majority of cases relate to the land-use change and forestry sectors.[27]

JUMA's climate litigation database specifically categorizes cases according to the biome involved, when explicitly mentioned in the claim as a 'relevant issue.'[28] As of August 2024, 34 climate litigation cases relate to the Amazon rainforest. The fact that over 42.5% of Brazilian cases directly or indirectly relate to the Amazon rainforest shows that the biome remains a 'protagonist' in domestic cases, central to the climate and socio-environmental agenda in the country.[29] This is unsurprising, considering that Brazil's GHG emissions are mainly linked to alterations in land use and management, particularly in the Amazon region. Figure 13.1 portrays the distribution of Amazon-related cases filed per year.

Climate-related cases about the Amazon rainforest commenced in 2017 and reached their zenith in 2020, with eleven cases filed that year. Subsequent years have consistently witnessed the submission of 5–6 cases annually, except for 2022, which saw only one new case filed. Figure 13.2 shows the status of these cases as of August 2024.

Presently, 13 cases have been decided. Seven of the concluded cases were resolved in favor of the plaintiffs—*PSB et al v Brazil (on Climate Fund)*,[30] *PSB et al v Brazil (on Amazon Fund)*,[31] *State of Rondônia et al v*

24 'Brazil Archives' (Sabin Center for Climate Change Law, Global *Climate Change Litigation Database*) <https://climatecasechart.com/non-us-jurisdiction/brazil/> accessed 2 August 2024.

25 Danielle de Andrade Moreira et al, 'Plataforma de Litigância Climática no Brasil' [Platform of Climate Litigation in Brazil] (nd) <https://litigancia.biobd.inf.puc-rio.br/> accessed 14 August 2024.

26 Joana Setzer & Lisa Benjamin, 'Climate Litigation in the Global South: Filing Gaps' (2020) 114 *AJIL Unbound* 56.

27 Danielle de Andrade Moreira et al, *Brazilian Climate Litigation Bulletin 2023* (JUMA/PUC-Rio 2023) 16, <www.juma.nima.puc-rio.br/_files/ugd/a8ae8a_c23cbedfe3ba42bdbe37d8650e727bd6.pdf> accessed 2 April 2024.

28 ibid.

29 ibid.

30 *PSB et al v Brazil (on Climate Fund)* (n 16).

31 *PSB et al v Brazil (on Amazon Fund)* ADO 59, STF Judgment of 16 August 2023.

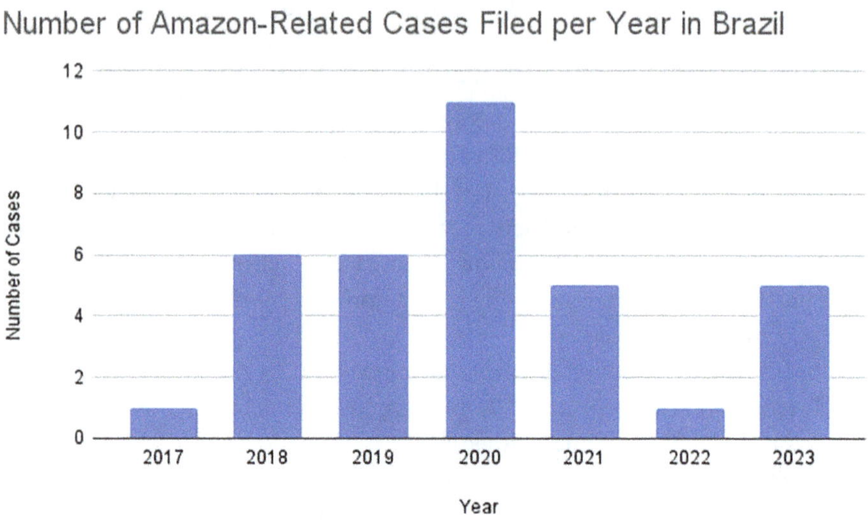


FIGURE 13.1 Development of Brazilian climate cases related to the Amazon rainforest

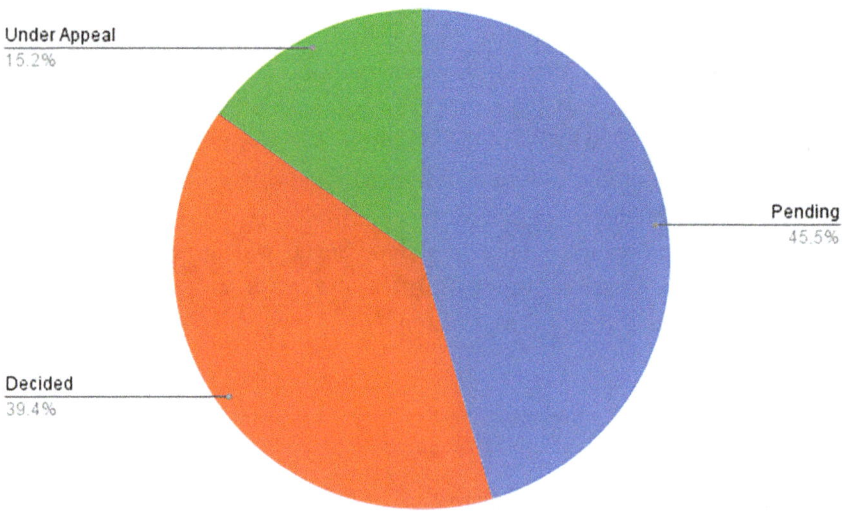


FIGURE 13.2 Status of Brazilian climate cases related to the Amazon rainforest

*Invaders of the Guajará-Mirim State Park,*[32] *Rede Sustentabilidade v Brazil (on Amazon Deforestation)*, *PSB et al v Brazil (on deforestation and human*

32 *State of Rondônia et al v Invaders of the Guajará-Mirim State Park*, ACP 7002381-27.2020.8.22.0015, Rondônia State Court Judgment of 21 November 2023.

*rights*),[33] *Jaci-Paraná Extractive Reserve and Guajará-Mirim State Park*,[34] *IBAMA v Souza Brilhante*[35]—while two cases, *Fabiano Contarato et al v Ricardo Salles*[36] and *PSB et al v Brazil (Federal environmental sanctioning process)*, were dismissed. *Rede Sustentabilidade v Brazil (on Amazon Deforestation)* and *Omission related to paralyzation of the PPCDAm* (ADPF 760) were partially upheld.[37] This section details some of the decisions in the aforementioned cases. The first instance decisions, some of which are under appeal, are discussed in the following thematic sections.

### 4.1 *Decided Climate Cases Related to the Amazon Rainforest*

In a thorough analysis of the 17 concentrated control cases related to the climate crisis (not all related to the Amazon rainforest), De Andrade Moreira et al identified a series of commonalities between them, including a strong grounding on the constitutional right to a healthy environment, associated with other related human rights.[38] A few of these specifically relate to the Amazon rainforest.[39] Their analysis further shows that nine cases discuss land use changes and their climate impacts, representing almost half of Brazil's GHG emissions.[40] The Amazon rainforest is at the core of most of these cases since 78.4% of national emissions from land use change happened in the Amazon

33 *PSB et al v Brazil (on deforestation and human rights) ADPF 760*, STF Judgment of 6 April 2022.

34 *State ADI 0804739-62.2021.8.22.0000 (Jaci-Paraná Extractive Reserve and Guajará-Mirim State Park)*, requested by the Public Prosecutor's Office on 1 May 2021, Judgment of 1 November 2021.

35 *IBAMA v Souza Brilhante (on ilegal wood storage)* ACP 1003478-16.2018.4.01.3100, Federal Court of Amapá, Judgment of 2 September 2022.

36 *Fabiano Contarato et al v Ricardo Salles*, PET 8351, Federal Supreme Court judgment of 20 August 2021.

37 *Rede Sustentabilidade v Brazil (on Amazon Deforestation)* ADO 54, Judgment of 1 April 2022.

38 De Andrade Moreira et al (n 28) 6.

39 *Rede Sustentabilidade v Brazil (on Amazon Deforestation)* ADO 54, Judgment of 1 April 2022; *PSB et al v Brazil (on Amazon Fund)* (n 33); *Partido dos Trabalhadores v Brazil (Fires in the Pantanal and the Amazon Forest)* ADPD 746 requested on 1 September 2020 to the Federal Supreme Court; *PSB et al v Brazil (on deforestation and human rights)* (n 35); *Rede Sustentabilidade v Institutional Security Cabinet and National Mining Agency (on Mining in Preserved Areas in the Amazon)* ADPF 921, filed on 9 December 2021 before the Federal Supreme Court.

40 De Andrade Moreira et al (n 24) 9. (citing *Sistema de Estimativas de Emissões de Gases de Efeito Estufa* (SEEG). *2021. Análise das emissões brasileiras de Gases de Efeito Estufa e suas implicações para as metas climáticas do Brasil 1970–2020.s.l.:* Observatório do Clima. <https://seeg.eco.br/wp-content/uploads/2023/03/SEEG9_DOC_ANALITICO_2021_FINAL.pdf > accessed 15 August 2024).

alone in 2020.[41] Thus, it is unsurprising that the climate cases already decided by the STF are directly or tangentially related to the Amazon rainforest. These were filed during a challenging political moment, characterized by backsliding of environmental and climate policies, which led to a rise in climate cases specifically.[42]

In *Fabiano Contarato et al v Ricardo Salles*, three congressmen called for an investigation into the former Minister of Environment in 2019, citing a breach of international climate commitments.[43] The case primarily relied on a lack of commitment to combating illegal deforestation in Amazonia. In August 2021, the STF closed the case following Salles' resignation, rendering it moot. As a result, the case lost its legal foundation.[44]

*PSB et al v Brazil (on Climate Fund)* and *PSB et al v Brazil (on Amazon Fund)* share a common thread, centering on the paralyzation of financing for projects linked to climate mitigation and adaptation, and anti-deforestation initiatives, respectively. These cases are intrinsically tied to the PNMC, with the Climate Fund and the Amazon Fund serving as pivotal mechanisms.[45] Despite the availability of funds in both, the Bolsonaro administration halted the allocation of resources to specific projects, prompting political parties from the opposition to file these cases. Situated within a series of constitutional control cases brought before the STF, these legal actions emphasize the imperative to safeguard the constitutional right to a healthy environment,[46] recognizing climate change as an inherent facet of this right.[47] This is particularly critical amid the ongoing climate crisis and Brazil's perceived failure to protect it.

The 2022 decision in *PSB et al (on Climate Fund)* marked a milestone in climate litigation. While the decision did not explicitly mention the Amazon biome, it holds profound implications for legal strategies addressing deforestation in

41 *Sistema de Estimativas de Emissões de Gases de Efeito Estufa (SEEG). 2021. [Análise das emissões brasileiras de Gases de Efeito Estufa e suas implicações para as metas climáticas do Brasil]* Observatório do Clima. https://seeg.eco.br/wp-content/uploads/2023/03/SEEG9 _ accessed April 2, 2024.

42 Meghie Rodrigues, 'Bolsonaro's Troubled Legacy for Science, Health and the Environment', *Nature* (27 September 2022)<www.nature.com/articles/d41586-022-03038-3> accessed 2 April 2024.

43 *Fabiano Contarato et al v Ricardo Salles* (n 37).

44 ibid.

45 Law No 12.114, of 9 December 2009, *Fundo Nacional sobre Mudança do Clima* [National Climate Change Fund].

46 De Andrade Moreira et al (n 24).

47 Délton Winter de Carvalho & Rafaela Santos Martins da Rosa, 'Climate Constitutionalism as a Foundation for Climate Litigation in Latin America' (2023) 16 *Journal of Human Rights Practice huad055* 71. See Rafaela Rosa, Chapter 17.

Brazil. Discussions during the public hearings extensively focused on the Amazon rainforest. In the decision, the STF affirmed the constitutional obligation of the executive branch to allocate and execute Climate Fund resources for mitigation. This mandate, grounded in the constitutional right to a healthy environment and the principle of separation of powers, establishes the government's duty to strategically allocate funds, directing them to areas where mitigation efforts are most imperative.[48]

Notably, the STF clarified the unique status of environmental treaties as a subset of human rights treaties, endowing them with a 'supranational' standing.[49] This 'supra-legality' grants these treaties a hierarchical superiority over ordinary laws.[50] Consequently, any Brazilian legislation or decree conflicting with the provisions of the Paris Agreement, potentially including the NDC presented by Brazil to the UNFCCC, is subject to nullification.[51] Any act or omission contravening this safeguard constitutes a direct violation of the Constitution and human rights. Hence, 'the constitutional duty to effectively allocate funds entails an obligation to address climate change' in harmony with the international commitments embedded within the climate change framework.[52]

In *State of Rondônia et al v Invaders of the Guajará-Mirim State Park*,[53] the court underscored the pivotal role of the Guajará-Mirim State Park—located within the Amazon rainforest—in preserving biodiversity, given the role of protected areas in curbing GHG emissions.[54] Moreover, the ruling elucidated the multifaceted impacts of deforestation on water security, climate stability, soil health, air quality, biodiversity, public health, intergenerational equity, and economic prosperity. Ultimately, the court concluded that the illegal occupation of the disputed areas ran counter to prevailing legislation prohibiting anthropization in ecologically sensitive areas. In November 2023, the court dismissed the defendant's appeal.[55]

Meanwhile, *Rede Sustentabilidade v Brazil (on Amazon Deforestation)*[56] and *PSB et al v Brazil (on deforestation and human rights)*[57] were judged jointly, as

48 Maria Antonia Tigre & Joana Setzer, 'Human Rights and Climate Change for Climate Litigation in Brazil and Beyond: An Analysis of the Climate Fund Decision' (2023) 54(4) *Georgetown JIL* 593, 596–597.

49 *PSB et al v Brazil (on Climate Fund)* (n 16).

50 ibid, §16.

51 Tigre & Setzer (n 50).

52 ibid. See also Délton Winter de Carvalho & Armando Rocha (Chapter 6).

53 *State of Rondônia et al v Invaders of the Guajará-Mirim State Park* (n 34).

54 ibid.

55 ibid.

56 *Rede Sustentabilidade v Brazil (on Amazon deforestation)* (n 39).

57 *PSB et al v Brazil (on deforestation and human rights)* (n 35).

both argued there was an unconstitutional omission by the federal government regarding the implementation of the policy to combat deforestation, namely by President Bolsonaro and Environmental Minister Salles. Both were filed by opposing political parties in 2019 and 2020 respectively. The rapporteur, Minister Carmen Lúcia, provided her vote in 2022, recognizing an 'unconstitutional state of things' regarding environmental matters and demanding the adoption and implementation of actions for deforestation control.[58] STF's plenary reached a decision in March 2024.[59] Considering that the Lula administration reenacted the PPCDAm and deforestation rates in the Amazon have since declined, Minister Carmen Lúcia's updated vote noted that the 'unconstitutional state of things' only partially remained. However, the decision was partially favorable, as most other Ministers did not vote to recognize the unconstitutional state of things.[60]

Minister Flávio Dino proposed opening extraordinary credit to guarantee the continuity of governmental actions to counter deforestation, and most Ministers accepted this proposition. Moreover, the decision provided that the federal government must (i) monitor the implementation of the deforestation control actions by environmental bodies; (ii) reduce 80% of deforestation by 2027 and 100% 2030; (iii) implement the 5th phase of the PPCDAm by 2027; (iv) include the PPCDAm in a schedule to receive funding by the Amazon Fund; and (v) adopt measures to strengthen environmental federal bodies and other relevant institutes, namely the Brazilian Institute for the Environment and Renewable Natural Resources (IBAMA), Institute Chico Mendes (ICMBio) and the National Indigenous Foundation (Funai); among others. This landmark decision reiterated the compromise of eliminating deforestation in the Amazon by 2030 and determined relevant measures to guarantee it, including the adoption of actions and deadlines.[61]

In *Jaci-Paraná Extractive Reserve and Guajará-Mirim State Park*,[62] a direct action of unconstitutionality was brought regarding a state law that reduced protected areas and further allowed for illegal occupation and deforestation

58 *Rede Sustentabilidade v Brazil* (*on Amazon deforestation*) (n 41).

59 ibid.

60 ibid.

61 The decision is dated March 14, 2024 and the summary was published in March 19, 2024. However, the full decision was not yet published at the time of the writing. The content of the decision was reported by Tiago Angelo, *Supremo manda União adotar medidas contra o desmatamento e abrir crédito* (Conjur, 2024) available at https://www.conjur.com.br/2024-mar-14/stf-manda-uniao-adotar-medidas-contra-desmatamento-e-abrir-credito-extraordinario/ accessed April 2, 2024.

62 *Jaci-Paraná Extractive Reserve and Guajará-Mirim State Park* (n 38).

to the detriment of the rights of traditional extractivist populations to persist. The removal of these areas directly impacted indigenous communities in voluntary isolation, and the law passed without any free, prior, and informed consultation and consent (FPIC), or technical studies carried out. In November 2021, the court declared specific provisions and an amendment to the law unconstitutional.[63] The ruling emphasized the absence of prior studies supporting the protected areas' disqualification, violating the principles of precaution, prevention, public participation, intergenerational equity, and avoiding environmental regression. It highlighted the government's duty to protect the environment. A separate vote from Judge Monico Neto emphasized the context of the climate emergency and the role of protected areas in Amazonia.[64]

In light of this, the vote highlighted an 'ecological (and climatic) unconstitutional state of affairs' in which the public authority demonstrates a profound and systematic institutional incapacity to manage environmental and climate policies. The vote further noted the role of the Amazon rainforest as a national heritage, as defined in the constitution, and one of the primary measures for effectively addressing the adverse effects of climate change, combating deforestation. The progressive loss of forest cover in the country has led to significant biodiversity loss, exacerbated adverse climate effects, and impacted indigenous and traditional cultures, thereby violating fundamental and intergenerational human rights outlined in the constitution.[65]

While there are not yet a plethora of decisions, insights can be drawn from these cases, underscoring the imperative to uphold international climate commitments, particularly in combating illegal deforestation in the Amazon. The decisions granted by Brazilian courts so far show a pronounced reliance on the constitutional right to a healthy environment, intricately linked with broader human rights considerations, as well as the interplay between national policy decisions and international obligations. Furthermore, these decisions highlight the multifaceted impacts of deforestation on various aspects of human rights, from water security to intergenerational equity. Collectively, these cases underscore the judiciary's pivotal role in safeguarding environmental and human rights, particularly in the context of the Amazon rainforest's ecological

63 ibid.

64 ibid.

65 See Walelasoetxeige Paiter Bandeira Surui, Guilherme Leal & Mariana Miranda, 'Judiciário reconhece crise climática em ação contra desmatamento na Amazônia' (*Jota*, 23 March 2022) <https://www.jota.info/opiniao-e-analise/artigos/judiciario-reconhece-emergencia-climatica-em-acao-contra-desmatamento-23032022> accessed 2 April 2024.

significance and the broader imperative to address climate change at both national and international levels.

### 4.2 *Themes Related to Climate Litigation in the Amazon Rainforest*

While climate cases related to the Amazon rainforest represent a predominant area of climate litigation in Brazil, there are various types of cases. Setzer and Winter de Carvalho categorize different strategies based on whether these seek to impose negative or positive obligations.[66] For instance, legal actions brought against governments aim to address their actions and inactions contributing to escalating deforestation and GHG emissions. These cases strive to prevent government engagement in activities that could exacerbate climate impacts or rollback crucial regulations. Moreover, government inaction prompts demand for positive obligations, urging the adoption, implementation, and enforcement of measures aimed at emission reduction. Additionally, litigants have contested the stagnation of specific climate governance mechanisms, which has been linked to a notable surge in deforestation rates. Following a global trend of rights-based climate litigation cases, which is especially prominent in the Global South, most cases rely on human rights.[67]

Building on this preliminary analysis, we have categorized Amazon-related climate cases based on six themes: (i) carbon credits and land grabbing, (ii) climate damages, (iii) illegal deforestation, (iv) administrative omissions, (v) project-specific authorization, (vi) forest fires. Figure 13.3 reflects how these are distributed.

#### 4.2.1 Carbon Credits and Land Grabbing

The first category of Amazon-related cases is carbon credits and land grabbing. This category encompasses five pending cases that intricately intertwine the issues of carbon projects and the encroachment upon protected lands inhabited by indigenous and other traditional populations.[68] One case relates to a contractual dispute on carbon credits.[69] These cases can be considered

66 Joana Setzer & Délton Winter de Carvalho, 'Climate Litigation to Protect the Brazilian Amazon: Establishing a Constitutional Right to a Stable Climate' (2021) 30(2) *RECIEL* 197, 199.

67 Maria Antonia Tigre & Melanie Jean Murcott, 'Developments, Opportunities, and Complexities in Global South Climate Litigation: Introduction to the Special Collection' (2023) *Journal of Human Rights Practice* https://doi.org/10.1093/jhuman/huad070 accessed 2 April 2024.

68 For more on climate cases related to indigenous communities, see Maria Antonia Tigre, 'Climate Change and Indigenous Groups: The Rise of Indigenous Voices in Climate Litigation' (2022) 9(3) *e-Publica* 214.

69 *Carbonext Tecnologia* (n 68). This case is an exception in this category—all other comments relate to the first five.

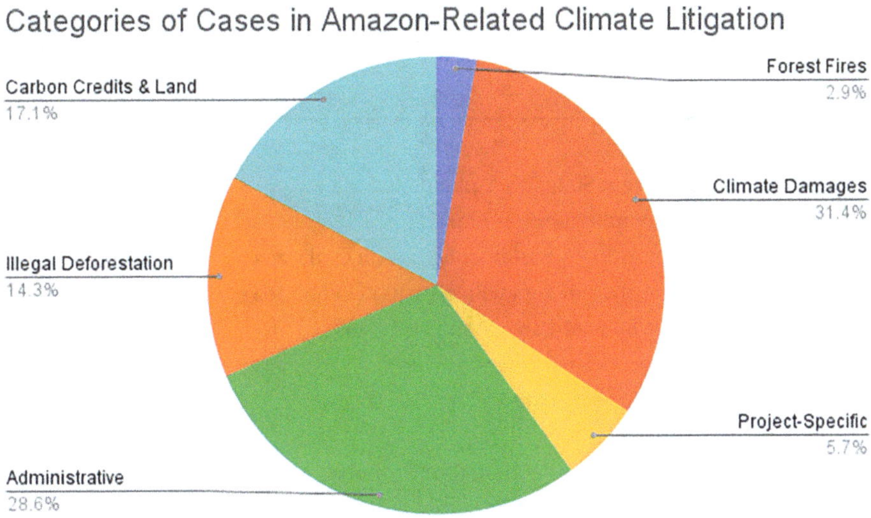


FIGURE 13.3 Categories of Brazilian climate cases related to the Amazon rainforest

land grabbing based on claims that private parties illegally appropriate profits from public lands based on the protection and preservation promoted by traditional populations residing there. The cases address the illegal overlap between carbon project areas and protected areas, as well as the emission of carbon credits for the conservation of such areas by private companies sold in voluntary carbon markets.

Notably, private entities sought to exploit protected public lands—such as Agro Extractivist Reserves (RESEX)—which are public areas occupied by traditional riverine communities (*ribeirinhos*) and other agro-extractivist communities without their consent. The cases were filed in 2021 and 2023 and are still pending. Among these legal challenges, one was initiated by two community associations of Extractivist Reserves in Marajó Island in Pará, while the remaining four were brought by the Public Defense of the State of Pará addressing projects in the Municipality of Portel. These cases underscore the deficiencies in existing policies and procedures that fail to adequately safeguard the rights of local or indigenous communities and ensure just transitions within the Amazon region.

All cases rely on the Brazilian Constitution, the Law of the National System of Protected Areas,[70] which regulates RESEX a protected area, the National Policy of Sustainable Development of Traditional Peoples and

70 Law No 9.985, of 18 de July 2000, *Sistema Nacional de Unidades de Conservação.*

TABLE 13.2 Cases related to carbon credits and land grabbing

| Case name | Year filed | Status |
|---|---|---|
| Carbonext Tecnologia em Soluções Ambientais Ltda v Amazon Imóveis (Voluntary Carbon Market)[a] | 2021 | Decided by lack of procedural interest |
| AMOREMA and AMORETGRAP v Sustainable Carbon et al[b] | 2021 | Pending |
| Public Defense of the State of Pará v Brazil AGFOR et al[c] | 2023 | Pending |
| Public Defense of the State of Pará v Associação dos Ribeirinhos e Moradores et al[d] | 2023 | Pending |
| Public Defense of the State of Pará v Floyd Promoção e Representação LTDA et al[e] | 2023 | Pending |
| Public Defense of the State of Pará v RMDLT Property Group et al[f] | 2023 | Pending |

a *Carbonext Tecnologia em Soluções Ambientais Lda. v Amazon Imóveis* (*Voluntary Carbon Market*). 44th Civil Court of São Paulo, Process No 1072768-63.2021.8.26.0100, Decision of 7 October 2021.

b *AMOREMA and AMORETGRAP v Sustainable Carbon at al* (*on voluntary carbon markets*) ACP 1045416-11.2021.4.01.3900, filed in 2021 before the Federal Court of Pará.

c *Public Defender's of the State of Pará v Brazil AGFOR et al* (Project 2552 carbon credits and 'forest carbon grabbing'), ACP 0806505-59.2023.8.14.0015, filed on 20 July 2023 before the State Court of Pará.

d *Public Defender's Office of the State of Pará v Associação dos Ribeirinhos e Moradores et al* (*Project 2620 carbon credits and 'forest carbon grabbing'*), ACP 0806464-92.2023.8.14.0015, filed on 19 July 2023 before the State Court of Pará.

e *Public Defender's Office of the State of Pará v Floyd et al* (*Project 981 carbon credits and 'forest carbon grabbing'*), ACP 0806631-12.2023.8.14.0015, filed on 25 July 2023 before the State Court of Pará.

f *Public Defender's Office of the State of Pará v RMDLT Property Group et al* (*Project 997 carbon credits and 'forest carbon grabbing'*), ACP 0806582-68.2023.8.14.0015, filed on 24 July 2023 before the State Court of Pará.

Communities,[71] the Brazilian Civil Code,[72] as the defendants would have contracted areas not belonging to them, which constitutes a civil infraction, and the Convention 169 of the International Labour Organization (ILO).[73] ILO

71 Decree No 6460, of 7 February 2007, *Política Nacional de Desenvolvimento Sustentável dos Povos e Comunidades Tradicionais* [National Policy of Sustainable Development of Traditional Peoples and Communities].

72 Law No 10.406, 10 January, *Código Civil* [Civil Code].

73 International Labour Organization (ILO) Convention No 169 concerning Indigenous and Tribal Peoples in Independent Countries, adopted 1989, ratified by Brazil through Decrees No 5.051/2004 and No 10.088/2019.

Convention 169 protects the rights of indigenous and other traditional populations to their collective areas and establishes their rights to FPIC regarding laws, policies, and projects that affect their territories.[74] The lawsuits proposed by the public defender's office also rely on the Convention of Biological Diversity,[75] as it affected the rights to traditional knowledge relating to the conservation and sustainable use of forests.

The first case was proposed by local associations (AMOREMA and AMORETGRAP), representing communities of the Federal Extractivist Reserves in Marajó Island, Pará. They argue that the area of three farms holding Project Ecomapuá, a carbon project registered in the VERRA, the largest global certification of carbon credits, totally or partially overlaps the two reserves.[76] Furthermore, they note that the defendants are not the project's owners due to the exclusive use by traditional populations granted through public concessions formalized between the federal government and the associations. As such, the project violates their rights and should be considered null.[77] They request, among others, information about the contracts signed, restitution of the benefits received by the defendants, compensation for material damages, and collective moral damage. Finally, they request that the defendants stop buying or selling carbon credits from inside or around the Mapuá and Terra Grande-Pracuúba Extractive Reserves and stop using the name and image of the extractivist populations, their associations, and the respective extractive reserves.

---

74 See Maria Antonia Tigre & Sarah Slinger, 'A Voice in the Development of Amazonia: The Constitutional Rights to Participation of Indigenous Peoples', in Lima et al (eds), *Indigenous Amazonia, Regional Development and Territorial Dynamics: Contentious Issues* (Springer, 2020).

75 Convention on Biological Diversity (adopted 5 June 1992, entered into force 29 December 1993), 1760 UNTS 79.

76 The project is registered in the Verra platform, <https://verra.org/project/vcs-program/>. Project details state that: 'The project activity Ecomapuá Amazon REDD Project represents a Reducing Emissions project from Deforestation and Degradation (REDD) through Avoided Unplanned Deforestation (AUD), in an area of 86,269.84 ha, located in 5 farms in Marajó Island, State of Pará, in northern Brazil. The present REDD project, through conservation measures, will avoid the predicted 4,253.14 ha of deforestation, equating to around 2,745,350 $tCO_2eq$ in Emissions Reductions over the 30 year project lifetime, not including Reductions for the project's efficiency, non-permanence risk buffer and displacement leakage factor.' The case was published in an investigative journalism report by Apública: Anna Beatriz Anjos, *Empresa vende créditos de carbono sobre terras públicas na Ilha do Marajó* (Agência Pública, 2022) <https://apublica.org/2022/05/empresa-vende-creditos-de-carbono-sobre-terras-publicas-na-ilha-do-marajo/> accessed April 2, 2024.

77 *AMOREMA & AMORETGRAP* (n 69).

The cases proposed by the Public Defenders' Office of Pará pertain to avoided deforestation in carbon projects, which allegedly overlap with five State Agroextrativist Settlement Projects (PEAEX) in Portel. The projects also have VERRA's verified carbon standard (VCS) certification.[78] In addition to overlapping public lands, the Public Defenders' Office argued that the private lands registered in the projects were previously canceled for illegalities. These cases were also brought against the Municipality of Portel for allowing the carbon projects despite their location in state-owned lands. As a preliminary matter, all cases request the recognition of the ownership of the lands by the traditional communities affected by the project overlapping their areas, the suspension of the projects, and an order preventing the defendants from entering the RESEX. Furthermore, they request the recognition of the right to the traditional territory, the invalidation of the projects and any legal transactions derived from them, an order to prohibit the defendants from entering the territories, a declaration that the Public Utility Decree issued by the Municipality of Portel is null and void, and an order to pay collective moral damages to the Eastern Amazon Fund in favor of the agro-extractivist communities of Portel.

In *AMOREMA e AMORETGRAP v Sustainable Carbon et al*, a preliminary decision considered the competency of the federal court in the matter, as the Inter-American Development Bank (IDB) is one of the defendants.[79] Federal courts are competent to address cases involving international bodies. However, no decision discussing merit has been taken in any of the cases.

The issue of consent in carbon projects is not novel, given previous allegations of violations of indigenous people's rights in Reducing Emissions from Deforestation and Forest Degradation (REDD+) initiatives[80] despite international safeguards adopted under the UNFCCC to protect the rights of indigenous and local populations.[81] Nonetheless, these cases reinforce the urgent need for improved, transparent, and equitable procedures and heightened due

78 *Public Defense of the State of Pará v Brazil AGFOR et al (Project 2552 carbon credits and 'forest carbon grabbing')* (n 72); *Public Defender's Office of the State of Pará v Associação dos Ribeirinhos e Moradores et al (Project 2620 carbon credits and 'forest carbon grabbing')* (n 73); *Public Defender's Office of the State of Pará v Floyd Promoção e Representação LTDA et and others (Project 981 carbon credits and 'forest carbon grabbing')* (n 74); *Public Defender's Office of the State of Pará v RMDLT Property Group and others (Project 997 carbon credits and 'forest carbon grabbing')* (n 75).

79 *AMOREMA & AMORETGRAP* (n 69).

80 Such as in CIFOR, Rights abuse allegations in the context of REDD+ readiness and implementation: A preliminary review and proposal for moving forward, 2017 https://doi.org/10.17528/cifor/006630.

81 UNFCCC, COP Decision No 1/CP.16.

diligence standards for carbon credit companies. Moreover, amidst ongoing discussions in the Brazilian Congress regarding a regulated carbon market bill (PL 2148/15 and others),[82] there is an opportunity to address these gaps and fortify the protection of traditional lands, ensure compliance with FPIC, and facilitate a just transition.

### 4.2.2 Climate Damages for Illegal Deforestation

The second category of cases relates to climate damages for illegal deforestation, which includes 11 cases. Among these, 10 have been proposed by the Brazilian Federal Institute for Environment and Renewable Natural Resources (IBAMA) and one by the Federal Public Prosecution's Office (MPF). All are Public Civil Actions (ACP s).[83] A first batch of nine lawsuits was proposed by IBAMA in 2018 and 2019, against different lumber companies. The cases follow the same legal arguments and relate to the exploitation of wood without a permit, seeking the recovery of the deforested area and the payment for the social cost of carbon (SCC). To calculate the SCC, these cases used the methodology of the Amazon Fund to estimate the cost of emissions based on the deforested areas in the Amazon, which considers 5 dollars per ton of carbon equivalent ($CO_2$eq) emissions.[84]

As of August 2024, eight cases had preliminary decisions with conflicting results. Four decisions were favorable to the plaintiffs and called on defendants to propose reforestation plans and pay for the SCC (*IBAMA v Souza Brilhante*,[85] *IBAMA v Seringal*,[86] *IBAMA v Floresta Verde*[87] and *IBAMA v Dirceu Kruger*).[88] In *IBAMA v Gabriel Madeiras* and *IBAMA v Silmar Gomes Moreira*, the first-degree decision was partially favorable, ordering the defendant to present reforestation plans but rejected the payment of the SCC. In *IBAMA v Madelin Madeireira Linhares*, the court rejected IBAMA's legal standing to bring

82 Projeto de Lei [Bill] nº 2.148, de 30 de junho de 2015 (Brazil).

83 Collective lawsuits which may be filed by the public prosecution, public defense, government bodies or an association constituted for more than one year with the objective to safeguard the environment or other collective rights.

84 *IBAMA v Souza Brilhante (on ilegal wood storage)* (n 89); *IBAMA v Madeireira Madevi (on ilegal wood storage)* (n 90); *IBAMA v Madelin Madeireira Linhares (on illegal wood storage)* (n 91); *IBAMA v Gabriel Madeiras (on illegal wood storage)* (n 92); *IBAMA v Alto Norte (on ilegal wood storage)* (n 93); *IBAMA v Silmar Gomes Moreira (on ilegal wood storage)* (n 94); *IBAMA v Madeira Nova Aliança (on illegal wood storage)* (n 95); *IBAMA v Floresta Verde (on ilegal wood storage)* (n 96); and *IBAMA v Seringal (on ilegal wood storage)* (n 97).

85 *IBAMA v Souza Brilhante (on illegal wood storage)* (n 89).

86 *IBAMA v Seringal (on illegal wood storage)* (n 97).

87 *IBAMA v Floresta Verde (on illegal wood storage)* (n 96).

88 *IBAMA v Dirceu Kruger (on illegal wood storage)* (n 99).

TABLE 13.3 Cases related to climate damages for illegal deforestation

| Case name | Year filed | Status |
|---|---|---|
| IBAMA v Souza Brilhante [a] | 2018 | Decided |
| IBAMA v Madeireira Madevi[b] | 2018 | Under appeal |
| IBAMA v Madelin Madeireira Linhares LTDA[c] | 2018 | Under appeal |
| IBAMA v Gabriel Madeiras[d] | 2018 | Under appeal |
| IBAMA v Alto Norte[e] | 2018 | Pending |
| IBAMA v Silmar Gomes Moreira[f] | 2018 | Under appeal |
| IBAMA v Madeira Nova Aliança[g] | 2019 | Pending |
| IBAMA v Floresta Verde[h] | 2019 | Under appeal |
| IBAMA v Seringal[i] | 2019 | Under appeal |
| Federal Public Prosecutor's Office et al v Dauro Parreira de Rezende[j] | 2021 | Pending |
| IBAMA v Dirceu Kruger[k] | 2023 | First Degree Decision |

a *IBAMA v Souza Brilhante (on illegal wood storage)* ACP 1003478-16.2018.4.01.3100, Federal Court of Amapá, Judgment of 2 September 2022.

b *IBAMA v Madeireira Madevi (on ilegal wood storage)* ACP 1000656-73.2018.4.01.3902, filed on 20 December 2018 before the Federal Court of Pará.

c *IBAMA v Madelin Madeireira Linhares (on illegal wood storage)* ACP 1001659-42.2018.4.01.4200, Federal Court of Roraima Judgment of 5 August 2020.

d *IBAMA v Gabriel Madeiras (on illegal wood storage)* ACP 1000185-42.2018.4.01.3907, Federal Court of Pará Judgment of 5 June 2019.

e *IBAMA v Alto Norte (on ilegal wood storage)* ACP 1000200-41.2018.4.01.3606, filed on 20 December 2018 before the Mato Grosso Federal Court.

f *IBAMA v Silmar Gomes Moreira (on ilegal wood storage)* ACP 1000469-62.2018.4.01.3903, filed on 19 December 2018 before the Federal Court of Pará.

g *IBAMA v Madeira Nova Aliança (on illegal wood storage)* ACP 1000275-31.2019.4.01.3902, filed on 28 January 2019 before the Federal Court of Pará.

h *IBAMA v Floresta Verde (on ilegal wood storage)* ACP 1000083-80.4.01.3908, Federal Court of Pará Judgment of 25 March 2020.

i *IBAMA v Seringal (on ilegal wood storage)* ACP 1000364-26.2019.4.01.3200, Federal Court of Amazonas, Judgment of 15 August 2023.

*J* *Federal Public Prosecutor's Office et al v Rezende (on deforestation and climate damage)* ACP 1005885-78.2021.4.01.3200, filed on 7 April 2021 before the 7th Federal Environmental and Agrarian Court of the Judiciary Section of Amazonas.

k *IBAMA v Dirceu Kruger (on illegal wood storage)* ACP 1037196-19.2023.4.01.3200, Federal Court in Amazonas Judgment of 18 July 2024.

the lawsuit, the only negative ruling in this sense.[89] *IBAMA v Souza Brilhante* has been decided and other decisions have been appealed.

89 *IBAMA v Madelin Madeireira Linhares (on illegal wood storage)* (n 91).

In *IBAMA v Madeireira Madevi*, in a preliminary decision, the court ordered (i) the suspension of the right to participate in financing lines offered by official credit establishments and (ii) the restriction of access to government tax incentives and tax benefits.[90] However, the federal judge stated that, for the time being, the use of the SCC for the purposes of decreeing the unavailability of assets was not feasible due to the lack of technical subsidies, and that the amount requested was, at first glance, disproportionate.

In *IBAMA v Floresta Verde*, the judge highlighted the importance of the Amazon in the constitution and treated climate damage as environmental damage.[91] In addition to the obligation of reforestation, the judge ruled in favor of the payment of damages of R$ 9.322.387,20, quoting environmental precedents of the Superior Court of Justice (STJ), which considered that despite restoration efforts, there are interim damages while the vegetation is not recovered.[92] In *IBAMA v Souza Brilhante,* the judge ruled in favor of IBAMA, initially only considering the reforestation plan. After a procedural appeal by IBAMA asking for clarifications, the judge ruled in favor of the payment of damages of R$ 1.447.650,20 per the requested SCC in considering the $CO_2$ emissions as one of the ecosystem services affected, 'the damage caused to the community by the polluter can be identified as the loss of nutrients and the soil itself, the impact on the local population, the loss of natural capital, an increase in carbon dioxide in the atmosphere, and a reduction in water availability.'[93] Both precedents utilize methodologies from CEPAL.[94]

On the other hand, in *IBAMA v Silmar Gomes Moreira,* the judge ordered the defendant to present reforestation plans and ordered the bank to block assets in the total amount of R$ 2.225.650,65 to guarantee the fulfillment of the decision. However, the decision does not address the SCC.

In 2021, the MPF proposed a similar lawsuit, *Federal Public Prosecutor's Office et al v Rezende,* regarding the illegal occupation and deforestation of federal public lands.[95] This case also includes climate damages, in addition to environmental damages and collective moral damages, and uses the same methodology

90 *IBAMA v Madeireira Madevi* (*on illegal wood storage*) (n 90).

91 *IBAMA v Floresta Verde* (*on illegal wood storage*) (n 96).

92 *Public Prosecutor's Office of the State of Minas Gerais v Rubens de Castro Maia*, Special Appeal No Resp 1180078/MG, Judgment of 2 December 2010 (Superior Court of Justice), Rapporteur: Minister Herman Benjamin.

93 *IBAMA v Souza Brilhante* (*on illegal wood storage*) (n 89).

94 José Eduardo Allatore et al, *El costo social del carbono: una visión agregada desde América Latina* (CEPAL 2019).

95 *Federal Public Prosecutor's Office et al v Rezende* (*on deforestation and climate damage*) (n 98).

as the previous IBAMA cases.[96] There was an intermediate decision by the federal court accepting its jurisdiction, but no decision on the merits has been made yet.[97]

Finally, *IBAMA v Dirceu Kruger* also addresses illegal deforestation in public lands and utilizes similar arguments but innovates by seeking a much higher amount in damages as the SCC is calculated based on the Organisation for Economic Co-operation and Development (OECD)'s CARBON RATE of sixty euros per $CO_2$eq.[98] Kruger is a cattle rancher which had already faced several administrative charges for illegal deforestation and fires, and had admitted to land-grabbing. In this case, IBAMA argued that climate damages are specific and independent from environmental damages. In 2024, a favorable first-degree preliminary decision recognized the climate damage and the amount claimed in the total amount of R$ 292,118,400.00. The decision accepted the OECD methodology used by IBAMA, because, according to the judge, 'although there are no definitive parameters for this quantification at the moment, I believe it is appropriate to consider the amount presented by the plaintiff, since it is taken from an OECD study and is in line with the academic discussions that the issue has sparked in Brazil.'[99] The preliminary decision froze assets in this amount until a final decision is made and prohibits Kruger from engaging in any commercial activities involving the deforested properties, as well as the rental or lending of agricultural equipment, under the penalty of a fine of R$ 1,000,000.00 for each violation. The sale or donation of bovine specimens or agricultural products is also prohibited. Thus, although a final decision is pending, this landmark decision awarded the highest level of damages for climate-related harms.

The strategy of including requests for climate damage builds on the polluter pays principle and on previous environmental litigation surrounding deforestation, which may be a powerful tool to deter further deforestation. Despite some preliminary decisions, a solid precedent has yet to be formed concerning these cases, especially from higher courts. The plea for climate damages is strengthened by Article 14 of the Brazilian National Council of Justice (CNJ) Resolution 433/2021,[100] which establishes that decisions regarding environmental impacts should consider impacts on global climate change. The CNJ is also

---

96 Maria Antonia Tigre, 'Guest Commentary: Brazilian's First Tort Climate Case for Illegal Deforestation in Amazonia' (*Climate Law—A Sabin Center Blog*, 16 June 2021) <https://blogs.law.columbia.edu/climatechange/2021/06/16/guest-commentary-brazilians-first-tort-climate-case-for-illegal-deforestation-in-amazonia/> accessesd 15 August 2024.

97 *Federal Public Prosecutor's Office et al v Rezende (on deforestation and climate damage)* (n 98).

98 *IBAMA v Dirceu Kruger (on illegal wood storage)* (n 99).

99 ibid.

100 Resolution No 433/2021 of the National Council of Justice (Brazil).

developing a protocol to assist judges with environmental decisions, which includes a section on the most adequate procedures to quantify climate damages.[101] The draft protocol notes that the valuation of damages per the amount of the Amazon Fund may be insufficient. Current studies place the cost of conserving the Amazon Rainforest closer to 20 USD per $CO_2$eq.[102]

### 4.2.3 Cases Related to Illegal Deforestation Policy

While most cases tangentially relate to illegal deforestation, we identified five cases that specifically relate to illegal deforestation in the Amazon rainforest as a policy measure. These cases were filed between 2020 and 2022. Two cases have been decided (*State of Rondônia et al v Invaders of the Guajará-Mirim State Park* and *Jaci-Paraná Extractive Reserve and Guajará-Mirim State Park*).[103] Most cases were filed by NGOs against the government. One case was filed by the state of Rondônia and the public prosecutor's office against invaders in a national park.

TABLE 13.4 Cases related to illegal deforestation policy

| Case name | Year filed | Status |
|---|---|---|
| IEA v Brazil[a] | 2020 | Pending |
| State of Rondônia et al v Invaders of the Guajará-Mirim State Park[b] | 2020 | Decided |
| Observatório do Clima v Minister of Environment et al[c] | 2021 | Pending |
| Jaci-Paraná Extractive Reserve and Guajará-Mirim State Park[d] | 2021 | Decided |
| IEA v Brazil et al (Chico Mendes Extraction Reserve)[e] | 2022 | Pending |

a *IEA v Brazil*, ACP 5048951-39.2020.4.04.7000, filed in 2020 before the 4th Regional Federal Regional Court of Curitiba.

b *State of Rondônia et al v v Invaders of the Guajará-Mirim State Park* (n 34).

c *Laboratório do Observatório do Clima v Minister of Environment et al*, ACP 1027282-96.2021.4.01.3200 (2021), filed on 26 October 2021 before the 7th Federal Environmental and Agrarian Court of the Judiciary Section of Amazonas.

d *Jaci-Paraná Extractive Reserve and Guajará-Mirim State Park* (n 36).

e *IEA v Brazil et al (Chico Mendes Extraction Reserve)* ACP 1012197-54.2022.4.01.3000, filed on 28 October 2022 before the 2nd Federal Civil and Criminal Court of the Judiciary Section of Acre.

101 CNJ, *Protocolo para Julgamento de Ações Ambientais*, forthcoming.

102 ibid.

103 These were discussed in Section 4.1 above (this Chapter).

These cases share a few common threads. First is the reliance on scientific evidence, prominently featuring available deforestation data and its pervasive impacts on climate change. This reliance is exemplified through sources like the INPE, which employs satellite-based monitoring systems to record deforestation trends. Furthermore, these cases underscore the intricate interplay between national policy frameworks and their implications at both regional and international levels. Additionally, they rely on fundamental rights, especially the constitutional right to a healthy environment. These overarching themes highlight the complexities inherent in addressing deforestation and emphasize the necessity of interdisciplinary approaches integrating scientific findings, policy considerations, and respect for fundamental rights in effective environmental governance. In essence, they question the government's failure to meet emissions targets set out in the PNMC[104] and, therefore, comply with action plans for preventing and controlling deforestation in Brazilian biomes,[105] including PPCDAm.

In *IEA v Brazil et al* (*Chico Mendes Extraction Reserve*),[106] an NGO filed a public civil action against the federal government, arguing the government had failed to comply with its action plans to prevent deforestation and mitigate and adapt to climate change, violating national law and fundamental rights. The case centers on illegal deforestation causing the majority of national GHG emissions to ensure that the PPCDAm aligns with the PNMC. The NGO requested an order compelling the government to comply with national climate law, reforest an area equivalent to what was deforested beyond the statutory limit, and allocate sufficient budgetary resources.[107] Furthermore, it uniquely requested the recognition of a new norm, the fundamental right to a stable climate for present and future generations. The plaintiffs argued that the recognition is justified given the magnitude of the climate crisis and how it affects fundamental rights. According to Setzer and Winter de Carvalho, the recognition is implicit and a 'logical consequence of integrating fundamental rights' in the Brazilian Constitution, building on synergies between more traditional rights expressly provided, such as the right to dignity, the right to life, freedom, equality, health, food, and housing, among others.[108]

104 Law No 12.187, of 29 December 2009, *Política Nacional sobre Mudança do Clima* [National Policy on Climate Change].

105 Decree No 9.578, of 22 November 2018.

106 *IEA v Brazil* (n 120).

107 ibid.

108 Setzer & Winter de Carvalho (n 66) 204. See also Délton Winter de Carvalho & Armando Rocha (Chapter 7).

A decision from the Federal Regional Court of the Fourth Region (TRF4) from December 2021[109]—focused on a preliminary matter of whether the case should be combined with another pending case—partially leaned towards this recognition, specifically differentiating between environmental cases and climate cases given its 'autonomous climate function'.[110] A decision on the merits is still pending.

In *Observatório do Clima v Ministério do Meio Ambiente e União Federal (Atualização do Plano Nacional sobre Mudança do Clima)*,[111] a network of 71 civil society organizations sued the government requesting that the PNMC be updated to the best available science and aligned with the seriousness of the climate emergency, ensuring an emissions reductions pathway that is consistent with the long-term temperature goal of the Paris Agreement. However, after changes in government, the process to update the PNMC was initiated with public participation, and the NGO and the Brazilian government reached a settlement.[112]

In *IEA v Brazil et al (Chico Mendes Extraction Reserve)*,[113] the plaintiffs state that deforestation in a protected area causes irreparable damage to the Amazon Rainforest and affects the rights and way of life of the traditional extractivist community, which is based on the sustainable exploitation of natural resources. Noting the deforestation reduction targets that are not being met, the plaintiffs emphasize the vital role of the forest in the carbon cycle and the additional emissions due to illegal deforestation. The plaintiffs call for full reparations and forest restoration, as well as compensation for climate damages, including moral damages, given the damage caused to the vulnerable populations of the extractivist communities living inside the protected area. The case is still pending. Despite ongoing legal proceedings, these cases collectively advocate for updated climate policies aligned with scientific evidence and the seriousness of the climate emergency, aiming for emissions reductions consistent with global goals like those outlined in the Paris Agreement.

#### 4.2.4 Cases Related to Administrative Omissions

The following category, cases related to administrative omissions related to deforestation policies, is the largest identified, with nine cases proposed

109 *IEA v Brazil* (n 120).

110 Maria Antonia Tigre, Délton Winter de Carvalho and Joana Setzer, 'IEA v Brazil: When a Court Accepts the Legally Disruptive Nature of Climate Change' (Climate Law—A Sabin Center Blog 2021) <https://blogs.law.columbia.edu/climatechange/2021/12/21/iea-v-brazil-when-a-court-accepts-the-legally-disruptive-nature-of-climate-change/> accessed 15 August 2024.

111 *Laboratório do Observatório do Clima v Minister of Environment et al* (n 122).

112 At the time of the writing, this had not been made public.

113 *IEA v Brazil et al (Chico Mendes Extraction Reserve)* (n 124).

TABLE 13.5 Cases related to administrative omissions

| Case name | Year filed | Status |
|---|---|---|
| Rede Sustentabilidade v Brazil (on Amazon deforestation)[a] | 2019 | Decided |
| Fabiano Contarato et al v Ricardo Salles (Accusation of the Former Minister of Environment for crimes of responsibility related to omissions in the Amazon rainforest)[b] | 2019 | Decided |
| PSB et al v Brazil (on Amazon Fund)[c] | 2020 | Decided |
| Partido dos Trabalhadores v Brazil (Fires in the Pantanal and the Amazon Forest)[d] | 2020 | Decided |
| PSB et al v Brazil (on Climate Fund)[e] | 2020 | Decided |
| PSB et al v Brazil (on deforestation and human rights)[f] | 2020 | Decided |
| PSB et al v Brazil (Federal environmental sanctioning process[g] | 2020 | Decided |
| Federal Public Prosecutor's Office v Brazil et al (on deforestation hotspots in the Amazon)[h] | 2020 | Decided |
| Federal Public Prosecutor's Office v Ricardo Salles et al[i] | 2020 | Pending |

a *Rede Sustentabilidade v Brazil (on Amazon deforestation)* (n 39).
b *Fabiano Contarato et al v Ricardo Salles* (n 37).
c *PSB et al v Brazil (on Amazon Fund)* (n 33).
d *Partido dos Trabalhadores v Brazil (Fires in the Pantanal and the Amazon Forest)* (n 39).
e *PSB et al v Brazil (on Climate Fund)* (n 16).
f *PSB et al v Brazil (on deforestation and human rights)* (n 35).
g *PSB et al v Brazil (Federal environmental sanctioning process)* ADPF 755, filed on 21 October 2020 before the Federal Supreme Court.
h *Federal Public Prosecutor's Office v Brazil et al (on deforestation hotspots in the Amazon)* ACP 1007104-63.2020.4.01.3200, filed in 2020 before the 7th Federal Environmental and Agrarian Court of the Judiciary Section of Amazonas.
i *Federal Public Prosecutor's Office v Ricardo Salles et al*, ACIA 1037665-52.2020.4.01.3400, filed on 6 July 2020 before the 8th Federal Court of the Judiciary Section of the Federal District.

in 2019 and 2020. This follows an overall trend in climate litigation in Brazil between 2018 and 2021, which was directed at tackling the omission and negligence regarding environmental and climate regulations under the Bolsonaro administration. Seven out of the cases in this category are constitutional control cases, including ADO (*Ação Direta de Inconstitucionalidade por Omissão*, Direct Action of Unconstitutionality by Omission) and ADPF (*Arguição de Descumprimento de Preceito Fundamental*, Action for the Failure to Comply with a Fundamental Precept). Concentrated constitutional control cases are adjudicated and decided directly by the STF.[114]

114 For an in-depth analysis of these cases, see De Andrade Moreira et al (n 28).

Among these cases, eight have been decided, ie, the cases relating to the paralyzation of the Climate Fund and the Amazon Fund, *Omission related to paralyzation of the PPCDAm* (ADPF 760), *Rede Sustentabilidade v Brazil* (*on Amazon deforestation*) and *Partido dos Trabalhadores v Brazil* (*Fires in the Pantanal and the Amazon Forest*). These have been described in section 4.1. *PSB et al v Brazil* (*Federal environmental sanctioning process*) was extinct without a merit decision. *Federal Public Prosecutor's Office v Ricardo Salles et al* (on the administrative impropriety of the former Minister of Environment and Federal Government related to omissions in the Amazon rainforest) is pending and one case has an unavailable status (under secrecy), i.e., *Federal Public Prosecutor's Office v Brazil et al* (*on deforestation hotspots in the Amazon*). *Federal Public Prosecution v Ricardo Salles et al* has lost its object, as noted above.

*PSB et al v Brazil* (*Federal environmental sanctioning process*) was proposed by four political parties in 2020. The plaintiffs argued that Federal Decree No 9.760/2019, edited by former President Bolsonaro, had paralyzed the environmental sanctioning process, mainly because of the conciliation stage it included and the impossibility of converting fines into environmental services. They highlighted that the conversion provided for in Federal Law No 9.605/1998, which provides for criminal and administrative sanctions for conduct harmful to the environment, is an important institute for fulfilling Brazil's commitment to the Paris Agreement. The justice-rapporteur, Minister Marco Aurélio, provided a vote considering the urgency and risk of the matter and requested the plenary to decide. However, the case was extinguished in December 2023 due to the loss of the object, as the Lula government revoked the decree.

Meanwhile, *Partido dos Trabalhadores v Brazil* (*Fires in the Pantanal and the Amazon Forest*) was proposed by the Labor Party (PT) due to unconstitutional omissions of the government in combating forest fires in both biomes. The arguments highlight how this scenario affects climate change and social and economic impacts, including on health and impacts on Amazon's flora and fauna. Therefore, the plaintiff argued that the omissions violated the fundamental rights to health, life and a balanced environment. They requested, preliminarily, the adoption of efforts to combat fires in the Pantanal and the Amazon Rainforest, especially to restructure the National System for Preventing and Combating Forest Fires (PREVFOGO) and implement the PPCDAm, in addition to the creation of similar action plans for other Brazilian biomes; the institution of an integrated public health project and veterinary medical treatment; the creation of a multidisciplinary commission to serve as an observatory for these measures and an explanation from the Ministry of the Environment on the budget execution of environmental protection programs in 2019 and 2020. They also requested recognition of the unconstitutionality of part of the environmental policy of the former executive branch due to omissions in the face of incidents of devastation of biomes, confirming the preliminary injunctions. Trials regarding the case commenced in December 2023, jointly with other similar lawsuits, *Rede Sustentabilidade v Brazil* (*on the Prevention of Forest Fires*)[115] and *PSL et al v Brazil et al.*[116] The case is currently pending a final decision, but there is a written vote by the Rapporteur, Minister André Mendonça, in favor of the request.

The cases above clearly illustrate a strategic pathway to combat omission to protect the environment under the former administration and demonstrate the importance of a robust and effective judiciary when other powers do not fulfill their constitutional obligations. Considering the government change, most lawsuits have lost their objective entirely or partially. Nonetheless, making final decisions emphasizing the importance of implementing environmental policies in Amazon may be critical to avoid future backsliding.

### 4.2.5 Cases Related to Activity Regulation

Two cases relate to the regulation of activities in the Amazon, both filed against the federal government. One case was filed by the Federal Public Prosecutor's Office, and the other by environmental NGOs and the Brazilian Association of Environmental Prosecutors (ABRAMPA). The first case, *Federal Public Prosecutor's Office v Brazil* (*Sugarcane zoning*), sought to make the government liable for publishing Presidential Decree No 10.084/2019, which revoked Federal Decree No 6.961/2009, establishing the zoning for agroecological sugarcane and prohibiting the planting of sugarcane in the Amazon region.

TABLE 13.6 Cases related to activity regulation

| Case name | Year filed | Status |
|---|---|---|
| Federal Public Prosecutor's Office v Brazil (Sugarcane zoning)[a] | 2019 | Under appeal |
| ISA et al v Brazil et al (Wood exportation)[b] | 2020 | Unavailable |

a *Federal Public Ministry v Brazil* (*Sugarcane zoning*), ACP 1016202-09.2019.4.01.3200, filed on 12 December 2019 before the 7th Federal Environmental and Agrarian Court of the Judiciary Section of Amazonas.

b *ISA et al v Brazil et al* (*Wood exportation*), ACP 1009665-60.2020.4.01.3200, filed on 4 June 2020 before the 7th Federal Environmental and Agrarian Court of the Judiciary Section of Amazonas.

115 *Rede Sustentabilidade v Brazil* (*on the Prevention of Forest Fires*) ADPF 743, filed on 17 September 2020.

116 *PSL et al v Brazil et al*, ADPF 755, filed on 21 October 2020.

The plaintiffs argued that the decree unjustifiably affected the ecologically balanced environment and made it more difficult for Brazil to comply with its NDC per the Paris Agreement, as the investigations showed that sugarcane production could provide environmental impacts without proper mitigation plans. The investigation was based on scientific research published in *Science Magazine*,[117] which concluded that sugarcane planting was unsustainable in the Amazon and Pantanal biomes. A preliminary ruling granted an injunction that suspended the effects of Presidential Decree No 10.084/2019 and determined that the Federal Government should take all measures to restore the effects of Federal Decree No 6.961/2009.[118] An appeal by the federal government against the preliminary decision was denied, but a final decision is still pending.

The second case, *ISA et al Brazil et al* (*Wood exportation*), requests the nullity of IBAMA's Interpretative Order 7036900/2020, which waived the need for an authorization issued by the agency for the export of wood products and by-products from native species, considering that an Exportation Forestry Origin Document (DOF) was sufficient. This interpretation understood that the previous regulation, Normative Instruction (IN) 15/2011, was no longer applicable, considering new regulations and an effort to streamline procedures. The IN established that those interested in obtaining an export authorization had to present, in person, at the IBAMA unit with jurisdiction over the customs warehouse, a series of documents proving that the goods were legal, submitting them to inspection and release. The plaintiffs challenged the order, arguing that only requesting the DOF is insufficient for the correct inspection, monitoring, and control of timber exports. Since the information in the DOF is entered by the interested parties themselves and not by IBAMA, it could be easily fraudulent. Consequently, the agency would have no way to verify its precision before the cargo is sent abroad. According to the proponents, this change was part of the deconstruction of public environmental policy in Brazil, which occurred under the previous administration, to the detriment of protective legislation.

The case is currently under secrecy; therefore, it was impossible to analyze if there were any decisions so far. Nonetheless, in another case, the STF Minister Alexandre de Moraes monocratically suspended the effects of IBAMA's Interpretative Order 7036900/2020.[119] This decision was part of Operation

117 Lucas Ferrante & Philip Martin Fernside, 'Amazon Sugar Cane: A Threat to the Forest' (2018) 359(6383) *Science* 1476.

118 Decree No 6.961, of 17 September 2009.

119 Fernando Couto Garcia, 'A Operação "Akuanduba", a LINDB e o Código Florestal' (*Conjur*, 25 May 2021) <https://www.conjur.com.br/2021-mai-25/garcia-operacao-akuanduba-lindb-codigo-florestal/> accessed 15 March 2024.

Akuanduba, an operation by the Federal Police investigating crimes in environmental organs. As in the previous decision, considering changes in the postures of the federal government and IBAMA, due to the new administration, it is unlikely that they would maintain the interpretation of Interpretative Order 7036900/2020 even if the decision is not maintained.

Both cases demonstrate the importance of litigation to prevent administrative rollbacks on environmental protection. Although there was no final decision, the preliminary decisions effectively suspended potentially harmful regulation.

#### 4.2.6 Cases Related to Forest Fires

Finally, one case relates to forest fires in the Amazon. This case is different from most of the cases detailed above, as it is a criminal case against a person who allegedly provoked a forest fire, affecting native vegetation of the Amazon Rainforest without authorization. The accused confessed to being a farmer who caused deforestation, seeking to open up pasture for cattle, and requested an agreement. The judge found the defendant guilty and sentenced him to four years and two months of imprisonment, and a fine.[120] The decision mentioned GHG emissions when it deliberated the crime of causing an illegal forest fire. Nonetheless, the Prosecution found the prison time insufficient and appealed; the appeal is still pending.

TABLE 13.7 Cases related to forest fires

| Case name | Year filed | Status |
|---|---|---|
| Federal Public Prosecutor's Office v Rogério[a] | 2017 | Under appeal |

a *Federal Public Prosecutor's Office v Rogério*, APOrd 0001306-46.2017.4.01.3200, filed on 29 September 2016 before the 7th Federal Environmental and Agrarian Court of the Judiciary Section of Amazonas.

## 5 Transnational Cases Related to the Brazilian Amazon Forest

In addition to the aforementioned Brazilian cases, relevant transnational cases have been proposed concerning supply chains and the violation of the duty

120 ibid.

of vigilance as it pertains to certain companies and their activities in the Brazilian Amazon rainforest. The United Nations Environment Program (UNEP) and the Sabin Center identify transnational litigation as a trend in global litigation.[121] The Grantham Institute of the London School of Economics identified addressing the deforestation value chain as a trend.[122] Transnational litigation can also be an effective and innovative way to address the root cause of environmental and climate change impacts by targeting the demand leading to such issues.

The *Envol Vert et al v Casino*[123] case was proposed by eleven environmental NGOs due to the Casino group's subsidiaries activities with the cattle industry in Brazil and Colombia. The supermarket chain's purchases allegedly provoke environmental and human rights harms, including deforestation. According to the plaintiffs, meat purchased by the subsidiaries originated from cattle raised in deforested areas in indigenous territories, and thus, these impacts also affected global climate change.

Meanwhile, in *Notre Affaire à Tous Les Amis de la Terre, and Oxfam France v BNP Paribas*,[124] environmental NGOs denounce a lack of transparency and clarity in the bank's plans and information regarding its investments and loans. While this case does not mention deforestation in the Amazon, it relies on commitments by the company, including the commitment to 'cease all financial support to companies that produce from oil and gas reserves in the Amazon and to those that develop related infrastructures.'[125]

Both cases are based on the French law on the duty of vigilance, which provides that specific companies must establish a plan to prevent the violation of human rights and environmental damage that may occur in the course of their business.[126] Although these cases are recent and yet to be decided, they provide alternative legal pathways toward protecting the Amazon rainforest, ensuring transparency and compliance beyond the Brazilian judiciary.

---

121 Michael Burger & Maria Antonia Tigre, *Global Climate Litigation Report: 2023 Status Review* (Sabin Center for Climate Change Law 2023) <https://scholarship.law.columbia.edu/sabin_climate_change/202/> accessed 15 August 2024.

122 Joana Setzer & Catherine Hingham, *Global Trends in Climate Change Litigation: 2023 Snapshot* (Grantham Research Institute on Climate Change and the Environment & Sabin Center for Climate Change Law 2023). < https://www.lse.ac.uk/granthaminstitute/wp-content/uploads/2023/06/Global_trends_in_climate_change_litigation_2023_snapshot.pdf> accessed 15 August 2024.

123 *Envol Vert et al v Casino* (2021), filed before the Saint-Étienne Judicial Court (France).

124 *Notre Affaire à Tous Les Amis de la Terre, and Oxfam France v BNP Paribas* (2023), filed before the Judicial Court of Paris (France).

125 ibid.

126 France, Law No 2017–399, of 27 March 2017, on the duty of vigilance of parent companies and prime contractors.

## 6 Conclusion

The drastic reduction in deforestation in the Brazilian Amazon in 2023 underscores the pivotal role of effective governance and implementation of policies like the PPCDAm, particularly through command and control measures. Climate litigation in Amazonia is still on the rise. However, several precedents have already clarified governmental responsibility and the government's duty to implement these policies. However, there is still much room to advance regarding the liability of corporations and people responsible for deforestation, other sources of GHG emissions and environmental infractions which impact the Amazon rainforest, its biodiversity and the local and global community through climate change. In addition, transparency and monitoring of implementation of the decisions is key to the effectiveness of climate change litigation. Other issues that can be considered by public policies and strategic climate litigation are: Consideration of climate change when authorizing legal deforestation, through authorizations of suppression of native vegetation (ASV), and the promotion of effective compensation; innovative approaches to restoration and the consideration of forests for adaptation and to avoid climate induced loss and damage.

Regarding the consideration of climate change when authorizing legal deforestation, according to an analysis by JUMA,[127] existing legislation is already sufficient to establish the consideration of climate variables in the processes of environmental licensing, including by strategic litigation. The same consideration could be applied to ASVs, as the government should consider climate change and other environmental criteria when authorizing deforestation, as well as establishing a limit to the concession of ASVs and proper compensation of the same area or vegetation. The Law of the Atlantic Rainforest (LMA, Federal Law No 11428/2006) stipulates that a destination of an equal area for conservation or restoration is required for the authorization of legal deforestation. The same logic could be extended to the Amazon region and the rest of the country, and strategic litigation could be a pathway to achieve this.

In addition, climate change lawsuits regarding deforestation could explore solutions that consider the supply chain of ecosystem restoration and not only the restoration of the area itself to strengthen future restoration and multiple benefits for the communities, to create alternatives for deforestation, such as agroforestry and bioeconomy. An example is the agreement (TAC) proposed by the Public Prosecution of Bahia, in which companies were held liable for

127 Danielle de Andrade Moreira (ed), *Litigância Climática no Brasil: Argumentos Jurídicos para a Inserção da Variável Climática no Licenciamento Ambiental* (Editora PUC-Rio 2021).

the deforestation in areas within their supply chains, and had to establish and maintain the Arboretum Project, a program that includes research, collection of seeds and a nursery of native vegetation managed by the Brazilian Forest Service.[128]

Finally, litigation in the Amazon could consider the important role of forests, particularly of the Amazon rainforest, for climate change adaptation, including the protection of water sources against the erosion of riverbeds and landslides. Another aspect could be to seek the liability of those who promote deforestation for climate change induced losses and damages, such as seeking reparations for communities affected by the droughts in the Amazon in 2023[129] in addition to compensation regarding climate damages to the global climate system. This approach would either prevent or seek specific reparations for the most vulnerable communities to climate change, advancing the climate justice agenda.

128 More information about the Project is available at https://www.programaarboretum.eco.br/quem-somos.

129 Ministry of Science, Technology and Innovation, 'Historic drought in the Amazon in 2023 was 30 times more likely due to climate change' (MCTI, 11 January 2024) <www.gov.br/mcti/pt-br/acompanhe-o-mcti/noticias/2024/01/seca-historica-na-amazonia-2023-foi-30-vezes-mais-provavel-devido-a-mudanca-do-clima> accessed 15 August 2024.

CHAPTER 14

# The Rights of Nature: Another Legal Avenue for Climate Litigation in Brazil?

*Fernanda Cavedon-Capdeville*, José Rubens Morato Leite**, Humberto Filpi*** and Tônia Dutra*****

## 1 Introduction

Latin America has become a source of ecocentric legal innovations, which reflect the complex relations of socio-ecological diversity in a scenario of high exposure to the climate crisis and colonialist models of nature exploitation. The strategies for responding to this crisis are inspired by the intrinsic connection of the region's traditional peoples with nature, influencing the manifestations of justice and law. The ecocentric turn of law in Latin America is expressed by ecological constitutionalism and the experiences of climate litigation articulating human and nature rights and invoking principles of ecological law. Nine climate cases related to rights of nature were identified in the region.[1] This typical climate litigation has been little studied to date, with

* PhD in Environmental Law. Post-doctoral researcher at the Federal University of Santa Catarina (UFSC). ORCID ID: 0000-0001-6839-1579.

** Professor of Environmental Law at the Law Faculty of the Federal University of Santa Catarina (UFSC), Research Productivity Scholarship from the National Council for Scientific and Technological Development, CNPq. ORCID ID: 0000-0001-6686-8441.

*** Master in Environmental Law. PhD researcher at the Federal University of Santa Catarina (UFSC).

**** PhD in Environmental Law. Post-doctoral researcher at the Federal University of Santa Catarina (UFSC), PDJ/CNPq.

1 *Center for Social Justice Studies et al v Presidency of the Republic et al* (*Atrato River*), Process No T-622/16, Judgment of 10 November 2016 (Constitutional Court of Colombia), available at <https://climatecasechart.com/non-us-case/atrato-river-decision-t-622-16-of-november-10-2016/>, *Future Generations v Ministry of the Environment et al* (2018) Process No 11001 22 03 000 2018 00319 00, Decision of 5 April 2018 (Supreme Court of Colombia), available at <https://climatecasechart.com/non-us-case/future-generation-v-ministry-environment-others/>; *Municipal Authorities v Ecuador* (*'Los Cedros'*), Case No 1149–19-JP/20, Judgment of 10 November 2021 (Constitutional Court of Ecuador), available at <https://www.garn.org/wp-content/uploads/2022/06/Los-Cedros-Decision-ENGLISH-Final.pdf>; *Herrera Carrion et al v Ministry of the Environment et al* (*'Mecheros' Case*), Process No 21201202000170, Judgment of 29 July 2021 (Sala Multicompetente de la Corte

 | DOI:10.1163/9789004690974_015

the categorizations and analysis carried out by Filpi,[2] Cavedon-Capdeville and others,[3] and Tigre and others[4] standing out.

This chapter proposes to address the possibility of integrating this ecocentric perspective into climate litigation in Brazil, inspired by the argument about rights of nature and the legal innovations of ecological law in Latin America, which are also being advanced in Brazil.[5] The following question guided the study: how do the recent developments of ecological law and rights of nature in Latin American climate litigation, fostered by the dialogue of courts, contribute to developing an ecocentric perspective in climate cases in Brazil? This analysis focuses on the Brazilian case *Costa Legal et al v Florianópolis et al* (*'Lagoa da Conceição'*),[6] the only Brazilian climate case to integrate the rights of nature perspective, based on an ecocentric interpretation of the constitutional

---

Provincial de Justicia de Sucumbíos), available at <https://climatecasechart.com/non-us-case/herrera-carrion-et-al-v-ministry-of-the-environment-et-al-caso-mecheros/>; *Baihua Caiga et al v PetroOriental SA*, Process No 22201202000469 (Family, Women, and Children Judicial Unit from Francisco de Orellana Canton of Ecuador), available at <https://climatecasechart.com/non-us-case/baihua-caiga-et-al-v-petrooriental-sa/>; Álvarez et al v Peru (Peruvian Amazon), Process No 00859-2020-0-1801-JR-DC01, filed on 16 December 2019 before the Superior Court of Lima, available at <https://climatecasechart.com/non-us-case/alvarez-et-al-v-peru/>; *Asociación Civil por la Justicia Ambiental et al v Province of Entre Ríos et al (Delta del Paraná Case)*, filed on 2 July 2020 before the Supreme Court of Justice of Argentina, available at <https://climatecasechart.com/non-us-case/asociacion-civil-por-la-justicia-ambiental-v-province-of-entre-rios-et-al/>; *Residents v Local Government*, Process No 572/2020, filed in 2020 before the 5th District Court in Administrative Matters of Mexico City (*'Xochimilco Wetlands Case'*); *Costa Legal et al v Florianópolis et al*, ACP No 5012843-56.2021.4.04.7200, filed on 19 May 2021 before the 6th Federal Court of Santa Catarina, available at <https://climatecasechart.com/non-us-case/ong-costa-legal-and-others-vs-municipality-of-florianopolis-and-others/>.

2 Humberto Filpi, *Litigância Climática Ecologizada: contribuições da América Latina* (Lumen Juris 2021).

3 Fernanda de Salles Cavedon-Capdeville, Valeria Berros, Humberto Filpi & Paola Villavicencio-Calzadilla 'An Ecocentric Perspective on Climate Litigation: Lessons from Latin America' (2023) *Journal of Human Rights Practice* 1.

4 Maria Antonia Tigre, Natalia Urzola & Alexandra Goodman, 'Climate Litigation in Latin America: Is the Region Quietly Leading a Revolution?' (2023) 14 *Journal of Human Rights and the Environment* 67.

5 On the theoretical development of ecological law in Brazil, see Eg José Rubens Morato Leite (ed), *Ecologização do Direito Ambiental Vigente* (2nd edn, Lumen Juris 2020). Ingo Wolfgang Sarlet & Tiago Fensteinseifer, *Direito Constitucional Ecológico: Constituição, Direitos Fundamentais e Proteção da Natureza* (7th edn, Thomson Reuters—Revista dos Tribunais 2021).

6 *Costa Legal et al v Florianópolis et al* (n 1). Documents of the case can be found at José Rubens Morato Leite, Melissa Ely Mello & Carolina Medeiros Bahia (ed), *Direito Ecológico na Prática: Ação Estrutural da Lagoa da Conceição* (AmoLer Editora 2023).

provisions and inspired by Latin-american climate caselaw, as well as the application of the Organic Law of Florianópolis which provides for the possibility to recognize juridical personality and rights to nature.[7]

The article is divided in two sections. Section 1 explores the legal and jurisprudential innovations related to ecological law and the rights of nature in Latin America that anchor the ecocentric perspective of climate litigation. Common features and key arguments of climate cases in Latin America that foster the development of this ecocentric perspective are systematized. Section 2 contextualizes the discussion in Brazil, considering ecocentric legal avenues to climate litigation. First, Brazilian case law reflecting ecological law arguments is highlighted. Second, the article explores the possibility of a nature's rights-based climate litigation in Brazil through the analysis of the *Lagoa da Conceição Case,* through the following criteria: (i) the ecocentric arguments, including rights of nature, (ii) the influence of the dialogue of courts in the development of the ecocentric perspective; and (iii) socio-ecological governance structures to manage ecosystems considered as subjects of rights. Even if the case is still pending, a preliminary injunction determined the creation of a Judicial Chamber for the Protection of *Lagoa da Conceição* aiming at presenting measures to address climate change impacts and designate a guardian of the rights and interests of the natural entity. These achievements confirm the viability of a nature's rights-based climate litigation in Brazil, inspired by case law and constitutional interpretation aligned with ecological law and experiences of climate litigation with an ecocentric perspective in Latin America.

## 2 Contributions from Ecological Law to Anchor the Ecocentric Perspective of Climate Litigation: Experiences from Latin America

Ecological law aims to respond to the climate crisis through a systemic and ecocentric approach based on a rationality more aligned to the complexities of social and nature interactions, indigenous and traditional communities' knowledge and ways of life, and the promotion of climate justice for human and non-human beings (Morato Leite and others, 2023). The main features of Ecological Law can be summarized in the following elements: (i) ecocentric approach, considering nature and its elements as subjects of rights; (ii) ecological justice perspective; (iii) intergenerational and interspecies solidarity; (iv) non-fragmented and ecosystem approach to regulation; (iv) nature-centered

7 Municipality of Florianópolis. Amendment to Organic Law No 47/2019. <https://leismunicipais.com.br/lei-organica-florianopolis-sc>, accessed 2 November 2023.

environmental protection; (v) ecological integrity as a fundamental principle; (vi) recognition of non-state-based sources of law, as the traditional knowledge from indigenous peoples; (vii) protection of the intrinsic and immaterial values of nature; (viii) ecological dimension of human rights (Bosselmann 2021; Garver 2021; Morato Leite 2020; Kotzé 2018; Capra and Mattei 2015). As presented in the following sections, these ecocentric perspectives of law have been developed in Latin America at both legislative and jurisprudential levels. However, there are still limits to their practical implementation, especially in relation the implementation of favourable rulings, as identified in *Center for Social Justice Studies et al v Presidency of the Republic et al* (Constitutional Court of Colombia); *Future Generations v Ministry of the Environment et al* (Supreme Court of Colombia). Despite the differing recognition and implementation levels, these perspectives inspire climate litigation in the region.

### 2.1 *The Latin American Ecological Constitutionalism and the Recognition of Rights of Nature*

Latin America has been the scenario of conflicts around 'political ecology' issues, opposing views on human/nature relations. Social movements' experiences in recognizing the ways of life of original peoples and traditional communities in a neo-extractivist context give rise to other approaches to nature, drawing attention to alternate possibilities of organizing life and understanding themselves as subjects and social groups.[8] The new Latin American constitutionalism[9] that comes from popular demands allowed the emergence of these approaches regarding the specificities of the region's peoples in their relationship with nature, as exposed by Wolkmer & Wolkmer.[10] Some constitutions (Eg Ecuador, Colombia, and Bolivia) present a multicultural perspective, open to different cultural approaches to nature. Other constitutional

---

8 Maristella Svampa, *Las fronteras del neoextractivismo en América Latina: Conflictos socioambientales, giro ecoterritorial y nuevas dependencias* (CALAS 2019).

9 Latin American new constitutionalism is a movement that comprises the constituent processes and constitutions that came after the period of dictatorships that fell on Latin America. These constitutional texts express the strong democratic demands of the moment, of concrete claims and realities, which have in common the attempt to subvert subordination to the capitalist world system. They are transformative constitutions anchored in mechanisms of popular participation and expression.

10 Antônio Carlos Wolkmer & Maria de Fátima Wolkmer, 'Pluralismo jurídico y constitucionalismo emancipador desde el sur', in Santos & Cunha (eds), *Colóquio Internacional Epistemologias do Sul: aprendizagens globais Sul-Sul, Sul-Norte e Norte-Sul*, vol. 2 (Centro de Estudos Sociais 2015).

texts indirectly address issues regarding the pluri-ethnic composition of Latin America, such as the Brazilian Constitution (1988).[11]

The Constitution of Colombia (1991)[12] presents an open perspective to the world visions of its original peoples, providing for the protection of ethnic and cultural diversity, as well as natural heritage. The right to a healthy environment, public participation, and the State's duty to protect environmental diversity and integrity were recognized (notably in arts 79 and 80), as well as the ecological function of property (art 58) and the internalization of a pluri-ethnic composition (art 7). Similar provisions are also identified in the constitutions of Argentina (1994), Uruguay (1996), Paraguay (1992), Peru (1979) and Venezuela (1999).[13] Chile is currently in the process of drafting a new constitutional text after the proposal of an ecological constitution recognizing the rights of nature was rejected in 2022.[14]

The constitutions of Ecuador (2008)[15] and Bolivia[16] are the greater examples of the new constitutionalism interculturality and ecocentric approach, recognizing new political subjects and rescuing ancestral ways of participation and non-anthropocentric values. These openings are part of a broader movement towards ecological law that was underway at the time in other parts of the world. The intrinsic connection between human beings and nature underlies and supports the interpretation of the constitutional text, which places this movement among the main lines of the so-called ecological constitutionalism. This approach considers the constitutional path as an appropriate means

11 Constitution of the Federative Republic of Brazil 1988 https://www.planalto.gov.br/ccivil_03/constituicao/constituicao.htm accessed 09 April 2024.

12 Political Constitution of the Republic of Colombia 1991 http://www.secretariasenado.gov.co/constitucion-politica accessed on 09 April 2024.

13 Constitution of the Argentine Nation 1994, art 41, https://www.argentina.gob.ar/normativa/nacional/ley-24430-804/texto accessed 09 April 2024; Constitution of the Oriental Republic of Uruguay 1967, art 47, https://parlamento.gub.uy/documentosyleyes/documentos/11/HTML accessed 09 April 2024 ; Constitution of the Republic of Paraguay 1992, arts 7 and 8 https://www.bacn.gov.py/archivos/9580/CONSTITUCION_ORIGINAL_FIRMADA.pdf accessed 09 April 2024 ; Political Constitution of Peru 1993, arts 66 to 69, https://www.congreso.gob.pe/Docs/constitucion/constitucion/index.html accessed 09 April 2024 ; Constitution of the Bolivarian Republic of Venezuela 1999, arts 127 to 129, http://historico.tsj.gob.ve/legislacion/crv.html accessed 09 April 2024.

14 Centro de Derecho Ambiental, *La propuesta de Constitución Ecológica de Chile: edición concordada* (University of Chile Faculty of Law 2022).

15 Constitution of the Republic of Ecuador 2008 https://www.asambleanacional.gob.ec/sites/default/files/documents/old/constitucion_de_bolsillo.pdf accessed 09 April 2024.

16 Political Constitution of the Plurinational State of Bolivia 2009 https://aaps.gob.bo/images/MarcoLegal/Leyes/CPE.pdf accessed 09 April 2024.

to integrate international perspectives and local values related to ecological protection.

Nature as a subject of rights and the principle of *Buen Vivir* in the Constitution of Ecuador (2008) result from these dialogues and the integration of distinct levels of knowledge and values. By declaring Nature/*Pachamama* as a subject of rights, the Constitution gives rise to a hybrid culture-nature entity, consistent with the original peoples, for whom relations with 'beings other than humans are part of their worldview. The Constitution of Bolivia also integrates the rights of *Pachamama* and the principle of *Buen Vivir*, advancing indigenous rights and legal pluralism. Although rights of nature were not included in the constitutional text, the Mother Earth Law (2010) recognized these rights, and the Integral Development Law (2012) regulated *Buen Vivir*.

Legal implications of ecological constitutionalism and the recognition of the rights of specific ecosystems have been built up through litigation, both in relation to constitutions recognizing the rights of nature (Ecuador) and ecocentric interpretation of constitutional provisions leading to the recognition of these rights (Eg Colombia). For example, the Constitutional Court of Ecuador highlights the constitutional double dimension of nature in *Santiago García Llorre case*, not only under the traditional paradigm of an object of law but also as an independent subject with its own right.[17] The Constitutional Court emphasizes the paradigm shift promoted by the constitutional system of 2008, which, in addition to considering nature as a subject of rights, gives transversality over the legal system as a whole to the rights recognized to *Pachamama*.

The ecocentric perspective emerging from the Andean constitutionalism and climate issues have been jointly considered since the World People's Conference on Climate Change and the Rights of Mother Earth that took place in Bolivia (2010). Thereafter, the confrontation of the climate crisis was nourished by ecological constitutionalism while the Courts subsidized its further development and adaptation to climate claims (see Section 2.2.).

In the *Atrato River* case, the Constitutional Court of Colombia recognized the constitution's ecological paradigm by adopting an ecocentric approach to interpreting constitutional provisions, such as the right to the environment.[18] The court points out that several rulings recognize the Colombian Constitution as 'ecological,' based on the superior interest of protecting the environment (§§ 4.7 and 5.3). The ecocentric approach, in turn, arises from this

17 *Santiago García Llore, Director Provincial Esmeraldas*, Process No 0507–12-EP, Judgment No 166–15-SEP-CC (24 June 2015) (Constitutional Court of Ecuador), available at <https://portal.corteconstitucional.gob.ec/FichaRelatoria.aspx?numdocumento=166-15-SEP-CC>.

18 *Center for Social Justice Studies et al v Presidency of the Republic et al* (*Atrato River*) (n 1).

interpretation (§ 5.9). Cultural and ethnic pluralism and ancestral knowledge integrate and support Colombian ecological constitutionalism (§ 5.10). The ecocentric perspective of the right to the environment expresses the ecological constitution paradigm for protecting biocultural diversity. Ethical and cultural pluralism guide the interpretation of constitutional provisions (§§ 5.10 and 5.58). The court recognizes a biocultural perspective of rights arising from the multi-ethnic dimension of the constitution that considers the interdependence between biological and cultural diversity.

Finally, the decision in *Future Generations* case is a benchmark in connecting the ecological interpretation of the constitutional provisions, recognizing the rights of nature, and the climate crisis.[19] The main argument for recognizing the Colombian Amazon as a subject of rights is that the constitutional text is an ecological constitution. The set of subjects of the right to the environment is broadened, encompassing all the planet's inhabitants, including ecosystems and other living beings (§ 11.3). This interpretation stems from the understanding that, in the court's jurisprudence, the analysis of constitutional provisions from a perspective that places the environment as a priority has resulted in an ecological constitution (§ 7).

The integration of interculturality, ancestral knowledge, and democratic practices have been inscribing the values of original peoples in the new constitutional design, offering the possibility of another logic of life in which living and knowing happen in an intertwined way. In this sense, Latin American ecological constitutionalism is a way to recognize a non-dualist perspective in relation to nature in the context of climate change and boost the ecocentric perspective in climate litigation, as discussed in the following section.

### 2.2 *The Ecocentric Perspective of Climate Litigation in Latin America: Common Features and Key Arguments*

One of the main trends in climate litigation in Latin America is the ecocentric approach, either by invoking the rights of nature or referring to the principles of ecological law. Nine climate cases identified in national jurisdictions, either resolved or pending, make specific reference to the rights of nature,[20] and arguments from ecological law are identified in other cases, as the principles of *in dubio pro natura* and ecological integrity and the ecocentric dimension of the right to the environment. This section highlights features and arguments of regional climate litigation that foster this ecocentric perspective.

19 *Future Generations v Ministry of the Environment et al* (n 1).

20 The nine cases are referenced in note 1.

Some stakeholders in climate litigation are pushing forward the ecocentric perspective in Latin America, especially traditional peoples who bring decolonial perceptions of nature, and children and young people, fostering intergenerational and interspecies solidarity. Of the nine climate cases invoking the rights of nature, five have children and young people as plaintiffs (*Future Generations, Mecheros, Peruvian Amazon, Delta del Paraná,* and *Xochimilco Wetlands*). They emphasize that children and the unborn, human and non-human, are under-represented in decisions that affect their future existence (*Delta del Paraná*). Fundamental rights include unborn children, and environmental degradation jeopardizes future life, not limited to human life (*Future Generations*, §§ 5.3 and 5.2). The intergenerational dimension of climate litigation in the region has an ecocentric approach, considering the future implications of the climate crisis for the entire community of life.

Four nature's rights-based climate cases were brought by indigenous peoples and/or traditional communities (*Atrato River, Mecheros, Baihua Caiga* and *Lagoa da Conceição*) and in others (Eg *Los Cedros*), even though they are not plaintiffs, their rights and connection with the ecosystems are invoked. As one of the groups most affected by climate change, indigenous peoples, inspired by jurisprudence and recognized rights on indigenous protection, have become central stakeholders of climate litigation.[21] In the *Atrato River* case, both human and nature rights are considered in interrelation with the rights of traditional communities, as cultural and ethnic pluralism support Colombian constitutionalism (§ 5.10).

Climate cases in Latin America generally focus on ecosystems essential to climate stability and the subsistence of traditional communities, while their ecological functions are also threatened by climate change. The ecosystem-based approach provides the opportunity to tackle litigation from an ecocentric perspective based on recognizing their rights and intrinsic value. All the climate cases invoking the rights of nature argument are focused on essential regional ecosystems. The ecosystem approach is also present in Brazilian climate litigation, as in the case *PSB et al v Brazil* (*on deforestation and human rights*).[22] Plaintiffs highlight that ecosystem services provided by the Amazon Forest, essential to climate stability, are affected by deforestation, the primary Brazilian source of emissions causing climate change.[23]

21 Maria Antonia Tigre, 'Climate Change and Indigenous Groups: The Rise of Indigenous Voices in Climate Litigation' (2022) 9 *e-Publica* 214.

22 *PSB et al v Brazil* (*on deforestation and human rights*), ADPF 760, Judgment of 6 April 2022, available at <https://climatecasechart.com/non-us-case/brazilian-socialist-party-and-others-v-brazil/>.

23 See Maria Antonia Tigre & Anna Maria Cárcamo (Chapter 13) in this book.

Many cases also focus on the impact of extractive activities on ecosystems and, therefore, on the climate system and the rights of those who depend on them. The *Wayuu Indigenous Communities v. Ministry of Home Affairs and others* (*'Bruno River Case'*),[24] addressing mining impacts, highlights the interdependence of ecological services provided by the river with the capacity of the Wayúu to adapt to climate change (§§ 1.5.7 and 3.8.1). This argument is also discussed in the *Wayúu Indigenous Community and others v. Ministry of Environment and others* (*'Cerrejón Mine Case'*),[25] considering the impacts of coal mining on ecosystems and associated rights of indigenous and Afro-Colombian communities. This ecosystem approach has fostered the development of legal arguments inspired by ecological law, as the *in dubio pro natura* principle, frequently invoked in climate cases, as in the decision of the *Los Cedros* case referring to the principle of favorability *pro natura*, which provides for applying law in a way that most favor enforcing the rights of nature (§40). The principles of ecological integrity and maintenance of ecological processes are also mentioned (*Bruno River, Cerrejón Mine, Baihua Caiga* and *Páramo de Santurbán*).[26]

The dialogue between human rights and the rights of nature leads to recognizing the ecocentric dimension of the right to the environment in Latin America, fostered by the *Advisory Opinion OC-23/17* of the Inter-American Court of Human Rights (IACtHR 2017), stating that the right to the environment protects the elements of the environment, regardless of their utility or the effects of their degradation on human beings, and recognizing nature as a legal interest in itself, whose importance extends to all living organisms (§ 62). This perspective was developed in Resolution 3/2021 related to the climate emergency by the Inter-American Commission on Human Rights (IACHR 2021), and could be reaffirmed by IACtHR in the Advisory Opinion regarding climate emergency and human rights, requested by Colombia and Chile in 2023, that should be adopted in 2024.[27] In Brazil, the injunction of 28 June 2020 in the

24 *Wayuu Indigenous Communities v Ministry of Home Affairs et al* (*'Bruno River Case'*), Process No SU-698/17, Judgment of 28 November 2017 (Constitutional Court of Colombia).

25 *Wayúu Indigenous Community et al v Ministry of Environment et al* (*'Cerrejón Mine Case'*), filed on 22 February 2019 before the Colombian Council of State, Process No 11001-0324-000-2019-00107-00, available at <https://climatecasechart.com/non-us-case/wayuu-indigenous-community-and-others-v-ministry-of-environment-and-others/>.

26 *Committee for the Defence of Water and the Páramo de Santurbán et al v Ministry of Environment and Sustainable Development et al* (*Páramo de Santurbán*case), Process No 680012333000-2020-00827-00, filed before the Contentious Administrative Court of Santander (Colombia).

27 *Request for an Advisory Opinion on the Climate Emergency and Human Rights submitted to the Inter-American Court of Human Rights by the Republic of Colombia and the Republic of*

case PSB *et al v Brazil* (*on Climate Fund*)[28] refers to *Advisory Opinion OC-23/17* to highlight that the right to the environment is also held by nature (§ 16).

Two strategies regarding the dialogue between human and nature's rights can be identified: (i) damages to ecosystems and/or the impacts of extractive activities on the climate and living beings lead to a joint violation of both rights, identified in Ecuador's climate cases as the *Los Cedros* case, in which the Constitutional Court recognized the violation of human and nature's rights (§ 242), or the *Mecheros* and *Baihua Caiga* cases, where plaintiffs claimed that the impacts of oil extraction in the Ecuadorian Amazon violate human and nature rights; (ii) the interpretation of human rights and the Constitution with an ecocentric approach supports the recognition of nature as a subject of rights, identified in the Colombia's climate cases, as in the *Atrato River* case in which the Constitutional Court of Colombia based the recognition of the river as a subject of rights in the Ecological Constitution, which recognizes biocultural rights that promote the joint protection of human beings and nature (§ 9.32). Also in the *Future Generations* case, the Supreme Court of Colombia, considering the damage to the ecological integrity of the Amazon, the consequences for the climate system and the rights of human and non-human beings, recognizes specific rights to the ecosystem. This line of argument can also be identified in the pending cases *Lagoa da Conceição* (see section 3.2); *Delta del Paraná* and *Álvarez et al v Peru*, requesting the recognition of rights to ecosystems based on an ecocentric interpretation of constitutional provisions.

Finally, socioecological governance structures are proposed in climate litigation to bridge the gap between legal innovations, such as rights of nature, and traditional environmental management structures. These structures include guardianship strategies to exercise the legal representation of ecosystems' rights (Eg *Rio Atrato, Delta del Paraná* and *Lagoa da Conceição*), as well as management plans and strategies integrating the perspectives of nature and future generations (Eg *Future Generations, Delta del Paraná* and *Lagoa da Conceição*).

From the elements highlighted, an ecocentric perspective is well developed in Latin American climate litigation, due to the contributions of ecological law, progressive constitutionalism on ecological grounds and the connections between human and nature rights. This ecocentric perspective could inspire litigation in Brazil, as analyzed in the following section.

---

*Chile*, request filed by Chile and Colombia on 9 January 2023, available at <https://www.corteidh.or.cr/docs/opiniones/soc_1_2023_en.pdf>.

28 PSB *et al v Brazil* (*on Climate Fund*), ADPF 708, Judgment of 7 January 2022, available at <https://climatecasechart.com/non-us-case/psb-et-al-v-federal-union/>.

## 3 Ecocentric Legal Avenues to Climate Litigation in Brazil

Based on the elements highlighted in Section 2, this section analyzes possible ecocentric legal avenues to climate litigation in Brazil from selected Brazilian case law inspired by ecological law and the analysis of the *Lagoa da Conceição* case, as the country's first experience on climate litigation integrating the rights of nature perspective.

### 3.1 *The Influence of Ecological Law on Brazilian Environmental Jurisprudence: Inspiring Features for Climate Litigation*

This section illustrates the evolutionary pathways of ecological law in Brazilian jurisprudence, which could foster ecocentric arguments in climate litigation. Beyond the rights of nature, other features of ecological law could be identified in Brazilian case law (whether climate cases or not), which creates a favorable context for developing an ecocentric approach to litigation and from which climate cases can draw inspiration. The analysis focuses on the non-exhaustive case law of the Federal Supreme Court (STF) and the Superior Court of Justice (STJ) that, even if not grounded in the rights of nature, invokes principles of ecological law and other ecocentric arguments.

Regarding the STF, the ecocentric perspective has been developed in *Public Prosecutor's Office v Governor of the State of Ceará* (*Vaquejada Case*),[29] in which the court pointed out the need to embrace the ecological dimension of the rule of law and adopt a biocentric approach of constitutional provisions (art 5, VII, §1). The ruling brings an ecocentric interpretation of dignity, broadened to include non-human beings, resulting from an ecocentric interpretation of the Constitution. This interpretation overcomes the anthropocentric and utilitarian perspective of nature and leads to the recognition that animals have dignity. Furthermore, ecocentric perspectives aligned with ecological law have been integrated into climate cases under the STF. In the case *PSB et al v Brazil* (*on Amazon Fund*),[30] concerning the Federal government's failure to adopt administrative measures concerning the Amazon Fund, plaintiffs allege a violation of Article 225 of the Federal Constitution, regarding the State's duties to preserve and restore ecological processes and promote the ecological management of ecosystems. The Court's decision dealt with the principle of

29 *Public Prosecutor's Office v Governor of the State of Ceará* (*Vaquejada Case*), ADI 4983 CE, Judgment of 6 October 2017, available at <https://jurisprudencia.stf.jus.br/pages/search/sjur366632/false>.

30 *PSB et al v Brazil* (*on Amazon Fund*), ADO 59, Judgment of 16 August 2023, available at <https://climatecasechart.com/non-us-case/psb-et-al-v-brazil/>.

non-regression on ecological matters that also apply for the fundamental rights in connection with environmental protection. Another argument invoked by the Court is the right to an 'ecological minimum.' In *PSB et al v Brazil* (*on Climate Fund*), international environmental treaties, including the Paris Agreement, have been placed on the same level as human rights treaties. The injunction of 28 June 2020 on this case refers to the *Advisory Opinion OC-23/17*, recognizing the ecocentric dimension of the right to the environment. Also, in the case *PSB et al v Brazil* (*on deforestation and human rights*),[31] plaintiffs pointed out that an ecologically balanced environment is essential not only for maintaining or promoting the quality of human life, but also for the very survival of all living beings. Ecological balance is under constitutional protection, which requires adequate protection for all the elements that are part of it.

From the jurisprudence of the STJ, this study highlights two outstanding elements of ecological law developed by the court: (i) the *in dubio pro natura* principle and (ii) the intrinsic value of nature and ecological dignity.

The *in dubio pro natura* principle, one of the main principles of ecological law,[32] had been well developed in the court's case law. According to this principle, when judges interpret and apply laws and evaluate environmental conflicts, they must choose the path that best guarantees essential ecological processes and biodiversity (Benjamin 2014), corresponding to an ecocentric interpretation of the *in dubio pro damnato* principle. By following the logic that, in doubt, the decision should be taken in favor of the injured party or the victim, the *in dubio pro natura* principle considers nature itself as the injured party whose protection should prevail. The STJ has invoked this principle to justify, for example, the reversal of the burden of proof,[33] to recognize ecological

31 *PSB et al v Brazil* (*on deforestation and human rights*), ADPF 760, Judgment of 6 April 2022, available at <https://climatecasechart.com/non-us-case/brazilian-socialist-party-and-others-v-brazil/>.

32 This principle was recognized in the IUCN World Declaration on the Environmental Rule of Law of 2016 <http://www2.ecolex.org/server2neu.php/libcat/docs/LI/MON-091064.pdf> accessed 30 October 2023.

33 Eg see *Public Prosecutor's Office of the State of Rio Grande do Sul v Amapá do Sul S/A*, Judgment of 25 August 2009, Special Appeal No REsp 972.902/RS, Rapporteur: Minister Eliana Calmon, available at <https://www.stj.jus.br/websecstj/cgi/revista/REJ.cgi/ATC?seq=5620750&tipo=51&nreg=200701758820&SeqCgrmaSessao=&CodOrgaoJgdr=&dt=20090914&formato=PDF&salvar=false>; *Alberto Pasqualini Refap S/A v Public Prosecutor's Office of the State of Rio Grande do Sul*, Judgment of 9 March 2010, Special Appeal No REsp 883.656/RS, Rapporteur: Minister Herman Benjamin; *Santo Antônio Energia S/A v FCB*, Judgment of 13 October 2020, Special Appeal No REsp 1818008/RO, Rapporteur: Minister Herman Benjamin.

non-pecuniary moral damage,[34] or the possibility of accumulating the order to restore the damaged ecosystems with pecuniary compensation.[35]

The STJ also recognized the intrinsic value of nature and all living beings in the case *Public Prosecutor's Office of the State of Minas Gerais v PPP*[36] addressing the deforestation of the biome *cerrado*. The court ruled that the victims of an environmental damage include the ecological processes themselves. The duty to repair the environmental damage safeguards the Brazilian flora because of the irreplaceable ecological services it provides to life in all its forms. Recognizing the duty to protect the flora, the court advanced the ecocentric interpretation of environmental law. It emphasized the relationship between ecological protection and life in a broad sense, which, therefore, encompasses human life. Finally, one of the most paradigmatic cases regarding ecocentric perspectives in Brazil is the *Maria Angelica Caldas Uliana v. State of São Paulo Treasury*,[37] in which the court advanced the concept by attributing dignity and rights to non-human animals. A violation of the ecological dimension of human dignity was recognized in a dispute involving the custody of a wild animal, a parrot, living in captivity. The ruling calls for a review of the anthropocentric and individualistic notion of human dignity and to move towards an ecological understanding of the dignity of life, which is in line with the ecocentric pattern. According to the court, non-human living beings are no longer just means for humans to guarantee their own dignity. A broader dignity inherent to the existence of all beings is recognized and complemented by corresponding rights. In a dialog of courts, the STJ references some of the afore-mentioned Latin American jurisprudence related to ecological constitutionalism and the rights to nature, such as the *Atrato River* case. The STJ mentioned the judgment of the *Rio Atrato* case in terms of recognising the rights of non-human beings

---

34 Eg *Brasilit Industry and Commerce Ltda et al v Public Prosecutor's Office of the State of Rio de Janeiro*, Judgment of 27 August 2013, Special Appeal No REsp 1.367.923/RJ, Rapporteur: Minister Humberto Martins.

35 *Public Prosecutor's Office of the State of Minas Gerais v Pedro Paulo Pereira*, Judgment of 14 August 2012, Special Appeal No 1.198.727/MG, Rapporteur: Minister Herman Benjamin, available at <https://www.stj.jus.br/websecstj/cgi/revista/REJ.cgi/ATC?seq=13806316&tipo=5&nreg=201001113499&SeqCgrmaSessao=&CodOrgaoJgdr=&dt=20130509&formato=PDF&salvar=false>.

36 ibid.

37 *Maria Angelica Caldas Uliana et al v State of São Paulo Treasury*, Judgment of the Superior Court of Justice of 21 March 2019, REsp (Special Appeal) 1.797.175/SP (Rapporteur: Justice Og Fernandes), available at <https://www.stj.jus.br/websecstj/cgi/revista/REJ.cgi/ITA?seq=1806039&tipo=0&nreg=201800312300&SeqCgrmaSessao=&CodOrgaoJgdr=&dt=20190328&formato=PDF&salvar=false&fbclid=IwAR33tDl5FlTBGayDQS5iUkveeJQblCjyNmFS8MDnHREhEKegqWLXWYeHyE>.

and for its redefinition of the relationship between human beings and nature based on a biocentric and not just anthropocentric approach to law.

The ecocentric elements highlighted in Brazilian jurisprudence demonstrate a favorable context for enhancing this perspective in climate litigation. An example is the case *Lagoa da Conceição*, which was inspired by some of the cases mentioned above to support the recognition of this natural entity as a subject of rights, as discussed in the following section.

### 3.2 *Brazilian Nature's Rights-Based Climate Litigation:* **ONG Costa Legal et al v Municipality of Florianópolis et al**

*Lagoa da Conceição* is a lagoon in the Municipality of Florianópolis, in the State of Santa Catarina, South of Brazil. Its landscape and ecosystems are intrinsically connected to the identity and history of the city and its traditional communities. Despite its ecological, economic, and sociocultural importance, this ecosystem has suffered a process of degradation, intensified by climate change. Decades ago, studies had already pointed out the lack of adequate governance to protect its ecological integrity. Nevertheless, the existence of a structural problem[38] became more evident when, after heavy rains and due to planning failures, a dam of a sewage treatment plant collapsed in 2021, causing the pollution of the lagoon at levels never seen before. This damage, combined with historical structural environmental problems and aggravated by the impacts of climate change, threatened the very existence of the Lagoon's ecosystems and living beings.

In response, a structural class action was filed by civil society in the Federal Court of Florianópolis in 2021, with legal advice from research groups of the Federal University of Santa Catarina (UFSC). The claim aims to protect *Lagoa da Conceição's* ecological integrity, based on its recognition as a subject of rights and the development of governance structures in a more participative and ecological way. There were other class actions, agreements, action plans, and working groups concerning *Lagoa da Conceição*.[39] However, structural

38 Marco Felix Jobim, 'A Previsão das Medidas Estruturantes no Artigo 139, IV, do Novo Código de Processo Civil Brasileiro', in Zaneti Jr (ed), *Repercussões do Novo CPC—Processo Coletivo* (JusPodivmv 2016); Edilson Vitorelli, 'Levando os Conceitos a Sério: Processo Estrutural, Processo Coletivo, Processo Estratégico e suas Diferenças' (2018) 284 *Revista de Processo* 333.

39 See, for example, *Public Prosecutor's Office v CASAN*, ACP 5004793-41.2021.4.04.7200, filed before the 6th Federal Court of Florianópolis. This is a public civil action concerning the environmental damage that occurred in January 2021, caused by the collapse of the stabilization lagoon (evapoinfiltration—LEI) that is part of the Lagoa da Conceição sewage treatment plant. The disaster resulted in the flooding and destruction of inhabited areas

problems persist, given the inability of governance schemes to guarantee the protection of the ecosystem and its associated rights. Hence, the plaintiffs alleged an 'organized irresponsibility scenario'[40] (Beck 1992) resulting from the inaction and lack of adequate risk assessment by public institutions, the fragmentation of the environmental management, and the weak public participation and cooperation of the involved stakeholders. In consequence, this nature's rights-based climate litigation seeks the development of a socioecological governance structure more aligned with the specificities of *Lagoa da Conceição* as a subject of rights, considering the effects of climate change as a transversal issue that aggravate the existent ecological harms. Furthermore, the plaintiffs argue that the governance of the lagoon should be considered through "ecocentric lens", both in terms of understanding the impacts of the adverse effects of climate change on the entire community of life in *Lagoa da Conceição*, and in designing the measures needed to respond to these impacts, taking into account the recognition of the rights of ecosystems that are essential to climate balance.

Climate issues were considered in three dimensions: (i) *Lagoa da Conceição* and the communities that depend on its ecosystems are threatened by the interactions between climate change, pre-existing ecological damage and structural problems on environmental governance, requiring legal-institutional arrangements that coordinate different sectors of policy and action (including climate), beyond the sectorization and fragmentation of ecosystem management.; (ii) the ecosystems of *Lagoa da Conceição* play a central role in tackling the increase of extreme events in coastal zones, as the ecological services provided by them are of vital importance to reduce risks and to better adapt to the adverse effects of climate change; and (iii) Inspired by other ecocentric climate cases in the region, recognizing nature's rights to ecosystems that are essential to climate balance and also threatened by extreme events can be an important strategy for facilitating adaptation and strengthening climate resilience for all forms of life.

The plaintiffs, relying on scientific studies and opinions from experts[41] argued that, in this context of environmental degradation, adverse effects of climate change and organized irresponsibility, new governance structures must be implemented, aligned to the premise that *Lagoa da Conceição* is a

and the lagoon beach, as well as the contamination of the lagoon's waters, with damage to its fauna and flora, and a risk to public health.

40 Ulrich Beck, *Risk Society. Towards a new Modernity* (Sage Publications 1992).

41 Expert's opinions can be access on José Rubens Morato Leite, Melissa Ely Mello & Carolina Medeiros Bahia (eds), *Direito Ecológico na Prática: Ação Estrutural da Lagoa da Conceição* (AmoLer Editora 2023).

subject of rights, and interlinked to the rights of traditional communities and future generations. They requested that *Lagoa da Conceição* should be recognized as a subject of the rights to exist and have its ecological services and vital cycles recovered and maintained.[42] The legal grounds of the claim are: (i) the ecocentric interpretation of the environmental constitutional provisions, (ii) the principles of ecological law invoked in Brazilian case law (see section 3.1), (iii) Latin American ecocentric case law, and (iv) the Organic Law of Florianópolis that provides for the rights of nature.[43] In line with the initiatives of other Brazilian municipalities,[44] the Organic Law of Florianópolis established the duty to promote harmony with nature, to preserve, repair, restore and enlarge natural ecosystems for human and non-human, including conferring rights to nature.

The Brazilian Constitution (1998) recognizes the ecologically balanced environment as a fundamental right and states the obligation to preserve and restore essential ecological processes (Article 225). Nevertheless, the plaintiffs argued for a more ecocentric interpretation of these provisions, inspired by the studies of Benjamin (2007) and experts' opinions supporting the claim, to consider nature and its elements as subjects of the right to the environment. Thus, the claim for the protection of *Lagoa da Conceição* is based on an interspecies,

---

42 *Costa Legal et al v Florianópolis et al*, ACP 5012843-56.2021.4.04.7200, filed on 19 May 2021 before the 6th Federal Court of Santa Catarina, available at <https://climatecasechart.com/non-us-case/ong-costa-legal-and-others-vs-municipality-of-florianopolis-and-others/>.

43 Translated by the authors: '*Art. 133.* The Municipality is responsible for promoting diversity and harmony with nature and to preserve, recover, restore and expand natural ecosystem processes, in order to provide the socio-ecological resilience of urban and rural environments, considering that the planning and management of natural resources should promote the sustainable management of common use resources and agroecological practices, in order to guarantee the quality of life of human and non-human populations, to respect the principles of good living and to grant nature the title of right. *Single paragraph.* The Public Authorities will promote public policies and environmental monitoring instruments so that nature acquires legal title and is considered in municipal budget programs and in government projects and actions, and decision-making must be supported by Science, use principles and nature conservation practices, observe the precautionary principle, and seek to involve the Legislative and Judiciary powers, the State and the Union, other municipalities in the Metropolitan Region and civil society organizations.' (Municipality of Florianópolis. Amendment to Organic Law No 47/2019. <https://leismunicipais.com.br/lei-organica-florianopolis-sc> accessed 02 november 2023).

44 The Municipalities of Guajará-Mirim (2023), of Cáceres (2023), Serro (2022), Florianópolis (2019), Paudalho (2018), Bonito (2017) have already recognized the rights of nature at its locals Law. <http://www.harmonywithnatureun.org/rightsOfNature/> accessed 02 november 2023.

intra and intergenerational solidarity's constitutional duty, as well as on the principle of ecological integrity and the protection of ecological dignity, following a *pro natura* imperative typical of ecological law.

Brazilian case law adopting principles of ecological law (section 3.1), the ecocentric interpretation of the right to the environment adopted by IACtHR, and the recognition of ecosystems' rights in Latin American climate cases were invoked to support the claim. The petition emphasized that the STF adopted an ecocentric perspective of the Constitution in the *Vaquejada Case*, recognizing the protection of dignity beyond human beings.[45] Seeking to promote the dialogue of courts, it was highlighted the paradigmatic *Advisory Opinion OC-23/17* (section 2.1) stating that the right to the environment protects the components of the environment for their intrinsic value, even in the absence of certainty about risks to human beings; and the tendency to recognize the rights of nature through jurisprudence and constitutional provisions.

Strengthening the dialogue with Latin American climate cases, plaintiffs mentioned that similar issues related to ecosystems affected by climate change were issued through an ecocentric perspective in countries such as Colombia and Argentina, where the rights of nature are not constitutionally recognized.[46] The main references were the decisions of the Colombian Constitutional Court in the *Atrato River* case and the Supreme Court of Colombia in the *Future Generations* case, recognizing Atrato River and Colombian Amazon as subjects of the rights to protection, conservation, maintenance, and restoration, and determining the adoption of judicial structural measures. The Colombian case law innovated in the ecocentric interpretation of the Constitution, recognized by the courts as an ecological constitution (section 2.1), giving rise to natural entities rights.

Reproducing common features of Latin American climate litigation (section 2.2), the ecocentric perspective is adopted in the *Lagoa da Conceição* case as an alternative to achieve greater protection for this ecosystem, which is both vulnerable and essential to cope with climate change impacts. The rights of nature are interlinked with the protection of human rights, especially of the traditional communities that depend on this ecosystem to preserve their way of life and livelihoods, boosting the ecocentric dimension of the right to the environment.

---

45 *Public Prosecutor's Office v Governor of the State of Ceará* (*Vaquejada Case*) (n 29).

46 *Center for Social Justice Studies et al v Presidency of the Republic et al* (n 1); *Future Generations v Ministry of the Environment et al* (n 1); and *Asociación Civil por la Justicia Ambiental et al v Province of Entre Ríos et al* (n 1).

From these legal and jurisprudential ecocentric arguments, plaintiffs requested the recognition of *Lagoa da Conceição* as a subject of the rights to existence, to have its ecological integrity preserved, and to the conservation, maintenance, and restoration of its essential ecological processes. They also asked to provide this natural entity the procedural right to participate in the governance structures proposed to its management, represented by a designated guardian.

The case also integrates an ecocentric perspective in the proposed socio-ecological governance structures to overcome the structural problem threatening *Lagoa da Conceição* ecological integrity and connected human rights. These proposals were inspired by other Latin American climate cases, as the governance measures performed in the Colombian cases mentioned above, and requested in the *Delta do Paraná* case, as the designation of a guardian to represent the *Lagoa da Conceição's* own interest and protect its rights. Socio-ecological governance was framed following four aspects: (i) non-fragmented and integral protection of the ecosystems and the communities that depend on it; (ii) coordinated efforts on multi-level and inter-agenda actions; (iii) new participatory governance structures; and (iv) the recognition of the rights of nature. Specific judicial measures were adopted to implement this model of socio-ecological governance: (i) the Lagoa da Conceição Judicial Protection Chamber (CJ-PLC), and (ii) the Judicial Protection Plan for Lagoa da Conceição (PJ-PLC).

Considering that the current structural problem was sufficiently demonstrated, including an 'organized irresponsibility scenario,' the Environmental Federal Judge of Florianópolis, by a preliminary injunction,[47] determined the creation of the Lagoa da Conceição Judicial Protection Chamber (CJ-PLC). The Chamber aims to advise on the adoption of structural measures necessary to guarantee the ecological integrity of the natural entity. After its creation, the composition of the CJ-PLC was approved, encompassing representatives from the plaintiff associations, the public entities, and other interested parties, including the Federal University of Santa Catarina (UFSC). The court homologated the CJ-PLC internal regulation, bringing points previously argued by the plaintiffs. For example, the elaboration of a Judicial Protection Plan for Lagoa da Conceição (PJ-PLC) which has among its objectives to propose measures to deal with climate change, and the designation of a guardian of the rights and interests of *Lagoa da Conceição*.[48] The Judicial Plan for the Protection of

47 See Morato Leite, Mello & Bahia (n 43) 112–118.

48 The Internal Regulation of Lagoa da Conceição Judicial Protection Chamber (CJ-PLC) can be consulted in Morato Leite, Mello & Bahia (n 43) 158–164.

Lagoa da Conceição (PJ-PLC) should, among other issues, establish guidelines and priorities related to the effectiveness of fundamental rights in a non-fragmented and systemic way, encompassing specific areas which include the climate aspect, and considering broad participation and consideration of human and non-human interests, including those of future generations.

A working group of experts at CJ-PLC was created, which is currently contributing to diagnosing the problems that threaten the ecological integrity of *Lagoa da Conceição*. Even if the case is still pending, these achievements demonstrate the potential of a nature's rights-based climate litigation in Brazil, inspired both by the Brazilian legal and jurisprudential frameworks aligned with Ecological Law and by the dialogue of courts and experiences of climate litigation with an ecocentric perspective in Latin America.

The innovative aspect of the case is that it approaches both its object, and the associated problem and measures aimed at resolving it through the lens of ecological law, based on a systemic, non-fragmented approach and focused on maintaining ecological processes and life cycles threatened by climate change on an ecocentric basis. As for the object, *Lagoa da Conceição* is considered in all its complexity, as a territory of interaction between human and non-human living beings anchored in a territory with socio-cultural and ecological dimensions. As for the problem and its solution, the arguments go beyond a specific damage or violation of rights. It considers the complex interactions between different layers of vulnerabilities and risks aggravated by an unconstitutional state of affairs that increases the exposure to climate impacts and compromises the capacity of ecosystems to perform their functions of prevention and mitigation of climate risks. The case, through the Judicial Protection Chamber, provides spaces for dialog and collaboration between governmental and social actors and for the integration of political agendas, which promotes the mainstreaming of climate issues in the management of *Lagoa da Conceição*. Finally, it proposes an innovative design for socio-ecological governance to address climate change with an ecocentric approach, considering the implications for the entire community of life and guaranteeing the representation of the whole community, including nature itself.

The rights of nature argument, in the cases in which it has been invoked, allowed to deal with the climate crises in specific ecological territories in a more than anthropocentric way, leading to new approaches capable of encompassing all the complex relations of interdependence between all living beings, human and non-human, with each other and with ecosystems, and how climate change affects these fragile connections. It has favored decision-making processes and spaces of dialogue that integrate the perspective of nature beyond its usefulness to human beings and the consideration of climate issues in a systemic, integrated, and non-fragmented way through the lens of ecological justice.

## 4 Conclusion

The emergence of the Latin American ecological constitutionalism fostered ecocentric legal perspectives that have been integrated in climate litigation, considering the present and future implications of the climate crisis for the entire community of life. Some common features of the ecocentric climate cases are (i) the focus on ecosystems protection, (ii) the intergenerational and interspecies solidarity, (iii) the recognition of legal personality to ecosystems and the articulation of human and nature rights, (iv) a dialogue among courts on ecocentric arguments, and (v) the integration of indigenous peoples and traditional communities' knowledges, culture, and intrinsic relation with nature.

Brazilian courts have been inspired by the ecocentric turn of law and paradigmatic ecocentric precedents in Latin American climate jurisprudence, such as the *Future Generations* case. Even if rights of nature have not yet been discussed as a central issue in Brazilian highest courts, both STJ and STF have built a favorable path to an ecocentric paradigm, including in climate cases. These courts emphasized the ecological dimension of the rule of law, the protection of an 'ecological minimum,' the ecological dimension of human dignity, the intrinsic value of nature, besides the developments based on the *in dubio pro natura* principle.

The *Lagoa da Conceição Case* brings to Brazilian litigation the contributions of ecological constitutionalism and nature's rights-based climate litigation from Latin America. Inspired by these ecocentric legal innovations and taking advantage of Brazilian case law based on ecological law, plaintiffs propose a broad interpretation of the constitutional provisions to consider nature as a subject of environmental rights. The case also fostered the dialogue of courts as a strategy to enrich ecocentric legal arguments and to inspire the proposals for socio-ecological governance structures. This dialogue has led to concrete achievements, such as creating a Judicial Protection Chamber, aiming to designate a guardian of the rights and interests of *Lagoa da Conceição*. This analysis shows a favorable context for developing an ecocentric perspective in climate litigation in Brazil, which stems from Brazilian case law inspired by ecological law and the dialogue of courts and nature's rights-based climate cases in Latin America.

# SECTION 5

## *Beyond the State: Climate Litigation and the Energy Transition*

CHAPTER 15

# The Role of Financial Institutions in Climate Litigation in Brazil

*Alessandra Lehmen**

## 1 Introduction

Climate finance is key to achieving the goals of the Paris Agreement, but the combined climate finance streams from public and private sources still fall significantly short of the trillions required to both redirect capital flows to low-carbon activities and to aid developing countries in transitioning to clean energy, executing their national climate strategies, and bolstering adaptation initiatives.[1]

In 2023, in a decision adopted by the Conference of the Parties (CoP) to the UNFCCC regarding the 'First Global Stocktake' (GST), it was established that the goal of 'Transitioning away from fossil fuels in energy systems, in a just, orderly and equitable manner, accelerating action in this critical decade, so as to achieve net zero by 2050 in keeping with the science.'[2] To achieve this goal, it is of the essence to develop alternatives to fossil fuel revenues, since historically transitions only happen when an alternative is technologically and economically viable. To that end, the First Global Stocktake decision adopted by the COP in Dubai also establishes a new, specific target to triple renewables and double energy efficiency by 2030,[3] and this will need to happen on a global scale and without increasing public debt for developing countries.

Reducing the cost of capital and creating innovative financial instruments that involve the public and private sectors is crucial. COP29 in Azerbaijan will

* Dual-qualified lawyer (Brazil and New York); President, Brazilian Bar Environmental Law Commission, Rio Grande do Sul Chapter; Law Professor, University of Caxias do Sul (UCS); ORCID No. 0000-0003-3073-5633.

1 Climate Policy Initiative, *Global Landscape of Climate Finance 2023* (2023) <https://www.climatepolicyinitiative.org/pt-br/publication/global-landscape-of-climate-finance-2023/> accessed 23 January 2024> accessed 1 August 2024.

2 UNFCCC, Decision No. FCCC/PA/CMA/2023/L.17 (First Global Stocktake) 13 December 2023, §28(d), available at <https://unfccc.int/sites/default/files/resource/cma2023_L17_adv.pdf> accessed 2 February 2024.

3 UNFCCC, Decision No. FCCC/PA/CMA/2023/L.17, §28(a).

 | DOI:10.1163/9789004690974_016

focus on climate finance, and will have much to deliver both in terms of establishing a New Collective Quantified Goal (NCQG) and in mobilizing finance to 'transition away from fossil fuels.'

Financial markets are, therefore, an essential source of funding for the transition to a low-carbon economy. Against this backdrop, the notion of financed emissions, i.e., greenhouse gas (GHG) emissions linked to investment and lending activities of financial institutions, has been increasingly scrutinized through climate litigation. Indeed, there is growing awareness that, without redirecting the flow of cash to less carbon-intensive activities, there is little chance of meeting the goals of the Paris Agreement. Grounds for financial climate litigation are diverse, and, to date, plaintiffs have challenged activities of different types of financial institutions. One such example took place in Brazil, where the world's first climate-related litigation involving a development bank was filed in 2022.[4]

Finance climate litigation has picked up pace in the past couple of years, and is likely to further expand. This article analyzes these developments. Section 2 addresses the issue of what counts as climate finance and draws a distinction between two possible meanings of climate finance, namely, the economy-wide scope of Article 2(1)(c) of the Paris Agreement and the Copenhagen target of mobilizing finance to developing countries. Section 3 addresses the notion of financed emissions and how they relate to climate litigation, explores finance-related climate litigation in Brazil, and maps out possible trends.

## 2 Definition of Climate Finance

Defining climate finance is far from simple, for two reasons: first, there is no consensus as to what counts as climate finance; and second, climate finance is an expression that is employed to convey two different, and sometimes contrasting, ideas—namely, the Copenhagen target of a contribution of US$100 billion per year by developed countries; and the broader, economy-wide scope of Article 2.1(c) of the Paris Agreement.

### 2.1 *What Counts as Climate Finance?*

According to the UNFCCC, climate finance refers to 'local, national or transnational financing,' encompasses 'public, private and alternative sources of

4 *Conectas Direitos Humanos v BNDES and BNDESPAR*, Federal Court of the Federal District, Process No 1038657-42.2022.4.01.3400, filed on 21 June 2022.

financing,' and seeks to support 'mitigation and adaptation actions that will address climate change.'[5]

The UNFCCC Standing Committee on Finance defines the aims of climate finance as 'reducing emissions and enhancing sinks of greenhouse gases', and 'reducing vulnerability of, and maintaining and increasing the resilience of, human and ecological systems to negative climate change impacts.'[6]

Despite efforts by the United Nations to create universal categories that promote transparency and accountability, there is still no consensus on what counts as climate finance, and these ambiguities make it harder to assess the amount of resources that have actually been mobilized for climate projects.

Data regarding climate finance flows are gathered through various methodologies, each with its own interpretations. Nevertheless, the overarching objective of amalgamating diverse sources is to attain a clearer understanding of the global scale of investment in this sphere.

A London School of Economics and Political Science explainer on climate finance[7] mentions that the state of climate finance is assessed by the UNFCCC Standing Committee Biennial Assessment,[8] and that the latter's principal sources include the Climate Policy Initiative's Global Landscape of Climate Finance[9] and the International Energy Agency's endeavors in tracking investments in zero- and low-emission vehicles.[10] However, much of the finance monitored by these initiatives comprises commitments rather than actual disbursements. This is owing to the methodologies involved in gathering data from major providers of finance, such as official development aid from governments and lending by development banks.

5 United Nations Climate Change, *Introduction to Climate Finance* (2023) <https://unfccc.int/topics/introduction-to-climate-finance#:~:text=Climate%20finance%20refers%20to%20local,that%20will%20address%20climate%20change> accessed 23 January 2024.

6 United Nations Climate Change, *Biennial Assessment and Overview of Climate Finance Flows* (2014), available at <https://unfccc.int/files/cooperation_and_support/financial_mechanism/standing_committee/application/pdf/2014_biennial_assessment_and_overview_of_climate_finance_flows_report_web.pdf> accessed 23 January 2024.

7 'What is climate finance?' (London School of Economics and Political Science, 2023), available at <www.lse.ac.uk/granthaminstitute/explainers/what-is-climate-finance-and-where-will-it-come-from />, accessed 23 January 2024.

8 United Nations Climate Change, Biennial Assessment and Overview of Climate Finance Flows (2022), available at <https://unfccc.int/topics/climate-finance/resources/biennial-assessment-and-overview-of-climate-finance-flows> accessed 23 January 2024.

9 Climate Policy Initiative, *Global Landscape of Climate Finance: A Decade of Data* (2022), available at <https://www.climatepolicyinitiative.org/pt-br/publication/global-landscape-of-climate-finance-a-decade-of-data/> accessed 23 January 2024.

10 International Energy Agency, *Global EV Outlook* (IEA 2023), available at <www.iea.org/reports/global-ev-outlook-2023> accessed 23 January 2024.

Another source of discrepancy is the fact that climate finance can be assessed through several criteria—for instance, by type of finance instruments (Eg development aid, equity, or debt); whether it is provided at market or concessional rates; by origin (from public, private, or blended instruments; whether it stems from national or subnational governments, development financial institutions (DFIs), private financial institutions or multilateral funds; by direction of finance flows (domestic, bilateral, or multilateral); or by the sector and purpose of the activities or assets funded, whether these are related to mitigation, adaptation, or loss and damage, and whether a project is considered only for the elements that genuinely have a climate objective. Another source of uncertainty is the assessment of whether climate finance is 'new and additional' under the 2009 Copenhagen Accord, as this is a concept that lacks a formal definition[11] and is, therefore, subject to interpretation.

Substantial further research is needed to understand the real-world impact of climate finance, particularly regarding its tangible contributions to climate change mitigation, adaptation, and sustainable development. Assessing financial value alone overlooks variations in costs for climate change solutions across regions or countries and fails to shed light on the efficacy of financial flows, such as their role in achieving emissions reductions, bolstering resilience, and promoting a just transition.

### 2.2 *Article 2(1)(c) of the Paris Agreement*

Methodology discrepancies aside, climate finance is an expression that has been used to convey two different, and sometimes contrasting, ideas: the first is the Copenhagen target of a contribution of US$100 billion per year by developed countries. The second, broader one, is the necessary mobilization of capital flows, public and private, to decarbonize the economy. Understanding what these two meanings have in common—and where they differ—is fundamental for the articulation and convergence of climate finance action needed to achieve the objectives of the Paris Agreement.

The first idea conveyed by the expression climate finance—that of aligning global financial flows with the objectives of limiting global warming to 1.5°C—is related to the first, but also, and mainly, with Article 2(1)(c) of the Paris Agreement, which establishes the objective of promoting financial flows consistent with a path of low greenhouse gas emissions and climate-resilient development.

---

11 United Nations Conference on Trade and Development, *'New and Additional' Climate Finance: a continuing lack of clarity* (UNCTAD 2015), available at <https://unctad.org/system/files/official-document/presspb2015d15_en.pdf> accessed 23 January 2024.

The Climate Policy Initiative's 2024 Global Landscape of Climate Finance[12] indicates that an annual investment of $10 trillion between 2030 and 2050—a five-fold increase—is necessary to mitigate the most severe consequences of climate change. The report estimates the cost of inaction at a whopping USD 2,328 trillion, based on 'direct economic impacts of increased weather-related and other uninsurable damages, increased production costs, productivity losses, and health costs.' The report points out that these projections are likely to be 'a dramatic underestimate as they do not capture capital losses caused by stranded assets, losses to nature and biodiversity, or those from increased conflict and human migration that cannot yet be reasonably costed.'[13]

According to the Intergovernmental Panel on Climate Change (IPCC) AR6 Synthesis Report, 'There is sufficient global capital to close the global investment gaps, but there are barriers to redirect capital to climate action'. The report adds that 'Barriers include institutional, regulatory and market access barriers, which can be reduced to address the needs and opportunities, economic vulnerability and indebtedness in many developing countries, ample global capital is available to bridge the investment gap required for climate action.'[14] The primary challenge lies, therefore, in aligning global capital towards climate-related endeavors, rather than merely securing additional funds for mitigation and adaptation efforts.

Article 2(1)(c) of the Paris Agreement aims to address this challenge by advocating for financial flows that support a trajectory towards low greenhouse gas emissions and climate-resilient development. Nevertheless, the wording of Article 2(1)(c) lacks specificity, leading to disagreements among countries regarding its scope and implementation.

The regulatory goal of Article 2(1)(c) of the Paris Agreement is comprehensive and encompasses both mitigation and adaptation efforts, potentially involving both domestic and international financial flows. It necessitates not only bolstering investments in climate-friendly projects such as renewable energy but also scaling back funding for carbon-intensive activities. Furthermore, it extends beyond governmental spending to encompass the private sector, including financial institutions, businesses, corporations, and investors.

Implementing Article 2(1)(c) of the Paris Agreement calls for economic and financial reforms, employing a variety of tools such as innovative policies and financial instruments like green procurement and climate-related bonds.

---

12 Climate Policy Initiative (n 1).

13 ibid.

14 IPCC, *Climate Change 2023: Synthesis Report. Contribution of Working Groups I, II and III to the Sixth Assessment Report of the Intergovernmental Panel on Climate Change* (IPCC 2023).

Additionally, ensuring equity requires tailoring the alignment of financial flows to the unique economic, financial, and social contexts of each country, with particular attention to the pursuit of sustainable development, poverty eradication, and just transition, especially in developing nations.

The idea of 'climate-resilient development' contained in Article 2(1)(c) of the Paris Agreement can be better understood from a double materiality perspective. The concept, introduced in 2019 by the European Commission,[15] considers how an economic activity impacts the climate and how it is impacted by climate, in a double matrix of financial materiality and outward materiality. In other words, it considers, on the one hand, the impacts of the activity on the climate system, and, on the other, the degree of exposure of the activity to climate risks, as well as resilience to these risks.

Despite making incremental strides, grappling with the role of Article 2(1)(c) of the Paris Agreement in broader climate negotiations, elucidating pivotal terms such as 'financial flows' and 'consistency,' and addressing concerns regarding countries' sovereignty all present formidable challenges for the international finance community as it seeks to forge ahead.

Defining 'consistency of financial flows' stands out as a crucial hurdle in implementing Article 2(1)(c) of the Paris Agreement. Countries diverge in their interpretations, employing terms like 'directing, orienting, aligning, shifting, steering, scaling up, scaling down and more.'[16] The Climate Policy Initiative points out that 'consistency of financial flows' can imply not only a focus on measuring green or brown flows, 'but also flows to assets and activities that neither contribute to GHG emission reductions nor increase them, that neither contribute to adaptation nor maladaptation.'[17] The IPCC adopts a broader perspective, encompassing all investments, regardless of their contribution to climate goals, including those facilitating transitional phases.[18]

---

15 Régis Gourdel, Irene Monasterolo, Nepomuk Dunz, Andrea Mazzocchetti, Laura Parisi, 'The Double Materiality of Climate Physical and Transition Risks in the Euro Area', European Central Bank—Working Paper No 2665 (May 2022), available at <https://www.ecb.europa.eu/pub/pdf/scpwps/ecb.wp2665~622858d454.en.pdf~622858d454.en.pdf> accessed 12 February 2024. Régis Gourdel, Irene Monasterolo, Nepomuk Dunz, Andrea Mazzocchetti, Laura Parisi.

16 Natalia Alayza, *What Is the Paris Agreement's Article 2.1(c) on Climate Finance, and Why Does it Matter? Key Questions, Answered* (World Resources Institute 2023), available at <https://www.wri.org/insights/article-2-1-c-paris-agreement-explained> accessed 11 February 2024.

17 Climate Policy Initiative, *Global Climate Finance: An Updated View 2018* (Climate Policy Initiative 2018), available at <https://climatepolicyinitiative.org/wp-content/uploads/2018/11/Global-Climate-Finance-An-Updated-View-2018.pdf> accessed 11 February 2024.

18 IPCC (n 12).

However, achieving 'consistency' also requires decision on actions to avoid. At least, States should share an understanding of how to diminish investments misaligned with climate objectives, such as financing fossil fuels, and the potential ramifications for domestic policies and national development.

As such, achieving the goals outlined in Article 2(1)(c) of the Paris Agreement requires a broad realignment of financial systems with sustainable development and international climate objectives. This entails ensuring that all forms of investments and financial activities, including those of the private sector, are in harmony with global climate goals.

The importance of these concepts in the real world is tremendous. The direction of capital flows is decisive in determining whether or not there is a chance of stopping the planet's current warming trajectory. The projects financial institutions choose to finance and the companies to which investors decide to allocate their capital hold the key to decarbonization of the economy, and, consequently, to the success or failure of the Paris Agreement's objectives.

### 2.3 *The Copenhagen Commitment and the New Collective Quantified Goal (NCQC)*

The second meaning of climate finance refers to the transfer of resources by developed countries to developing countries, and originated in 2009, at COP15. In Copenhagen, developed countries made a commitment to contribute 100 billion dollars per year, between 2020 and 2025, for mitigation and adaptation in the countries that are most vulnerable to climate change. It was also established that these 100 billion must be new and additional, balanced between mitigation and adaptation, and include private sources. While Article 2(1)(c) of the Paris Agreement encompasses all financial flows for signatory nations, the NCQG specifically focuses on financial assistance to developing countries.

As seen, Article 2(1)(c) of the Paris Agreement stands as a holistic objective within the Paris Agreement aimed at tackling climate change. However, its effective implementation requires consideration of the entire agreement, particularly other financial objectives contemplated in the text. There is, therefore, a need for alignment between Article 2(1)(c) and the forthcoming New Collective Quantified Goal (NCQG), an update of the Copenhagen commitment that is slated for establishment at COP29 in 2024.[19] The NCQG will establish a fresh financial target surpassing the current commitment of developed States to collectively provide $100 billion annually for climate finance.

19 United Nations Climate Change, *New Collective Quantified Goal on Climate Finance*, available at <https://unfccc.int/NCQG> accessed 11 February 2024.

Crucially, the mandate to adopt the NCQG emphasizes the necessity of considering the needs and priorities of developing States. These latter have voiced concerns that discussions on Article 2(1)(c) of the Paris Agreement might divert attention from this focal point or impose conditions that hinder access to financial support.

Negotiators must take these concerns seriously as they chart a path forward. From a Global South perspective, it is important to consider that States have distinct development trajectories, requirements, and agendas. Crafting policies and mechanisms to synchronize their financial flows must acknowledge this diversity. Nonetheless, given that Article 2(1)(c) represents a global endeavor, inquiries will emerge regarding the criteria for action and the necessity of uniform policies and regulations across all States, and whether failure to promote reform will hamper their ability to access climate finance.

Another matter of particular interest for developing States is the link between climate finance and debt. This is a twofold process: on the one hand, flows of climate finance can result in further indebtedness; on the other hand, increasingly larger amounts of capital and investment are required for States to cope with the adverse effects of climate change, particularly those in the Global South.

To tackle the climate crisis effectively, immediate attention must be directed towards resolving the debt crisis prevalent in the Global South. This involves implementing debt relief measures alongside the provision of new, additional, and sufficient grant-based climate finance. Finance is indispensable to assist vulnerable nations in adapting to climate change impacts, addressing loss and damage beyond adaptation capacity, and navigating the climate transition.

Another key finding of the Climate Policy Initiative's 2024 Global Landscape of Climate Finance reinforces the need for innovative financial instruments and the importance of blended capital, urging 'renewed emphasis on the strategic use of public funds and other concessional finance to mobilize significantly more private capital:' DFIs provide 57% of all public finance, and 17% of public finance to least developed countries (LDC s) is provided at market rates, further driving LDC s into debt.[20]

The allocation of climate finance from the Global North to the Global South forms the cornerstone of the international cooperation framework for climate action under the UNFCCC and its Paris Agreement. It is firmly rooted in the UNFCCC principle of common but differentiated responsibilities and respective capabilities (CBDRC). Furthermore, acceleration and worsening of the

20 Climate Policy Initiative (n 10).

adverse effects of climate change disproportionately affect countries in the Global South, putting the debate on the operationalization of the loss and damage fund agreed upon at COP27[21] in the spotlight.

In short, decarbonization of the economy requires concerted climate financing initiatives, whether through the transfer of resources to developing countries agreed in 2009 in Copenhagen, or through the indispensable redirection of capital flows to low-carbon activities.

## 3 Climate Litigation Involving Financial Institutions

### 3.1 *Financed Emissions*

The rise in financial climate litigation is unsurprising, given that financial flows play a central role in achieving the goals of the Paris Agreement. The recent surge in climate-related lawsuits, with a heightened risk of legal actions targeting financial market participants, has been anticipated over the past few years. The Network for Greening the Financial System (NGFS) highlights a noticeable trend where courts increasingly grant plaintiffs standing and rule in favor of them in climate-related litigation.[22]

Against this backdrop, financed emissions are a key concept for climate litigation involving financial institutions. According to Jain and Pathak, financed emissions are 'emissions resulting from investments and financial activities, including loans, investments and portfolios.'[23]

The latest IPCC Sixth Assessment Report (AR6)[24] provides insights into investment and financial flows. It asserts the existence of a climate financing deficit, highlighting a persistent misallocation of global capital. Moreover, it identifies significant inequalities in financial access as exacerbating the prospects for a fair and global transition to a low-carbon future. Additionally, the sluggish execution of commitments by States and stakeholders within the

21 United Nations Climate Change, *Sharm el-Sheikh Implementation Plan* (2022), available at <https://unfccc.int/sites/default/files/resource/cop27_auv_2_cover%20decision.pdf> accessed 2 February 2024.

22 Network for Greening the Financial System, *Climate-related litigation: Raising awareness about a growing source of risk* (2021), available at <https://www.ngfs.net/sites/default/files/medias/documents/climate_related_litigation.pdf accessed 12 February 2024.

23 Ankit Jain & Devansh Pathak, *Tackling 'financed emissions' as the gateway to a greener economy* (World Economic Forum 2023), available at <https://www.weforum.org/agenda/2023/05/financed-emissions-could-be-a-gateway-to-a-greener-economy/> accessed 12 February 2024.

24 IPCC (n 12).

financial sector to enhance climate finance fails to align with the pressing call for bold climate initiatives or the compelling economic incentives—such as performance gains and improved resilience—supporting such actions. Climate litigation has been employed as a strategic means to accelerate these changes.

The carbon footprint of financial institutions comprises not only financing, but also equity and bond underwriting and direct equity participation. The Financial Times reported that 'More than one-third of the $669bn of financing provided to oil, gas and coal companies in 2022 by the world's 60 biggest banks was through underwriting bonds and equities sold on to investors, rather than loans made by the banks themselves, according to a tally by non-profits including Urgewald and the Rainforest Action Network,' adding that, in a bid to avoid double standards, 'the Science-Based Targets Initiative, a voluntary oversight body that signs off on the integrity of banks' net zero goals, … could reject joint targets that give underwriting a lower weighting than lending.'[25]

Beyond the assessment of project-based emissions, it is vital to note that the financial sector carries an important dimension of systemic risk. Analysis of climate risks and opportunities by financial institutions is particularly relevant, as these have the potential to be transmitted to the production chain through financed projects.

Mao, Wei, and Ren posit that 'Climate change has recently been recognized as a potential driver of systemic risk, and its shocks to the financial system are expected to materialize in the near future,' adding that 'it is of great importance to understand the implications for the macroprudential regulation of climate change in order to enable central banks and supervisors to achieve their financial stability objectives.'

It is also necessary to consider how the transmission mechanisms between the financial and the real sectors of the economy translate to sustainable and climate finance. Caldecott and others posit that said transmission mechanisms include 'the cost of capital faced by firms when raising finance; access to liquidity, which affects corporate operations, planning, and refinancing, particularly when under financial pressure; and the financial sector's role in changing corporate practices.'[26]

25 Kenza Bryan, 'Investment Banks Squabble over Carbon Footprint of Underwriting Deals' (*Financial Times*, 7 July 2023) <https://www.ft.com/content/ca549b24-ece5-46c2-85fb-5fe1aa24d296> accessed 27 January 2024.

26 Ben Caldecott, Alex Clark, Elizabeth Harnett, Krister Koskelo, Christian Wilson & Felicia Liu, 'Sustainable Finance and Transmission Mechanisms to the Real Economy', University of Oxford Smith School of Enterprise and the Environment Working Paper 22–04, available at <https://www.smithschool.ox.ac.uk/sites/default/files/2022-04/Sustainable

Climate litigation involving financial institutions is as diverse as the climate finance environment itself: grounds for financial climate litigation include taxonomy criteria,[27] bond acquisitions, sustainable investment claims, as well as financing and equity portfolios, and, to date, plaintiffs have challenged activities carried out by different types of financial institutions, namely a commercial bank,[28] an asset management firm,[29] a central bank,[30] and a development bank.[31] Of these examples, only the latter case was filed in the Global South[32]—more specifically, in Brazil—, but all can potentially be replicated across jurisdictions, as they fall into rather broad categories concerning either financed emissions or greenwashing related to misinformation and disinformation that can be adapted to different legal systems.

### 3.2 *Finance-Related Climate Litigation in Brazil*

The JUMA-NIMA litigation database, developed by the Pontifical University of Rio de Janeiro, compiles all climate-related cases in Brazil, and indicates that, as of this writing, only two climate cases filed in the country have banks as defendants: *AMOREMA e AMORETGRAP v Sustainable Carbon and others*,[33] which

-Finance-and-Transmission-Mechanisms-to-the-Real-Economy.pdf> accessed February 11 2024.

27 Greenpeace et al v Commission, Process No T-214/23, filed before the General Court of the European Union, available at <https://climatecasechart.com/non-us-case/greenpeace-and-others-v-commission/>, accessed 11 February 2024.

28 *Notre Affaire à Tous Les Amis de la Terre, and Oxfam France v BNP Paribas* (2023), Judicial Court of Paris (France), available at <https://climatecasechart.com/non-us-case/notre-affaire-a-tous-les-amis-de-la-terre-and-oxfam-france-v-bnp-paribas/> accessed February 11 2024.

29 'Verbraucherschützer verklagen die DekaBank wegen Nachhaltigskeitsfonds' (Finanz Business, 15 February 2021), available at <https://finanzbusiness.de/nachrichten/banken/article12763163.ece> accessed 11 February 2024.

30 *ClientEarth v Belgian National Bank*, filed in April 2021, available at <https://climatecasechart.com/non-us-case/clientearth-v-belgian-national-bank/#:~:text=Summary%3A,other%20greenhouse%2Dgas%20intensive%20companies> accessed 11 February 2024.

31 Conectas Direitos Humanos v BNDES and BNDESPAR (n 4).

32 According to a report by the Columbia Sabin Center for Climate Change Law, 'Global South cases represent only 8.3% of the total cases documented. (...) In terms of jurisdictions, Brazil has the highest proportion of cases at 39%, followed by Mexico at 10.5%, Indonesia at 7.1%, and Colombia at 6.7%.' Maria Antonia Tigre, Climate Litigation in the Global South: Mapping Report (Sabin Center for Climate Change Law, 2024), available at <https://scholarship.law.columbia.edu/cgi/viewcontent.cgi?article=1231&context=sabin_climate_change> accessed 1 August 2024.

33 AMOREMA and AMORETGRAP v Sustainable Carbon at al (on voluntary carbon markets), ACP 1045416-11.2021.4.01.3900, filed in 2021 before the Federal Court of Pará.

challenges 'green land-grabbing' associated with carbon credit projects; and *Conectas Direitos Humanos v BNDES and BNDESPAR*,[34] which seeks information and governance improvements with regard to the climate policies of the Brazilian development banks' equity investment arm. The latter case, *Conectas*, touches directly on the role of financial institutions in the decarbonization of the economy, and is the first climate lawsuit in the world involving a development bank. In June 2023, in its seventy-eight session, the United Nations General Assembly adopted the Note by the Secretary-General A/78/255, 'Promotion and protection of human rights in the context of climate change', transmitting the Report of the former Special Rapporteur on the Promotion and Protection of Human Rights in the Context of Climate Change, Ian Fry, and highlighting the case to illustrate the assertion that 'Banks have become the target of climate change litigation for funding projects that are not consistent with reducing greenhouse gas emissions.'[35] The document also mentions that 'In 2022, a Brazilian NGO, Conectas Direitos Humanos, filed a claim against the Brazilian National Bank for Economic and Social Development and BNDESPAR, its investment arm, which is responsible for managing the Bank's shareholdings in various Brazilian companies,' and that the claim aims at obtaining a court-mandated 'plan establishing rules and mechanisms to commit their investments and divestments to the reduction of greenhouse gas emissions by the companies they finance.'[36] Moreira refers to the case as 'a paradigmatic example of a systemic corporate case'.[37]

In *Conectas*, the plaintiff argues that the allocation of financial resources from public institutions (such as development banks) to companies in the productive sector must comply with criteria of maximum return to the sustainable development of the country from an economic, social, and environmental point of view. This is especially relevant, according to the plaintiff, when such

34 *Conectas Direitos Humanos v BNDES and BNDESPAR* (n 4).

35 United Nations General Assembly, *Note by the Secretary-General A/78/255, 'Promotion and protection of human rights in the context of climate change'* (2023), available at <https://documents.un.org/doc/undoc/gen/n24/213/32/pdf/n2421332.pdf> accessed 31 July 2024.

36 Office of the United Nations High Commissioner for Human Rights, UN Doc A/78/255, Report of the Special Rapporteur on the Promotion and Protection of Human Rights in the Context of Climate Change, Ian Fry (2023), available at <https://www.ohchr.org/en/documents/thematic-reports/a78255-report-special-rapporteur-promotion-and-protection-human-rights> accessed 31 January 2024.

37 Danielle de Andrade Moreira, Carolina de Figueiredo Garrido, Juliana Chermont Pessoa Lopes, Paula Máximo de Barros Pinto, Victória Lourenço de Carvalho e Gonçalves, Luciana Tse Chaves Garcia Rego, Maria Eduarda Garambone Sydenstricker & Ana Paula Ricci, *Panorama da Litigância Climática no Brasil: Relatório de 2024* (JUMA/PUC-Rio, 2024).

allocation of funds is provided under conditions that are generally more favorable than those practiced by the market, whether through financing or shareholding. The claim maintains that BNDESPAR invests public resources, that it maintains equity positions in sectors that are among the most carbon-intensive in the Brazilian economy, and that these two circumstances require that the climate issue is incorporated into the defendants' operations in an effective and transparent way.

The claim further maintains that preventing climate change from reaching unacceptable levels is a basic prerequisite for the environmental sustainability of economic and social development, and therefore, when selecting companies in which to acquire equity, BNDESPAR has a duty towards Brazilian society to consider the investees' track record of sustainability and their exposure different categories of climate risks, such as those arising from the asset exposure to physical risks or from unpreparedness for the transition to a low-carbon economy. An expert opinion rendered by the Center for Integrated Study on the Environment and Climate Change of the Federal University of Rio de Janeiro, presented as evidentiary support,[38] found that at least 65% of the equity held by BNDESPAR is concentrated in carbon-intensive companies. The calculation was based on an analysis of reports published by the companies and comprises a sample of 85% of the investment portfolio of BNDESPAR as of March 2021, represented by ten companies from the oil and gas, electricity, meat production, mining, and pulp and paper sectors.

The legal basis for the claim includes Brazilian obligations under the Paris Agreement, as embodied in its submitted nationally determined contribution (NDC); Articles 37, 170 (VI), 174 and 225 of the Brazilian Constitution; Articles 3, 4(I), 6, 8 and 11 of the National Policy on Climate Change (Law No 12,187/09, regulated by Decree No 9,578/18); the Brazilian National Adaptation Plan, established by Ministry of the Environment Ordinance No 150/2016; Articles 116 and 154 of Law No 6,404/76 (Code of Corporations); Articles 186 and 187 of the Civil Code, the UN Guiding Principles for Business and Human Rights, which had been explicitly incorporated to the National Guidelines for Business and Human Rights through Decree No 9,571/18; Article 1(4) and (6) of Law No 13,874/2019 (Economic Freedom Law); Law No 12,527/11 (Access to Information Law); the sustainability requirements established by Law No 13,303/16; the duty to respect the integrity of the climate system provided for in Article 1(I) of the Forest Code; socio-environmental and climate standards issued by Brazilian regulators, e.g. the Central Bank of Brazil (BACEN) and the securities

38 Emilio Lèbre La Rovere et al, *Expert opinion rendered in Conectas Direitos Humanos v BNDES and BNDESPAR* (2022).

regulator (CVM); the United Nations Global Compact, especially Sustainable Development Goal (SDG) 13; and the rules of the Green Climate Fund (GCF).

With regard to the role of financial institutions in countering the climate crisis, the case builds on the 'alignment bullseye' approach proposed by the Climate Policy Initiative and the Institute for Climate Economics, according to which banks should at least 'do no harm' ('all activities should neither hinder nor be counterproductive to the achievement of climate objectives and should be consistent with long-term national sustainable and low-GHG, climate-resilient development pathways'); then support Paris-consistent climate co-benefits ('prioritize activities with direct or indirect mitigation and adaptation co-benefits that are consistent with the national attainment of the long-term goals of the Paris Agreement'), and, finally, reach a stage in which they foster transformative outcomes ('prioritize activities … that reduce the barriers to and support the large-scale, systemic and structural changes needed for the transition of economic, social and natural systems across and within national economies).'[39]

The case adds another layer of arguments beyond the rights-based approach typically prevalent in the Global South[40] by framing climate obligations of financial institutions in terms of ESG (Environmental, Social, and Governance) regulation newly enacted in Brazil, of the fiduciary duties applicable under Brazilian Corporate Law, and of climate stewardship expectations.

ESG is not a new concept,[41] but rose to prominence in recent years. Climate change is an important part of ESG, which, in turn, is becoming increasingly regulated, implying it can also be used in litigation in case of noncompliance. While it is true that ESG still involves a good deal of self-regulation, there is a clear global trend of increasing ESG regulation.

In Brazil, ESG regulations and standards have been increasingly targeting climate change topics. Several recent developments regarding ESG regulation

---

39 Ian Cochran & Alice Pauthier, 'A Framework for Alignment with the Paris Agreement: Why, What and How for Financial Institutions?', I4CE Discussion Paper (2019), available at <https://unfccc.int/sites/default/files/resource/Aligning%20with%20the%20Paris%20Agreement%20-%20Part%201%20-%20CPI-I4CE.pdf> accessed 2 January 2024.

40 Jaqueline Peel & Jolene Lin,'Transnational Climate Litigation: The Contribution of the Global South' (2019) 113 *AJIL Unbound* 679.

41 See, generally, The Global Compact, *Who Cares Wins—Connecting Financial Markets to a Changing World* (2004), available at <https://d306pr3pise04h.cloudfront.net/docs/issues_doc%2FFinancial_markets%2Fwho_cares_who_wins.pdf>, accessed February 14 2024; United Nations Environment Programme Finance Initiative, *A legal framework for the integration of environmental, social and governance issues into institutional investment*, (2005), available at <https://www.unepfi.org/wordpress/wp-content/uploads/2022/07/Freshfields-A-legal-framework-for-the-integration-of-ESG-issues-into-institutional-investment.pdf>, accessed February 14 2024.

are noteworthy. Resolution No 59/2021 of the Brazilian Securities Regulator (CVM) adopts a 'comply-or-explain' regulatory approach to order public companies to periodically disclose climate information, or explain the reasons for failing to adopt measures in this regard. Similarly, in 2021, the Central Bank of Brazil launched a package of regulations on sustainability criteria applicable to rural credit, on regulation of social, environmental and climate risk, and on the annual disclosure, by financial institutions, of a standardized Social, Environmental and Climate Risks and Opportunities Report (the GRSAC Report).[42]

Beyond newer ESG regulation, the legal duty to expressly consider climate criteria in a company's operations also derives from the fiduciary duty applicable under Brazilian law. This happens on two levels.

First, the 1976 Brazilian Law of Corporations establishes that both the controlling shareholder (Article 116) and the board (Article 154) must wield their power in order to make the company fulfill its social function, and has duties and responsibilities towards shareholders and the community. In other words, controlling shareholders have responsibilities to incorporate externalities into the business.

Second, the guidelines from the Institute of Climate Stewardship apply to institutional investors, who are responsible for making sound investment decisions regarding the assets in which their clients invest. Public company shareholders have been increasingly vocal with regard to information and measures related to climate policies.[43]

Another argument used in the case is that incorporation of climate issues into BNDESPAR operations must take place from a double materiality perspective, considering, on the one hand, how BNDESPAR is affected by climate change, and, on the other hand, how BNDESPAR affects climate change. This was highlighted by the expert opinion presented as evidentiary support: in the court document, La Rovere states that 'lack of knowledge of climate risks relevant to the investment portfolio, as well as their impact on the environment and Brazilian society (double materiality), can compromise the risk management process and strategic planning of BNDESPAR.'[44]

42 Central Bank of Brazil, *Sustainability* (2021), available at <https://www.bcb.gov.br/estabilidadefinanceira/sustentabilidade> accessed 13 January 2024.

43 Latin American Climate Lawyers Initiative for Mobilizing Action and Fundação Getulio Vargas, *Climate Stewardship in Brazil: A Guide for Investors* (2022), available at <https://laclima.org/wp-content/uploads/2022/08/climate-stewardship-guide-brazil-LACLIMA-FGVSP.pdf>, accessed 13 January 2024.

44 La Rovere (n 38).

### 3.3 *Trends and Possibilities*

Finance-related climate litigation shows no signs of receding. The London School of Economics Grantham Institute's *Global Trends in Climate Change Litigation: 2024 Snapshot* report finds that 'Cases that challenge the flow of finance to projects and activities that are not aligned with climate action have continued to increase in number and diversity.' The report further notes that 'turning off the taps' cases may be filed against public or private financial institutions, or a combination of the two, aiming at underscoring of incorporating climate risk analysis in financial decision-making, 'increasing the cost of capital for high-emitting activities to the point where such activities become economically unviable, even if they remain legally permissible.'[45]

Batoudaki mentions that an analysis of Sustainalytics data for fifteen large banks shows that the number of cases related to the environmental and carbon impact of products increased twelvefold between 2020 and 2023, adding that 'legal risk may become a much larger concern as we approach 2030, a milestone year for transition plans to net zero by 2050.'[46] In Brazil, climate litigation has been gaining traction since 2020, but is far less frequent than environmental litigation at large. This means there are possibilities for expansion and for testing new arguments and theses.

A distinctive feature of climate litigation in the Global South is a prevalence of rights-based claims, and this holds generally true in Brazil. Achieving the Paris Agreement's goals, however, is unattainable without involvement of the private sector. It is likely, therefore, that climate litigation strategies will increasingly focus on non-state actors. As ESG standards and obligations continue to evolve into mandatory and increasingly stringent requirements worldwide, arguments that challenge specific, measurable ESG obligations are likely to be further explored in climate litigation.

These may include duties related to fiduciary responsibility, liability in supply chains (both direct and indirect), disclosure requirements, and prevention of corporate greenwashing. Such arguments not only reinforce existing obligations but also provide clarity and granularity to broader principles and rights-based approaches. As we have posited, 'rights-based approaches can

---

45 Joana Setzer & Catherine Higham, *Global Trends in Climate Litigation: 2024 Snapshot* (Grantham Research Institute on Climate Change and the Environment 2024) available at <https://www.lse.ac.uk/granthaminstitute/wp-content/uploads/2024/06/Global-trends-in-climate-change-litigation-2024-snapshot.pdf>.

46 Theodora Batoudaki, 'Double Trouble: The Rise of Greenwashing and Climate Litigation for Banks' (*Sustainalytics*, 26 January 2024), available at <https://www.sustainalytics.com/esg-research/resource/investors-esg-blog/double-trouble--the-rise-of-greenwashing-and-climate-litigation-for-banks> accessed January 27 2024.

provide a robust framework in which to argue such cases,' while ESG litigation can challenge 'specific obligations, helping overcome procedural hurdles typically found in climate cases, such as those related to attribution, standing, and justiciability.'[47]

In this vein, private financial institutions are often publicly-traded companies, which means they are also prone to being challenged by investors on the basis of their ESG performance. This two-pronged exposure to scrutiny means that new litigation strategies can arise from non-governmental organizations, clients, investors, and significant shareholders who are troubled by a disparity between a bank's declared strategy and its tangible advancement towards achieving its net-zero objectives.

Another trend to watch is that concerning a disconnect between disclosures and practice, either leading to greenwashing litigation or to the practice dubbed as 'greenhushing', in which market players refrain from making sustainability statements to prevent scrutiny. This can prove harder with time, as disclosure requirements have been multiplying, and disclosures that used to be voluntary are now increasingly mandatory. A heightened degree of disclosures entails increased scrutiny of information that is made available by companies, expanding the basis for greenwashing litigation. In sum, more disclosure means more information, and more information means shedding more light on greenwashing.

The above mentioned flourishing of climate-related rules and regulations has been unfolding in three fronts. First, there has been a significant rise in unilateral climate measures with cross-border effects on global value chains, most of them stemming from the European Union, with significant impacts in Brazil. Second, there has been a rise in sustainability and climate reporting standards, both mandatory, such as the CS3D proposal, CSRD, and ESRS, and voluntary, such as ISSB IFRS S1 and S2, that are also affecting actors along global value chains. Third, other types of climate-related regulations or proposals, namely recent developments regarding anti-deforestation (EUDR), greenwashing (GCD), carbon border adjustment (CBAM), sustainable taxonomy (EUST), antitrust (EU Sustainability Guidelines), and environmental crime (ECD), and capital requirements (CRD) are bound to impact financial institutions and finance-related climate litigation.

This creates a perfect storm of sorts, that is due to elicit responses from countries that want to preserve their competitiveness—particularly from large exporters of commodities like Brazil—that will necessarily reverberate across

47 Alessandra Lehmen, 'Advancing Climate Litigation in Brazil' (2022) 22(8) *German Law Journal* 1471.

corporate activity. The Porter hypothesis,[48] which posits that strict environmental regulations can induce efficiency and encourage innovations that help improve commercial competitiveness, can also be put to the test: will more regulation level the playing field and eliminate unfair advantages and free-riding, or, to the contrary, will it create overlapping requirements that are increasingly harder to navigate?

In Brazil, some responses to this wave of regulation, albeit quite timid, have taken place. One such example is the issuance of a self-regulatory rule by the Federation of Banks of Brazil (FEBRABAN), comprised of large commercial banks and later joined by the Brazilian development bank, stating that they will no longer finance meat producers involved in illegal deforestation.[49]

Also, it is interesting to note that greenwashing litigation, both judicial and administrative, has been flourishing around the world, but not as much in Brazil. This is somewhat counterintuitive, as Brazil has regulation that is rather protective of consumers, and, relative to other jurisdictions, imposes fewer procedural hurdles with regard to standing and access to justice. Moving forward, with more disclosure requirements that affect global value chains entering into force, there may be a change to this scenario.

Lastly, another matter to keep track of is the issue of materiality and its impacts on litigation: as seen above, *Conectas* challenges the Brazilian development bank's equity portfolio both in terms of whether it is a sound investment and on its impacts on climate. Whether different standards of materiality will impact climate litigation remains to be seen: interoperability among standards is still low, meaning there is ample room for conflict and overlaps, and, while the European initiatives adopt double materiality, the ISSB frameworks settled for single materiality. In Brazil, the ISSB has been already endorsed by the Brazilian securities regulator (CVM), through Resolution No 193/2023, and by the Federal Council of Accountants (CFC). Adopting single materiality affects enforcement and litigation prospects in the sense that perhaps there will be less information available to scrutinize. This is, however, unlikely to affect core climate arguments, meaning that challenging an activity's impacts on climate will remain possible under other legal grounds.

Establishing a definitive pattern for finance-related climate litigation is challenging due to the diverse range of climate-related cases and legal frameworks

48 Michael E Porter, 'America's Green Strategy' (1991) 264(4) *Scientific American* 168.

49 Federation of Banks of Brazil, *Banks establish self-regulatory rule for bovine meat chain* (2023), available at <https://portal.febraban.org.br/noticia/3935/pt-br/#:~:text=The%20new%20rule%2C%20approved%20in,2025%2C%20the%20non%2Dacquisition%20of> accessed 13 February 2024.

involved, but these developments may prompt additional climate litigation against banks, offering litigants further legal grounds for their claims. Consequently, we anticipate that legal and reputational risks related to climate litigation will continue to rise for financial institutions.

## 4 Conclusion

Climate finance will remain at the top of the climate agenda priorities for the foreseeable future, as decarbonization does not happen in a financial vacuum: net-zero will only be achieved when financial flows converge towards it. Indeed, achieving the goals of the Paris Agreement, both economy-wide and related to financing the transition in developing countries, requires a comprehensive reorientation of financial systems towards sustainable development and global climate targets. This involves alignment of all types of investments and financial products and activities, including those originating from the private sector, with overarching global climate objectives.

The current shortfall of climate finance and the substantial disparities in access to finance hinder the prospects of a fair and comprehensive transition to a low-carbon future. The slow progress in making finance flows consistent with the goals of the Paris Agreement is misaligned with the urgent need for ambitious climate action. Climate litigation has emerged as a strategic tool to expedite these transformations, and legal grounds for finance-related litigation are highly likely to continue to develop and expand in the near- to mid-term.

## Conflict of Interests

The author is outside counsel to the Plaintiff in *Conectas*.

CHAPTER 16

# The State's Duty to Pursue the Highest Possible Ambition

*by Filling Regulatory Gaps on Corporate Climate Responsibilities*

*Guilherme J. S. Leal**

## 1 Introduction

The 1992 United Nations Framework Convention on Climate Change (UNFCCC) requires its Parties to 'take *precautionary* measures to anticipate, prevent or minimize the causes of climate change and mitigate its adverse effects.'[1] Since then, the precautionary principle has gained wide acceptance in the field of risk regulation, being incorporated into various legal acts (such as Brazil's National Policy on Climate Change, passed by Law No 12,187/09) and applied by courts to hold both public and private actors accountable for their failures in exercising precaution when so required. The problem, however, is that there are dozens of definitions of precaution, and, as Sunstein put it, 'they are not compatible with one another.'[2] Not surprisingly, this has instigated many scholars to search for 'significant variations in how the [precautionary] principle is formulated, interpreted and implemented,' as pointed out by Fisher, who perceived an academic endeavour to spot 'precaution everywhere.'[3] Finding variations in the application of the precautionary principle is not problematic per se, for the flexibility of the outcomes that can be achieved through a precaution-based decision-making is of the essence of this principle. But the randomness of the results is rather troublesome and incompatible with

* Guilherme J. S. Leal is an environmental and climate change lawyer with over 20 years of practice in Brazil. He holds a master's degree in Energy Law from the University College London, UK, and in Environmental Law from the George Washington University, USA. He lectures on Environmental Law and Climate Change Law in postgraduate courses at the Pontifical Catholic University of Rio de Janeiro, Brazil.

1 United Nations Framework Convention on Climate Change (adopted 9 May 1992, entered into force 21 March 1994) 1771 *UNTS* 107, art 3(3).

2 Cass Sunstein, *Laws of Fear: Beyond the Precautionary Principle* (CUP 2008) 18.

3 Elizabeth Fisher, 'Precaution, Precaution Everywhere: Developing a 'Common Understanding' of the Precautionary Principle in the European Community' (2002) 9(1) *Maastricht Journal of European and Comparative Law* 7.

 | DOI:10.1163/9789004690974_017

this process' rationale. Yet, many inconsistencies are found in the application of this principle, including in Brazil, where Justice Fux, of the Federal Supreme Court (STF), once complained that 'the precautionary principle is employed indiscriminately as a black box from which various legal outcomes can be drawn.'[4]

In the realm of climate change, *ambition* is the new black box. Ambitious mitigation pledges can be spotted everywhere. Indeed, as scientific consensus on the climate emergency is being built around robust evidence that the world is falling short in the efforts required to limit global warming to 1.5°C,[5] the idea of ambition permeates virtually every aspect of modern society, including political discourses;[6] social claims;[7] economic assessments;[8] business plans;[9] judicial disputes;[10] and laws and regulations.[11] However, it is hard

---

4 *ANPT et al v Brazil*, ADI 4066, Judgment of 24 August 2017, available at <https://redir.stf.jus.br/paginadorpub/paginador.jsp?docTP=TP&docID=14452232&prcID=2607856>.

5 Lee et al, 'Summary for Policymakers', in IPCC, *Climate Change 2023: Synthesis Report. Contribution of Working Groups I, II and III to the Sixth Assessment Report of the Intergovernmental Panel on Climate Change* (IPCC 2023), mentioning that it is 'likely that warming will exceed 1.5°C during the 21st century and make it harder to limit warming below 2°C'.

6 Ministério do Meio Ambiente e Mudança do Clima (MMA), 'Marina anuncia na ONU correção da meta climática brasileira: Compromisso retoma ambição apresentada no Acordo de Paris, alterada pelo governo anterior', *Notícias* (1 November 2023) available at <https://www.gov.br/mma/pt-br/noticias/marina-anuncia-na-onu-correcao-da-meta-climatica-brasileira>.

7 Tatjana Stankovic, Jon Hovi & Tora Skodvin, 'The Paris Agreement's Inherent Tension between Ambition and Compliance' (2023 10 *Humanities and Social Sciences Communications* 550 ('Parties to the Paris Agreement face mounting social pressure to raise their ambition').

8 World Economic Forum (WEF), 'Bold Measures to Close the Climate Action Gap: A Call for Systemic Change by Governments and Corporations' (2024) available at <https://www3.weforum.org/docs/WEF_Bold_Measures_to_Close_the _Climate_Action_Gap_2024.pdf> ("Governments must urgently close the gaps in national ambition and action").

9 The Science-Based Targets initiative (SBTi), for example, is a collaboration between several entities that aim to "lead the way to a net-zero economy, boost innovation and drive sustainable growth by setting ambitious, science-based emissions reduction targets" (available at <https://sciencebasedtargets.org/>).

10 In 2022, the IPCC acknowledged that, if successful, climate litigation 'can lead to an increase in a country's overall ambition to tackle climate change' (Pathak et al, 'Technical Summary', in *Climate Change 2022: Mitigation of Climate Change. Contribution of Working Group III to the Sixth Assessment Report of the Intergovernmental Panel on Climate Change* (CUP 2023) 125.

11 Eg Brazil's Interministerial Committee on Climate Change's (ICCC) Resolution No. 5/23 ('Provides for the correction of Brazil's Nationally Determined Contribution (NDC) to the Paris Agreement aiming at reestablishing the level of ambition of the NDC presented in 2015, in terms of the absolute values of GHG').

to identify amongst all those usages a common understanding of the term, mainly because, as it stands now, the idea of ambition is predominantly self-determined. Therefore, ambition, like precaution, is at risk of being 'employed indiscriminately,' as Justice Fux put it.

The development of a common understanding of ambition is challenging, for it is a multifaced issue of global scale, underpinned by conflicting interests of all possible natures. Indeed, the urgent call for ambitious transformations to push the world towards a meaningful and just transition to a low-carbon society stems from manifold factors, ranging from science-based proofs revealing that a point of no return for action is looming[12] to value-based demands for behavioural changes to tackle a 'moral crisis' posed by climate change.[13] Somewhere within this large spectrum of driving forces behind climate ambition lies the Paris Agreement, an international treaty whereby its Parties have committed to pursue ambitious measures to mitigate GHG emissions.[14] Accordingly, 'to strengthen the global response to the threat of climate change,'[15] States shall 'prepare, communicate and maintain' successive Nationally Determined Contributions (NDC s) according to their 'highest possible ambition,' as well as 'pursue domestic mitigation measures' to enforce at the national level those self-imposed obligations.[16]

Therefore, for climate ambition undertaken at the international sphere to be translated into obligations at the national and subnational levels, States ought to take effective domestic measures, which may include, *inter alia*, substantial revision of the legal landscape on climate change and the creation of new regulations to inform GHG emitters' behaviours, both public and private. This is critical to enforce the Paris Agreement and related instruments, especially in jurisdictions rooted in the civil law tradition (such as Brazil), where conducts are primarily guided by a systemic body of written acts passed by the Legislative branch and regulated by the Executive branch.[17]

---

12 António Guterres, 'Point World towards Solutions, Show Need to End Global Heating with Cold, Hard Facts, Secretary-General Tells Intergovernmental Panel on Climate Change', UN Doc SG/SM/21722 (13 March 2023) ('Our world is at a crossroads—and our planet is in the crosshairs. We are nearing the point of no return; of overshooting the internationally agreed limit of 1.5°C of global warming. We are at the tip of a tipping point').

13 Rafidah Rahman, 'Active Inaction: Why the Climate Crisis is a Moral Crisis' (2022) 28(1) *Local Environment* 1.

14 UN, *Adoption of the Paris Agreement* (Decision 1/CP.21, Annex), FCCC/CP/2015/10/Add.1 (2016).

15 Paris Agreement, art 2.

16 Paris Agreement, arts 4(2) and 4(3).

17 Following the civil law tradition, the Judicial branch does not create laws, but rather construes the laws and regulations passed by the Legislative and Executive branches,

However, there is a serious 'implementation gap' between NDCs and domestic actions, as revealed by the first global stocktake under the Paris Agreement.[18] According to Hale et al, regulation may help filling this gap, mostly with regards to corporate responsibilities: 'net-zero regulations—understood here as rules that require firms to align to the mitigation goals in Articles 2 and 4 of the Paris Agreement by reducing emissions in the near term to reach a long-term state of net zero—are a critical piece of the broader "implementation gap" identified in the first global stocktake.'[19] Thus, regulating corporate climate ambition is arguably a key measure to shape expected conducts and enforce them.

Brazil's National Policy on Climate Change is in place since 2009, but it lacks clear-cut rules ordering private companies to mitigate or neutralise GHG emissions. Although this act has set a relevant legal framework, its general aspirational provisions fail to put forward explicit commands to inform GHG emitters' conducts. In December 2024, the National Congress passed the Law No 15,042/24, creating the Brazilian Emission Trading Scheme (BETS), an important step in that direction. But the Law is yet to be regulated and the subject may become a contentious political field, so it is hard to foresee when this regulation will be approved. Besides, the incumbent President Lula da Silva's administration is striving to pass a cross-cutting climate plan with comprehensive strategies on mitigation and adaptation. This plan is expected to lay down multi-sectorial directives on these subjects, but it is not possible to foresee whether it will be fully operational at once. Against this backdrop, in the short term, corporate climate litigation in Brazil is less likely to be grounded on breaches of direct climate change regulation, and more likely to rely on general goals and principles of climate policies and plans, as well as analogies with environmental law cases. This is a challenging situation for the Judiciary, which may be at

ordering their application according to its interpretation. Despite its basis in the civil law tradition, Brazil's judicial system has been influenced to some extent by the common law's use of precedents. In this regard, case law has contributed to the development of the Brazilian environmental law in the last few decades and is likely to influence the shaping of climate change law.

18 UN, *Outcome of the first global stocktake* (Decision 1/CMA.5), FCCC/PA/CMA/2023/16/Add.1 (2024).

19 Thomas Hale, Thom Wetzer, Selam Kidane Abebe, Myles Allen, Amir Amel-Zadeh, John Armour, Kaya Axelsson, Ben Caldecott, Lucilla Dias, Sam Frankhauser, Benjamon Franta, Cameron Hepburn, Kennedy Mbeva, Lavanya Rajamani, Steve Smith & Rupert Stuart-Smith, 'Turning a Groundswell of Climate Action into Ground Rules for Net Zero' (2024) 14 *Nature Climate Change* 306.

risk of being accused of being politically motivated to stand up as a climate activist or to back off as a climate laggard.

This chapter argues that the Paris Agreement's normative account of 'ambition', being informed by the 'highest possible' standard set forth in Article 4(3), and the States' duty to 'pursue domestic mitigation measures' under Article 4(2), may serve, in Brazil, as legal grounds to force both Legislative and Executive branches to employ their best efforts to enact, within the boundaries of their powers, climate laws and regulations as domestic mitigation measures, especially in view of their 'constitutional normative duty to protect fundamental rights,' as recognised by the STF.

## 2 Climate Ambition and Regulation

Article 4(2) of the Paris Agreement states that its 'Parties shall pursue domestic mitigation measures'[20] to ultimately achieve the 'highest possible ambition' set forth in Article 4(3).[21] The use of the term 'shall pursue' implies a deliberate choice by the Parties to create an obligation of conduct that compels States to carry out all appropriate measures to push them towards the non-binding mitigation target established in their NDC s. In this context, regulation is a critical means to fulfil climate ambition, for it bridges the gap between broad pledges undertaken at the international level and concrete conducts required at the domestic level.

### 2.1 *States' Duty to Pursue the Highest Possible Ambition through Regulation*

Although the term 'ambition' had 'entered the lexicon of international climate law,' Duvic-Paoli argues that its concept 'remains poorly understood.'[22] Some

20 Paris Agreement, art 4(2). Each Party shall prepare, communicate and maintain successive nationally determined contributions that it intends to achieve. Parties shall pursue domestic mitigation measures, with the aim of achieving the objectives of such contributions.

21 Paris Agreement, art 4(3). Each Party's successive nationally determined contribution will represent a progression beyond the Party's then current nationally determined contribution and reflect its highest possible ambition, reflecting its common but differentiated responsibilities and respective capabilities, in the light of different national circumstances.

22 Leslie-Anne Duvic-Paoli, 'International Law: A Discipline of Ambition' (2023) 36(2) *Leiden Journal of International Law* 233. See also Eckard Rehbinder, 'Ambition as a Legal Concept in the Paris Agreement and Climate Litigation: Some Reflections' (2022) 52

scholars have sought to provide a detailed examination of the matter, but, while this chapter acknowledges the valuable classifications proposed by some of them,[23] Mayer's analysis of two alternative approaches seems particularly useful for the purposes of this chapter. He addresses ambition as (i) 'expected outcome,' ie the mitigation target intended to be achieved by a State within a certain timeframe, and (ii) 'level of effort,' ie a standard of conduct to be carried out by a State as means to achieve a target.[24] The latter approach will inform this study about the States' duty to enact regulations in order to fulfil ambitious mitigation goals.

Ambition as 'expected outcome' is essentially a *target*. According to Hilson, 'a climate target will invariably be expressed as a numeric figure, often as a percentage reduction from a baseline year, and for the most part to be achieved by a certain date.'[25] Understanding climate ambition as a combination of a 'substantive numeric target' and 'the time at which it is to be reached,'[26] (i) on one hand, can be a practical way to scrutinise emission reduction trajectories, but, (ii) on the other hand, can be problematic, given, for example, the lack of consensus about what 'substantive' means. Defining the relevance of a mitigation target can be controversial, particularly because of its self-determined nature. Indeed, under the Paris Agreement, sovereign States have a large margin of discretion when setting their targets based on their 'common but differentiated responsibilities and respective capabilities, in the light of different national circumstances.'[27] Eventually, this 'denotes whichever ambition a state decides for itself is its highest possible ambition,' as Zahar observes.[28] And this subject can be even more difficult when it enters into the discussion about the extent to

*Environmental Policy and Law* 377 ('the content and meaning of "ambition" are far from being agreed upon').

23 Eg Alexander Zahar, 'Collective Obligation and Individual Ambition in the Paris Agreement' (2020 9(1) *Transnational Environmental* Law 165.

24 Benoit Mayer, 'The "Highest Possible Ambition" on Climate Change Mitigation as a Legal Standard' (2024) 73(2) *ICLQ* 285.

25 Chris Hilson, 'Hitting the Target? Analysing the Use of Targets in Climate Law' (2020) 32(2) *Journal of Environmental Law* 195–220.

26 For instance, Stiell argues that 'renewed ambition means commitments marked by specific and concrete targets and milestones that will deliver the unprecedented social and economic transition to keep 1.5°C alive, even if we temporarily breach that limit over the next five years' (Simon Stiell, 'Ambitious and Accelerated Climate Action: A Blueprint for Course Correction', *UN Chronicle* [19 September 2023] available at <https://www.un.org/en/un-chronicle/ambitious-and-accelerated-climate-action-blueprint-course-correction>).

27 Paris Agreement, art 4(3).

28 Zahar (n 23).

which a State's ambitious target would express its 'fair share' on a global scale.[29] In any event, regardless of the ambition rate defined by a State, it will not constitute a binding obligation of result under the Paris Agreement. Article 4(2) establishes that the 'domestic mitigation measures' to be adopted by States have 'the purpose of achieving' the NDCs' objectives, which denotes a merely aspirational nature of this provision. In other words, Article 4(2) does not aim to guarantee, as a direct result of its implementation, the achievement of the targets set in the NDCs; rather, it is meant to ensure the appropriate means to such end. As Rajamani observes, the phrase 'intends to achieve' alludes to a good faith expectation that each Party will succeed in reaching the desired contributions, without, however, requiring the expected outcome.[30] Therefore, ambition as 'expected outcome' does not create a binding obligation of result.

Ambition as 'level of effort' is a standard of conduct. Mayer explains that this approach refers to 'the stringency of the measures taken and the significance of the resulting economic and social burden.'[31] From this perspective, climate ambition is not about setting high numeric targets, but acting with the best efforts to contribute 'to strengthen the global response to the threat of climate change.'[32] In this regard, Voigt maintains that 'the concept of "highest possible ambition" expresses a standard of conduct to be exercised by Parties,' which must 'take all appropriate measures according to their capabilities ("best efforts") in order to progressively ("ongoing") achieve the protection of the interests or rights concerned.'[33] The phrase 'shall pursue' used in Article 4(2) indicates an intentional decision by the Parties to impose a legally binding duty on States, which ought to take all necessary actions to move towards the intended mitigation goal. This *pursuit* is mandatory.[34] As Rajamani put it,

29 ibid.

30 This legitimate expectation of material outcome is consistent with the principle of good faith. Regarding this matter, it is important to highlight the Vienna Convention on the Law of Treaties (promulgated in Brazil by Decree No 7,030/09), which, 'noting that the principles of free consent and of good faith and the *pacta sunt servanda* rule are universally recognized,' establishes that 'every treaty in force is binding upon the parties to it and must be performed by them in good faith' (Article 26).

31 Mayer (n 24).

32 Paris Agreement, art 2(1).

33 Christina Voigt, 'The Power of the Paris Agreement in International Climate Litigation' (2023) 32(2) *RECIEL* 237.

34 The Brazilian version of the Paris Agreement was approved by the Decree No 9.073/17. As it reads: '*As Partes devem adotar medidas de mitigação domésticas*,' which can be translated as follows: "The Parties shall adopt domestic mitigation measures'. This language is arguably more stringent than the English version, which, instead of 'shall *adopt*,' says 'shall *pursue*.' This seems to be simply a case of inaccurate translation, especially

amongst the 'many treasures to be mined in this carefully negotiated text,'[35] it must be highlighted the compulsory nature of the following actions once they are tied to the modal verb 'shall': 'prepare, communicate, and maintain' successive NDC s, and 'pursue domestic mitigation measures.' Thus, while ambition as 'expected outcome' gives rise to a good faith expectation of result, ambition as 'level of effort' creates a binding obligation of conduct (or due diligence).[36]

As Voigt points out, 'the achievement itself [of the NDC s's objectives] does not become legally binding, but Parties are under the obligation to design measures that are necessary, meaningful and, indeed, effective to function as a means to this end.'[37] For this obligation to be met, States must act with due care, which can be expressed through a myriad of measures that will vary from country to country, according to their particularities. Voigt further explains that the abovementioned obligation 'implies that Parties will need to engage in legislative and political processes with the purpose of establishing, administrating and enforcing such measures.'[38] Such *engagement*, one would add, seems to represent Article 4(2)'s duty to '*pursue* domestic mitigation measures.' Thus, it could be argued that, under the Paris Agreement, for the 'highest possible ambition' standard to be fulfilled, States must act to enable, in the best possible way and taking into account the urgency of the climate crisis, governance mechanisms that integrate climate change into their policymaking, across multiple levels and fields, as well as enforcement instruments, seeking to achieve the NDC s' goals.

In this context, regulation is a key 'domestic mitigation measure.' To secure an economically viable, legally sound, socially equitable, and environmentally

considering that the Portuguese version follows the English's wording: '*As partes devem prosseguir as medidas de atenuação interna*' (European Union, *Jornal Oficial da União Europeia*, L 282, vol 59, 19 October 2016, p 7). In any case, both the 'adoption' and the 'pursuit' of domestic mitigation measures are aimed at 'achieving the objectives' of the NDC s. Therefore, while the fulfilment of the obligation to adopt or to seek such mitigation measures at the domestic level does not guarantee, as a result of their implementation, the full achievement of the targets set in the NDC s, it surely must ensure the appropriate means to this end.

35 Lavanya Rajamani, 'Ambition and Differentiation in the 2015 Paris Agreement: Interpretative Possibilities and underlying Politics' (2016) 65(2) *ICLQ* 497. See also Lavanya Rajamani, 'The 2015 Paris Agreement: Interplay between Hard, Soft and Non-Obligations' (2016) 28 *Journal of Environmental Law* 354, and Peter Lawrence & Daryl Wong, 'Soft Law in the Paris Climate Agreement: Strength or Weakness?' (2017) 26 *RECIEL* 280.

36 Benoit Mayer, 'International Law Obligations Arising in relation to Nationally Determined Contributions' (2018) 7(2) *Transnational Environmental Law* 256.

37 Voigt (n 33).

38 ibid.

responsible pathway to decarbonising the economy, States must seek to implement proper regulations. Hence, revising the regulatory framework on climate change and setting rules to guide both public and private conducts are pivotal steps for enabling the enforceability of the Paris Agreement, particularly in jurisdictions rooted in the civil law tradition (such as Brazil), where actions are primarily—although not exclusively—governed by a body of written acts passed by the Legislative branch (laws) and regulated by the Executive branch (regulations, which embrace presidential decrees and a myriad of administrative acts issued by governmental bodies).

Regulating climate change is not a simple task, mainly because it must take place in a context of deep 'transformation of economic, political and legal frameworks and institutions that enable and sustain low greenhouse gas emissions development,'[39] which varies across different jurisdictions and legal cultures. Furthermore, it must be acknowledged that the 'architectures' of regulation, as Gunningham put it,[40] has significantly evolved in the last decades, so there is no room for 'one size fits all' regulatory solution. Climate change is a cross-cutting topic that needs a multi-dimensional approach, and regulation must suit such need. Hence, the States' duty to pursue the highest possible ambition through regulation entails the idea that, under their domestic legal systems, they must employ their best efforts to adopt proper regulatory architectures to tackle climate change in each of and all its dimensions.

### 2.2 *Implementation Gap and Corporate Voluntary Ambition*

Translating broad, international commitments into concrete, domestic measures is crucial for ensuring progress towards the Paris Agreement's long-term goals. By turning aspirational targets into legally binding obligations, regulation, under proper architectures, may serve as a key driver of meaningful action in reducing emissions and mitigating climate change. Furthermore, it has a critical role in the allocation of climate responsibilities and the shaping of diligent conducts to be followed by State and non-State actors. But, notwithstanding the relevance of regulation and other domestic measures for the Paris Agreement's purposes, in 2023, the first global stocktake revealed that 'policies implemented by the end of 2020 are projected to result in higher global greenhouse gas emissions than those implied by the nationally determined

39 ibid.

40 Neil Gunningham, 'Environment Law, Regulation and Governance: Shifting Architectures' (2009) 21(2) *Journal of Environmental Law* 179.

contributions, indicating an implementation gap.'[41] This finding reflects a complex reality created by manifold reasons. Amongst them, there are, for example, States where governments fail to enforce existing laws and policies,[42] and to pass regulations with clear commands to guide GHG emitters and stakeholders' conducts.[43] These shortcomings hinder the effectiveness of national efforts to meet climate goals, underscoring the need for more precise and enforceable legal mechanisms to bridge the gap between pledges and actions in the implementation of the Paris Agreement. In this regard, Decision 1/CMA.5 calls Parties 'to take action to urgently address this [*implementation*] gap.'[44]

Meanwhile, at least part of the regulatory vacuum is being filled by voluntary commitments undertaken by private companies and often framed as Environmental, Social, and Governance (ESG) policies[45] or Corporate Environmental Responsibility (CER) initiatives. As Gunningham points out, a conventional definition of CER' implies 'voluntary and unenforceable action beyond that which is required by law.'[46] But, he adds, such measures are taken 'as a response to public pressures and social expectations.'[47] Therefore, although voluntary initiatives aim at demonstrating a company's dedication to addressing climate change and its willingness to lead beyond regulatory mandates, self-imposed burdens often reflect one's surrender to economic pressures or social expectations.[48] But regardless of the motives that may prompt a company to pursue ESG and CER initiatives, by setting their own targets and pledging to achieve net-zero emissions, for example, they eventually comply with external wills

41 UN, *Outcome of the first global stocktake* (Decision 1/CMA.5), FCCC/PA/CMA/2023/16/Add.1 (2024).

42 Reinhold Gallmetzer, 'Providing Evidence to Support Strategic Climate Enforcement and Litigation', in Rodríguez-Garavito (ed), *Litigating the Climate Emergency: How Human Rights, Courts, and Legal Mobilization Can Bolster Climate Action* (CUP2022) 255.

43 For example, Decision 1/CMA.5 '*recognizes* the role of the private sector and *highlights* the need to strengthen policy guidance, incentives, regulations and enabling conditions to reach the scale of investments required to achieve a global transition towards low greenhouse gas emissions and climate-resilient development' (UN [n 41]).

44 UN (n 41).

45 Lei Lei &Dayong Zhang, 'ESG and Corporate Climate Actions', in Wu, Zhang & Ji (eds), *Climate Finance. Climate Change and Energy Transition* (Springer 2024) 227.

46 Neil Gunningham, 'Corporate Environmental Responsibility: Law and the Limits of Voluntarism', in McBarnet (ed), *The New Corporate Accountability: Corporate Social Responsibility and the Law* (CUP 2007) 476.

47 ibid.

48 Analysing NDC's ambition, Duvic-Paoli observes that, 'seen as a response to global challenges, ambition is wanted and needed: COP decisions call for 'stronger and more ambitious climate action,' thus, 'at best, declarations of ambition offer a proof of good will and a commitment to co-operate.' Duvic-Paoli (n 22).

and position themselves as proactive actors in the fight against climate change, in the absence of stringent regulatory frameworks. Thus, while regulatory structures are still developing, voluntary initiatives may play a crucial role in advancing climate goals and setting benchmarks for corporate responsibility. In this vein, Hale et al notice that, 'despite their shortcomings, voluntary commitments can, under the right conditions, pave the way for mandatory rules. Indeed, in the climate realm, we are already starting to see the beginnings of such a "conveyor belt".'[49]

In the context of climate change, a central element in assessing a company's commitment is its *ambition*. While this does not refer to the 'highest possible ambition' standard of Article 4(3)—which is directed to States in the context of the preparation, communication, and maintenance of their NDCs—ambition is nonetheless widely expected from the corporate sector.[50] In this context, the Science Based Targets initiative (SBTi) stands as one of the leading frameworks that translates the Paris Agreement's goals into actionable, company-specific mitigation plans, operating under the slogan 'driving ambitious corporate climate action.'[51] This initiative provides businesses with a structured pathway for emissions reduction in line with the Paris Agreement's objectives and has been embraced by thousands of companies globally. Such quality standards play a critical role in shaping the ambition level of corporate climate commitments and significantly influence best practices within the market.[52]

Notwithstanding the role of private initiatives in 'pav[ing] the way for mandatory rules'[53] and enhancing corporate engagement in the decarbonisation of the economy and the energy transition, the appropriateness of several technical methodologies used to assess the contribution of voluntary mitigation actions to the objectives of the Paris Agreement have come under scrutiny. Much of the criticism against voluntary initiatives stems from a perceived lack of transparency, with claims regarding restricted access to the information and

49 Hale et al (n 19).

50 See, for example: United Nations High-Level Expert Group on the Net Zero Emissions Commitments of Non-State Entities, *Integrity Matters: Net Zero commitments by Businesses, Financial Institutions, Cities and Regions* (2023) available at <https://www.un.org/sites/un2.un.org/files/high-level_expert_group_n7b.pdf> ('Non-state actors must lobby for positive climate action and not against it. By working with governments to create strong standards, non-state actors can help create an ambition loop and ensure a level playing field for ambitious net zero pledges and to further de-risk a speedy transition and maximise the economic benefits of rigorous net zero alignment').

51 SBTi (available at https://sciencebasedtargets.org/).

52 Hale et al (note 19).

53 ibid.

data employed in formulating companies' mitigation plans.[54] Furthermore, concerns have been raised in Brazil over the reportedly insufficient attention to social impacts and the rights and interests of Indigenous communities, particularly in the context of carbon credit generation projects within the voluntary market—which have, in some instances, resulted in judicial disputes.[55] And some governmental bodies have also joined the choir of critics to the voluntary carbon market and taken a stance to slow down negotiations for carbon credits originated from projects in Indigenous lands. In April 2024, Brazil's federal body responsible for protecting Indigenous peoples' interests (FUNAI) issued a public statement 'advising indigenous peoples not to proceed with negotiations on carbon credit projects with private entities,' which has come along with a key remark: 'while guidelines and regulations are not in place.'[56]

My purpose in raising these disputes is not to discuss the merits or legitimacy of their claims (although, incidentally, they seem to be rather extreme), but to illustrate that complex issues, such as climate change, are inherently contentious, with litigation likely to escalate, mainly in the vacuum of regulations. In light of this, while voluntary initiatives generate collective benefits and should be encouraged, regulation may enhance dispute resolution. Undoubtably, there is 'an unprecedented regulatory challenge' ahead of us, while 'policymakers, regulators and companies will need to turn the groundswell of voluntary action into rigorous, cohesive and fair ground rules for the economy.'[57] However, Hale et al highlight that mandatory rules would provide

---

54 Anders Bjørn, Joachim Peter Tilsted, Amr Addas & Shannon Lloyd, 'Can Science-Based Targets Make the Private Sector Paris-Aligned? A Review of the Emerging Evidence' (2022) 8 *Current Climate Change Reports* 53, and Mark Roelfsema, Takeshi Kuramochi & Michel den Elzen, 'Comparing the ambition of EU companies with science-based targets to EU regulation-imposed reductions' (2024) 21 *npj Climate Action* 3.

55 *AMOREMA and AMORETGRAP v Sustainable Carbon at al*, ACP 1045416-11.2021.4.01.3900, filed in 2021 before the Federal Court of Pará, available at <https://climatecasechart.com/non-us-case/amorema-e-amoretgrap-vs-sustainable-carbon-and-others-carbon-credits-and-extractive-reserves/>.

56 FUNAI, *Posicionamento da Funai sobre créditos de carbono em terras indígenas* (1 April 2024) available at <https://www.gov.br/funai/pt-br/assuntos/noticias/2024/posicionamento-da-funai-sobre-creditos-de-carbono-em-terras-indigenas>. In this same vein, on 8 August 2024, the Federal Public Prosecutor's Office in the State of Amazonas issued a Legal Recommendation (No 1/24), advising public and private entities to suspend ongoing carbon credit projects in indigenous lands 'while regulations on the subject are not in force' (Ministério Público Federal (MPF), 'MPF recomenda suspensão de todas as atividades de crédito de carbono/REDD+ em territórios no Amazonas' [8 August 2024] available at <https://www.mpf.mp.br/am/sala-de-imprensa/noticias-am/mpf-recomenda-suspensao-de-todas-as-atividades-de-credito-de-carbono-redd-em-territorios-no-amazonas>).

57 Hale et al (n 19).

benefits: (i) 'they are less readily reversible;' (ii) mandatory rules level the playing field;' and (iii) 'mandatory rules can be enforced legally, while voluntary systems largely rely on public scrutiny and reputational risk to drive action.'[58]

## 3 The Brazilian State's Duty to Regulate on Climate Change

Brazil, as a leading developing country, plays a major role in the international climate change regime, and, at the domestic level, has its own National Policy on Climate Change, approved in 2009. Other nationwide, climate-related rules have been enacted ever since, but, while they might have strengthened some comprehensive, framework goals and principles, the Brazilian climate law still lacks clear-cut commands ordering private companies to mitigate or neutralize GHG emissions at a national, multi-sectorial level. As mentioned, BETS' law has been passed very recently and is not yet operational. Thus, taking into account the Brazilian State's 'constitutional duty to protect fundamental rights' (as ruled by the STF), provided their omission, a case can be made for compelling both the Legislative and Executive branches to employ their best efforts to adopt proper laws and regulations on corporate climate responsibilities.

### 3.1 *The Brazilian Climate Change Legal Landscape*

As mentioned, Brazil's climate change law lacks binding, clear-cut rules compelling private companies to mitigate GHG emissions. This does not mean that the Brazilian regulators have been completely negligent about climate mitigation in business. But the subject has been governed in a limited manner. To illustrate this, this chapter outlines some of the highlights of the Brazilian climate change legal landscape, including (i) the international regime embraced by the domestic law; (ii) the climate change policy at the national level; (iii) chief market-driven regulations; and (iv) a new cross-cutting climate plan the incumbent administration seeks to put in force.

#### 3.1.1 UN Climate Regime and the Brazilian NDC

Brazil is a Party to the UNFCCC and related treaties, ie 1997 Kyoto Protocol and 2015 Paris Agreement.[59] Therefore, the UN Climate Regime has been

58 ibid.

59 Brazil has incorporated the UN Climate Regime into the domestic legislation through the following acts: (i) the UNFCCC: Executive Decree No 2,652/98; (ii) the Kyoto Protocol: Executive Decree No 5,445/05; and (iii) the Paris Agreement: Executive Decree No 9,073/17.

incorporated into Brazil's domestic law, and its provisions are binding at all federative levels (federal, state, and municipal). Furthermore, 'the commitments undertaken by Brazil through the UNFCCC, the Kyoto Protocol, and other climate change-related documents to which it eventually becomes a signatory' must be taken into account, as framework directives, in the interpretation and implementation of the 2009 National Policy on Climate Change.[60] Such commitments include the obligations laid down in the Paris Agreement and the Brazilian NDCs.

Under its Paris Agreement's duties, Brazil has communicated to the UNFCCC secretariat four NDC versions: (i) in 2015, President Dilma Rousseff's administration submitted the Brazilian intended Nationally Determined Contribution (iNDC), which, under the paragraph 22 of Decision 1/CP.21, was converted into NDC once Temer's administration presented, in 2016, Brazil's instrument of ratification of the agreement;[61] (ii) in 2020, Bolsonaro's administration put forward an 'updated' version of the NDC, less ambitious than the previous one, which give rise to criticisms and litigation;[62] (iii) in 2022, Bolsonaro's administration presented a 'second updated' version of the NDC;[63] and (iv) in 2023, Lula's administration submitted the third update of the NDC.[64] A new NDC was submitted to the UNFCCC secretariat in 2024, in the context of COP29.

---

60 Law No 12,187/09, art 5(I).

61 The NDC and related 'updated versions' are available at <https://www.gov.br/mma/pt-br/assuntos/mudanca-do-clima/NDC>. In the original NDC, Brazil took into account the estimated levels of GHG emissions in 2005 (2.1 $GtCO_2eq$) to commit to pursue an economy-wide reduction of 37 percent by 2025 (thereby reaching the amount of 1.3 $GtCO_2eq$) and, as an indicative contribution, of 43 percent by 2030 (1.2 $GtCO_2eq$).

62 According to this new document, the 2025 target (37 percent reduction) was maintained and the 2030 target (43 percent reduction), rather than indicative contribution, became a commitment. Moreover, the new NDC stated that these goals would be 'compatible with an indicative long-term objective of reaching climate neutrality in 2060.' This 2060 net-zero pledge was anticipated to 2050, as explained in a letter submitted on 31 October 2021 to the UNFCCC secretariat. This NDC was widely criticised because, although it presented the same reduction targets, revisions of the 2005 baseline led to increases in the absolute emissions (See Caio Borges, Caroline Prolo & Emilio Lèbre La Rovere, *Análise Científica e Jurídica da nova Contribuição Nacionalmente Determinada (NDC) Brasileira ao Acordo de Paris* (2021) available at <https://climaesociedade.org/wp-content/uploads/2022/06/Analise-Cientifica-e-Juridica-da-nova-Contribuicao-Nacionalmente-Determinada-NDC-Brasileira-ao-Acordo-de-Paris-1-1.pdf>).

63 This version confirmed the 2025 mitigation pledge (37 percent reduction), raised the 2030 target (from 43 to 50 percent reduction), and highlighted its 'long-term objective to achieve climate neutrality by 2050.'

64 Based on the 2005 emissions, it reaffirmed (i) the commitment of reaching the total amount of 1.3 $GtCO_2eq$ by 2025 (48,4% reduction) and of 1.2 $GtCO_2eq$ by 2030 (53,1% reduction); and (ii) the 'long-term objective to achieve climate neutrality by 2050.'

The domestic effects and enforceability of the Paris Agreement and NDC s have already been recognised by the Brazilian Judiciary. In 2022, in a case challenging the 2020 version of Brazil's NDC, the 4th Panel of the 3rd Region's Court of Appeals held that (i) the Paris Agreement, when incorporated into the Brazilian legal system by Executive Decree No 9,073/17, has been granted the status of law under the national legal system; and (ii) the NDC, rather than being exclusively a diplomatic act to which Brazil would be bound in the international sphere, is primarily an internal act, enforceable and justiciable at the domestic level.[65] And in 2022, the STF further strengthened the legal clout of environmental law treaties (such as the Paris Agreement). In a landmark ruling on the government's negligence in the management of the National Fund on Climate Change, the court held that environmental law treaties are a type of human rights treaty and, therefore, must enjoy a 'supra-legal' status, which places them above ordinary laws passed by the Legislative branch.[66] Thus, in Brazil, the Paris Agreement has a 'supra-legal' status, above the National Policy on Climate Change.

Despite the Judiciary's recognition of the 'supra-legal' status of the Paris Agreement and the enforceability and justiciability of this treaty and the NDC at the domestic level, these obligations primarily apply to States, which bear direct responsibilities under the treaty's provisions. When it comes to private companies, however, the application of such obligations is far more challenging and would require more expansive interpretations of the relevant provisions. Furthermore, the four 'versions' of the NDC have a common excerpt: 'the ["economy-wide absolute"] targets will be translated into policies and measures to be detailed and implemented.' This provision, along with Article 4(3) of the Paris Agreement, strengthens the idea that the Brazilian State has the duty to pursue proper regulations addressing multi-sectorial mitigation.

#### 3.1.2 National Climate Change Policy

Brazil's Constitution, promulgated in 1988, does not make explicit reference to the protection of the climate, but it enshrines fundamental, intergenerational environmental rights. In this regard, Article 225 states that 'all have the right to an ecologically balanced environment, an asset of common use and essential

---

65 *Six Youths v Minister of Environment et al*, Popular Action No 5008035-37.2021.4.03.6100, filed on 13 April 2021 before the 14th Federal Civil Court of São Paulo, Judgment of 7 June 2024, available at <https://climatecasechart.com/non-us-case/six-youths-v-minister-of-environment-and-others/>.

66 *PSB et al v Brazil (on Climate Fund)*, ADPF 708, Judgment of 7 January 2022, available at <https://climatecasechart.com/non-us-case/psb-et-al-v-federal-union/>.

to a healthy quality of life, and both the government and the society have the duty to defend and preserve it for present and future generations.' Notwithstanding the lack of explicit reference in the Constitution to the protection of the climate system, the STF has already recognised the government's constitutional duty to promote it.[67]

Furthermore, climate-related issues have been incorporated, explicitly and implicitly, into national and subnational legislation, as either a central or incidental element. Although some laws and regulations have addressed climate change as a core subject, climate change law is generally understood within the broader context of environmental law.[68] Scotford and Minas have suggested a very useful classification of climate legislation (ie direct or indirect),[69] which this chapter applies below for practical purposes.

The National Policy on Climate Change (passed by Law No 12,187/09) is the most obvious example of 'direct climate legislation,' for its 'primary purpose (...) is to achieve climate policy objectives.'[70] This act created a comprehensive framework for tackling climate change in Brazil, providing for key concepts, principles, guidance, objectives, directives, instruments, and institutional arrangements. Amongst its provisions, Article 3 is noteworthy, for it (i) enshrines the prevention and precautionary principles in its *chapeau*, and (ii) states that 'everyone has the duty to (...) reduce the impacts of anthropogenic interference on the climate system' (item I), and that 'measures to foresee, avoid, or minimise the identified causes of climate change' must be carried out (item II).[71] While it could be argued that these provisions reflect an effort to establish fundamental guidelines to be followed by 'everyone' (Article 3(I) of the National Policy on Climate Change), it is equally plausible to contend that they remain broad and programmatic, lacking the operational specificity

67 ibid.

68 Joana Setzer, Guilherme Leal & Caio Borges, 'Climate Change Litigation in Brazil: Will Green Courts Become Greener?', in Alogna, Bakker & Gauci (eds), *Climate Change Litigation: Global Perspectives* (Brill 2021) 143.

69 Eloise Scotford & Stephen Minas, 'Probing the Hidden Depths of Climate Law: Analysing National Climate Change Legislation' (2018) 28(1) *RECIEL* 67.

70 ibid.

71 Direct climate legislation also comprises laws that explicitly take into account climate change issues, even though they were designed for non-climate purposes. The 2012 Forest Code (Law No 12,651/12), one of Brazil's main environmental laws, is such an example. It includes, amongst its guiding principles, Brazil's sovereign commitment to preserve the integrity of the climate system for the benefit of present and future generations (Article 1-A, sole paragraph, I). Additionally, the National Energy Policy (Law No 9,478/1997) lays down, amongst its objectives, the goal to 'mitigate emissions of GHG and pollutants in the energy and transport sectors' (Article 1, XVIII).

required to impose concrete obligations on private companies. This absence of clear regulatory content seems to undermine attempts to hold the private sector accountable under the current climate framework.[72] The new Law No 15,042/24 (BETS) will be key for establishing and implementing private companies' mitigation targets, but, as mentioned, it is yet to be regulated.

Other laws 'intersect with climate change but do not address it explicitly.' According to the definition established by Scotford and Minas, they may be regarded as 'indirect climate legislation.' This is the case, for example, of the 1981 National Environmental Policy (Law No 6,938/81), which laid down a nationwide framework for comprehensive environmental protection. This act provides for, *inter alia*, a strict civil liability regime (regardless of fault) for environmental damages, whereby direct and indirect polluters may be compelled to bear the cost of repairing environmental damages and compensating those affected thereby. Under such regime, courts have been applying a far-reaching definition of 'indirect polluter.' In this regard, according to Brazil's High Court of Justice, 'to determine the cause of an urban-environmental damage and hold co-defendants jointly and severally liable, the following persons must be treated equally: whoever acts; whoever fails to act when should have acted; whoever is indifferent to others' actions; whoever remains in silence when should have denounced; whoever finances others' actions; and whoever enjoys benefits from others' actions.'[73] Anyone who falls into this vast array of conditions and persons may be held liable, not only strictly, but also jointly and severally.

Despite being an environmental law per se, the National Environmental Policy is the legal foundation for Brazil's main climate change lawsuits. Therefore, in climate change litigation, the Brazilian courts are likely to consider environmental law precedents, where the legal concepts of damages, causation and liability have been extensively examined in disputes involving pollution. In this vein, it is worth noting that, according to Resolution No 433/21 of the National Council of Justice, 'when holding one liable for environmental damage, the judge must consider, amongst other aspects, the impact of this damage on global climate change.' However, the translation of the environmental strict, joint and several liability regime to climate-related cases must be made

72 In 2010, the federal environmental agency (IBAMA) enacted an administrative rule (Normative Instruction No. 12/10) determining that mitigation and compensation of GHG emissions should be assessed within the environmental permitting processes. However, such norm not only failed to lay down concrete guidance on such matters, but have never been consistently applied by IBAMA.

73 Superior Court of Justice, Special Appeal No 1.071.741-SP (Rapporteur: Justice Herman Benjamin) Judgment of 24 March 2009, available at <https://www.stj.jus.br/websecstj/cgi/revista/REJ.cgi/ATC?seq=4715617&tipo=0&nreg>.

*cum grano salis*, and regulation could help define proportional measures in this regard.

### 3.1.3 Market-Driven Climate Regulation

With the rise of corporate voluntary pledges in the last years, and the need of information to allow society and stakeholders to scrutinise them, several corporate socially responsible conducts became subject to regulation. To some extent, this represents a typical evolution of guidelines that, as they gain legitimacy and recognition as best practices, are subsequently incorporated by the State as new binding legal standards. As a result, this transformation enhances the positive externalities of these practices and help separating climate leaders from climate laggards,[74] thereby contributing to broader societal benefits. Such initiatives are mainly related to the enhancement of transparency measures and the disclosure of information on ESG practices and climate-related risks and opportunities.

In this regard, the following norms are noteworthy: (i) in 2021, the National Monetary Council (NMC) and the Brazilian Central Bank (BCB) passed a package of norms binding to all financial institutions operating in Brazil, regulating the financial institutions' duties (i.a) to elaborate 'Social, Environmental and Climate Responsibility Policies,' laying down principles and directives to inform their activities and decisions (NMC Resolution No 4,945/21), and (i.b) to manage and disclose climate-related risks and opportunities concerning their activities, according to the TCFD's recommendations[75] (NMC Resolution No 4,943/21, BCB Resolution No 139/21, and BCB Normative No 153/21);[76] (ii) also in 2021, the Brazilian Securities and Exchange Commission (CVM) enacted its Resolution No 59/21 (reissued with amendments in 2022, through Resolution No 87/22), establishing substantial innovations in the informational regime

74 Neil Gunningham & Darren Sinclair, *Leaders and Laggards: Next-Generation Environmental Regulation* (1st edn, Greenleaf 2002).

75 Financial Stability Board's Task Force on Climate-Related Financial Disclosures (TCFD), *Final Report: Recommendations of the Task Force on Climate-related Financial Disclosures* (2017) available at <https://assets.bbhub.io/company/sites/60/2021/10/FINAL-2017-TCFD-Report.pdf>.

76 It is also worth noting that, in 2014, following the first NMC regulation on the matter (Resolution No 4,327/14), the Brazilian Federation of Banks (FEBRABAN) published its Normative Act SARB No 14/14, setting forth the banking sector's self-regulation programme for the development and implementation of socio-environmentally responsible policies. After an amendment that took place in 2020 (by means of FEBRABAN's Deliberation No 31/20), the obligation to follow the TCFD's recommendations was incorporated into that Normative Act.

for issuers of securities;[77] and (iii) in 2023, CVM issued its Resolution No 193, concerning the preparation and disclosure of sustainability-related financial information reports, based on the international standards issued by the International Sustainability Standards Board (ISSB)[78]—at first, the preparation and disclosure of reports based on ISSB standards will be voluntary, but, for publicly traded companies, this will become mandatory starting in 2026.

Such rules, as seen, regulate the duty to disclose information about climate risks and actions taken to address them. But they do not establish mitigation targets to be achieved by the regulated entities. The idea of setting forth GHG emissions ceilings was introduced in Brazil in 2017, by the National Biofuels Policy (RenovaBio).[79] In a nutshell, under this Law, the National Council of Energy Policy establishes annual emissions reduction targets for the downstream distribution sector, and, on an annual basis, such targets are allocated amongst individual fuel distributers according to their market shares. Individual targets are met through the verified acquisition of certified biofuel credits (Credit Decarbonisation by Biofuels—CBIO). Thus, the RenovaBio scheme has a very limited scope, insofar as its application is bound to fuel distributors, and no other sector.

In fact, due to this aspect, in February 2024, a political party filed a lawsuit in the STF challenging this Law, on the grounds that it overburdens a single sector in a disproportionate manner and breaches the principle of equity, by failing to regulate other key GHG emitters.[80] The STF has not yet decided on the merit

77 According to this Resolution, issuers of securities must regularly inform CVM, amongst other issues: (i) whether they disclose ESG information in an annual report or any other document; (ii) of the methodology and standard followed in the preparation of such report; (iii) whether the report is audited or scrutinised by a third, independent entity (which must be identified); (iv) the website where the report can be found; (v) whether the report considers key ESG performance indicators, and what the applicable material indicators are; (vi) whether the report considers the Sustainable Development Goals (SDGs); (vii) whether their reports consider the TCFD's recommendations or financial disclosures recommendations from other recognised entities that are related to climate issues; and (viii) whether they carry out GHG inventories, indicating, if applicable, the scope of emissions and the website where additional information on this subject can be found. If they fail to meet such disclosure obligations, the issuers of securities must present proper justifications.

78 ISSB issued two standards: (i) IFRS S1 General Requirements for Disclosure of Sustainability-related Financial Information, and (ii) IFRS S2 Climate-related Disclosures (ISSB, *ISSB issues inaugural global sustainability disclosure standards* [26 June 2023] available at <https://www.ifrs.org/news-and-events/news/2023/06/issb-issues-ifrs-s1-ifrs-s2/>.

79 Law No 13,576/17.

80 *PRD v Brazil (RenovaBio and Unlawful Interference in Economic Activity)*, ADI 7596, filed on 5 February 2024 before the STF, available at <https://climatecasechart.com/non-us-case/adi-7596-renovabio-and-unlawful-interference-in-economic-activity/>.

of the case, but, considering the terms of the initial pleading, important rulings on equality and proportionality in the definition of emission reduction targets are likely to place, which could have significant implications for the BETS law.

This law establishes a comprehensive cap-and-trade system. According to its text, installations and emission sources that emit more than (i) 10,000 tonnes of $CO_2$eq per year must submit annual emissions reports to the government; and (ii) 25,000 tonnes of $CO_2$eq per year must not only submit such reports but also adhere to caps to be set forth by the government. The cap will be established through a National Allocation Plan, which will involve: (i) defining a nationwide maximum emission threshold (excluding agribusiness) to be adhered to during a specified period (Commitment Period); and (ii) allocating allowances to installations and facilities emitting more than 25,000 tonnes of $CO_2$eq per year (at first, via free allocation, then, through auction processes), while ensuring total emissions do not exceed this limit. The law provides for the possibility of purchasing a limited quantity, to be defined in regulations, of carbon credits generated from certified projects in the voluntary market. Besides, a new governance framework will be regulated within the federal government dedicated to regulating, implementing, and overseeing the BETS. The law also addresses penalties to be imposed on those who violate its provisions, ranging from fines to suspension of activities and licenses.

The law will not enter into force immediately; there will be a period of up to two years for its regulation to be approved, followed by a phase that may take around three years to operationalise the necessary instruments for the full implementation of the regulated market in Brazil.

#### 3.1.4 The Prospect of a Cross-Cutting Climate Plan

The cross-cutting approach to the climate agenda was at the core of President Lula' 2022 campaign. Following his victory in the runoff, this pledge swiftly materialized in 2023 and 2024, with nearly all government ministries receiving directives on the issue. Many ministries were integrated into the Interministerial Committee on Climate Change (ICCC), established by Decree No 11,550/23 with the purpose of defining guidelines for Brazil's climate change policies. In its inaugural meeting in September 2023, the ICCC endorsed a comprehensive climate package comprising resolutions that included, *inter alia*, mandates for updating the National Policy for Climate Change, as well as the National Plan on Climate Change (Climate Plan).[81]

81 ICCC Resolution No 3/23.

Brazil's first (and only) Climate Plan was issued in 2008 and has never been revised—which prompted the filling of a lawsuit against the government, in 2021, seeking a new Climate Plan.[82] The incumbent Lula's administration embraced this task and initiated dialogues with public and private actors aiming to lay down a draft. The Climate Plan will consolidate 'the strategies, plans, and goals of the federal Executive Branch for the achievement of the objectives of the National Policy on Climate Change and the NDC goals' (ICCC Resolution No 3/23, Article 1). It will contain at least three sections: (i) mitigation, which will feature detailed Sectoral Mitigation Plans, outlining strategies tailored to different sectors; (ii) adaptation, which will also incorporate Sectoral Adaptation Plans, designed to enhance resilience across various sectors; and (iii) cross-cutting strategies, which will integrate overarching approaches and instruments aimed at achieving the objectives outlined in the preceding sections. This includes addressing the socioeconomic impacts of transitioning to climate neutrality by 2050, as well as addressing losses and damages linked to extreme climate events.

Therefore, the Climate Plan will establish fundamental guidelines that will have a significant impact on the private sector. However, it is not possible to foresee whether it will be fully operational at once. Should further regulations be required, and probably will, corporate climate litigation in Brazil is less likely to be grounded on breaches of direct climate change regulation, and more likely to rely on general goals and principles of the climate policies and plans, as well as analogies with environmental law cases.

### 3.2 *The State's Constitutional Duty to Regulate Climate Change*

Article 3 of the National Policy for Climate Change states that, when carrying out measures to achieve this policy's goals, the government will take into account a general duty to act on reducing the impacts deriving from anthropogenic interference with the climate. In addition, the government is required to take measures to anticipate, prevent and minimise human contributions to climate change, where there is reasonable scientific and technical consensus. Such measures must take into consideration, Eg (i) the different

82 *Laboratório do Observatório do Clima v Minister of Environment et al*, ACP 1027282-96.2021.4.01.3200, filed on 26 October 2021 before the 7th Federal Environmental and Agrarian Court of the Judiciary Section of Amazonas, available at <https://climatecasechart.com/non-us-case/laboratorio-do-observatorio-do-clima-v-environmental-ministry-and-brazil/>.

socio-economic contexts in which they are implemented; (ii) the different burdens on corporations and affected communities, as well as (iii) the individual responsibilities of those who emit greenhouse gases and those who suffer the impacts of climate change. By neglecting such provisions, the government may be in breach of its duty of care.

In 2022, the STF issued a landmark ruling on the government's negligence in the management of the National Fund on Climate Change. The government's omissions were highlighted by the Minister Barroso, who (i) pointed out the 'non-functioning' of the Fund and 'the failure to allocate its substantial resources for the adoption of measures to mitigate climate change, in violation of the right to a healthy environment (Federal Constitution, art 225), and international commitments to which Brazil is a Party (Federal Constitution, Article 5(2));' (ii) highlighted the 'collapse of public policies to combat climate change, undoubtedly aggravated by the Executive's omission;' and, (iii) in recognising that 'treaties on environmental law [hence, including the Paris Agreement] constitute a subset of human rights treaties,' emphasised that 'there is no legally valid option to simply omit action in combating climate change.'[83] As a result, for the first time in Brazil, it was concluded that there is a 'constitutional, supra-legal, and legal duty of the Union and elected representatives (...) to combat climate change'[84] and that, in the case under analysis, this duty was not fulfilled by the federal Executive.

In this context, the STF recognised the fundamental right to the integrity of the climate system,[85] essential to the right to an ecologically balanced environment, and the public authorities have a duty to 'ensure the effectiveness of this right,' according to Article 225 of the Constitution and Brazil's international commitments, including those undertaken within the Paris Agreement's regime.

As Justice Weber held in a dispute about the government's negligence regarding the Amazon Fund, the constitutional duty to ensure the effectiveness of the fundamental right to the integrity of the climate system requires the State to protect 'both the normative framework, which encompasses primary and secondary legislative activities (such as regulations), and the material provision of essential factual measures to enable the realization of fundamental rights.'[86] Regarding the immediate normative application of fundamental

83 *PSB et al v Brazil* (*on Climate Fund*).

84 ibid.

85 On this topic, see Ingo Sarlet, Gabriel Wedy & Tiago Fensterseifer, *Curso de Direito Climático* (Thomson Reuters 2023) 150.

86 *PSB et al v Brazil* (*on Amazon Fund*), ADO 59, Judgment of 16 August 2023, available at <https://climatecasechart.com/non-us-case/psb-et-al-v-brazil/>.

rights, Minister Weber clarified that, (i) even though such implementation 'does not directly depend on legislative acts, it requires the Executive to create the necessary conditions for its fulfilment, through both normative and factual protective measures;' and (ii) 'the protection of fundamental rights guaranteed by the Constitution sometimes requires, for their effectiveness, the enactment of administrative and legislative regulatory norms.'[87]

Therefore, tied to the aforementioned 'constitutional, supra-legal, and legal duty of the Union and elected representatives (...) to combat climate change' is the 'constitutional normative duty to protect fundamental rights,' which implies 'the enforceability of the exercise of necessary public constitutional competencies to provide the structural and material conditions for the fulfilment of those rights.'[88] Hence, it is the responsibility of the State, notably the Legislative and Executive branches, to create an appropriate regulatory framework for the effective implementation of the fundamental right to the integrity of the climate system, as guaranteed by the Constitution, domestic law, and international commitments. In the *PSB et al v Brazil* (*on Amazon Fund*) case, the STF found a 'normative state of unconstitutionality' in the actions of prevention and control of deforestation and the reduction of greenhouse gases resulting therefrom, which, according to the Court, contradicts the international and national commitments undertaken by the Brazilian State.

In light of this, considering that the effective protection of the fundamental right to the integrity of the climate system involves achieving the objectives established in the NDC, Article 4(2) of the Paris Agreement, when referring to 'domestic mitigation measures,' encompasses, *inter alia*, 'the immediate normative application of fundamental rights,' which, as seen, 'requires the Executive to create the necessary conditions for its fulfilment, through both normative and factual protective measures.' In this regard, as emphasised by Minister Weber, it is evident 'the role of the Administrator, even more so than that of the Legislator, as responsible for the imperatives of protection, materialised in normative commands (primary and secondary) and in basic factual provisions for the fulfilment of rights.'[89]

## 4 Conclusion

As seen, ambition is the new black box. Like the precautionary principle, it is at risk of being 'employed indiscriminately,' as Justice Fux put it. Therefore,

87 ibid.

88 ibid.

89 ibid.

it is critical to pursue a common understanding on this term. This is not the purpose of this chapter, but it tries to address the matter based on the concept that 'ambition' can be treated as 'expected outcome' (ie the mitigation target intended to be achieved by a State within a certain timeframe), and 'level of effort' (ie a standard of conduct to be carried out by a State as means to achieve a target). This latter approach informed the analysis of the States' duty to pursue the highest possible ambition through regulation, which would entail the idea that, under their domestic legal systems, they must employ their best efforts to adopt proper regulatory architectures to tackle climate change in a multi-dimensional manner.

The Paris Agreement's Article 4(2) states that its 'Parties shall pursue domestic mitigation measures' to ultimately achieve the 'highest possible ambition' standard set forth in Article 4(3). The use of the term 'shall pursue' alludes to a deliberate choice to create an obligation of conduct that requires States to carry out all appropriate measures to push them towards the non-binding mitigation target established in their NDCs. In this context, regulation is a critical means to fulfil climate ambition, for it bridges the gap between broad pledges undertaken at the international level and concrete conducts required at the domestic level.

According to Voigt, under the Paris Agreement's obligation to pursue the 'highest possible ambition,' States 'need to plan their climate strategies holistically and within a long-term period.'[90] In Brazil, Lula's administration is showing signs of efforts to give climate change a holistic approach, through an unprecedented cross-cutting planning. Notwithstanding, to avoid inertia or setbacks by the incumbent and next governments, it is crucial that the regulation of Brazil's NDC is recognised not merely as a discretionary act, but as a duty arising from both the Constitution and the National Policy for Climate Change, as well as the Paris Agreement, namely Article 4(2). This provision establishes the obligation to communicate successive NDCs to the UNFCCC secretariat, as well as to adopt domestic measures to achieve the objectives of the communicated NDCs.

On such grounds, both the Legislative and Executive branches can be forced to employ their best efforts to enact, within the boundaries of their powers, climate laws and regulations as domestic mitigation measures, especially in view of their 'constitutional normative duty to protect fundamental rights,' recognised by the STF, which implies 'the enforceability of the exercise of necessary public constitutional competencies to provide the structural and material conditions for the fulfilment of those rights.'

90 Voigt (n 33).

CHAPTER 17

# Climate Damage and Tort Law in Brazilian Climate Litigation

*Rafaela Martins da Rosa**

## 1 Introduction

The sense of urgency for ambitious climate action has never been higher.[1] The year 2024 ended with robust scientific indicators that reinforce the information from the Intergovernmental Panel on Climate Change (IPCC) in its latest Synthesis Report[2] regarding the limited time window for adopting truly effective actions in slowing the pace of the harmful escalation of anthropogenic climate change, boosted in this period by the conditions of the El Niño phenomenon.[3] The current language is that there is a boiling stage,[4] what in the Brazilian scenario was represented by a historic drought in the Amazon, and the passage of torrential rains followed by unprecedented floods in the southern region.[5]

* Federal Judge at the 4th Regional Federal Court

1 The Copernicus Climate Change Service (C3S) stated that the year 2024 was the hottest on record. Copernicus information can be found at https://www.copernicus.eu/en/news/news/copernicus-global-climate-report-2024-confirms-last-year-warmest-record-first-ever-above.> Accessed on: March 3, 2025.

2 IPCC, *Climate Change 2023: Synthesis Report. Contribution of Working Groups I, II and III to the Sixth Assessment Report of the Intergovernmental Panel on Climate Change* (IPCC 2023).

3 'NOAA declares the arrival of El Niño' (National Oceanic and Atmospheric Administration, 8 June 2023), available at <https://www.weather.gov/news/230706-ElNino>, accessed on 12 November 2023.

4 'Hottest July ever signals "era of global boiling has arrived" says United Nation's chief' (United Nations 27 July 2023), available at <https://news.un.org/en/story/2023/07/1139162>, accessed on 12 November 2023.

5 'Reporting on the historic drought in the Amazon' (New York Tymes, 19th October 2024), available at <https://www.nytimes.com/2024/10/19/world/americas/south-america-drought-amazon-river.html>, accessed on 3 March 2025. Torrential rains passed through southern Brazil in May 2024: https://www.washingtonpost.com/world/2024/05/06/brazil-flooding-leaves-dozens-dead/>, accessed on 3, March 2025.

 | DOI:10.1163/9789004690974_018

Last year also presented discouraging reports of mitigation gaps,[6] insufficient and precarious adaptation measures,[7] and record spending on losses and damages,[8] with finance flows running against the urgency.[9]

At the same time, the lack of effectiveness or enforcement of the bases on which the international legal regime on climate change is founded have never been as clear. Similarly, the difficulties in imposing compliance with the necessary mitigating and adaptive actions, whether on public agents or private entities, are obvious. In light of the increased difficulties in making concrete advances, multiple initiatives have emerged to attempt to reverse humanity's journey toward the climate precipice.

In the legal field, reformulations or re-readings of the norms and tools of current legal regimes are escalating,[10] appropriately accommodating the reality and complexity[11] of climate change in applicable legal precepts, promoting possible disruptions compatible with the rule of law.[12] Additionally, there is an increasing demand[13,14] for awareness regarding the impact of climate

6 UNFCCC Secretariat, 'Nationally Determined Contributions under the Paris Agreement. Synthesis Report by the secretariat', 28 October 2024, Doc No FCCC/PA/CMA/2024/10, available at < https://unfccc.int/documents/641792>. United Nations Environment Programme, *Emissions Gap Report 2024: No more hot air ... please!* (UNEP 2024), available at < https://www.unep.org/resources/emissions-gap-report-2024>.

7 United Nations Environment Programme, Adaptation Gap Report 2024*: Come hell and high water* (UNEP 2024), available at <https://www.unep.org/resources/adaptation-gap-report-2024>.

8 Rebecca Newman & Illan Noy, 'The Global Costs of Extreme Weather that Are Attributable to Climate Change (2023) 14 *Nature Communications* 6103.

9 Simon Black, Ian Parry & Nate Vernon-Lin, 'Fossil Fuel Subsidies Surged to Record $7 Trillion' (IMF Blog, 24 August 2023) available at <https://www.imf.org/en/Blogs/Articles/2023/08/24/fossil-fuel-subsidies-surged-to-record-7-trillion>.

10 Michael B Gerrard & Joseph A MacDouglad, 'An Introduction to Climate Change Liability Litigation and a View to the Future' (2013) 20(1) *Connecticut Insurance Law Journal* 153, 162.

11 Richard J Lazarus, 'Super Wicked Problems and Climate Change: Restraining the Present to Liberate the Future' (2009) 94 *Cornell Law Review* 1153.

12 Elizabeth Fisher, Eloise Scotford & Emily Barritt, 'The Legally Disruptive Nature of Climate Change (2017) 80(2) *The Modern Law Review* 173.

13 Cinnamon Piñon Carlarne, 'The Essential Role of Climate Litigation and the Courts in Averting Climate Crisis', in Mayer & Zahar (eds), *Debating Climate Law* (CUP 2023) 111.

14 Mary C Wood, 'On the Eve of Destruction: Courts Confronting the Climate Emergency' (2022) 97(1) *Indiana Law Journal* 239.

litigation on strategic climate governance.[15] Climate cases encourage judges' decisions to be increasingly assertive when dealing with the climate emergency.[16]

The process of re-reading the precepts of normative systems to seek legally effective protection in climate matters is noticeable in the Brazilian legal environment, as is the movement for these theoretical and normative developments to be accepted in judicial decisions. Openness to the application of these resignifications depends on the courts' progressive stances to understand the complexity of climate science, and incorporate it as an indelible part of their judicial commands.[17]

Although many reflections on legal reinterpretations of climate phenomena are in full swing in Brazil, as the contributions of this collective work indicate, this chapter will focus on just one of them. The application of civil liability for damage to the climate system in the Brazilian litigation scenario will be the subject of analysis, detailing the reasons why its handling in cases should be a protagonist and a new frontier in the use of litigation as a tool to promote climate justice. Furthermore, the reasons why the Brazilian example can serve as inspiration and reference for other legal systems and their respective Courts are detailed.

Over the last three years, in Brazil it has been consolidated (in scholarship and in the case law of the Federal Supreme Court, STF) the interpretation of the constitutional protection enshrined in the human right to a balanced environment for present and future generations as incorporating protection of the climate system, evolving Brazilian environmental constitutionalism to climate constitutionalism.[18] This interpretation took shape in paradigmatic

15 For an overview of climate litigation around the world in 2023, see Joana Setzer & Catherine Higham, *Global Trends in Climate Litigation: 2024 Snapshot* (Grantham Research Institute on Climate Change and the Environment 2024) available at <https://www.lse.ac.uk/granthaminstitute/wp-content/uploads/2024/06/Global-trends-in-climate-change-litigation-2024-snapshot.pdf>.

16 César Rodríguez-Garavito (ed), *Litigar a Emergência Climática: A Mobilização Cidadã perante os Tribunais para Enfrentar a Crise Ambiental e Assegurar Direitos* Básicos (FGV Editora 2022).

17 Maria Antonia Tigre, Natalia Urzola & Alexandra Goodman, 'Climate Litigation in Latin America: Is the Region Quietly Leading a Revolution?' (2023) 14 *Journal of Human Rights and the Environment* 67.

18 Regarding environmental constitutionalism, see James May & Erin Daly, *Global Environmental Constitutionalism* (CUP 2015). On the evolution towards climate constitutionalism, see James May & Erin Daly, 'Global Climate Constitutionalism and Justice in the Courts', in Jaria-Manzano & Borras (eds), *Research Handbook on Global Climate Constitutionalism* (Edward Elgar 2019) 235. Detailing the phenomenon of climate constitutionalism in Latin America, see Délton Winter de Carvalho & Rafaela Martins da Rosa, 'Climate

decisions concluded by the STF in 2022 and 2023 (ie *PSB and others v Brazil* (*on Climate Fund*),[19] and *PSB and others v Brazil* (*on Amazon Fund*),[20] which reflect the Court's maturity in reading the protection due in climate matters through the lens of constitutionally protected human rights in Brazil. This decisions promoted an assertive interpretation of the recognition of climate protection as an integral part of the intergenerationl right to a balanced environment,[21] understood as a fundamental human right, and highlighted transjudicialism[22] by referring to climate precedents from other courts and the control of conventionality with the Inter-American system of human rights (applying the terms of the Recommendation No 123/2022 made by the Brazilian National Council of Justice, CNJ).[23] When referring to Inter-American Court of Human Rights precedents, the STF also endorses the understanding of the extraterritoriality of the obligation to preserve the human right to a healthy environment and the duty to avoid the production of damage.[24]

Based on the recognition that the protection of the climate system is included in the content of the fundamental right to a healthy environment, the climate system is, at the same time, established as a legal asset subject to constitutional protection in Brazil. Consequently, its violation or threat of violation compels the handling of civil liability, because civil liability regime in

---

Constitutionalism as a Foundation for Climate Litigation in Latin America' (2024) 16(1) *Journal of Human Rights Practice* 71.

19 *PSB et al v Brazil* (*on Climate Fund*), ADPF 708, Judgment of 7 January 2022, available at <https://climatecasechart.com/non-us-case/psb-et-al-v-federal-union/>.

20 *PSB et al v Brazil* (*on Amazon Fund*), ADO 59, Judgment of 16 August 2023, available at <https://climatecasechart.com/non-us-case/psb-et-al-v-brazil/>.

21 Danielle de Andrade Moreira, Ana Lucia B Nina, Carolina de Figueiredo Garrido & Maria Eduarda Segovia Barbosa Neves, 'Rights-Based Climate Litigation in Brazil: An Assessment of Constitutional Cases Before the Brazilian Supreme Court' (2024) 16(1) *Journal of Human Rights Practice* 47.

22 Regarding the origin of the term transjudicialism, see Anne-Marie Slaughter, 'A Tipology of Transjudicial Communication' (1995) 29 *University of Richmond Law Review* 99.

23 Available at <https://atos.cnj.jus.br/atos/detalhar/4305>.

24 This extraterritoriality was also highlighted by STF's Minister Cármen Lúcia, in her vote on *PSB et al v Brazil* (*on deforestation and human rights*). ADPF 760, Judgment of 6 April 2022, available at https://climatecasechart.com/non-us-case/brazilian-socialist-party-and-others-v-brazil/: 'The big question raised is the planetary responsibility that the Forest lends to the care of the Planet's climatic condition, because if its location indisputably subjects it to national sovereignty, but carbon emissions enter the atmosphere, subjecting it to the sovereignty of whoever it is. It emerges from its Brazilian sovereign care corresponding duty towards all humanity due to the impact that its preservation represents on the survival of all beings on the Planet.'

matters of environmental damage in Brazil, unlike many other legal regimes, is constitutional in scope.[25]

In Brazil, tort law to environmental issues derives directly from a constitutional norm. Article 225(3) of the Brazilian Constitution enshrines triple responsibility (civil, criminal and administrative) for all those whose conduct violates the environment. Tort law in environmental and climate matters, therefore, is a liability under public law and part of the constitutional regime, which makes the Brazilian liability system unique.

In this context, Brazilian climate litigation related to climate damage starts from the necessary assimilation that the institute of civil liability is a legal tool capable of removing from the plane of abstraction or mere moral rhetoric the principal notion about finalistic and not merely procedural duties of care on climate matters, allowing its requirement of applicability in the examination of cases submitted for consideration by domestic courts. The civil liability regime that already exists in Brazil for dealing with environmental matters makes it possible for the endless discussions about climate justice to stop being so ethereal and gain application in climate litigation.

It is also this regime that has extraordinary potential to contribute to undermining the persistence of colonialist practices in the North-South relationship, and fulminating in a logic such as that donations from significant emitters (whether public or private entities), supposedly remove legal obligations to respond for damaging the climate system. Civil liability for climate damage is an instrument that will certainly reveal that the principle of not causing harm, or not continuing to cause harm, does not just have a moral or rhetorical sense.[26] Causing damage to the climate system and continuing to do so is an unlawful act. This act is subject to judicial liability, and this is what the handling of tort law in Brazil is largely about.

Clearly, to enable the maximum potential of civil liability for climate damage is capable of offering to climate litigation, there is a need for skillful theoretical (doctrine), normative (law) and jurisprudential (precedents) maturity to facilitate the coherent application of its premises in the context of actions that discuss climate damage.

At the current moment, in climate tort law cases in *common law* systems, there is a general resistance to understanding the elementary notion of climate damage as damage to the climate system considered in itself, in an autonomous

25 José Joaquim Gomes Canotilho, Ingo Wolfgang Sarlet & Gilmar Mendes, *Comentários à Constituição do Brasil* (3rd edn, Saraiva 2023).

26 Marco Grasso & Richard Heede, 'Time to Pay the Piper: Fossil Fuel Companies' Reparations for Climate Damages' (2023) 6(5) *One Earth* 459.

and demonstrable way (as pure ecological environmental damage), regardless of personal or property injuries. Climate damage is the damage directly suffered by the climate system, materialized by its warming from anthropogenic emissions. It is the most relevant category of damage that exists, because this occurrence undermines the functionality of the climate system, on which humanity depends as a premise of existence.

Some judges from other jurisdictions are reluctant to recognize what would be a duty subject to civil liability in climate matters, perfectly described by New Zealand judges in the *Smith v Fonterra Co-Operative Group Limited*[27] case as the 'new tort,' suggested as a 'breach of duty' (the duty to 'cease contributing to damage to the climate system'). As described below, in the opposite direction, this evolution in interpretation is already a reality in the Brazilian tort law system.

Brazil, whether on a theoretical level, in current regulations and in norms originating from its own Judiciary, or in concrete cases decided or in progress on responsibility for climate damage, indicates that it has assimilated that climate damage directly suffered by the climate system is a damage of a unique type, which affects the functionality of the climate system as a planetary totality considered. The civil liability regime for climate damage, therefore, will certainly require dialogue between the courts and climate science,[28] as detailed as follows.

This chapter is structured in this way. Section 2, after this introduction, addresses the fundamental importance of the legal category of damage for advances in effectiveness in climate litigation. Section 3 analyzes the notion of climate damage, as well as its specificities, and the reception and adherence of the tort law regime for environmental damage to climate damage in Brazil. It is reinforced how the conjunction between doctrine, norms, and jurisprudence is receptive to the concept of climate damage, and its independence and autonomy in the analysis of indirect damages that affect people and property. Section 4 addresses the importance of this distinction within the scope of the judicial system by Resolution No 433 of the National Council of Justice. Section 5 analyzes the current and future prospects of litigation over climate damage. Section 6 highlights prospective implications from the consolidation of the

27 *Smith v Fonterra Co-Operative Group Limited et al*, [2020] NZHC 419, [2021] NZCA 552 & [2022] NZSC 35, Judgment of the High Court of New Zealand of 7 February 2024, available at <https://climatecasechart.com/non-us-case/smith-v-fonterra-co-operative-group-limited/>.

28 Jessica A Wentz, Delta Merner, Benjamin Franta, Alessandra Lehmen & Peter C Frumhoff, 'Research Priorities for Climate Litigation' (2023) 11(1) *Earth's Future* 1.

concept of climate damage, notably in the possible causal links between direct climate damage and losses and damages associated with climate change. In conclusion, it is reinforced that the civil liability regime for Brazilian climate damage can be a progressive example of how to reconcile the rule of law with the effectiveness of climate litigation in promoting justice.

## 2 The Fundamental Importance of Damages for the Advancement of Climate Litigation

Climate litigation moves through many avenues and explores multiple possible approaches.[29,30] Despite the increasing handling of numerous ways based on the most varied legal institutes, tort law arguments have emerged since the early stages of doctrinal discussions on the phenomenon,[31] as well as the arguments of demands in judicial courts on the subject.[32,33]

In common law jurisdictions, there is a prevailing view that limits the use of tort law to private law and the relationship between private rights.[34] It is not surprising that the liability regime for damages, even when it involves environmental damage, is still predominantly anchored in the respective civil codes.[35]

---

29 United Nations Environment Programme, *Global Climate Litigation Report: 2023 Status Review* (UNEP 2023).

30 Joana Setzer & Catherine Higham, *Global Trends in Climate Change Litigation: 2023 Snapshot* (Grantham Research Institute on Climate Change and the Environment 2023).

31 David Grossman, 'Warming Up to a Not So Radical Idea: Tort-based Climate Change Litigation' (2003) 28(1) *Columbia Journal of Environmental Law* 1.

32 Daniel A Farber, 'Basic Compensation for the Victims of Climate Change' (1 December 2006) University of California, Berkeley Public Law Research Paper No 954357, available at <https://ssrn.com/abstract=954357>.

33 'Nevertheless, the very attempt to run it may yield benefits for the tort system. As this section argues, the effort to fit the major of all collective action problems into the traditional paradigm of tort reveals much about how that paradigm more generally needs to shift.' Douglas A Kysar, 'What Climate Change Can Do About Tort Law' (2011) 41(1) *Environmental Law* 1.

34 Maria Lee, Climate Change Tort (28 August 2015) available at <https://ssrn.com/abstract=2695107 or http://dx.doi.org/10.2139/ssrn.2695107>.

35 In a different sense, the STF, when judging Theme 0999, highlighted that environmental damage does not correspond to a mere civil offense, so that it enjoys special attention for the benefit of all the community, therefore prevailing the constitutional principles of protection, preservation, and reparation of the environment. See *Public Prosecutor's Office et al v Orleir Messias Cameli et al*, Special Appeal No RE 654.833/AC, Theme 0999, Judgment of 20 April 2020, available at <https://portal.stf.jus.br/processos/detalhe.asp?incidente=4130104>.

Visible damages are required in specific or determinable people, which can be concretely demonstrated.[36] There is, therefore, an attachment to substance, which reflects an attachment to procedure, on issues of legitimacy (standing). These are conceptual barriers that make it extremely difficult to deal with civil liability in climate matters. In paradigmatic first demands based on civil liability, following the example of *Native Village of Kivalina v. ExxonMobil Corp*,[37] the still incipient development of climate attribution science also made the success of cases even more difficult.[38]

However, the institute of civil liability has always permeated the argumentative bases of climate litigation for a fundamental reason. Regardless of the legal tradition it is anchored, and the level of openness to discussions of public law, at its base lies one of the most relevant categories in law, damage, and one of the most prominent principles in law, the no harm principle.[39]

Damage is a central category to any attempt at legal regulation that aims to enable the legal system to act and react in the face of conduct considered unacceptable, whether to people or to natural or built elements in the surrounding area. Regardless of the legal system or the tradition on which it is based, damage is a central and indispensable element, insofar as it is only from the observation of its occurrence or threat of occurrence that it can, strictly speaking, be discussed about the imputation of measures with recognized legal coercion.[40]

As Kysar and Farber have already reflected, while civil liability only focuses on private relationships and private damages, it is not very capable of dealing with climate issues.[41,42] On the contrary, when civil liability for damages is conceived as a public law regime, protecting public and common goods, such as the climate system, it reveals itself to be an indispensable tool for advancing climate litigation. This is already the vision in the Brazilian civil liability system for damage to the environment, and now with the recognition of the climate system as part of the environment, responsibility for damage to the

36 Peter Cane, *The Anatomy of Tort Law* (Hart Publishing, 1997).

37 *Native Village of Kivalina & City of Kivalina v ExxonMobil Corp*, Supreme Court of the United States, Case No 12–1072, available at <https://climatecasechart.com/case/native-village-of-kivalina-v-exxonmobil-corp/>.

38 Henry Weaver & Douglas A Kysar, 'Courting Disaster: Climate Change and the Adjudication of Catastrophe' (2017) 93(1) *Notre Dame Law Review* 295, 329.

39 Sandrine Maljean-Dubois, 'The No-Harm Principle as the Foundation of International Climate Law', in Mayer & Zahar (eds.), *Debating Climate Law* (CUP 2023) 15.

40 Paulo de Bessa Antunes, *Dano Ambiental: Uma Abordagem Conceitual* (2nd edn, Atlas 2015).

41 Kysar (n 33).

42 Daniel A Farber, 'Tort Law in the Era of Climate Change, Katrina and 9/11: Exploring Liability for Extraordinary Risks' (2009 43 *Valparaíso University Law Review* 1075.

climate system will make use of an already consolidated trajectory of legal understanding.

Therefore, in the context of climate change, the damage that would first need well understanding is the damage directly affected by the set of natural resources and their interactions, specifically what climate change law calls, based on the reading of the IPCC's scientific concepts, the climate system, as an indivisible totality. At the basis of any evolution in the handling of tort law would be the requirement to make the damage to the macro-good climate system the protagonist, and not the damage that people and property have indirectly suffered, are suffering, or will suffer as a consequence of the ongoing climate damage (the warming of the climate system).

The evolution of responsibility for climate damage relies on the significant advances in climate attribution science and source attribution science.[43] With the proper handling of these advances, in their translation into legal proceedings, it is possible to conclude how much the problem of climate change is collective, the sum of actions (public and private) that cause unique damage to the climate system. This unique damage, with advances in source attribution science, makes it possible to identify and individualize emission sources, as well as mitigation efforts.

The possibility of individualizing emission mitigation duties in the judicial decision, for example, also shows the importance of conventional and constitutional arguments (many of those grouped as rights-based arguments)[44] being able to connect in specific cases with arguments of liability for damages. It is no coincidence, as Peel and Osofsky have already highlighted, that the judicial decisions in the landmark *Urgenda Foundation v. State of the Netherlands*[45] and also in the first decision on *Milieudefensie et al. v. Royal Dutch Shell plc.*[46]

---

43 Michael Burger, Jessica Wentz,& Radley Horton, 'The Law and Science of Climate Change Attribution' (2020) 45(1) *Columbia Journal of Environmental Law* 57.

44 Juan Auz, 'Human Rights-Based Climate Litigation in Latin America' ('Oxford Human Rights Hub Blog', 14 April 2021) accessed 11 November 2023.

45 As Peel and Osofsky observed, 'while Urgenda pursued a number of different lines of argument in the case (including alleging breaches of constitutional rights under the Dutch Constitution, of human rights under the European Convention on Human Rights, and of the Netherlands' obligations under international and European climate change law), the Court's decision centred on the general negligence provisions of the Dutch Civil Code,' Jacqueline Peel, Hari Osofsky & Anita Foerster, 'A "Next Generation" of Climate Change Litigation? An Australian Perspective' (2017) 9(3) *Oñati Socio-Legal Series* 275.

46 As mentioned in the first decision on the *Milieudefensie case*, 'every emission of $CO_2$ and other [GHG], anywhere in the world and caused in any way, contributes to this damage and its increase.' *Milieudefensie et al v Royal Dutch Shell plc*, ECLI:NL:RBDHA:2021:5339,

cases, judges defined concrete (individualized) mitigation duties imposed, respectively, on a public entity[47] and a private entity based on the reading and handling of civil wrongdoing and liability standards to civil duties not to cause harm to the environment.[48] More recently, the Belgian court in *vzw Klimaatzaak v Kingdom of Belgium et al* also used the civil norm of liability for damages to individually define the mitigation effort in Belgium and some regions of the country.[49] The Belgian judges, in fact, expressly differentiated the damage to the environment as result of GHG emissions (direct climate damage) from the indirect damages that the warming of the climate system caused and will cause to people. These cases reinforce the central role of the legal category of damage to the climate system as a way of rationalizing individual duties imposed by judicial decisions.

The theoretical and normative application by the courts that places the damage to the climate system as damage of an autonomous nature and affecting the planet is welcomed in the Brazilian legal regime and jurisprudence. This is because since the legal regime on damage to the environment and its liability was structured, the doctrine and decisions of the Brazilian courts assumed the autonomy of damage to the value in itself of the environment, and states that a damage to the environment would be both a damage to the environment itself and, indirectly, could also be damage to people and property specifically

The Hague District Court, Judgment of 26 May 2021, para 4.4.37, available at <http://climatecasechart.com/climate-change-litigation/non-us-case/milieu defensie-et-al-v-royal-dutch-shell-plc/>.

47 This was also the legal understanding established by the Administrative Court of Paris when considering the dispute proposed by Notre Affaire à Tous and others, in the decision handed down on February 3, 2021. On that occasion, the Administrative Court of Paris recognized that the French State, in the commitments not respected as part of the first carbon budget foreseen in the regulation that was questioned by the fact, should be considered responsible for part of what the French Administrative Court called 'ecological damage linked to the direct impact of excess gas emissions greenhouse effect on global warming.' The damage referred to by the judges there, as happened in *Milieudefensie*, is the damage directly imposed on the macro-legal climate system, insofar as the French court stated that this damage would directly relate to the impact that excess French emissions will have in global warming. See *Notre Affaire à Tous Les Amis de la Terre, and Oxfam France v BNP Paribas* (2023), Judicial Court of Paris (France), available at <https://climatecasechart.com/non-us-case/notre-affaire-a-tous-les-amis-de-la-terre-and-oxfam-france-v-bnp-paribas/>.

48 See also Tim Baxter, 'Urgenda-Style Climate Litigation Has Promise in Australia' (2017) 32(3) *Australian Environment Review* 70.

49 *vzw Klimaatzaak v Kingdom of Belgium et al*, Process No 2021/AR/15gs, 2022/AR/737 & 2022/AR/891, Judgment of the Court of Appeals of 30 November 2023, available at <https://climatecasechart.com/non-us-case/vzw-klimaatzaak-v-kingdom-of-belgium-et-al/>.

affected by the environmental damage.[50] This acceptance now allows concrete advances to be observed in litigation related to civil liability for climate damage, and how this assimilation process occurs is the subject of attention in the following topic.

## 3 The Concept and Specificities of Climate Damage and Its Adherence to the Brazilian Tort Law for Environmental Damage

This topic is divided into a few items. First, the concept of damage to the climate system is clarified and, afterwards, the specificities of this concept and its framing to the liability regime for environmental damage in Brazil are detailed.

### 3.1 *Conceptualizing Damage to the Climate System*

The application of civil liability for climate damage depends, as a premise, on understanding what is conceptualized as climate damage, as damage that results from the intolerable interference of GHG caused by anthropogenic emissions in the functioning of the climate system.

When the 'inaugural norm' of international climate change law was drafted[51] (ie the United Nations Framework Convention on Climate Change, UNFCCC), the treaty aimed to reproduce the consensus in the scientific community, raising the intergenerational protection of the climate system to the status of protected by the international legal regime of climate change.[52] The climate system was posited, in respect and endorsement of the scientific description, as a global, systemic unit with dynamic behavior resulting from the dilated spatio-temporal interactions of all its components (atmosphere, oceans, cryosphere, land surface, and biosphere).[53]

---

50 Antonio Herman Benjamin, 'Responsabilidade Civil pelo Dano Ambiental' (1998) 3(9) *Revista de Direito Ambiental* 48.

51 David Freestone, 'The United Nations Framework Convention on Climate Change—The Basis for the Climate Change Regime', in Carlarne, Gray & Tarasofsky, (eds). The Oxford Handbook of International Climate Change Law (OUP 2016) 97.

52 The Preamble of the UNFCCC states that the change in the Earth's climate system and its negative effects are a common concern of humanity, implying that States Parties are collectively determined to 'protect the climate system for present and future generations.'

53 The climate system is defined as the totality of the atmosphere, hydrosphere, biosphere and geosphere and their interactions. The term 'hydrosphere' is used in the text to designate, together, both the oceans and the area of ice or cryosphere. The climate system is identified and named by the IPCC in AR1 as the interactive junction of the atmosphere, the oceans, the ice or cryosphere, the geosphere, and the biosphere. See Houghton,

The main objective of the convent was to avoid dangerous anthropogenic interference with the climate system (article 2). The Brazilian regulatory framework incorporated the intergenerational protection of the climate system in alignment with the ratification of international climate norms.[54]

In Brazil, by translating the core of the scientific transposition and possible meanings of the term environment, since the original wording of article 225, a multidimensional legal concept has also been adopted.[55] It was understood that the term environment would encompass both natural and artificial aspects, as well as the so-called historical and cultural elements of the surroundings, and this has been repeatedly stated in the doctrine and jurisprudence of the Brazilian apex courts.[56]

Thus, the concept of environment for Brazilian law is even broader than the concept of climate system, which is limited to the sum and interactions of the natural elements that compose it (atmosphere, oceans, cryosphere, land surface, and biosphere). The notion of climate system does not consider, for example, the cultural environment, which is component of the broad concept of environment adopted in the Brazilian constitutional and infra-constitutional legal regime.[57] Similar understanding seems to have been adopted by the United Nations General Assembly (UNGA) in Resolution

---

Jenkins & Ephraums (eds), *Climate Change—The Scientific Assessment* (CUP 1991), available at <https://www.ipcc.ch/report/ar1/wg1/>, accessed 8 November 2023.

54 Federal Law No 12,187/2009 (National Policy on Climate Change, PNMC), referred to the same nomenclature as the Convention, the requirement for intergenerational protection of the climate system as an objective of the Brazilian climate change policy. The legal duty of everyone to act for the benefit of present and future generations was established to reduce the impacts resulting from anthropogenic interference with the climate system (art 3). Furthermore, the Brazilian Forest Code, materialized by Law no 12,651/2012, in its article 1, 'A', sole paragraph, stated that the forestry legal framework would meet, among its principles, the principle of integrity of the climate system for the well-being of present and future generations. This incorporation of the climate system as a legal asset then began to be endorsed by the jurisprudence of the Brazilian Superior Court of Justice (STJ), and enshrined by the STF in the precedents cited in the introduction.

55 Tiago Fensterseifer & Ingo Wolfgang Sarlet, *Direito Constitucional Ambiental: Constituição, Direitos Fundamentais e Proteção do Ambiente* (2nd edn, Revista dos Tribunais 2012) 45.

56 Ana Maria Moreira Marchesan, *A Tutela do Patrimônio Cultural sob o Enfoque do Direito Ambiental* (Livraria do Advogado 2007).

57 Article 216 of the Brazilian Constitution sets out that the cultural environment as part of the comprehensive concept of environment. Several Brazilian statutory norms complement this constitutional provision, namely Decree-Law No 25/37, Decree-Law No 4,146/42 (which provides for the protection of fossil deposits), Law No 3,924/61 (on archaeological heritage), Law No 7,542/86 (on underwater heritage), Law No 12,343/10 (National Culture Plan Law), and Law No 13,018/14 (Living Culture Policy Law).

No A/77/L58, when requesting an advisory opinion from the International Court of Justice (ICJ) on the obligations of States with respect to climate change. In the two initial questions formulated, the climate system was expressed mentioned as part of the concept of environment, referring to the request to 'duties to protect the climate system and other parts of the environment,' and the legal consequences applicable to those who cause damage to the climate system.[58]

From the condition of the climate system as a legal asset worthy of protection, and as an inseparable part of the concept of environment, comes the consideration of legal autonomy already understood as public environmental damage (gender), as well as incident to climate damage (species).

In the international normative context, since the World Charter for Nature of 1982,[59] the intrinsic value of the environment and the need for its preservation as a legal asset in itself have already been affirmed. Still a year before the UNFCCC was drawn up, the UN Security Council approved Resolution 687, on the damage caused by Iraq to Kuwait following the invasion that triggered the Gulf War.[60] This Resolution, by providing for the applicable legal liability regime, distinguished and separated personal damage from ecological damage, establishing, as the doctrine states, reparation obligations for both.[61,62,63] Farber reflects that this Resolution innovated within the scope of the international legal regime, precisely to the extent that it expressly provided for the possibility of compensation for damage to the environment itself.[64]

In legislation subsequent to the UNFCCC, it is also seen that the autonomy[65] of the environmental legal good is praised when conceptualizing its respective

58 UNGA Res 77/276 (29 March 2023) 'Request for an Advisory Opinion of the International Court of Justice on the Obligations of States in respect of Climate Change', UN Doc A/77/L.58, available at <https://www.icj-cij.org/sites/default/files/case-related/187/187-20230412-app-01-00-en.pdf>.

59 Available at <https://digitallibrary.un.org/record/39295>, accessed on 12 September 2023.

60 UNSC Resolution 687 (8 April 1991) UN Doc S/RES/687.

61 Cymie Payne, 'UN Commission Awards Compensation for Environmental and Public Health Damage from 1990–91 Gulf War' (2005) 9(25) *Insights*, available at <https://www.asil.org/insights/volume/9/issue/25/un-commission-awards-compensation-environmental-and-public-health-damage >, accessed 10 November 2023.

62 Daniel A Farber, 'Basic Compensation for Victims of Climate Change' (2007) 155 *University of Pennsylvania Law Review* 1605.

63 Philippe Sands, Jacqueline Peel, Adriana Fabra & Ruth McKenzie, *Principles of International Environmental Law* (3rd edn, CUP 2012) 724–725.

64 Farber (n 61).

65 Eg according to Article 1246 of the French Civil Code, 'any person responsible for ecological damage is obliged to compensate it'. Article 1248 of the Civil Code of France provides that 'action for compensation for ecological damage is open to any person with the capacity and right to act, such as (...) associations approved or created at least five years ago,

harm. Directive 2004/35/CE of the European Parliament and the Council, for example, defines the concept of damage to the environment as an intrinsic value, regardless of any harm to people, whether in their health or well-being, whether in your assets.[66] In the words of the Directive, 'ecological damage' would translate into a 'significant and measurable adverse change in the state of a natural asset or the quality of its services.'

The Brazilian tort law for environmental damage endorses this understanding.[67] The expression 'environmental damage' in Brazil is considered damage from more than one dimension. It encompasses both damage directly affected by the environment in itself[68] (which has an autonomous liability regime) and damages that derive from harmful effects on the environment on other protected assets (people, such as life, health, well-being, material, and intangible heritage).[69]

Consequently, in specifying climate damage as a type of diffuse environmental damage that affects the set of elements of the climate system, the planetary character of the climate system is recognized, and the impossibility that climate damage can be divided into spaces or territorial jurisdictions of lesser extent. Consequently, the threat or violation of this right is also a violation on a scale that is not merely transboundary, but essentially global or planetary.

It is understood that climate damage is damage on a planetary scale, requiring planetary judges[70] and planetary litigation.[71] Even if the injury or violation is questioned before a domestic court, it is necessary to understand that it is dealing with a global legal asset.

---

in date of initiation of the process, which aims to protect nature and the defense of the environment.'

66 Directive 2004/35/EC of the European Parliament and of the Council, of 21 April 2004, on environmental responsibility in terms of prevention and repair of environmental damage.

67 Álvaro Luiz Valery Mirra, *Ação Civil* Pública *e a Reparação do Dano ao Meio Ambiente* (2nd Juarez de Oliveira 2004).

68 A similar understanding is also shared in Portugal: see JJ Gomes Canotilho, *Introdução ao Direito do Ambiente* (Universidade Aberta 1998) 25; Carla Amado Gomes, 'De Que Falamos Quando Falamos de Dano Ambiental? Direito, Mentiras e Crítica' (2010) 17 *Revista de Ciê*ncias Empresariais e Jurídicas 11, 12.

69 *LDC-SEV Bioenergia v Jos*é Maria Chagas Damasceno, Special Appeal No REsp 1.373.788/SP, Judgment of the STJ of 3 June 2014, Rapporteur: Paulo de Tarso Sanseverino, available at <https://www.stj.jus.br/websecstj/cgi/revista/REJ.exe/ITA?seq=1327704&tipo=0&nreg=201300708472&SeqCgrmaSessao=&CodOrgaoJgdr=&dt=20140610>.

70 Herman Benjamin 'Laudato Si, a Ecologização da Justiça Social e o Juiz Planetário' (2021) 7(2) *Journal of Institutional Studies* 560.

71 Louis J Kotzé, '*Neubauer et al. versus Germany*: Planetary Climate Litigation for the Anthropocene? (2021) 22(8) *German Law Journal* 1423.

This can materialize, for example, in each case of illegal deforestation or forest fire, when it is argued that these conducts added to emissions that add to the direct damage on the climate system. Also emissions that add to the damage always will be important in the assessment of those projected to occur outside the area of domestic jurisdiction, but from products such as fuels extracted for subsequent export. When considering damage to the climate system as a global damage, domestic judges would always evaluate public and private decisions related to all scopes of emissions.[72] As the Queensland Land Court accurately summarized in *Waratah Coal Pty Ltd v Youth Verdict Ltd et al* when not recommending the approval of a new coal mine in the country: 'this case is about Queensland coal, mined in Queensland, and exported from Queensland to be burnt in power stations to generate electricity. Wherever the coal is burnt the emissions will contribute to environmental harm, including in Queensland.'[73,74]

This certainty comes from scientific information that confirms the natural causality (the linear relationship) between anthropogenic emissions and warming of the climate system as a whole. And this natural causality becomes the legal causality required to attribute responsibility for contributing to climate damage.

### 3.2 *The Certainty of the Natural (and Legal) Causality of Climate Damage*

With regard to the causal link of climate damage, and its requirement for proof in court, the Brazilian regime once again harmonizes the evidentiary basis from scientific information summarized by the IPCC, with the legal requirement of causality for attribution of responsibility. Climate damage identifies a single type of causal source as originating and linearly responsible for the deleterious impact on the functionality of the climate system. The skillful action

---

72 Understanding the global nature of climate damage and the analysis of emissions exported to other countries was the subject of detailed analysis by the Queensland Land court in the *Waratah Coal* case: *Waratah Coal Pty Ltd v Youth Verdict Ltd et al*, [2020] QLC 33; [2021] QLC 4; [2021] QLC 36; [2022] QLC 3; [2022] QLC 4, Queensland Land Court Judgment of 25 November 2022, available at <https://climatecasechart.com/non-us-case/youth-verdict-v-waratah-coal/>.

73 ibid 72.

74 The same certainty was recently affirmed by the Oslo District Court in *The North Sea Fields Case*, when demanding an administrative assessment from the Norwegian authorities on fossil combustion emissions (occurring in other countries) from fuels extracted in the North Sea. *The North Sea Fields Case*, App No 23-099330TVI-TOSL/05, Oslo District Court, Judgment of 16 May 2024, available at <https://climatecasechart.com/non-us-case/the-north-sea-fields-case-greenpeace-nordic-and-nature-youth-v-energy-ministry/>.

and conduct that causes harmful and direct anthropogenic interference in the climate system is identified in the emission of GHG into the atmosphere. This is the human action that triggers a harmful cascade movement in all other components of the climate system.[75]

Since August 2021, the scientific consensus and the use of the expression 'established fact' by the IPCC[76] have been established when designating that the warming of the climate system is generated because of (is caused by) emitting anthropogenic GHG. This is the most important conclusion for legal purposes from the science of climate change attribution. Because it is in the linear and direct causality between the anthropic source and the deleterious effects felt, in its planetary unit, by the climate system.

This causal proof meets the causal link assumptions required in environmental matters in the Brazilian liability system. Liability for environmental damage (which includes climate damage) is objective in the Brazilian regime, and all it takes to demonstrate the causal link is recognition of the ability of the activity to carry out the damage, contribute to, or even exacerbate the risk of damage.[77]

Capable climate-damaging activity is an activity that generates GHG emissions or suppresses sinks. In Brazil, these conducts are considered potentially

75 This understanding was highlighted by Justice Brian Preston in *Gray v The Minister for Planning and Ors*. AUSTRALIA: 'There is a causal link between the Project's cumulative GHG emissions and climate change and its consequences. Project cumulative GHGs are emissions that will contribute to the global total of GHG concentrations in the atmosphere. Total global GHG concentrations will affect the climate system and impact climate change. The Project's cumulative GHG emissions are therefore likely to contribute to future changes to the climate system and the impacts of climate change.' *Gray v The Minister for Planning and Ors*, Case No 40870/2006, New South Wales Land and Environment Court, Decision of 27 November 2006, available at <http://climatecasechart.com/non-us-case/gray-v-minister-planning-ors/>.

76 IPCC, Climate Change 2021: The Physical Science Basis. Contribution of Working Group I to the Sixth Assessment Report of the Intergovernmental Panel on Climate Change (CUP 2021) 68, available at <https://www.ipcc.ch/ report/ar6/wg1/#TS>.

77 According to Article 14, in its first paragraph, of the National Environmental Policy Law, Law No 6,938/81, the polluter is obliged, regardless of the existence of fault, to compensate or repair the damage caused to the environment and to third parties affected by his activity. The Public Ministry of the Union and States will have the legitimacy to propose civil and criminal liability actions for damage caused to the environment. This legal provision is interpreted by the STJ as enshrining objective liability, informed by the theory of integral risk, with the causal link being the binding factor that allows the risk to be integrated into the unity of the act. See *Emilia Mary Melato Gomes v Mineração Rio Pomba Cataguases Ltda,* Special Appeal No REsp 1.374.284/MG, Judgment of 30 September 2014, available at https://www.jusbrasil.com.br/jurisprudencia/stj/864823848/inteiro-teor-864823858.

polluting actions because the concept of pollution already adopted by Brazilian legislation is broad, and recognizes as pollutants both those that degrade the environment itself, and indirectly the health or well-being of people, as well as substances that directly cause harm to people.[78]

The classification of GHG as polluting agents arises from their ability to cause changes in the functionality of the climate system, regardless of measurements of the impact on human beings. The Brazilian understanding of the notion of pollution, within the scope of Climate Change Law, refers to the assimilation of the capacity of GHG to affect and, therefore, deregulate, by concentrating and not dispersing in one of the components of the system, the atmosphere, the entire way the climate system works, which directly and linearly depends on a level of concentration of GHG so as not to heat up at an accelerated rate.

In the Brazilian environmental regulatory regime and framework, since 1981, even before the Federal Constitution of 1988, the conception of what could be legally considered as pollution has already gone far beyond a restricted anthropocentric view. Article 14 of Law No 6938/81 defines pollution, in its article 3, the degradation that affects the environmental quality itself.[79] Humanity as a whole is indirectly affected by the disruption to the functionality of the climate system (today, a shock that is of an existential nature), and this is the scientific data that, related to the legal notion, definitively places GHG in the condition of pollutants.[80]

---

78 This is the meaning of Article 3 of the National Environmental Policy Law (Law No 6,938/81). Pollution is the degradation of environmental quality resulting from activities that directly or indirectly: (a) harm the health, safety and well-being of the population; (b) create adverse conditions for social and economic activities; (c) adversely affect the biota; (d) affect the aesthetic or sanitary conditions of the environment; (e) release materials or energy that do not comply with established environmental standards.

79 Paulo Affonso Leme Machado, *Direito Ambiental Brasileiro* (7th edn, Malheiros 1998).

80 Materializing these different dimensions of pollution (direct and indirect) implied by the emission of GHG, the decision handed down by the Federal Court of Rio Grande do Sul in August 2022, in the context of a climate case that postulated the cancellation of licensing for a coal mine project in the State. Among the reasons that justified the nullity of the way in which the administrative procedure was being carried out, the Federal Judge from Rio Grande do Sul expressly noted, in a separate section, that the impact of the project's emissions on the climate system had not been considered by the administrative authority, as of an analysis of the same as alignment with the demands of the Paris Agreement and the nationally determined contribution, regarding the lack of administrative analysis of the impact of emissions on human health, in violation of the guidelines proposed by Conama Resolution No 491/2018. By stating this, the decision highlights that there is a distinct analysis of the notion of pollution as an affectation of the functionality of the climate system in its entirety, which runs in parallel and concomitantly with a more restrictive analytical perspective on the consideration of direct affectation on human health due to GHG

Considering the damage to the climate system as a global and intrinsically diffuse damage also has repercussions on the legitimacy to legally process requests for accountability.

### 3.3 *Legitimacy to Sue over Climate Damage and Responsibility to Respond as a Polluter*

Furthermore, as a damage of a diffuse nature, the active procedural legitimacy to claim responsibility for direct climate damage in court is broad, guaranteeing both individuals and communities the right of access to judicial remedies. In Brazil, legislation and precedents recognize wide legitimacy for taking actions that aim to protect the environment, and that question responsibility for damage to the environment. This broad legitimacy applies to climate damage as a type of environmental damage. Civil society organizations (as envisaged in the European context by the Aarhus Convention), institutions such as public prosecutors and public lawyers, as well as individuals interested in holding agents responsible for causing damage to the climate system, can do so.

Just as the legitimacy for those bringing the actions is broad, as climate damage is damage of a diffuse nature, which results from a sum of actions (public and private, individual and collective), the Brazilian regulatory regime establishes the duty of everyone to respond jointly and severally for this diffuse damage. Consequently, plaintiffs have the ability to choose to sue one or another person responsible, so that their individual contribution to the damage can be measured (with the help of the science of source attribution) and duly held responsible. Each company emitting GHG, and every agent that promotes deforestation can be sued to respond in their individual contribution to the climate damage, even if the damage results from this sum of contributions. Brazilian doctrine and jurisprudence enshrine passive solidarity and optional joinder between all (public or private agents) who contribute to damage (calling them direct and indirect polluters).[81]

---

emissions. Precisely the macro and integral analysis of the impact on the functionality of the climate system due to the emitted anthropic action is the analysis that shapes the notion of climate damage as damage of equal dimension and of concrete measurement. See *Associação Gaúcha et al v Copelmi Mineração et al* (*Nova Seival Thermal Power Plant*), ACP 5030786-95.2021.4.04.7100, filed on 19 May 2020 before the 9th Federal Court of Rio Grande do Sul, available at <https://climatecasechart.com/non-us-case/instituto-preservar-et-al-v-copelmi-mineracao-ltda-and-ibama/>.

81 Public or collective civil action for environmental damage can be filed against a polluter, a natural or legal person, under public or private law, responsible, directly or indirectly, for an activity that causes environmental degradation (Law No 6,898/ 91, art 3[IV]), jointly obligated to pay compensation, through the formation of an optional joint venture (see

The responsibility of each and every one of them is possible to be questioned based on the certainty that it is human emissions, in their sum of contributions, that are linearly causing the intolerable warming of the climate system.

The Brazilian system of civil liability for environmental damage is receptive to the fact that there are many agents (public and private) responsible for a sum of conducts that result in climate damage. Diffuse environmental damage (which climate damage is a specie) has always been recognized by court's in Brazil as operating under 'the empire of dispersion of the causal nexus'[82] due to the plurality of individual causing sources, dispersed temporally and geographically.

Brazilian Law recognizes that environmental damage has the ability to present cumulative or synergistic effects. Specifically regarding climate damage, the duty to determine the participation of individual causal sources for GHG emissions arises from an express provision in Brazilian federal climate law, which sets out the duty to weigh individual responsibilities regarding the origin of emission sources and the effects caused on the climate.[83]

In Brazil, individualized responsibility is palpable for direct climate damage to the extent that it is possible to estimate how an individual act has affected or intends to affect the carbon stock chain, or exhaust the budget compatible with scientific demands endorsed by the STF.[84] Based on the certainty about general causality, brought as an unequivocal fact by the IPCC, it is possible to go ahead with the analysis and use of research arising from the science of attributing emission sources.

---

*Public Prosecutor's Office of the State of Mato Grosso v Clélio Nogueira Cunha*, Special Appeal No REsp 884.150/MT, Judgment of the STJ of 19 June 2008, Rapporteur: Minister Luiz Fux, available at <https://processo.stj.jus.br/SCON/jurisprudencia/toc.jsp?livre=%28RESP.clas.+e+%40num%3D%22884150%22%29+ou+%28RESP+adj+%22884150%22%29.suce>). According to the STJ, 'For the purpose of determining the causal link in environmental damage, those who do it, those who do not do it when they should do it, those who allow it to do it, those who do not care if they do it, those who finance it to do it, and those who benefit when others do it are equated.' See *Public Prosecutor's Office v Schneider*, Special Appeal No 650.728-SC, Judgment of of the Superior Court of Justice of 2 December 2009, Rapporteur: Minister Herman Benjamin, available at <https://climatecasechart.com/non-us-case/public-prosecutors-office-v-h-carlos-schneider-sa-comercio-e-industria-others/>.

82 Benjamin (n 69).

83 National Policy on Climate Change (Law No 12,187/2009), art 3(III).

84 In the judgment of case *PSB and others v Brazil* (*on Climate Fund*), the STF recognized that the Paris Agreement has supralegal normative force at the domestic level. Complying with the scientific demand that makes the goals of the Agreement viable is a law that can be required in Brazil.

In summary, the basis of the liability regime for environmental damage in Brazil is the adherent and receptive to the assessment of climate damage as a type of environmental damage that affects a specific diffuse asset (the climate system). This responsibility is considered objective[85] and requires full reparation under the Brazilian legal regime. Both direct polluters (emitting agents) and indirect polluters (for example banks financing emitting activities, public agents omitted in their duty of inspection, among others) may be sued as polluters (defendants).

Therefore, the direct climate damage, truly of a planetary dimension, is perceived and separated from the many other types of damage that affect other legal assets (life, health, property, etc.) and that directly they have a greater or lesser causal relationship with the increase in anthropogenic climate change (they are indirect climate damage).

The separate division and analysis in the litigation of damage to the climate system from indirect damage (which people and property suffer) is supported by doctrine and judicial decisions in Brazil. It should be noted that direct damage to the climate system, in this sense, does not include that caused to natural and legal persons, individually considered, and to their own and individual material or moral assets, as reflex ('ricochet') damage resulting from activities broadcasters. Although evidently subject to repair, such damages caused 'through' the environment are considered individual damages and not collective or diffuse damages, as also recognized by the STJ, which qualifies these damages as 'private environmental damages.'[86]

Finally, the demonstration of the re-reading of the tort law regime for environmental damage to accommodate the particularities of civil liability in climate matters has just been consolidated by the Brazilian Judicial Power itself. By editing a specific Resolution on the National Policy of the Judiciary in environmental matters, one topic is dedicated to establishing concrete guidelines to guide the actions of Brazilian judges in climate litigation about climate damage. This junction is detailed in the following item.

---

85 The Brazilian specific regime of environmental civil liability is based on the enshrinement of responsibility objective of the environmental degrader, that is, responsibility that does not depend on the agent's fault, based on the simple risk or the simple fact of the activity causing the environmental damage. This is precisely what is prescribed by Article 225(3) of the Constitution and Article 14(1) of Law No 6,938/1981.

86 Álvaro Mirra, 'Responsabilidade Civil Ambiental e a Jurisprudência do STJ' (2019) 20(48) *Cadernos Jurídicos* 47, and *Participação, Processo Civil e Defesa do Meio Ambiente* (Letras Jurídicas 2011) 441.

## 4 The Assimilation of the Concept of Climate Damage by the Brazilian National Council of Justice (CNJ)

In October 2021, the National Council of Justice (CNJ) issued Resolution No 433, establishing the National Policy of the Judiciary for the Environment. This Resolution addresses a wide range of environmental topics, but one of the central axes of the Policy incorporates climate protection as part of the National Policy of the Judiciary for the Environment.

This Resolution created the subject of climate litigation as a sub-subject of Environmental Law in the table of procedural classes of actions in Brazil,[87] and also established in Article 12 the possibility that the amounts charged in convictions for environmental crimes be applied to actions to mitigate climate change.

In its Article 14, Resolution No 433 consolidated the understanding of climate damage summarized here: it determined the duty of analysis by Brazilian courts, in convictions for environmental damage, of the impact of environmental damage on global climate change (the analysis of damage to climate system).

As a way of providing Brazilian judges with technical elements and to guide the concrete application of the Resolution, at the end of 2022 the National Council of Justice held a public consultation.[88] In the Call Notice for the aforementioned public consultation, the Council expressly stated that the Brazilian Judiciary, when carrying out the consultation, sought to be guided by appropriate scientific criteria (and cited the science of attribution in climate litigation), to ensure the slick environmental repair.

Subsequently, in July 2023, the presidency of the CNJ established an interinstitutional working group to monitor the implementation of Article 14 of Resolution No 433. This working group conducted a public hearing to collect economic measurement references for emissions and sink losses and prepared the Judgment Protocol for Environmental actions. The first scope, delivered in September 2023 and with the use determined by CNJ Recommendation No 145/2023, reinforced the reliability and validity of the use as a means of evidence in environmental actions of satellite images and remote sensing.[89]

The second scope, approved by the Council's board in October 2024, was commissioned to summarize the contributions received in the consultation and public hearing and provides judges with guidelines to base decisions on

---

87 The concept of climate litigation adopted by the Brazilian Unified Procedural Table was the concept adopted by Unep in the Reports on the status of global climate litigation. The subject of climate change was included as a sub-subject of Environmental Law, receiving the code 15008, https://www.cnj.jus.br/sgt/consulta_publica_assuntos.php.

88 The full Public Consultation Notice carried out by the National Council of Justice can be accessed at: https://www.cnj.jus.br/poder-judiciario/consultas-publicas/quantificacao-de-danos-ambientais/.

89 Available at <https://atos.cnj.jus.br/atos/detalhar/5278>.

quantifying climate damage. These guidelines, exposed in the CNJ Resolution No. 156 of October 2024, tend to harmonize decisions about measuring climate damage in similar situations, since the increase in the handling of climate disputes regarding responsibility for climate damage is already notable in Brazil, as detailed in the following item.

## 5 Tort Law for Climate Damage Currently in Brazilian Climate Litigation

In a survey by researchers of the current situation of Brazilian climate litigation, the handling of actions bas-ed on civil liability for climate damage is already identified as a rapidly growing movement.[90] Litigation based on civil liability for climate damage has been highlighted as the second highest number of occurrences.

Right now, handling civil liability for climate damage in legal actions is still preferably focused on practices of illegal deforestation or forest fires in Brazilian biomes. The reason for the strategic use of litigation based on liability for climate damage in forest injuries arises from the fact that emissions from deforestation are the main source of Brazilian GHG emissions,[91] and that deforestation is mostly illegal[92] in Brazil, so that discussions on the legality of the conduct that generated the damage dissipates, as does any margin of tolerability for regular emissions. Furthermore, it is concerned with containing the

90 See Danielle de Andrade Moreira, Carolina de Figueiredo Garrido, Juliana Chermont Pessoa Lopes, Paula Máximo de Barros Pinto, Victória Lourenço de Carvalho e Gonçalves, Luciana Tse Chaves Garcia Rego, Maria Eduarda Garambone Sydenstricker & Ana Paula Ricci, *Panorama da Litigância Climática no Brasil: Relatório de 2024* (JUMA/PUC-Rio 2024).

91 On March 22, 2023, the SEEG Report (Greenhouse Gas Emission Estimation System) was released, which analyzed the numbers of Brazilian emissions from 1970 to 2021, and the implications for the climate goals assumed by Brazil before the UNFCCC. The document was produced by the Climate Observatory with the contribution of IPAM (Amazon Environmental Research Institute) and other partner entities. The Report reports that Brazil emitted 2.4 billion gross tons of GHG in 2021, an increase of 12.5% compared to 2020, when the country had emitted 2.1 billion tons. Land use changes accounted for the majority of Brazilian gross emissions in 2021: 1.18 billion tons of $CO_2$ equivalent, representing 49% of the national total that year. The majority of gross emissions (92%) are caused by changes in land use, the majority of which consist of deforestation in the Amazon biome, which concentrates 77% (911 MtCO2e) of the sector's gross emissions in 2021. Full SEEG Report available at <https://www.oc.eco.br/wp-content/uploads/2023/03/SEEG-10-anos-v4.pdf>, accessed on 3 September 2023.

92 According to the Annual Report on Deforestation in Brazil—RAD 2022, more than 76 thousand deforestation alerts were validated and published by MapBiomas Alerta in the period evaluated. Of this total, signs of irregularities/illegalities were found in more than 98% of the alerts issued. The full Annual Deforestation Report (RAD) 2022 published by MapBiomas available at <http://alerta.mapbiomas.org/relatorio>, accessed 3 November 2023.

escalation of deforestation and the real risk of reaching the point of no return in the Amazon Forest and triggering its savannization.[93,94]

Thus, at the end of 2018 and beginning of 2019, following specific actions since then, the first cases centered on claims for responsibility for climate damage were filed narrating forest wood deposits without documentation of origin. The actions were filed in different courts in Brazilian states.[95,96]

---

93 Nico Wunderling, Arie Staal, Boris Sakschewski, Marina Hirota, Obbe A Tuinenburg, Jonathan F Donges, Henrique MJ Barbosa & Ricarda Winkelmann, (2022). 'Recurrent Droughts Increase Risk of Cascading Tipping Events by Outpacing Adaptive Capacities in the Amazon Rainforest' (2022) 119(32) *Environmental Sciences* e2120777119.

94 The historic drought experienced by the Amazon region in 2023 was even pointed out as factual evidence of the proximity of reaching its point of no return. Nils Bochow & Niklas Boers. 'The South American Monsoon Approaches a Critical Transition in Response to Deforestation' (2023) 9(40) *Science Advances* 1.

95 *IBAMA v Alto Norte (on ilegal wood storage)*, ACP 1000200-41.2018.4.01.3606, filed on 20 December 2018 before the Federal Court of Juína, available at <https://climatecasechart.com/non-us-case/federal-environment-agency-ibama-v-alto-norte-industria-comercio-e-exportacao-de-madeiras-ltda/>; *IBAMA v Souza Brilhante (on illegal wood storage)*, ACP 1003478-16.2018.4.01.3100, filed on 19 December 2018 before the Federal Court of Amapá, Judgment of 2 September 2022, available at <https://climatecasechart.com/non-us-case/federal-environment-agency-ibama-v-souza-brilhante-eireli/>; *IBAMA v Silmar Gomes Moreira (on illegal wood storage)*, ACP 1000469-62.2018.4.01.3903, filed on 19 December 2018 before the Federal Court of Pará (Altamira), available at <https://climatecasechart.com/non-us-case/federal-environmental-agency-ibama-v-silmar-gomes-moreira/>; *IBAMA v Seringal (on illegal wood storage)*, ACP 1000364-26.2019.4.01.3200, filed on 28 January 2019 before the Federal Court of Amazonas, Judgment of 15 August 2023, available at <https://climatecasechart.com/non-us-case/federal-environmental-agency-ibama-v-seringal-industria-e-comercio-de-madeiras-eireli/>; *IBAMA v Madeireira Madevi (on illegal wood storage)*, ACP 1000656-73.2018.4.01.3902, filed on 20 December 2018 before the Federal Court of Pará, available at <https://climatecasechart.com/non-us-case/federal-environment-agency-ibama-v-madeireira-madevi-ltda/>; *IBAMA v Madelin Madeireira Linhares (on illegal wood storage)*, ACP 1001659-42.2018.4.01.4200, filed on 20 December 2018 before the federal Court of Roraima, Judgment of 5 August 2020, available at <https://climatecasechart.com/non-us-case/federal-environment-agency-ibama-v-madelin-madeireira-linhares-ltda/>; *IBAMA v Madeira Nova Aliança (on illegal wood storage)*, ACP 1000275-31.2019.4.01.3902, filed on 28 January 2019 before the Federal Court of Pará, available at <https://climatecasechart.com/non-us-case/federal-environment-agency-ibama-v-madeira-nova-alianca-ltda/>; *IBAMA v Floresta Verde (on illegal wood storage)*, ACP 1000083-80.2019.4.01.3908, filed on 4 February 2019 before the Federal Court of Pará, Judgment of 25 March 2020, available at <https://climatecasechart.com/non-us-case/federal-environment-agency-ibama-v-industria-comercio-e-exportacao-de-madeiras-floresta-verde-ltda/>; *IBAMA v Gabriel Madeiras (on illegal wood storage)*, ACP 1000185-42.2018.4.01.3907, filed on 19 December 2018 before the Federal Court of Pará, Judgment of 5 June 2019, available at <https://climatecasechart.com/non-us-case/federal-environmental-agency-ibama-v-gabriel-industria-e-comercio-madeiras-eireli/>; *IBAMA v Siderúrgica São Luiz et al (on 'coal irregular origin')*, Process No. 1010603-35.2019.4.01.3800, filed on 2 July 2019 before the 15th Federal Civil Court of Minas Gerais, available at <https://climatecasechart.com/non-us-case/federal-environmental-agency-ibama-v-siderurgica-sao-luiz-ltda-and-martins/>.

96 *Federal Public Prosecutor's Office et al v Rezende (on deforestation and climate damage)*, ACP 1005885-78.2021.4.01.3200, filed on 7 April 2021 before the 7th Federal Environmental

In these actions, it was alleged that, among the dimensions of deleterious effects that derive from deforestation and subsequent illegal storage of wood is the harmful contribution to the warming of the climate system. The sum of illegal emissions is claimed to cause direct damage to the climate system, insofar as deforestation deprives the power of absorption of carbon from the forest and also causes the release of carbon through the loss of forest cover.

The postulations explain that the environmental damage resulting from deforestation or fire is not limited to the loss of vegetation and its impacts on the local ecosystem or biodiversity. In addition to these harmful consequences, the actions result in GHG emissions, and these emissions contribute to the warming of the global climate system. These emissions add to the climate damage directly suffered by the climate system. They, therefore, argue that the climate damage resulting from these emissions and losses from sinks must be covered by the civil liability regime in environmental matters.

In quantifying the damage, these cases, in addition to postulating the duty to restore areas, a duty that would derive from the environmental damage to the vegetation itself, added demands for compensation obligations (duty to pay for climate damage), estimated based on emissions generated by infringing conduct. They reinforce that the duty to fully repair environmental damage is consolidated in Brazilian jurisprudence, and used as a reference for charging for emissions and losses from sinks, the value of the social cost of carbon or the value of the Amazon Fund. Tree favorable decisions have already been handed down in these cases,[97,98] and others are still awaiting a decision on the merits.

In the first decisions on *IBAMA v Souza Brilhante (on illegal wood storage)* and *IBAMA v Floresta Verde (on illegal wood storage)*, judges listed the harmful effects that the conduct of illegal deforestation produced, mentioning,

---

and Agrarian Court of the Judiciary Section of Amazonas, available at <https://climatecasechart.com/non-us-case/ministerio-publico-federal-v-de-rezende/>.

97 *IBAMA v Souza Brilhante (on illegal wood storage)* (n 94), and *IBAMA v Floresta Verde (on illegal wood storage)* (n 94), both cases already referring to responsibility for climate damage.

98 One of the recent lawsuits filed to claim specific responsibility for climate damage is *IBAMA v Dirceu Kruger (on illegal wood storage)*, ACP 1037196-19.2023.4.01.3200, filed on 12 September 2023 before a Federal Court in Amazonas, Judgment of 18 July 2024, available at <https://climatecasechart.com/non-us-case/ibama-v-dirceu-kruger-illegal-deforestation-in-the-amazon-and-climate-damage/>. The plaintiff explains that climate damage is precisely the damage caused to the climate system, and that climate damage is characterized by the release of GHG emissions from deforestation. The plaintiff recognizes that the effects of the reported climate damage spread throughout Brazil, with global spread as well. The plaintiff considers that illegal emitters of GHG must be condemned to internalize the negative externality they produce to the detriment of society, and that liability litigation allows for individualized compensation due to the agent's illegitimate contribution to climate damage. The decision handed down in July 2024 recognized the merits of the claim for damages for climate change, and set compensation at R$292 million.

among others, the loss of soil nutrients, the decrease in water availability, and the illegal increase in carbon dioxide in the atmosphere. The decisions stated that compensation for the damage should, therefore, include the value of these emissions. By recognizing that the conduct caused emissions into the atmosphere, and that these emissions need to be part of the duty to repair the environmental damage, Brazilian judges assimilate the global character of the climate system, and the global character of the damage to the climate system.

When the climate dimension of the damage adds to the environmental damage, that is, for the repercussion that the emissions generated and lost sinks add to the ongoing damage to the climate system, this also represents a significant economic impact. The sum of the emission values, as well as the repair cost that incorporates the emissions, will be reflected not only in the final convictions, but also in the judicial anticipatory measures, whether to stop the harmful conduct or to guarantee the reserve of amounts that can be paid the full reparation owed by those convicted.

It is common to observe in these cases decisions about embargoes of the areas, blocking of bank accounts and constriction of assets, and also prohibition of access to bank financing for activities.[99] The judicial granting of precautionary measures such as these has the power to effectively contain the advance of deforestation in forests, stop the escalation of emissions that result from cutting down trees, and ensure that there are resources to cover all the duties imposed upon convictions.

These cases, in summary, are consolidating the analysis of responsibility for direct climate damage in Brazil. This sedimentation will probably have effects on other economic sectors with significant emissions in the country. Currently, a bill is being processed[100] to define the maximum emission limits of the activities prioritized by Federal Law No 12,187/2009 and adequate to comply with the Brazilian most recently nationally determined contribution. Certainly, emissions from these sectors may be questioned in legal actions as to whether they are within the defined limits and decarbonization targets, or

99 For example, in *IBAMA v Alto Norte* (n 94), on the preliminary decision, the judge accepted the requests for unavailability of assets (blocked bank accounts, restricted vehicles, among others), suspended the right to participate in bank financing lines, and restricted access to tax benefits granted by the public authorities. He justified his decision by stating his fear that at the end of the action there will be no way to recover the environment and return to the *status quo ante*.

100 The project for law (PL) number 412 of 2022 intends to regulate the Brazilian emissions reduction market. Available at <https://www25.senado.leg.br/web/atividade/materias/-/materia/151967>.

whether they may be considered unlawful or abuse of rights and thus contributing to cumulative effect of climate damage.[101]

Finally, the consolidation of civil liability for climate damage in Brazil also allows mechanisms to be activated that relate direct damage (warming the climate system) to losses and damages associated. That is, once the individual contribution of agents to the damage to the climate system is recognized, parts of the costs spent to prevent and repair damages that derive from climate damage and that affect people and property, can evidently be questioned in the Brazilian courts.

## 6 Future Perspectives: Connections between Contributions to Direct Climate Damage and Responsibilities for Indirect Climate Damage

As Kysar rightly reflected, judges must avoid the temptation to shy away from tort claims that are significant, complex or politically sensitive issues such as climate change. As worrying as they may be. Apparently, Kysar reinforced that these moments are precisely when the illicit act may be most necessary.[102]

The consolidation of the climate damage in Brazil will imply two main developments in the expected evolution of civil liability. These developments will require the Brazilian judiciary to mature the dialogue with the sciences of climate change attribution and source attribution, so tort law already in force in the country can accommodate the complexities in climate matters.

First, it must be recognized that climate damage is damage that is projected in a synergistic and continuous way. This recognition of climate damage with a cumulative and permanent effect will probably reinforce scrutiny on the environmental licensing of all projects that intend to add emissions to this damage that is occurring. The tort law's efficacy regime will certainly also be used as a

101 The institute of the abuse of rights is present in Article 187 of the Civil Code, which says that 'The holder of a right who, when exercising it, manifestly exceeds the limits imposed by its economic or social purpose, by the good-faith or good customs.'

102 Douglas A Kysar, 'The Public Life of Private Law: Tort Law as a Risk Regulation Mechanism' (2018) 9(1) *European Journal of Risk Regulation* 48.

climate risk regulation.[103,104] Above all, it will require understanding that this damage is heading towards irreversibility.[105]

Future climate damage is irreversible damage, so civil liability will deal with the concrete measures necessary to avoid the scope of this irreversible damage. Considering the recognition of objective liability in Brazil for those who degrade the environment, arising from the simple risk or the simple fact of the activity degrading, regardless of the agent's guilt or the regularity of the conduct, judicial scrutiny is expected to be strict on conduct that intends to add emissions to the climate system, worsening the ongoing synergistic and cumulative damage.

Furthermore, there is certainly potential to be explored in Brazilian litigation (as well as in litigation in other countries) that establishes causal link between contributions (past, current or projected) to direct climate damage (agents that add up emissions and add up to warming), and indirect climate damages or losses and damages associated with climate change.

The individual or collective damages that people or communities are experiencing due to direct climate damage in progress will certainly support the filing of demands that connect the portions of responsibility of certain emitting agents (for example large producers of fossil fuels or agricultural products), with the duty to contribute proportionally to the cost of indirect climate damage, whether current or projected future damage. These connections are precisely what is expected from the evolution of civil liability for climate matters, and it will be possible as long as the legal categories of direct damage to the climate system and indirect damages that result from are well understood.

---

103 Article 225 of the Constitution, when establishing the intergenerational responsibility for preserving the environment, also prescribes that public authorities must control the production, commercialization, and use of techniques that pose substantial risks to life, quality of life and the environment. The Constitution also guarantees the preservation of essential ecological processes and prohibits practices that put ecological functions at risk. See Délton Winter de Carvalho, *Gestão Jurídica Ambiental* (2nd edn, Revista dos Tribunais 2021) 157–158.

104 In the case filed by Greenpeace Argentina, the author alleged that the opening of new oil exploration in the Argentinian Sea will cause climate damage due to the State's failure to fulfill its duty of care and protection of the collective good at risk. It would be an essential requirement to analyze cumulative climate impacts, considering all GHG emissions, including exported emissions, to fully assess the responsibility for the State's omissions. See *Greenpeace Argentina et al v Argentina et al*, FMP 105/2022, filed before the Federal Court of Mar de la Plata, available at <http://climatecasechart.com/non-us-case/greenpeace-argentina-et-al-v-argentina-et-al/>.

105 A careful review of the precedents in *Milieudefensie* and *vzw Klimaatzaak* reveals that the judges in these cases ruled on the risk of imminent or future climate damage, on the risk of reaching points of no return and on the irreversibility of damage to the climate system. Based on the risk of future damage, they decided to individualize the efforts of agents (public and private) to contribute to preventing irreversible climate damage globally.

On the international scene, even without a final decision, the *Luciano Liiuya v RWE AG*,[106] pending before a German court, and *Asmania et al v Holcim*,[107] in Court of Switzerland, are paradigmatic examples of the causal relationships that can be sought in the Courts between contributions to direct climate damage (in these cases, past or historical contributions based on historical emissions studies, such as Heede's studies), and the legal duty to repair indirect climate damage, or request fund to provide adaptation measures.[108]

Both initials of these cases connect the individual historical percentage contributions (of RWE AG and Holcim) in emissions already released into the atmosphere, as an argumentative basis for invoking proportional civil reparation duties. These cases work on the individual historical contribution of corporations to direct climate damage (to the warming of the global climate system), as a measure of individualization of civil liability to help fund measures that reduce plaintiffs' losses and damages.

As Tigre and Wewerinke-Singh pointed out, the German Court already recognizes a damage in the 'global neighborhood,' in light of the global impact of GHG emissions. The Court also acknowledged that RWE's emissions are not solely responsible for the flood risk (the alleged indirect damage risk to Luciano property), but sufficient for RWE AG to be partially liable for the existing risk. As such, the Court deemed that partial causation cannot be excluded.[109]

This partial causation comes precisely from the certainty that all emissions matter because they all add to the damage and enhance the harmful effects that are suffered by communities and people. In the Brazilian system, equally significant emitters—national or foreign (for example, in the agricultural production chains and even in the production of coal, oil, and gas)—can obviously be questioned in court to contribute jointly to the cost of amounts that Brazilian people and communities have spent or will spend to alleviate damages generated from the warming of the climate system.

This is because Brazilian legislation understands degradation of environmental quality as both damage to the environment (and therefore damage to the climate system), and also personal and property damage that derives from.

---

106 *Luciano Lliuya v RWE AG*, Case No 2 O 285/15, filed before the District Court of Essen Regional Court, available at <https://climatecasechart.com/non-us-case/lliuya-v-rwe-ag/>.

107 *Asmania et al v Holcim*, filed before the Cantonal Court of Zug (Kantonsgericht Zug), available at <https://climatecasechart.com/non-us-case/four-islanders-of-pari-v-holcim/>.

108 Richard Heede, 'Carbon Majors: Accounting for Carbon and Methane Emissions 1854–2010' (Climate Mitigation Services 2014), available at <https://climateaccountability.org/pdf/MRR%209.1%20Apr14R.pdf> and <https://climateaccountability.org/carbon-majors/>.

109 Maria Antônia Tigre & Margaretha Wewerinke-Singh, 'Beyond the North-South Divide: Litigation's Role in Resolving Climate Change Loss and Damage Claims' (2023) 32(3) *RECIEL* 385.

People and their property injured or at risk of suffering damage can also take legal action against polluters seeking liability. The joint action is optional in cases on liability in environmental matters in Brazil, and authors who suffer indirect climate damage (Eg property damage, personal injury, or death) can choose who they demand liability claims for.

Furthermore, objective liability and the theory of full risk are already applied by Brazilian Courts not only with regard to environmental damage itself, such as collective or public damage (the direct climate damage), but also to individual damages caused to individuals and legal entities, as a result of attacks on the environment (individual or private damage caused 'through' the environment).[110] The path to the use of civil liability in matters of indirect climate damage is evidently open, and it appears that Brazil is capable of emerging as a protagonist of civil liability for climate-related losses and damages. The coming years will tell.

## 7 Final Considerations

In Brazilian law, what this text demonstrates is that responsibility for environmental damage already caused, years ago, the reformulation of the tort law regime to a constitutional and public law basis. Brazil respected international standards at its domestic level, and created an autonomous liability system for environmental damage per se and autonomous for personal damage.

In Brazil, therefore, the use of tort law regime for climate damage, recognized as a specific type or dimension of environmental damage, is an example that materializes the necessary legal evolution that accommodates the fight against climate change in legal tools applicable by judicial courts.

The hope is that the rationality and handling of civil liability for direct climate damage, affecting the climate system, already underway in Brazil, will awaken theorists and scholars from other contexts, as well as allow judges from other courts, to observe how legal arguments applying liability for climate damage are built on solid foundations, which respect international norms and remove the claim of climate justice in courts from a simple rhetorical plane.

Courts and scholars in other jurisdictions have already realized that barriers will have to be overcome. This chapter sought to demonstrate that they are far from insurmountable, and that global warming calls also for effective climate litigation.

---

110 See *Emilia Mary Melato Gomes v Mineração Rio Pomba Cataguases Ltda* (n 77); or LDC-SEV *Bioenergia v José Maria Chagas Damasceno* (n 69).

CHAPTER 18

# Just Transition Litigation in Brazil

*Luiz Ormay Jr* *

## 1 Introduction: What Is Just Transition and Why Do We Need to Talk about It

In the history of human evolution, energy usage has been a crucial means for our species to overcome challenges and adapt to various conditions on the planet. Indeed, the concept of energy is semantically simple but carries extremely complex implications, especially in contemporary society.

Although this chapter does not aim to delve into a historical digression or philosophical reflection on the subject, it is important to highlight that the use of energy marked human civilization, especially from the Industrial Revolution onwards.

During this period, the widespread use of fossil fuels became one of the key features shaping the dominant societal model we have today. Furthermore, empirical data suggests that the use of fossil fuels has not stopped yet, and will not stop soon. In fact, it seems that it will keep a pivotal role in the years (or decades) of transition into carbon-neutral economies.

Although its large-scale usage dates back to the 18th century, it was in the mid-19th century that this expansion became exponential, reaching records year after year. According to the most recent data, in 2022, 36,8 gigatons of carbon dioxide were emitted into the planet's atmosphere considering only energy generation.[1]

Being carbon dioxide a greenhouse gas (GHG), its high concentration in the atmosphere is a major cause of global warming and climate change. According to the Intergovernmental Panel on Climate Change (IPCC):

> Anthropogenic greenhouse gas emissions have increased since the pre-industrial era, driven largely by economic and population growth, and are now higher than ever. This has led to atmospheric concentrations of carbon dioxide, methane and nitrous oxide that are unprecedented

* PhD candidate at the University of Brasília, lcormay@lopesormayjr.adv.br, ORCID No. 0009-0006-1750-9374.

1 International Energy Agency, *CO2 Emissions in 2022* (IEA 2023), available at <https://iea.blob.core.windows.net/assets/3c8fa115-35c4-4474-b237-1b00424c8844/CO2Emissionsin2022.pdf>.

 | DOI:10.1163/9789004690974_019

> in at least the last 800,000 years. Their effects, together with those of other anthropogenic drivers, have been detected throughout the climate system and are extremely likely to have been the dominant cause of the observed warming since the mid-20th century.[2]

With that said, the only viable path to curb the scenario of global warming and climate change is through the reduction of global GHG emissions. However, due to the way our economies work worldwide, this task is not straightforward for several reasons.

Exploiting oil and gas is extremely profitable and has allowed transnational corporations to accumulate significant capital and power. Additionally, a whole chain of activities linked to fossil fuels generates jobs and taxes. Therefore, a sudden break with the dominant energy model prevailing since the Industrial Revolution is unlikely.

Actually, there is a certain consensus that the path to necessary change will occur through a just transition, a process of energy transition where society moves away from the use of fossil fuels and shifts toward the use of sustainable sources while taking care of economic and social consequences of this change:

> A just transition incorporates key principles, such as respect and dignity for vulnerable groups, the creation of decent jobs, social protection, employment rights, fairness in energy access and use, and social dialogue and democratic consultation with the relevant stakeholders, while coping with the effects of asset-stranding and the transition to green and clean economies.[3]

This expression is commonly used to express the idea of a transition to a low-carbon economy in which the benefits and burdens of climate impacts and action on climate change are shared fairly among different sectors of

---

2 Intergovernmental Panel on Climate Change, *Climate Change 2014: Synthesis Report. Contribution of Working Groups I, II and III to the Fifth Assessment Report of the Intergovernmental Panel on Climate Change* (IPCC 2015) 151ff.

3 Denton, Halsnæs et al, 'Accelerating the transition in the context of sustainable development', in Shukla et al (eds), *Climate Change 2022: Mitigation of Climate Change. Contribution of Working Group III to the Sixth Assessment Report of the Intergovernmental Panel on Climate Change* (CUP 2023) 1727ff.

society, and in which everyone is given a voice in decision-making processes that will affect their lives and livelihoods.[4]

The 'just transition' concept emerged in the 1980s when US trade unions advocated for transition policies to protect jobs affected by new regulations on water and air pollution and in recent years, it has become widespread in the context of addressing climate change. This popularity is due to the fact that just transition is a potential mechanism to reduce GHG emissions without incurring a high social and economic cost.

For instance, a recent study made by the International Renewable Energy Agency (IRENA) stated that the socioeconomic benefits coming from a more accelerated energy transition through progressive policies could provide 40 million jobs in the electricity sector by 2050.[5]

In 2021, during the 26th United Nations Climate Change Conference, the concept of energy transition gained greater prominence, being mentioned twice in the Glasgow Climate Pact.

However, as much as it may seem like a simple idea, practice demonstrates that just transition execution is highly complex. The first issue is that a just energy transition plan can vary significantly depending on the characteristics of each country. For example, discussing a just transition in the United States is different from discussing it in South Africa.

Another issue is when economic and political groups benefiting from the fossil fuel chain appropriate the concept of a just transition to implement their own agendas. By using the discourse of the need to prioritize jobs and energy security, these groups shape legislation to ensure that the just transition is neither a transition nor just and primarily benefits fossil fuels.

At the same time, legislation is key to address climate change as it plays a critical role in achieving net-zero emissions.[6] This is why it is so important to talk about energy transition. We need to be vigilant about the pretexts created to hinder the implementation of a truly just energy transition program as this mechanism is crucial for addressing climate change.

---

4 Joana Setzer & Catherine Higham, *Global Trends in Climate Change Litigation: 2023 Snapshot* (Grantham Research Institute on Climate Change and the Environment 2023).

5 International Renewable Energy Agency, World Energy Transitions Outlook 2023: 1.5°C Pathway, vol. 2 (IREA 2023), available at <https://www.irena.org/Publications/2023/Jun/World-Energy-Transitions-Outlook-2023>.

6 Merner, Benjamin, Ercole, Keuschnigg, Kunik, Martínez Toral, Peterson, Setzer, Sokol, Tandon & Turowski, 'Comparative Analysis of Legal Mechanisms to Net-Zero: Lessons from Germany, the United States, Brazil, and China' (2024) 15(1) *Carbon Management* 1.

## 2 Setting the Scene: Just Transition Legislation in Brazil as a Trigger for Litigation

From a positive law perspective, few statutes have been adopted in Brazil formally aimed to regulate 'just transition', which, however, have rather contributed to extending coal-based energy production. Understanding this legislative process is key to understanding litigation in this context.

In fact, more than half of the energy produced in Brazil derives from coal, oil, and gas—which are also the most subsidized sources of energy in Brazil. In 2021, there were around 60 billion dollars and specifically in energy generation 150 million dollars were spent on coal alone while renewable sources received less than three times that amount.[7]

Some geographic factors specific to Brazil can explain this. Even though it increased by 23% between 2018 and 2021, coal represents only 2.7% of the electricity generation supply and is geographically restricted to the southern region of the country.[8] Still, coal burning represented 30% of GHG emissions in the National Interconnected System.[9]

However, although the IPCC has been stating that the use of coal should fall by at least 80% between 2020 and 2030, in Brazil there are several attempts to increase the use of coal under the umbrella of 'just transition' bills. To understand this regulation of coal use in the context of just transition, one must bear in mind that, according to the Instituto de Estudos Socioeconômicos, Brazil's coal industry is only economically viable due to large subsidies provided by the government which are largely paid by consumers through their electricity bills.[10] These subsidies are scheduled to end in 2027,[11] which helps explain the increasing lobbying from the industry. As such, in August 2021, the Ministry of Mines and Energy presented the Program for the Sustainable Use of National Mineral Coal, which defends the installation of new coal-based thermoelectric plants in the south of Brazil.[12]

---

7 Instituto de Estudos Socioeconômicos, *Subsídios aos Combustíveis Fósseis no Brasil: Conhecer, Avaliar, Reformar* (IES 2022), available at <https://grauna.org.br/wayback/httpswwwinescorgbr_public/20220921182359mp_/https://www.inesc.org.br/wp-content/uploads/2018/06/Estudo_completo_Inesc.pdf>.

8 Despite that insignificance in terms of energy generation, the socio environmental impact caused by the coal industry is massive. See <https://coalwatch.org>.

9 Instituto de Estudos Socioeconômicos (n 7).

10 Instituto de Estudos Socioeconômicos (n 7).

11 Federal Law No 10.438/2002.

12 See <https://www.gov.br/mme/pt-br/destaques/gt-sc/relatorio-1/relatorio_gt_sc_vf-002.pdf>.

This document is the product of intense lobbying by coal companies in the State of Santa Catarina (the most coal-rich in the country) in reaction to a series of indications that the subsidies would not be renewed. In 2019, the *Tribunal de Contas da União* (Court of Auditors of the Union, or 'TCU') analyzed coal subsidies and stated that maintaining them is contradictory with the goal of reducing GHG:

> In summary, subsidies for national mineral coal are contradictory in relation to the effort to reduce greenhouse gas emissions, as provided for in the Paris Agreement, since:
> (i) mineral coal is the fossil energy source with the highest level of greenhouse gas emissions in the generation of thermoelectricity according to current environmental licensing requirements;
> (ii) national mineral coal thermoelectric plants do not provide the complementarity to face the intermittency of non-conventional renewables, so that the subsidies applied to national mineral coal cause the displacement of other energy sources that are more efficient from an environmental point of view in the matrix electricity, such as renewables.[13]

In 2022, Federal Law No 14,299/22 was approved by the National Congress and regulates for the first time just transition in Brazil. Despite its name, it does not establish an energy transition program, but rather extends the use of coal until 2040, when it schedules the closure of thermoelectric plans the state of Santa Catarina.

In 2022, Decree No 11,127/22 was adopted and aims to regulate the Just Energy Transition Program Council, a body that has so far only had one meeting and approved only its operating rules, having not taken any type of decision or at least had a discussion about energy transition.

Also in 2022, the state of Santa Catarina approved Law No 18,330/22 on just transition for coal. Just like the former Federal Law, this latter state statutory law suggests an energy transition plan, but actually establishes various forms of economic incentives for the coal industry and sets out a regime of exclusion of environmental liability for the operators in this industry.

In general, by not establishing a deadline for the coal phase out and by guaranteeing incentives/benefits and promotion of activities in the coal production chain, it distorts the concept of 'Just Energy Transition' and contributes to the continued emissions of coal based GHG.

---

13 Judgment No 1530/2019, of 3 July 2019 (Plenary Session), Process No 008.692/2018-1 (RA Auditing Report), Rapporteur: Judge Aroldo Cedraz.

Finally, on November 30, 2023, the Chamber of Deputies of the Brazilian Congress approved a project that regulates the use of offshore energy potential (PL 576/2021). Although it regulates offshore energy (mainly wind energy), in the last moment of voting a clause allowing to contract coal-fired thermoelectric plants by the year 2050 was added and approved. The project still needs to be voted on by the Federal Senate, but the chances are high that a new statute 'dressed' as an energy transition will benefit coal in the country.

In short, the Brazilian legislation on just transition is formally concerned with the topic, but in fact, it rather allow for an extended operation of coal-based thermoelectric plants. The semantics used to not accurately describe the content of positive law. In this light, it is not unfair to qualify these statutes as 'just transition greenwashing', as they are used not for the purpose of reducing GHG emissions and combating climate change, but instead to establish benefits for the fossil fuel industry. Accordingly, civil society movements[14] and some political parties filed two lawsuits before the Federal Supreme Court (STF), alleging the unconstitutionality of these statutes.

This follows a thread of a growing climate litigation scenario that is happening in Brazilian judiciary in the last few years.[15]

## 3 Just Transition on Trial: the Federal Supreme Court

It is well known that the Brazilian Constitution is long and detailed, has a strong programmatic content, and is includes a vast array of legal principles (namely, in relation to the protection and the preservation of the environment). This explains why the Constitution is fertile ground for climate and environmental litigation targeting just transition statutes, especially if one bears in mind the STF's case law and the constitutional scholarship that emphasize the direct applicability of fundamental rights and the normative binding force legal principles established in the Constitution.

Besides that, the Brazilian legal system is very peculiar, as the Constitution adopted a mix of the American (or diffuse) and the Austrian (or concentrated) systems of review of constitutionality. In this context, the STF holds a very broad subject matter jurisdiction, including the competence to decide on first instance various issues regarding the interpretation and application of the Constitution in general and fundamental rights more specifically.

14 Ie Instituto Internacional Arayara and Observatório do Clima.

15 Setzer & Higham (n 4).

This broad subject matter jurisdiction explains the legal and political protagonism of the STF due to the nature of the cases it rules. Although this has always been a constant, in recent years, the STF has become the center of political debate in several cases decided by it.

Among the several decisions taken by the STF, there is a group of seven lawsuits judged in the first half of 2022, which became known as 'the green agenda' and brought the STF to the forefront of the environmental debate. This set of lawsuits resulted from a strong coordination between non-governmental organizations and political parties, which came together to defend environmental policies.

So far, some of the lawsuits are still pending, but overall the message conveyed in the Supreme Court's judgments was that it would not tolerate, under the Constitution, a setback in environmental policies or the adoption of measures or policies that increase the contribution of Brazil to climate change—*PSB et al v Brazil (on deforestation and human rights)*,[16] *PSB et al v Brazil (on Climate Fund)*,[17] or *Rede Sustentabilidade v Brazil (on the 'Pacote Verde')*.[18] Obviously, this does not mean that any environmental or climate litigation will be successful, but still, it emphasizes the core importance placed upon the environment and climate protection by the STF.

In fact, this grassroots movement gathering civil society and political parties followed a global trend and initiated a new branch of environmental and climate rights defense in the country and paved the way for just transition litigation in Brazil. They were brought to the STF, namely in the first couple of review of constitutionality lawsuits: just like the green agenda, both cases resulted from the mobilization of civil society and political parties, and this union of perspectives happened not only because political parties are fundamental agents of change in a democracy, but also because the Brazilian Constitution allows them to file lawsuits directly at the STF to challenge a statute's constitutionality.[19]

Just transition litigation in Brazil was inaugurated by two cases: *Rede Sustentabilidade et al v Brazil (on Jorge Lacerda Thermoelectric Complex)*[20] and *Rede*

16 *PSB et al v Brazil (on deforestation and human rights)*, ADPF 760, Judgment of 6 April 2022.

17 *PSB et al v Brazil (on Climate Fund)*, ADPF 708, Judgment of 7 January 2022.

18 *Rede Sustentabilidade v Brazil (on the 'Pacote Verde')*, ADPF 651, Judgment of 28 April 2022.

19 Article 103 of the Constitution lists political parties as one of the few entities that can challenge a statute's constitutionality directly before the STF.

20 *Rede Sustentabilidade et al v Brazil (on Jorge Lacerda Thermoelectric Complex)*, ADI 7095, filed on 10 March 2022.

*Sustentabilidade v State of Santa Catarina (on Just Energy Transition)*,[21] which are constitutional lawsuits that argue the unconstitutionality of statutes as they contradict the fundamental right to an ecologically balanced and healthy environment, inclusive of a dimension of a healthy atmosphere. Even though the lawsuits were brought against statutes from different levels (Federal Law No 14,299/22 and State Law No 18,330/22), the distortion of the concept of just transition by the legislators was carried out in a very similar way in both.

Both the claims can be classified as 'just transition litigation', which can be defined as lawsuits raising questions over the justice and fairness of measures adopted to deliver climate action according to the most recent criteria developed by the academy.[22]

The decision to litigate these cases before the STF was made for several reasons. The first is that given the absence of discussion and social participation in the legislative process (in fact, procedural rights of participation related to the environment were devised for administrative processes), the judiciary became a powerful instrument for public scrutiny of statutory laws, and a place in which civil society (through *amicus curiae* briefs or public hearings) can actively participate in the debate.

The second reason is that climate litigation has proven to be an important instrument for increasing State's climate ambitions. In the Sixth Assessment Report, the IPCC recognized that climate litigation has influenced the outcome and ambition of climate governance and that climate litigation is an important mechanism to influence climate policy outside of the formal United Nations Framework Convention on Climate Change (UNFCCC) processes.[23,24] This suggests that bringing a climate change-related case before a court is far from being pointless, since it can actually trigger State action and ambition.

The third reason is that climate change litigation is not a desire, but rather a need. In other words, it is a duty of each of us as human beings to fight for the preservation of our planet, in that sense the Brazilian Constitution states that defending the environment is a collective duty.[25] Also, in the case of Brazilian

---

21 *Rede Sustentabilidade v State of Santa Catarina (on Just Energy Transition)*, ADI 7332, filed on 29 December 2022.

22 Setzer & Higham (n 4).

23 Setzer & Higham (n 4).

24 Michael Burger & Maria Antonia Tigre, *Global Climate Litigation Report: 2023 Status Review* (Sabin Center for Climate Change Law & UNEP 2023).

25 Article 225 of the Brazil Constitution states that 'Everyone has the right to an ecologically balanced environment, an asset for the common use of the people and essential to a healthy quality of life, imposing on the Public Power and the community the duty to defend and preserve it for present and future generations.'

just transition statutes, there were no other effective means to face the deliberate encouragement of the most polluting fossil fuel using a false just transition plan.

At the same time, the new rules adopted and mentioned before seriously enhance Brazil's contribution to GHG concentration in the Earth's atmosphere. As seen above, those statutes not only encourage the use of coal for energy generation, but also falsely, but effectively, occupy the just transition regulatory space, which should be filled by a plan that actually represents just transition. This was perceived by civil society movements, who were concerned with the fact that 'false' or 'inaccurately labeled' just transition statutes would prevent the authorities from adopting a proper regulatory framework aimed at promoting a model of just transition in Brazil.

The fourth reason is that by bringing lawsuits that challenge the just transition plan presented by the government, civil society movements and political parties send a clear message to state and federal decision-makers that these movements and parties would act as watchdogs of the constitutional legal order and of the climate and environmental impact of laws, regulations, and other decisions adopted at the state or the federal level. This kind of lawsuit can be defined as strategic climate litigation because the claimant`s intention goes beyond what is formally requested in the motion. In fact, this kind of litigation aims to push climate policies forward.[26] internal and external actors that there is resistance, a fight for the environment, and that the decision to approve these legislations goes against the Brazilian constitutional order.

Although the two lawsuits were filed in 2022, there is no decision yet. However, some events deserve to be highlighted. In *Rede Sustentabilidade v State of Santa Catarina* (*on Just Energy Transition*), the Federal Public Prosecutor's Office presented a statement recognizing the unconstitutionality of some of the bill's provisions. Of course the Federal Public Prosecutor is not a judge (in the Brazilian legal system, he merely provides an objective reading of the existing provisions of the Constitution and other statutory norms and regulations, in defense of the rule of law), but his position is not neutral in terms of outcome of a judicial process: if the Federal Public Prosecutor sides with and brings arguments in favor of the applicants, this may be suggestive of what will be the future decision of the STF.

In *Rede Sustentabilidade et al v Brazil* (*on Jorge Lacerda Thermoelectric Complex*), in order to have more information and a better understanding of the case, Justice Gilmar Mendes (responsible for the case) determined that the

26 Joana Setzer & Catherine Higham, *Global Trends in Climate Change Litigation: 2022 Snapshot* (Grantham Research Institute on Climate Change and the Environment 2022).

Ministry of Mines and Energy (MME), the Ministry of Environment and Climate Change (MMA) and the National System Operator (ONS) should provide more information specifically on the obligation to contract energy generated by the Jorge Lacerda Thermoelectric Complex (which is powered by coal). In response, the MMA said the following:

> With this observation, it seems to us that article 4 of Law 14,299/2022, by creating the Just Energy Transition Program exclusively for the coal region of the State of Santa Catarina without reducing carbon dioxide emissions and without aligning with the goals of neutrality anchored in the two provisions of the United Nations Framework Convention on Climate Change. In addition to the conflicting aspect with these global pacts, its application generates a distortion when the application of the commented norm should have been foreseen for the entire national territory, which leads us to strongly agree with the arguments presented by the ADIN applicants regarding the unconstitutionality of the aforementioned law.[27]

Accordingly, instead of aligning with the defendants, the MMA suggested to the Supreme Court that it should rule in favor of the applicants.[28] Although there is no deadline for the judgment, all the necessary steps have already been completed. It is now up to the reporting Justices to request the Supreme Court's Chief a date for judgment.

Putting the just transition statutes under judicial scrutiny was surprising to some extent, but it was also an act of climate defense, an act of resistance, and an act of hope: an act of defense of a truly just transition; an act of resistance by giving voice to all those who are concerned with the contribution of Brazil to GHG emissions worldwide; and an act of hope, as it believes that the Brazilian Supreme Court will judge these cases in their favor, and thus pressure state and federal authorities to be more ambitious in their just transition plans.

Although it is always difficult to hint what a court's ruling will be, one can say that if the STF follows the environmental trend adopted in recent years, it is very likely that the lawsuits will be upheld and the just transition policies will be declared unconstitutional.

---

27 *Rede Sustentabilidade et al v Brazil* (*on Jorge Lacerda Thermoelectric Complex*), 'Statement of the Minister of the Environment and Climate Change'.

28 Although the MMA's opinion is non-binding, it can influence the Court's decision.

## 4 Conclusion

Despite the many warnings science has been making to humanity about the dangers of climate change and the recognized urgency to act to reduce GHG emissions, in general terms it seems that we are far from reaching the climate goals recommend by the scientific community, especially the IPCC. As a matter of fact, in some cases we are acting in the opposite way by keeping investing instead of phasing out the use of fossil fuels.

In this scenario, it's important to keep talking and demanding a 'just energy transition' program as it is one of the valuable mechanisms to reduce GHG emissions and tackle climate change while reducing socioeconomics consequences during the process. We also must be careful about the 'just transition' plans created by governments because sometimes they can be just another greenwashing tool.

This is what happened in Brazil with legislation that, instead of establishing a democratic and effective 'just energy transition' program, only cares about the coal industry by giving it subsidies and not even setting up a mandatory deadline for coal usage. Due to that and following the global trend,[29] the 'just transition litigation' emerged in Brazil with two constitutional lawsuits—*Rede Sustentabilidade et al v Brazil (on Jorge Lacerda Thermoelectric Complex)* and *Rede Sustentabilidade v State of Santa Catarina (on Just Energy Transition)*—against these statutes.

The cases brought by civil society and political parties seek to push the governments (both federal and state) to adjust the 'just energy transition' plans to align them with GHG emissions reduction goals instead of giving more incentives and subsidies to the coal industry. None of the motions had any ruling until this moment, but both the STF's precedents and the arguments presented by the parties give reasons to believe that the Court will recognize the unconstitutionality of the 'just transition' statutes.

Beyond any doubts, it would be better that the legislative power, together with civil society, elaborate a just transition program that put Brazil on the right path to net zero; unfortunately, up until now, the only statutes that were approved go the wrong way. In this way, it seems that the future of the Brazilian 'just energy transition' will be decided by courts.

---

29 Setzer & Higham (n 4).

APPENDIX

# Table of Cases

## International Courts and Tribunals

### *Inter-American Court of Human Rights*

***Baraona Bray v Chile (Preliminary Objections, Merits, Reparations and Costs)***

Judgment of Nov 24, 2022, IACtHR, Series C No 481, available at https://www.corteidh.or.cr/docs/casos/articulos/seriec_481_ing.pdf

***Case of the Xucuru Indigenous People and their Members v Brazil***

Judgment of Feb 5, 2018, IACtHR Series C No 346, available at https://www.corteidh.or.cr/docs/casos/articulos/seriec_346_ing.pdf

***Case of Airton Honorato et al v Brazil***

Judgment of Nov 27, 2023, IACtHR Series C No 508, https://www.corteidh.or.cr/docs/casos/articulos/seriec_508_esp.pdf

***Compulsory Membership in an Association Prescribed by Law for the Practice of Journalism (Articles 13 and 29 American Convention on Human Rights***

Advisory Opinion OC-5/85, IACtHR Series A No 5 (13 November 1985) available at https://www.corteidh.or.cr/docs/opiniones/seriea_05_esp.pdf

***Environment and Human Rights (State Obligations in Relation to the Environment in the Context of the Protection and Guarantee of the Rights to Life and to Personal Integrity—Interpretation and Scope of Articles 4(1) and 5(1) of the American Convention on Human Rights)***

Advisory Opinion OC-23/17, IACtHR Series A No 23 (15 November 2017) available at https://www.corteidh.or.cr/docs/opiniones/seriea_23_ing.pdf

***Habitantes de La Oroya v Peru (Excepciones Preliminares, Fondo, Reparaciones y Costas)***

Judgment of Nov 27, 2023, IACtHR Series C No 511, available at https://www.corteidh.or.cr/docs/casos/articulos/seriec_511_esp.pdf

***Habitantes de La Oroya v Peru (Excepciones Preliminares, Fondo, Reparaciones y Costas)***

Case No 12.718, IACommHR Decision of 19 November 2020

***Indigenous Communities of The Lhaka Honhat (Our and) Association v Argentina***

Judgment of Feb 6, 2020, IACtHR Series C No 420, available at https://www.corteidh.or.cr/docs/casos/articulos/seriec_400_ing.pdf

***Kawas-Fernández v Honduras (Merits, Reparations and Costs)***

Judgment of April 3, 2009, IACtHR Series C No 196, available at <https://www.corteidh.or.cr/docs/casos/articulos/seriec_196_ing.pdf>

 | DOI:10.1163/9789004690974_020

*Request for an Advisory Opinion on the Climate Emergency and Human Rights Submitted to the Inter-American Court of Human Rights by the Republic of Colombia and the Republic of Chile*

Request filed by Chile and Colombia on 9 January 2023, available at https://www.corteidh.or.cr/docs/opiniones/soc_1_2023_en.pdf

### *International Tribunal for the Law of the Sea*

*Request for an Advisory Opinion submitted by the Commission of Small Island States on Climate Change and International Law*

Advisory Opinion (21 May 2024) ITLOS Case No 31, Request filed on 12 December 2022, available at https://www.itlos.org/fileadmin/itlos/documents/cases/31/Advisory_Opinion/C31_Adv_Op_21.05.2024_orig.pdf

### *International Court of Justice*

*Accordance with International Law of the Unilateral Declaration of Independence in respect of Kosovo*

Advisory Opinion (23 July 2010) ICJ Rep 403, available at https://www.icj-cij.org/case/141

*Certain Questions Concerning Diplomatic Relations* (*Honduras v Brazil*)

Order of 12 May 2010 (Discontinuance), ICJ Rep 303, available at https://www.icj-cij.org/case/147

*Legal Consequences arising from the Policies and Practices of Israel in the Occupied Palestinian Territory*

Advisory Opinion (14 July 2024) available at https://www.icj-cij.org/case/186

*Legal Consequences for States of the Continued Presence of South Africa in Namibia (South West Africa) notwithstanding Security Council Resolution 276 (1970)*

Advisory Opinion (21 June 1971) ICJ Rep 16, available at https://www.icj-cij.org/case/53

*Legal Consequences of the Construction of a Wall in the Occupied Palestinian Territory*

Advisory Opinion (9 July 2004) ICJ Rep 136, available at https://www.icj-cij.org/case/131

*Legal Consequences of the Separation of the Chagos Archipelago from Mauritius in 1965*

Advisory Opinion (25 February 2019) ICJ Rep 95, available at https://www.icj-cij.org/case/169

*Request for an Advisory Opinion of the ICJ on the Obligations of States in Respect of Climate Change*

UNGA Res 77/276 (29 March 2023) 'Request for an Advisory Opinion of the International Court of Justice on the Obligations of States in respect of Climate Change', UN Doc A/77/L.58, available at https://www.icj-cij.org/sites/default/files/case-related/187/187-20230412-app-01-00-en.pdf

### *European Court of Human Rights*

***Duarte Agostinho et al v Portugal et al***

Judgment [GC] of 9 April 2024, App no 39371/20, available at https://climatecasechart.com/non-us-case/youth-for-climate-justice-v-austria-et-al/

***Verein KlimaSeniorinnen Schweiz et al v Switzerland***

Judgment [GC] of 9 April 2024, App no 53600/20, available at https://climatecasechart.com/non-us-case/union-of-swiss-senior-women-for-climate-protection-v-swiss-federal-council-and-others/

### *Court of Justice of the European Union*

***Greenpeace et al v Commission***

*Greenpeace et al v European Commission*, Case No T-214/23, filed on 18 April 2023 before the General Court of the Court of Justice of the European Union, available at https://climatecasechart.com/non-us-case/greenpeace-and-others-v-commission/

### *Human Rights Committee*

***Daniel Billy et al v Australia (Torres Strait Islanders Petition)***

Views adopted on 23 September 2022, Communication No CCPR/C/135/D/3624/2019, submitted in 13 May 2019, available at https://climatecasechart.com/non-us-case/petition-of-torres-strait-islanders-to-the-united-nations-human-rights-committee-alleging-violations-stemming-from-australias-inaction-on-climate-change/#:~:text=On%20September%2023%2C%202022%2C%20the,private%20life%2C%20family%20and%20home

## Domestic Courts in Brazil

### *Federal Supreme Court*

***ADEPOL-Brasil v President of the Court of Justice of the State of São Paulo***

*Associação dos Delegados de Polícia do Brasil—ADEPOL-Brasil v Presidente do Tribunal de Justiça do Estdo de São Paulo*, ADI 5240 SP, Judgment of 20 August 2015, Raporteur: MInister Luiz Fux, available at < https://redir.stf.jus.br/paginadorpub/paginador.jsp?docTP=TP&docID=10167333>

***ANPT et al v Brazil***

*Associação Nacional dos Procuradores do Trabalho (ANPT) e Associação Nacional dos Magistrados da Justiça do Trabalho (ANAMATRA) v União Federal.* ADI 4066, Judgment of 24 August 2017, Rapporteur: Minister Rosa Weber, available at https://redir.stf.jus.br/paginadorpub/paginador.jsp?docTP=TP&docID=14452232&prcID=2607856

***Antônio de Andrade Ribeiro Junqueira v Presidente da República***

Decision of 17 November 1995, Process No MS 22.164, Rapporteur: Minister Celso de Mello

***Banco Bradesco S/A v Luciano Cardoso Santos***

*Banco Bradesco S/A v Luciano Cardoso Santos*, Extraordinary Appeal No 466.343-1, Judgment of 3 December 2008, Rapporteur: Minister Gilmar Mendes, available at https://redir.stf.jus.br/paginadorpub/paginador.jsp?docTP=AC&docID=595444

***Banco Bradesco S/A v Vera Lúcia B de Albuquerque et al***

*Banco Bradesco S/A v Vera Lúcia B de Albuquerque et al*, Special Appeal No RE 466.343-1 SP, Judgment of 3 December 2008, Rapporteur: Minister Gilmar Mendes

***Banco Itaú v Armando Segabinazzi***

*Banco Itaú v Armando Luiz Segabinazzi*, Special Appeal No 349703, Judgment of 13 December 2008, Rapporteur: Minister Carlos Britto, available at https://redir.stf.jus.br/paginadorpub/paginador.jsp?docTP=AC&docID=595406

***Comercial Cesa S/A v Public Prosecutor's Office***

*Comercial Cesa S/A v Ministério Público Federal*, AgReg-AgIn 777.502 RS, Judgment of 28 September 2010, Rapporteur: Minister Ellen Gracie

***Fabiano Contarato et al v Ricardo Salles***

*Fabiano Contarato Randolph Rodrigues e Joenia Batista v Ricardo Salles (Minister of the Environment)*, PET 8351, filed on 22 August 2019 before the Federal Supreme Court, Judgment of 20 August 2021, Rapporteur: Minister Edson Fachin, available at https://climatecasechart.com/non-us-case/fabiano-contarato-randolph-rodrigues-and-joenia-batista-v-ricardo-salles/

***Fundação Nacional do Índio v IMA***

*Fundação Nacional do Índio (FUNAI) v Instituto do Meio Ambiente de Santa Catarina (IMA)*. Special Appeal No 1017365 SC, Judgment of 27 September 2023, Rapporteur: Minister Edson Fachin, available at https://www.conjur.com.br/dl/fa/fachin-indios1.pdf

***Governor of the State of Paraíba v Parliament of Paraíba***

*Governador do Estado da Paraíba v Assembleia Legislativa do Estado da Paraíba*, ADI 6957, Judgment of 17 December 2022, Rapporteur: Minister Edson Fachin, available at https://jurisprudencia.stf.jus.br/pages/search/sjur474285/false

***Habeas Corpus 143988***

Habeas Corpus No 143988, Order of 24 August 2020, Rapporteur: Minister Edson Fachin

***Indigenous Genocide Law Case***

*Articulação dos Povos Indígenas do Brasil (APIB), Partido Socialismo e Liberdade (PSL) e Rede Sustentabilidade v União Federal*, ADI 7582, filed in December 2023 before the Federal Supreme Court, available at https://climatecasechart.com/non-us-case/adi-7582-indigenous-genocide-law/

***Partido dos Trabalhadores v Brazil (Fires in the Pantanal and the Amazon Forest)***

ADPF 746, requested by Partido dos Trabalhadores on 1 September 2020, available at https://climatecasechart.com/non-us-case/adpf-746-fires-in-the-pantanal-and-the-amazon-forest/

***Partido Progressista v Presidente da República***

*Partido Progressista v Presidente da República*, ADC 42, Judgment of 21 February 2018, Rapporteur: MInister Luiz Fux, available at https://jurisprudencia.stf.jus.br/pages/search/sjur408490/false

***PPS v Brazil***

*Partido Popular Socialista v União Federal.* ADI 26, Judgment of 13 June 2019, Rapporteur: Minister Celso de Mello, available at https://redir.stf.jus.br/paginadorpub/paginador.jsp?docTP=TP&docID=748686816&pr

***PRD v Brazil (RenovaBio and Unlawful Interference in Economic Activity)***

*Partido Renovação Democática v União Federal.* ADI 7596, filed on 5 February 2024 before the STF, available at https://climatecasechart.com/non-us-case/adi-7596-renovabio-and-unlawful-interference-in-economic-activity/

***PSB et al v Brazil (on Amazon Fund)***

*Partido Socialista Brasileiro (PSB), Partido Socialismo e Liberdade (PSOL), Partido dos Trabalhadores (PT) e Rede Sustentabilidade v União Federal.* ADO 59, Judgment of 16 August 2023, Rapporteur: Minister Rosa Weber, available at https://climatecasechart.com/non-us-case/psb-et-al-v-brazil/

***PSB et al v Brazil (on Climate Fund)***

*Partido Socialista Brasileiro (PSB), Partido Socialismo e Liberdade (PSOL), Partido dos Trabalhadores (PT) e Rede Sustentabilidade v União Federal.* ADPF 708, Judgment of 7 January 2022, Rapporteur: Minister Luís Roberto Barroso, available at https://climatecasechart.com/non-us-case/psb-et-al-v-federal-union/

***PSB et al v Brazil (on deforestation and human rights)***

*Partido Socialista Brasileiro (PSB), Rede Sustentabilidade, Partido Democrático Trabalhista (PDT), Partido Verde, Partido dos Trabalhadores (PT), Partido Socialismo e Liberdade (PSOL) e Partido Comunista do Brasil (PCdoB) v União Federal.* ADPF 760, Judgment of 6 April 2022, Rapporteur: Minister Cármen Lúcia, available at https://climatecasechart.com/non-us-case/brazilian-socialist-party-and-others-v-brazil/

***PSB et al v Brazil (on Electrobras Privatization)***

*Partido Socialista Brasileiro (PSB), Partido Socialismo e Liberdade (PSOL), Rede Sustentabilidade, Partido dos Trabalhadores (PT), Partido Democrático Trabalhista (PDT) e Partido Comunista do Brasil (PCdoB) v União Federal.* ADI 6932, filed on 15 July 2021, available at https://climatecasechart.com/non-us-case/adi-6932-eletrobras-privatization/

***PSB et al v Brazil (Federal environmental sanctioning process)***

*Partido Socialista Brasileiro (PSB), Partido Socialismo e Liberdade (PSOL), Partido dos Trabalhadores (PT) e Rede Sustentabilidade v União Federal,* ADPF 755, filed on 21 October 2020, available at https://climatecasechart.com/non-us-case/adpf-755-federal-environmental-sanctioning-process/

***PSL v Brazil et al (on Arrest Warrant)***

*Partido Socialismo e Liberdade v União Federal et al*, ADPF 347 DF, Judgment of 9 September 2015, Rapporteur: Minister Marco Aurélio, available at https://portal.stf.jus.br/processos/detalhe.asp?incidente=4783560

***PSL et al v Brazil et al (Pantanal Wildfires)***

*Partido Socialismo e Liberdade (PSL), Partido Socialismo e Liberdade (PSOL), Partido Socialista Brasileiro (PSB), Partido dos Trabalhadores (PT) e Rede Sustentabilidade v União Federal, Estado do Mato Grosso e Estado do Mato Grosso do Sul*, ADPF 857, filed on 22 June 2021, available at https://climatecasechart.com/non-us-case/adpf-857-pantanal-wildfires/

***PSL v Ceará State Council of the Environment***

*Partido Socialismo e Liberdade (PSOL) v Conselho Estadual do Meio Ambiente do Ceará*, ADI 6288 CE, Judgment of 23 November 2020, Rapporteur: Minister Rosa Weber, available at https://redir.stf.jus.br/paginadorpub/paginador.jsp?docTP=TP&docID=754566819

***Public Prosecutor's Office v Governor of the State of Bahia***

*Procurador-Geral da República v Governador do Estado da Bahía*, ADI 5014 BH, Judgment of 13 November 2023, Rapporteur: Minister Dias Toffoli, available at https://redir.stf.jus.br/paginadorpub/paginador.jsp?docTP=TP&docID=774332617

***Public Prosecutor's Office v Governor of the State of Ceará***

*Procurador-Geral da República v Governador do Estado do Ceará*, ADI 4615 CE, Judgment of 20 September 2019, Rapporteur: Milnister Roberto Barroso, available at https://redir.stf.jus.br/paginadorpub/paginador.jsp?docTP=TP&docID=751257523

***Public Prosecutor's Office v Governor of the State of Ceará (Vaquejada Case)***

*Procurador-Geral da República v Governador do Estado do Ceará*, ADI 4983 CE, Judgment of 6 October 2017, Rapporteur: Minister Marco Aurélio, available at https://jurisprudencia.stf.jus.br/pages/search/sjur366632/false

***Public Prosecutor's Office v Governor of the State of Mato Grosso***

*Procurador-Geral da República v Governador do Estado de Mato Grosso*, ADI 4.529 MT, Judgment of 22 November 2022, Rapporteur: Minister Rosa Weber, available at https://redir.stf.jus.br/paginadorpub/paginador.jsp?docTP=TP&docID=764658040

***Public Prosecutor's Office v Governor of the State of Rio de Janeiro***

*Procurador-Geral da República v Governador do Estado do Rio de Janeiro*, AgReg ADI 2950-9 RJ, Judgment of 6 October 2004, Rapporteur: Minister Eros Grau

***Public Prosecutor's Office v Governor of the State of Santa Catarina***

*Procurador-Geral da República v Governador do Estado de Santa Catarina*, ADI 6650 SC, filed on 18 December 2020, Judgment of 27 April 2021, Rapporteur: Minister Cármen Lúcia, available at https://www.jusbrasil.com.br/jurisprudencia/stf/1203199122/inteiro-teor-1203199189

***Public Prosecutor's Office et al v Orleir Messias Cameli et al***

*Ministério Público Federal & Fundação Nacional do Índio* (*FUNAI*) *v Orleir Messias Cameli, Marmud Cameli Cia. & Abraão Cândido da Silva*, Special Appeal No RE 654.833/AC, Theme 0999, Judgment of 20 April 2020, Rapporteur: Minister Alexandre de Moraes, available at https://portal.stf.jus.br/processos/detalhe.asp?incidente=4130104

***Public Prosecutor's Office v President of the Republic***

*Procuradora-Geral da República v Presidente da República*, ADPF 623 DF, Judgment of 22 May 2023, Rapporteur: Minister Rosa Weber, available at https://redir.stf.jus.br/paginadorpub/paginador.jsp?docTP=TP&docID=769273788

***Public Prosecutor's Office v President of the Republic et al***

*Procurador-Geral da República v Presidente da República & Congresso Nacional*, ADI 5617, Judgment of 15 March 2018, Rapporteur: Minister Edson Fachin, available at https://jurisprudencia.stf.jus.br/pages/search/sjur391945/false

***Public Prosecutor's Office v President of the Republic* (*on gender identity*)**

*Procuradora-Geral da República v Presidente da República*, ADI 4275, Judgment of 1 March 2018, Rapporteur: Minister Edson Fachin, available at https://jurisprudencia.stf.jus.br/pages/search/sjur399205/false

***Public Prosecutor's Office of the State of São Paulo v Sindicato da Indústria de Material Plástico do Estado de São Paulo***

*Procurador-Geral do Estado de São Paulo v Sindicato da Indústria de Material Plástico do Estado de São Paulo*, Special Appeal No RE 732.686 SP, 19 Judgment of October 2017, Rapporteur: Minister Luiz Fux, available at https://jurisprudencia.stf.jus.br/pages/search/repercussao-geral9422/false

***Raposa Serra do Sol***

Judgment of 30 April 2009, Petition No 3388/RR, popular action filed by Augusto Affonso Botelho Neto against Brazil on 20 April 2005

***Rede Sustentabilidade v Brazil* (*on Amazon Deforestation*)**

*Rede Sustentabilidade v União Federal*, ADO 54, filed on 21 August 2019 before the Federal Supreme Court, Judgment of 1 April 2022, Rapporteur: Minister Cármen Lúcia, available at https://climatecasechart.com/non-us-case/ado-54-amazon-deforestation/

***Rede Sustentabilidade v Brazil* (*on the 'Pacote Verde'*)**

*Rede Sustentabilidade v União Federal*. ADPF 651, Judgment of 28 April 2022, Rapporteur: Minister Cármen Lúcia, available at https://portal.stf.jus.br/processos/detalhe.asp?incidente=5853176

***Rede Sustentabilidade v Brazil* (*on the Prevention of Forest Fires*)**

Rede Sustentabilidade v União Federal, ADPF 743, filed on 17 September 2020, available at https://portal.stf.jus.br/processos/detalhe.asp?incidente=6007933

***Rede Sustentabilidade v Institutional Security Cabinet and National Mining Agency (on Mining in Preserved Areas in the Amazon)***
*Rede Sustentabilidade v Gabinete de Segurança Institucional da Presidência da República & Agência Nacional de Mineração*, ADPF 921, requested by Rede Sustentabilidade on 9 December 2021

***Rede Sustentabilidade v National Environmental Council (on CONAMA Resolutions)***
*Rede Sustentabilidade v Conselho Nacional do Meio Ambiente (CONAMA)*, ADPF 747, 748 and 749, filed on 2 October 2020, Judgment of 14 December 2021, Rapporteur: Minister Rosa Wever, available at https://climatecasechart.com/non-us-case/workers-party-vs-national-environment-council-adpf-749-on-conama-resolutions/

***Rede Sustentabilidade v State of Santa Catarina (on Just Energy Transition)***
*Rede Sustentabilidade v Estado de Santa Catarina.* ADI 7332, filed on 29 December 2022, available at https://climatecasechart.com/non-us-case/adi-7332-policy-for-just-energy-transition-of-the-state-of-santa-catarina/

***Rede Sustentabilidade et al v Brazil (on Jorge Lacerda Thermoelectric Complex)***
*Rede Sustentabilidade, Partido Socialismo e Liberdade (PSOL) e Partido Socialista Brasileiro (PSB) v União Federal.* ADI 7095, filed on 10 March 2022, available at https://climatecasechart.com/non-us-case/adi-7095-complexo-termeletrico-jorge-lacerda/

***São Bernardo Ônibus Ltda v Belo Horizonte Environment Secretary***
*São Bernardo Ônibus Ltda v Secretário Municipal do Meio Ambiente de Belo Horizonte*, Special Appeal RE 194.704 MG, Judgment of 24 October 2017, Rapporteur: Minister Carlos Velloso

***SERTESP et al v Brazil et al***
*Sindicato das Empresas de Rádio e Televisão no Estado de São Paulo (SERTESP) & Ministério Público Federal v União Federal & Federação Nacional dos Jornalistas (FENAJ)*, Special Appeal No 511.961, Judgment of 17 June 2009, Rapporteur: Minister Gilmar Mendes, available at https://redir.stf.jus.br/paginadorpub/paginador.jsp?docTP=AC&docID=605643

***STC v Court of Justice of the State of Rio Grande do Sul (on gender identity)***
*STC v Oitava Câmara Cível do Tribunal de Justiça do Estado do Rio Grande do Sul*, Extraordinary Appeal No 670.422, Judgment of 18 August 2018, Rapporteur: Minister Dias Toffoli, available at https://jurisprudencia.stf.jus.br/pages/search/sjur420306/false

### *Superior Court of Justice*

***Brasilcom et al v Ministério de Minas e Energia***
*Brasilcom et al v Ministério de Minas e Energia*, MS 27093/DF (2020/0306047), Decision of 10 December 2022, Rapporteur: Minister Gurgel de Faria, available at https://climatecasechart.com/non-us-case/brasilcom-et-al-v-ministerio-de-minas-e-energia/

***Alberto Pasqualini Refap S/A v Public Prosecutor's Office of the State of Rio Grande do Sul***

*Alberto Pasqualini Refap S/A v Public Prosecutor's Office of the State of Rio Grande do Sul*, Judgment of 9 March 2010, Special Appeal No REsp 883.656/RS, Rapporteur: Minister Herman Benjamin, available at https://scon.stj.jus.br/SCON/pesquisar.jsp?i=1&b=ACOR&O=JT&livre=%27RESP%27.clas.+e+@num=%27883656%27&thesaurus=JURIDICO&fr=veja

***Brasilit Industry and Commerce Ltda et al v Public Prosecutor's Office of the State of Rio de Janeiro***

*Brasilit Indústria e Comércio Ltda et al v Ministério Público do Estado do Rio de Janeiro*, Special Appeal No REsp 1.367.923/RJ, Judgment of 27 August 2013, Rapporteur: Minister Humberto Martins, available at https://www.jusbrasil.com.br/jurisprudencia/stj/24158298/inteiro-teor-24158299

***Emilia Mary Melato Gomes v Mineração Rio Pomba Cataguases Ltda***

*Emilia Mary Melato Gomes v Mineração Rio Pomba Cataguases Ltda*, Special Appeal No REsp 1.374.284/MG, Judgment of 30 September 2014, Rapporteur: Minister Luis Felipe Salomão, available at https://www.jusbrasil.com.br/jurisprudencia/stj/864823848/inteiro-teor-864823858

***LDC-SEV Bioenergia v José Maria Chagas Damasceno***

*LDC-SEV Bioenergia v José Maria Chagas Damasceno*, Special Appeal No REsp 1.373.788/SP, Judgment of the STJ of 3 June 2014, Rapporteur: Minister Paulo de Tarso Sanseverino, available at https://www.stj.jus.br/websecstj/cgi/revista/REJ.exe/ITA?seq=1327704&tipo=0&nreg=201300708472&SeqCgrmaSessao=&CodOrgaoJgdr=&dt=20140610

***Maia Filho v IBAMA***

*Maia Filho v Instituto Brasileiro do Meio Ambiente e dos Recursos Naturais*, Special Appeal No 1000.731-RO, Judgment of 25 August 2009, Rapporteur: Minister Herman Benjamin, available at https://climatecasechart.com/non-us-case/maia-filho-v-environmental-federal-agency-ibama/

***Maria Angelica Caldas Uliana v State of São Paulo Treasury***

*Maria Angelica Caldas Uliana v State of São Paulo Treasury*, Judgment of the Superior Court of Justice of 21 March 2019, Special Appeal No REsp 1.797.175/SP, Rapporteur: Minister Og Fernandes, available at https://www.stj.jus.br/websecstj/cgi/revista/REJ.cgi/ITA?seq=1806039&tipo=0&nreg=201800312300&SeqCgrmaSessao=&CodOrgaoJgdr=&dt=20190328&formato=PDF&salvar=false&fbclid=IwAR33tDl5FlTBGayDQS5iUkveeJQblCjyNmFS8MDnHREhEKegqWLXWYeHyE

***Public Prosecutor's Office of the State of Mato Grosso v Clélio Nogueira Cunha***

*Ministério Público Estado do Mato Grosso v Clélio Nogueira Cunha*, Special Appeal No REsp 884.150/MT, Judgment of 19 June 2008, Rapporteur: Minister Luiz Fux, available at https://processo.stj.jus.br/SCON/jurisprudencia/toc.jsp?livre=%28RESP.clas.+e+%40num%3D%22884150%22%29+ou+%28RESP+adj+%22884150%22%29.suce

***Public Prosecutor's Office v Schneider***

*Public Prosecutor's Office v H Carlos Schneider S/A Comércio e Indústria et al*, Special Appeal No REsp 650.728-SC, Judgment of 2 December 2009, Rapporteur: Minister Herman Benjamin, available at https://climatecasechart.com/non-us-case/public-prosecutors-office-v-h-carlos-schneider-sa-comercio-e-industria-others/

***Public Prosecutor's Office of the State of Minas Gerais v Pedro Paulo Pereira***

*Ministério Público do Estado de Minas Gerais v Pedro Paulo Pereira*, Judgment of 14 August 2012, Special Appeal REsp No 1.198.727/MG, Rapporteur: Minister Herman Benjamin, available at https://www.stj.jus.br/websecstj/cgi/revista/REJ.cgi/ATC?seq=13806316&tipo=5&nreg=201001113499&SeqCgrmaSessao=&CodOrgaoJgdr=&dt=20130509&formato=PDF&salvar=false

***Public Prosecutor's Office of the State of Minas Gerais v Rubens de Castro Maia***

*Ministério Público do Estado de Minas Gerais v Rubens de Castro Maia*, Special Appeal No REsp 1180078/MG, Judgment of 2 December 2010, Rapporteur: Minister Herman Benjamin

***Public Prosecutor's Office of the State of Rio Grande do Sul v Amapá do Sul S/A***

*Ministério Público do Estado do Rio Grande do Sul v Amapá do Sul S/A*, Judgment of 25 August 2009, Special Appeal No REsp 972.902/RS, Rapporteur: Minister Eliana Calmon, available at https://www.stj.jus.br/websecstj/cgi/revista/REJ.cgi/ATC?seq=5620750&tipo=51&nreg=200701758820&SeqCgrmaSessao=&CodOrgaoJgdr=&dt=20090914&formato=PDF&salvar=false

***Public Prosecutor's Office of the State of São Paulo v Public Treasury of the State of São Paulo***

*Ministério Público do Estado de São Paulo v Fazenda do Estado de São Paulo*, Special Appeal No REsp 1.071.741-SP, Judgment of 24 March 2009, Rapporteur: Minister Herman Benjamin, available at https://www.stj.jus.br/websecstj/cgi/revista/REJ.cgi/ATC?seq=4715617&tipo=0&nreg

***Santo Antônio Energia S/A v FCB***

*Santo Antônio Energia S/A v FCB*, Judgment of 13 October 2020, Special Appeal No REsp 1818008/RO, Rapporteur: Minister Herman Benjamin

### *Court of Auditors*

***Judgment No 1539/2019***

Judgment No 1530/2019, of 3 July 2019 (Plenary Session), Process No 008.692/2018-1 (RA Auditing Report), Rapporteur: Judge Aroldo Cedraz, available at https://pesquisa.apps.tcu.gov.br/documento/acordao-completo/*/NUMACORDAO%253A1530%2520ANOACORDAO%253A2019%2520COLEGIADO%253A%2522Plen%25C3%25A1rio%2522/DTRELEVANCIA%2520desc%252C%2520NUMACORDAOINT%2520desc/0

### *Federal District*

***Conectas Direitos Humanos v BNDES and BNDESPAR***

*Conectas Direitos Humanos v BNDES Participações S.A.* (*BNDESPAR*) *and Banco Nacional de Desenvolvimento Econômico e Social* (*BNDES*), Federal Court of the Federal District, Process No. 1038657-42.2022.4.01.3400, filed on 21 June 2022, available at https://climatecasechart.com/non-us-case/conectas-direitos-humanos-v-bndes-and-bndespar/

***Federal Public Prosecutor's Office v Ricardo Salles et al***

*Ministério Público Federal v Ricardo Salles e União Federal* (*Ação de Improbidade Administrativa*) ACIA 1037665-52.2020.4.01.3400, filed on 6 July 2020 before the 8th Federal Court of the Judiciary Section of the Federal District, available at https://climatecasechart.com/non-us-case/federal-public-prosecutors-office-v-ricardo-salles-and-federal-union/

### *State of Acre*

***IEA v Brazil et al* (*Chico Mendes Extraction Reserve*)**

*Instituto de Estudos Amazónicos v União Federal, Instituto Nacional do Meio Ambiente e dos Recursos Naturais Renováveis* (*IBAMA*) *& Instituto Chico Mendes de Conservação da Biodiversidade* (*ICMBio*) ACP 1012197-54.2022.4.01.3000, filed on 28 October 2022 before the 2nd Federal Civil and Criminal Court of the Judiciary Section of Acre, available at https://climatecasechart.com/non-us-case/institute-of-amazonian-studies-v-federal-union-and-federal-environmental-agencies-ibama-and-icmbio-chico-mendes-extraction-reserve/

### *State of Amapá*

***IBAMA v Souza Brilhante* (*on illegal wood storage*)**

*Instituto Brasileiro do Meio Ambiente e dos Recursos Renováveis v V. de Souza Brilhante EIRELI*, ACP 1003478-16.2018.4.01.3100, filed on 19 December 2018 before the Federal Court of Amapá, Judgment of 2 September 2022, available at https://climatecasechart.com/non-us-case/federal-environment-agency-ibama-v-souza-brilhante-eireli/

### *State of Amazonas*

***Arayara et al v ANP et al***

*Instituto Arayara de Educação e Cultura para a Sustentabilidade, Articulação dos Povos Indígenas do Brasil* (*APIB*) *e Terra Indígena Rio dos Pardos Aldeia Kupli v Agência Nacional do Petróleo, Gás Natural e Biocombustíveis* (*ANP*), *Instituto Brasileiro do Meio Ambiente e dos Recursos Naturais Renováveis* (*IBAMA*) *e União Federal*, ACP 1049493-58.2023.4.01.3200, filed in December 2023 before the 3rd Federal Civil Court of the Judiciary Section of Amazonas, available at https://climatecasechart.com/non-us

-case/instituto-arayara-apib-and-rio-dos-pardos-indigenous-land-kupli-village-vs-anp-ibama-federal-government-and-others/

***Federal Public Ministry v Brazil (Sugarcane zoning)***

*Ministério Público Federal v União Federal*, ACP 1016202-09.2019.4.01.3200, filed on 12 December 2019 before the 7th Federal Environmental and Agrarian Court of the Judiciary Section of Amazonas, available at https://climatecasechart.com/non-us-case/federal-public-ministry-vs-federal-union-zoning-of-sugar-cane/

***Federal Public Prosecutor's Office v Brazil et al (on deforestation hotspots in the Amazon)***

*Ministério Público Federal v União Federal, Instituto Brasileiro do Meio Ambiente e dos Recursos Naturais Renováveis (IBAMA), Instituto Chico Mendes da Biodiversidade (ICMBio) and Fundação nacional dos Povos Indígenas (Funai)*, ACP 1007104-63.2020.4.01.3200, filed in 2020 before the 7th Federal Environmental and Agrarian Court of the Judiciary Section of Amazonas, available at https://climatecasechart.com/non-us-case/ministerio-publico-federal-v-ibama/

***Federal Public Prosecutor's Office v Rogério***

*Ministério Público Federal v Rogério*, APOrd 0001306-46.2017.4.01.3200, filed on 29 September 2016 before the 7th Federal Environmental and Agrarian Court of the Judiciary Section of Amazonas, available at https://climatecasechart.com/non-us-case/federal-public-prosecutors-office-vs-rogerio-forest-fire/

***Federal Public Prosecutor's Office et al v Rezende (on deforestation and climate damage)***

*Ministério Público Federal e Instituto Nacional de Colonização e Reforma Agrária (INCRA) v Dauro Parreiras de Rezende (on deforestation and climate damage)*, ACP 1005885-78.2021.4.01.3200, filed on 7 April 2021 before the 7th Federal Environmental and Agrarian Court of the Judiciary Section of Amazonas, available at https://climatecasechart.com/non-us-case/ministerio-publico-federal-v-de-rezende/

***IBAMA v Dirceu Kruger (on illegal wood storage)***

*Instituto Brasileiro do Meio Ambiente e dos Recursos Naturais Renováveis (IBAMA) v Dirceu Kruger*, ACP 1037196-19.2023.4.01.3200, filed on 12 September 2023 before a Federal Court in Amazonas, Judgment of 18 July 2024, available at https://climatecasechart.com/non-us-case/ibama-v-dirceu-kruger-illegal-deforestation-in-the-amazon-and-climate-damage/

***IBAMA v Seringal (on illegal wood storage)***

*Instituto Brasileiro do Meio Ambiente e dos Recursos Renováveis v Seringal Indústria e Comércio de Madeiras EIRELI*, ACP 1000364-26.2019.4.01.3200, filed on 28 January 2019 before the Federal Court of Amazonas, Judgment of 15 August 2023, available at https://climatecasechart.com/non-us-case/federal-environmental-agency-ibama-v-seringal-industria-e-comercio-de-madeiras-eireli/

***ISA et al v Brazil et al (Wood exportation)***

*Instituto Socioambiental (ISA), Associação Brasileira dos Membros do Ministério Público de Meio Ambiente (ABRAMPA) e Greenpeace Brasil v União Federal e Instituto Brasileiro do Meio Ambiente e dos Recursos Naturais Renováveis (IBAMA)*, ACP 1009665-60.2020.4.01.3200, filed on 4 June 2020 before the 7th Federal Environmental and Agrarian Court of the Judiciary Section of Amazonas, available at https://climatecasechart.com/non-us-case/isa-abrampa-and-greenpeace-v-brazil/ and at https://judicialportal.informea.org/sites/default/files/court-case/ACP-ISA-1009665-60.2020.4.01.3200.pdf

***Laboratório do Observatório do Clima v Minister of Environment et al***

*Laboratório do Observatório do Clima v Ministério do Meio Ambiente e União Federal*, ACP 1027282-96.2021.4.01.3200, filed on 26 October 2021 before the 7th Federal Environmental and Agrarian Court of the Judiciary Section of Amazonas, available at https://climatecasechart.com/non-us-case/laboratorio-do-observatorio-do-clima-v-environmental-ministry-and-brazil/

### *State of Ceará*

***Instituto Verdeluz et al v Portocem et al (on installation of a thermoelectric plant in Pecém)***

*Instituto Verdeluz, Conselho Indígena do Povo Anacé de Japiman and Associação Indígena do Povo Anacé da Aldeia Planalto Cauipe v Portocem Geração de Energia, S.A., Secretaria do Meio Ambiente do Estado do Ceará (SEMACE), Instituto Brasileiro do Meio Ambiente (IBAMA) and Fundação Nacional do Índio (FUNAI)*, ACP 5003643-89.2022.4.02.5116, filed in 2022 before the Federal Court in Ceará (Brazil), available at https://climatecasechart.com/non-us-case/instituto-verdeluz-and-others-v-portocem-geracao-de-energia-sa-and-semace/

### *State of Mato Grosso*

***IBAMA v Alto Norte (on illegal wood storage)***

*Instituto Brasileiro do Meio Ambiente (IBAMA) v Alto Norte Indústroa, Comércio e Exportação de Madeiras Lda.*, ACP 1000200-41.2018.4.01.3606, filed on 20 December 2018 before the Federal Court of Juína, available at https://climatecasechart.com/non-us-case/federal-environment-agency-ibama-v-alto-norte-industria-comercio-e-exportacao-de-madeiras-ltda/

### *State of Minas Gerais*

***IBAMA v Siderúrgica São Luiz et al (on 'coal irregular origin')***

*Instituto Brasileiro do Meio Ambiente (IBAMA) v Siderúrgica São Luiz and Geraldo Magela Martins*, Process No 1010603-35.2019.4.01.3800, filed on 2 July 2019 before the 15th Federal Civil Court of Minas Gerais, available at https://climatecasechart.com/non-us-case/federal-environmental-agency-ibama-v-siderurgica-sao-luiz-ltda-and-martins/

### *State of Pará*

***AMOREMA and AMORETGRAP v Sustainable Carbon at al***

*Associação dos Moradores da Reserva Extrativista Mapuá (AMOREMA) and Associação dos Moradores da Reserva Extrativista Terra Grande-Pracuúba (AMORETGRAP) v Sustainable Carbon (on voluntary carbon markets).* ACP 1045416-11.2021.4.01.3900, filed in 2021 before the Federal Court of Pará, available at https://climatecasechart.com/non-us-case/amorema-e-amoretgrap-vs-sustainable-carbon-and-others-carbon-credits-and-extractive-reserves/

***IBAMA v Floresta Verde (on illegal wood storage)***

*Instituto Brasileiro do Meio Ambiente e dos Recursos Naturais Renováveis v Indúsria, Comércio e Exportação de Madeiras Floresta Verde, Lda.*, ACP 1000083-80.2019.4.01.3908, filed on 4 February 2019 before the Federal Court of Pará, Judgment of 25 March 2020, available at https://climatecasechart.com/non-us-case/federal-environment-agency-ibama-v-industria-comercio-e-exportacao-de-madeiras-floresta-verde-ltda/

***IBAMA v Gabriel Madeiras (on illegal wood storage)***

*Instituto Brasileiro do Meio Ambiente e dos Recursos Naturais Renováveis v Gabriel Indústria e Comércio de Madeiras EIRELI*, ACP 1000185-42.2018.4.01.3907, filed on 19 December 2018 before the Federal Court of Pará, Judgment of 5 June 2019, available at https://climatecasechart.com/non-us-case/federal-environmental-agency-ibama-v-gabriel-industria-e-comercio-madeiras-eireli/

***IBAMA v Madeira Nova Aliança (on illegal wood storage)***

*Instituto Brasileiro do Meio Ambiente e dos Recursos Naturais Renováveis v Madeira Nova Aliança Lda.*, ACP 1000275-31.2019.4.01.3902, filed on 28 January 2019 before the Federal Court of Pará, available at https://climatecasechart.com/non-us-case/federal-environment-agency-ibama-v-madeira-nova-alianca-ltda/

***IBAMA v Madeireira Madevi (on illegal wood storage)***

*Instituto Brasileiro do Meio Ambiente e dos Recursos Naturais Renováveis v Madeireira Madevi Lda.*, ACP 1000656-73.2018.4.01.3902, filed on 20 December 2018 before the Federal Court of Pará, available at https://climatecasechart.com/non-us-case/federal-environment-agency-ibama-v-madeireira-madevi-ltda/

***IBAMA v Silmar Gomes Moreira (on illegal wood storage)***

*Instituto Brasileiro do Meio Ambiente e dos Recursos Naturais Renováveis v Silmar Gomes Moreira*, ACP 1000469-62.2018.4.01.3903, filed on 19 December 2018 before the Federal Court of Pará (Altamira), available at https://climatecasechart.com/non-us-case/federal-environmental-agency-ibama-v-silmar-gomes-moreira/

***Public Defender's Office of the State of Pará v Associação dos Ribeirinhos e Moradores et al (Project 2620 carbon credits and 'forest carbon grabbing')***

*Defensoria Pública do Estado do Pará v Associação dos Ribeirinhos e Moradores, Sindicato dos Produtores Rurais de Portel, Amigos dos Ribeirinhos Assessoria Ambiental EIRELI, Brazil AGFOR LLC, and Municipality of Portel*, ACP 0806464-92.2023.8.14.0015, filed on 19 July 2023 before the State Court of Pará, available at https://climatecasechart

.com/non-us-case/public-defenders-office-of-the-state-of-para-vs-associacao-dos-ribeirinhos-e-moradores-and-others-project-2620-carbon-credits-and-forest-carbon-grabbing/

***Public Defender's Office of the State of Pará v Brazil AGFOR et al (Project 2252 carbon credits and 'forest carbon grabbing')***

*Defensoria Pública do Estado do Pará v Brazil AGFOR, Michael Edward Greene, Jonas Akila Morioka, Amigos dos Ribeirinhos Assessoria Ambiental EIRELI, Associação dos Ribeirinhos e Moradores, BLB Florestal Preservação no Brasil, Ltda., and Municipality of Portel*, ACP 0806505-59.8.14.0015, filed on 20 July 2023 before the State Court of Pará, available at https://climatecasechart.com/non-us-case/public-defenders-office-of-the-state-of-para-vs-brazil-agfor-llc-and-others-project-2252-carbon-credits-and-forest-carbon-grabbing/

***Public Defender's Office of the State of Pará v Floyd et al (Project 981 carbon credits and 'forest carbon grabbing')***

*Defensoria Pública do Estado do Pará v Floyd Promoção e Representação, Ltda., Avoided Deforestation Project (Manaus) Limited, Brazil AGFOR LLC, Michael Edward Greene e Jonas Akila Morioka*, ACP 0806631-12.2023.8.14.0015, filed on 25 July 2023 before the State Court of Pará, available at https://climatecasechart.com/non-us-case/public-defenders-office-of-the-state-of-para-vs-floyd-promocao-e-representacao-ltda-and-others-project-981-carbon-credits-and-forest-carbon-grabbing/

***Public Defender's Office of the State of Pará v RMDLT Property Group et al (Project 997 carbon credits and 'forest carbon grabbing')***

*Defensoria Pública do Estado do Pará v RMDLT Property Group, Brazil Property Group Compra Venda e Locação de Imóvel Ltda., Brazil AGFOR LLC, AGFOR Empreendimentos, Michael Edward Greene, and Municipality of Portel*, ACP 0806582-68.2023.8.14.0015, filed on 24 July 2024 before the State Court of Pará, available at https://climatecasechart.com/non-us-case/public-defenders-office-of-the-state-of-para-vs-rmdlt-property-group-and-others-project-997-carbon-credits-and-forest-carbon-grabbing/

### *State of Paraná*

***IEA v Brazil***

*Instituto de Estudos Amazónicos (IEA) v União Federal.* ACP No. 5048951-39.2020.4.04.7000, filed on 8 October 2020 before the 4th Federal Regional Court of Curitiba, Decision of 7 December 2021, available at https://climatecasechart.com/non-us-case/institute-of-amazonian-studies-v-brazil/

### *State of Rio de Janeiro*

***Public Prosecutor's Office of the State of Rio de Janeiro v Niterói (Neighborhood Impact Study)***

*Ministério Público Federal do Estado do Rio de Janeiro v Município de Niterói.* ACP No 0006155-57.2013.8.19.0002, filed on 31 January 2013 before the Civil Court of Niterói, available at https://climatecasechart.com/non-us-case/public-prosecutors-office-of-the-state-of-rio-de-janeiro-vs-municipality-of-niteroi-neighborhood-impact-study/

### *State of Rio Grande do Sul*

***Associação Gaúcha et al v Copelmi Mineração et al (Nova Seival Thermal Power Plant)***

*Associação Gaúcha de Proteção ao Ambiente Natural (AGAPAN), Instituto Gaúcho de Estudos Ambientais (INGÁ), Instituto Preservar, Cooperativa Agroecológica Nacional Terra e Vida Lda, Coonattera, Bionatur and Centro de Educação Popular e Agroecologia (CEPPA) v Copelmi Mineração Lda. and Instituto Brasileiro do Meio Ambiente e dos Recursos Naturais e Renováveis (IBAMA)*, ACP 5030786-95.2021.4.04.7100, filed on 19 May 2020 before the 9th Federal Court of Rio Grande do Sul, available at https://climatecasechart.com/non-us-case/instituto-preservar-et-al-v-copelmi-mineracao-ltda-and-ibama/

***Arayara v Copelmi Mineração et al (on hydrological risks)***

*Instituto Arayara de Educação e Cultura v Copelmi Mineração Lda., Fundação Estadual de Proteção Ambiental Henrique Luis Roessler (FEPAM) and Agência Nacional de Águas (ANA)*, ACP 5069057-47.2019.4.04.710, filed on 10 September 2020 before the Court of Justice of Rio Grande do Sul, available at https://climatecasechart.com/non-us-case/arayara-association-of-education-and-culture-vs-copelmi-mineracao-ltda-and-fepam-guaiba-mine-project-and-hydrological-risks/

***Arayara et al v Copelmi Mineração et al (Mina Guaíba project)***

*Instituto Arayara de Educação e Cultura, Associação Indígena Poty Guarani, Conselho de Articulação do Povo Guarani and Comunidade da Aldeia Guarani Guajayvi v Copelmi Mineração Lda., Fundação Nacional do Índio (FUNAI) and Fundação Estadual de Proteção Ambiental Henrique Luis Roessler (FEPAM)*, ACP 5069057-47.2019.4.04.7100 (Federal Court), filed on 1 October 2019 before the 9th Federal Court of Rio Grande do Sul, Judgment of 1 February 2022, available at https://climatecasechart.com/non-us-case/arayara-association-of-education-and-culture-and-others-v-funai-copelmi-mineracao-ltda-and-fepam-mina-guaiba-project-and-affected-indigenous-communities/

***Arayara et al v Copelmi et al (Mina Guaíba project and affected communities)***

*Instituto Internacional Arayara e Colônia de Pescadores Z-5 v Copelmi Mineração Ltda e Fundação Estadual de Proteção Ambiental (FEPAM)* ACP 5044993-20.2019.8.21.0001 / 5125450-05.2020.8.21.0001, filed on 27 September 2019 before the 10th Public Court of Porto Alegre, available at https://climatecasechart.com/non-us-case/instituto-internacional-arayara-and-fishermens-colony-z-5-v-copelmi-mineracao-ltda-and-fepam-mina-guaiba-project-and-affected-communities/

***Public Prosecutor's Office of the State of Rio Grande do Sul v State of Rio Grande do Sul et al (on carbochemical complex)***

*Ministério Público do Estado de Rio Grande do Sul v Estado de Rio Grande do Sul and Fundação Estadual de Proteção Ambiental Henrique Luis Roessler (FEPAM)*, ACP

9065931-65.2019.8.21.0001 and 5091523-82.2019.8.21.0001, filed on 1 September 2019, available at https://climatecasechart.com/non-us-case/public-ministry-of-the-state-of-rio-grande-do-sul-vs-state-of-rio-grande-do-sul-and-fepam-carbochemical-complex/

***Public Prosecutor's Office of the State of Rio Grande do Sul v Municipality of Eldorado do Sul et al (Eldorado Master Plan)***

*Procurador-Geral de Justiça do Rio Grande do Sul v Município de Eldorado do Sul e Câmara Municipal de Eldorado do Sul,* ADI 0007238-31.2021.8.21.7000, filed in 22 January 2021 before the Court of Justice of Rio Grande do Sul, Judgment of 10 December 2021, available at https://climatecasechart.com/non-us-case/state-adi-0007238-3120218217000-eldorado-do-sul-master-plan/

### *State of Rondônia*

***Jaci-Paraná Extractive Reserve and Guajará-Mirim State Park***

*State ADI 0804739-62.2021.8.22.0000 (Jaci-Paraná Extractive Reserve and Guajará-Mirim State Park)*, requested by the Public Prosecutor's Office on 1 May 2021, Judgment of 1 November 2021, available at https://climatecasechart.com/non-us-case/state-adi-0804739-6220218220000-jaci-parana-extractive-reserve-and-guajara-mirim-state-park/

***State of Rondônia et al v Invaders of the Guajará-Mirim State Park***

*Estado de Rondônia e Ministério Público do Estado de Rondônia v Todos os Invasores Encontrados no Parque Estadual de Guajará-Mirim e na sua Zona de Amortecimento,* ACP 7002381-27.2020.8.22.0015, filed on 27 October 2020 before the State Court of Rondônia, Judgment of 21 November 2023, available at https://climatecasechart.com/non-us-case/state-of-rondonia-and-public-prosecutors-office-of-the-state-of-rondonia-vs-invaders-of-the-guajara-mirim-state-park-and-its-amortization-zone-illegal-occupation-of-the-guajara-mirim-state-park/

### *State of Roraima*

***IBAMA v Madelin Madeireira Linhares (on illegal wood storage)***

*Instituto Brasileiro do Meio Ambiente e dos Recursos Naturais Renováveis v Madelin Madeireira Linhares Lda.*, ACP 1001659-42.2018.4.01.4200, filed on 20 December 2018 before the federal Court of Roraima, Judgment of 5 August 2020, available at https://climatecasechart.com/non-us-case/federal-environment-agency-ibama-v-madelin-madeireira-linhares-ltda/

### *State of Santa Catarina*

***Costa Legal et al v Florianópolis et al***

*ONG Costal Legal, Associação Florianopolitana das Entidades Comunitárias (UFECO) e Associação Pachamama v Município de Florianópolis, Fundação Municipal do Meio Ambiente (FLORAM), Estado de Santa Catarina, Instituto do Meio Ambiente de Santa Catarina (FATMA), Companhia Catarinense de Águas e Saneamento (CASAN) e Agên-*

*cia de Regulação de Serviços Públicos de Santa Catarina* (*ARESC*). ACP No 5012843-56.2021.4.04.7200, filed on 19 May 2021 before the 6th Federal Court of Santa Catarina, available at https://climatecasechart.com/non-us-case/ong-costa-legal-and-others-vs-municipality-of-florianopolis-and-others/

***Public Prosecutor's Office v CASAN***

*Ministério Público Federal v Companhia Catarinense de Águas e Saneamento* (*CASAN*), ACP 5004793-41.2021.4.04.7200, filed before the 6th Federal Court of Florianópolis

### *State of São Paulo*

***Carbonext v Amazon Imóveis* (*Voluntary Carbon Market*)**

*Carbonext Tecnologia em Soluções Ambientais Lda. v Amazon Imóveis* (*Voluntary Carbon Market*). 44th Civil Court of São Paulo, Process No. 1072768-63.2021.8.26.0100, Decision of 7 October 2021, available at https://climatecasechart.com/non-us-case/carbonext-tecnologia-em-solucoes-ambientais-ltda-v-amazon-imoveis-voluntary-carbon-market/

***Six Youths v Minister of Environment et al***

*Thalita Silva e Silva, Marcelo dos Santos Rocha, Walelasoetxeige Paiter Bandeira Surui, Paulo Ricardo Brito dos Santos, Paloma Costa Oliveira e Daniel Augusto Araújo Gonçalves Holanda v Ricardo de Aquino Salles, Ernesto Henrique Fraga Araújo e União Federal*, Popular Action No 5008035-37.2021.4.03.6100, filed on 13 April 2021 before the 14th Federal Civil Court of São Paulo, Judgment of 7 June 2024, available at https://climatecasechart.com/non-us-case/six-youths-v-minister-of-environment-and-others/

### *State of Sergipe*

***Federal Public Prosecutor's Office v Brazil et al* (*Sea advance and coastal erosion*)**

*Ministério Público Federal v União Federal, Instituto Brasileiro do Meio Ambiente e dos Recursos Naturais Renováveis, Estado do Sergipe, Agência Ambiental do Sergipe e Outros*. ACP 0800002-72.2014.4.05.8502, filed on 29 January 2024 before the Sergipe 5th Federal Court, available at https://climatecasechart.com/non-us-case/federal-public-prosecutors-office-mpf-v-brazil-and-others-sea-advance-and-coastal-erosion/

## Domestic Cases (Other Jurisdictions)

### *Argentina*

***Asociación Civil por la Justicia Ambiental et al v Province of Entre Ríos et al* (*Delta del Paraná Case*)**

*Asociación Civil por la Justicia Ambiental, Úrsula Weisburd, Florentina Boeykens, Gala Verzeñassi Moller, Augusto Farre Araguás & Álvaro Weisburd v Provincia de Entre Ríos Y Otros*, filed on 2 July 2020 before the Supreme Court of Justice of Argentina, available at https://climatecasechart.com/non-us-case/asociacion-civil-por-la-justicia-ambiental-v-province-of-entre-rios-et-al/

***Greenpeace Argentina et al v Argentina et al***

*Fundación Greenpeace Argentina, Surfrider Argentina, Asociación de Surf de Argentina, Fundación Patagonia Natural, Asociación Civil Medio Ambiente Responsable (Organización Mar), Kula Earth Asociación Civil, Asociación de Surfistas de Necochea, Asociación de General Alvardo de Surf, Asociación Argentina de Abogados y Abogadas Ambientalistas & Ecos de Mar v Estado Nacional, Secretaría de Energía de la Nación & Ministerio de Ambiente, Desarrollo Sostenible y Cambio Climático*, FMP 105/2022, filed before the Federal Court of Mar de la Plata, available at http://climatecasechart.com/non-us-case/greenpeace-argentina-et-al-v-argentina-et-al/

## *Australia*

***Bushfire Survivors for Climate Action Inc v Environmental Protection Authority***

*Bushfire Survivors for Climate Action Inc v Environmental Protection Authority*, [2021] NSWLEC 92; [2020] NSWLEC 152, 26 August 2021 (Land and Environment Court of New South Wales), available at https://climatecasechart.com/non-us-case/bushfire-survivors-for-climate-action-incorporated-v-environment-protection-authority/

***Gray v The Minister for Planning and Ors***

*Gray v The Minister for Planning and Ors*, Case No 40870/2006, New South Wales Land and Environment Court, Decision of 27 November 2006, available at http://climatecasechart.com/non-us-case/gray-v-minister-planning-ors/

***Waratah Coal Pty Ltd v Youth Verdict Ltd et al***

*Waratah Coal Pty Ltd v Youth Verdict Ltd, The Bimblebox Alliance Inc, John and Susan Brinnand & Chief Executive, Department of Environment and Science*, [2020] QLC 33; [2021] QLC 4; [2021] QLC 36; [2022] QLC 3; [2022] QLC 4, Queensland Land Court Judgment of 25 November 2022, available at https://climatecasechart.com/non-us-case/youth-verdict-v-waratah-coal/

## *Belgium*

***ClientEarth v Belgian National Bank***

*ClientEarth v Belgian National Bank*, filed in April 2021, available at https://climatecasechart.com/non-us-case/clientearth-v-belgian-national-bank/#:~:text=Summary%3A,other%20greenhouse%2Dgas%20intensive%20companies

***VZW Klimaatzaak v Kingdom of Belgium et al***

*VZW Klimaatzaak v Kingdom of Belgium, the Walloon Region, the Flemish Region, and the Brussels-Capital Region*, Process No 2021/AR/15gs, 2022/AR/737 & 2022/AR/891, Judgment of the Court of Appeals of 30 November 2023, available at https://climatecasechart.com/non-us-case/vzw-klimaatzaak-v-kingdom-of-belgium-et-al/

### *Colombia*

***Center for Social Justice Studies 'Tierra Digna' v Presidency of the Republic et al* (*Atrato River*)**

*Center for Social Justice Studies 'Tierra Digna' v Presidency of the Republic & Minister of the Interior*, Process No T-622/16, Judgment of 10 November 2016 (Constitutional Court), available at https://climatecasechart.com/non-us-case/atrato-river-decision-t-622-16-of-november-10-2016/

***Committee for the Defence of Water et al v Ministry of Environment and Sustainable Development et al* (*Páramo de Santurbán case*)**

*Committee for the Defence of Water and the Páramo de Santurbán v Ministry of Environment and Sustainable Development et al* (*Páramo de Santurbán case*), Process No 680012333000-2020-00827-00, filed before the Contentious Administrative Court of Santander

***Future Generations v Ministry of the Environment et al***

*José Daniel Rodríguez Peña, Félix Jeffry Rodríguez Peña, Claudia Andrea Lozano Barragán, Acxan Duque Guerrero, Antoine Philippart Marín, Victoria Alexandra Arenas Sánchez, Ariadna Haydar Chams, Carmen Elena Rosales García, Adrián Santiago Cruz Rodríguez, Danna Valentina Cruz Rodríguez, Aderly Rolando Chamorro Rubio, Yuli Maryerly Correa Fonque, Andrés Mauricio Salamanca Mancera, Catalina María Bohórquez Carvajal, Aymara Cuevas Ramírez, Laura Jiménez Ospina, Juan Darío Medina Carreño, Candelaria Valencia Arango, Yurshell Yanishey Rodríguez Hooker, Violeta Posada Riaño, María Camila Bustos Ortíz, Pablo Cavanzo Piñeros, Jesús David Medina Carreño, Valentina Rozo Ángel y Gabriela Eslava Bejarano v Presidencia de la República de Colombia, Ministerio de Ambiente y Desarrollo Sostenible, Ministerio de Agricultura y Desarrollo Rural, Unidad Administrativa Especial Parques Nacionales Naturales, Corporación para el Desarrollo Sostenible del Norte y el Oriente Amazónico, Corporación para el Desarrollo Sostenible del Sur de la Amazonía, Corporación para el Desarrollo Sostenible de la Macarena, las alcaldías de los municipios de San Vicente del Caguán, Cartagena del Chairá, San José del Guaviare, Calamar, La Macarena, Puerto Leguízamo, Solano, Uribe, El Retorno, Puerto Guzmán, Puerto Rico, Miraflores, Florencia y Vistahermosa; y a las gobernaciones de Amazonas, Caquetá, Guainía, Guaviare, Putumayo y Vaupés*, Process No 11001 22 03 000 2018 00319 00, Decision of 5 April 2018 (Supreme Court of Colombia), available at https://climatecasechart.com/non-us-case/future-generation-v-ministry-environment-others/

***Liliana Andrea García Ávila et al v Ministerio de Ambiente y Desarrollo et al***

*Liliana Andrea García Ávila et al v Ministerio de Ambiente y Desarrollo et al*, Process No 25000 2341 000 2023 00614 00, Administrative Court of Cundinamarca, Judgment of 7 July 2023

***Wayúu Indigenous Communities* (*Bruno River Case*)**

*Wayúu Indigenous Communities v Ministry of Home Affairs et al*, Process No SU-698/17, Judgment of 28 November 2017 (Constitutional Court of Colombia)

***Wayúu Indigenous Communities* (*'Cerrejón Mine Case'*)**

*Wayúu Indigenous Community et al v Ministry of Environment et al*, filed on 22 February 2019 before the Colombian Council of State, Process No 11001-0324-000-2019-00107-00, available at https://climatecasechart.com/non-us-case/wayuu-indigenous-community-and-others-v-ministry-of-environment-and-others/

### *Ecuador*

***Baihua Caiga et al v PetroOriental SA***

*Baihua Caiga et al v PetroOriental SA*, Process No 22201202000469 (Family, Women, and Children Judicial Unit from Francisco de Orellana Canton of Ecuador), available at https://climatecasechart.com/non-us-case/baihua-caiga-et-al-v-petrooriental-sa/

***Herrera Carrion et al v Ministry of the Environment et al* (*'Mecheros' Case*)**

*Herrera Carrion et al v Ministry of the Environment et al*, Process No 21201202000170, Judgment of 29 July 2021 (Sala Multicompetente de la Corte Provincial de Justicia de Sucumbíos), available at https://climatecasechart.com/non-us-case/herrera-carrion-et-al-v-ministry-of-the-environment-et-al-caso-mecheros/

***Municipal Authorities v Ecuador* (*'Los Cedros'*)**

*Municipal Authorities v Ecuador*, Case No 1149-19-JP/20, Judgment of 10 November 2021 (Constitutional Court of Ecuador), available at https://www.garn.org/wp-content/uploads/2022/06/Los-Cedros-Decision-ENGLISH-Final.pdf

***Santiago García Llore, Director Provincial Esmeraldas***

*Santiago García Llore, Director Provincial Esmeraldas*, Process No 0507-12-EP, Judgment No 166-15-SEP-CC (24 June 2015) (Constitutional Court of Ecuador), available at https://portal.corteconstitucional.gob.ec/FichaRelatoria.aspx?numdocumento=166-15-SEP-CC

### *France*

*Envol Vert et al v Casino* (2021)

*Envol Vert, Sherpa, Canopée, Notre Affaire à Tous, France Nature Environnement, Mighty Earth, Comissão Pastoral da Terra* (CPT), *Coordenação das Organizações Indígenas da Amazônia Brasileira* (COIAB), *Federação dos Povos Indígenas do Pará* (FEPIPA), *Federação das Organizações e Povos Ind°igenas do Mato Grosso* (FEPOIMT) *& Organización Nacional de los Pueblos Indígenas de la Amazonia Colombiana* (OPIAC) *v Casino*, filed before the Saint-Étienne Judicial Court, available at https://climatecasechart.com/non-us-case/envol-vert-et-al-v-casino/

***Notre Affaire à Tous et al v BNP Paribas***

*Notre Affaire à Tous, Les Amis de la Terre, and Oxfam France v BNP Paribas*, filed in 2023 before the Judicial Court of Paris (France), available at https://climatecasechart.com/non-us-case/notre-affaire-a-tous-les-amis-de-la-terre-and-oxfam-france-v-bnp-paribas/

### *Germany*

***Neubauer et al v Germany***

Cases No BvR 2656/18, 1 BvR 78/20, m1 BvR 96/20 and 1 BvR 288/20, Judgment od 24 March 2021 (Constitutional Court), available at https://www.bundesverfassungsgericht.de/SharedDocs/Entscheidungen/EN/2021/03/rs20210324_1bvr265618en.html

***Luciano Lliuya v RWE AG***

Case No 2 O 285/15, filed before the District Court of Essen Regional Court, available at https://climatecasechart.com/non-us-case/lliuya-v-rwe-ag/

### *Ireland*

***Friends of the Irish Environment v Ireland***

*Friends of the Irish Environment v The Government of Ireland*, Case 2017 No 793 JR, Judgment of 19 September 2019 (High Court of Ireland), available at https://climatecasechart.com/non-us-case/friends-of-the-irish-environment-v-ireland/

### *Mexico*

***Greenpeace v Instituto Nacional de Ecología y Cambio Climático***

*Greenpeace v Instituto Nacional de Ecología y Cambio Climático*, Amparo 159/2022, Decision of 15 December 2022 (11th Collegiate Court of the First Circuit in Administrative Matters), available at https://climatecasechart.com/non-us-case/greenpeace-v-instituto-nacional-de-ecologia-y-cambio-climatico-and-others/

***Xochimilco Wetlands Case***

*Residents v Local Government*, Process No 572/2020, filed in 2020 before the 5th District Court in Administrative Matters of Mexico City

### *Netherlands*

***Milieudefensie et al v Royal Dutch Shell plc***

*Milieudefensie et al v Royal Dutch Shell plc*, ECLI:NL:RBDHA:2021:5339, The Hague District Court, Judgment of 26 May 2021, available at http://climatecasechart.com/climate-change-litigation/non-us-case/milieu defensie-et-al-v-royal-dutch-shell-plc/

***Urgenda v State of the Netherlands***

*Stichting Urgenda v State of the Netherlands*, ECLI:NL:HR(2019(2007, Hoge Raad, 19/00135, Supreme Court, Judgment of 20 December 2019

### *New Zealand*

***Smith v Fonterra Co-Operative Group Limited et al***

*Michael John Smith v Fonterra Co-Operative Group Limited, Genesis Energy Limited, Dairy Holdings Limited, New Zealand Steel Limited, Z Energy Limited, Chanel Infrastructure NZ Limited & BT Mining Limited*, [2020] NZHC 419, [2021] NZCA 552

& [2022] NZSC 35, Judgment of the High Court of New Zealand of 7 February 2024, available at https://climatecasechart.com/non-us-case/smith-v-fonterra-co-operative-group-limited/

### *Norway*

***The North Sea Fields Case***

*Greenpeace Nordic & Natural og Ungdom v Energy Ministry*, App No 23-099330TVI-TOSL/05, Oslo District Court, Judgment of 16 May 2024, available at https://climatecasechart.com/non-us-case/the-north-sea-fields-case-greenpeace-nordic-and-nature-youth-v-energy-ministry/

### *Pakistan*

***Leghari v Pakistan***

*Asghar Leghari v Federation of Pakistan*, Process No WP 25501/201, Supreme Court, Judgment of 25 January 2018, available at https://climatecasechart.com/non-us-case/ashgar-leghari-v-federation-of-pakistan/

### *Peru*

Álvarez et al v Peru

Álvarez et al v Peru, Process No 00859-2020-0-1801-JR-DC01, filed on 16 December 2019 before the Superior Court of Lima, available at https://climatecasechart.com/non-us-case/alvarez-et-al-v-peru/

### *Switzerland*

***Asmania et al v Holcim***

*Asmania et al v Holcim*, filed before the Cantonal Court of Zug (Kantonsgericht Zug), available at https://climatecasechart.com/non-us-case/four-islanders-of-pari-v-holcim/

### *United States of America*

***Juliana v United States***

Juliana v United States, Case No 24-684, Petition initially filed on 9 June 2017, available at https://climatecasechart.com/case/juliana-v-united-states/

# Index


access to justice 9, 20, 22, 24, 31–32, 149, 169, 171–173, 177–182, 334
Action Plan for the Prevention and Control of Deforestation in the Legal Amazon (PPCDAm) 51, 91, 97, 135, 211–212, 235, 263–264, 266, 269, 272, 284, 287, 292
activism 3, 10, 12, 42, 92, 195, 202
advisory opinions 5, 8, 18, 24, 31, 35, 81–83, 126*n*5, 127*n*8, 128, 140–168, 238*n*63, 245, 247–248, 255, 302–303, 305, 310, 372
Agro Extractivist Reserves (RESEX) 275, 278
Amazon rainforest 7–8, 16–17, 20, 24, 33, 36–37, 41, 60, 64, 77, 95, 97, 107, 134–135, 175, 208, 211, 235, 260–263, 265–275, 283–287, 290–293, 301, 360, 382
Amazon Fund 39, 51, 82, 90*n*25, 170, 197, 267, 269*n*40, 270, 272, 278–279, 283, 286–287, 304, 358, 363, 383
American Convention on Human Rights (ACHR) 17, 19, 26, 31, 125–126, 142*n*18, 152*n*66, 153*n*70, 165
  Article 26 5, 24, 30, 127–129

biodiversity 2, 7, 17, 24, 35, 48, 55, 72, 90, 119, 217, 230, 239, 253–254, 260, 265, 271, 292, 305, 383
  biodiversity conservation 26
  biodiversity loss 95*n*34, 192, 195, 223, 240–241, 273, 321
biome 2, 36, 48–49, 59–60, 95*n*31, 107, 197, 233–234, 236–237, 239, 249, 252, 256, 262–263, 266–267, 270, 284, 287–289, 306, 381
Brazilian Institute for the Environment and Renewable Natural Resources (IBAMA) 13, 16, 91, 52*n*17, 212, 234–235, 269–282, 289–290 353*n*72, 382*n*95, 383–384
Bolsonaro, Jair 14, 26, 50, 92, 98, 107, 212, 261, 270, 272, 286–287, 349

carbon neutral 15, 24, 26, 38, 40, 389, 398
carbon credits 37–38, 49*n*9, 52, 89, 274–279, 354–355,
civil liability 52, 59–60, 62–66, 234*n*41, 352, 362–367, 369–370, 374*n*77, 378–379, 381, 383, 385–388
climate attribution science 367–368, 375, 385
climate change 1, 3, 5, 7*n*42, 9, 12, 13, 16–17, 20, 22–23, 30, 32, 39, 40, 43, 47–48, 50–53, 55–59, 61, 63, 65–67, 69, 72–74, 79, 81, 83–85, 89, 91, 97, 111–113, 116–117, 119, 121–127, 133–137, 139–142, 144–147, 149, 157, 160–162, 172–173, 178, 180, 187–195, 201, 207–208, 210, 212, 214, 216–220, 222, 226*n*17, 227*n*20, 232, 234–235, 239–240, 245–246, 248, 251, 257, 263*n*9–10, 274, 282, 284–285, 287, 291, 296, 301–302, 307, 310–312, 324–328, 331–332, 336, 344–345, 348, 351–352, 355, 357, 360, 362*n*15, 366, 367*n*38–42, 370–373, 375–376, 378–380, 385–286, 388–391, 394–396, 398–399
  mitigation 2, 4, 6, 8, 9*n*33, 11, 15, 18, 24–26, 28, 35–38, 40*n*121, 41–42, 49, 55*n*35, 60, 76–77, 86–87, 90, 92, 94, 99–107, 115, 120, 129, 156, 169–171, 174–175, 179, 182, 196, 199, 203, 207, 213, 216, 221, 233*n*40, 247, 249, 252, 255–256, 258–259, 260–262, 265–266, 270–271, 289, 312, 319–321, 323, 330, 337–343, 346–347, 349–350, 352*n*72, 354, 356, 358–359, 361, 368–369, 387*n*208, 390*n*3
  adaptation 6, 8, 11, 25–26, 31, 33, 35, 37, 49, 68, 71, 76, 90, 93–94, 107, 120, 128–129, 170–171, 175–176, 179, 181–182, 196, 198–200, 202–204, 233*n*40, 246*n*7, 247, 249–250, 252–255, 258, 260*n*1, 266, 270, 292–293, 299, 308, 317, 319–323, 329, 339, 356, 361, 387
Climate Fund 6*n*21, 9, 11–12, 15–16, 17*n*60, 19, 23, 27, 29–30, 39, 51, 55, 77, 81, 86, 91, 93, 94–96, 100*n*54, 106–107, 112–113, 118–124, 136–138, 170, 196–198, 265*n*16, 267, 270–271, 286–287, 303, 305, 330, 357*n*83, 363, 395
climate governance 3, 7–8, 42, 68, 89, 93, 119, 142, 220–221, 237–238, 261–263, 274, 292, 303, 307–308, 328, 330, 345, 396

climate justice 5, 7, 9, 24–25, 27, 31, 41–43, 49, 59–60, 66, 87*n*13–14, 141*n*12, 124*n*14, 149, 169–172, 174, 178–179, 181–182, 187, 189, 196, 198–203, 205, 217, 221–222, 229, 231, 233, 241, 255, 293, 362, 364, 366, 388, 402
climate stability 26, 30–31, 51, 54, 56, 58, 72, 84, 111, 119, 125–129, 132–139, 271, 301,
compensation 21, 27, 40, 50, 52, 62, 164, 170–171, 204, 234–235, 277, 285, 292–293, 306, 352, 366*n*32, 372, 377*n*81, 383–384
Constitution 22–23, 25, 27, 48, 65, 67–68, 70, 73–77, 79–80, 83–84, 91, 94, 111, 118, 122–123, 126, 129, 131, 135, 137–139, 164, 205, 206*n*16, 213, 215–216, 219, 226, 230, 231*n*30, 233*n*36, 235, 237*n*59, 238, 241*n*77, 248*n*22, 251, 253, 265, 271, 273, 275, 281, 284, 298–300, 303, 310, 351, 358–359, 368*n*45, 371*n*57, 376, 394–397
  Art 225 19, 21, 24, 26, 30, 35, 38, 41, 49, 53–55, 61, 71–72, 78, 82, 121, 130, 132–134, 136, 197–198, 225, 231–233, 250, 265, 304, 309, 329, 350, 357, 364, 371, 379*n*85, 386*n*103, 396*n*25
constitutional control 76, 270, 286
Convention 169 of the International Labour Organization (ILO) 214, 276–277
Convention of Biological Diversity 249*n*28, 277
corporate climate litigation 25, 39, 339, 356,

damages 21–22, 26, 56, 58–59, 62, 66, 170, 172, 174, 176, 179, 204, 264, 291, 303, 321, 352, 363
  climate damages 16, 25, 37, 39–40, 49, 52, 63–64, 193, 233–234, 274, 279–283, 285, 292–293,356, 360–362, 364–372, 374–375, 377–388, 411
  material damages 277, 373, 379
  moral damages 63, 65, 237, 277–278, 281, 285, 306, 379
decolonization 196
deforestation 8, 13, 15–16, 37, 39, 50–52, 55, 60, 64–66, 75, 77, 78, 80–81, 87–88, 90–91, 95–100, 106–107, 120, 134–135, 174–176, 197, 204, 207–209, 211–212, 234–235, 238, 260–274, 277–287, 290–293, 301, 305–306, 333–334, 374, 377, 381–384, 395, 404, 406, 411, 414
deregulation 6, 9, 12, 14–16, 23, 42, 49, 186, 261
duty to protect the environment (*See also* duty to protect flora) 55, 76, 84, 121, 137–138, 211, 225, 246*n*10, 247, 250–251, 258, 273, 298, 306, 309,

enforcement 15, 28, 52, 56, 68, 91, 151, 165, 261, 274, 334, 343, 345, 361
energy transition 38–41, 52, 123, 196, 210, 240, 317, 345–346, 389–394, 396–399, 407
environmental constitutionalism (*See also* ecological constitutionalism) 131*n*26, 224*n*4, 294, 297, 299, 300, 303, 306, 313, 362
environmental crimes 97, 256, 290, 380
environmental impact assessment (EIA) 16, 25, 52, 56, 59, 61, 78, 213–214, 247
environmental litigation (link with) 61ff 17, 25, 34, 48–49, 53, 56, 58, 66, 113, 136, 138, 187, 198–199, 224, 266, 282, 332, 395
environmental permit 75, 79, 352*n*72
environmental rights (*See* right to a healthy environment) 5, 7, 20, 38, 72, 84, 87, 121, 207, 211, 230, 313, 350,
extractivist community 234, 238, 269, 272–273, 277, 285

fair share 9*n*33, 55*n*35, 342
federal constitution 15, 20, 27, 48, 67, 70, 91, 111, 118, 126, 129, 131, 133, 135, 137, 139, 205, 215, 225*n*10, 231, 275, 284, 298, 329, 357, 371, 376, 394, 397
  Article 225 (*See* right to a healthy environment) 19, 21, 24, 26, 30, 38, 41, 49, 53–55, 71, 78, 82, 121, 130, 132, 134, 136, 197, 231*n*30, 232–233, 250, 265, 281, 304, 309, 350, 364, 396*n*25
Federal Supreme Court (STF) 9, 12–13, 15, 19, 21–22, 27, 29, 31, 39, 41, 51*n*13, 52*n*19, 54–55, 71, 74–80, 81*n*85, 82, 90*n*25, 91, 93, 95–96, 112, 116, 118–124, 129–131, 137–139, 150–157, 170, 174–176, 187, 197, 208–211, 213, 215–217, 219, 232, 234, 238–239, 265, 265, 270–72, 286, 304, 310, 313, 337, 340, 348, 350–351, 354, 357–359, 362–363, 366, 371, 378, 394–399, 402–407
financial institutions 24, 26, 39, 43, 52, 317–321, 323, 325–333, 335, 346, 353

Forest Code (*See also* Law of Protection of Native Vegetation) 50, 133, 251, 258, 266, 329, 351*n*71, 371
forest fires 37, 41, 175, 180, 185, 208, 211, 274, 287–288, 290, 374, 403, 406, 411
free, prior and informed consent (FPIC) 34, 205, 273, 277, 279
future generations (*See also* intergenerational equity) 10, 15, 24, 34–35, 42, 53, 63–65, 71, 81, 87–88, 91, 117, 121, 135, 138, 149, 201–202, 217, 223–237, 239, 241–242, 251, 262–263, 265, 284, 294*n*1, 297, 300, 303, 309–310, 312–313, 351, 362, 370–371, 296, 419

gender 24, 32, 149, 152–155, 165, 179, 185, 193–194, 372, 406–407
Glasgow Leaders' Declaration on Forests and Land Use 265
global emissions 1, 8, 48*n*4, 60, 227, 260, 264, 390
Global South 2–5, 7, 10, 15, 28, 32*n*100, 42, 47, 53, 57, 86–87, 89–90, 95, 107, 112, 122, 169, 175–776, 189, 191–192, 195, 199, 202, 239, 255, 267*n*27, 274, 324–325, 327, 330, 332

human rights 2*n*3, 9, 22*n*85, 29, 32, 42, 50–51, 80, 86, 88, 90, 107–108, 112, 115, 118, 123, 125, 137–139,150–159, 163, 165, 182, 192–195, 197, 199, 202, 204, 208, 211, 217, 223–229, 237–241, 266*n*24, 269, 271, 274, 286, 291, 297, 328–329, 350, 362, 368, 3395–396, 401, 402, 404
  fundamental rights 20–21, 54–55, 67, 70, 75, 78–79, 82–84, 87, 91, 97–98, 105–106, 111, 118, 121–122, 124, 127, 130–132, 134–138, 187, 216, 235, 273, 284, 287, 301, 305, 309, 312, 340, 357–359, 363, 394, 396
  right to dignity 34, 232, 284
  right to life 20, 34, 72, 75, 81–82, 111, 116, 126, 130–131, 135, 142*n*18, 156, 203, 205, 230, 232, 241*n*77, 284, 287, 400
  right to freedom 135, 284
  right to equality 135, 284
  right to health 34, 79, 81–82, 111, 116, 119, 135, 187, 205, 232, 242, 271, 284, 287
  right to food 111, 116–117, 135, 187, 284
  right to housing 116–117, 135, 284
  right to a healthy environment 5, 16–18, 20–21, 24, 26, 30–31, 37–38, 41, 54, 66, 70*n*14, 76, 78 ,81, 94, 111, 113, 117, 119–122, 125–132, 134–135, 137–139, 142, 149, 201, 225*n*11, 231, 241, 245, 250, 256–258, 265, 269–271, 273, 284, 298, 357, 363
  right to a stable climate 6*n*21, 11, 15, 17, 19–21, 54, 62, 91, 97, 129, 134–136, 139, 201, 235, 250*n*40, 270, 274*n*67, 284
  rights of nature 24, 34, 37–38, 54, 89, 131, 231–232, 234, 236, 294–304, 306, 309–313

IEA *v Brazil* 17, 23, 30, 35–36, 51*n*13, 53*n*24, 91, 96, 107, 129, 134, 136*n*42, 138–139, 232–235, 283–285, 410, 414
indigenous people 10, 35, 193, 196, 226, 230, 233*n*39, 238*n*60, 278, 297, 313
  indigenous communities 19*n*71, 24, 33, 127*n*6, 191–192, 194–195, 201, 203–206, 210, 213, 217, 220, 222, 237, 273, 274–275, 296, 301–302, 347, 400, 419
  indigenous rights 16, 24, 33–35, 37, 97, 117, 201–202, 204–205, 207–208, 210–217, 219–222, 234, 239, 242, 275, 277–278, 299, 301–302, 347
  indigenous territories 33, 192, 195, 202–203, 206–207, 211–212, 219–220, 222, 277, 291
Institute Chico Mendes (ICMBio) 96*n*25, 212, 272, 410–411
International Court of Justice (ICJ) 18, 36, 141, 143–146, 150–151, 155, 160–168, 247–248, 255,, 372, 401
International Tribunal for the Law of the Seas (ITLOS) 8, 18, 35, 141–147, 150–151, 155, 245, 247–248, 255, 401
INPE (National Institute for Space Research) 261, 284
Inter-American Development Bank (IDB) 278
Inter-American Human Rights System (IAHRS) 84, 116
  Inter-American Commission on Human Rights (IACHR) 83, 128, 163, 195*n*32, 302
  Inter-American Court of Human Rights (IACtHR) 5, 17, 24, 30*n*98, 31, 33, 35, 37, 81–83, 126–127, 128–133,135, 139, 142, 147–148, 150–159, 165, 233, 237–239, 302, 310, 363, 400–401

intergenerational equity 34, 89, 223, 225, 228–229, 231, 271, 273
Intergovernmental Panel on Climate Change (IPCC) 1, 8, 28, 40, 87, 92, 94–95, 97, 101, 104, 107, 113, 200, 203, 321–322, 325, 337, 338*n*12, 360, 368, 370, 374–375, 378, 389–390, 392, 396, 399
international courts 2, 26, 31, 42, 67n**, 70*n*14, 123–124, 140–141, 143–144, 150, 157, 159, 161, 163, 165, 167, 227*n*18, 400

judicial activism 12, 42
judicial discretion 4, 30–31, 76, 143
just transition 275, 279

Latin America 5, 6, 9–10, 22, 28, 54, 67, 70, 83, 89, 149, 186, 221, 238, 270*n*48, 294–298, 300–303, 306, 309–313, 331*n*43, 362, 368*n*44
land grabbing 37, 274–276, 282, 328
Law of the Atlantic Rainforest (LMA) 292
Law of the National System of Protected Areas 275
loss and damage 175*n*25, 196, 264, 292–293, 320, 324–325, 356, 361, 366, 383, 385–388

mangroves 2, 8, 13, 36, 41, 50, 237, 251–252, 254–256, 258
marine 24, 26, 141, 236–237, 250, 252, 254,
  marine protection 35–36, 142, 245–249, 251, 253, 255, 257, 259
  marine habitat 2, 8, 35–36
maritime zone 8, 250, 253–254
Ministry of the Environment 87, 136, 169, 252, 287, 294*n*1, 297, 300*n*19, 302, 310*n*46, 329, 419–420
Monist Constitutional Architecture 5

National Council of Justice (CNJ) 156*n*78, 211, 238*n*63, 263, 283, 380
  Resolution 433/2021 40, 52–53, 282
National Indigenous Foundation (Funai) 16*n*59, 19*n*71, 33*n*105, 212–214, 216, 272, 347, 403, 406, 411–412, 415
National Climate Change Policy (Política Nacional de Mudanças Climáticas, PNMC) 48, 52, 55–56, 91–93, 97, 120, 136, 198, 212, 235, 251, 266, 270, 284–285, 329, 336, 339, 348, 350–351, 356, 359, 371*n*54, 378*n*83
National Policy on the Environment (Política Nacional do Meio Ambiente, PNMA) 48, 56, 72, 93, 235, 251, 253–254, 258, 266, 352
National System for Preventing and Combating Forest Fires (PREVFOGO) 287
Natural Sinks 2, 19, 26, 128
Nationally Determined Contributions (NDC s) 15, 18–20, 88, 92, 98, 114–115, 120, 122, 139, 175, 249, 263–266, 271, 289, 329, 337–340, 340*n*20–21, 342–343, 345–346, 348–350, 256, 258–259, 361*n*6
non-governmental organizations (NGO s) 12, 20–23, 58, 66, 91, 97, 144–145, 147–148, 201, 204, 283–285, 288, 291, 328, 333, 395

ocean 35, 145*n*36, 236, 247–249, 252, 254, 258*n*87, 259, 370–371
  ocean acidification 8, 246, 253

Pantanal Forests 2, 20, 175–176, 2080–209, 211, 269, 286–287, 289, 403, 405
Paris Agreement 6, 9, 11, 15, 17–19, 24, 26, 29–30, 33–34, 29, 42, 48, 52, 54–55, 87–88, 92, 111–124, 134, 137–139, 149, 156, 175, 187, 197, 212, 218, 241, 247, 249, 263, 265–266, 271, 285, 287, 289, 305, 317–318, 320–325, 337*n*7, 338–346, 348–350, 357–359, 361*n*6, 376*n*80, 378*n*84, 393
political party 21, 119, 123, 241, 270, 272, 287, 354
polluter-pays principle 62–63, 65, 149
Popular Class Action 56, 175
poverty 24, 32, 115, 117, 185, 194, 200, 231, 322
precaution principle 56, 61, 149, 211, 273, 309, 336–337, 351, 358
prevention principle 56, 61, 211, 273, 351
protected areas 80*n*78, 175, 206, 252, 263–264, 271–273, 275, 285
*PSB et al v Brazil* (*on Amazon Fund*) (*See also* ADO 59) 39, 51*n*13, 81–82, 90*n*25, 170*n*8–9, 197, 267, 269–271, 286–287, 303–304, 357–358, 363, 404

*PSB et al v Brazil* (*on Climate Fund*) (*See also* ADPF 708) 9, 11–12, 15–16, 19, 23, 27, 29–31, 39, 51*n*13, 55, 77*60*, 70, 81, 86, 90–91, 93–97, 106–107, 112, 118–119, 121–124, 136–139, 170, 196–198, 265*n*16, 267, 270–271, 286–287, 303, 305, 350, 363, 395, 404
*PSB et al v Brazil* (*on deforestation and human rights*) (*See also* ADPF 760) 51, 77, 78*n*66, 81, 91, 97, 106–107, 208, 211, 232, 268–269, 271, 286, 301, 305, 363, 395, 404
Public Civil Action 21–23, 56, 59, 134, 174, 177*n*31, 207, 234, 279, 307, 377
public defender
  Public Defenders' Office 20–22, 170, 172, 174, 177, 181–182, 276–278, 413–414
public participation 9, 27–28, 82, 83*n*102, 87, 106, 148, 177–179, 253, 273, 298
public prosecutor 50*n*10, 58
  Public Prosecutor's Office 13–14, 20–23, 36, 52*n*17, 76*n*55–56, 78*n*69, 79*n*72–75, 82*n*94, 170, 172, 174–175, 177, 181–182, 205, 208–209, 211–212, 231*n*31, 256, 258, 269*n*35, 280–283, 286–288, 290, 304–307, 310*n*45, 347*n*56, 366*n*35, 377*n*81, 382*n*96, 397, 403, 405–406, 408–411, 414–417

race 24, 32, 149, 179, 185, 188, 191–194, 231*n*30
REDD+ 52, 264, 277–278, 347*n*56
regulatory gaps 39, 262, 336
rights-based litigation 5*n*15, 6*n*21, 19–20, 24, 50*n*11, 54, 66, 75*n*50, 87*n*13, 112*n*8, 113, 117, 266*n*24, 274, 296, 307–308, 312–313, 332, 363*n*21, 368
rule of law 12*n*43, 20, 22, 68–69, 141, 257, 304, 305*n*32, 313, 361, 366, 397
San Salvador Protocol 127
  Article 11 5, 126

scientific evidence 28, 32, 85–90, 97–99, 101–102, 104–107, 284–285, 289, 337
sea level rise 2, 8, 13, 36, 176, 203, 233*n*40, 237, 246, 253, 257–259
separation of powers 2, 4, 9–10, 12, 15, 24, 27–28, 42, 67–69, 71, 73, 75–77, 79–80, 84, 120, 137, 197, 231*n*31, 271
setbacks (in policies) (*See* deregulation) 6, 9, 12, 14–16, 23, 26, 42, 49, 50, 58–59, 66, 186, 261, 359
social and economic development 2, 26, 194, 328–330, 287
social cost of carbon (SCC) 279, 281–282, 383,
standing 5, 21–23, 40, 55, 58*n*50, 128, 131, 170, 174, 231*n*31, 236*n*52, 242, 279, 319, 325, 333–334, 367
Superior Court of Justice (STJ) 13, 36, 64, 90*n*22, 151–152, 174, 216, 256–258, 281, 304–306, 313, 352*n*73, 371*n*54, 373*n*69, 375*n*77, 377*n*81, 379, 407–408
systematic content analysis 99–101, 106

tort law 25, 39–40, 282*n*97, 360, 364–368, 370, 373, 379, 381, 385, 388
traditional knowledge 202, 221–222, 277, 296, 313
transnational climate litigation 2*n*3, 3, 37, 53*n*25, 89*n*20, 115*n*23, 121, 136, 239–242, 262, 290–291, 330*n*40

unconstitutional state of things 78, 272–273
United Nations Framework Convention on Climate Change (UNFCCC) 18, 30, 34, 80, 111*n*1, 113*n*12, 133, 137, 139, 190, 246–247, 249–250, 252, 263, 265–266, 271, 278, 317–319, 324, 336, 348–349, 359, 361*n*6, 370, 372, 381*n*91, 396, 398

vulnerable groups 10, 24, 26, 32–33, 40, 116, 178, 181, 191, 193–194, 390

water security 271, 273
wood storage (illegal) 52*n*17, 234*n*41, 269*n*36, 279*n*85–89, 280, 281*n*91–94, 282*n*99, 382*n*95, 383, 410–413, 416

www.ingramcontent.com/pod-product-compliance
Lightning Source LLC
LaVergne TN
LVHW012051011026
849162LV00017B/139